# FANTASY FOOTBALL HANDBOOK
## 1997/98

# FANTASY FOOTBALL HANDBOOK
## 1997/98

## Bruce Smith

P.G. & E. Chandler
335 Lakeside Drive
Denton, Texas 76208
Tel. (940) 321-1468

HarperCollins*Publishers*

First published in 1997
by HarperCollins*Publishers*
London

© Bruce Smith 1997

1 3 5 7 9 8 6 4 2

A CIP catalogue record for this book is
available from the British Library

ISBN 0 00 218798 1

Photographs supplied courtesy of Allsport

Printed in Great Britain by
The Bath Press

# Contents

## The Author

Bruce Smith is an award winning journalist and author. He has written over 150 books on a variety of subjects. He is editor of *Football Decision* – the professional football clubs own magazine – and also *Stadium & Arena Management* magazine. His most popular annual publications include the *FA Carling Premiership Pocket Annual* and *Grand Prix Formula 1 Pocket Annual*.

His hobbies include all sports especially football and basketball and he can often be found cheering on Stevenage Borough and London Towers on most weekends.

# Introduction

THE FANTASY FOOTBALL HANDBOOK is designed to help you get the most out of your particular game of fantasy football management. It contains all the facts and figures you need to create your own fantasy team. It centres on the twenty teams who will take their place in the 1997-98 FA Premier League and the 430 or so players who will make up the squads of these teams. The facts and figures regarding the team players are possibly the most comprehensive available in any publication and come from my own Premiership database.

How you play the game is your decision and the aim here is not to tell you who to pick but more to outline the individual strengths and weaknesses of teams, managers and their players. Taking this in combination with the various information listed and your understanding of the way your fantasy league operates, you should stand a more than reasonable chance of success.

But fantasy management, just like the real thing, requires time, effort, skill and a good deal of luck – as mentioned above a thorough understanding of the way your league works is vitally important and with this you can start to formulate tactics and the best way to use players to their full.

Because of the wide range of games available, this handbook does not aim to go into detail about any one version. However it does start by outlining the various types of game there are and provides you with some useful strategies that you might want to employ to take full advantage.

Following this you will find selections of teams from a couple of the bigger newspaper versions of the game and you may want to think about using these as your foundation stones. Beware though, players change, as does their form, and it is not just the initial team you pick that is important but also the way you handle the likes of transfers and injuries during the course of the season. It is up to you, and only you, to stay on top of your games. Absolutely no slacking allowed!

Beyond this you will find the Club Guide and this aims to provide you with background information on what the team achieved last year and who were the stars and, perhaps more importantly, who their stars will be in the 1997-98 season. This is followed by a detailed look at each *club v club* home record in the Premiership since its inception and a listing of transfers throughout the 1996-97 season, right up to July 1st 1997.

The Player Directory provides profiles of around 470 players who will make up the bulk of the squads of the 20 Premiership teams during the season. This is supplemented with three years' worth of facts and figures that will provide you with their underlying performance profile – you want the best for your team but you also want those who perform the most consistently. These Form Factors will help you choose. Note that all these figures, like all those given in this Handbook, relate specifically to FA Carling Premiership matches unless otherwise stated.

Finally there is a player by player summary of how each of the squad players competed last season, with a detailed analysis of appearances numbers.

In short, you'll find everything you need to choose and maintain your fantasy team and players. Now go and find your own luck and with skill, who knows? You could be on the road to a championship season. Here's hoping!

## Acknowledgments

A special word of thanks to David Tavener, Barry Robinson, Jim Bluck and Mark Webb for the help and expertise they provided in collating material for this book.

## Deadlines

Football is a fast moving game especially when it comes to the pre-season. As far as transfers go the deadline date set in this book was 12th July and only moves that had actually been signed and registered at that point have been included.

## Contact

If you have any suggestions regarding details you would like to see in future editions of this book then please direct them to me at the following address:

Bruce Smith,
PO Box 382
St Albans,
Herts
AL2 3JD

Alternatively you can email me at:

Bruce-Smith@msn.com

Printable suggestions only please!

**Game Guide**

# Choosing and Using

NATIONAL NEWSPAPERS provide possibly the simplest and most effective way to play fantasy football. Indeed, if the bug really takes you, most newspapers have fantasy games going all year round that allow you to try cricket and Formula 1, for instance, at times when the football season does actually stop.

These fantasy leagues normally start a few weeks into the season and, although it is generally a good idea to start at this point, you can enter the fun at any time of the year.

The other common way of playing is by taking the play-by-mail approach and take part in one of the many leagues that can be found by looking through the ads and small ads in the back of soccer magazines. The frequency at which these run varies and, although most run in tandem with the football season, they can often run out of season.

There is also a third method which is becoming ever more popular and that is the On-Line Fantasy League. These are leagues run along similar lines to the above which are being set up on the Internet and allow you to interact more directly. Larger newspaper organisations are doing this as a common method to supplement their paper editions.

What is best? It's a matter of personal preference of course and largely depends on how much time you can spare and how seriously you are willing to take it. The newspaper versions are normally less complex in nature and also more accessible because they tend to be based solely on actual events and players. The performance of your team is based on how your players performed, or didn't perform, in their matches each weekend. This means that it is possible for you to calculate the points your players scored if you wish or simply wait for them to be published in the paper during the following week.

In these versions of games it is often just a matter of selecting a team, registering it and making sure you manage any transfers that are permissible to best effect.

Play by Mail editions can offer a greater depth of play and often allow you to take account of other options. Players may not be generally available and have to be selected from an overall pool of players that the league's Gamesmaster (he's the organiser) originates and can only be with one team at a time and are therefore bought and sold by making bids. Some games go even further and allow you to develop a whole infrastructure around your team and include stadiums and boardroom decisions to name but two! It is not my intention to go that far down the line in this book – I'm afraid if you want to build a two-tier stand you will need to get help elsewhere – here I intend to concentrate on players, managers and clubs!

Play-by-Mail, rather obviously, also relies on you having to send in weekly sheets (Turnsheets) and then wait for the result to come back. If you miss the deadline you could find yourself slipping. Many of these leagues also allow you to contact other managers in your league by publishing a list of contact numbers in a weekly circular.

On-Line versions allow you to make changes right up to the posted deadlines and results are also posted back to you more quickly. Their rules follow similar lines to the ones in any associated publications but quite often differ in several fundamental ways. For instance you may be able to register a squad of players rather than just a single team of players.

If you have only tried one version, it is worth experimenting with the other just to see if it is more suitable to what you want and expect out of playing a game of fantasy football. Details for these are readily available in newspapers and magazines and it is simply a matter of contacting the telephone number or address shown and awaiting a reply.

All versions of the game cost money to play and this may not just be the cost of a stamp or two, so take this into account when you are selecting the game of your choice.

Whichever version of fantasy football you decide to opt for, it cannot be overstressed how important it is for you to be familiar with its rules. Sometimes this can take a while and, despite plenty of study work and scouring the competition rule book, it often only fully falls into place when you have played your brand of game for a while.

No matter what version of the game you are opting for – get yourself organised. You will start collecting bits of paper and making notes everywhere and the best place for these and any other paperwork is in a suitable folder or filing system. It is no fun looking for bits of paper and scribbled notes when you have a deadline to meet – I have proved this on many occasions.

If you are using a folder or a good filing system, keep room at the start of it to record all the vital information you will need to have at your fingertips. This includes phone number, address and often a PIN number.

Let's now look at team selection and strategy in some detail. Much of what follows is written with the newspaper version of fantasy football games in mind. However salient points concerning the Play-by-Mail games are included at the appropriate points.

## Planning

Once you have decided what type of game you are opting for, you should get things underway.

The key to good planning is this:
*Start early, register late.*

By starting to plan as early as possible you are giving yourself time to succeed. Get the new rules as soon as they come out and make yourself fully conversant with them. Jot down notes and key items that you might otherwise forget or miss and start to think about how best you can use the limitations the rules impose to your best advantage.

The Leagues will give you a deadline by which time your team must be registered. They will impress upon you the need to do this as early as possible. Why? To ensure you get the best players available. Well yes that is certainly the case where there is only a limited set of players to select from and you want to ensure you have the best in your teams. But in the bigger games run by the daily nationals in which all players are available to you, it is just a matter of administration. They want you to get your entry in to ensure they keep the rush at the end to a minimum. This is understandable but if you are playing through a newspaper, do as I say and get your entry in at the last moment as this could, and probably will, suit you. The reason behind this tactic will become clearer as we progress.

## Team Names

It may come to you in a flash or you may spend all your time fretting about what to call your team. Many Play-by-Mail games allow you to choose a real team name like Arsenal, Barcelona or Stevenage – but to do this you have to be first in because the more popular teams, such as the three examples given, go quickly. If your name is already taken then the next available name is given to you.

In general, newspapers allow you to select your own team names and this is where you can be wonderfully creative or dreadfully dull. 'Money Blaggers United' is a bit more entertaining than 'Brucies Team'. Some of the names that caught my eye during the 1996-97 season were:

Heaven Eleven
Runaway Seahorses
Kendodsdadsdogisdead

I'd Rather be in SW19
Hartlepoolaregoingup

If you do well enough to get into the top listings you may well find your name, and your team's, appearing in the regular listings printed in respective newspapers – you can't do a lot about the former (especially if your name is Smith) so be really creative about the second. Watch out for the obvious though, make sure you don't exceed the number of characters permissible in the name and don't be offensive.

## The Players

There are normally a number of restrictions that will apply when you decide to select your team. To prevent you simply naming 11 players from the Manchester United starting line-up, there are normally two simple rules to follow:

1. There is a limited amount of money for you to spend on players.
2. There is a limit to the number of players from one team you can pick.

Each of the players who will be listed as starters in your league are assigned a transfer value. This value is what you have to spend to secure them for your team, and there is always an upper limit or ceiling on what you are allowed to spend. The amount available can depend on what the prices assigned for each player are, these figures can vary a good deal from league to league. The upper limit of some games for the 1996-97 season was as much as £35 million and this may well increase to perhaps £40 million for the 1997-98 season.

The players per club restriction prevents you snapping up all of your players from one or two clubs, even if the budget allowed you to do so. The number of players limit can again vary between the leagues, but two seems to be fairly normal.

In essence these two simple, but fundamental rules make the game one that makes you think and really does start to test your knowledge of football. The key about the second basic rule is that the club a player is allocated to is the one he was with at the time the player lists were printed and distributed. This means that he may well have actually transferred to another club during the course of time between the list being printed and the season getting underway. This is something you can use to your advantage and is why I mentioned earlier that you should leave your entry to the last possible moment. For example when your player list was published, Teddy Sheringham might still have been playing for Tottenham but then started the season with Manchester United. For all playing purposes, Sheringham would still be regarded as a Tottenham player, so in this respect you could effectively have three Manchester United players in your own fantasy team, even if the limit was two!

There is also often another restriction that is imposed, in that you must make your selection from position categories. In this case players are categorised by their position – the categories are normally:

    Goalkeepers
    Fullbacks
    Centre Backs
    Midfielders
    Strikers

Your 11 team players have to come from these areas and there can be restrictions such that your 11 players may be selected as:

| | |
|---|---|
| Goalkeepers | 1 |
| Fullbacks | 2 |
| Centre Backs | 2 |
| Midfielders | 4 |
| Strikers | 2 |

This is in playing terms a 4-4-2 formation but in fantasy football would be referred to as a 1-2-2-4-2 formation.

All this will provide you with some debate. Firstly you'll scream and marvel at some of the valuations put on players and this is where your bargain hunting ability comes into play. On the other hand, though, you'll find that some players get assigned funny classifications which can work to your benefit. For example, if a player that you and I would regard as an out-and-out striker is listed as a midfield player. Identifying these *irregularities,* for want of a better word, allows you to run with what is effectively a 4-3-3 formation. They can also mean you score a lot more points. A free-scoring midfield player may get more points than a similar player classed as a striker who is supposed to score. Examples where confusion could occur are players such as Matt Le Tissier and Dennis Bergkamp. Other positions to watch are full-backs classified as midfielders, especially when their own teams like to use wing-backs.

Beware though because it can operate in reverse where a midfielder is classified as a striker and therefore doesn't seem to pick up as many points for your team as he should.

Some leagues, especially those of an on-line nature, allow you to register a whole squad of players. In these cases you will have more money available to spend – say £55 million, but will still face the other limitations already outlined.

# Registering

Once you have done your ground work, made your selections and named your team, you will need to register it. Again the documentation that will have been supplied with the starter pack you originally requested will contain the information on how to do this. The two traditional methods are by filling out a registration form or by calling a hotline phone number.

Whatever method you go for, make sure you have all the facts and figures to hand. Players are allocated identification numbers that will need to be recorded, as well as their values. Double check your values and the total because if you go over the limit your application will be rejected and you could miss the start of the season.

## Under Way

Once the season is under way, the rules of the game will determine what you can, and can't, do. Transfers will have an important role to play and these are discussed in a little more detail later on. You may also decide to keep track of your own players and how they are scoring for your team. This will certainly help you identify who might need to leave the club!

If you are in a Play-By-Mail league then your scores and associated facts and figures will be posted back to you. If you are in an On-Line version you can log on to your particular web site and find out how well you are doing. Newspaper versions of the game will generally print the full list of players available in their game once a week and alongside the players they will normally list how many points they did or didn't score the previous week and their running aggregate total. Using this you can keep a list of how well you are doing, simply by checking the numbers. Another option often available is the premium-priced hotline where you can use your game PIN to access your own standing and details.

Some versions, such as the *Interactive Team Football* run by *The Times* in conjunction with *Sky Sports* allows you to update and see your performance on your TV screen, via the Astra satellite in combination with a touch-tone telephone.

## Scoring

How you score points again relies on the manner in which your league is run. The most basic, simplest and often therefore the most popular might go something like this:

For every goal scored by any player
    – 3 points
For any assist by any of your players
    – 2 points
For every clean sheet kept by your goalkeeper or defender
    –2 points
For every goal conceded by your goalkeeper or defender
    – 1 point

These criteria are applied to each member of your team to give them their weekly totals – which can be positive or negative. This is added to the previous week's values to provide a total aggregate score. The higher your aggregate score, the nearer the top of the league you will be.

# Selecting and Managing the Team

YOU WILL ULTIMATELY develop your own method of picking a team and this will probably depend on how much time you can spend studying the form of individual players. The most obvious way to start is to go for all the big name players and use this as a reference point that you can work back from as you will almost certainly be over budget. The real expertise comes from being able to pick out 'winners' – that's players breaking on to the scene who score points and are good value for money.

Possibly the most exciting find last season from a fantasy football point of view was Ole Gunnar Solskjaer. A virtual unknown when he arrived in England from Norwegian side Molde where he had spent just one season, having been brought by them from a Norwegian third division side! Others might be easier to predict – Emile Heskey for example, who I had in my side.

A strategy that is employed by many other players is to spend a big chunk of their money on attackers and then do as best as they can with the money that is left over. This is fine in theory but my view is that while you want a top scorer in your side you also want all your other players to contribute to the team performance and not effectively loose

you points by low scores or even negative scores. It can prove false economics and this should be borne out in some of the examples that follow on below.

The player and team outlines in this book should allow you to come up with some real gems but a good way to start is to look at past performances.

## Getting Value for Money

One method to see just how well either your players, potential or otherwise, have performed is to do a little homework when the year's final results are published. Some players can earn excellent points one week only to lose them again the next. The true value of a player is not just his total number of points at the end of the season, but how much of your budget he cost you to obtain those points. In these cases I calculate what I call the player's PPM – that stands for Points Per Million. I divide the number of points the player scored by the amount he cost. This can provide some interesting results.

Consider Alan Shearer – the Premiership's all-time top scorer and a guaranteed 25 goals plus per season. In one newspaper his end of season total was 85. However, Shearer is always going to be one of the most expensive you can buy – £8 million in this particular game. This gave him a PPM of 10.63. His closest rival was Ian Wright who had a better PPM of 12.03 and his total of 71 points cost over £2 million less at £5.9 million. The decision here is to decide whether the extra 16 points are worth the additional £2.1 million. In reality it would probably be better to spend the £2.1 to get a better player elsewhere in the team.

Using this method it is clear that Ole Gunnar Solskjaer was probably the buy of the season with his 59 points costing just £2.8 million and giving a PPM factor of

## Categorically the Best

### Goalkeepers

| | £m | Pts | PPM |
|---|---|---|---|
| Nigel Martyn | 2.50 | 37 | 14.80 |
| Mark Bosnich | 3.00 | 28 | 9.33 |
| Pavel Srnicek | 2.40 | 19 | 7.92 |
| David Seaman | 3.10 | 24 | 7.74 |
| Tim Flowers | 2.60 | 18 | 6.92 |
| Peter Schmeichel | 3.40 | 22 | 6.47 |
| Neil Sullivan | 2.00 | 12 | 6.00 |
| David James | 3.10 | 18 | 5.81 |

### Full Backs

| | £m | Pts | PPM |
|---|---|---|---|
| Stig Bjornebye | 2.10 | 41 | 19.52 |
| Robbie Elliott | 2.40 | 37 | 15.42 |
| Alan Wright | 3.20 | 48 | 15.00 |
| Steve Staunton | 2.90 | 35 | 12.07 |
| Fernando Nelson | 3.30 | 39 | 11.82 |
| Nigel Winterburn | 3.30 | 38 | 11.52 |
| Lee Dixon | 3.40 | 36 | 10.59 |
| Jason McAteer | 3.60 | 30 | 8.33 |

### Centre Backs

| | £m | Pts | PPM |
|---|---|---|---|
| Ugo Ehiogu | 3.10 | 49 | 15.81 |
| David Wetherall | 2.70 | 33 | 12.22 |
| Lucas Radebe | 2.30 | 27 | 11.74 |
| Martin Keown | 3.30 | 38 | 11.52 |
| Tony Adams | 3.60 | 36 | 10.00 |
| Darren Peacock | 2.90 | 26 | 8.97 |
| Colin Hendry | 2.90 | 25 | 8.62 |
| Steve Bould | 3.20 | 28 | 8.75 |
| Philippe Albert | 3.40 | 26 | 7.65 |

### Midfielders

| | £m | Pts | PPM |
|---|---|---|---|
| Gary McAllister | 2.00 | 37 | 18.50 |
| Kevin Gallacher | 2.50 | 40 | 16.00 |
| Emile Heskey | 2.60 | 40 | 15.38 |
| Marcus Gayle | 2.30 | 33 | 14.35 |
| Mark Pembridge | 2.30 | 32 | 13.91 |
| Juninho | 3.40 | 41 | 12.06 |
| David Beckham | 3.00 | 34 | 11.33 |
| Aljosa Asanovic | 2.60 | 28 | 10.77 |
| Robert Lee | 3.20 | 29 | 9.06 |
| Paul Merson | 2.90 | 26 | 8.97 |
| Matt Le Tissier | 4.70 | 33 | 7.02 |
| Benito Carbone | 3.60 | 25 | 6.94 |
| Steve McManaman | 4.20 | 26 | 6.19 |

### Strikers

| | £m | Pts | PPM |
|---|---|---|---|
| OG Solskjaer | 2.80 | 59 | 21.07 |
| Ian Wright | 5.90 | 71 | 12.03 |
| Steve Claridge | 3.60 | 41 | 11.39 |
| Mark Hughes | 3.70 | 42 | 11.35 |
| Chris Sutton | 4.10 | 45 | 10.98 |
| Dion Dublin | 4.70 | 50 | 10.64 |
| Alan Shearer | 8.00 | 85 | 10.63 |
| Dwight Yorke | 6.10 | 59 | 9.67 |
| Robbie Fowler | 7.20 | 65 | 9.03 |
| Dennis Bergkamp | 5.40 | 48 | 8.89 |
| Les Ferdinand | 6.70 | 59 | 8.81 |
| Eric Cantona | 6.50 | 57 | 8.77 |
| Gianfranco Zola | 5.70 | 44 | 7.72 |
| Stan Collymore | 6.80 | 43 | 6.32 |

just £2.8 million and giving a PPM factor of 21.07. You won't get him for £2.8 million now though.

The tables on the left show how the best players in each category performed.

That said there are bargains to be had and if you have a computer spreadsheet available to you can set up a worksheet so that you can monitor players performances to date and see which are earning the points for minimal costs. These should be the targets of any transfers you undertake.

## Best Not

The above method allows you to start making selections based on how well the players were actually performing in your own league, but how does that relate to what is actually perceived of their performance. There is one way to examine this which can have a practical benefit.

The Professional Footballer's Association (PFA) vote for their best player every year – not only that they also vote for their team of the year and I have listed their 1996-97 choice below and including the value they were assigned and the points they returned, had I chosen them in my particular league (which I didn't!).

## PFA Team Performance

| Player | Team | £ (m) | Pts |
|---|---|---|---|
| David Seaman | Arsenal | 3.1 | 24 |
| Gary Neville | Man. Utd | 3.4 | 27 |
| Stig Bjornebye | Liverpool | 2.1 | 41 |
| Tony Adams | Arsenal | 3.6 | 36 |
| Mark Wright | Liverpool | 3.4 | 21 |
| David Beckham | Man. Utd | 3.0 | 34 |
| Steve McManaman | Liverpool | 4.2 | 26 |
| Roy Keane | Man. Utd | 2.8 | 8 |
| David Batty | N'castle | 2.5 | 2 |
| Alan Shearer | N'castle | 8.0 | 85 |
| Ian Wright | Arsenal | 5.9 | 71 |
| *Totals* | | 42.0 | 375 |

In my league the total of 375 points would have put me in the top 10 but would also have put me £7.0 million over budget! Equally it includes three players from Arsenal, Liverpool and Manchester United. However, the team provides a good starting point to work from and, looking retrospectively, to determine what changes can be made to maximise points and get under budget.

Looking straight through the team we can see that both Roy Keane and David Batty provided poor returns – just seven points in total from an outlay of £5.3 million.

From my basic list of top PPM performers above I would immediately substitute both for Kevin Gallacher and Emile Heskey – that's 80 points for £5.1 million. Also Gary McAllister is better PPM value than Steve McManaman and saves more money. The semi-revised team looks like this:

| Player | Team | £ (m) | Pts |
|---|---|---|---|
| David Seaman | Arsenal | 3.1 | 24 |
| Gary Neville | Man. Utd | 3.4 | 20 |
| Stig Bjornebye | Liverpool | 2.1 | 40 |
| Tony Adams | Arsenal | 3.6 | 37 |
| Mark Wright | Liverpool | 3.4 | 24 |
| David Beckham | Man. Utd | 3.0 | 34 |
| Gary McAllister | Coventry | 2.0 | 37 |
| Kevin Gallacher | Blackburn | 2.5 | 40 |
| Emile Heskey | Leicester | 2.6 | 40 |
| Alan Shearer | Newcastle | 8.0 | 71 |
| Ian Wright | Arsenal | 5.9 | 62 |
| *Totals* | | *39.6* | *435* |

| Player | Team | £ | Pts |
|---|---|---|---|
| Nigel Martyn | Leeds Utd | 2.5 | 37 |
| Alan Wright | Aston Villa | 3.2 | 48 |
| Stig Bjornebye | Liverpool | 2.1 | 41 |
| Ugo Ehiogu | Aston Villa | 3.1 | 49 |
| David Wetherall | Leeds Utd | 2.7 | 33 |
| David Beckham | Man. Utd | 3.0 | 34 |
| Gary McAllister | Coventry | 2.0 | 37 |
| Kevin Gallacher | Blackburn | 2.5 | 40 |
| Emile Heskey | Leicester | 2.6 | 40 |
| OG Solskjaer | Man. Utd | 2.8 | 59 |
| Ian Wright | Arsenal | 5.9 | 71 |
| *Totals* | | *32.6* | *489* |

Now I would have won my league with this points total but I am still over budget and still have three Arsenal players. Who can I get rid of? David Seaman missed a large chunk of last season through injury so had less time to score points. This should be borne in mind but the best value goalkeeper was Nigel Martyn who scored 37 points at £2.5 million.
In defence Ugo Ehiogu hauled in 39 points for £3.1 million and David Wetherall returned 33 points for £2.7 million. I'd also put in Alan Wright in place of Gary Neville who is more expensive but has a much better points return value.

Replacing at centre back and fullback still leaves the team well over budget. A large chunk of this can be saved by getting rid of Alan Shearer or Ian Wright but this will mean the sacrifice of some points.

On last years figures there is only one contender and this is Ole Gunnar Solskjaer. The final team selection would therefore be:

Amazing – 489 points for £32.6 million – a table-topping team. Of course it is certain that the above players won't all perform to the levels they did in 1996-97 to earn these points. Equally Solskjaer will cost a lot more this season and there might be a re-classification of Kevin Gallacher from midfield to striker. Despite that I would suggest that at least half this team will have a similar performance and if you have the skills to identify another Solskjaer in the making you will be well on your way to a winning season.

## Private Selection

The above method is fine if you have direct access to all players in your league. This is normally the case when you are playing in a newspaper or magazine league. However it is often not the case when you are playing one of the Play-by-Mail leagues. In many of these games you will be required to join an auction for players when the league is about to get underway.

How the auction is held will depend on your league. It may involve placing bids, it may be on a first come first serve basis

**Fantasy Football Handbook**

– but whichever it is, you can prepare yourself in much the same way, although you will need to have back-up players available in your base selection list just in case one or more of your bids fails.

If you join a league that is already underway then you will probably be supplied with a set of players by the league. This is your starting point and it will be up to you to watch your league's transfer market so that you can mould your own team in the fullness of time. Hey, just like the real thing!

## Transfers

Transfer polices vary from league to league. Some allow you to do them all the time. In many Play-by-Mail leagues you simply bid and bid and hope that they are accepted by the managers who currently own the rights to the players. The policy of newspaper and magazine games vary as well. Some allow you to make them only a few times per season and then there may be a limit on the number of players you can transfer, while others allow you to make transfers on a weekly basis, again with an upper limit on the number you can make. In all cases you can only make transfers that will keep you within your budget. Thus if there are two players totalling £6 million that you want for your team, you must first transfer out two players to that value or more.

If you are only allowed limited transfers then you need to plan and pick wisely – don't make a change for changes sake!

If you are only allowed a limited number of transfers over a season then there are two reasons why you might consider making a change to your starting line-up. Firstly you have an injured player

to replace and secondly you have a player who is not doing the business.

In the case of injured players think carefully. An injured player is not earning you points but equally he isn't costing you points! If you have a midfield player who has scored a total of 30 points for you up to Christmas and then breaks a leg is it really worth getting rid of him? If you refer back to the lists presented earlier you'll see that there aren't too many midfield players who score 30 points at the end of the season let alone half way through it! This is one reason why it is worth keeping track of points scored by players other than those on your team – so that you have the best possible choices available to you when you want to replace an injured or a poor performing player.

Remember that in both of these cases you'll only earn the points that the player scores after you assigned him to your team. Games that allow just the occasional updates often add new players to their lists at the same point to take account of any new arrivals, so keep abreast of the transfer market and how well these players have been performing.

In Leagues that allow weekly transfers you can make them for all the above reasons but you can also use them for tactical reasons. Consider the team that we arrived at before and is listed below again:

| Player | Team | £ (m) | Pts |
|--------|------|-------|-----|
| Nigel Martyn | Leeds Utd | 2.5 | 37 |
| Alan Wright | Aston Villa | 3.2 | 48 |
| Stig Bjornebye | Liverpool | 2.1 | 41 |
| Ugo Ehiogu | Aston Villa | 3.1 | 49 |
| David Wetherall | Leeds Utd | 2.7 | 33 |
| David Beckham | Man. Utd | 3.0 | 34 |
| Gary McAllister | Coventry | 2.0 | 37 |
| Kevin Gallacher | Blackburn | 2.5 | 40 |
| Emile Heskey | Leicester | 2.6 | 40 |
| OG Solskjaer | Man. Utd | 2.8 | 59 |
| Ian Wright | Arsenal | 5.9 | 71 |
| *Totals* | | *32.6* | *489* |

Consider what might happen when Arsenal play Leeds United. Here the team will have three of its own players in opposition. Striker Ian Wright comes up against centre back David Wetherall and goalkeeper Nigel Martyn. There are winner and loser conflicts amongst your own team here. If Ian Wright scores then both Martyn and Wetherall are going to lose points. If Wright (and Arsenal) are shut out then Martyn and Wetherall score points but Wright doesn't.

The sensible option here might be to transfer Ian Wright out and look for a replacement for a week. If you have been keeping track of players then you will have the ready-made replacement.

Obviously in these matters it pays to keep track of the fixture list a week or two ahead but you can also look beyond and into the fixture list if you are clever enough. And we are.

In the Club Guide you will find a list of each club's Premiership home records against the other 19 teams that make up the Premier League for 1997-98. Tradition plays a big part in results and if you scour through the fixtures as they come you will find out how teams have traditionally fared against each other. Take Liverpool v Chelsea. Liverpool have a 100% home record against Chelsea over the last five years of the Premiership. Manchester United have a 100% record over Southampton at Old Trafford. Therefore if you have Chelsea players going away to Liverpool players, you may want to consider making some short- term transfers. The same goes for any Southampton players you have, when United are about to take them on at home.

The listing opposite provides you with what I call some home bankers – these are matches in the past five years that have always favoured the home team!

## Keeping Track

Part of the fun behind playing fantasy football is to check out how your team are going and to plan ahead – the reasons for which have already been outlined above. Play-by-Mail games will normally send you a sheet each week showing you just how your players and your team are doing.

Newspaper versions of the game will publish the weekly and aggregate performances of players to date and, if you're good enough, your name and the teams in their top performers list.

If you don't play the transfer market at all, preferring to let your team 'ride', then you can simply total up the aggregates for your players as and when you want to get your points totals at any one time.

However, if you are planning on a game where you will be hyper-active in the transfer market then you will need to keep on top of the administrative management of the team so that you can

# Home Bankers

| Match /Event | P | W | D | L | F | A | Pts | % |
|---|---|---|---|---|---|---|---|---|
| Liverpool v Chelsea | 5 | 5 | 0 | 0 | 14 | 4 | 15 | 100.00 |
| Manchester United v Southampton | 5 | 5 | 0 | 0 | 12 | 4 | 15 | 100.00 |
| Blackburn Rovers v Newcastle United | 4 | 4 | 0 | 0 | 5 | 1 | 12 | 100.00 |
| Manchester United v West Ham United | 4 | 4 | 0 | 0 | 8 | 1 | 12 | 100.00 |
| Newcastle United v Aston Villa | 4 | 4 | 0 | 0 | 13 | 5 | 12 | 100.00 |
| Newcastle United v Coventry City | 4 | 4 | 0 | 0 | 15 | 0 | 12 | 100.00 |
| Newcastle United v Everton | 4 | 4 | 0 | 0 | 8 | 1 | 12 | 100.00 |
| Newcastle United v Wimbledon | 4 | 4 | 0 | 0 | 14 | 2 | 12 | 100.00 |
| Arsenal v Sheffield Wednesday | 5 | 4 | 1 | 0 | 11 | 4 | 13 | 86.67 |
| Arsenal v Southampton | 5 | 4 | 1 | 0 | 13 | 7 | 13 | 86.67 |
| Blackburn Rovers v Chelsea | 5 | 4 | 1 | 0 | 10 | 2 | 13 | 86.67 |
| Blackburn Rovers v Sheffield Wednesday | 5 | 4 | 1 | 0 | 12 | 3 | 13 | 86.67 |
| Blackburn Rovers v Southampton | 5 | 4 | 1 | 0 | 9 | 4 | 13 | 86.67 |
| Blackburn Rovers v Wimbledon | 5 | 4 | 1 | 0 | 11 | 4 | 13 | 86.67 |
| Everton v Southampton | 5 | 4 | 1 | 0 | 12 | 2 | 13 | 86.67 |
| Leeds United v Everton | 5 | 4 | 1 | 0 | 9 | 2 | 13 | 86.67 |
| Leeds United v Wimbledon | 5 | 4 | 1 | 0 | 11 | 3 | 13 | 86.67 |
| Manchester United v Arsenal | 5 | 4 | 1 | 0 | 6 | 0 | 13 | 86.67 |
| Manchester United v Coventry City | 5 | 4 | 1 | 0 | 11 | 1 | 13 | 86.67 |
| Manchester United v Sheffield Wednesday | 5 | 4 | 1 | 0 | 12 | 3 | 13 | 86.67 |
| Manchester United v Tottenham Hotspur | 5 | 4 | 1 | 0 | 9 | 2 | 13 | 86.67 |
| Leeds United v West Ham United | 4 | 3 | 1 | 0 | 6 | 2 | 10 | 83.33 |
| Newcastle United v Chelsea | 4 | 3 | 1 | 0 | 9 | 3 | 10 | 83.33 |
| Newcastle United v West Ham United | 4 | 3 | 1 | 0 | 8 | 1 | 10 | 83.33 |
| Southampton v Newcastle United | 4 | 3 | 1 | 0 | 8 | 4 | 10 | 83.33 |
| West Ham United v Southampton | 4 | 3 | 1 | 0 | 9 | 5 | 10 | 83.33 |
| Wimbledon v Nottingham Forest | 4 | 3 | 1 | 0 | 5 | 2 | 10 | 83.33 |
| Aston Villa v Liverpool | 5 | 4 | 0 | 1 | 9 | 5 | 12 | 80.00 |
| Aston Villa v Wimbledon | 5 | 4 | 0 | 1 | 15 | 2 | 12 | 80.00 |
| Blackburn Rovers v Coventry City | 5 | 4 | 0 | 1 | 17 | 7 | 12 | 80.00 |
| Blackburn Rovers v Liverpool | 5 | 4 | 0 | 1 | 14 | 6 | 12 | 80.00 |
| Liverpool v Aston Villa | 5 | 4 | 0 | 1 | 12 | 5 | 12 | 80.00 |
| Liverpool v Leeds United | 5 | 4 | 0 | 1 | 13 | 1 | 12 | 80.00 |
| Liverpool v Sheffield Wednesday | 5 | 4 | 0 | 1 | 8 | 2 | 12 | 80.00 |
| Manchester United v Wimbledon | 5 | 4 | 0 | 1 | 11 | 4 | 12 | 80.00 |
| Tottenham Hotspur v Southampton | 5 | 4 | 0 | 1 | 12 | 5 | 12 | 80.00 |
| Blackburn Rovers v West Ham United | 4 | 3 | 0 | 1 | 10 | 7 | 9 | 75.00 |
| Everton v West Ham United | 4 | 3 | 0 | 1 | 6 | 2 | 9 | 75.00 |
| Liverpool v Newcastle United | 4 | 3 | 0 | 1 | 10 | 8 | 9 | 75.00 |
| Newcastle United v Arsenal | 4 | 3 | 0 | 1 | 6 | 2 | 9 | 75.00 |
| Newcastle United v Sheffield Wednesday | 4 | 3 | 0 | 1 | 9 | 5 | 9 | 75.00 |

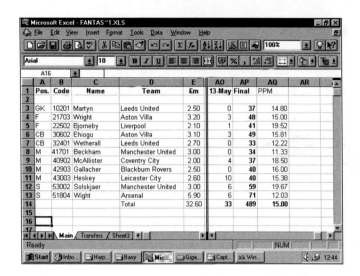

| | A | B | C | D | E | | AO | AP | AQ | AR | |
|---|---|---|---|---|---|---|---|---|---|---|---|
| 1 | Pos. | Code | Name | Team | £m | | 13-May | Final | PPM | | |
| 2 | | | | | | | | | | | |
| 3 | GK | 10201 | Martyn | Leeds United | 2.50 | | 0 | 37 | 14.80 | | |
| 4 | F | 21703 | Wright | Aston Villa | 3.20 | | 3 | 48 | 15.00 | | |
| 5 | F | 22502 | Bjorneby | Liverpool | 2.10 | | 1 | 41 | 19.52 | | |
| 6 | CB | 30602 | Ehiogu | Aston Villa | 3.10 | | 3 | 49 | 15.81 | | |
| 7 | CB | 32401 | Wetherall | Leeds United | 2.70 | | 0 | 33 | 12.22 | | |
| 8 | M | 41701 | Beckham | Manchester United | 3.00 | | 0 | 34 | 11.33 | | |
| 9 | M | 40902 | McAllister | Coventry City | 2.00 | | 4 | 37 | 18.50 | | |
| 10 | M | 42903 | Gallacher | Blackburn Rovers | 2.50 | | 0 | 40 | 16.00 | | |
| 11 | M | 43003 | Heskey | Leicester City | 2.60 | | 10 | 40 | 15.38 | | |
| 12 | S | 53002 | Solskjaer | Manchester United | 3.00 | | 6 | 59 | 19.67 | | |
| 13 | S | 51804 | Wight | Arsenal | 5.90 | | 6 | 71 | 12.03 | | |
| 14 | | | | Total | 32.60 | | 33 | 489 | 15.00 | | |
| 15 | | | | | | | | | | | |
| 16 | | | | | | | | | | | |

keep track of your players and the points that they are accumulating for you.

There are several ways to do this. If you have access to a computer you might be able to set everything up on a spreadsheet – such as the one shown above. This is simple if you don't plan too many transfers but you will need to think carefully about the design of the spreadsheet if you plan to make regular dealings. Remember, you will need to keep track of the points, positive or negative, that players accumulated for you prior to their departure. This book isn't a spreadsheet primer, but one way to do this is to create a worksheet for each of the players you use with a cell for each week of the season. Into each cell add points at the appropriate time and total these to be carried forward into a main summary worksheet.

This same method can be used for the pen and paper approach and you may find a ruled hardback book convenient for this.

Fantasy Football Handbook

# Top Performers

The following lists should give you an even better indication as to the sort of players you should be selecting. Remember that it is not necessarily the best individual players that win the most points, but those that work with their team. The best goalkeeper in the world is not going to score as many points behind a leaky defence as he will by playing behind a watertight one!

The points totals given are my own rounded figures based on how the players performed across some of the top newspaper based fantasy leagues. They are generally rounded up to the nearest five and only players who score 10 points or more across the course of the season are included.

## GOALKEEPERS

| Name | Club | Pts |
|---|---|---|
| MARTYN | Leeds U. | 40 |
| BOSNICH | Aston Villa | 30 |
| SEAMAN | Arsenal | 25 |
| SCHMEICHEL | Manchester U. | 25 |
| JAMES | Liverpool | 20 |
| SRNICEK | Newcastle U. | 20 |
| FLOWERS | Blackburn R. | 15 |
| HISLOP | Newcastle U. | 15 |
| OAKES | Aston Villa | 10 |
| OGRIZOVIC | Coventry City | 10 |
| TAYLOR | Southampton | 10 |
| WALKER | Tottenham H. | 10 |
| MIKLOSKO | West Ham U. | 10 |
| HEALD | Wimbledon | 10 |

## FULL BACKS

| Name | Club | Pts |
|---|---|---|
| WRIGHT | Aston Villa | 50 |
| KELLY | Leeds U. | 45 |
| WINTERBURN | Arsenal | 40 |
| BJORNEBYE | Liverpool | 40 |
| DIXON | Arsenal | 35 |
| STAUNTON | Aston Villa | 35 |
| BERG | Blackburn R. | 30 |
| LE SAUX | Blackburn R. | 30 |
| PETRESCU | Chelsea | 30 |
| McATEER | Liverpool | 30 |
| NEVILLE G. | Manchester U. | 30 |
| WATSON | Newcastle U. | 30 |
| HINCHCLIFFE | Everton | 25 |
| BARTON | Newcastle U. | 25 |
| BERESFORD | Newcastle U. | 25 |
| IRWIN | Manchester U. | 20 |
| POWELL C. | Derby County | 15 |
| DORIGO | Leeds U. | 15 |
| HALLE | Leeds U. | 15 |
| NOLAN | Sheffield W. | 15 |
| BENALI | Southampton | 15 |
| CUNNINGHAM | Wimbledon | 15 |
| KIMBLE | Wimbledon | 15 |
| HALL | Coventry City | 10 |

| | | | | | |
|---|---|---|---|---|---|
| ATHERTON | Sheffield W. | 10 | **MIDFIELD** | | |
| AUSTIN | Tottenham H. | 10 | *Name* | *Club* | *Pts* |
| EDINBURGH | Tottenham H. | 10 | GALLACHER | Blackburn R. | 45 |
| | | | McALLISTER | Coventry City | 40 |
| **CENTRE BACKS** | | | BECKHAM | Manchester U. | 35 |
| *Name* | *Club* | *Pts* | PEMBRIDGE | Sheffield W. | 35 |
| EHIOGU | Aston Villa | 50 | LE TISSIER | Southampton | 35 |
| KEOWN | Arsenal | 40 | ASANOVIC | Derby County | 30 |
| BOULD | Arsenal | 35 | SPEED | Everton | 30 |
| WETHERALL | Leeds U. | 35 | McMANAMAN | Liverpool | 30 |
| ADAMS | Arsenal | 30 | LEE | Newcastle U. | 30 |
| RADEBE | Leeds U. | 30 | SHERWOOD | Blackburn R. | 25 |
| ALBERT | Newcastle U. | 30 | DI MATTEO | Chelsea | 25 |
| PEACOCK | Newcastle U. | 30 | CARBONE | Sheffield W. | 25 |
| HENDRY | Blackburn R. | 25 | NIELSEN | Tottenham H. | 25 |
| WRIGHT | Liverpool | 25 | SINTON | Tottenham H. | 25 |
| MAY | Manchester U. | 25 | GIGGS | Manchester U. | 25 |
| DICKS | West Ham U. | 25 | TOWNSEND | Aston Villa | 20 |
| BILIC | Everton | 25 | BOWYER | Leeds U. | 20 |
| SCIMECA | Aston Villa | 20 | PARKER | Leicester City | 20 |
| SOUTHGATE | Aston Villa | 20 | BARNES | Liverpool | 20 |
| WALSH | Leicester City | 20 | BERGER | Liverpool | 20 |
| PERRY | Wimbledon | 20 | BUTT | Manchester U. | 20 |
| DAISH | Coventry City | 15 | BEARDSLEY | Newcastle U. | 20 |
| SHORT | Everton | 15 | HUGHES | West Ham U. | 20 |
| UNSWORTH | Everton | 15 | EARLE | Wimbledon | 20 |
| ELLIOTT | Leicester City | 15 | PLATT | Arsenal | 15 |
| MATTEO | Liverpool | 15 | DAILLY | Derby County | 15 |
| JOHNSEN | Manchester U. | 15 | WALLACE | Leeds U. | 15 |
| CAMPBELL | Tottenham H. | 15 | LENNON | Leicester City | 15 |
| MARSHALL | Arsenal | 10 | REDKNAPP | Liverpool | 15 |
| WILLIAMS | Coventry City | 10 | MAGILTON | Southampton | 15 |
| WATSON | Everton | 10 | ANDERTON | Tottenham H. | 15 |
| BABB | Liverpool | 10 | BERKOVIC | West Ham U. | 15 |
| RUDDOCK | Liverpool | 10 | PARLOUR | Arsenal | 14 |
| PALLISTER | Manchester U. | 10 | VIEIRA | Arsenal | 10 |
| NEWSOME | Sheffield W. | 10 | JOHNSON | Aston Villa | 10 |
| STEFANOVIC | Sheffield W. | 10 | FLITCROFT | Blackburn R. | 10 |
| WALKER | Sheffield W. | 10 | WILCOX | Blackburn R. | 10 |
| LUNDEKVAM | Southampton | 10 | SALAKO | Coventry City | 10 |
| NEILSON | Southampton | 10 | POWELL | Derby County | 10 |
| VAN GOBBEL | Southampton | 10 | KEANE | Manchester U. | 10 |
| CALDERWOOD | Tottenham H. | 10 | POBORSKY | Manchester U. | 10 |
| SCALES | Tottenham H. | 10 | OAKLEY | Southampton | 10 |

| | | |
|---|---|---|
| HOWELLS | Tottenham H. | 10 |
| MONCUR | West Ham U. | 10 |

## STRIKERS

| Name | Club | Pts |
|---|---|---|
| SHEARER | Newcastle U. | 90 |
| WRIGHT | Arsenal | 75 |
| FOWLER | Liverpool | 65 |
| YORKE | Aston Villa | 60 |
| SOLSKJAER | Manchester U. | 60 |
| BERGKAMP | Arsenal | 50 |
| DUBLIN | Coventry City | 50 |
| COLLYMORE | Aston Villa | 45 |
| SUTTON | Blackburn R. | 45 |
| HUGHES | Chelsea | 45 |
| ZOLA | Chelsea | 45 |
| CLARIDGE | Leicester City | 45 |
| STURRIDGE | Derby County | 40 |
| HESKEY | Leicester City | 40 |
| EKOKU | Wimbledon | 40 |
| FERGUSON | Everton | 35 |
| COLE | Manchester U. | 35 |
| ASPRILLA | Newcastle U. | 35 |
| SHERINGHAM | Manchester U. | 35 |
| GAYLE | Wimbledon | 35 |
| VIALLI | Chelsea | 30 |
| WARD | Derby County | 30 |
| DEANE | Leeds U. | 30 |
| BOOTH | Sheffield W. | 30 |
| OSTENSTAD | Southampton | 30 |
| STUART | Everton | 25 |
| HIRST | Sheffield W. | 25 |
| WHELAN | Coventry City | 20 |
| MARSHALL | Leicester City | 20 |
| HOLDSWORTH | Wimbledon | 20 |
| RUSH | Leeds U. | 15 |
| IVERSEN | Tottenham H. | 10 |

# Final Tables and Scorers 96-97

## FA Carling Premiership 1996-97

| | | HOME | | | | | AWAY | | | | | |
|---|---|---|---|---|---|---|---|---|---|---|---|---|
| | P | W | D | L | F | A | W | D | L | F | A | Pts |
| Manchester United | 38 | 12 | 5 | 2 | 38 | 17 | 9 | 7 | 3 | 38 | 27 | 75 |
| Newcastle United | 38 | 13 | 3 | 3 | 54 | 20 | 6 | 8 | 5 | 19 | 20 | 68 |
| Arsenal | 38 | 10 | 5 | 4 | 36 | 18 | 9 | 6 | 4 | 26 | 14 | 68 |
| Liverpool | 38 | 10 | 6 | 3 | 38 | 19 | 9 | 5 | 5 | 24 | 18 | 68 |
| Aston Villa | 38 | 11 | 5 | 3 | 27 | 13 | 6 | 5 | 8 | 20 | 21 | 61 |
| Chelsea | 38 | 9 | 8 | 2 | 33 | 22 | 7 | 3 | 9 | 25 | 33 | 59 |
| Sheffield Wednesday | 38 | 8 | 10 | 1 | 25 | 16 | 6 | 5 | 8 | 25 | 35 | 57 |
| Wimbledon | 38 | 9 | 6 | 4 | 28 | 21 | 6 | 5 | 8 | 21 | 25 | 56 |
| Leicester City | 38 | 7 | 5 | 7 | 22 | 26 | 5 | 6 | 8 | 24 | 28 | 47 |
| Tottenham Hotspur | 38 | 8 | 4 | 7 | 19 | 17 | 5 | 3 | 11 | 25 | 34 | 46 |
| Leeds United | 38 | 7 | 7 | 5 | 15 | 13 | 4 | 6 | 9 | 13 | 25 | 46 |
| Derby County | 38 | 8 | 6 | 5 | 25 | 22 | 3 | 7 | 9 | 20 | 36 | 46 |
| Blackburn Rovers | 38 | 8 | 4 | 7 | 28 | 23 | 1 | 11 | 7 | 14 | 20 | 42 |
| West Ham United | 38 | 7 | 6 | 6 | 27 | 25 | 3 | 6 | 10 | 12 | 23 | 42 |
| Everton | 38 | 7 | 4 | 8 | 24 | 22 | 3 | 8 | 8 | 20 | 35 | 42 |
| Southampton | 38 | 6 | 7 | 6 | 32 | 24 | 4 | 4 | 11 | 18 | 32 | 41 |
| Coventry City | 38 | 4 | 8 | 7 | 19 | 23 | 5 | 6 | 8 | 19 | 31 | 41 |
| Sunderland | 38 | 7 | 6 | 6 | 20 | 18 | 3 | 4 | 12 | 15 | 35 | 40 |
| Middlesbrough | 38 | 8 | 5 | 6 | 34 | 25 | 2 | 7 | 10 | 17 | 35 | 39 |
| Nottingham Forest | 38 | 3 | 9 | 7 | 15 | 27 | 3 | 7 | 9 | 16 | 32 | 34 |

*Middlesbrough deducted 3 points for failing to fulfil fixture.*

## FA Carling Premiership Top Scorers by Club

| Club | Scorers |
|---|---|
| Arsenal | Wright 23, Bergkamp 12, Merson 6 |
| Aston Villa | Yorke 17, Milosevic 9, Johnson 4 |
| Blackburn Rovers | Sutton 11, Gallacher 10, Sherwood 3, Flitcroft 3 |
| Chelsea | Vialli 9, M. Hughes 8, Zola 8 |
| Coventry City | Dublin 13, Whelan 6, McAllister 6 |
| Derby County | Sturridge 11, Ward 8, Asanovic 6 |
| Everton | Ferguson 10, Speed 9, Stuart 5, Unsworth 5 |

| | |
|---|---|
| Leeds United | Deane 5, Sharpe 5, Bowyer 4 |
| Leicester City | Claridge 12, Heskey 10, Marshall 8 |
| Liverpool | Fowler 18, Collymore 12, McManaman 7 |
| Manchester United | Solskjaer 18, Cantona 11, Beckham 8 |
| Middlesbrough | Ravanelli 16, Juninho 12, Beck 5 |
| Newcastle United | Shearer 25, Ferdinand 16, R. Elliott 7 |
| Nottingham Forest | Campbell 6, Haaland 6, Pearce 5 |
| Sheffield Wednesday | Booth 10, Hirst 6, Pembridge 6, Carbone 6 |
| Southampton | Le Tissier 13, Ostenstad 9, Berkovic 4, Evans 4, Magilton 4 |
| Sunderland | Russell 4, Stewart 4, Gray 3, Ball 3, Bridges 3 |
| Tottenham Hotspur | Sheringham 7, Iversen 6, Sinton 6 |
| West Ham United | Kitson 8, Dicks 6, Hartson 5 |
| Wimbledon | Ekoku 11, Gayle 8, Earle 7 |

## FA Carling Premiership Top Scorers

| Player | Club | Goals | All-time Total |
|---|---|---|---|
| Alan SHEARER | Newcastle United | 25 | 137 |
| Ian WRIGHT | Arsenal | 23 | 94 |
| Robbie FOWLER | Liverpool | 18 | 83 |
| Ole Gunnar SOLSKJAER | Manchester United | 18 | 18 |
| Dwight YORKE | Aston Villa | 17 | 48 |
| Les FERDINAND | Newcastle United | 16 | 101 |
| Fabrizio RAVANELLI | Middlesbrough | 16 | 16 |
| Dion DUBLIN | Coventry City | 13 | 43 |
| Matt LE TISSIER | Southampton | 13 | 80 |
| Dennis BERGKAMP | Arsenal | 12 | 23 |
| Stan COLLYMORE | Liverpool | 12 | 49 |
| Steve CLARIDGE | Leicester City | 12 | 12 |
| JUNINHO | Middlesbrough | 12 | 12 |
| Eric CANTONA | Manchester United | 11 | 70 |
| Efan EKOKU | Wimbledon | 11 | 42 |
| Dean STURRIDGE | Derby County | 11 | 11 |
| Chris SUTTON | Blackburn Rovers | 11 | 59 |

## FA Carling Premiership Players Used

| | | Total | Start | Sub | Snu | Ps |
|---|---|---|---|---|---|---|
| 1 | Liverpool | 462 | 418 | 44 | 146 | 44 |
| 2 | Middlesbrough | 465 | 418 | 47 | 142 | 47 |
| 3 | Aston Villa | 472 | 418 | 54 | 136 | 54 |
| 4 | Newcastle United | 472 | 418 | 54 | 135 | 54 |
| 5 | Southampton | 472 | 418 | 54 | 136 | 54 |
| 6 | Leeds United | 473 | 418 | 55 | 135 | 55 |
| 7 | Everton | 474 | 418 | 56 | 134 | 56 |
| 8 | Blackburn Rovers | 478 | 418 | 60 | 130 | 60 |
| 9 | Coventry City | 478 | 418 | 60 | 130 | 60 |
| 10 | Tottenham Hotspur | 481 | 418 | 63 | 127 | 63 |
| 11 | Leicester City | 482 | 418 | 64 | 126 | 64 |
| 12 | Nottingham Forest | 482 | 418 | 64 | 126 | 64 |

| | | | | | | | |
|---|---|---|---|---|---|---|---|
| 13 | Arsenal | 484 | 418 | 66 | 124 | 66 | |
| 14 | Chelsea | 489 | 418 | 71 | 119 | 71 | |
| 15 | Wimbledon | 491 | 418 | 73 | 117 | 73 | |
| 16 | Sunderland | 492 | 418 | 74 | 116 | 74 | |
| 17 | Manchester United | 493 | 418 | 75 | 115 | 75 | |
| 18 | West Ham United | 500 | 418 | 82 | 108 | 82 | |
| 19 | Derby County | 505 | 418 | 87 | 103 | 87 | |
| 20 | Sheffield Wednesday | 510 | 418 | 92 | 98 | 92 | |

# Nationwide League Division 1 1996-97

| | P | W | D | L | F | A | Pts | |
|---|---|---|---|---|---|---|---|---|
| Bolton Wanderers | 46 | 28 | 14 | 4 | 100 | 53 | 98 | P |
| Barnsley | 46 | 22 | 14 | 10 | 76 | 55 | 80 | P |
| Wolverhampton W. | 46 | 22 | 10 | 14 | 68 | 51 | 76 | |
| Ipswich Town | 46 | 20 | 14 | 12 | 68 | 50 | 74 | |
| Sheffield United | 46 | 20 | 13 | 13 | 75 | 52 | 73 | |
| Crystal Palace | 46 | 19 | 14 | 13 | 78 | 48 | 71 | P |
| Portsmouth | 46 | 20 | 8 | 18 | 59 | 53 | 68 | |
| Port Vale | 46 | 17 | 16 | 13 | 58 | 55 | 67 | |
| QPR | 46 | 18 | 12 | 16 | 64 | 60 | 66 | |
| Birmingham City | 46 | 17 | 15 | 14 | 52 | 48 | 66 | |
| Tranmere Rovers | 46 | 17 | 14 | 15 | 63 | 56 | 65 | |
| Stoke City | 46 | 18 | 10 | 18 | 51 | 57 | 64 | |
| Norwich City | 46 | 17 | 12 | 17 | 63 | 68 | 63 | |
| Manchester City | 46 | 17 | 10 | 19 | 59 | 60 | 61 | |
| Charlton Athletic | 46 | 16 | 11 | 19 | 52 | 66 | 59 | |
| West Bromwich Albion | 46 | 14 | 15 | 17 | 68 | 72 | 57 | |
| Oxford United | 46 | 16 | 9 | 21 | 64 | 68 | 57 | |
| Reading | 46 | 15 | 12 | 19 | 58 | 67 | 57 | |
| Swindon Town | 46 | 15 | 9 | 22 | 52 | 71 | 54 | |
| Huddersfield Town | 46 | 13 | 15 | 18 | 48 | 61 | 54 | |
| Bradford City | 46 | 12 | 12 | 22 | 47 | 72 | 48 | |
| Grimsby Town | 46 | 11 | 13 | 22 | 60 | 81 | 46 | R |
| Oldham Athletic | 46 | 10 | 13 | 23 | 51 | 66 | 43 | R |
| Southend | 46 | 8 | 15 | 23 | 42 | 86 | 39 | R |

Play-off final:   Crystal Palace v Sheffield United: 1-0 at Wembley Stadium.

# Nationwide League Division 2 1996-97

| | P | W | D | L | F | A | Pts | |
|---|---|---|---|---|---|---|---|---|
| Bury | 46 | 24 | 12 | 10 | 62 | 38 | 84 | P |
| Stockport County | 46 | 23 | 13 | 10 | 59 | 41 | 82 | P |
| Luton Town | 46 | 21 | 15 | 10 | 71 | 45 | 78 | |
| Brentford | 46 | 20 | 14 | 12 | 56 | 43 | 74 | |
| Bristol City | 46 | 21 | 10 | 15 | 69 | 51 | 73 | |
| Crewe Alexandra | 46 | 22 | 7 | 17 | 56 | 47 | 73 | P |

| | P | W | D | L | F | A | Pts | |
|---|---|---|---|---|---|---|---|---|
| Blackpool | 46 | 18 | 15 | 13 | 60 | 47 | 69 | |
| Wrexham | 46 | 17 | 18 | 11 | 54 | 50 | 69 | |
| Burnley | 46 | 19 | 11 | 16 | 71 | 55 | 68 | |
| Chesterfield | 46 | 18 | 14 | 14 | 42 | 39 | 68 | |
| Gillingham | 46 | 19 | 10 | 17 | 60 | 59 | 67 | |
| Walsall | 46 | 19 | 10 | 17 | 54 | 53 | 67 | |
| Watford | 46 | 16 | 19 | 11 | 45 | 38 | 67 | |
| Millwall | 46 | 16 | 13 | 17 | 50 | 55 | 61 | |
| Preston North End | 46 | 18 | 7 | 21 | 49 | 55 | 61 | |
| Bournemouth | 46 | 15 | 15 | 16 | 43 | 45 | 60 | |
| Bristol Rovers | 46 | 15 | 11 | 20 | 47 | 50 | 56 | |
| Wycombe Wanderers | 46 | 15 | 10 | 21 | 51 | 56 | 55 | |
| Plymouth Argyle | 46 | 12 | 18 | 16 | 47 | 58 | 54 | |
| York City | 46 | 13 | 13 | 20 | 47 | 68 | 52 | |
| Peterborough United | 46 | 11 | 14 | 21 | 55 | 73 | 47 | R |
| Shrewsbury Town | 46 | 11 | 13 | 22 | 49 | 74 | 46 | R |
| Rotherham | 46 | 7 | 14 | 25 | 39 | 70 | 35 | R |
| Notts County | 46 | 7 | 14 | 25 | 33 | 59 | 35 | R |

# Nationwide League Division 3 1996-97

| | P | W | D | L | F | A | Pts | |
|---|---|---|---|---|---|---|---|---|
| Wigan Athletic | 46 | 26 | 9 | 11 | 84 | 51 | 87 | P |
| Fulham | 46 | 25 | 12 | 9 | 72 | 38 | 87 | P |
| Carlisle United | 46 | 24 | 12 | 10 | 67 | 44 | 84 | P |
| Northampton Town | 46 | 20 | 12 | 14 | 67 | 44 | 72 | P |
| Swansea City | 46 | 21 | 8 | 17 | 62 | 58 | 71 | |
| Chester City | 46 | 18 | 16 | 12 | 55 | 43 | 70 | |
| Cardiff City | 46 | 20 | 9 | 17 | 56 | 54 | 69 | |
| Colchester United | 46 | 17 | 17 | 12 | 62 | 51 | 68 | |
| Lincoln City | 46 | 18 | 12 | 16 | 70 | 69 | 66 | |
| Cambridge United | 46 | 18 | 11 | 17 | 53 | 59 | 65 | |
| Mansfield Town | 46 | 16 | 16 | 14 | 47 | 45 | 64 | |
| Scarborough | 46 | 16 | 15 | 15 | 65 | 68 | 63 | |
| Scunthorpe | 46 | 18 | 9 | 19 | 59 | 62 | 63 | |
| Rochdale | 46 | 14 | 16 | 16 | 58 | 58 | 58 | |
| Barnet | 46 | 14 | 16 | 16 | 46 | 51 | 58 | |
| Leyton Orient | 46 | 15 | 12 | 19 | 50 | 58 | 57 | |
| Hull City | 46 | 13 | 18 | 15 | 44 | 50 | 57 | |
| Darlington | 46 | 14 | 10 | 22 | 64 | 78 | 52 | |
| Doncaster United | 46 | 14 | 10 | 22 | 52 | 66 | 52 | |
| Hartlepool | 46 | 14 | 9 | 23 | 53 | 66 | 51 | |
| Torquay United | 46 | 13 | 11 | 22 | 46 | 62 | 50 | |
| Exeter City | 46 | 12 | 12 | 22 | 48 | 73 | 48 | |
| Brighton & Hove Alb | 46 | 13 | 10 | 23 | 53 | 70 | 47 | |
| Hereford United | 46 | 11 | 14 | 21 | 50 | 65 | 47 | R |

# Club Guide

# Arsenal

THE MANAGER MAY have changed but the system that has made Arsenal such a wonderfully organised side in the past decade remains. Last season the Gunners possessed the Premiership's meanest defence – they conceded just 32 goals in their 38 Premiership matches.

What makes that all the more impressive is that they were without both skipper Tony Adams and David Seaman for eight and 14 games respectively. Both players are automatic selections not just for their team but also their country and it begs the question whether they might have had an even bigger say in the outcome of the Premier League title race last season if both had been fully fit.

Arsenal lost key games last year, not least to both Manchester United and Newcastle United at home – and both these sides denied them a place in the Champions' League for the 1997-98 season. Also Fortress Highbury simply failed to provide its normal invincibility – the Gunners lost four matches at their North London home – as many as they did on the road. More pointedly they also conceded more goals at home – 18 against 14 away – which could suggest that the days when teams defended in depth at Highbury have long gone. In truth this probably isn't the case, Arsenal's success last season, especially away from home was in playing a classic counter attack game soaking up pressure and then using the blinding pace of both Wright and Bergkamp to switch defence into offense.

But while the Gunners' defence remains ever tight because they have a system that works for them, their problem was their inability to provide important goals from other players when the flowing source of Ian Wright and Dennis Bergkamp dried up. Manager Arsène Wenger has been looking to right this with a series of high profile signings in the close season and the promise of more to come.

In 1996-97 Wenger kept faith with the wing-back system introduced by George Graham and continued, to a large extent, by Bruce Rioch. The Frenchman though is known to prefer a flat back-four system and this has been a feature of his previous sides, be it a 4-4-2 or 4-3-3 system.

What will not change is the scrooge-like nature of the Arsenal defence and you can take any of the regulars from here and place them in your fantasy team with the knowledge that they will almost certainly score you points on most weekends. Seaman, Adams and Keown will provide the base but whether Dixon or Winterburn will retain their places in even the medium term may be open to debate. The arrival of £1million teenager Mathew Upson from Luton Town and Gilles Grimandi from Monaco will increase pressure for places.

# Club Data File

## Responsibility

Top Scorers:   Ian Wright (23),
              Dennis Bergkamp (12)

Sent-Off:     Tony Adams (twice)
              Ian Wright, Dennis
              Bergkamp, John Hartson

## Usage 1996-97

Squad:        31 players used

Substitutes:  66 used, 124 not used

## Players 1996-97

Most Used Subs:   Ray Parlour (13),
                 Paul Shaw (7)

Most SNU:        John Lukic (20),

Mathew Rose † (12)

Most Subbed:   Dennis Bergkamp (8),
              John Hartson †(8),
              Stephen Hughes (6)

## Five Year Premiership Form

|       | P  | W  | D  | L  | F  | A  | Pts | Ps |
|-------|----|----|----|----|----|----|-----|----|
| 92-93 | 42 | 15 | 11 | 16 | 40 | 38 | 56  | 10 |
| 93-94 | 42 | 18 | 17 | 7  | 53 | 28 | 71  | 4  |
| 94-95 | 42 | 13 | 12 | 17 | 52 | 49 | 51  | 12 |
| 95-96 | 38 | 17 | 12 | 9  | 49 | 32 | 63  | 5  |
| 96-97 | 38 | 19 | 11 | 8  | 62 | 32 | 68  | 3  |

**Key**
SNU = Subs Not Used
† No longer with club
PWDLFA in *italics* denotes Football League.

In midfield Patrick Vieira was one of the finds of last season and provides the perfect link between defence and attack – don't expect too many goals though. Indeed goals from the middle of the pitch has been one of the problems facing the Gunners in recent seasons. Just 17 from recognised midfield players in 1996-97.

It is up front where Arsenal will continue to win. One can't help think that if Ian Wright curbed his temper and was available to play in all Arsenal matches, that he would be challenging Alan Shearer for top scorer in the Premier League every season. Wrighty came close last season but only because Shearer suffered with an injury. Bergkamp was the Gunners' best player last term and may well eclipse his performances in the 1997-98 season, not least because he was joined by former club-mate and fellow Dutch international Marc Overmars. Blindingly fast and with a great touch, he has suffered with injuries but looks to have recovered. Someone said to me that the injury had lost him a yard of pace. My reply was that he was now only two yards faster than most other players.

# Arsène Wenger

With less than a season in charge at Highbury Arsène Wenger has already set about establishing himself as one of the most respected and innovative managers in the Premiership. He has won respect wherever he has been in charge and was the mentor of England coach Glenn Hoddle. He never really made an impact as a player playing in lower leagues being joining division one club Strasbourg at the age of 29.

Having gained a degree in Economics he joined Strasbourg as youth coach and moved up to the reserve team before leaving to take control at Nancy – via a spell at Cannes – to become the youngest manager in France. His exploits took him to Monaco where he won the championship and had success in various cups. He turned down Bayern Munich to join J-League club Grampus Eight and after two seasons moved to Highbury.

# Arsenal v Record

| Opponents | 92/3 | 93/4 | 94/5 | 95/6 | 96/7 | P | W | D | L | F | A | Pts | % |
|---|---|---|---|---|---|---|---|---|---|---|---|---|---|
| Aston Villa | 0-1 | 1-2 | 0-0 | 2-0 | 2-2 | 5 | 1 | 2 | 2 | 5 | 5 | 5 | 33.33 |
| Barnsley | - | - | - | - | - | 0 | 0 | 0 | 0 | 0 | 0 | 0 | 0.00 |
| Blackburn Rovers | 0-1 | 1-0 | 0-0 | 0-0 | 1-1 | 5 | 1 | 3 | 1 | 2 | 2 | 6 | 40.00 |
| Bolton Wanderers | - | - | - | 2-1 | - | 1 | 1 | 0 | 0 | 2 | 1 | 3 | 100.00 |
| Chelsea | 2-1 | 1-0 | 3-1 | 1-1 | 3-3 | 5 | 3 | 2 | 0 | 10 | 6 | 11 | 73.33 |
| Coventry City | 3-0 | 0-3 | 2-1 | 1-1 | 0-0 | 5 | 2 | 2 | 1 | 6 | 5 | 8 | 53.33 |
| Crystal Palace | 3-0 | - | 1-2 | - | - | 2 | 1 | 0 | 1 | 4 | 2 | 3 | 50.00 |
| Derby County | - | - | - | - | 2-2 | 1 | 0 | 1 | 0 | 2 | 2 | 1 | 33.33 |
| Everton | 2-0 | 2-0 | 1-1 | 1-2 | 3-1 | 5 | 3 | 1 | 1 | 9 | 4 | 10 | 66.67 |
| Leeds United | 0-0 | 2-1 | 1-3 | 2-1 | 3-0 | 5 | 3 | 1 | 1 | 8 | 5 | 10 | 66.67 |
| Leicester City | - | - | 1-1 | - | 2-0 | 2 | 1 | 1 | 0 | 3 | 1 | 4 | 66.67 |
| Liverpool | 0-1 | 1-0 | 0-1 | 0-0 | 1-2 | 5 | 1 | 1 | 3 | 2 | 4 | 4 | 26.67 |
| Manchester United | 0-1 | 2-2 | 0-0 | 1-0 | 1-2 | 5 | 1 | 2 | 2 | 4 | 5 | 5 | 33.33 |
| Newcastle United | - | - | 2-1 | 2-3 | 2-0 | 0-1 | 4 | 2 | 0 | 2 | 6 | 5 | 6 | 50.00 |
| Sheffield Wednesday | 2-1 | 1-0 | 0-0 | 4-2 | 4-1 | 5 | 4 | 1 | 0 | 11 | 4 | 13 | 86.67 |
| Southampton | 4-3 | 1-0 | 1-1 | 4-2 | 3-1 | 5 | 4 | 1 | 0 | 13 | 7 | 13 | 86.67 |
| Tottenham Hotspur | 1-3 | 1-1 | 1-1 | 0-0 | 3-1 | 5 | 1 | 3 | 1 | 6 | 6 | 6 | 40.00 |
| West Ham United | - | 0-2 | 0-1 | 1-0 | 2-0 | 4 | 2 | 0 | 2 | 3 | 3 | 6 | 50.00 |
| Wimbledon | 0-1 | 1-1 | 0-0 | 1-3 | 0-1 | 5 | 0 | 2 | 3 | 2 | 6 | 2 | 13.33 |
| Totals | | | | | | 101 | 44 | 35 | 22 | 143 | 90 | 167 | 55.12 |

## Transfers In and Out

| Mth | Player | Signed From | Fee | Notes |
|---|---|---|---|---|
| Aug-96 | Patrick Vieira | Milan | £3,500,000 | |
| Aug-96 | Remi Garde | Strasbourg | Free | |
| Jan-97 | Nicolas Anelka | Paris St Germain | Undisclosed | |
| Mar-97 | Alex Manninger | Casino Salzburg | £500,000 | |
| May-97 | Mathew Upson | Luton Town | £1,200,000 | Rising to £2,000,000 |
| Jun-97 | Marc Overmars | Ajax | £7,000,000 | |
| Jun-97 | Emmanuel Petit | Monaco | £3,000,000 | |
| Jun-97 | Gilles Grimandi | Monaco | £2,000,000 | |
| Jun-97 | Luis Bo Morte | Sporting Lisbon | £1,750,000 | |
| Jun-97 | Alberto Mendez | FC Feucht (Germany) | £200,000 | |

| Mth | Player | Signed For | Fee | Notes |
|---|---|---|---|---|
| Aug-96 | Paul Dickov | Manchester City | £1,000,000 | |
| Aug-96 | Chris Coffey | Crewe Alexandra | Free | |
| Oct-96 | Eddie McGoldrick | Manchester City | £300,000 | |
| Oct-96 | Mark Flatts | Watford | Monthly Contract | |
| Nov-96 | David Hillier | Portsmouth | £250,000 | |
| Dec-96 | Noel Imber | Woking | Free | |
| Jan-97 | Andy Linighan | Crystal Palace | £110,000 | |
| Jan-97 | Paul Read | Wycombe Wanderers | £35,000 | |
| Feb-97 | John Hartson | West Ham United | £3,200,000 | Could rise to £5,000,000 |
| Mar-97 | Steve Morrow | QPR | £500,000 | |
| May-97 | Mathew Rose | QPR | £500,000 | |
| Jun-97 | Paul Merson | Middlesbrough | £5,000,000 | |
| Jun-97 | Lee Harper | QPR | £125,000 | Rising to £250,000 |

# Aston Villa

WINNING THE Coca Cola Cup, reaching the semi-finals of the FA Cup and a rise of 14 places in the Premiership was always going to be a tough act for Brian Little's Aston Villa side to follow and, with early exits from all the cup competitions, it could be argued that, in many respects, the 1996-97 campaign was a disappointing time for the club. However, dig deeper into the facts and you see that a year of consolidation was also a year of building for Villa.

In defence they had the second best record in the Premiership and the players here performed with outstanding ability. Attack though was a different matter altogether with just 47 goals and only two of their strike-force into double figures. The arrival of Stan, The Man, Collymore will provide other options and presumably more goals.

It was the central back-three for Villa though that were simply outstanding throughout with Ugo Ehiogu, like wing-back Alan Wright, playing in every minute of every game, and big fantasy points earners throughout the season. Gareth Southgate, again with injury problems, missed a third of the season but his team conceded just six goals when he was absent. Perhaps the real revelation was the encouraging development of Riccardo Scimeca who provided excellent cover in the centre of defence. This could be his year to make the final breakthrough and he may have a cheap valuation as such.

Eighteen clean sheets was an excellent record, especially given that the goal keeping honours were shared by Mark Bosnich and Michael Oakes and it may not be a foregone conclusion that Bosnich will always have the nod for the number one position during the season. Of the two buys Little made at the start of 1996-97, Fernando Nelson was the most successful playing as a wing-back.

In midfield much was promised but it didn't quiet live up to the expectations of the previous season. Mark Draper – an important player for Villa – never really got going and failed to score the sort of goals he did at Leicester. Ian Taylor was one of the real unsung heroes of Villa last year, quietly turning in point scoring performances throughout. It might have been the arrival of Sasa Curcic, seen as a threat to his place, that was an ignition factor. Curcic though couldn't hold down a first team place and may be under pressure himself since the arrival of Collymore and with Taylor in good form. The evergreen Andy Townsend added his usual grafting stability but these three players contributed just four goals to the Villa cause.

# Club Data File

## Responsibility

Top Scorers:  Dwight Yorke (17),
              Savo Milosevic (9)

Sent-Off:     Mark Draper,
              Steve Staunton

## Usage 1996-97

Squad:        25 players used

Substitutes:  54 used, 136 not used

## Players 1996-97

Most Used Subs:   Julian Joachim (12),
                  Tommy Johnson (10)

Most SNU:     Julian Joachim (21),
              Scott Oakes (17),
              Gareth Farrelly (15)

Most Subbed:  Sasa Curcic (10),
              Mark Draper (10),
              Savo Milosevic (8)

## Five Year Premiership Form

|       | P  | W  | D  | L  | F  | A  | Pts | Ps |
|-------|----|----|----|----|----|----|-----|----|
| 92-93 | 42 | 21 | 11 | 10 | 57 | 40 | 74  | 2  |
| 93-94 | 42 | 15 | 12 | 15 | 46 | 50 | 57  | 10 |
| 94-95 | 42 | 11 | 15 | 16 | 51 | 56 | 48  | 18 |
| 95-96 | 38 | 18 | 9  | 11 | 52 | 35 | 63  | 4  |
| 96-97 | 38 | 17 | 10 | 11 | 47 | 34 | 61  | 5  |

Will Brian Little go for a three-striker attack is the question. Dwight Yorke will certainly get the nod – a superbly skilful player who might have had more than his 17 Premiership goals had he not had to wait until the end of September to get going. The powerful Collymore looks an ideal foil for the quick and nimble Yorke and, despite his much published problems at Liverpool, he still managed 12 goals in his 30 appearances to finish second top scorer at Anfield.

# Brian Little

Brian Little has helped transform Villa in recent seasons. Having played for the club during the previous decade and won full England recognition, he made some of his first steps into coaching as Middlesbrough's youth team coach. After a brief time in charge at Wolves he moved onto Darlington where he saw them go out of the Football League and then bounce straight back as Conference champions.

His reputation was enhanced as manager at Leicester City when he won promotion to the Premiership before a somewhat controversial move to Villa Park in November 1994. Having guided them to a Coca-Cola Cup win in 1996, he is one of those managers who always calls it as it is and rarely makes excuses.

But where does that leave Milosevic? A prolific goalscorer while in his native Belgrade, he is certainly gifted but, despite finding himself in great positions, often fails to deliver. After two seasons in England he has the experience of the games and should he rediscover a more consistent touch in front of goal he would be worthy of consideration. It remains a question mark though and of the three Villa central striker he must be seen as the odd-one out. Much the same can be said of Julian Joachim who promised so much – but Joachim is a regular squad player and has youth on his side. This is a big season for both players and one might spark.

# Aston Villa v Record

| Opponents | 92/3 | 93/4 | 94/5 | 95/6 | 96/7 | P | W | D | L | F | A | Pts | % |
|---|---|---|---|---|---|---|---|---|---|---|---|---|---|
| Arsenal | 1-0 | 1-2 | 0-4 | 1-1 | 2-2 | 5 | 1 | 2 | 2 | 5 | 9 | 5 | 33.33 |
| Barnsley | - | - | - | - | - | 0 | 0 | 0 | 0 | 0 | 0 | 0 | 0.00 |
| Blackburn Rovers | 0-0 | 0-1 | 0-1 | 2-0 | 1-0 | 5 | 2 | 1 | 2 | 3 | 2 | 7 | 46.67 |
| Bolton Wanderers | - | - | - | 1-0 | | 1 | 1 | 0 | 0 | 1 | 0 | 3 | 100.00 |
| Chelsea | 1-3 | 1-0 | 3-0 | 0-1 | 0-2 | 5 | 2 | 0 | 3 | 5 | 6 | 6 | 40.00 |
| Coventry City | 0-0 | 0-0 | 0-0 | 4-1 | 2-1 | 5 | 2 | 3 | 0 | 6 | 2 | 9 | 60.00 |
| Crystal Palace | 3-0 | - | 1-1 | - | | 2 | 1 | 1 | 0 | 4 | 1 | 4 | 66.67 |
| Derby | - | - | - | - | 2-0 | 1 | 1 | 0 | 0 | 2 | 0 | 3 | 100.00 |
| Everton | 2-1 | 0-0 | 0-0 | 1-0 | 3-1 | 5 | 3 | 2 | 0 | 6 | 2 | 11 | 73.33 |
| Leeds United | 1-1 | 1-0 | 0-0 | 3-0 | 2-0 | 5 | 3 | 2 | 0 | 7 | 1 | 11 | 73.33 |
| Leicester City | - | - | 4-4 | - | 1-3 | 2 | 0 | 1 | 1 | 5 | 7 | 1 | 16.67 |
| Liverpool | 4-2 | 2-1 | 2-0 | 0-2 | 1-0 | 5 | 4 | 0 | 1 | 9 | 5 | 12 | 80.00 |
| Manchester United | 1-0 | 1-2 | 1-2 | 3-1 | 0-0 | 5 | 2 | 1 | 2 | 6 | 5 | 7 | 46.67 |
| Newcastle United | - | 0-2 | 0-2 | 1-1 | 2-2 | 4 | 0 | 2 | 2 | 3 | 7 | 2 | 16.67 |
| Sheffield Wednesday | 2-0 | 2-2 | 1-1 | 3-2 | 0-1 | 5 | 2 | 2 | 1 | 8 | 6 | 8 | 53.33 |
| Southampton | 1-1 | 0-2 | 1-1 | 3-0 | 1-0 | 5 | 2 | 2 | 1 | 6 | 4 | 8 | 53.33 |
| Tottenham Hotspur | 0-0 | 1-0 | 1-0 | 2-1 | 1-1 | 5 | 3 | 2 | 0 | 5 | 2 | 11 | 73.33 |
| West Ham United | - | 3-1 | 0-2 | 1-1 | 0-0 | 4 | 1 | 2 | 1 | 4 | 4 | 5 | 41.67 |
| Wimbledon | 1-0 | 0-1 | 7-1 | 2-0 | 5-0 | 5 | 4 | 0 | 1 | 15 | 2 | 12 | 80.00 |
| Totals | | | | | | 101 | 49 | 29 | 23 | 145 | 86 | 176 | 58.09 |

## Transfers In and Out

| Mth | Player | Signed From | Fee | Notes |
|---|---|---|---|---|
| Aug-96 | Sasa Curcic | Bolton Wanderers | £4,000,000 | |
| May-97 | Stan Collymore | Liverpool | £7,000,000 | |
| Jun-97 | Simon Grayson | Leicester City | £1,350,000 | |

| Mth | Player | Signed For | Fee | Notes |
|---|---|---|---|---|
| Sep-96 | Andrew Mitchell | Chesterfield | Non-Contract | |
| Oct-96 | Paul McGrath | Derby County | £100,000 | Rising to £200,000 |
| Oct-96 | Franz Carr | Reggiana | Free | |
| Mar-97 | Carl Tiler | Sheffield United | £650,000 | |
| Mar-97 | Phil King | Swindon Town | Free | |
| Jun-97 | Gareth Farrelly | Everton | £700,000 | |

# Barnsley

WITH JUST ONE win from their last ten games of the 1995-96 season, Barnsley were few people's tip for promotion in 1996-97, but it happened and the Tykes become the 24th club to have featured in the Premier League.

The pre-season started with Danny Wilson releasing nine players and drafting in six, although only one, Matt Appleby, cost the Yorkshire club a fee. Wilson's starting line-up for the first Division One fixture of the season saw seven changes from the one which ended the 1995-96 season and the impact was immediate as a succession of results stormed Barnsley to the top of the Nationwide League. The League Managers Association voted Wilson their Manager of the Year in May and he will be hoping that his close season buys – which include many players who will be unknown to most footballing fans – can repeat the business at the start of the 1997-98 season.

Selecting players from any newly promoted team is difficult, especially when the team have never played in the Premier League before. It is also made more difficult when virtually unknown foreign players are drafted in. In many respects you are taking a chance and a gamble – but that is what managers do when they set about building a team for a new challenge. Ask Danny Wilson!

However a couple of Barnsley's campaign last season featured players with some Premiership experience. The arrival of the Foreign Legion at Middlesbrough was the Tykes' gain in that they picked up John Hendrie for a song, and he went on to score 15 times in 36 appearances. Paul Wilkinson also arrived from Teeside on a free transfer and missed just one game, contributing nine goals. However, both these players failed to feature with any significance in the 1995-96 Middlesbrough side, a fact that ultimately lead to their departure for Oakwell. Will Danny Wilson keep faith in them or will he blood one of his new signings instead? Georgi Hristov has arrived from Partizan Belgrade, having helped his club to a third successive championship. Just 21-years old, Barnsley paid £1.5 million for his services – a club record – and it can't have been for him to sit on the bench. Expect his partner to be either Hendrie or Wilkinson.

In midfield Barnsley have a powerhouse in Neil Redfearn, who finished as the club's top-scorer with 17 goals from 43 games – six from the spot (the fourth consecutive season he has reached double figures). That record alone should ensure him his place in the side  and expect him to line up alongside another new signing – Mark Tinkler. A

# Club Data File

## Responsibility

Top Scorers: Neil Redfearn (17), John Hendrie (15)

Sent off: Darren Sheridan

## Usage 1996-97

Squad: 21 players used

Substitutes: 64 used, 76 not used

## Players 1996-97

Most Used Subs: Martin Bullock (23), Clint Marcelle (13), Andy Liddle (13)

Most SNU: Jovo Bosancic (20), Martin Bullock (15), Andy Liddell (9)

Most Subbed: Andy Liddle (10), Clint Marcelle (10), Jovo Bosancic (9)

## Five Year Premiership Form

| | P | W | D | L | F | A | Pts | Ps |
|---|---|---|---|---|---|---|---|---|
| 92-93 | 46 | 17 | 9 | 20 | 56 | 60 | 60 | 13 |
| 93-94 | 46 | 16 | 7 | 23 | 55 | 67 | 55 | 18 |
| 94-95 | 46 | 20 | 12 | 14 | 63 | 52 | 72 | 6 |
| 95-96 | 46 | 14 | 18 | 14 | 60 | 66 | 60 | 10 |
| 96-97 | 46 | 22 | 14 | 10 | 76 | 55 | 80 | 2 |

*all games in Football League.*

South African international, Eric Tinkler plays in the Paul Ince mould and should make a big impact in Yorkshire. Clint Marcelle could be another player to hold his own in the Premiership.

# Danny Wilson

Voted Manager of the Year by his peers in May 1997, Wilson will surely be worthy of the vote again if he has secured Barnsley's status in the Premiership come the end of 1997-98. His success is all the more remarkable given that the Barnsley job is the first time he has occupied the hot-seat. Originally in the role of player/manager, Wilson moved to Oakwell from Sheffield Wednesday for £200,000 in the summer of 1993 and played close on a hundred games in the Tykes' midfield.

Having started his playing career at Wigan, he joined Bury on a free transfer and went to Hillsborough via Chesterfield, Forest, Scunthorpe, Brighton and Luton, making over a century of appearances for all these clubs bar Forest and Scunthorpe United.

At the back Ales Krizan will be challenging for his place since his close season arrival from Marimor Branik. A Slovakian international, he could partner Arjan De Zeeuw who was a near ever-present last season. Matt Appleby is another option and may feature as a sweeper or as part of a central back three.

Nick Eaden has been Barnsley's most consistent performer in recent years and the right-back position is pretty much his own property. He featured in all 46 Nationwide League games last year just like goalkeeper Dave Watson, who managed 17 clean sheets last season. That will be a lot more difficult in 1997-98 but he will be an important member of the squad.

Other squad members to watch out for include Martin Bullock, Andy Liddle and Jovo Bosanovic. Other than that, the two key players for Barnsley who should certainly be considered for your team are Neil Redfearn and Mark Tinkler.

# Barnsley v Record

First season in the Premiership for Barnsley, therefore they have no Premier League record against any of the clubs they will face this season.

## Transfers In and Out

| Mth | Player | Signed From | Fee | Notes |
|---|---|---|---|---|
| Oct-96 | John Hendrie | Middlesbrough | £250,000 | |
| Dec-96 | Shaun Dennis | Raith | Trial | |
| Feb-97 | Steve Tweed | Hibs | Trial | |
| Mar-97 | Tony Bullock | Leek Town | £20,000 | |
| Jun-97 | Georgi Hristov | Partizan Belgrade | £1,500,000 | |
| Jun-97 | Eric Tinkler | Cagliari | £650,000 | |
| Jun-97 | Ales Krizan | Maribor Branik | £450,000 | |
| Jun-97 | Lars Lees | Bayer Leverkusen | £250,000 | |

| Mth | Player | Signed For | Fee | Notes |
|---|---|---|---|---|
| Aug-96 | Brendan O'Connell | Charlton | £125,000 | |
| Mar-97 | Glynn Hurst | Notts Co | Trial | |

# Blackburn Rovers

HAVING SPENT millions on creating a Premiership winning side, Blackburn Rovers' fans saw it all but fall away with the departure of just one player – Alan Shearer. As the England skipper became the world's most expensive player at that time, he took with him the main bulk of the Rovers' goals. The first player to 100 Premiership goals, and thirty plus with them each year, he was a very hard act to follow.

The other half of the SAS act was still ready to go on stage though and Chris Sutton has seemingly fully recovered from the injury problems that beset him the previous year. His 11 goals in just 25 games was just about 25% of the team's goals. Indeed last season was almost a regeneration of the Rovers' forward line with Kevin Gallacher hopefully recovered fully from two broken legs and just a goal behind Sutton from his 36 games. With the added boost of Scotland caps, Gallacher, and indeed Sutton, could prove a valuable source of fantasy points at a respectable cost.

With Shearer gone, the backbone of the side centred around goalkeeper Tim Flowers and centre-half Colin Hendry. Flowers, with a recall to the England squad, continues to be a top performer. Although he missed just two games last season, this was his longest spell out and, along with Everton's Neville Southall, he heads the list of all-time Premier League appearances – 195 from a possible 202.

Hendry turned in some fine performances in the middle and Graeme Le Saux came back from his long injury lay-off. Le Saux was soon back to form and scoring fantasy points and, while his future at the club is the continual subject of debate, he will be an automatic choice wherever he goes. Hendry will be looking to recapture that championship winning form as soon as possible and that may be on the cards following an operation on a long-term groin injury during the close season.

In fact consistency, or rather the lack of it, in performance was one of the major factors in Blackburn's season. Last season's new boy from Greece George Donis possesses amazing speed but couldn't establish himself in a side which at last saw the return of Jason Wilcox from his lay-off. Stuart Ripley continues to remain an enigma that might be re-vitalised under new managership.

A full season will have helped Gary Flitcroft bed in while Graham Fenton will be looking to have more involvement this time around. They might be interesting and cost efficient buys.

Blackburn, who were for so long in real danger of being relegated, survived largely on their home form having managed just one win on the road – at

# Club Data File

## Responsibility

Top Scorers:  Chris Sutton (11),
Kevin Gallacher (10)

Sent-Off:  Tim Sherwood

## Usage 1996-97

Players:  26 players used

Substitutes:  60 used, 130 not used

## Players 1996-97

Most Used Subs:  George Donis (11),
Graham Fenton (8),
Stuart Ripley (8)

Most SNU:  Shay Given (36),
Nicky Marker (22)

Most Subbed:  Kevin Gallacher (10),
Garry Flitcroft (8),
Per Pedersen (8)

## Five Year Premiership Form

|  | P | W | D | L | F | A | Pts | Ps |
|---|---|---|---|---|---|---|---|---|
| 92-93 | 42 | 20 | 11 | 11 | 68 | 46 | 71 | 4 |
| 93-94 | 42 | 25 | 9 | 8 | 63 | 36 | 84 | 2 |
| 94-95 | 42 | 27 | 8 | 7 | 80 | 39 | 89 | 1 |
| 95-96 | 38 | 18 | 7 | 13 | 61 | 47 | 61 | 7 |
| 96-97 | 38 | 9 | 15 | 14 | 42 | 43 | 42 | 13 |

# Roy Hodgson

Roy Hodgson created a name for himself on the continent despite being almost unknown in his home country, England. In fact it is doubtful many fans will have heard of him before he took Switzerland through to the World Cup finals in the USA in 1994.

Hodgson did in fact spend two years in charge at Bristol in the early Eighties, sandwiched in between spells in Sweden where he managed Halmstads, Obebro and Malmo.

In 1990 he moved to Switzerland and to a position with Xamax Neuchatel before being offered, and accepting, the Swiss national job in 1995. His success ultimately saw him move to Italy and a degree of success with Internazionale. But after 15 years on the road, Blackburn will benefit from his knowledge of the game and also from the fact that he is a manager known to some of the world's leading stars.

Everton on New Year's Day. After a season in which they have had to soldier in the knowledge that a new guy was on his way – although it was never quiet clear who it would be for a long period – Rovers have at last got their man, even if he wasn't their first choice.

A fully fit defence will help their cause and Flowers, Le Saux and Hendry will be expensive but good points-earning buys, as will most of the team's rearguard. Up front the SAS will be altered to the GAS where Gallacher and Sutton might find new team-mates joining them. The midfield still misses David Batty and might well be the weak link.

New manager Roy Hodgson will surely put the Blackburn boat in order and will no doubt be looking to add some talent of his own. With this in mind it might be worth only considering players who are sure to be in the side – those fringe players who might be tempting as potential come-gooders might be the ones to suffer.

# Blackburn Rovers v Record

| Opponents | 92/3 | 93/4 | 94/5 | 95/6 | 96/7 | P | W | D | L | F | A | Pts | % |
|---|---|---|---|---|---|---|---|---|---|---|---|---|---|
| Arsenal | 1-0 | 1-1 | 3-1 | 1-1 | 0-2 | 5 | 2 | 2 | 1 | 6 | 5 | 8 | 53.33 |
| Aston Villa | 3-0 | 1-0 | 3-1 | 1-1 | 0-2 | 5 | 3 | 1 | 1 | 8 | 4 | 10 | 66.67 |
| Barnsley | - | - | - | - | - | 0 | 0 | 0 | 0 | 0 | 0 | 0 | 0.00 |
| Bolton Wanderers | - | - | - | 3-1 | | 1 | 1 | 0 | 0 | 3 | 1 | 3 | 100.00 |
| Chelsea | 2-0 | 2-0 | 2-1 | 3-0 | 1-1 | 5 | 4 | 1 | 0 | 10 | 2 | 13 | 86.67 |
| Coventry City | 2-5 | 2-1 | 4-0 | 5-1 | 4-0 | 5 | 4 | 0 | 1 | 17 | 7 | 12 | 80.00 |
| Crystal Palace | 1-2 | - | 2-1 | - | | 2 | 1 | 0 | 1 | 3 | 3 | 3 | 50.00 |
| Derby County | - | - | - | - | 1-2 | 1 | 0 | 0 | 1 | 1 | 2 | 0 | 0.00 |
| Everton | 2-3 | 2-0 | 3-0 | 0-3 | 1-1 | 5 | 2 | 1 | 2 | 8 | 7 | 7 | 46.67 |
| Leeds United | 3-1 | 2-1 | 1-1 | 1-0 | 0-1 | 5 | 3 | 1 | 1 | 7 | 4 | 10 | 66.67 |
| Leicester City | - | - | 3-0 | - | 2-4 | 2 | 1 | 0 | 1 | 5 | 4 | 3 | 50.00 |
| Liverpool | 4-1 | 2-0 | 3-2 | 2-3 | 3-0 | 5 | 4 | 0 | 1 | 14 | 6 | 12 | 80.00 |
| Manchester United | 0-0 | 2-0 | 2-4 | 1-2 | 2-3 | 5 | 1 | 1 | 3 | 7 | 9 | 4 | 26.67 |
| Newcastle United | - | 1-0 | 1-0 | 2-1 | 1-0 | 4 | 4 | 0 | 0 | 5 | 1 | 12 | 100.00 |
| Sheffield Wednesday | 1-0 | 1-1 | 3-1 | 3-0 | 4-1 | 5 | 4 | 1 | 0 | 12 | 3 | 13 | 86.67 |
| Southampton | 0-0 | 2-0 | 3-2 | 2-1 | 2-1 | 5 | 4 | 1 | 0 | 9 | 4 | 13 | 86.67 |
| Tottenham Hotspur | 0-2 | 1-0 | 2-0 | 2-1 | 0-2 | 5 | 3 | 0 | 2 | 5 | 5 | 9 | 60.00 |
| West Ham United | - | 0-2 | 4-2 | 4-2 | 2-1 | 4 | 3 | 0 | 1 | 10 | 7 | 9 | 75.00 |
| Wimbledon | 0-0 | 3-0 | 2-1 | 3-2 | 3-1 | 5 | 4 | 1 | 0 | 11 | 4 | 13 | 86.67 |
| Totals | | | | | | 101 | 66 | 17 | 18 | 195 | 92 | 215 | 70.96 |

## Transfers In and Out

| Mth | Player | Signed From | Fee | Notes |
|---|---|---|---|---|
| Feb-97 | Per Pedersen | OB | £2,500,000 | |

| Mth | Player | Signed For | Fee | Notes |
|---|---|---|---|---|
| Aug-96 | Michael Holt | Preston NE | Free | |
| Aug-96 | Bobby Mimms | Crystal Palace | Non-Contract | |
| Feb-97 | Richard Hope | Darlington | Free | |
| May-97 | Shay Given | Newcastle United | Tribunal | |

# Bolton Wanderers

PROMOTION, RELEGATION, promotion. Bolton Wanderers go into the 1997-98 season hoping to break the sequence and establish themselves as a team worthy of a place in the Premier League. They, of the three promoted sides, have the recent experience both in management and in players. And of course they will start the season in a magnificent new stadium on the outskirts of Horwich.

After dropping out of the Premiership at the end of the 1995-96 season, manager Colin Todd parted with two of the side's most wanted players, with the sale of Sasa Curcic to Aston Villa and Alan Stubbs to Celtic for a combined fee of £7.5 million. Around £2.5 million of that income was used to entice Michael Johansen and Per Frandsen to Burnden Park from Copenhagen.

Apart from that there was little tinkering with a side that was about to set off and score 100 remarkable goals in the Nationwide League and become runaway champions with five games to spare. Indeed only a last minute equaliser by Tranmere prevented Bolton breaking 100 points for the season as well.

Up front it was the dynamic duo of John McGinlay and Nathan Blake who went on to share 43 league goals. Scottish international McGinlay claimed 24 for himself in 43 games. It was a welcome

bonus for the striker who had managed just six goals in that relegation season of 1995-96 – and Blake managed just one in his 18 games. A full season together has clearly benefited both and they will need to be watched during 1997-98.

At the back it was the vastly experienced Chris Fairclough around whom Todd built his team. Fairclough was an ever-present and also weighed in with eight goals of his own, which is very impressive for a centre half and many more goals than he scored in a season while at Nottingham Forest, Leeds United and Tottenham Hotspur. Goals though have always come relatively easily for Fairclough, who managed 23 in nearly 200 appearances for Leeds.

Although Keith Branagan featured in the majority of Bolton's league games, and has proved a brave and reliable number one for Wanderers in recent years, he may find his position between the sticks challenged by Gavin Ward, who featured in 10 of Bolton's games when the Republic of Ireland international was injured. He proved a more than adequate replacement and is waiting in the wings.

At the time of writing, Bolton look to be losing the services of Gundi Bergsson and this may force Todd into the transfer market or to revert to a more traditional flat back four with Gerry Taggart playing

# Club Data File

## Responsibility

Top Scorers:  John McGinlay (24),
Nathan Blake (19)

Sent Off:  Nathan Blake, Keith
Branagan, Gerry Taggart

## Usage 1996-97

Squad:  23 players used

Substitutes:  64 used, 76 not used

## Players 1996-97

Most Used Subs:  Dave Lee (12),
Andy Todd (9),
Scott Taylor (9)

Most SNU:  Scott Taylor (13),
Andy Todd (10),
Michael Johansen (8)

Most Subbed:  Michael Johansen (11),
Per Frandsen (8),
Scott Sellars (7)

## Five Year Premiership Form

|       | P  | W  | D  | L  | F   | A  | Pts | Ps |
|-------|----|----|----|----|-----|----|-----|----|
| 92-93 | 46 | 27 | 9  | 10 | 80  | 41 | 90  | 2  |
| 93-94 | 46 | 16 | 7  | 23 | 63  | 64 | 59  | 14 |
| 94-95 | 42 | 20 | 12 | 14 | 67  | 45 | 77  | 3  |
| 95-96 | 38 | 8  | 5  | 25 | 39  | 71 | 29  | 20 |
| 96-97 | 46 | 28 | 14 | 4  | 100 | 53 | 98  | 1  |

*Football League seasons in italics*

alongside Fairclough. Taggart only missed a few games last season and has the experience to form a strong backbone with Fairclough. Watch out too for Steve McAnespie, who had his 1996-97 limited

## Colin Todd

As a player Colin Todd ranked amongst the best, especially when he played under the guidance of Brain Clough at Derby County. A skilful defender who was cool and composed on the ball, he will require those three attributes on the managerial bench during the 1997-98 campaign.

Todd formed a lengthy managerial partnership as assistant to Bruce Rioch although he had held the reins himself for a while at Middlesbrough before renewing his ties with Rioch at Bolton. After Rioch left for Arsenal, Todd took on the role in tandem with Roy McFarland before being given the job outright and leading Bolton to the championship. The 1997-98 season will be his first in sole charge of a Premiership club.

by injury, and Bryan Small.

Frandsen, Lee, Sellars and Jamie Pollock could well form the basis of the Bolton midfield and the last two have good Premiership experience. Indeed Sellars had an outstanding season and knows from his time at Blackburn and Newcastle what it takes to succeed in the top division. John Sheridan may also get his chance to revitalise his Premiership credentials, having joined the club from Sheffield Wednesday mid-way through last season. While McGinlay and Blake were top scorers, Alan Thompson also helped himself to 11 goals in 34 games from the left side and this may ensure that he is first in the midfield pecking order when Todd makes his first selections.

The gap between the Premier League and Nationwide League can be a big one to bridge, a fact that many teams have experienced to their dismay in recent years. However, Derby County and Leicester City have proved it can be traversed and Bolton will be looking to do it this time around but will need their key players to maintain their Nationwide championship winning form.

# Bolton Wanderers v Record

| Opponents | 92/3 | 93/4 | 94/5 | 95/6 | 96/7 | P | W | D | L | F | A | Pts | % |
|---|---|---|---|---|---|---|---|---|---|---|---|---|---|
| Arsenal | - | - | - | 1-0 | - | 1 | 1 | 0 | 0 | 1 | 0 | 3 | 100.00 |
| Aston Villa | - | - | - | 0-2 | - | 1 | 0 | 0 | 1 | 0 | 2 | 0 | 0.00 |
| Barnsley | - | - | - | - | - | 0 | 0 | 0 | 0 | 0 | 0 | 0 | 0.00 |
| Blackburn Rovers | - | - | - | 2-1 | - | 1 | 1 | 0 | 0 | 2 | 1 | 3 | 100.00 · |
| Chelsea | - | - | - | 2-1 | - | 1 | 1 | 0 | 0 | 2 | 1 | 3 | 100.00 |
| Coventry City | - | - | - | 1-2 | - | 1 | 0 | 0 | 1 | 1 | 2 | 0 | 0.00 |
| Crystal Palace | - | - | - | - | - | 0 | 0 | 0 | 0 | 0 | 0 | 0 | 0.00 |
| Derby County | - | - | - | - | - | 0 | 0 | 0 | 0 | 0 | 0 | 0 | 0.00 |
| Everton | - | - | - | 1-1 | - | 1 | 0 | 1 | 0 | 1 | 1 | 1 | 33.33 |
| Leeds United | - | - | - | 0-2 | - | 1 | 0 | 0 | 1 | 0 | 2 | 0 | 0.00 |
| Leicester City | - | - | - | - | - | 0 | 0 | 0 | 0 | 0 | 0 | 0 | 0.00 |
| Liverpool | - | - | - | 0-1 | - | 1 | 0 | 0 | 1 | 0 | 1 | 0 | 0.00 |
| Manchester United | - | - | - | 0-6 | - | 1 | 0 | 0 | 1 | 0 | 6 | 0 | 0.00 |
| Newcastle United | - | - | - | 1-3 | - | 1 | 0 | 0 | 1 | 1 | 3 | 0 | 0.00 |
| Sheffield Wednesday | - | - | - | 2-1 | - | 1 | 1 | 0 | 0 | 2 | 1 | 3 | 100.00 |
| Southampton | - | - | - | 0-1 | - | 1 | 0 | 0 | 1 | 0 | 1 | 0 | 0.00 |
| Tottenham Hotspur | - | - | - | 2-3 | - | 1 | 0 | 0 | 1 | 2 | 3 | 0 | 0.00 |
| West Ham United | - | - | - | 0-3 | - | 1 | 0 | 0 | 1 | 0 | 3 | 0 | 0.00 |
| Wimbledon | - | - | - | 1-0 | - | 1 | 1 | 0 | 0 | 1 | 0 | 3 | 100.00 |
| Totals | | | | | | 19 | 5 | 4 | 10 | 16 | 31 | 19 | 33.33 |

# Transfers In and Out

| Mth | Player | Signed From | Fee | Notes |
|---|---|---|---|---|
| Aug-96 | Per Frandsen | Copenhagen | £1,250,000 | |
| Aug-96 | Michael Johansen | Copenhagen | £1,250,000 | |
| Nov-96 | Jamie Pollock | Middlesbrough | £1,500,000 | |
| Dec-96 | John Sheridan | Sheffield Wednesday | £180,000 | |
| Dec-96 | Martin Johansen | FC Copenhagen | Non-Contract | |
| May-97 | Neil Cox | Middlesbrough | £1,500,000 | |

| Mth | Player | Signed For | Fee | Notes |
|---|---|---|---|---|
| Aug-96 | Sasa Curcic | Aston Villa | £4,000,000 | |
| Aug-96 | Fabian de Freitas | Osasuna | £250,000 | |
| Sep-96 | Wayne Burnett | Huddersfield | Unknown | |
| Mar-97 | Aidan Davison | Bradford | Free | |

# Chelsea

STAMFORD BRIDGE could well be one of the most exciting places to be during the 1997-98 season. Last season's FA Cup win could well provide further fuel to a talented band of players that will have been further strengthened by the arrival of several more who have every chance of succeeding in the Premier League. Add to this the close season completion of building works at the ground that will turn The Bridge into one of the most atmospheric in the country. The Kings Road could well be swinging once again.

With many new signings before the start of last season, it was amazing that Ruud Gullit was able to get them to blend into a Cup winning side so quickly. Gullit himself suffered from injury that limited his appearances and, even fully fit, the days of the Dutch manager as a player must be in doubt. As a mentor to bring the younger Chelsea talent on there may be no one better but that will surely be limited to the reserves.

At the back there will be an interesting battle for the number one spot where the Blues have four 'keepers with considerable experience. Dimitri Kharine was established as the first choice but injury ended his season and, after Kevin Hitchcock had covered for a while, Frode Grodas arrived to establish himself as the

main man. However, the £2.25 million arrival of Dutch number two Ed De Gouy from Feyenoord will throw a spanner in the works. De Gouy has not left Rotterdam to be number two at Chelsea so where does that leave Grodas, Kharine and Hitchcock? Be careful if you fancy a Chelsea 'keeper in your team!

There are a good number of players who will remain first choice selections – Di Matteo, Clarke, Mark Hughes, Leboeuf, Wise, Petrescu and Zola are amongst them. Scott Minto might have been added to that list but he opted for a Bosman style transfer to Benfica in the close season.

Many established players will be under pressure from the arrival of several other players, which include international defenders in the form of Bernard Lambourde (Bordeaux), Gustavo Poyet (Real Zaragoza) and the highly talented Celestine Babayaro, a Nigerian left-back from Anderlecht. These players are likely to compete with Burley, Duberry, Myers, Newton, Morris and Sinclair. Danny Granville is also tipped for full England international honours in the years ahead and will be pressing for his place while Jody Morris was one of the successes in the England Under-20 side that played in the international tournament in Malaysia during the close season.

# Club Data File

## Responsibility

Top Scorers:  Gianluca Vialli (9),
Mark Hughes (8),
Gianfranco Zola (8)

Sent-Off:  Frode Grodas
Frank Leboeuf

## Usage 1996-97

Squad:  32 players used

Substitutes:  71 used, 119 not used

## Players 1996-97

Most Used Subs:  Ruud Gullit (6),
Jody Morris (6)

Most SNU:  Nick Colgan (15),
Frode Grodas (9),
Jody Morris (8),
Mark Nicholls (8)

Most Subbed:  Craig Burley (8),
Paul Hughes (6),
Scott Minto (6),
Andy Myers (6)

## Five Year Premiership Form

|       | P  | W  | D  | L  | F  | A  | Pts | Ps |
|-------|----|----|----|----|----|----|-----|----|
| 92-93 | 42 | 14 | 14 | 14 | 51 | 54 | 56  | 11 |
| 93-94 | 42 | 13 | 12 | 17 | 49 | 53 | 51  | 14 |
| 94-95 | 42 | 13 | 15 | 14 | 50 | 55 | 54  | 11 |
| 95-96 | 38 | 12 | 14 | 12 | 46 | 44 | 50  | 11 |
| 96-97 | 38 | 16 | 11 | 11 | 58 | 55 | 59  | 6  |

# Ruud Gullit

Quite possibly the best player to come out of Holland since Johan Cruyff and, just like him, has also made the conversion to management with what looks like considerable ease. Taking a philosophical attitude to almost everything, he seems almost unaffected by the pressure that so many other managers seem to suffer. A great thinker, he has also made a considerable impact when employed as a game analyst with the BBC. The sort of person you could listen to talking about football all night.

He started his career at Haarlem before moving to Feyenoord and PSV. His major success came at Milan before they sold him to Sampdoria where he had such a good year that it prompted Milan to re-sign him. His arrival at Chelsea as a signing by Glenn Hoddle was a watershed day in the history of Chelsea. He was captain of the Dutch side that won the European Championship in 1988.

Up front the tall Norwegian striker Tore Andre Flo has been added to the squad and may be offered as a foil for Mark Hughes and Gianfranco Zola to play off.

Goals will always come from Zola and Hughes – both have great scoring records down the years. Interestingly it was Gianluca Vialli who notched most in the league last year but, if he remains at Chelsea, his chances may again be limited. Elsewhere Frank Leboeuf has taken on the role of penalty taker and this added to his tally of six goals last season – a number matched from the centre of midfield by Roberto Di Matteo.

All-in-all the Chelsea squad offers some of the most attractive signings you could make for your fantasy team. However it also provides some real selection problems – not just for you but Ruud boy as well!

# Chelsea v Record

| Opponents | 92/3 | 93/4 | 94/5 | 95/6 | 96/7 | P | W | D | L | F | A | Pts | % |
|---|---|---|---|---|---|---|---|---|---|---|---|---|---|
| Arsenal | 1-0 | 0-2 | 2-1 | 1-0 | 0-3 | 5 | 3 | 0 | 2 | 4 | 6 | 9 | 60.00 |
| Aston Villa | 0-1 | 1-1 | 1-0 | 1-2 | 1-1 | 5 | 1 | 2 | 2 | 4 | 5 | 5 | 33.33 |
| Barnsley | - | - | - | - | - | 0 | 0 | 0 | 0 | 0 | 0 | 0 | 0.00 |
| Blackburn Rovers | 0-0 | 1-2 | 1-2 | 2-3 | 1-1 | 5 | 0 | 2 | 3 | 5 | 8 | 2 | 13.33 |
| Bolton Wanderers | - | - | - | 3-2 | | 1 | 1 | 0 | 0 | 3 | 2 | 3 | 100.00 |
| Coventry City | 2-1 | 1-2 | 2-2 | 2-2 | 2-0 | 5 | 2 | 2 | 1 | 9 | 7 | 8 | 53.33 |
| Crystal Palace | 3-1 | - | 0-0 | - | | 2 | 1 | 1 | 0 | 3 | 1 | 4 | 66.67 |
| Derby County | - | - | - | - | 3-1 | 1 | 1 | 0 | 0 | 3 | 1 | 3 | 100.00 |
| Everton | 2-1 | 4-2 | 0-1 | 0-0 | 2-2 | 5 | 2 | 2 | 1 | 8 | 6 | 8 | 53.33 |
| Leeds United | 1-0 | 1-1 | 0-3 | 4-1 | 0-0 | 5 | 2 | 2 | 1 | 6 | 5 | 8 | 53.33 |
| Leicester City | - | - | 4-0 | - | 2-1 | 2 | 2 | 0 | 0 | 6 | 1 | 6 | 100.00 |
| Liverpool | 0-0 | 1-0 | 0-0 | 2-2 | 1-0 | 5 | 2 | 3 | 0 | 4 | 2 | 9 | 60.00 |
| Manchester United | 1-1 | 1-0 | 2-3 | 1-4 | 1-1 | 5 | 1 | 2 | 2 | 6 | 9 | 5 | 33.33 |
| Newcastle United | - | 1-0 | 1-1 | 1-0 | 1-1 | 4 | 2 | 2 | 0 | 4 | 2 | 8 | 66.67 |
| Sheffield Wednesday | 0-2 | 1-1 | 1-1 | 0-0 | 2-2 | 5 | 0 | 4 | 1 | 4 | 6 | 4 | 26.67 |
| Southampton | 1-1 | 2-0 | 0-2 | 3-0 | 1-0 | 5 | 3 | 1 | 1 | 7 | 3 | 10 | 66.67 |
| Tottenham Hotspur | 1-1 | 4-3 | 1-1 | 0-0 | 3-1 | 5 | 2 | 3 | 0 | 9 | 6 | 9 | 60.00 |
| West Ham United | - | 2-0 | 1-2 | 1-2 | 3-1 | 4 | 2 | 0 | 2 | 7 | 5 | 6 | 50.00 |
| Wimbledon | 4-2 | 2-0 | 1-1 | 1-2 | 2-4 | 5 | 2 | 1 | 2 | 10 | 9 | 7 | 46.67 |
| Totals | | | | | | 101 | 43 | 34 | 24 | 148 | 108 | 163 | 53.80 |

# Transfers In and Out

| Mth | Player | Signed From | Fee | Notes |
|---|---|---|---|---|
| Nov-96 | Gianfranco Zola | Parma | £4,500,000 | |
| Nov-96 | Frode Grodas | Lillestroem | Free | |
| Mar-97 | Celestine Babayaro | Anderlecht | £2,250,000 | Signed in April but joining in July |
| Mar-97 | Danny Granville | Cambridge United | £300,000 | |
| Mar-97 | Paul Parker | Fulham | Free | |
| May-97 | Gustavo Poyet | Real Zaragoza | Free | |
| May-97 | Tore Andre Flo | SK Brann | £300,000 | |
| Jun-97 | Ed De Goey | Feyenoord | £2,250,000 | |
| Jun-97 | Bernard Lambourde | Bordeaux | £1,500,000 | |

| Mth | Player | Signed For | Fee | Notes |
|---|---|---|---|---|
| Aug-96 | Anthony Barness | Charlton Athletic | £165,000 | |
| Aug-96 | Zeke Rowe | Peterborough United | Free | |
| Aug-96 | Nigel Spackman | Sheffield United | Free | |
| Aug-96 | Russell Kelly | Darlington | Non-Contract | |
| Nov-96 | John Spencer | QPR | £2,500,000 | |
| Dec-96 | Terry Phelan | Everton | £850,000 | |
| Dec-96 | Gavin Peacock | QPR | £800,000 | Rising to £1,000,000 |
| Jun-97 | Scott Minto | Benfica | Free | |

# Coventry City

IT WAS ANOTHER season when the Great Escape was performed by the Sky Blues. Nine times in the past 30 years Coventry have managed to beat the Big 'D' on the last day of the season – sooner or later the odds have to go the other way. Will it be the 1997-98 season?

The 1996-97 season started with the arrival of Gary McAllister from Leeds United, a £3 million acquisition of one of the best midfield players and most consistent performers in recent seasons. It came as a shock that he should leave the security of Elland Road but he was no doubt prompted by the chance to play alongside his former Scottish team-mate Gordon Strachan. McAllister was an ever-present but even his considerable expertise wasn't the turning point.

In truth the Coventry midfield perhaps relied too much on experience and the ageing legs of those who provided it. Kevin Richardson had won league championship medals at Aston Villa and Arsenal – but time is not on his side either.

So where will the revival come from? The arrival of Darren Huckerby from Newcastle before the transfer deadline could be regarded as one of the best buys of the season. A highly talented player, who can run at defences and score goals, he will be the shining light in the side.

Noel Whelan is amongst the best in the land on his day and, if he can further develop his role with Huckerby, the basis may be there. The departure of Eion Jess and Peter Ndlovu was surprising, especially the latter who was always hailed as one of the stars of the future. Over the past couple of seasons John Salako has struggled to find the consistency that made him an England international player when he was at Crystal Palace and his one goal from 24 appearances was another reason why Coventry struggled.

Individual rather than team performances must be the key if you fancy any Coventry City players in your team. Steve Ogrizovic may be the oldest goalkeeper in the Premiership but he also remains one of the best. Anything less than top class performances from him in recent seasons would probably have meant that this particular entry wouldn't have been written. But the defence in front of him remains suspect. Gary Breen, who signed from Birmingham at the start of 1997, made a number of basic errors late in the season that cost the Sky Blues goals.

Elsewhere the likes of Paul Williams, Paul Telfer and Richard Shaw have stood out in a struggling team at times and may represent good buys if you are willing to take a gamble.

But out of all these players Dion

# Club Data File

### Responsibility

Top Scorers: Dion Dublin (13),
Noel Whelan (6),
Gary McAllister (6)

Sent-Off: Liam Daish, Dion Dublin
(twice), Noel Whelan,
Brian Borrows

### Usage 1996-97

Squad: 31 players used

Substitutes: 60 used, 130 not used

### Players 1996-97

Most Used Subs: Peter Ndlovu (10),
Brian Borrows (7)

Most SNU: John Filan (37),
Willie Boland (13),
Gordon Strachan (9)

Most Subbed: Eion Jess (10),
Noel Whelan (9)
Darren Huckerby (7)

### Five Year Premiership Form

|       | P  | W  | D  | L  | F  | A  | Pts | Ps |
|-------|----|----|----|----|----|----|-----|----|
| 92-93 | 42 | 13 | 13 | 16 | 52 | 57 | 52  | 15 |
| 93-94 | 42 | 14 | 14 | 14 | 43 | 45 | 56  | 11 |
| 94-95 | 42 | 12 | 14 | 16 | 44 | 62 | 50  | 16 |
| 95-96 | 38 | 8  | 14 | 16 | 42 | 60 | 38  | 16 |
| 96-97 | 38 | 9  | 14 | 15 | 38 | 54 | 41  | 17 |

# Gordon Strachan

Having been on the masthead as player/coach at the start of the 1996-97 season, Gordon Strachan found his job title had changed to one of player/manager in the November of 1996 as Big Ron Atkinson was moved 'upstairs' to that ubiquitous position of 'Director of Football'.

Strachan's influence on his side was considerable, no more so than when he was on the pitch playing alongside his players. This was particularly true towards the end of the season when he turned in some inspiring performances. Even so he featured in just nine games and seven of those came from the subs' bench. As such, his playing days are almost gone and it will be his performances from the bench and in the transfer market that will hold the key. The acquisition of Darren Huckerby was inspired and, if he can continue to unearth realistically priced finds, Coventry may soldier on for more seasons to come.

Dublin probably remains the most vital of them all. When he is present it seems to lift the team and, at Highfield Road, the crowd. His 14 goals were remarkable given that his team only just escaped relegation and the fact that he occasionally played at centre-half; but, beyond that his performances earned him many man of the match awards for his side. The only blot on his landscape was a seven match ban due to two sending-off offences. Had he been available for those games then Coventry's end of season nightmare might have been simply a bad dream.

# Coventry City v Record

| Opponents | 92/3 | 93/4 | 94/5 | 95/6 | 96/7 | P | W | D | L | F | A | Pts | % |
|---|---|---|---|---|---|---|---|---|---|---|---|---|---|
| Arsenal | 0-2 | 1-0 | 0-1 | 0-0 | 1-1 | 5 | 1 | 2 | 2 | 2 | 4 | 5 | 33.33 |
| Aston Villa | 3-0 | 0-1 | 0-1 | 0-3 | 1-2 | 5 | 1 | 0 | 4 | 4 | 7 | 3 | 20.00 |
| Barnsley | - | - | - | - | - | 0 | 0 | 0 | 0 | 0 | 0 | 0 | 0.00 |
| Blackburn Rovers | 0-2 | 2-1 | 1-1 | 5-0 | 0-0 | 5 | 2 | 2 | 1 | 8 | 4 | 8 | 53.33 |
| Bolton Wanderers | - | - | - | 0-2 | | 1 | 0 | 0 | 1 | 0 | 2 | 0 | 0.00 |
| Chelsea | 1-2 | 1-1 | 2-2 | 1-0 | 3-1 | 5 | 2 | 2 | 1 | 8 | 6 | 8 | 53.33 |
| Crystal Palace | 2-2 | - | 1-4 | - | | 2 | 0 | 1 | 1 | 3 | 6 | 1 | 16.67 |
| Derby County | - | - | - | - | 1-2 | 1 | 0 | 0 | 1 | 1 | 2 | 0 | 0.00 |
| Everton | 0-1 | 2-1 | 0-0 | 2-1 | 0-0 | 5 | 2 | 2 | 1 | 4 | 3 | 8 | 53.33 |
| Leeds United | 3-3 | 0-2 | 2-1 | 0-0 | 2-1 | 5 | 2 | 2 | 1 | 7 | 7 | 8 | 53.33 |
| Leicester City | - | - | 4-2 | - | 0-0 | 2 | 1 | 1 | 0 | 4 | 2 | 4 | 66.67 |
| Liverpool | 5-1 | 1-0 | 1-1 | 1-0 | 0-1 | 5 | 3 | 1 | 1 | 8 | 3 | 10 | 66.67 |
| Manchester United | 0-1 | 0-1 | 2-3 | 0-4 | 0-2 | 5 | 0 | 0 | 5 | 2 | 11 | 0 | 0.00 |
| Newcastle United | - | 2-1 | 0-0 | 0-1 | 2-1 | 4 | 2 | 1 | 1 | 4 | 3 | 7 | 58.33 |
| Sheffield Wednesday | 1-0 | 1-1 | 2-0 | 0-1 | 0-0 | 5 | 2 | 2 | 1 | 4 | 2 | 8 | 53.33 |
| Southampton | 2-0 | 1-1 | 1-3 | 1-1 | 1-1 | 5 | 1 | 3 | 1 | 6 | 6 | 6 | 40.00 |
| Tottenham Hotspur | 1-0 | 1-0 | 0-4 | 2-3 | 1-2 | 5 | 2 | 0 | 3 | 5 | 9 | 6 | 40.00 |
| West Ham United | - | 1-1 | 2-0 | 2-2 | 1-3 | 4 | 1 | 2 | 1 | 6 | 6 | 5 | 41.67 |
| Wimbledon | 0-2 | 1-2 | 1-1 | 3-3 | 1-1 | 5 | 0 | 3 | 2 | 6 | 9 | 3 | 20.00 |
| Totals | | | | | | 101 | 33 | 33 | 35 | 115 | 116 | 132 | 43.56 |

# Transfers In and Out

| Mth | Player | Signed From | Fee | Notes |
|---|---|---|---|---|
| Aug-96 | Reggie Genaux | Standard Liege | £1,000,000 | |
| Nov-96 | Darren Huckerby | Newcastle United | £1,000,000 | |
| Jan-97 | Gary Breen | Birmingham City | £2,500,000 | |
| Jan-97 | Alex Evtushok | Dnepr | £800,000 | |

| Mth | Player | Signed For | Fee | Notes |
|---|---|---|---|---|
| Aug-96 | Ally Pickering | Stoke City | £280,000 | |
| Aug-96 | Jonathan Gould | Bradford | Free | |
| Jan-97 | Reggie Genaux | Udinese | £800,000 | |

# Crystal Palace

CRYSTAL PALACE START their third season in six years as an FA Premier League side. A reasonable statistic on its own but when you throw in the caveat that they have been relegated at the end of the previous two Premiership seasons, it is no wonder that most Palace fans have their fingers crossed and will be saying a third-time luck prayer under their breath.

The Eagles soared high via the play-offs thanks to a wondrous last minute effort by the jewel in their crown – David Hopkin. And they will look to the omens pointing out that Leicester City gained their promotion in similar fashion at the end of 1995-96 against them and went on to consolidate their position and win the Coca-Cola League Cup. Lightning doesn't often strike twice in the same place and Palace's future may depend on the ability to retain Hopkin, with so many of the bigger clubs sniffing around, and also their ability and willingness to pay for top class players.

While Steve Coppell basked in the Wembley play-off victory, the season started with Dave Bassett at the helm and he was very active in the transfer market prior to the start of the 1996-97 season. Long-serving 'keeper Nigel Martyn went to Leeds in exchange for £2.25 million and five other players also departed. Martyn was replaced by Chris Day from Spurs for an initial £225,000. Other

players to cost a fee were Kevin Muscat at £200,000 and Carlo Nash from non-league side Clitheroe for £35,000.

Tottenham were less than happy over Day's departure but with the chance of first team football, the England Under-21 keeper was happy with the move to start with. By the end of the season it was the remarkable form of Carlo Nash – their non-league find – who had made inroads to the number one spot, playing in 21 games. The twist didn't end there because just prior to the start of the 1997-98 season Coppell secured the signature of Watford goalkeeper Kevin Miller as Chris Day moved the other way. Miller will undoubtedly start the season as number one but Nash may well battle through again given the chance – that particular rivalry promises to be interesting.

The arrival of Andy Linighan from Arsenal in January 1997 did a lot to help Palace's push into those final play-off places. His experience as a Premiership player with Arsenal will be a major boost to the Eagles as they look for a way to shut-out the Premiership strikers. Other potentials for a central defensive role include David Tuttle, Robert Quinn and Dean Gordon. Leif Anderson may also come to the fore if he overcomes the shoulder injury that inhibited his chances in 1996-97 but the main role alongside Linighan could be that of Kevin Muscat,

# Club Data File

## Responsibility

Top Scorers: Bruce Dyer (17),
David Hopkin (13),
Neil Shipperley (12)

Sent Off: Dougie Freedman, Kevin
Muscat, Ray Houghton, Andy
Roberts

## Usage 1996-97

Squad: 29 players used

Substitutes: 100 used, 30 not used

## Players 1996-97

Most Used Subs: George Ndah (20),
Leon McKenzie (17),
Dougie Freedman (11)

Most SNU: Robert Quinn (8),
Carl Veart (5)

Most Subbed: Bruce Dyer (23),
Dougie Freedman (12),
Neil Shipperley (8)

## Five Year Premiership Form

|  | P | W | D | L | F | A | Pts | Ps |
|---|---|---|---|---|---|---|---|---|
| 92/93 | 42 | 11 | 16 | 15 | 48 | 61 | 49 | 20 |
| 93/94 | 46 | 27 | 9 | 10 | 73 | 46 | 90 | 1 |
| 94/95 | 42 | 11 | 12 | 19 | 34 | 49 | 45 | 19 |
| 95/96 | 46 | 20 | 15 | 11 | 67 | 48 | 75 | 3 |
| 96/97 | 46 | 19 | 14 | 13 | 78 | 48 | 71 | 6 |

*Football League seasons in italics*

# Steve Coppell

As a player Steve Coppell will always be synonymous with Manchester United whilst as a manager it would appear that his name will be forever associated with Crystal Palace. His place in the Palace history books is assured after returning for the final couple of months of the season, following an astonishing change of heart at Manchester City, to guide the Eagles into the Premiership for a second time. He has been there once before with them in charge of the their 42 game season in the 1992-93 season.

When Coppell took over at Palace in June 1984 he became the youngest manager in the League. He took them into the old Division One via the play-offs and to the FA Cup final – only to lose to his former Manchester United in a replay. After dropping out of the Premiership in 1993, Coppell resigned but it was just a matter of time until he returned home.

Marc Edworthy was the only ever-present in the Palace side last season and has developed into one of the most solid right-backs around. If he can maintain his form in the Premiership, he could find himself in the limelight.

Up front the partnership of Bruce Dyer, Dougie Freedman and Neil Shipperley supplied 42 of Palace's 72 Division One goals and they were well supported from midfield by 13 strikes from David Hopkin. Of the front three only Freedman hasn't had Premiership experience. Dyer will need to do better than the one goal he scored in his 16 games of the 1994-95 season, but it is Neil Shipperley, with a reasonably proven scoring rate with 20 goals in his 103 outings for Chelsea and Southampton, who may well provide the main thrust of the Eagles' offence. Experience as ever will be the key and, while Ray Houghton may not expect to add many more games to his 105 Premiership total, he will provide an invaluable foil for Hopkin when the going gets tough.

# Crystal Palace v Record

| Opponents | 92/3 | 93/4 | 94/5 | 95/6 | 96/7 | P | W | D | L | F | A | Pts | % |
|---|---|---|---|---|---|---|---|---|---|---|---|---|---|
| Arsenal | 1-2 | - | 0-3 | - | - | 2 | 0 | 0 | 2 | 1 | 5 | 0 | 0.00 |
| Aston Villa | 1-0 | - | 0-0 | - | - | 2 | 1 | 1 | 0 | 1 | 0 | 4 | 66.67 |
| Barnsley | - | - | - | - | - | 0 | 0 | 0 | 0 | 0 | 0 | 0 | 0.00 |
| Blackburn Rovers | 3-3 | - | 0-1 | - | - | 2 | 0 | 1 | 1 | 3 | 4 | 1 | 16.67 |
| Bolton Wanderers | - | - | - | - | - | 0 | 0 | 0 | 0 | 0 | 0 | 0 | 0.00 |
| Chelsea | 1-1 | - | 0-1 | - | - | 2 | 0 | 1 | 1 | 1 | 2 | 1 | 16.67 |
| Coventry City | 0-0 | - | 0-2 | - | - | 2 | 0 | 1 | 1 | 0 | 2 | 1 | 16.67 |
| Derby County | - | - | - | - | - | 0 | 0 | 0 | 0 | 0 | 0 | 0 | 0.00 |
| Everton | 0-2 | - | 1-0 | - | - | 2 | 1 | 0 | 1 | 1 | 2 | 3 | 50.00 |
| Leeds United | 1-0 | - | 1-2 | - | - | 2 | 1 | 0 | 1 | 2 | 2 | 3 | 50.00 |
| Leicester City | - | - | 2-0 | - | - | 1 | 1 | 0 | 0 | 2 | 0 | 3 | 100.00 |
| Liverpool | 1-1 | - | 1-6 | - | - | 2 | 0 | 1 | 1 | 2 | 7 | 1 | 16.67 |
| Manchester United | 0-2 | - | 1-1 | - | - | 2 | 0 | 1 | 1 | 1 | 3 | 1 | 16.67 |
| Newcastle United | - | - | 0-1 | - | - | 1 | 0 | 0 | 1 | 0 | 1 | 0 | 0.00 |
| Sheffield Wednesday | 1-1 | - | 2-1 | - | - | 2 | 1 | 1 | 0 | 3 | 2 | 4 | 66.67 |
| Southampton | 1-2 | - | 0-0 | - | - | 2 | 0 | 1 | 1 | 1 | 2 | 1 | 16.67 |
| Tottenham Hotspur | 1-3 | - | 1-1 | - | - | 2 | 0 | 1 | 1 | 2 | 4 | 1 | 16.67 |
| West Ham United | - | - | 1-0 | - | - | 1 | 1 | 0 | 0 | 1 | 0 | 3 | 100.00 |
| Wimbledon | 2-0 | - | 0-0 | - | - | 2 | 1 | 1 | 0 | 2 | 0 | 4 | 66.67 |
| Totals | | | | | | 42 | 12 | 15 | 15 | 43 | 48 | 51 | 40.48 |

# Transfers In and Out

| Mth | Player | Signed From | Fee | Notes |
|---|---|---|---|---|
| Aug-96 | Chris Day | Tottenham Hotspur | £225,000 | Rising to £425,000 plus £100,000 on an England appearance |
| Aug-96 | Bobby Mimms | Blackburn Rovers | Non-Contract | |
| Aug-96 | Kevin Muscat | S. Melbourne | £200,000 | |
| Sep-96 | Mike Lunsmann | Hertha Berlin | Trial | |
| Oct-96 | Neil Shipperley | Southampton | £1,000,000 | |
| Nov-96 | Dean Wordsworth | Bromley | unknown | |
| Jan-97 | Andy Linighan | Arsenal | £110,000 | |
| Jun-97 | Kevin Miller | Watford | £1,550,000 | |

| Mth | Player | Signed For | Fee | Notes |
|---|---|---|---|---|
| Aug-96 | Jamie Vincent | Crewe | £25,000 | Rising to £70,000 |
| Sep-96 | Bobby Mimms | Preston | Non-Contract | |
| Jun-97 | Chris Day | Watford | £250,000 | |

# Derby County

CANNON FODDER – that is probably what most on-lookers would have thought on Derby's arrival in the Premiership last season. Instead they provided more cannon balls than fodder and blasted their way through to establish themselves as a rather good Premier League outfit. Much of that was down to the rather astute purchasing power of manager Jim Smith, not just in purchasing the likes of Christian Dailly (£1 million), Croatian Aljosa Asanovic (£950,000) and Dane Jacob Laursen (£500,000) but in the off-loading of players to make way for those of Premiership standard.

Laursen and Dailly provided the backbone of the side and with 36 appearances each, were top performers for the Rams. By the end of the season Dailly's value had risen greatly and his consistency did not go unnoticed as Scotland handed him his first cap. One of Smith's shrewdest move was to take veteran defender Paul McGrath from Aston Villa, and his experience proved vital, although his services were not retained at the end of the season.

The star of the show though was the Croat Aljosa Asanovic who would have a case to claim that it was he in fact who was the best foreign import last season – not Zola, not Di Matteo or any other name you care to throw into the pot. His

passing and awareness on the ball were outstanding. The only blemish and an item that might still remain in question for the coming season would be is ability to play through games – he was subbed eleven times in all last season. Nevertheless he must be high on your list of consideration.

The Powells – Darryl and Chris – were other consistent performers. However, the players that had played such a vital role in Derby's rise out of the Nationwide League, typically Simpson, van Der Laan, Willems and Yates all struggled to hold down a first team place with any regularity. These are players that you might have considered last year but should now have question marks against their names.

Another player to catch the eye in the big league was the home-grown talent of Dean Sturridge. Small and bustling with a powerful shot, his nine goals made him joint top scorer in the league for County and the subject of £7 million transfer speculation throughout the close season. He may not be as cheap this season as he was last but he will be worth checking.

The other player in the goals was Igor Stimac although he occasionally drew the headlines for other reasons and played in a third fewer games than Sturridge.

Smith's buys towards the end of the season add interesting spice to possible

# Club Data File

## Responsibility

Top Scorers: Dean Sturridge (11),
Ashley Ward (8),
Aijosa Asanovic (6)

Sent-Off: Darryl Powell,
Christian Dailly

## Usage 1996-97

Squad: 30 players used

Substitutes: 87 used, 103 not used

## Players 1996-97

Most Used Subs: Paul Simpson (19),
Marco Gabbiadini (9),
Lee Carsley (9)

Most SNU: Martin Taylor (28),
Paul Simpson (12),

Most Subbed: Aljosa Asanovic (11),
Jacob Laursen (7),
Robin Van Der Laan (7),
Ron Willems (7)

## Five Year Premiership Form

|        | P  | W  | D  | L  | F  | A  | Pts | Ps |
|--------|----|----|----|----|----|----|-----|----|
| 92-93  | 46 | 19 | 9  | 18 | 68 | 57 | 66  | 8  |
| 93-94  | 46 | 20 | 11 | 15 | 73 | 68 | 71  | 6  |
| 94-95  | 46 | 18 | 12 | 16 | 66 | 51 | 66  | 9  |
| 95-96  | 46 | 21 | 16 | 9  | 71 | 51 | 79  | 2  |
| 96-97  | 38 | 11 | 13 | 14 | 45 | 58 | 46  | 12 |

*Football League seasons in italics*

# Jim Smith

Jim Smith could rightly be described as a man for all seasons. He has been a football league club manager for some 26 years now and been in charge for well over 100 games, making him by far the league's most experienced manager. That's two great records but there is also another, perhaps unenviable, one: three of the clubs he has previously played for – Aldershot, Halifax and Lincoln – lost their league status, although Lincoln made it back up the ladder.

One of the most liked managers in the game, Derby County is Smith's eighth managerial challenge. Before he arrived at the Baseball Ground he had taken charge at Boston, Colchester, Blackburn, Birmingham, Oxford, Newcastle and Portsmouth, but it is at Derby where he has had his greatest success and once again proved his nose for unearthing bargains.

international 'keeper, arrived and played in the final games of the season after Russell Hoult had tended goal for most of the other games. And from Costa Rica the arrival of Paulo Wanchope and Mauricio Solis went un-noticed until Wanchope scored one of the goals of the season as Derby turned over Manchester United in their own house. Wanchope could be a real bargain.

Asanovic, Dailly, Laursen and Sturridge will remain the pick of the crop and all well worthy of selection but the Derby team has a couple of other potential gems that could make big points, trouble is which ones?

# Derby County v Record

| Opponents | 92/3 | 93/4 | 94/5 | 95/6 | 96/7 | P | W | D | L | F | A | Pts | % |
|---|---|---|---|---|---|---|---|---|---|---|---|---|---|
| Arsenal | - | - | - | - | 1-3 | 1 | 0 | 0 | 1 | 1 | 3 | 0 | 0.00 |
| Aston Villa | - | - | - | - | 2-1 | 1 | 1 | 0 | 0 | 2 | 1 | 3 | 100.00 |
| Barnsley | - | - | - | - | - | 0 | 0 | 0 | 0 | 0 | 0 | 0 | 0.00 |
| Blackburn Rovers | - | - | - | - | 0-0 | 1 | 0 | 1 | 0 | 0 | 0 | 1 | 33.33 |
| Barnsley | - | - | - | - | - | 0 | 0 | 0 | 0 | 0 | 0 | 0 | 0.00 |
| Chelsea | - | - | - | - | 3-2 | 1 | 1 | 0 | 0 | 3 | 2 | 3 | 100.00 |
| Coventry City | - | - | - | - | 2-1 | 1 | 1 | 0 | 0 | 2 | 1 | 3 | 100.00 |
| Crystal Palace | - | - | - | - | - | 0 | 0 | 0 | 0 | 0 | 0 | 0 | 0.00 |
| Everton | - | - | - | - | 0-1 | 1 | 0 | 0 | 1 | 0 | 1 | 0 | 0.00 |
| Leeds United | - | - | - | - | 3-3 | 1 | 0 | 1 | 0 | 3 | 3 | 1 | 33.33 |
| Leicester City | - | - | - | - | 2-0 | 1 | 1 | 0 | 0 | 2 | 0 | 3 | 100.00 |
| Liverpool | - | - | - | - | 0-1 | 1 | 0 | 0 | 1 | 0 | 1 | 0 | 0.00 |
| Manchester United | - | - | - | - | 1-1 | 1 | 0 | 1 | 0 | 1 | 1 | 1 | 33.33 |
| Newcastle United | - | - | - | - | 0-1 | 1 | 0 | 0 | 1 | 0 | 1 | 0 | 0.00 |
| Sheffield Wednesday | - | - | - | - | 2-2 | 1 | 0 | 1 | 0 | 2 | 2 | 1 | 33.33 |
| Southampton | - | - | - | - | 1-1 | 1 | 0 | 1 | 0 | 1 | 1 | 1 | 33.33 |
| Tottenham Hotspur | - | - | - | - | 4-2 | 1 | 1 | 0 | 0 | 4 | 2 | 3 | 100.00 |
| West Ham United | - | - | - | - | 1-0 | 1 | 1 | 0 | 0 | 1 | 0 | 3 | 100.00 |
| Wimbledon | - | - | - | - | 0-2 | 1 | 0 | 0 | 1 | 0 | 2 | 0 | 0.00 |
| Totals | | | | | | 19 | 8 | 6 | 5 | 25 | 22 | 30 | 52.63 |

# Transfers In and Out

| Mth | Player | Signed From | Fee | Notes |
|---|---|---|---|---|
| Aug-96 | Christian Dailly | Dundee United | £1,000,000 | |
| Oct-96 | Paul McGrath | Aston Villa | £100,000 | Rising to £200,000 |
| Mar-97 | Paulo Wanchope | CS Heridiano | £600,000 | |
| Mar-97 | Mauricio Solis | CS Heridiano | £600,000 | |
| Mar-97 | Mart Poom | FC Flora Tallinn | £500,000 | |
| May-97 | Jonathan Hunt | Birmingham City | £500,000 | |
| May-97 | Stefano Eranio | Milan | Free | |

| Mth | Player | Signed For | Fee | Notes |
|---|---|---|---|---|
| Aug-96 | David Preece | Cambridge United | Free | |
| Aug-96 | Steve Sutton | Birmingham City | Free | |
| Oct-96 | Paul Parker | | Released | |
| Nov-96 | Jason Kavanagh | Wycombe Wanderers | £20,000 | |
| Nov-96 | Paul Parker | Sheffield United | Monthly Contract | |
| Dec-96 | Ian Ashbee | Cambridge United | Free | |
| Jan-97 | Will Davies | Cobh Rangers | Free | |
| May-97 | Darren Wassall | Birmingham City | £100,000 | |

# Everton

FOR THE PRE-SEASON and opening games there was so much optimism amongst Evertonians and you could understand why. FA Cup winners in May 1995, an improvement in Premiership form and a couple of large investments in the transfer market seemed to be the foundations upon which Joe Royle was building a side capable of going all the way.

In particular Paul Gerrard was signed from Oldham for £1 million and Royle raided Leeds to snap up Gary Speed for £3.5 million. An early season win over Newcastle United was followed by a tremendous 2-2 draw at Old Trafford where the Toffeemen had become the first side to score at Manchester United in the league in 1996! But it was the calm before the storm and Everton hit a slump in form that ended their season all too prematurely. Even the arrival of Nicky Barmby for £5.75 million failed to re-ignite the players and ultimately Joe Royle decided he'd had enough.

Everton weren't helped by non-availability of players. Andrei Kanchelskis, their leading scorer the previous season but with just three league goals to his credit this time around, departed to Fiorentina for £8 million while the injury to Andy Hinchcliffe deprived them of the precision left-sided play that had recently earned the player a call-up to the England side.

Despite this there are (once again) positive signs for the 1997-98 season. Key to this will be the arrival from West Ham of Slaven Bilic. A star player with the Hammers during 1996-97, he is likely to be a long-term replacement for the 35-year old Dave Watson who finished the season as player/manager at Goodison. His linking with a fit again Unsworth and the ever dependable Earl Barrett should provide a formidable barrier in front of a formidable goalkeeper. Or perhaps that should be two 'keepers. The arrival of Paul Gerrard raised a few eyebrows when it happened, not least because he is so highly rated and it seemed strange that he would be prepared to play second fiddle to Neville Southall. That indeed he did, featuring in just five of Everton's games, but Southall remains on of the all-time greats and, with Tim Flowers, has played in more Premier League games than anyone else.

In midfield, Gary Speed will again be the main focus of play for Everton and only suspension caused him to miss out on one game last season, while Joe Parkinson will be looking to recapture the form that eluded him for much of the year.

Up front Everton always look likely to be a threat, on paper at least. Duncan

# Club Data File

## Responsibility

Top Scorers: Duncan Ferguson (10),
Gary Speed (9)

Sent-Off: Duncan Ferguson,
David Unsworth

## Usage 1996-97

Squad: 31 players used

Substitutes: 56 used, 134 not used

## Players 1996-97

Most Used Subs: Michael Branch (12),
Tony Grant (7),
Graham Stuart (6)

Most SNU: Paul Gerrard (30),
Marc Hottiger (22),
Paul Rideout (15)

Most Subbed: Michael Branch (7), Nick
Barmby (5),
Andrei Kanchelskis (5),
Claus Thomsen (5)

## Five Year Premiership Form

|  | P | W | D | L | F | A | Pts | Ps |
|---|---|---|---|---|---|---|---|---|
| 92-93 | 42 | 15 | 8 | 19 | 53 | 55 | 53 | 13 |
| 93-94 | 42 | 12 | 8 | 22 | 42 | 63 | 44 | 17 |
| 94-95 | 42 | 11 | 17 | 14 | 44 | 51 | 50 | 15 |
| 95-96 | 38 | 17 | 10 | 11 | 64 | 44 | 61 | 6 |
| 96-97 | 38 | 10 | 12 | 16 | 44 | 57 | 42 | 15 |

Ferguson averaged a goal every three games last season and might have

# Howard Kendall

It seemed that every available name had been linked with the job at Goodison Park before Howard Kendall returned for what is his third spell as the manager in charge of Everton. No-one can doubt that Kendall is amongst the all-time Everton greats. He has been involved in three championship seasons with them, both as player and manager. He played in the side that took the title in 1969-70 and managed the team in the triumphant years of both 1984-85 and 1986-87.

Having been tempted to Spain and Athletic Bilbao, he returned to take control of Manchester City but returned to Goodison in November 1990. He was in charge of the side that struggled during the first Premiership season (1992-93) and inevitably parted for Sheffield United, whom he took to the Wembley play-off final. Now he has been tempted back to Everton again.

notched more had his inevitable flirt with trouble not earned him suspension. It must also be considered a big season for Nick Barmby, looking to firmly establish himself at Goodison Park and to force his way back into the thoughts of Glenn Hoddle and the England national side where he looked like being a fixture.

The real source of fantasy players at good prices might be found in the Everton youngsters. Richard Dunn, Michael Branch and Michael Ball are amongst the best prospects in the country. Keep an eye on them and watch out for the new signings there will ultimately be with the arrival of a new manager – if Howard Kendall can be called that.

# Everton v Record

| Opponents | 92/3 | 93/4 | 94/5 | 95/6 | 96/7 | P | W | D | L | F | A | Pts | % |
|---|---|---|---|---|---|---|---|---|---|---|---|---|---|
| Arsenal | 0-0 | 1-1 | 1-1 | 0-2 | 0-2 | 5 | 0 | 3 | 2 | 2 | 6 | 3 | 20.00 |
| Aston Villa | 1-0 | 0-1 | 2-2 | 1-0 | 0-1 | 5 | 2 | 1 | 2 | 4 | 4 | 7 | 46.67 |
| Barnsley | - | - | - | - | - | 0 | 0 | 0 | 0 | 0 | 0 | 0 | 0.00 |
| Blackburn Rovers | 2-1 | 0-3 | 1-2 | 1-0 | 0-2 | 5 | 2 | 0 | 3 | 4 | 8 | 6 | 40.00 |
| Bolton Wanderers | - | - | - | 3-0 | | 1 | 1 | 0 | 0 | 3 | 0 | 3 | 100.00 |
| Chelsea | 0-1 | 4-2 | 3-3 | 1-1 | 1-2 | 5 | 1 | 2 | 2 | 9 | 9 | 5 | 33.33 |
| Coventry City | 1-1 | 0-0 | 0-2 | 2-2 | 1-1 | 5 | 0 | 4 | 1 | 4 | 6 | 4 | 26.67 |
| Crystal Palace | 0-2 | - | 3-1 | - | | 2 | 1 | 0 | 1 | 3 | 3 | 3 | 50.00 |
| Derby County | - | - | - | - | 1-0 | 1 | 1 | 0 | 0 | 1 | 0 | 3 | 100.00 |
| Leeds United | 2-0 | 1-1 | 3-0 | 2-0 | 0-0 | 5 | 3 | 2 | 0 | 8 | 1 | 11 | 73.33 |
| Leicester City | - | - | 1-1 | - | 1-1 | 2 | 0 | 2 | 0 | 2 | 2 | 2 | 33.33 |
| Liverpool | 2-1 | 2-0 | 2-0 | 1-1 | 1-1 | 5 | 3 | 2 | 0 | 8 | 3 | 11 | 73.33 |
| Manchester United | 0-2 | 0-1 | 1-0 | 2-3 | 0-2 | 5 | 1 | 0 | 4 | 3 | 8 | 3 | 20.00 |
| Newcastle United | - | 0-2 | 2-0 | 1-3 | 2-0 | 4 | 2 | 0 | 2 | 5 | 5 | 6 | 50.00 |
| Sheffield Wednesday | 1-1 | 0-2 | 1-4 | 2-2 | 2-0 | 5 | 1 | 2 | 2 | 6 | 9 | 5 | 33.33 |
| Southampton | 2-1 | 1-0 | 0-0 | 2-0 | 7-1 | 5 | 4 | 1 | 0 | 12 | 2 | 13 | 86.67 |
| Tottenham Hotspur | 1-2 | 0-1 | 0-0 | 1-1 | 1-0 | 5 | 1 | 2 | 2 | 3 | 4 | 5 | 33.33 |
| West Ham United | - | 0-1 | 1-0 | 3-0 | 2-1 | 4 | 3 | 0 | 1 | 6 | 2 | 9 | 75.00 |
| Wimbledon | 0-0 | 3-2 | 0-0 | 2-4 | 1-3 | 5 | 1 | 2 | 2 | 6 | 9 | 5 | 33.33 |
| Totals | | | | | | 101 | 40 | 28 | 33 | 142 | 121 | 148 | 48.84 |

# Transfers In and Out

| Mth | Player | Signed From | Fee | Notes |
|---|---|---|---|---|
| Aug-96 | Paul Gerrard | Oldham Athletic | £1,000,000 | Rising to £1,500,000 |
| Oct-96 | Nick Barmby | Middlesbrough | £5,750,000 | |
| Dec-96 | Terry Phelan | Chelsea | £850,000 | |
| Jan-97 | Claus Thomsen | Ipswich Town | £900,000 | |
| May-97 | Slaven Bilic | West Ham United | £4,500,000 | |
| Jun-97 | Gareth Farrelly | Aston Villa | £700,000 | |

| Mth | Player | Signed For | Fee | Notes |
|---|---|---|---|---|
| Aug-96 | Matthew Woods | Chester City | Free | |
| Sep-96 | Chris Knight | Erith & Bel. | Free | |
| Nov-96 | Matt Jackson | Birmingham City | £500,000 | |
| Nov-96 | Jason Kearton | Crewe Alex. | Free | |
| Nov-96 | Peter Holcroft | Swindon Town | Free | |
| Dec-96 | Vinny Samways | Las Palmas | £600,000 | |
| Jan-97 | Andrei Kanchelskis | Fiorentina | £8,000,000 | |
| Jan-97 | Anders Limpar | Birmingham City | £100,000 | |
| Jan-97 | Neil Moore | Norwich City | Free | |
| Feb-97 | John Ebbrell | Sheffield United | £1,000,000 | |

# Leeds United

WITH GEORGE GRAHAM back on the Premiership scene and in control at Leeds United, the cynics might say that you need look no further for the meanest and best organised defence. Indeed the tail end of United's season look that way with 12 clean sheets in the last 18 games and five during December alone.

The trouble was that scoring goals at the other end was almost equally as difficult and indeed the Leeds fans would often sing "We'll score again, don't know where, don't know when..." to the tune of 'White Cliffs of Dover'. In fact they scored just 28 goals and that was three fewer than bottom of the table Nottingham Forest – United finished with just three goals at home in their last eight games!

United's defensive shoring up was implemented largely by Howard Wilkinson before he departed with the acquisition of goalkeeper Nigel Martyn from Crystal Palace. Martyn played in all but one of Leeds' games and, with experience, will probably take over the England jersey in the fullness of time.

However, not even Martyn could prevent United conceding ten goals in their first five games. Wilkinson went and Graham arrived and although the defeats continued early-on, the boat had been well and truly turned around by the December.

In addition to Martyn, Garry Kelly was another consistent performer and has proved his worth in recent seasons for both Leeds and fantasy team. Tony Dorigo will remain a prospective pick but his last two seasons have been blighted with injury.

Other signings that Wilkinson made before his departure included Ian Rush, Lee Sharpe and Lee Bowyer. Rush has signalled his intention to move on and may already have done so by the time you read this. Lee Sharpe was constantly linked with Arsenal while Graham was there while Lee Bowyer is one of the best young talents around. This would suggest that both will figure in Graham's rebuilding plans. Bowyer may well form a thriving midfield partnership with Gunner Halle who was one of Graham's own signings and the addition of Molenaar and Laurent may have prompted the close-season departure of Carlton Palmer. If not, then he may find his opportunities limited.

The problems for Leeds United look to be in attack and more arrivals are likely here. Derek Lilley came from Greenock Morton before the transfer deadline and showed flashes in his six games that he might have what it takes to succeed at the top. But like so many Leeds players he didn't get on the scoresheet and just how much United struggled here is reflected in

# Club Data File

## Responsibility

Top Scorers: Brian Deane (5),
Lee Sharpe (5)

Sent-Off: Carlton Palmer

## Usage 1996-97

Squad: 31 players used

Substitutes: 56 used, 134 not used

## Players 1996-97

Most Used Subs: Andy Gray (6),
Mark Jackson (6)

Most SNU: Mark Beeney (37),
Ian Harte (21),
Mark Ford (13)

Most Subbed: Andy Couzens (7),
Rod Wallace (7),
Mark Ford (6)

## Five Year Premiership Form

|       | P  | W  | D  | L  | F  | A  | Pts | Ps |
|-------|----|----|----|----|----|----|----|----|
| 92-93 | 42 | 12 | 15 | 15 | 57 | 62 | 51 | 17 |
| 93-94 | 42 | 18 | 16 | 8  | 65 | 39 | 70 | 5  |
| 94-95 | 42 | 20 | 13 | 9  | 59 | 38 | 73 | 5  |
| 95-96 | 38 | 12 | 7  | 19 | 40 | 57 | 43 | 13 |
| 96-97 | 38 | 11 | 13 | 14 | 28 | 38 | 46 | 11 |

# George Graham

One of the most successful managers of the last ten years, George Graham will probably be most remembered for the bung allegations that ultimately lead to his dismissal from Arsenal and a world wide ban for one year.

He is one of the few to win all English honours both as a player (with Chelsea, Arsenal and Manchester United) and a manager (with Arsenal). He won the double as a member of the 1970-71 side and also played in their Fairs Cup-winning side.

In the 1988-89 season he was manager of the side that won 2-0 at Anfield to snatch the title from Liverpool in what ranks as one of the most dramatic games of football ever played. The Gunners repeated the feat two seasons later despite having points deducted and went on to complete the first ever domestic cup double in 1993.

Expect him to take Leeds back to the top with a game play that is based on solid defence.

the fact that Lee Sharpe and Brian Deane were joint top scorers with just five goals a piece.

Deane spent most of last season playing wide on the right and it might be that he will revert to the more familiar role in the centre forward position in an effort to rekindle the scoring record he had while with Sheffield United.

The 1997-98 season looks like being another one where Graham continues his re-organisation, scouring for young talent that will see Leeds through the next ten years. As such the only players you should really consider are those who look well established and integral to Leeds United under George Graham. In this respect Martyn and Kelly in defence will keep clean sheets, Sharpe and Bowyer in midfield will also score goals. There is no real outstanding prospect in attack at present but watch the 'arrivals lounge' at Elland Road.

# Leeds United v Record

| Opponents | 92/3 | 93/4 | 94/5 | 95/6 | 96/7 | P | W | D | L | F | A | Pts | % |
|---|---|---|---|---|---|---|---|---|---|---|---|---|---|
| Arsenal | 3-0 | 2-1 | 1-0 | 0-3 | 0-0 | 5 | 3 | 1 | 1 | 6 | 4 | 10 | 66.67 |
| Aston Villa | 1-1 | 2-0 | 1-0 | 2-0 | 0-0 | 5 | 3 | 2 | 0 | 6 | 1 | 11 | 73.33 |
| Barnsley | - | - | - | - | - | 0 | 0 | 0 | 0 | 0 | 0 | 0 | 0.00 |
| Blackburn Rovers | 5-2 | 3-3 | 1-1 | 0-0 | 0-0 | 5 | 1 | 4 | 0 | 9 | 6 | 7 | 46.67 |
| Bolton Wanderers | - | - | - | 0-1 | | 1 | 0 | 0 | 1 | 0 | 1 | 0 | 0.00 |
| Chelsea | 1-1 | 4-1 | 2-3 | 1-0 | 2-0 | 5 | 3 | 1 | 1 | 10 | 5 | 10 | 66.67 |
| Coventry City | 2-2 | 1-0 | 3-0 | 3-1 | 1-3 | 5 | 3 | 1 | 1 | 10 | 6 | 10 | 66.67 |
| Crystal Palace | 0-0 | - | 3-1 | - | | 2 | 1 | 1 | 0 | 3 | 1 | 4 | 66.67 |
| Derby County | - | - | - | - | 0-0 | 1 | 0 | 1 | 0 | 0 | 0 | 1 | 33.33 |
| Everton | 2-0 | 3-0 | 1-0 | 2-2 | 1-0 | 5 | 4 | 1 | 0 | 9 | 2 | 13 | 86.67 |
| Leicester City | - | - | 2-1 | - | 3-0 | 2 | 2 | 0 | 0 | 5 | 1 | 6 | 100.00 |
| Liverpool | 2-2 | 2-0 | 0-2 | 1-0 | 0-2 | 5 | 2 | 1 | 2 | 5 | 6 | 7 | 46.67 |
| Manchester United | 0-0 | 0-2 | 2-1 | 3-1 | 0-4 | 5 | 2 | 1 | 2 | 5 | 8 | 7 | 46.67 |
| Newcastle United | - | 1-1 | 0-0 | 0-1 | 0-1 | 4 | 0 | 2 | 2 | 1 | 3 | 2 | 16.67 |
| Sheffield Wednesday | 3-1 | 2-2 | 0-1 | 2-0 | 0-2 | 5 | 2 | 1 | 2 | 7 | 6 | 7 | 46.67 |
| Southampton | 2-1 | 0-0 | 0-0 | 1-0 | 0-0 | 5 | 2 | 3 | 0 | 3 | 1 | 9 | 60.00 |
| Tottenham Hotspur | 5-0 | 2-0 | 1-1 | 1-3 | 0-0 | 5 | 2 | 2 | 1 | 9 | 4 | 8 | 53.33 |
| West Ham United | - | 1-0 | 2-2 | 2-0 | 1-0 | 4 | 3 | 1 | 0 | 6 | 2 | 10 | 83.33 |
| Wimbledon | 2-1 | 4-0 | 3-1 | 1-1 | 1-0 | 5 | 4 | 1 | 0 | 11 | 3 | 13 | 86.67 |
| Totals | | | | | | 101 | 53 | 29 | 19 | 148 | 84 | 188 | 62.05 |

# Transfers In and Out

| Mth | Player | Signed From | Fee | Notes |
|---|---|---|---|---|
| Aug-96 | Lee Sharpe | Manchester United | £4,500,000 | |
| Nov-96 | Tommy Knarvik | IL Skjerjard | Free | |
| Dec-96 | Gunnar Halle | Oldham Athletic | £400,000 | |
| Jan-97 | Robert Molenaar | FC Volendam | £1,000,000 | |
| Mar-97 | Pierre Laurent | Bastia | £500,000 | |
| Mar-97 | Derek Lilley | Greenock Morton | £500,000 | May rise to £700,000 |
| May-97 | Anton Drobnjak | Bastia | £4,000,000 | |
| May-97 | David Robertson | Rangers | £500,000 | |
| Jun-97 | Jimmy Floyd Hasselbaink | Boavista | £2,000,000 | |
| Jun-97 | Bruno Riberio | Vitoria Setubal | £500,000 | |
| Jun-97 | Alf Inge Haaland | Nottingham Forest | Tribunal | |

| Mth | Player | Signed For | Fee | Notes |
|---|---|---|---|---|
| Feb-97 | Paul Beesley | Manchester City | £500,000 | |
| Feb-97 | Robert Bowman | Rotherham United | Free | |
| Mar-97 | Mark Tinkler | York City | Undisclosed | |

# Leicester City

GIVEN THAT the Foxes have made a habit of jumping back and forwards between the Premier League and Nationwide League in recent seasons, it was perhaps not surprising that Martin O'Neill's side were made firm favourites to go straight back down again last season. Oh dear – how wrong. Chalk up a ninth place finish, a Coca Cola Cup win and a place in next season's UEFA Cup and there were some rather red faces around amongst the pundits!

Leicester were a surprise package and a delightful one at that. Equally they have some players who need serious consideration for any fantasy side, not least because they are good and they will also probably be available for reasonable amounts of fantasy cash!

There were a few eyebrows raised when O'Neill started to deal in the transfer market. Out went top scorer Iwan Roberts and Brian Carey, and in came Ian Marshall, Muzzy Izzet, Spencer Prior and 'keeper Kasey Keller at a combined price of £3 million. In retrospect the arrivals proved to be very useful buys, but arguably the best buy of all could have come prior to the transfer deadline in March when Matt Elliot was signed from Oxford United for £1.6 million. He slotted into the back-line with ease and provided a commanding figure and coming within a whisper of winning a quarter final FA Cup tie at Chelsea.

Kasey Keller added stability in goal, where the long-term future of Kevin Poole must be in doubt. Having played in all of their promotion winning games, he featured just seven times last season. Keller, after a slightly shaky start, grew in confidence as the season went on and, USA international commitments apart, should be almost ever-present. The presence of Elliot in front of him will help the Leicester cause. However the close season departure of full-back Simon Grayson to Aston Villa will be a blow but will be balanced by the return from injury of Robert Ullathorne, who had his season cut short just minutes into his debut.

Muzzy Izzet was languishing in the reserves at Chelsea but settled into the Foxes' midfield alongside the likes of Lennon and the exceptional Garry Parker, whose passing remains amongst the best to be seen. This is a player who can play and is worth the entrance fee alone to my mind.

Pontus Kaamark moved to Filbert Street in November 1995 but failed to capture a regular place on the bench, let alone the starting line-up. However, his performances in man marking Juninho in the Cola Cup final games will have served notice to O'Neill.

# Club Data File

## Responsibility

| Top Scorers: | Steve Claridge (12), |
| | Emile Heskey (10), |
| | Ian Marshall (8) |

Sent-Off:    Steve Walsh

### Usage 1996-97

Squad:       31 players used

Substitutes: 64 used, 126 not used

### Players 1996-97

Most Used Subs:  Jamie Lawrence (13),
                 Garry Parker (9),
                 Stuart Campbell (6)

Most SNU:     Kevin Poole (31),
              Mark Robins (18),
              Jamie Lawrence (16)

Most Subbed:  Scott Taylor (9),
              Steve Claridge (7),
              Muzzy Izzet (6)

### Five Year Premiership Form

|       | P  | W  | D  | L  | F  | A  | Pts | Ps |
|-------|----|----|----|----|----|----|-----|----|
| 92-93 | 46 | 22 | 10 | 14 | 71 | 64 | 76  | 6  |
| 93-94 | 46 | 19 | 16 | 11 | 72 | 59 | 73  | 4  |
| 94-95 | 42 | 6  | 11 | 25 | 45 | 80 | 29  | 21 |
| 95-96 | 46 | 19 | 14 | 13 | 66 | 60 | 71  | 5  |
| 96-97 | 38 | 12 | 11 | 15 | 46 | 54 | 47  | 9  |

*Football league results in italics*

Up front Emile Heskey continued to pave his way towards what could well be a full international cap in the future. Watching him play, it is hard to believe

# Martin O'Neill

Full of passion, Martin O'Neill spends his time living every kick and movement of his players. He is the sort of manager you would probably choose to talk football with, because he lives and breaths the game.

A dynamic player with Nottingham Forest where he won a championship, two League Cups and a European Cup and a cupboard full of caps for Northern Ireland. He learnt his managerial trade at the footballing bastions of Grantham and Shepshed before enjoying outstanding success at Wycombe, taking them to two FA Trophy triumphs at Wembley, a Conference title and promotion to the Football League.

Eventually he answered the call of Norwich City and, although he didn't see the season out with them, he did with Leicester and took them through to triumph in the Coca-Cola Cup.

that he is still just 19-years of age. He was a near ever-present playing wide on the left in a midfield/attacking role that saw him net 10 goals, just two fewer than Steve Claridge. Claridge you feel should play with a Zimmer Frame but he is another player who has grown in stature in the past season and his ability to run straight at, and often through, defences, was a highlight of his season – and one that invariably ended with a goal.

An interesting gamble was the £1 million signing of Steve Guppy. Martin will not agree with me that he is a gamble, knowing how well he played under him when Wycombe Wanderers won through into the Football League. Newcastle United were tempted but he remained at Port Vale before O'Neill stepped in. Guppy, a former bailiff, could be unlocking a few more doors if he has the confidence to come through.

There are plenty of ifs and buts with players in the Leicester squad. But that is what being a manager is all about and the Ifs on quite a few of the names above will almost certainly outweigh the buts.

# Leicester City v Record

| Opponents | 92/3 | 93/4 | 94/5 | 95/6 | 96/7 | P | W | D | L | F | A | Pts | % |
|---|---|---|---|---|---|---|---|---|---|---|---|---|---|
| Arsenal | - | - | 2-1 | - | 0-2 | 2 | 1 | 0 | 1 | 2 | 3 | 3 | 50.00 |
| Aston Villa | - | - | 1-1 | - | 1-0 | 2 | 1 | 1 | 0 | 2 | 1 | 4 | 66.67 |
| Barnsley | - | - | - | - | - | 0 | 0 | 0 | 0 | 0 | 0 | 0 | 0.00 |
| Blackburn Rovers | - | - | 0-0 | - | 1-1 | 2 | 0 | 2 | 0 | 1 | 1 | 2 | 33.33 |
| Bolton Wanderers | - | - | - | - | - | 0 | 0 | 0 | 0 | 0 | 0 | 0 | 0.00 |
| Chelsea | - | - | 1-1 | - | 1-3 | 2 | 0 | 1 | 1 | 2 | 4 | 1 | 16.67 |
| Coventry City | - | - | 2-2 | - | 0-2 | 2 | 0 | 1 | 1 | 2 | 4 | 1 | 16.67 |
| Crystal Palace | - | - | 0-1 | - | | 1 | 0 | 0 | 1 | 0 | 1 | 0 | 0.00 |
| Derby County | - | - | - | - | 4-2 | 1 | 1 | 0 | 0 | 4 | 2 | 3 | 100.00 |
| Everton | - | - | 2-2 | - | 1-2 | 2 | 0 | 1 | 1 | 3 | 4 | 1 | 16.67 |
| Leeds | - | - | 1-3 | - | 1-0 | 2 | 1 | 0 | 1 | 2 | 3 | 3 | 50.00 |
| Liverpool | - | - | 1-2 | - | 0-3 | 2 | 0 | 0 | 2 | 1 | 5 | 0 | 0.00 |
| Manchester United | - | - | 0-4 | - | 2-2 | 2 | 0 | 1 | 1 | 2 | 6 | 1 | 16.67 |
| Newcastle United | - | - | 1-3 | - | 2-0 | 2 | 1 | 0 | 1 | 3 | 3 | 3 | 50.00 |
| Sheffield Wednesday | - | - | 0-1 | - | 1-0 | 2 | 1 | 0 | 1 | 1 | 1 | 3 | 50.00 |
| Southampton | - | - | 4-3 | - | 2-1 | 2 | 2 | 0 | 0 | 6 | 4 | 6 | 100.00 |
| Tottenham Hotspur | - | - | 3-1 | - | 1-1 | 2 | 1 | 1 | 0 | 4 | 2 | 4 | 66.67 |
| West Ham United | - | - | 1-2 | - | 0-1 | 2 | 0 | 0 | 2 | 1 | 3 | 0 | 0.00 |
| Wimbledon | - | - | 3-4 | - | 1-0 | 2 | 1 | 0 | 1 | 4 | 4 | 3 | 50.00 |
| Totals | | | | | | 40 | 12 | 11 | 17 | 50 | 63 | 47 | 39.17 |

# Transfers In and Out

| Mth | Player | Signed From | Fee | Notes |
|---|---|---|---|---|
| Aug-96 | Kasey Keller | Millwall | £900,000 | |
| Aug-96 | Ian Marshall | Ipswich Town | £800,000 | |
| Aug-96 | Spencer Prior | Norwich City | £600,000 | |
| Sep-96 | Sascha Lennart | Royal Antwerp | Free | |
| Oct-96 | Stuart Slater | Ipswich Town | Non-Contract | |
| Oct-96 | Lee Farrell | Lincoln City | Monthly Contract | |
| Jan-97 | Matt Elliott | Oxford United | £1,600,000 | |
| Feb-97 | Steve Guppy | Port Vale | £850,000 | Could rise to £1,000,000 |
| Feb-97 | Robert Ullathorne | Osasuna | £600,000 | |

| Mth | Player | Signed For | Fee | Notes |
|---|---|---|---|---|
| Aug-96 | Mark Blake | Walsall | Free | |
| Jan-97 | Phil Gee | Hednesford Town | Free | |
| Feb-97 | Paul Hyde | Leyton Orient | Non-Contract | |
| Mar-97 | Paul Hyde | Leyton Orient | Free | |
| Jun-97 | Simon Grayson | Aston Villa | £1,350,000 | |

# Liverpool

IT IS FAST approaching a decade since the championship of England last rested in Anfield. A decade ago, that would have been unthinkable and the clock is now ticking on its return, in the form of the Premier League, to the red of Merseyside. On balance it would seem that Liverpool have largely lost the knack of winning the really big crunch games, that particular pendulum having swung in the direction of Old Trafford – the 3-1 home defeat by United virtually ensured the championship returned to Manchester.

Yet the players are there. It would not be difficult to believe that names such as Fowler, McManaman, Redknapp, Barnes and James will have been some of the most popular selections on any fantasy manager's wish list. Since John Barnes was dropped towards the end of the season there has been speculation that his days at Anfield are numbered – that may well be the case and may make him a player to be avoided in your selection. Yet the cases for the others remain good.

David James ended the season under a cloud after a series of mishaps that cost his team. His consistency throughout the past years though has been exceptional and he was once again an ever-present for the team, but his 12 clean sheets were probably less than he would have anticipated. Stig Inge Byornebye was the only other ever-present and he featured as a wing-back with Jason McAteer, who missed just one game.

The central three changed throughout the season with only Mark Wright a generally consistent factor. His partners included Babb, Matteo, Ruddock and Scales (who departed for Tottenham). The long-term injury to Rob Jones, such a revelation in the 1995-96 season, didn't help but one suspects that a more settled back three will help the Reds in 1997-98, and David James for that matter.

In midfield McManaman missed just one game and injury limited Jamie Redknapp's chances – when fit, both must be prime considerations. As must be new arrival Oyvind Leonhardsen a £3.5 million signing from Wimbledon. A seasoned Norwegian international, Leonhardsen will add the bite in the Liverpool midfield that they may have been lacking in recent seasons. His non-stop running style should also help him fit into the fluent short passing game that is the Anfield hallmark. He could be a major success.

Patrik Berger may have been another popular choice but ten of his 23 games came from the bench. However, he may find himself with the opportunity to play a more forward role now that Stan Collymore has departed for Villa. Collymore, despite his much publicised problems at Anfield, still finished as the

# Club Data File

## Responsibility

Top Scorers: Robbie Fowler (18),
Stan Collymore (12),
Steve McManaman (7)

Sent-Off: Robbie Fowler

### Usage 1996-97

Squad: 25 players used

Substitutes: 44 used, 146 not used

### Players 1996-97

Most Used Subs: Patrik Berger (10),
Stan Collymore (5),
Mark Kennedy (5),
Jamie Redknapp (5)

Most SNU: Mark Kennedy (20),
Neil Ruddock (17),
Lee Jones (15)

Most Subbed: Stan Collymore (9),
Patrik Berger (5)

### Five Year Premiership Form

|       | P  | W  | D  | L  | F  | A  | Pts | Ps |
|-------|----|----|----|----|----|----|-----|----|
| 92-93 | 42 | 16 | 11 | 15 | 62 | 55 | 59  | 6  |
| 93-94 | 42 | 17 | 9  | 16 | 59 | 55 | 60  | 8  |
| 94-95 | 42 | 21 | 11 | 10 | 65 | 37 | 74  | 4  |
| 95-96 | 38 | 20 | 11 | 7  | 70 | 34 | 71  | 3  |
| 96-97 | 38 | 19 | 11 | 8  | 62 | 37 | 68  | 4  |

side's second top scorer with 12 goals from 30 games and that slack will need to be taken up by someone.

The bulk of the goals will come from Robbie Fowler, whose 18 last season

## Roy Evans

When Roy Evans was appointed manager in January 1994 he represented a change back to the famous 'Boot Room' methods that had brought the likes of Shankly, Paisley and Fagin so much success down the years. His first full season saw Liverpool succeed in the League Cup, beating Bolton in the final, while the following season a defeat by Manchester United prevented another triumph in the FA Cup.

The pedigree of the Boot Room and the knowledge it has passed on through some of the greatest managers in the history of the game is important, not least because Evans had only limited action as a first team professional footballer, making just nine appearances for Liverpool as a left-back.

represented over a goal every two games. He missed the final run-in after being sent off following a tussle in the derby game with Everton and also drew criticism for withdrawing from England's tour to France. Who plays alongside Fowler? Berger would seem the early choice unless there are new arrivals at Anfield prior to the start of the season to join the likes of Oyvind Leonhardsen. Paul Ince was a name being touted at the time of writing but this would leave the Liverpool squad overflowing with central players. It would however add additional bite in an area where it has been largely absent.

Fowler will be a regular goalscorer throughout the season and should be well up any list of fantasy strikers. McManaman will also add to his tally with assists but also goals – seven last year. Berger added six strikes but, beyond that, the goals were rather sparser around the team. Redknapp found the net three times, but he, like McManaman, is more a maker of goals than a scorer.

# Liverpool v Record

| Opponents | 92/3 | 93/4 | 94/5 | 95/6 | 96/7 | P | W | D | L | F | A | Pts | % |
|---|---|---|---|---|---|---|---|---|---|---|---|---|---|
| Arsenal | 0-2 | 0-0 | 3-0 | 3-1 | 2-0 | 5 | 3 | 1 | 1 | 8 | 3 | 10 | 66.67 |
| Aston Villa | 1-2 | 2-1 | 3-2 | 3-0 | 3-0 | 5 | 4 | 0 | 1 | 12 | 5 | 12 | 80.00 |
| Barnsley | - | - | - | - | - | 0 | 0 | 0 | 0 | 0 | 0 | 0 | 0.00 |
| Blackburn Rovers | 2-1 | 0-1 | 2-1 | 3-0 | 0-0 | 5 | 3 | 1 | 1 | 7 | 3 | 10 | 66.67 |
| Bolton Wanderers | - | - | - | 5-2 | | 1 | 1 | 0 | 0 | 5 | 2 | 3 | 100.00 |
| Chelsea | 2-1 | 2-1 | 3-1 | 2-0 | 5-1 | 5 | 5 | 0 | 0 | 14 | 4 | 15 | 100.00 |
| Coventry City | 4-0 | 1-0 | 2-3 | 0-0 | 1-2 | 5 | 2 | 1 | 2 | 8 | 5 | 7 | 46.67 |
| Crystal Palace | 5-0 | | 0-0 | - | | 2 | 1 | 1 | 0 | 5 | 0 | 4 | 66.67 |
| Derby County | - | | - | - | 2-1 | 1 | 1 | 0 | 0 | 2 | 1 | 3 | 100.00 |
| Everton | 1-0 | 2-1 | 0-0 | 1-2 | 1-1 | 5 | 2 | 2 | 1 | 5 | 4 | 8 | 53.33 |
| Leeds United | 2-0 | 2-0 | 0-1 | 5-0 | 4-0 | 5 | 4 | 0 | 1 | 13 | 1 | 12 | 80.00 |
| Leicester City | - | | 2-0 | - | 1-1 | 2 | 1 | 1 | 0 | 3 | 1 | 4 | 66.67 |
| Manchester United | 1-2 | 3-3 | 2-0 | 2-0 | 1-3 | 5 | 2 | 1 | 2 | 9 | 8 | 7 | 46.67 |
| Newcastle United | - | 0-2 | 2-0 | 4-3 | 4-3 | 4 | 3 | 0 | 1 | 10 | 8 | 9 | 75.00 |
| Sheffield Wednesday | 1-0 | 2-0 | 4-1 | 1-0 | 0-1 | 5 | 4 | 0 | 1 | 8 | 2 | 12 | 80.00 |
| Southampton | 1-1 | 4-2 | 3-1 | 1-1 | 2-1 | 5 | 3 | 2 | 0 | 11 | 6 | 11 | 73.33 |
| Tottenham Hotspur | 6-2 | 1-2 | 1-1 | 0-0 | 2-1 | 5 | 2 | 2 | 1 | 10 | 6 | 8 | 53.33 |
| West Ham United | - | 2-0 | 0-0 | 2-0 | 0-0 | 4 | 2 | 2 | 0 | 4 | 0 | 8 | 66.67 |
| Wimbledon | 2-3 | 1-1 | 3-0 | 2-2 | 1-1 | 5 | 1 | 3 | 1 | 9 | 7 | 6 | 40.00 |
| Totals | | | | | | 101 | 62 | 23 | 16 | 196 | 86 | 209 | 68.98 |

## Transfers In and Out

| Mth | Player | Signed From | Fee | Notes |
|---|---|---|---|---|
| Aug-96 | Patrik Berger | B. Dortmund | £3,250,000 | |
| Jan-97 | Bjorn Tore Kvarme | Rosenborg | Free | |
| Mar-97 | Jorgen Nielsen | Hvidovre | £400,000 | |
| Jun-97 | Oyvind Leonhardsen | Wimbledon | £3,500,000 | |

| Mth | Player | Signed For | Fee | Notes |
|---|---|---|---|---|
| Aug-96 | Iain Brunskill | Bury | Free | |
| Aug-96 | Lee Bryden | Darlington | Free | |
| Aug-96 | David Lamour | Doncaster | Free | |
| Aug-96 | Steve Pears | Hartlepool | Free | |
| Dec-96 | John Scales | Tottenham Hotspur | £2,600,000 | |
| Dec-96 | Phil Charnock | Crewe Alexandra | Unknown | |
| Dec-96 | Ashley Neal | Huddersfield Town | Free | |
| May-97 | Stan Collymore | Aston Villa | £7,000,000 | |

# Manchester United

FOUR TITLES IN five years, including two Doubles, really just shows that you don't have to look too far in a Manchester United team for players that will earn you points. The silverware that has rolled in at Old Trafford in recent years has been almost a fantasy come true in itself!

However, even if your budget extended that far and the rules of your particular game allow, the facts are that not one United player played in every game last season and only seven players managed to break the 30 barrier – this out of a squad that saw 28 players used at some point.

Cantona, who played in 36 games was one of those players but last season was not his best and he has now of course gone into retirement. The other player matching his record was Michael Schmeichel who should be well to the top of your list of potential goalkeepers. He naturally benefits like other 'keepers who play behind solid defences in that it gives them less to do. In this respect United did change considerably and only Gary Neville and Ronnie Johnsen provided a near common core. Gary Neville continued to enhance his reputation and his progress seems to have, quite rightly, installed him as an England selection. Johnsen included five appearances as sub in his 31 games but proved more than adequate cover both at the centre of defence and in midfield when required.

Gary Pallister may now be nearing the end of his career at Old Trafford and may in the not too distant future follow in the footsteps of Steve Bruce, but as his career comes to an end, the 1997-98 season could see Phil Neville fully establish himself alongside his brother Gary in the back line, both for United and England. David May will also be pushing for the regular inclusion that was very nearly rewarded in an England appearance last season and Dennis Irwin has been one of the most underrated in his role anywhere.

There are an abundance of riches in the midfield and David Beckham will feature high on many lists, at a price, but there may be cheaper picks elsewhere, not least in Nicky Butt whose five goals from midfield proved valuable and more than the disappointing three that Ryan Giggs provided – his poor finishing remains the only blemish in his game. We might too have expected more from Karel Poborsky who was subbed in 10 of the 15 games he started and sat out a further 15 games.

Up front United have so many options. Not the least of these is the arrival of Teddy Sheringham, who is regarded as the replacement for Cantona. But Sheringham is a totally different player to the Frenchman and we may see a slightly

# Club Data File

## Responsibility

Top Scorers: Ole Gunnar Solskjaer (18)
Eric Cantona (11),
David Beckham (8)

Sent-Off: Roy Keane

## Usage 1996-97

Squad: 28 players used

Substitutes: 75 used, 115 not used

## Players 1996-97

Most Used Subs: Brian McClair (15),
Andy Cole (10),
Paul Scholes (8),
Ole Gunnar Solskjaer (8)

Most SNU: Raimond
Van Der Gouw (34),
Brian McClair (16),
Karel Poborsky (15)

Most Subbed: Ole Gunnar Solskjaer (11)
Karel Poborsky (10),
Nicky Butt (8)

## Five Year Premiership Form

|       | P  | W  | D  | L | F  | A  | Pts | Ps |
|-------|----|----|----|---|----|----|-----|----|
| 92-93 | 42 | 24 | 12 | 6 | 67 | 31 | 84  | 1  |
| 93-94 | 42 | 27 | 11 | 4 | 80 | 38 | 92  | 1  |
| 94-95 | 42 | 26 | 10 | 6 | 77 | 28 | 88  | 2  |
| 95-96 | 38 | 25 | 7  | 6 | 73 | 35 | 82  | 1  |
| 96-97 | 38 | 21 | 12 | 5 | 76 | 44 | 75  | 1  |

different system that also allocates a spot for England new boy Paul Scholes.

The goals last season came from Ole Gunnar Solskjaer – 18 in his 33

# Alex Ferguson

It is almost written down in folklore now that Alex Ferguson was probably only one FA Cup defeat away from being shown his marching orders at Old Trafford. That is almost ancient history now and Ferguson is certainly the most successful manager of recent times. In nearly 11 years in charge he has won nine major trophies and only one season has been barren – the first. Perhaps the nine haul shouldn't come as a surprise – he did the same trawl when he was with Aberdeen.

Ferguson took over from Ron Atkinson in November 1986 and his partnership with Brian Kidd has reaped dividends ever since, bringing the club its first championship in over 25 years and now having secured four of the five Premiership titles available.

Premiership games and an excellent return for his first season. Will Andy Cole now finally get a full run in the side? The rumours continue to surround possible transfers and do the circuit a little too often, leading you to believe he may be playing elsewhere before the end of the season.

The problem in selecting United players is that they will be expensive but also, because of the schedule of games they will face in 1997-98 with the Champions' League and domestic cups, not all players will be available to score points. Of course they will not lose you any. If you are looking towards Old Trafford for a couple of big buys then choose those who are going to play a major role both in games and in performances.

**Fantasy Football Handbook**

# Manchester United v Record

| Opponents | 92/3 | 93/4 | 94/5 | 95/6 | 96/7 | P | W | D | L | F | A | Pts | % |
|---|---|---|---|---|---|---|---|---|---|---|---|---|---|
| Arsenal | 0-0 | 1-0 | 3-0 | 1-0 | 1-0 | 5 | 4 | 1 | 0 | 6 | 0 | 13 | 86.67 |
| Aston Villa | 1-1 | 3-1 | 1-0 | 0-0 | 0-0 | 5 | 2 | 3 | 0 | 5 | 2 | 9 | 60.00 |
| Barnsley | - | - | - | - | - | 0 | 0 | 0 | 0 | 0 | 0 | 0 | 0.00 |
| Blackburn Rovers | 3-1 | 1-1 | 1-0 | 1-0 | 2-2 | 5 | 3 | 2 | 0 | 8 | 4 | 11 | 73.33 |
| Bolton Wanderers | - | - | - | 3-0 | | 1 | 1 | 0 | 0 | 3 | 0 | 3 | 100.00 |
| Chelsea | 3-0 | 0-1 | 0-0 | 1-1 | 1-2 | 5 | 1 | 2 | 2 | 5 | 4 | 5 | 33.33 |
| Coventry City | 5-0 | 0-0 | 2-0 | 1-0 | 3-1 | 5 | 4 | 1 | 0 | 11 | 1 | 13 | 86.67 |
| Crystal Palace | 1-0 | - | 3-0 | - | | 2 | 2 | 0 | 0 | 4 | 0 | 6 | 100.00 |
| Derby County | - | - | - | - | 2-3 | 1 | 0 | 0 | 1 | 2 | 3 | 0 | 0.00 |
| Everton | 0-3 | 1-0 | 2-0 | 2-0 | 2-2 | 5 | 3 | 1 | 1 | 7 | 5 | 10 | 66.67 |
| Leeds United | 2-0 | 0-0 | 0-0 | 1-0 | 1-0 | 5 | 3 | 2 | 0 | 4 | 0 | 11 | 73.33 |
| Leicester City | - | - | 1-1 | - | 3-1 | 2 | 1 | 1 | 0 | 4 | 2 | 4 | 66.67 |
| Liverpool | 2-2 | 1-0 | 2-0 | 2-2 | 1-0 | 5 | 3 | 2 | 0 | 8 | 4 | 11 | 73.33 |
| Newcastle United | - | 1-1 | 2-0 | 2-0 | 0-0 | 4 | 2 | 2 | 0 | 5 | 1 | 8 | 66.67 |
| Sheffield Wednesday | 2-1 | 5-0 | 1-0 | 2-2 | 2-0 | 5 | 4 | 1 | 0 | 12 | 3 | 13 | 86.67 |
| Southampton | 2-1 | 2-0 | 2-1 | 4-1 | 2-1 | 5 | 5 | 0 | 0 | 12 | 4 | 15 | 100.00 |
| Tottenham Hotspur | 4-1 | 2-1 | 0-0 | 1-0 | 2-0 | 5 | 4 | 1 | 0 | 9 | 2 | 13 | 86.67 |
| West Ham United | - | 3-0 | 1-0 | 2-1 | 2-0 | 4 | 4 | 0 | 0 | 8 | 1 | 12 | 100.00 |
| Wimbledon | 0-1 | 3-1 | 3-0 | 3-1 | 2-1 | 5 | 4 | 0 | 1 | 11 | 4 | 12 | 80.00 |
| Totals | | | | | | 101 | 71 | 24 | 6 | 194 | 57 | 237 | 78.22 |

# Transfers In and Out

| Mth | Player | Signed From | Fee | Notes |
|---|---|---|---|---|
| Aug-96 | Karel Poborsky | Slavia Prague | £3,500,000 | |
| Aug-96 | Ole Gunnar Solskjaer | Molde | £1,500,000 | |
| Aug-96 | Jordi Cruyff | Barcelona | £1,400,000 | |
| Jun-97 | Teddy Sheringham | Tottenham Hotspur | £3,500,000 | |

| Mth | Player | Signed For | Fee | Notes |
|---|---|---|---|---|
| Aug-96 | Lee Sharpe | Leeds United | £4,500,000 | |
| Aug-96 | Jorvan Kirovski | Borussia Dortmund | Free | |

P.G. & E. Chandler
335 Lakeside Drive
Denton, Texas 76208
Tel. (940) 321-1468

# Newcastle United

DESPITE THE BIG spending, the honours continued to elude the Toon Army last season but, with Dalglish in charge, it is surely just a matter of time before the silverware starts popping up at St. James' Park. Dalglish engineered a Premiership title at Blackburn Rovers, showing that it is possible to spend and create a team. However, despite the break-the-bank attitude that prevailed under Kevin Keegan, there would seem to be a basic underlying foundation in Newcastle, much of which is centred around the less expensive stars.

This point should be borne in mind when selecting players that are based at Newcastle. Dalglish is very much his own man and we can expect there to be a number of comings and goings as he builds what will be a team that will almost certainly be constructed around a more solid formation.

The key then is to look at who Dalglish brings in. At the time of writing only Shay Given, the Republic of Ireland international, and number two at Blackburn Rovers, had been signed. This would suggest that Given will be given the number one spot that has been so problematic at Newcastle. Either Srnicek or Hislop may be allowed to go.

David Batty and Alan Shearer were both signed by Dalglish when he was in charge at Ewood Park and both players would walk into any Premiership side. Both offer full quality and along with Given will form the backbone of the side that is likely to be completed in the central defensive position by Steve Howey. Howey missed much of last season through injury and, providing he overcomes this fully, he will regain his place and turn in the performances.

Darren Peacock missed just two games last season and, if no further additions in this central role are made, might get the nod over Phillipe Albert. But my sneaking feeling is that Dalglish may go about restructuring his back line and that might include a more involved role for Warren Barton, who wasn't favoured by Keegan towards the end of his reign.

In midfield Robert Lee finally seems to have started to carry his undoubted ability through a whole season. Too often in recent years he has started strongly only to wane in the final couple of months. Another potential points scorer. He may be joined by Des Hamilton who Dalglish prised away from Bradford City for £1.5 million before the transfer deadline. Hamilton only managed three non-playing appearances on the substitutes' bench before the end of last season but he must be in the manager's main plans (even if he will cost £8,000 extra per game for his first 80 games as a United player!).

# Club Data File

## Responsibility

Top Scorers: Alan Shearer (25),
Les Ferdinand (16),
Robbie Elliott (7)

Sent-Off: David Batty,
Keith Gillespie

## Usage 1996-97

Squad: 24 players used

Substitutes: 54 used, 135 not used

## Players 1996-97

Most Used Subs: Lee Clark (16),
Keith Gillespie (9),
Faustino Asprilla (7)

Most SNU: Shaka Hislop (22),
Peter Beardsley (12),
Lee Clark (12)

Most Subbed: Faustino Asprilla (12),
Les Ferdinand (8),
Keith Gillespie (8)

## Five Year Premiership Form

|  | P | W | D | L | F | A | Pts | Ps |
|---|---|---|---|---|---|---|---|---|
| 92-93 | 46 | 29 | 4 | 8 | 85 | 37 | 93 | 1 |
| 93-94 | 42 | 23 | 8 | 11 | 82 | 41 | 77 | 3 |
| 94-95 | 42 | 20 | 12 | 10 | 67 | 47 | 72 | 6 |
| 95-96 | 38 | 24 | 6 | 8 | 66 | 37 | 78 | 2 |
| 96-97 | 38 | 19 | 11 | 8 | 73 | 40 | 68 | 2 |

*Football league numbers in italics*

# Kenny Dalglish

King Kenny! As a player and as a manager he has had few peers and trying to cram all of his successes into a couple of paragraphs scarcely does him justice. Suffice to say that he remains Scotland's most capped player (102) and won four Scottish championships and four cups with Celtic. Moving to England, he won five Football League titles, one FA Cup, four League Cups and two Champions' Cups.

His managerial success has been equally glittering although it began in the most difficult circumstances in the wake of the Heysel disaster. Nevertheless his first season ended with the coveted Double and followed on with two more titles and an FA Cup triumph. After quitting mid-way through the 1991 season for personal reasons, he returned a year later at Blackburn Rovers and won promotion to the Premiership and the Premier League title itself just three years later. He moved on to Tyneside mid-way through last season, taking over from Kevin Keegan.

Up front there could be Ferdinand and Gillespie to play alongside Shearer. Ginola made the move to Spurs but it's an interesting fact that even if star players do leave a club in the coming months, they will almost certainly prove to be hits wherever else they may go so including them in your plans may not be as daft as it might first seem. Gillespie is an exciting player and missed only four of Newcastle's games last season.

With a place in the Champions' League, one point to bear in mind is the rather small nature of the Newcastle squad – made so because of Keegan's disbanding of the United reserves. One assumes that this will be re-instated by Dalglish and that new arrivals might not just include first team players but squad players he feels are stars in the making. Don't be surprised if a few more Ewood Park players move across the Pennines.

# Newcastle United v Record

| Opponents | 92/3 | 93/4 | 94/5 | 95/6 | 96/7 | P | W | D | L | F | A | Pts | % |
|---|---|---|---|---|---|---|---|---|---|---|---|---|---|
| Arsenal ... ... ... ... ... ... - | | 2-0 | 1-0 | 2-0 | 1-2 | 4 | 3 | 0 | 1 | 6 | 2 | 9 | 75.00 |
| Aston Villa ... ... ... ... ... - | | 5-1 | 3-1 | 1-0 | 4-3 | 4 | 4 | 0 | 0 | 13 | 5 | 12 | 100.00 |
| Barnsley ... ... ... ... ... ... - | | - | - | - | - | 0 | 0 | 0 | 0 | 0 | 0 | 0 | 0.00 |
| Blackburn Rovers ... ... ... - | | 1-1 | 1-1 | 1-0 | 2-1 | 4 | 2 | 2 | 0 | 5 | 3 | 8 | 66.67 |
| Bolton Wanderers ... ... ... - | | - | - | 2-1 | | 1 | 1 | 0 | 0 | 2 | 1 | 3 | 100.00 |
| Chelsea ... ... ... ... ... - | | 0-0 | 4-2 | 2-0 | 3-1 | 4 | 3 | 1 | 0 | 9 | 3 | 10 | 83.33 |
| Coventry City ... ... ... ... - | | 4-0 | 4-0 | 3-0 | 4-0 | 4 | 4 | 0 | 0 | 15 | 0 | 12 | 100.00 |
| Crystal Palace ... ... ... ... - | | - | 3-2 | - | | 1 | 1 | 0 | 0 | 3 | 2 | 3 | 100.00 |
| Derby County ... ... ... ... - | | - | - | - | 3-1 | 1 | 1 | 0 | 0 | 3 | 1 | 3 | 100.00 |
| Everton ... ... ... ... ... - | | 1-0 | 2-0 | 1-0 | 4-1 | 4 | 4 | 0 | 0 | 8 | 1 | 12 | 100.00 |
| Leeds United ... ... ... ... - | | 1-1 | 1-2 | 2-1 | 3-0 | 4 | 2 | 1 | 1 | 7 | 4 | 7 | 58.33 |
| Leicester City ... ... ... ... - | | - | 3-1 | - | 4-3 | 2 | 2 | 0 | 0 | 7 | 4 | 6 | 100.00 |
| Liverpool ... ... ... ... ... - | | 3-0 | 1-1 | 2-1 | 1-1 | 4 | 2 | 2 | 0 | 7 | 3 | 8 | 66.67 |
| Manchester United ... ... - | | 1-1 | 1-1 | 0-1 | 5-0 | 4 | 1 | 2 | 1 | 7 | 3 | 5 | 41.67 |
| Sheffield Wednesday ... ... - | | 4-2 | 2-1 | 2-0 | 1-2 | 4 | 3 | 0 | 1 | 9 | 5 | 9 | 75.00 |
| Southampton ... ... ... ... - | | 1-2 | 5-1 | 1-0 | 0-1 | 4 | 2 | 0 | 2 | 7 | 4 | 6 | 50.00 |
| Tottenham Hotspur ... ... - | | 0-1 | 3-3 | 1-1 | 7-1 | 4 | 1 | 2 | 1 | 11 | 6 | 5 | 41.67 |
| West Ham United ... ... ... - | | 2-0 | 2-0 | 3-0 | 1-1 | 4 | 3 | 1 | 0 | 8 | 1 | 10 | 83.33 |
| Wimbledon ... ... ... ... ... - | | 4-0 | 2-1 | 6-1 | 2-0 | 4 | 4 | 0 | 0 | 14 | 2 | 12 | 100.00 |
| *Totals* ... ... ... ... ... ... | | | | | | 80 | 58 | 14 | 8 | 189 | 63 | 188 | 78.33 |

## Transfers In and Out

| *Mth* | *Player* | *Signed From* | *Fee* | *Notes* |
|---|---|---|---|---|
| Mar-97 | Des Hamilton | Bradford City | £1,500,000 | Plus £8,000 per game to a maximum of £800,000 |
| Mar-97 | Bjarni Gudjonsson | IA Akranes | £500,000 | |
| May-97 | Shay Given | Blackburn Rovers | Contested | |

| *Mth* | *Player* | *Signed For* | *Fee* | *Notes* |
|---|---|---|---|---|
| Oct-96 | Chris Holland | Birmingham City | £600,000 | |
| Nov-96 | Darren Huckerby | Coventry City | £1,000,000 | |
| Feb-97 | Paul Kitson | West Ham United | £2,300,000 | |
| Jun-97 | Lee Clark | Sunderland | £2,500,000 | |

# Sheffield Wednesday

LAST SEASON BEGAN with a real bang for the Hillsborough side, who topped the table for a number of weeks before the rest of the Premier League caught David Pleat's side in their sights. Wednesday couldn't do wrong in those opening weeks of the season but, while the bubble did burst in September, the Owls management and their supporters will have learnt a lot about the players they have and, in particular, a couple of new names coming through the ranks.

Those changes to the squad started in the summer with Andy Booth, Scott Oakes, Matt Clarke and Wayne Collins moving to Hillsborough. At £2.75 million Booth, from Huddersfield, became Wednesday's joint highest purchase. As the season progressed Pleat delved deeper into the transfer market twice more to sign Italian Benito Carbone for £3 million and Peterborough's David Billington for £500,000. The Owls recouped £4.5 million in a clearout which included free transfers for former England players Waddle and Woods.

The name that made the headlines though was the home-grown and local teenager Richie Humphreys, who opened his account with a marvellous goal during a 2-1 win over Aston Villa. Humphreys' early season form was a great boost for the club as they awaited the return from an achilles injury of England striker David Hirst. Humphreys, perhaps not surprisingly couldn't readily maintain the form all the way through the season but his 29 appearances show he is one worth watching this time around, even if 15 of those did come from the subs' bench.

On the striking front it was Andy Booth who ultimately repaid some of his fee by finishing as Wednesday's leading scorer with 10 goals from his 35 games, so much so that the future of David Hirst must be under consideration.

At the back Kevin Pressman remained in impressive form and Des Walker at times looked almost rejuvenated in his defensive duties. He, like two other team-mates, did fall foul of the referee's red card. While his was a little harsh, the dismissals of Hirst and the debutant Clarke (in the Wednesday goal) were almost farcical. But such are the events that comprise football. Walker developed an excellent understanding with Dejan Stefanovic in their first full season together so expect at least the same again this season.

Peter Atherton remains one of the most consistent and consistently under-rated performers in the Premiership. No fuss but he invariable plays the captain's role to the full, leading by example and Coventry City must be wondering why they let him go in the summer of 1994.

The other new boys did good as well.

# Club Data File

## Responsibility

Top Scorers: Andy Booth (10),
David Hirst (6),
Mark Pembridge (6),
Benito Carbone (6)

Sent-Off: Matt Clarke, David Hirst,
Des Walker

## Usage 1996-97

Squad: 25 players used

Substitutes: 92 used, 98 not used

## Players 1996-97

Most Used Subs: Regi Blinker (18),
Ritchie Humphreys (15),

Most SNU: Scott Oakes (12)
Matt Clarke (37),
Steve Nicol (9),
Scott Oakes (9)

Most Subbed: Benito Carbone (11),
David Hirst (11),
Ritchie Humphreys (11)

## Five Year Premiership Form

|       | P  | W  | D  | L  | F  | A  | Pts | Ps |
|-------|----|----|----|----|----|----|-----|----|
| 92-93 | 42 | 15 | 14 | 13 | 55 | 51 | 59  | 7  |
| 93-94 | 42 | 16 | 16 | 10 | 76 | 54 | 64  | 7  |
| 94-95 | 42 | 13 | 12 | 17 | 49 | 57 | 51  | 13 |
| 95-96 | 38 | 10 | 10 | 18 | 48 | 61 | 40  | 15 |
| 96-97 | 38 | 14 | 15 | 9  | 50 | 51 | 57  | 7  |

# David Pleat

A well respected manager, Pleat has courted his own share of controversy, which ultimately cost him his job at Tottenham. After a promising start to his playing career, which started at Nottingham Forest, following England Schoolboy and Youth honours, he joined Luton where a broken leg and back problems hampered him. In 1971 he started on his managerial trail as a player/manager at Nuneaton before he joined the backroom staff at Luton as a coach. Pleat finally got the top job at Kenilworth Road in 1978.

Having taken Luton up through the Third and Second into the First Division, Pleat will perhaps be best remembered for his galloping celebration on the Maine Road pitch on the day they survived relegation in 1983. He was later to return to Luton after an unsuccessful spell at Leicester, but in between had a moderately successful time at Tottenham who he took to an FA Cup final in 1987 when they lost to Coventry. He was appointed as Wednesday's manager in July 1995.

The experience of Benito Carbone was probably something that Pleat had in mind when he sought his services. If marks were given for how much skill, touch and energy was displayed in a game, this guy would win all the awards. The only blemish is his ability to last the pace – he was Wednesday's most subbed player last season (11 times).

The dreadlocked Regi Blinker had his role to play even if much of it was from the bench. Wednesday will be looking for him to deliver more during 1997-98.

Other players that played a significant, if not full, part in Wednesday's campaign last year that might do even better this time around include Graham Hyde, Scott Oakes and Guy Whittingham. Steve Nicol will also probably go well again for this season, and the next...

Wednesday's disciplinary record, despite three players being dismissed, was generally good as they had the second lowest number of cautions and this, if repeated, should ensure they generally have a full squad to select from – barring injuries of course.

# Sheffield Wednesday v Record

| Opponents | 92/3 | 93/4 | 94/5 | 95/6 | 96/7 | P | W | D | L | F | A | Pts | % |
|---|---|---|---|---|---|---|---|---|---|---|---|---|---|
| Arsenal | 1-0 | 0-1 | 3-1 | 1-0 | 0-0 | 5 | 3 | 1 | 1 | 5 | 2 | 10 | 66.67 |
| Aston Villa | 1-2 | 0-0 | 1-2 | 2-0 | 2-1 | 5 | 2 | 1 | 2 | 6 | 5 | 7 | 46.67 |
| Barnsley | - | - | - | - | - | 0 | 0 | 0 | 0 | 0 | 0 | 0 | 0.00 |
| Blackburn Rovers | 0-0 | 1-2 | 0-1 | 2-1 | 1-1 | 5 | 1 | 2 | 2 | 4 | 5 | 5 | 33.33 |
| Bolton Wanderers | - | - | - | 4-2 | | 1 | 1 | 0 | 0 | 4 | 2 | 3 | 100.00 |
| Chelsea | 3-3 | 3-1 | 1-1 | 0-0 | 0-2 | 5 | 1 | 3 | 1 | 7 | 7 | 6 | 40.00 |
| Coventry City | 1-2 | 0-0 | 5-1 | 4-3 | 0-0 | 5 | 2 | 2 | 1 | 10 | 6 | 8 | 53.33 |
| Crystal Palace | 2-1 | - | 1-0 | - | | 2 | 2 | 0 | 0 | 3 | 1 | 6 | 100.00 |
| Derby | - | - | - | - | 0-0 | 1 | 0 | 1 | 0 | 0 | 0 | 1 | 33.33 |
| Everton | 3-1 | 5-1 | 0-0 | 2-5 | 2-1 | 5 | 3 | 1 | 1 | 12 | 8 | 10 | 66.67 |
| Leeds United | 1-1 | 3-3 | 1-1 | 6-2 | 2-2 | 5 | 1 | 4 | 0 | 13 | 9 | 7 | 46.67 |
| Leicester City | - | - | 1-0 | - | 2-1 | 2 | 2 | 0 | 0 | 3 | 1 | 6 | 100.00 |
| Liverpool | 1-1 | 3-1 | 1-2 | 1-1 | 1-1 | 5 | 1 | 3 | 1 | 7 | 6 | 6 | 40.00 |
| Manchester United | 3-3 | 2-3 | 1-0 | 0-0 | 1-1 | 5 | 1 | 3 | 1 | 7 | 7 | 6 | 40.00 |
| Newcastle United | - | 0-1 | 0-0 | 0-2 | 1-1 | 4 | 0 | 2 | 2 | 1 | 4 | 2 | 16.67 |
| Southampton | 5-2 | 2-0 | 1-1 | 2-2 | 1-1 | 5 | 2 | 3 | 0 | 11 | 6 | 9 | 60.00 |
| Tottenham Hotspur | 2-0 | 1-0 | 3-4 | 1-3 | 2-1 | 5 | 3 | 0 | 2 | 9 | 8 | 9 | 60.00 |
| West Ham United | - | 5-0 | 1-0 | 0-1 | 0-0 | 4 | 2 | 1 | 1 | 6 | 1 | 7 | 58.33 |
| Wimbledon | 1-1 | 2-2 | 0-1 | 2-1 | 3-1 | 5 | 2 | 2 | 1 | 8 | 6 | 8 | 53.33 |
| Totals | | | | | | 101 | 41 | 37 | 23 | 163 | 123 | 160 | 52.81 |

# Transfers In and Out

| Mth | Player | Signed From | Fee | Notes |
|---|---|---|---|---|
| Aug-96 | Orlando Trustfull | Feyenoord | £750,000 | |
| Aug-96 | Scott Oakes | Luton Town | £425,000 | Rising to £750,000 |
| Sep-96 | Dave Hercock | Cambridge City | Free | Five-figure fee after 10 appearances |
| Oct-96 | Benito Carbone | Internazionale | £3,000,000 | |
| Mar-97 | David Billington | Peterborough United | £500,000 | May rise to £1,000,000 |

| Mth | Player | Signed For | Fee | Notes |
|---|---|---|---|---|
| Aug-96 | Richard Baker | Linfield | £40,000 | |
| Aug-96 | David Faulkner | Darlington | Free | |
| Sep-96 | Chris Waddle | Falkirk | Free | |
| Oct-96 | Paul Sykes | Bradford PA | Free | |
| Dec-96 | John Sheridan | Bolton Wanderers | £180,000 | |
| Jan-97 | Mark Bright | Sion | £70,000 | |
| Mar-97 | Sam Sharman | Hull City | Free | |

# Southampton

FOR THE THIRD successive season, Southampton will start a Premiership campaign with a new manager in charge of team matters. David Jones, who produced a good deal of success at the unfashionable Stockport County, is the latest incumbent of the south coast job. And what a job he has!

Since the inception of the Premier League, Southampton have only once finished inside the top ten and, despite the arrival of Graeme Souness as manager in time for the 1996-97 season, few predicted that the trend was about to change. But there was optimism as Saints fans saw more new arrivals in one month than they probably had done for several seasons combine – and that might have been one of the reasons behind their fluctuating form as the new players and new ideas took so long to gel. How else can you explain a 6-3 win over Manchester United in a year the Reds won the title, followed by a 7-1 thrashing at the hands of Everton?

Souness though brought in several key signings who could serve new manager Jones well. For a start he invested £1.3 million in Galatasary defender Ulrich Van Gobbel, £1 million in Eyal Berkovic from Haifa Maccabi, and a further £2 million on Egil Ostenstad and Claus Lundekvam. On the credit side around £3m was collected from the sale of Richard Hall

and Tommy Widdrington, while veterans Bruce Grobbelaar and Mark Walters also left the Dell. Of all those it was Berkovic who really caught the eye and his departure to Upton Park and the claret and blue of West Ham will be a real disappointment to the Dell faithful.

But the first thing Jones did was ensure that the mercurial Matt Le Tissier signed a new four year deal which means he sees out his career in his adopted home town. Le Tissier of course provides the focal point of the team – often so brilliant for his team he has never quiet had the success when he dons the England shirt as he did once again during 1996-97. He remains an enigma in much the same way as John Barnes in that respect but unlike Barnes he has never had the full run of a sequence of games. For the Saints he remains the main man and is only one of three Premiership players who can boast that they hold both the Premiership appearance and goalscoring record for their clubs (the other two being Dean Holdsworth of Wimbledon and Teddy Sheringham – who was at Tottenham).

Egil Ostenstad ran 'The-Tiss' close for top scorer, blasting home ten goals in his 30 games and these included a memorable hat-trick in that 6-3 whipping of Manchester United. Ulrich Van Gobbel added bite to the midfield when required and may have been an ever-present had

# Club Data File

## Responsibility

Top Scorers: Matt Le Tissier (13),
Egil Ostenstad (9)

Sent-Off: Francis Benali, Jason
Dodd, Barry Venison,
Ulrich Van Gobbel

## Usage 1996-97

Squad: 32 players used

Substitutes: 54 used, 136 not used

## Players 1996-97

Most Used Subs: Robbie Slater (8),
Gordon Watson (8)

Most SNU: Dave Beasant (20),
Neil Maddison (16),
Steve Basham (14),
Neil Moss (14)

Most Subbed: Eyal Berkovic (11),
Mathew Oakley (11),
Simon Charlton (8),
Matt Le Tissier (8)

## Five Year Premiership Form

|       | P  | W  | D  | L  | F  | A  | Pts | Ps |
|-------|----|----|----|----|----|----|-----|----|
| 92-93 | 42 | 13 | 11 | 18 | 54 | 61 | 50  | 18 |
| 93-94 | 42 | 12 | 7  | 23 | 49 | 66 | 43  | 18 |
| 94-95 | 42 | 12 | 18 | 12 | 61 | 63 | 54  | 10 |
| 95-96 | 38 | 9  | 11 | 18 | 34 | 52 | 38  | 17 |
| 96-97 | 38 | 10 | 11 | 17 | 50 | 56 | 41  | 16 |

# Dave Jones

It was the sequence of games that took Stockport County to the semi Finals of the Coca-Cola League Cup that threw Dave Jones into the spotlight. His almost calm demeanour on the touch line as he watched his side sweep away top teams in their pursuit of more and more giant killings. That Coca-Cola run included a quarter final disposal of Southampton at the Dell after a 2-2 draw in Stockport, something that obviously drew him to the attention of those who now pay his wages.

Jones took over at County in March 1995 and in his first full season in charge they finished ninth in Division Two and last season, despite the cup distractions, they finished second to earn automatic promotion to Division One of the Nationwide League.

Prior to County, Jones' only managerial experience was at non-league Morecambe where he was also a player after a career that started at Everton and went to Preston NE via Coventry and Hong Kong.

he not had a couple of handfuls of yellow cards and a red one to earn sizeable suspensions.

At the back it was Maik Taylor, a signing from Barnet, who looked to be edging in front of the experienced Dave Beasant for the position in goal. Elsewhere in the team Jim Magilton played in all but one of the Premier League games and continues to prove such a stalwart to the club while Ken Monkou, Alan Neilson, Matthew Oakley and Jason Dodd where amongst several other players who couldn't hold down the regular spots they had been used to. And here lies the rub – which players will the new manager hold sway with and who will he let go? No doubt there will also be new additions and these could be worthy of consideration. The saving grace is how close to the start of pre-season training he arrived at the Dell so it may be some time into the season before he starts to tinker with players and the team. Le Tissier will almost certainly continue to be the star and the goalscorer.

# Southampton v Record

| Opponents | 92/3 | 93/4 | 94/5 | 95/6 | 96/7 | P | W | D | L | F | A | Pts | % |
|---|---|---|---|---|---|---|---|---|---|---|---|---|---|
| Arsenal | 2-0 | 0-4 | 1-0 | 0-0 | 0-2 | 5 | 2 | 1 | 2 | 3 | 6 | 7 | 46.67 |
| Aston Villa | 2-0 | 4-1 | 2-1 | 0-1 | 0-1 | 5 | 3 | 0 | 2 | 8 | 4 | 9 | 60.00 |
| Barnsley | - | - | - | - | - | 0 | 0 | 0 | 0 | 0 | 0 | 0 | 0.00 |
| Blackburn Rovers | 1-1 | 3-1 | 1-1 | 1-0 | 2-0 | 5 | 3 | 2 | 0 | 8 | 3 | 11 | 73.33 |
| Bolton Wanderers | - | - | - | 1-0 | | 1 | 1 | 0 | 0 | 1 | 0 | 3 | 100.00 |
| Chelsea | 1-0 | 3-1 | 0-1 | 2-3 | 0-0 | 5 | 2 | 1 | 2 | 6 | 5 | 7 | 46.67 |
| Coventry City | 2-2 | 1-0 | 0-0 | 1-0 | 2-2 | 5 | 2 | 3 | 0 | 6 | 4 | 9 | 60.00 |
| Crystal Palace | 1-0 | - | 3-1 | - | | 2 | 2 | 0 | 0 | 4 | 1 | 6 | 100.00 |
| Derby County | - | - | - | - | 3-1 | 1 | 1 | 0 | 0 | 3 | 1 | 3 | 100.00 |
| Everton | 0-0 | 0-2 | 2-0 | 2-2 | 2-2 | 5 | 1 | 3 | 1 | 6 | 6 | 6 | 40.00 |
| Leeds United | 1-1 | 0-2 | 1-3 | 1-1 | 0-2 | 5 | 0 | 2 | 3 | 3 | 9 | 2 | 13.33 |
| Leicester City | - | - | 2-2 | - | 2-2 | 2 | 0 | 2 | 0 | 4 | 4 | 2 | 33.33 |
| Liverpool | 2-1 | 4-2 | 0-2 | 1-3 | 0-1 | 5 | 2 | 0 | 3 | 7 | 9 | 6 | 40.00 |
| Manchester United | 0-1 | 1-3 | 2-2 | 3-1 | 6-3 | 5 | 2 | 1 | 2 | 12 | 10 | 7 | 46.67 |
| Newcastle United | - | 2-1 | 3-1 | 1-0 | 2-2 | 4 | 3 | 1 | 0 | 8 | 4 | 10 | 83.33 |
| Sheffield Wednesday | 1-2 | 1-1 | 0-0 | 0-1 | 2-3 | 5 | 0 | 2 | 3 | 4 | 7 | 2 | 13.33 |
| Tottenham Hotspur | 0-0 | 1-0 | 4-3 | 0-0 | 0-1 | 5 | 2 | 2 | 1 | 5 | 4 | 8 | 53.33 |
| West Ham United | - | 0-2 | 1-1 | 0-0 | 2-0 | 4 | 1 | 2 | 1 | 3 | 3 | 5 | 41.67 |
| Wimbledon | 2-2 | 1-0 | 2-3 | 0-0 | 0-0 | 5 | 1 | 3 | 1 | 5 | 5 | 6 | 40.00 |
| Totals | | | | | | 101 | 40 | 31 | 30 | 146 | 121 | 151 | 49.83 |

# Transfers In and Out

| Mth | Player | Signed From | Fee | Notes |
|---|---|---|---|---|
| Aug-96 | Graham Potter | Stoke City | £250,000 | Rising to £500,000 |
| Aug-96 | Robbie Slater | West Ham Utd | £250,000 | |
| Aug-96 | Richard Dryden | Bristol City | £150,000 | |
| Sep-96 | Eyal Berkovic | Maccabi Tel Aviv | £1,000,000 | |
| Sep-96 | Egil Ostenstad | Viking Stavanger | £800,000 | |
| Sep-96 | Claus Lundekvam | SK Brann | £400,000 | |
| Sep-96 | Russell Watkinson | Woking | Free | |
| Oct-96 | Ulrich van Gobbel | Galatasary | £1,300,000 | |
| Nov-96 | Aly Dia | (no club) | Monthly Contract | |
| Dec-96 | Maik Taylor | Barnet | £500,000 | |
| Mar-97 | Mike Evans | Plymouth Argyle | £500,000 | |

| Mth | Player | Signed For | Fee | Notes |
|---|---|---|---|---|
| Aug-96 | Bruce Grobbelaar | Plymouth Argyle | Free | |
| Oct-96 | Neil Shipperley | Crystal Palace | £1,000,000 | |
| Nov-96 | Neil Heaney | Manchester City | £500,000 | |
| Nov-96 | Frankie Bennett | Bristol Rovers | £15,000 | |
| Dec-96 | Sam Stockley-Phillips | Barnet | Free | |
| Jan-97 | Gordon Watson | Bradford City | £550,000 | |
| Feb-97 | Graham Potter | WBA | £150,000 | Could rise to £300,000 |
| Feb-97 | Nathan Blamey | Shrewsbury Town | Free | |
| Jun-97 | Eyal Berkovic | West Ham United | £1,750,000 | |

# Tottenham Hotspur

GOING, GOING, GONE pretty much sums up another dismal season for the white half of north London and given the departure of Teddy Sheringham to Manchester United and another spate of pre-season injuries involving Anderton (who else?) and even Allan Neilsen it is difficult to see anything other than another season of anonymity for Tottenham.

The only light on the horizon was the new six year contract signed by Sol Campbell – one of England's brightest talents. The failure to lure new players to White Hart Lane during the close season simply added to the pain of most Spurs supporters even though the big names were linked to them before they went elsewhere. The vain attempt to sign Brazilian Juninho was typical and led one broadsheet writer to suggest they were also seeking to lure Pele out of retirement and capture Aretha Franklin.

Even at the start of the 1995-96 season manager Gerry Francis was subdued in the transfer market as he released several fringe players and brought in Allan Nielsen from Brondby for £1.65 million. Tottenham suffered terribly with injuries not least to Gary Mabbutt, Chris Armstrong, Teddy Sheringham and Darren Anderton. Indeed Mabbutt, Armstrong and Anderton failed to complete a season of games between them when all would have almost certainly be regarded as first choice selections when the Premiership got under way in August.

That pre-season dip was the end of Gerry Francis' movement in the transfer market and it is generally overlooked that he spent close on £10 million two months later on, to bring Steffen Iversen, John Scales and Ramon Vega to White Hart Lane. Scales was troubled by injury straight away and Vega was sent off in only his second game. Iversen at least showed the way when he scored Spurs' first league hat trick for over two years Sunderland in March.

Sol Campbell competed in all 38 Premier League games for Spurs and can be regarded as their most outstanding player with the ability to anticipate well, intercept and pass without fuss. It is fair to say that he would probably walk straight into any Premiership team. Behind him Ian Walker missed just one game last season and forced his way into the England squad, but even his form couldn't help when the ball bounced over him against Liverpool and he was on the end of one or two disastrous results. Around them Clive Wilson struggled against nippy opposition and Dean Austin found it hard to find the form that had made him a regular in previous seasons. David Howells was, like Campbell, one of the season's few successes and this under-rated player is worth considering.

# Club Data File

## Responsibility

Top Scorers:    Teddy Sheringham (7),
Steffen Iversen (6),
Andy Sinton (6)
Allan Nielsen (6)

Sent-Off:    Ramon Vega

## Usage 1996-97

Squad:    32 players used

Substitutes:    63 used, 127 not used

## Players 1996-97

Most Used Subs:   Ronny Rosenthal (16),
Jason Dozzell (7),
Stuart Nethercott (7)

Most SNU:    Espen Baardsen (36),
Stuart Nethercott (19),
Rory Allen (12)

Most Subbed:    Andy Sinton (9),
Allan Nielsen (8),
Darren Anderton (7)

## Five Year Premiership Form

|  | P | W | D | L | F | A | Pts | Ps |
|---|---|---|---|---|---|---|---|---|
| 92-93 | 42 | 16 | 11 | 15 | 60 | 66 | 59 | 8 |
| 93-94 | 42 | 11 | 12 | 19 | 54 | 59 | 45 | 15 |
| 94-95 | 42 | 16 | 14 | 12 | 66 | 58 | 62 | 7 |
| 95-96 | 38 | 16 | 13 | 9 | 50 | 38 | 61 | 8 |
| 96-97 | 38 | 13 | 7 | 18 | 44 | 51 | 46 | 10 |

Despite the injuries, many of the previously better known Spurs players failed to take opportunities. Ruel Fox found himself on the bench on a dozen

# Gerry Francis

As a player Gerry Francis was one of the best. He helped QPR to promotion in 1973 and then to the runner-up spot in the old Division One in 1976. A proven England international he won 12 caps and was soon made national captain. However, a serious injury prematurely ended his playing career at its peek. Not to be deterred, he took over at Bristol Rovers as manager and won the Third Division Championship in 1991. A year later he was back at Loftus Road in the role of manager and immediately transformed their playing fortunes on a shoestring budget.

In 1994 he moved across London to White Hart Lane as Spurs appointed him to shore up a leaky defence that had become a symbol of the Ossie Ardiles' reign. He took the club to an FA Cup semi-final shortly after.

occasions, while Stuart Nethercott was an unused sub on no less than 19 occasions.

Andy Sinton provided additional firepower up front in the long-term absence of Armstrong and Sheringham weighed in with six priceless goals.

While the failure to add any new names other than David Ginola, and the departure of Sheringham, will have hogged the headlines in the build up to the start of the 1997-98 season, a worrying factor will be how their injured players recover and where the goals will come from. Last season Tottenham drew just seven of their games and lost 18 – something that was only matched by relegated Sunderland

In any fantasy side Campbell will always be a major contender as will Scales and Walker. Anderton might be another but not until his has proved his fitness. Beyond that there might be a few well priced players, especially amongst those recent signings who might be surprise packages – barring injury.

# Tottenham Hotspur v Record

| Opponents | 92/3 | 93/4 | 94/5 | 95/6 | 96/7 | P | W | D | L | F | A | Pts | % |
|---|---|---|---|---|---|---|---|---|---|---|---|---|---|
| Arsenal | 1-0 | 0-1 | 1-0 | 2-1 | 0-0 | 5 | 3 | 1 | 1 | 4 | 2 | 10 | 66.67 |
| Aston Villa | 0-0 | 1-1 | 3-4 | 0-1 | 1-0 | 5 | 1 | 2 | 2 | 5 | 6 | 5 | 33.33 |
| Barnsley | - | - | - | - | - | 0 | 0 | 0 | 0 | 0 | 0 | 0 | 0.00 |
| Blackburn Rovers | 1-2 | 0-2 | 3-1 | 2-3 | 2-1 | 5 | 2 | 0 | 3 | 8 | 9 | 6 | 40.00 |
| Bolton Wanderers | - | - | - | 2-2 | | 1 | 0 | 1 | 0 | 2 | 2 | 1 | 33.33 |
| Chelsea | 1-2 | 1-1 | 0-0 | 1-1 | 1-2 | 5 | 0 | 3 | 2 | 4 | 6 | 3 | 20.00 |
| Coventry City | 0-2 | 1-2 | 1-3 | 3-1 | 1-2 | 5 | 1 | 0 | 4 | 6 | 10 | 3 | 20.00 |
| Crystal Palace | 2-2 | - | 0-0 | - | | 2 | 0 | 2 | 0 | 2 | 2 | 2 | 33.33 |
| Derby | - | - | - | - | 1-1 | 1 | 0 | 1 | 0 | 1 | 1 | 1 | 33.33 |
| Everton | 2-1 | 3-2 | 2-1 | 0-0 | 0-0 | 5 | 3 | 2 | 0 | 7 | 4 | 11 | 73.33 |
| Leeds United | 4-0 | 1-1 | 1-1 | 2-1 | 1-0 | 5 | 3 | 2 | 0 | 9 | 3 | 11 | 73.33 |
| Leicester City | - | - | 1-0 | - | 1-2 | 2 | 1 | 0 | 1 | 2 | 2 | 3 | 50.00 |
| Liverpool | 2-0 | 3-3 | 0-0 | 1-3 | 0-2 | 5 | 1 | 2 | 2 | 6 | 8 | 5 | 33.33 |
| Manchester United | 1-1 | 0-1 | 0-1 | 4-1 | 1-2 | 5 | 1 | 1 | 3 | 6 | 6 | 4 | 26.67 |
| Newcastle United | - | 1-2 | 4-2 | 1-1 | 1-2 | 4 | 1 | 1 | 2 | 7 | 7 | 4 | 33.33 |
| Sheffield Wednesday | 0-2 | 1-3 | 3-1 | 1-0 | 1-1 | 5 | 2 | 1 | 2 | 6 | 7 | 7 | 46.67 |
| Southampton | 4-2 | 3-0 | 1-2 | 1-0 | 3-1 | 5 | 4 | 0 | 1 | 12 | 5 | 12 | 80.00 |
| West Ham United | - | 1-4 | 3-1 | 0-1 | 1-0 | 4 | 2 | 0 | 2 | 5 | 6 | 6 | 50.00 |
| Wimbledon | 1-1 | 1-1 | 1-2 | 3-1 | 1-0 | 5 | 2 | 2 | 1 | 7 | 5 | 8 | 53.33 |
| Totals | | | | | | 101 | 42 | 27 | 32 | 146 | 119 | 153 | 50.50 |

# Transfers In and Out

| Mth | Player | Signed From | Fee | Notes |
|---|---|---|---|---|
| Nov-96 | Steffen Iversen | Rosenborg | £2,700,000 | |
| Dec-96 | John Scales | Liverpool | £2,600,000 | |
| Jan-97 | Ramon Vega | Cagliari | £3,750,000 | |

| Mth | Player | Signed For | Fee | Notes |
|---|---|---|---|---|
| Aug-96 | Chris Day | Crystal Palace | £225,000 | Rising to £425,000 plus £100,000 on an England appearance |
| Sep-96 | Gerard McMahon | Stoke City | £450,000 | |
| Sep-96 | Andy Turner | Portsmouth | £250,000 | |
| Nov-96 | Jason Cundy | Ipswich Town | £200,000 | |
| Feb-97 | Kevin Scott | Norwich City | £250,000 | |
| Jun-97 | Teddy Sheringham | Manchester United | £3,500,000 | |

# West Ham United

HAVING FAILED miserably with some of his foreign signings, Hammers' manager Harry Redknapp went back into the transfer market before the 1997 deadline and made some very useful purchases, repeating the feat during the close season. So much so that, when you look at the side on paper, they have some real talent and, if it should click, then Slaven Bilic might just be wondering why he left for Everton.

West Ham's main problems last season were in scoring goals and stringing together two consecutive wins, something which was achieved just twice during the whole season. Prior to Christmas, the Hammers had won just four league games but had picked up a creditable draw at Newcastle and rescued a point at home to Manchester United after trailing by two goals late in the game. However all that changed when Redknapp broke the Hammers' bank to sign John Hartson and Paul Kitson from Arsenal and Newcastle respectively. The two weighed in with 12 goals in the final 13 games as the East End delighted in their aggressive but skilful play. The two got off the mark in a marvellous 4-3 win over Spurs, Kitson scoring a hat-trick and he might have had a second if he had not missed a penalty. Even with this late burst, it was still Julian Dicks who finished as the Hammers' top scorer!

With confidence, the Hartson/Kitson duo could, indeed should, continue where they left off, but Hartson will need to watch his disciplinary record – he was the first Premiership player to be suspended last season. All this means that Iain Dowie may well be the odd one out of the Hammers offense and may move on to yet another club.

At the back Ludo Miklosko missed just two games and has the confidence and presence that all great 'keepers need. But it was the now departed Slaven Bilic who was the rock and his service will be missed even though Richard Hall finally made his mark in the final eight games almost a year after signing for the club having been blighted by injury on his arrival. The departure of Bilic may mean that Rio Ferdinand has his chance to get a regular place and so aid his development as an England star of the (perhaps not too distant) future.

Maybe it is his disciplinary record but Julian Dicks really should be an England international (no I am not a West Ham supporter!). He has performed consistently well for the Hammers down the years and last season was no different, playing in 31 games and netting six times. This combination of defensive duties and goals is common for Dicks and should be borne in mind.

# Club Data File

## Responsibility

| | |
|---|---|
| Top Scorers: | Paul Kitson (8), Julian Dicks (6), John Hartson (5) |
| Sent-Off: | Marc Rieper, Michael Hughes |

## Usage 1996-97

| | |
|---|---|
| Squad: | 35 players used |
| Substitutes: | 82 used, 108 not used |

## Players 1996-97

| | |
|---|---|
| Most Used Subs: | Frank Lampard (10), Stan Lazaridis (9), Hugo Porfirio (8) |

| | |
|---|---|
| Most SNU: | Les Sealey (22), Frank Lampard (15), Keith Rowland (11) |
| Most Subbed: | Ian Bishop (9), Keith Rowland (8), John Moncur (7) |

### Five Year Premiership Form

| | P | W | D | L | F | A | Pts | Ps |
|---|---|---|---|---|---|---|---|---|
| 92-93 | 46 | 26 | 10 | 10 | 81 | 41 | 88 | 2 |
| 93-94 | 42 | 13 | 13 | 16 | 47 | 58 | 52 | 13 |
| 94-95 | 42 | 13 | 11 | 18 | 44 | 48 | 50 | 14 |
| 95-96 | 38 | 14 | 9 | 15 | 43 | 52 | 51 | 10 |
| 96-97 | 38 | 10 | 12 | 16 | 39 | 48 | 42 | 14 |

In the middle Steve Lomas – another arrival – should help bolster the skills of John Moncur and the prompting of Ian

# Harry Redknapp

Harry Redknapp is West Ham through and through, having played there in a distinguished career, often as an old-fashioned winger. He played in more than 170 games but never won any major honours – a semi final League Cup defeat by Stoke City in 1971 being the nearest he came.

He began on the managerial front as an assistant to Bobby Moore at Oxford City before he moved on to Bournemouth and guided them to an Associate Members Cup win and a third division championship title in 1987. Having suffered a serious car injury, he returned to nurture his son Jamie and move on to Liverpool. His chance at Upton Park came as assistant to Billy Bonds in 1991, whom he eventually replaced as manager.

Bishop, while a wide lying role could help Stan Lazaridis to build on his development in the last two years, by supplying the type of swinging crosses that John Hartson is capable of creating havoc from. However, it is the arrival of Eyal Berkovic that could most excite and invigorate the Hammers' middle lands and maybe put at risk the positions of one or two of the Upton Park stalwarts.

In short West Ham could provide some useful players for your own team and at reasonable prices.

# West Ham United v Record

| Opponents | 92/3 | 93/4 | 94/5 | 95/6 | 96/7 | P | W | D | L | F | A | Pts | % |
|---|---|---|---|---|---|---|---|---|---|---|---|---|---|
| Arsenal ... ... ... ... ... | - | 0-0 | 0-2 | 0-1 | 1-2 | 4 | 0 | 1 | 3 | 1 | 5 | 1 | 8.33 |
| Aston Villa ... ... ... ... | - | 0-0 | 1-0 | 1-4 | 0-2 | 4 | 1 | 1 | 2 | 2 | 6 | 4 | 33.33 |
| Barnsley ... ... ... ... ... | - | - | - | - | - | 0 | 0 | 0 | 0 | 0 | 0 | 0 | 0.00 |
| Blackburn Rovers ... ... ... | - | 1-2 | 2-0 | 1-1 | 2-1 | 4 | 2 | 1 | 1 | 6 | 4 | 7 | 58.33 |
| Bolton Wanderers ... ... ... | - | - | - | 1-0 | | 1 | 1 | 0 | 0 | 1 | 0 | 3 | 100.00 |
| Chelsea ... ... ... ... ... | - | 1-0 | 1-2 | 1-3 | 3-2 | 4 | 2 | 0 | 2 | 6 | 7 | 6 | 50.00 |
| Coventry City ... ... ... ... | - | 3-2 | 0-1 | 3-2 | 1-1 | 4 | 2 | 1 | 1 | 7 | 6 | 7 | 58.33 |
| Crystal Palace ... ... ... ... | - | - | 1-0 | - | | 1 | 1 | 0 | 0 | 1 | 0 | 3 | 100.00 |
| Derby County ... ... ... ... | | - | - | - | 1-1 | 1 | 0 | 1 | 0 | 1 | 1 | 1 | 33.33 |
| Everton ... ... ... ... ... | - | 0-1 | 2-2 | 2-1 | 2-2 | 4 | 1 | 2 | 1 | 6 | 6 | 5 | 41.67 |
| Leeds United ... ... ... ... | - | 0-1 | 0-0 | 1-2 | 0-2 | 4 | 0 | 1 | 3 | 1 | 5 | 1 | 8.33 |
| Leicester City ... ... ... ... | | - | 1-0 | - | 1-0 | 2 | 2 | 0 | 0 | 2 | 0 | 6 | 100.00 |
| Liverpool ... ... ... ... ... | - | 1-2 | 3-0 | 0-0 | 1-2 | 4 | 1 | 1 | 2 | 5 | 4 | 4 | 33.33 |
| Manchester United ... ... - | | 2-2 | 1-1 | 0-1 | 2-2 | 4 | 0 | 3 | 1 | 5 | 6 | 3 | 25.00 |
| Newcastle United ... ... ... | - | 2-4 | 1-3 | 2-0 | 0-0 | 4 | 1 | 1 | 2 | 5 | 7 | 4 | 33.33 |
| Sheffield Wednesday ... ... - | | 2-0 | 0-2 | 1-1 | 5-1 | 4 | 2 | 1 | 1 | 8 | 4 | 7 | 58.33 |
| Southampton ... ... ... ... | - | 3-3 | 2-0 | 2-1 | 2-1 | 4 | 3 | 1 | 0 | 9 | 5 | 10 | 83.33 |
| Tottenham Hotspur ... ... - | | 1-3 | 1-2 | 1-1 | 4-3 | 4 | 1 | 1 | 2 | 7 | 9 | 4 | 33.33 |
| Wimbledon ... ... ... ... ... | - | 0-2 | 3-0 | 1-1 | 0-2 | 4 | 1 | 1 | 2 | 4 | 5 | 4 | 33.33 |
| Totals ... ... ... ... ... ... | | | | | | 80 | 31 | 24 | 25 | 106 | 96 | 117 | 48.75 |

# Transfers In and Out

| Mth | Player | Signed From | Fee | Notes |
|---|---|---|---|---|
| Aug-96 | Florin Raducioiu | Espanyol | £2,400,000 | |
| Nov-96 | Scott Mean | Bournemouth | £100,000 | |
| Nov-96 | Les Sealey | Leyton Orient | Free | |
| Feb-97 | John Hartson | Arsenal | £3,200,000 | Could rise to £5,000,000 |
| Feb-97 | Paul Kitson | Newcastle United | £2,300,000 | |
| Mar-97 | Steve Lomas | Manchester City | £1,600,000 | May rise to £2,000,000 |
| Jun-97 | Eyal Berkovic | Southampton | £1,750,000 | |
| Jun-97 | Andrew Impey | QPR | £1,200,000 | |

| Mth | Player | Signed For | Fee | Notes |
|---|---|---|---|---|
| Aug-96 | Robbie Slater | Southampton | £250,000 | |
| Aug-96 | Scott Canham | Brentford | £25,000 | Rising to £60,000 |
| Aug-96 | Dale Gordon | Bournemouth | Free | |
| Aug-96 | Alvin Martin | Leyton Orient | Free | |
| Oct-96 | Tony Cottee | Selangor | £750,000 | |
| Oct-96 | Adrian Whitbread | Portsmouth | £250,000 | |
| Nov-96 | Peter Shilton | Leyton Orient | Monthly Contract | |
| Dec-96 | Ilie Dumitrescu | Club America | £800,000 | |
| Jan-97 | Florin Raducioiu | Espanyol | £1,600,000 | |
| Jan-97 | Kenny Brown | Birmingham City | £75,000 | |
| Jan-97 | Danny Shipp | Coleraine | £30,000 | |
| Feb-97 | Steve Jones | Charlton Athletic | £400,000 | |
| Mar-97 | Steve Mautone | Reading | £250,000 | |
| Mar-97 | Mark Bowen | Shimizu S-Pulse | Free | |
| May-97 | Slaven Bilic | Everton | £4,500,000 | |

      **Fantasy Football Handbook**

# Wimbledon

LAST SEASON looked to be promising Wimbledon so much as it unfolded, but in the end it fell away as games, and a relatively small squad, took their toll on the team's bid to emulate the 1998 FA Cup winning side. There only remained the heart-break of two semi-final defeats and a UEFA cup position lost through a slide down the Premiership table from the second position they once occupied.

It had started so differently. The 'experts' were rubbing their hands with glee as the Dons failed to either score or pick up a single point from their first three Premiership games. Manager Joe Kinnear made few changes to his squad during the summer and, while there were no big money sales, he bought modestly in spending £1.8 million on taking Ben Thatcher from Millwall and an initial £125,000 on Fulham's Darren Jupp.

The Dons finally broke their duck and from there they never really looked back as they went off on a seven match winning streak. The streak continued to a 14 match unbeaten run but caved in three days before Christmas at Villa Park as Villa meted out a 5-0 thrashing. Having appeared almost impregnable prior to that match, Wimbledon were never to fully recover.

Wimbledon's real boost in that opening half of the season was their ability to find the back of the net – 33 goals in their opening 19 league games, as compared to just 16 times from the final 19 games. Much of this was down to the electric form of Robbie Earle and why he hasn't had the recognition at international level remains one of life's great mysteries.

But that is often the case with Wimbledon players who find themselves playing terrific football but only getting recognition after they have moved on. In fact you might like to try naming an international side of players who found their feet at the club.

Up front it was Efan Ekoku who finished as top scorer with 11 goals from 30 games; interestingly he was also their most substituted man – 17 times in all. Close behind him in the netting stakes came Marcus Gayle who was subbed on 12 occasions – Joe Kinnear is clearly a man who likes to defend a lead perhaps! Dean Holdsworth found himself on the other end of that arrangement, being used as a sub in 15 matches, but he remains the Dons' all-time Premiership scorer.

Andy Clarke had started the season in the line-up against Manchester United and set a new record. It was his 100th Premiership appearance for the Dons – his 50th as a starter – the previous 50 had all come from the bench to make him the Premier League's most used sub!

# Club Data File

## Responsibility

Top Scorers: Efan Ekoku (11),
Marcus Gayle (8),
Robbie Earle (7)

Sent-Off: Vinnie Jones

## Usage 1996-97

Squad: 25 players used

Substitutes: 73 used, 113 not used

## Players 1996-97

Most Used Subs: Mick Harford (10),
Peter Fear (9),
Jon Goodman (7)

Most SNU: Paul Heald (23),
Mick Harford (15),
Brendan Murphy (13)

Most Subbed: Efan Ekoku (17),
Marcus Gayle (12),
Oyvind Leonhardsen (8)

## Five Year Premiership Form

| | P | W | D | L | F | A | Pts | Ps |
|---|---|---|---|---|---|---|---|---|
| 92-93 | 42 | 14 | 12 | 16 | 56 | 55 | 54 | 12 |
| 93-94 | 42 | 18 | 11 | 13 | 56 | 53 | 65 | 6 |
| 94-95 | 42 | 15 | 11 | 16 | 48 | 65 | 56 | 9 |
| 95-96 | 38 | 10 | 11 | 17 | 55 | 70 | 41 | 14 |
| 96-97 | 38 | 15 | 11 | 12 | 49 | 46 | 56 | 8 |

That opening game was also the one where 'keeper Neil Sullivan found himself lobbed by Beckham from the half way line. But Kinnear didn't lose faith

## Joe Kinnear

Joe Kinnear was appointed the Dons' manager at the start of 1992 having previously held the position of coach and assistant manager at the club. His managerial career started at Doncaster Rovers where he started as an assistant to Dave Mackay, ultimately taking over as manager for a three month period at the end of the 1988-89 season.

Kinnear played most of his professional football at Tottenham, making the full-back position his own and playing over 300 games in a period from 1963 to 1975. A Republic of Ireland international he won medals in the FA Cup, the League Cup (twice) and UEFA Cup with Spurs, before injury ended his career during a spell at Brighton.

with him and Sullivan finished with 36 games under his belt.

At the back Neil Ardley and Chris Perry formed a formidable barrier and will be the main foundation for the 1997-98 season. Ben Thatcher should have recovered from the injury that ended his season after just nine games and will be worth consideration.

Kenny Cunningham missed just two games while Vinnie Jones continued to give the Dons their bite. Indeed bite was something that had changed. After having the worst disciplinary record in 1995-96 they finished top of the fair Play league at the end of 1996-97 as they had far fewer bookings than any other side in the Premiership and just one player, predictably Jones, dismissed.

# Wimbledon v Record

| Opponents | 92/3 | 93/4 | 94/5 | 95/6 | 96/7 | P | W | D | L | F | A | Pts | % |
|---|---|---|---|---|---|---|---|---|---|---|---|---|---|
| Arsenal | 3-2 | 0-3 | 1-3 | 0-3 | 2-2 | 5 | 1 | 1 | 3 | 6 | 13 | 4 | 26.67 |
| Aston Villa | 2-3 | 2-2 | 4-3 | 3-3 | 0-2 | 5 | 1 | 2 | 2 | 11 | 13 | 5 | 33.33 |
| Barnsley | - | - | - | - | - | 0 | 0 | 0 | 0 | 0 | 0 | 0 | 0.00 |
| Blackburn Rovers | 1-1 | 4-1 | 0-3 | 1-1 | 1-0 | 5 | 2 | 2 | 1 | 7 | 6 | 8 | 53.33 |
| Bolton Wanderers | - | - | - | 3-2 | | 1 | 1 | 0 | 0 | 3 | 2 | 3 | 100.00 |
| Chelsea | 0-0 | 1-1 | 1-1 | 1-1 | 0-1 | 5 | 0 | 4 | 1 | 3 | 4 | 4 | 26.67 |
| Coventry City | 1-2 | 1-2 | 2-0 | 0-2 | 2-2 | 5 | 1 | 1 | 3 | 6 | 8 | 4 | 26.67 |
| Crystal Palace | 4-0 | - | 2-0 | - | | 2 | 2 | 0 | 0 | 6 | 0 | 6 | 100.00 |
| Derby County | - | - | - | - | 1-1 | 1 | 0 | 1 | 0 | 1 | 1 | 1 | 33.33 |
| Everton | 1-3 | 1-1 | 2-1 | 2-3 | 4-0 | 5 | 2 | 1 | 2 | 10 | 8 | 7 | 46.67 |
| Leeds United | 1-0 | 1-0 | 0-0 | 2-4 | 2-0 | 5 | 3 | 1 | 1 | 6 | 4 | 10 | 66.67 |
| Leicester City | - | - | 2-1 | - | 1-3 | 2 | 1 | 0 | 1 | 3 | 4 | 3 | 50.00 |
| Liverpool | 2-0 | 1-1 | 0-0 | 1-0 | 2-1 | 5 | 3 | 2 | 0 | 6 | 2 | 11 | 73.33 |
| Manchester United | 1-2 | 1-0 | 0-1 | 2-4 | 0-3 | 5 | 1 | 0 | 4 | 4 | 10 | 3 | 20.00 |
| Newcastle United | - | 4-2 | 3-2 | 3-3 | 1-1 | 4 | 2 | 2 | 0 | 11 | 8 | 8 | 66.67 |
| Nottingham Forest | 1-0 | - | 2-2 | 1-0 | 1-0 | 4 | 3 | 1 | 0 | 5 | 2 | 10 | 83.33 |
| Sheffield Wednesday | 1-1 | 2-1 | 0-1 | 2-2 | 4-2 | 5 | 2 | 2 | 1 | 9 | 7 | 8 | 53.33 |
| Southampton | 1-2 | 1-0 | 0-2 | 1-2 | 3-1 | 5 | 2 | 0 | 3 | 6 | 7 | 6 | 40.00 |
| Totals | | | | | | 101 | 44 | 26 | 31 | 148 | 124 | 158 | 52.15 |

# Transfers In and Out

| Mth | Player | Signed From | Fee | Notes |
|---|---|---|---|---|
| Jun-97 | Ceri Hughes | Luton Town | £350,000 | Rising to £750,000 |

| Mth | Player | Signed For | Fee | Notes |
|---|---|---|---|---|
| Aug-96 | Hans Segers | Wolverhampton W. | Non-Contract | |
| Sep-96 | Gary Elkins | Swindon Town | £100,000 | |
| Jun-97 | Oyvind Leonhardsen | Liverpool | £3,500,000 | |

# Player Directory

# Guide to the Player Directory

THE PLAYER DIRECTORY contains details of over 470 potential Premiership footballers and provides vital three-season form information which will help you make your fantasy selections. Each entry follows the same format, although there are some differences for goalkeeper entries and these are outlined below. Use the *Player Directory* information along with that provided in the *Team Directory* and the various tables throughout this book to ensure you get the best value from your purchasing budget. Remember that you are seeking consistent performers and sometimes the big-name players can obscure the performances of the majority of the players who provide the backbone of their team.

## Star Ratings

Each entry starts with the player's name and the club he was registered with at the time of writing. This is followed by his position and a star rating. Ratings are out of five: a player who has ❶❷❸❹❺ is considered a top buy, while a rating of a ❶ suggests that he probably isn't worth considering for your team! However don't immediately dismiss any player. A rating can also mean that he is simply unlikely to be in the side's starting line-up. Read the text because, should an injury thrust the player into the limelight,

you could find yourself with a real bargain on your hands!

This information is followed by the player's full name and date/place of birth. The body of the entry is the pen pic – a profile of the player which summarises his strengths and weaknesses, together with some general information regarding his performances last season.

## Form Factors

*Form Factors* provide the hard stats behind the player in the Premiership for the previous three-season period. Note that only Premiership details are listed here, thus if a player has been out of the top flight, or has missed a year, the seasons listed might not be concurrent and may not finish with the 1996-97 season. This is especially true of course with the three promoted teams. However, more detailed figures relating to all players including the promoted teams can be found in the section headed *Appearance Fact File*. This includes details you are unlikely to find elsewhere, including how many times a player was subbed last year, for example.

Back to the *Player Directory*: The format and information differ according to the position in which the player plays. For example, a goalkeeper entry concentrates on goals conceded and clean sheets as opposed to an entry for a forward, which concentrates on goals scored and the percentage of the goals he gets for his team.

Nevertheless the arrangement is straightforward and provides some basic information about the number of games the player appeared in, both as a starter and as a sub, along with details on the number of yellow and red cards they accumulated. Remember that red cards mean missed matches and yellow cards can mean suspensions as well. As a rule of thumb, five yellow cards will earn the recipient a suspension.

The key to these stats is as follows:

**Tot**    Total appearances for the season
**St**    Starting appearances
**Sb**    Sub appearances
**Y**    Yellow cards received
**R**    Red cards received

These figures are provided for all players and are followed by a look inside the numbers and an attempt to analyse the player's contribution to his team for each season. These are done on a strict season-by-season basis even if the player has played for two Premiership clubs in a season. In this case the numbers for the season are combined and the percentages calculated from the combined figures where appropriate.

There are therefore two possible sets of information. For all outfield players (not goalkeepers) the following information is provided:

**GP**    Game Percentage – this is the percentage of the Premiership games the player played in for that season. Thus a player with a 50.00 rating here would have played in half of the team's Premier League games.

**GG**    Game Goals – this is the number of games a player takes to score a goal. A rating of 5.25 would means the player scores a goal every 5.25 games. A figure of 0.00 indicates no goals.

**GF**    Goals For – the goals the player's team scored in the season.

**GS**    Goals Scored – the goals the player scored that season.

**TGR**    Team Goal Ratio – the percentage of the team's goals that the player scored.

Goalkeeper summaries concentrate on the number of goals they have or haven't conceded as the case may be. The key here is:

**GA**    Goals Against – the goals the 'keeper's team conceded in the relevant season.

**GkA**    Goals 'Keeper Against – the number of goals that the goalkeeper conceded for the season.

**GAp**    Goals/Appearance Ratio – the average number of goals the 'keeper concedes in a game.

**CS**    Clean Sheets – the number of occasions the 'keeper didn't concede a goal in a game.

**SO**    Shut Outs – the most number of full games in succession a goalkeeper went without conceding a goal.

**Rp**    Repeated – How often the shut-out was repeated.

## An Example

An example *Form Factors* entry can be seen overleaf. From this we can see that the player played for Arsenal in the Premiership during the past three seasons. Most of the time the player started games but the yellow and red card count shows that a large number of games could have been lost through suspensions in this period.

| | GA | GkA | GAp | CS | SO | Rp |
|---|---|---|---|---|---|---|
| 94-95 | 56 | 43 | 1.43 | 6 | 2 | 0 |
| 95-96 | 35 | 34 | 0.89 | 13 | 2 | 0 |
| 96-97 | 34 | 17 | 0.85 | 9 | 2 | 0 |
| Total | 125 | 94 | 1.07 | 28 | 6 | |

## Form Factors

| Season | Team | Tot | St | Sb | Y | R |
|---|---|---|---|---|---|---|
| 94-95 | Arsenal | 27 | 27 | 0 | 4 | 1 |
| 95-96 | Arsenal | 21 | 21 | 0 | 4 | 1 |
| 96-97 | Arsenal | 28 | 27 | 1 | 5 | 2 |
| Total | | 76 | 75 | 1 | 13 | 4 |

| | GP | GG | GF | GS | TGR |
|---|---|---|---|---|---|
| 94-95 | 64.29 | 9.00 | 52 | 3 | 5.77 |
| 95-96 | 55.26 | 21.00 | 49 | 1 | 2.04 |
| 96-97 | 73.68 | 9.33 | 62 | 3 | 4.84 |
| Averages | 64.41 | 13.11 | 54.33 | 2.33 | 4.22 |

The final line is simply a totalling of the figure above with an overall average given for the GAp total. ∎

The total averages on the final line show that the 76 games played during the three seasons amounted to a little over 64% of the club's Premiership games with the player scoring a goal on average every 13th game or so – this accounting for 4.22% of the team's goals during the three-year period.

Below is the second half of the *Form Factors* entry as it might appear for a goalkeeper. From the first line – season 1994-95 – we can see that his team conceded 56 goals, 43 of which the 'keeper was in goal for. This worked out to an average of 1.43 goals per game. Obviously this figure (GAp) is a key one as it tells you a lot about the 'keeper and his defence. The lower this figure the better for your fantasy team!

Beyond that we can see that there were six clean sheets in those games and the longest shut out was two games and this wasn't repeated.

## ADAMS, Tony

# Arsenal ❶❷❸❹❺ CB

Fullname: Anthony Alexander Adams
DOB: 10-10-66 Romford, Essex

Nagging injury problems during the past two seasons have limited Adams' time in the Gunners side. His ability to play through the pain however, during vital games for both club and country, has earned him considerable respect in the game.

Regarded as Mr Arsenal, Adams was the England captain throughout Euro 96 and showed a new side to his football last season under manager Arsène Wenger, often joining the attack and scoring three Premiership goals – his best season tally ever.

He joined Arsenal on Schoolboy forms in 1984 and led them to the championship in 1989 and '91. Captained the club to a unique FA Cup and Coca Cola Cup double in 1993 as well as successive appearances in the Cup Winners' Cup finals of 1994 and '95.

Despite his injury problems he has played in over 70% of Arsenal's Premiership games and as the 1997-98 season got under way was just five appearances short of his 400th League appearance for the club. Tends to average at least one suspension a year but an in-form Adams means an in-form Arsenal and generally the meanest defence in the Premiership, plus big Fantasy points for those who are willing to have him on their side!

*Tony Adams*

## Form Factors

| Season | Team | Tot | St | Sb | Y | R |
|--------|------|-----|-----|-----|-----|-----|
| 94-95 | Arsenal | 27 | 27 | 0 | 4 | 1 |
| 95-96 | Arsenal | 21 | 21 | 0 | 4 | 1 |
| 96-97 | Arsenal | 28 | 27 | 1 | 5 | 2 |
| Total | | 76 | 75 | 1 | 13 | 4 |

| | GP | GG | GF | GS | TGR |
|--------|-----|-----|-----|-----|-----|
| 94-95 | 64.29 | 9.00 | 52 | 3 | 5.77 |
| 95-96 | 55.26 | 21.00 | 49 | 1 | 2.04 |
| 96-97 | 73.68 | 9.33 | 62 | 3 | 4.84 |
| Averages | 64.41 | 13.11 | 54.33 | 2.33 | 4.22 |

## ALBERT, Philippe

# Newcastle U. ❶❷❸ CB

Fullname: Philippe Albert
DOB: 10-08-67 Bouillon, Belgium
    After joining the club from Anderlecht
for £2.65 million in the summer of 1994,
Albert became a favourite with the fans,
roaming forward as part of the
adventurous Newcastle playing style. A
serious knee injury curtailed his first
season on New Year's Day at Leeds
United and Newcastle appeared to
struggle without his presence at the back.
    A full international, the Belgian uses
his 6'3" height when moving forward at
corners and free-kicks and his long legs
get him up into some unlikely attacking
situations. Although he only managed
two Premiership goals in 1996-97, his hit
rate, at just over a goal every nine games,
makes a handy contribution to the coffers.
    Albert started all 27 of his 1996-97
appearances and can be expected to be at
the heart of the Newcastle defence in
1997-98. Under Kevin Keegan
Newcastle's style of play dictated that he
was at the wrong end of the field for a
fantasy player – that should change for
Dalglish's first full season in charge.

## Form Factors

| Season | Team | Tot | St | Sb | Y | R |
|--------|------|-----|-----|-----|-----|-----|
| 94-95 | Newcastle | 17 | 17 | 0 | 4 | 1 |
| 95-96 | Newcastle | 23 | 19 | 4 | 5 | 0 |
| 96-97 | Newcastle | 27 | 27 | 0 | 6 | 0 |
| Total | | 67 | 63 | 4 | 15 | 1 |

| | GP | GG | GF | GS | TGR |
|--------|-----|-----|-----|-----|-----|
| 94-95 | 40.48 | 8.50 | 67 | 2 | 2.99 |
| 95-96 | 60.53 | 5.75 | 66 | 4 | 6.06 |
| 96-97 | 71.05 | 13.50 | 73 | 2 | 2.74 |
| Averages | 57.35 | 9.25 | 68.67 | 2.67 | 3.93 |

## ALLEN, Graham

# Everton ❶ FB

Fullname: Graham Allen
DOB: 08-04-77 Franworth
    Twenty-year-old Bolton-born defender
who worked his way through the ranks at
Goodison Park before making an unusual
Premiership debut last Boxing Day
during a 4-2 defeat at Middlesbrough. He
replaced the injured Dave Watson after 14
minutes but then 14 minutes from time
was replaced himself by Marc Hottiger. A
former England Youth player, he was an
unused sub on eight occasions and, at just
20 years of age, has time on his side.

## Form Factors

| Season | Team | Tot | St | Sb | Y | R |
|--------|------|-----|-----|-----|-----|-----|
| 96-97 | Everton | 1 | 0 | 1 | 0 | 0 |
| Total | | 1 | 0 | 1 | 0 | 0 |

| | GP | GG | GF | GS | TGR |
|--------|-----|-----|-----|-----|-----|
| 96-97 | 2.63 | 8.50 | 44 | 0 | 0.00 |
| Averages | 2.63 | 8.50 | 44.00 | 0.00 | 0.00 |

## ALLEN, Rory

# Tottenham H. ❶ S

Fullname: Rory Allen
DOB: 17-10-77 Beckenham
    One of several youngsters at White
Hart Lane to have made progress into the
first team last season without firmly
establishing a permanent place in the
side. Made his debut in September 1996
and followed it four days later with the
opening goal in Tottenham's 2-1 home
defeat by Newcastle. He ended the season
with twelve games under his belt and four
goals to his credit. Lean figure who
joined Spurs as a trainee in July 1994,
being made up to full professional two
years later. Has great potential but will
need to curb his bookability with referees

– a yellow card every three games on average.

## Form Factors

| Season | Team | Tot | St | Sb | Y | R |
|--------|------|-----|----|----|----|----|
| 96-97 | Tottenham | 12 | 9 | 3 | 4 | 0 |
| Total | | 12 | 9 | 3 | 4 | 0 |

| | GP | GG | GF | GS | TGR |
|--------|------|------|------|------|------|
| 96-97 | 31.58 | 6.00 | 44 | 2 | 4.55 |
| Averages | 31.58 | 6.00 | 44.00 | 2.00 | 4.55 |

# ANDERSEN, Leif

## Crystal Palace ❶ CB

Fullname: Leif Erik Andersen
DOB: 19-04-71 Fredrickstad, Norway

A strong central defender who joined Palace in January 1996, signing from Norwegian club Moss for £120,000. At 6' 5" he is a dominant central defender and not surprisingly often involved in corner and free-kick situations around the opponents' penalty area. Was a near ever-present either in the team or on the bench during the end of the 1995-96 season but was unable to command a first team position last season, featuring in just 14 of Palace's games – seven as a substitute. His five starting appearances came in consecutive games in which Palace were unbeaten and included two 6-1 victories! In the later part of the season a shoulder injury needed an operation and, competing with David Tuttle, Robert Quinn and a fit-again Dean Gordon, he may find it equally hard to secure a Premiership place.

# ANDERTON, Darren

## Tottenham H. ❶❷❸❹ M

Fullname: Darren Robert Anderton
DOB: 03-03-72 Southampton

After hitting a level of consistency which earned him a regular place in the England set-up, he has been hit by a series of injuries which have completely devastated his past two seasons, although he stayed fit long enough to play in Euro '96. Anderton has managed just 24 Premiership games over the past two seasons but, when fully fit, will not only set up a high percentage of goals but will also score his fair share.

A player who normally assumes a wide role, he has terrific pace and possesses good sleight of foot that almost lures defenders towards him for them only to find the ball and him already gone.

He first came to national prominence on the back of Portsmouth's run to the FA Cup semi-finals and, after struggling early on, became very influential at White Hart Lane and should be considered for any fantasy team, provided he can regain full fitness.

## Form Factors

| Season | Team | Tot | St | Sb | Y | R |
|--------|------|-----|----|----|----|----|
| 94-95 | Tottenham | 37 | 37 | 0 | 3 | 0 |
| 95-96 | Tottenham | 8 | 6 | 2 | 0 | 0 |
| 96-97 | Tottenham | 16 | 14 | 2 | 4 | 0 |
| Total | | 61 | 57 | 4 | 7 | 0 |

| | GP | GG | GF | GS | TGR |
|--------|------|------|------|------|------|
| 94-95 | 88.10 | 7.40 | 66 | 5 | 7.58 |
| 95-96 | 21.05 | 4.00 | 50 | 2 | 4.00 |
| 96-97 | 42.11 | 5.33 | 44 | 3 | 6.82 |
| Averages | 50.42 | 5.58 | 53.33 | 3.33 | 6.13 |

## ANELKA, Nicolas

# Arsenal ❶❷❸ S

Fullname: Nicolas Anelka
DOB: 14-03-80 Versailles

There was uproar in France when the French Under-21 international was signed from Paris St. Germain towards the end of last season. The 17-year-old was at the end of his junior contract and Arsène Wenger took advantage of the Bosman Ruling to snatch the player regarded as one of the most exciting to have come out of France.

The lanky striker/winger made only nine appearances for the PSG first team but had impressed clubs all over Europe with his talents, with Barcelona and Atletico Madrid just two of the sides chasing him before Arsenal signed him on a six-year deal.

Made four substitute appearances for the Gunners at the tail end of the season and may have to settle for a bench role before establishing himself.

With the lack of senior strikers at Arsenal, Anelka may well be given a run in the first team if he impresses.

## Form Factors

| Season | Team | Tot | St | Sb | Y | R |
|--------|--------|-----|----|----|---|---|
| 96-97 | Arsenal | 4 | 0 | 4 | 0 | 0 |
| Total | | 4 | 0 | 4 | 0 | 0 |

| | GP | GG | GF | GS | TGR |
|--------|-------|------|-------|------|------|
| 96-97 | 10.53 | 0.00 | 62 | 0 | 0.00 |
| Averages | 10.53 | 0.00 | 62.00 | 0.00 | 0.00 |

## APPLEBY, Matty

# Barnsley ❶ M

Fullname: Matthew Wilfred Appleby
DOB: 16-04-72 Middlesbrough

Impressing most last season in his role as sweeper, Appleby played in Barnsley's first 25 games before small injuries sidelined him for the odd game here and there – still managed to chalk up 35 starts though.

Started his career at Newcastle where he played 20 league games and made his first and only mark on the Premiership in the black and white of United when he played against Coventry in the 1993-94 season. After that he was consigned to the backwaters of Darlington on a free transfer before Barnsley gambled £250,000 for him in the summer of 1996. It was a gamble that paid off and Appleby will look to prove his former Premier League employers wrong in 1997-98.

## Form Factors

| Season | Team | Tot | St | Sb | Y | R |
|--------|-----------|-----|----|----|---|---|
| 93-94 | Newcastle | 1 | 1 | 0 | 0 | 0 |
| Total | | 1 | 1 | 0 | 0 | 0 |

| | GP | GG | GF | GS | TGR |
|--------|------|------|-------|------|------|
| 93-94 | 2.38 | 0.00 | 82 | 0 | 0.00 |
| Averages | 2.38 | 0.00 | 82.00 | 0.00 | 0.00 |

*Neil Ardley*

with his ability with the ball a feature of his play.

He made his 100th Premiership appearance last season and, if he can maintain last season's form, will be a regular in the Wimbledon starting line-up in 1997-98.

## Form Factors

| Season | Team | Tot | St | Sb | Y | R |
|--------|------|-----|----|----|----|----|
| 94-95 | Wimbledon | 14 | 9 | 5 | 1 | 0 |
| 95-96 | Wimbledon | 6 | 4 | 2 | 1 | 0 |
| 96-97 | Wimbledon | 34 | 33 | 1 | 1 | 0 |
| Total | | 54 | 46 | 8 | 3 | 0 |

| | GP | GG | GF | GS | TGR |
|--------|-----|------|-------|------|------|
| 94-95 | 33.33 | 14.00 | 48 | 1 | 2.08 |
| 95-96 | 15.79 | 0.00 | 55 | 0 | 0.00 |
| 96-97 | 89.47 | 17.00 | 49 | 2 | 4.08 |
| Averages | 46.20 | 10.33 | 50.67 | 1.00 | 2.05 |

## ARMSTRONG, Chris

### Tottenham H.  ❶❷❸        S

Fullname:   Christopher Peter Armstrong
DOB:        19-06-71 Newcastle

A striker who found himself criticised during his early days at Tottenham, not least because of his poor scoring form as part of the Crystal Palace side that were relegated at the end of the 1994-95 season. He responded well though with 15 goals from 36 Premiership matches in his first season at White Hart Lane and looked to be forming a formidable partnership with Teddy Sheringham. This was hindered last season by an injury that limited him to just 12 games, but he still managed five goals.

Armstrong joined Spurs from Crystal Palace for a club record £4.5m in July 1994, having previously been on the books of Wrexham and Millwall. When fully fit, should prove one of the top strikers in the Premiership.

## ARDLEY, Neal

### Wimbledon  ❶❷❸❹    M

Fullname:   Neal Christopher Ardley
DOB:        01-09-72 Epsom

Another outstanding player from the Wimbledon training camp, Ardley is versatile enough to be comfortable in midfield or defence. A spate of injuries, including hamstring problems, in 1995-96 limited his first team opportunities but last season he featured in all but four of the Dons' games in the Premier League.

At 25-years old Ardley has started to play some of the best games of his career

*Aijosa Asanovic*

# Derby County ❶❷❸❹❺    M

Fullname:  Aijosa Asanovic
DOB:      14-12-65

Yugoslavian international who joined Derby County in the summer of 1996 on the advice of Derby team-mate Igor Stimac, who suggested that manager Jim Smith snap him up from Hadjuk Split. An experienced, well-travelled and stylish player who is good on the ball, he agreed to a move to the Midlands for a bargain £1 million. He had an excellent first season at the Baseball Ground where he missed just four Premiership matches and scored six times from his midfield position. He was however the most substituted player in the Derby team, which may suggest that the pace of the Premiership took its toll. If that is the case we might be in for an even better season from one of the best foreign players in the Premier League.

## Form Factors

| Season | Team | Tot | St | Sb | Y | R |
|---|---|---|---|---|---|---|
| 96-97 | Derby Co. | 34 | 34 | 0 | 3 | 0 |
| Total | | 34 | 34 | 0 | 3 | 0 |

| | GP | GG | GF | GS | TGR |
|---|---|---|---|---|---|
| 96-97 | 89.47 | 5.67 | 45 | 6 | 13.33 |
| Averages | 89.47 | 5.67 | 45.00 | 6.00 | 13.33 |

## Form Factors

| Season | Team | Tot | St | Sb | Y | R |
|---|---|---|---|---|---|---|
| 94-95 | C. Palace | 40 | 40 | 0 | 6 | 0 |
| 95-96 | Tottenham | 36 | 36 | 0 | 5 | 0 |
| 96-97 | Tottenham | 12 | 12 | 0 | 2 | 0 |
| Total | | 88 | 88 | 0 | 13 | 0 |

| | GP | GG | GF | GS | TGR |
|---|---|---|---|---|---|
| 94-95 | 95.24 | 5.00 | 34 | 8 | 23.53 |
| 95-96 | 94.75 | 2.50 | 50 | 15 | 30.00 |
| 96-97 | 31.58 | 2.40 | 55 | 5 | 11.36 |
| Averages | 73.87 | 3.30 | 46.33 | 9.33 | 21.63 |

## ASPRILLA, Tino

# Newcastle U.  ❶❷❸❹    S

Fullname:  Faustino Hernon Asprilla
DOB:       10-11-69 Colombia

The Colombian international arrived at Newcastle in a blaze of publicity in February of 1996 and brought a reputation for great skill coupled with a 'star' personality. He was known to English fans through his European exploits at Parma.

His overall form has resulted in 10 of his 38 appearances coming from the subs bench. However there have been glimpses of the defence-cracking skills and if his manager can find a way of getting the best from him over more games, he holds great potential as a fantasy player.

His quick turn on the ball, weaving runs and subtle feints make him a joy to watch, although the delight of the football fans has yet to be matched by true match-winning performances while his inconsistency tends to infuriate all those who admire him.

## Form Factors

| Season | Team | Tot | St | Sb | | Y | R |
|--------|------|-----|----|----|----|----|----|
| 95-96 | Newcastle | 14 | 11 | 3 | | 2 | 0 |
| 96-97 | Newcastle | 24 | 17 | 7 | | 1 | 0 |
| Total | | 38 | 28 | 10 | | 3 | 0 |

| | GP | GG | GF | GS | TGR |
|--------|------|------|------|------|------|
| 95-96 | 36.84 | 4.67 | 66 | 3 | 4.55 |
| 96-97 | 63.16 | 6.00 | 73 | 4 | 5.48 |
| Averages | 50.00 | 5.33 | 69.50 | 3.50 | 5.01 |

Tino Asprilla

## ATHERTON, Peter

### Sheffield W. ❶❷❸ FB

Fullname: Peter Atherton
DOB: 06-04-70 Orrell

Has proved to be an excellent signing for Sheffield Wednesday with the one time England Under-21 international winning the Player of the Year award at the end of his first season at Hillsborough. Atherton has played with great consistency since picking up that award, resulting in his promotion to captain of the Owls. Over the past three seasons he has been a rock in the Wednesday defence, mostly at the centre of it, playing in a remarkable 96% of their Premiership matches and missing just one game last season. Began his career with five seasons at Wigan Athletic before making a £300,000 move to Coventry City in 1991. In the summer of 1994 he signed for Wednesday and will pass the 200 appearance mark of Premiership matches early in the 1997-98 season.

### Form Factors

| Season | Team | Tot | St | Sb | Y | R |
|---|---|---|---|---|---|---|
| 94-95 | Sheffield W. | 41 | 41 | 0 | 5 | 0 |
| 95-96 | Sheffield W. | 35 | 35 | 0 | 6 | 0 |
| 96-97 | Sheffield W. | 37 | 37 | 0 | 7 | 0 |
| Total | | 113 | 113 | 0 | 18 | 0 |

| | GP | GG | GF | GS | TGR |
|---|---|---|---|---|---|
| 94-95 | 97.62 | 41.00 | 49 | 1 | 2.04 |
| 95-96 | 92.11 | 0.00 | 48 | 0 | 0.00 |
| 96-97 | 97.37 | 18.50 | 50 | 2 | 4.00 |
| Averages | 95.70 | 19.83 | 49.00 | 1.00 | 2.01 |

## AUSTIN, Dean

### Tottenham H. ❶❷ FB

Fullname: Dean Barry Austin
DOB: 26-04-70 Hemel Hempstead

Right-sided defender who, after three years of being a regular in the Spurs' defence, found his opportunities restricted during 1996-97 but nevertheless has still played in over half of Spurs' games since joining the club.

A tenacious defender who links well with the midfield but seldom finds time to go forward himself, as supported by his record of no goals in 124 Premiership appearances! A one time apprentice with Watford, he made his Football League debut with Southend United after two seasons with non-leaguers St. Albans City. Joined Tottenham for £750,000 in June 1992, following in the footsteps of Justin Edinburgh.

### Form Factors

| Season | Team | Tot | St | Sb | Y | R |
|---|---|---|---|---|---|---|
| 94-95 | Tottenham | 24 | 23 | 1 | 5 | 0 |
| 95-96 | Tottenham | 28 | 28 | 0 | 8 | 0 |
| 96-97 | Tottenham | 15 | 13 | 2 | 3 | 0 |
| Total | | 67 | 64 | 3 | 16 | 0 |

| | GP | GG | GF | GS | TGR |
|---|---|---|---|---|---|
| 94-95 | 57.14 | 0.00 | 66 | 0 | 0.00 |
| 95-96 | 73.68 | 0.00 | 50 | 0 | 0.00 |
| 96-97 | 39.47 | 0.00 | 44 | 0 | 0.00 |
| Averages | 56.77 | 0.00 | 53.33 | 0.00 | 0.00 |

## BAARDSEN, Espen

### Tottenham H. ❶ GK

Fullname: Espen Baardsen
DOB: 07-12-77 San Rafael, Ca.

A goalkeeper and imposing figure at 6'5", who was recommended to Tottenham Hotspur by one of his predecessors at White Hart Lane, Erik

Thorstvedt. Made his first team debut towards the end of the 1996-97 season during a 2-0 defeat at Liverpool and also played in the final match of the season against Coventry.

Born in San Rafael California, he was at college there prior to joining Spurs but is hardly a novice, having already played international football with Norway at Under-21 level despite having also played for the USA at Under-18 level! Likely to continue as understudy to Ian Walker for 1997-98.

## Form Factors

| Season | Team | Tot | St | Sb | Y | R |
|---|---|---|---|---|---|---|
| 96-97 | Tottenham | 2 | 1 | 1 | 0 | 0 |
| Total | | 2 | 1 | 1 | 0 | 0 |

| | GA | GkA | GAp | CS | SO | Rp |
|---|---|---|---|---|---|---|
| 96-97 | 51 | 2 | 1.00 | 0 | 0 | 0 |
| Total | 51 | 2 | 1.00 | 0 | 0 | – |

# BABAYARO, Celestine

# Chelsea ❶❷ FB

Fullname:  Celestine Babayaro
DOB:        29-08-78 Nigeria
One of Ruud Gullit's major close season signings, Babayaro cost £2.25 million from Belgium side Anderlecht. A Nigerian international, he played in their Olympic Gold Medal winning side and scored three goals from his accustomed left wing-back position.

At just 18 years old, he is a good technical player and, despite being just 5' 7" tall, very good in the air. He speaks fluent English and should have no trouble settling in at Stamford Bridge, especially given that he joined Anderlecht when just 15 years old. Has signed on a five-year contract.

# BABB, Phil

# Liverpool ❶❷❸❹ CB

Fullname:  Phillip Andrew Babb
DOB:        30-11-70 London
A well-balanced defender with enough skill to bring the ball out of defence and to take part in Liverpool's passing game. He wasn't holding down a regular place in the team last season but can act as cover in different positions. In 1996-97 he put in 22 appearances, one from the bench, and stayed on the bench twice. His heading ability makes him a potential danger at set pieces but, although he used to score regularly at previous club Bradford City, he only scored his first goal for Liverpool last year.

Babb moved from Bradford to Coventry, where he looked in a different class. Liverpool made him the most expensive British centre-half in September 1995 when they signed him for £3.6 million.

He was a member of Jack Charlton's Ireland side that earned a place in the 1994 World Cup finals and he played throughout the tournament.

Babb can look forward to a similar season in 1997-98 as part of a squad which should be competing for honours again.

## Form Factors

| Season | Team | Tot | St | Sb | Y | R |
|---|---|---|---|---|---|---|
| 94-95 | Liverpool | 34 | 33 | 1 | 3 | 1 |
| 95-96 | Liverpool | 28 | 28 | 0 | 2 | 0 |
| 96-97 | Liverpool | 22 | 21 | 1 | 5 | 0 |
| Total | | 84 | 82 | 2 | 10 | 1 |

| | GP | GG | GF | GS | TGR |
|---|---|---|---|---|---|
| 94-95 | 80.95 | 0.00 | 65 | 0 | 0.00 |
| 95-96 | 73.68 | 0.00 | 70 | 0 | 0.00 |
| 96-97 | 57.89 | 22.00 | 62 | 1 | 1.61 |
| Averages | 70.84 | 7.33 | 65.67 | 0.33 | 0.54 |

## BALL, Michael

# Everton ❶❷ M

Fullname: Michael Ball
DOB: 02-10-77 Liverpool
    Teenager who became the first player named Ball to feature on an Everton team sheet in 30 years when he made his Everton debut as a second-half substitute during a 1-0 win over Tottenham in April 1997. Went on to make five appearances before the season was out, three of them as a substitute. Born on Merseyside, Ball is an England Under-18 international player who has been nicknamed 'Iceman' by some of the coaches at Goodison Park for his coolness on the ball. Very versatile, the 19-year-old can play in defence or in midfield and has an enormous throw-in that will no doubt be looking for the head of Duncan Ferguson in years to come.

## Form Factors

| Season | Team | Tot | St | Sb | Y | R |
|---|---|---|---|---|---|---|
| 96-97 | Everton | 5 | 2 | 3 | 1 | 0 |
| Total | | 5 | 2 | 3 | 1 | 0 |

| | GP | GG | GF | GS | TGR |
|---|---|---|---|---|---|
| 96-97 | 13.16 | 0.00 | 44 | 0 | 0.00 |
| Averages | 13.16 | 0.00 | 44.00 | 0.00 | 0.00 |

## BARMBY, Nicky

# Everton ❶❷❸❹ FB

Fullname: Nicholas Jonathan Barmby
DOB: 11-02-74 Hull
    Since making his first team debut for Tottenham Hotspur in September 1992, he has become one of the costliest players in English football. An exceptional player who can play up front or just behind the attack. Progressed through the ranks not only with Spurs but also with England to become a full international in 1995. Scored 26 goals in 108 games for Spurs before moving to Middlesbrough, due to homesickness, for £5.25 million but after just 14 months was on the move again to Everton for £5.75 million.

    He made 25 appearances for Everton last season but scored only three goals. Career may not have taken off quite as spectacularly as expected but he has the potential to be a valuable member of any fantasy team.

## Form Factors

| Season | Team | Tot | St | Sb | Y | R |
|---|---|---|---|---|---|---|
| 95-96 | Middlesbro' | 32 | 32 | 0 | 4 | 0 |
| 96-97 | Middlesbro' | 10 | 10 | 0 | 0 | 0 |
| 96-97 | Everton | 25 | 22 | 3 | 0 | 0 |
| Total | | 67 | 64 | 3 | 4 | 0 |

| | GP | GG | GF | GS | TGR |
|---|---|---|---|---|---|
| 95-96 | 84.21 | 4.57 | 35 | 7 | 20.00 |
| 96-97 | 26.32 | 10.00 | 51 | 1 | 1.96 |
| 96-97 | 65.79 | 6.25 | 44 | 4 | 9.09 |
| Averages | 58.77 | 6.94 | 43.33 | 4.00 | 10.35 |

## BARNES, John

### Liverpool ❶❷❸ M

**Fullname:** John Charles Bryan Barnes
**DOB:** 07-11-63 Jamaica, W Indies
Jamaican-born, but with 79 caps for England, Barnes has spent ten years at Anfield since his £900,000 move from Watford.

Having made his name as a left winger, especially through one famous individual goal against Brazil for England, he has put his experience and passing skill to use in left and central midfield for Liverpool. His other important role over the past two seasons has been as captain.

He started 34 Premiership games in 1996-97 and came on as a sub once but missed the end of the season. His tally of four goals is fairly typical and he scores about every nine games.

Barnes has won two league titles, one FA cup winners medal and a League Cup winners medal while at Anfield but it's uncertain whether he'll now get a chance to add to these in a new-look Liverpool.

### Form Factors

| Season | Team | Tot | St | Sb | Y | R |
|---|---|---|---|---|---|---|
| 94-95 | Liverpool | 38 | 38 | 0 | 0 | 0 |
| 95-96 | Liverpool | 36 | 36 | 0 | 0 | 0 |
| 96-97 | Liverpool | 35 | 34 | 1 | 0 | 0 |
| Total | | 109 | 108 | 1 | 0 | 0 |

| | GP | GG | GF | GS | TGR |
|---|---|---|---|---|---|
| 94-95 | 90.48 | 5.43 | 65 | 7 | 10.77 |
| 95-96 | 94.74 | 12.00 | 70 | 3 | 4.29 |
| 96-97 | 92.11 | 8.75 | 62 | 4 | 6.45 |
| Averages | 92.44 | 8.73 | 65.67 | 4.67 | 7.17 |

## BARRETT, Earl

### Everton ❶❷❸❹ FB

**Fullname:** Earl Delisser Barrett
**DOB:** 28-04-67 Rochdale
A big favourite of former Everton manager Joe Royle under whom he also played at Oldham Athletic. Was troubled by injury during his first full season at Goodison Park but returned to peak condition in 1996-97 and missed just two Premiership matches – giving 100% throughout. Began his career with Manchester City and had a loan spell at Chester City before making 217 appearances for Oldham. He also became an England international whilst at Boundary Park. Went to Aston Villa for £1.7 million where he played 143 games and teamed up again with Royle in January 1995. Speedy, good tackler and fine man-marker, he will be a vital part of an Everton revival in 1997-98. Seldom booked, he last scored for Villa in February 1993 against...Everton!

### Form Factors

| Season | Team | Tot | St | Sb | Y | R |
|---|---|---|---|---|---|---|
| 94-95 | Everton | 17 | 17 | 0 | 1 | 1 |
| 95-96 | Everton | 8 | 8 | 0 | 1 | 0 |
| 96-97 | Everton | 36 | 36 | 0 | 1 | 0 |
| Total | | 61 | 61 | 0 | 3 | 1 |

| | GP | GG | GF | GS | TGR |
|---|---|---|---|---|---|
| 94-95 | 40.48 | 0.00 | 44 | 0 | 0.00 |
| 95-96 | 21.05 | 0.00 | 64 | 0 | 0.00 |
| 96-97 | 94.74 | 0.00 | 44 | 0 | 0.00 |
| Averages | 52.09 | 0.00 | 50.67 | 0.00 | 0.00 |

## BARTON, Warren

# Newcastle U. ❶❷❸❹ FB

Fullname: Warren Dean Barton
DOB: 19-03-69 Stoke Newington
After 180 league appearances with
Wimbledon, Barton joined Newcastle in
July 1995 as the UK's most expensive
full-back at £4.5 million. He was a team
regular in the Keegan era but in 1996-97
he totalled only 18 appearances, four of
those coming from the subs bench.

Barton's busy tackling combines with
some poise on the ball so it's not
surprising that he was used as a midfield
player during 1996-97 but, with
tremendous competition in the Newcastle
team, it's as a squad player, filling in for
injuries and suspensions, that Barton is
perhaps more likely to find a role.

## Form Factors

| Season | Team | Tot | St | Sb | Y | R |
|---|---|---|---|---|---|---|
| 94-95 | Wimbledon | 39 | 39 | 0 | 4 | 0 |
| 95-96 | Newcastle | 31 | 30 | 1 | 3 | 0 |
| 96-97 | Newcastle | 18 | 14 | 4 | 1 | 0 |
| Total | | 88 | 83 | 5 | 8 | 0 |

| | GP | GG | GF | GS | TGR |
|---|---|---|---|---|---|
| 94-95 | 92.86 | 19.50 | 48 | 2 | 4.17 |
| 95-96 | 81.58 | 0.00 | 66 | 0 | 0.00 |
| 96-97 | 47.37 | 18.00 | 73 | 1 | 1.37 |
| Averages | 73.93 | 12.50 | 62.33 | 1.00 | 1.85 |

## BARTRAM, Vince

# Arsenal ❶ GK

Fullname: Vincent Lee Bartram
DOB: 07-08-68 Birmingham
Bartram is one of several goalkeepers
on Arsenal's books. The former England
schoolboy international was a £400,000
signing in the summer of 1994 from
Bournemouth, for whom he made 132
league appearances. He made just 11
appearances for the Gunners during 1994-
95 when David Seaman was injured and
conceded 49 goals during that time with
two clean sheets. In the 1995-96 season
he had the substitute 'keeper spot to
himself but made the bench as a non-
playing player on 15 occasions – then-
manager Bruce Rioch preferring to use a
third outfield player.

The return of John Lukic further
limited chances and he made the bench
on just nine occasions as cover for Lukic
himself. Bartram's first team
opportunities are likely to remain few and
far between in the future and he is
unlikely to score many points as an
Arsenal player.

## Form Factors

| Season | Team | Tot | St | Sb | Y | R |
|---|---|---|---|---|---|---|
| 94-95 | Arsenal | 11 | 11 | 0 | 0 | 0 |
| Total | | 11 | 11 | 0 | 0 | 0 |

| | GA | GkA | GlA | CS | SO | Rp |
|---|---|---|---|---|---|---|
| 94-95 | 49 | 18 | 1.64 | 2 | 2 | 0 |
| Averages | 49 | 18 | 1.64 | 2 | 2 | – |

## BATTY, David

# Newcastle U. ❶❷❸❹❺   M

Fullname: David Batty
DOB: 02-12-68 Leeds

When Batty made his way to Newcastle after stints at Leeds United and Blackburn Rovers (both championship winning teams), he cost Kevin Keegan £4.5 million and many doubted whether he was worth it. However, it is important to reflect on the fact that Batty has been a linchpin in two championship winning sides at Leeds and Blackburn. He is now established at Newcastle, starting and finishing 32 games last season.

Batty has not only made central midfield his own at St James' Park but he's also forced his way into Glenn Hoddle's England set up with some energetic and aggressive displays. Although capable of moving forward, he perhaps lacks the final killer pass or shot, preferring to move the ball on. He certainly makes things happen around him and looks set to be a regular in the 1997-98 side. His terrier-like tackling can go wrong against pacier opposition. This resulted in a few too many yellow cards last season, yet surprising to many, his red card at Chelsea was the first of his career. A must for consideration.

### Form Factors

| Season | Team | Tot | St | Sb | Y | R |
|---|---|---|---|---|---|---|
| 94-95 | Blackburn | 5 | 4 | 1 | 2 | 0 |
| 95-96 | Blackburn | 23 | 23 | 0 | 5 | 0 |
| 95-96 | Newcastle | 11 | 11 | 0 | 2 | 0 |
| 96-97 | Newcastle | 32 | 32 | 0 | 10 | 1 |
| Total | | 71 | 70 | 1 | 19 | 1 |

| | GP | GG | GF | GS | TGR |
|---|---|---|---|---|---|
| 94-95 | 11.90 | 0.00 | 80 | 0 | 0.00 |
| 95-96 | 89.47 | 17.00 | 61 | 2 | 3.27 |
| 96-97 | 84.42 | 32.00 | 73 | 1 | 1.37 |
| Averages | 61.93 | 24.5 | 71.33 | 1.00 | 1.55 |

## BEARDSLEY, Peter

# Newcastle U.   ❶❷   M

Fullname: Peter Andrew Beardsley
DOB: 18-01-61 Newcastle

Coming to the end of his playing career and linked with moves to manage other clubs, Beardsley is a footballing enigma. Despite his obvious talent he was released by both the Merseyside giants and often ignored by England. He played 147 times for Newcastle in his first stint with the club and 131 in a highly successful Liverpool side, earning two League Championship medals and one FA Cup medal.

Kevin Keegan paid Everton £1.4 million for the 32 year-old England player in July 1993, banking on his experience at top clubs and unquenchable zest for the game. Beardsley has delivered everything asked of him, continually knocking on the England door with yet another outstanding performance. In 1996-97 he put in 25 appearances, three from the subs bench, scoring once every five games. Beardsley may still be able to contribute important performances, perhaps more and more from the subs bench and, from his position just behind the front players, he is always a good bet to score the odd goal.

### Form Factors

| Season | Team | Tot | St | Sb | Y | R |
|---|---|---|---|---|---|---|
| 94-95 | Newcastle | 34 | 34 | 0 | 3 | 0 |
| 95-96 | Newcastle | 35 | 35 | 0 | 6 | 0 |
| 96-97 | Newcastle | 25 | 22 | 3 | 3 | 0 |
| Total | | 94 | 91 | 3 | 12 | 0 |

| | GP | GG | GF | GS | TGR |
|---|---|---|---|---|---|
| 94-95 | 80.95 | 2.62 | 67 | 13 | 19.40 |
| 95-96 | 92.11 | 3.89 | 66 | 9 | 13.64 |
| 96-97 | 65.79 | 5.00 | 73 | 5 | 6.85 |
| Averages | 79.62 | 3.83 | 68.67 | 9.00 | 13.30 |

*David Beasant*

## BEASANT, Dave

# Southampton ❶ GK

Fullname: David John Beasant
DOB: 20-03-59 Willesden

Beasant started the 1996-97 season as Southampton's first choice between the posts, but lost out to Maik Taylor midway through the season.

Started the season as the second oldest 'keeper in the Premiership and it wasn't his best season as he conceded on average 1.71 goals per game in his 13 appearances – compared to his total Premier League average of 1.41 goals per game.

Started his career at Wimbledon where he played close on 400 senior games, his performances earning him a move to Newcastle that didn't really work out. After four years at Chelsea, he re-found his form at Southampton.

Having been voted the Saints Player of the Year at the end of 1995-96, Beasant managed just two clean sheets last season and may now be nearing the end of his Premiership career.

## Form Factors

| Season | Team | Tot | St | Sb | Y | R |
|--------|------|-----|-----|-----|-----|-----|
| 94-95 | Southampton | 13 | 12 | 1 | 0 | 0 |
| 95-96 | Southampton | 36 | 36 | 0 | 0 | 0 |
| 96-97 | Southampton | 14 | 13 | 1 | 0 | 0 |
| Total | | 63 | 61 | 2 | 0 | 0 |

| | GA | GkA | GAp | CS | SO | Rp |
|--------|-----|-----|-----|-----|-----|-----|
| 94-95 | 63 | 16 | 1.23 | 4 | 2 | 0 |
| 95-96 | 52 | 49 | 1.36 | 10 | 2 | 2 |
| 96-97 | 56 | 24 | 1.71 | 2 | 1 | 0 |
| Total | 171 | 89 | 1.41 | 16 | 5 | – |

# BECKHAM, David

## Manchester U. ❶❷❸❹❺    M

David Beckham

Fullname: David Beckham
DOB: 02-05-75 Leytonstone

Last season started with that goal and David Beckham's profile was lifted another notch and into a footballing name not just in England, but around the world with that goal – when he lobbed Wimbledon's Neil Sullivan from the halfway line to score the first of many 'wonder goals'.

He plays for United as a right-sided midfielder and is a hardworking and aggressive tackler as well as precociously talented passer. He can also be dangerous at free kicks around the area and when whipping in corners.

Born in the east-end of London, Beckham came through the ranks at Old Trafford and, despite his tender age at 22-years old, is already regarded as one of the finest midfielders in the Premiership. He ended 1996-97 as an England regular and looks set to be at the heart of his club and national side for years to come.

Beckham was named in the PFA Premiership team of the year and awarded PFA Young Player Of The Year Award for 1996-97. He was runner up in the senior Player Of The Year Award, behind England star Alan Shearer. Beckham played 36 games in 1996-97, three as sub, scoring eight goals. If he can keep his aggression under control and the yellow cards to a minimum, Beckham will surely have another outstanding season in 1997-98.

## Form Factors

| Season | Team | Tot | St | Sb | Y | R |
|--------|------|-----|-----|-----|-----|-----|
| 94-95 | Man. Utd | 4 | 2 | 2 | 0 | 0 |
| 95-96 | Man. Utd | 33 | 26 | 7 | 5 | 0 |
| 96-97 | Man. Utd | 36 | 33 | 3 | 6 | 0 |
| Total | | 73 | 61 | 12 | 11 | 0 |

| | GP | GG | GF | GS | TGR |
|--------|-----|-----|-----|-----|-----|
| 94-95 | 9.52 | 0.00 | 77 | 0 | 0.00 |
| 95-96 | 86.84 | 4.71 | 73 | 7 | 9.59 |
| 96-97 | 94.74 | 4.50 | 76 | 8 | 10.53 |
| Averages | 63.70 | 3.07 | 75.33 | 5.00 | 6.71 |

## BEENEY, Mark

# Leeds United    ❶   GK

Fullname: Mark Raymond Beeney
DOB: 30-12-67 Tunbridge Wells
  Goalkeeper who learned his trade at the lower levels for a number of years prior to a £350,000 move to Leeds United in April 1993 from Brighton & Hove Albion. The deal represented a handsome profit for the south coast club who bought him two years earlier for £30,000. Has the rare distinction of having played for two sides no longer in the Football League, Aldershot (on loan) and Maidstone United. Began his career with Kent side Gillingham. Made just one Premiership appearance during 1996-97 (a goalless draw with Derby County) and sat out the other 37 on the bench. Also played in a Coca Cola Cup tie and is likely to remain as backup for Nigel Martyn during the 1997-98 season.

## Form Factors

| Season | Team | Tot | St | Sb | Y | R |
|---|---|---|---|---|---|---|
| 93-94 | Leeds Utd | 22 | 22 | 0 | 0 | 0 |
| 95-96 | Leeds Utd | 10 | 10 | 0 | 0 | 1 |
| 96-97 | Leeds Utd | 1 | 1 | 0 | 0 | 0 |
| Total | | 33 | 33 | 0 | 0 | 1 |

| | GA | GkA | GAp | CS | SO | Rp |
|---|---|---|---|---|---|---|
| 93-94 | 39 | 20 | 0.91 | 9 | 3 | 0 |
| 95-96 | 57 | 15 | 1.50 | 3 | 2 | 0 |
| 96-97 | 38 | 0 | 0.00 | 1 | 1 | 0 |
| Total | 134 | 35 | 1.06 | 13 | 6 | – |

## BENALI, Francis

# Southampton   ❶❷   FB

Fullname: Francis Vincent Benali
DOB: 30-12-68 Southampton
  Francis Benali could be described as 'Mr Southampton'. Signed as a trainee in 1987, he has played over 250 senior games for the club and only Matt Le Tissier has played more Premier League games for the Saints. Despite his appearance record, he is still waiting to score his first senior goal for the club!
  A defender who can also play in midfield, he is often noted for his hard-tackling style that in itself invariably leads to cards and suspensions. Having received 11 cautions in 1994-95, he had just the three in 1996-97, but his dismissal against West Ham in only the third game of the season for serious foul play, was his third in the Premiership in five seasons. He was also sent off against Reading in the Cup and he missed a dozen games last year due to suspension – five of them in one block.

## Form Factors

| Season | Team | Tot | St | Sb | Y | R |
|---|---|---|---|---|---|---|
| 94-95 | Southampton | 35 | 32 | 3 | 11 | 0 |
| 95-96 | Southampton | 30 | 29 | 1 | 6 | 0 |
| 96-97 | Southampton | 18 | 14 | 4 | 3 | 1 |
| Total | | 83 | 75 | 8 | 20 | 1 |

| | GP | GG | GF | GS | TGR |
|---|---|---|---|---|---|
| 94-95 | 83.33 | 0.00 | 61 | 0 | 0.00 |
| 95-96 | 78.95 | 0.00 | 34 | 0 | 0.00 |
| 96-97 | 47.37 | 0.00 | 50 | 0 | 0.00 |
| Averages | 69.88 | 0.00 | 48.33 | 0.00 | 0.00 |

# Newcastle U. ❶❷❸ FB

Fullname: John Beresford
DOB: 04-09-66 Sheffield

A fast, skilful left back Beresford loves to get forward and join in the attack, something that endeared him to the gung-ho style of play that was the trademark of the Kevin Keegan era. All was fine until he fell out of favour with the former manager after a touch line exchange. Since then, and with the arrival of Kenny Dalglish, he has had to fight for his place and last season he started in just half of the 38 match campaign.

Beresford started as an apprentice at Manchester City before moving across the Pennines to Barnsley on a free transfer. Following a century of games for the Tykes he hit the south coast and had an equally successful stint at Portsmouth before Newcastle paid £650,000 for his services in the summer of 1992. Now with over 100 Premiership appearances under his belt, he may be nearing the end of his playing days in the top flight.

## Form Factors

| Season | Team | Tot | St | Sb | Y | R |
|---|---|---|---|---|---|---|
| 94-95 | Newcastle | 33 | 33 | 0 | 7 | 0 |
| 95-96 | Newcastle | 33 | 32 | 1 | 6 | 1 |
| 96-97 | Newcastle | 19 | 18 | 1 | 4 | 0 |
| Total | | 85 | 83 | 2 | 17 | 1 |

| | GP | GG | GF | GS | TGR |
|---|---|---|---|---|---|
| 94-95 | 78.57 | 0.00 | 67 | 0 | 0.00 |
| 95-96 | 86.84 | 0.00 | 66 | 0 | 0.00 |
| 96-97 | 86.84 | 0.00 | 73 | 0 | 0.00 |
| Averages | 84.09 | 0.00 | 68.67 | 0.00 | 0.00 |

# Blackburn Rovers ❶❷❸ FB

Fullname: Henning Berg
DOB: 01-09-69 Eidsvell

One of the best tackling defenders in the Premiership, Berg has been one of Blackburn Rovers' most consistent players since signing from Lillestrom for £400,000 in December 1992.

Normally a right-sided defender, injury to Ian Pearce during 1995-96 saw him convert to a more central defensive role – a position he plays for Norway.

He has missed just four Premiership games in the past three seasons. He is comfortable in possession of the ball and his accurate passing is a notable aspect of his game. Doesn't always get forward despite his crossing ability.

## Form Factors

| Season | Team | Tot | St | Sb | Y | R |
|---|---|---|---|---|---|---|
| 94-95 | Blackburn | 40 | 40 | 0 | 2 | 1 |
| 95-96 | Blackburn | 38 | 38 | 0 | 5 | 1 |
| 96-97 | Blackburn | 36 | 36 | 0 | 3 | 0 |
| Total | | 114 | 114 | 0 | 10 | 2 |

| | GP | GG | GF | GS | TGR |
|---|---|---|---|---|---|
| 94-95 | 95.24 | 40.00 | 80 | 1 | 1.25 |
| 95-96 | 100.00 | 0.00 | 61 | 0 | 0.00 |
| 96-97 | 94.74 | 18.00 | 42 | 2 | 4.76 |
| Averages | 96.66 | 19.33 | 61.00 | 1.00 | 2.00 |

## BERGER, Patrik

## Liverpool ❶❷❸❹ M

Fullname: Patrik Berger
DOB: 10-11-73 Prague

Liverpool signed the powerful Czech international after he featured in Euro '96, despite being hampered by sickness. He took time to settle in initially but put in some promising performances towards the end of the season, scoring six useful goals in the Premiership and looking the part in Liverpool's European ties. As well as coming on from the subs' bench 10 times in his 23 appearances, Berger was also an unused sub an additional nine times.

He played for arch rivals Sparta and Slavia Prague, joined German champions Borussia Dortmund in the summer of 1995 and helped them retain the Bundesliga, before moving to the Premiership.

Berger can play on the left or in central midfield and his left foot has regularly found the net for the Czech Republic. He is likely to get a good run in the team during 1997-98 and is more than likely to make an impact on the scoresheet.

### Form Factors

| Season | Team | Tot | St | Sb | Y | R |
|---|---|---|---|---|---|---|
| 96-97 | Liverpool | 23 | 13 | 10 | 0 | 0 |
| Total | | 23 | 13 | 10 | 0 | 0 |

| | GP | GG | GF | GS | TGR |
|---|---|---|---|---|---|
| 96-97 | 60.53 | 3.83 | 62 | 6 | 9.68 |
| Averages | 60.53 | 3.83 | 62.00 | 6.00 | 9.68 |

## BERGKAMP, Dennis

## Arsenal ❶❷❸❹❺ S

Fullname: Dennis Nicolaas Bergkamp
DOB: 18-05-69 Amsterdam

Bergkamp remains the Gunners' record signing, having joined for £7.5m in July 1995 from Internazionale. The Dutch maestro, a product of the Ajax youth policy, has proved to be the most skilful Arsenal player since Liam Brady with exceptional control and distribution skill.

Bergkamp possesses a terrific shot and can be devastating from free-kicks around the goal. A Dutch international who was in their Euro '96 squad, he needs just a couple more goals to become Holland's top scorer of all time. May already have broken that record however, he has a fear of flying and invariably is missing from games that are played outside of western Europe.

Likes to play just behind the main striker and has averaged a goal every three games since his arrival at Highbury and his sublime touch on the ball ensures that he will record a large number of assists during any season.

Last season he added more bite to his game and has shown that it is possible to combine skill and aggression at the very highest level of the game.

### Form Factors

| Season | Team | Tot | St | Sb | Y | R |
|---|---|---|---|---|---|---|
| 95-96 | Arsenal | 33 | 33 | 0 | 5 | 0 |
| 96-97 | Arsenal | 29 | 28 | 1 | 6 | 0 |
| Total | | 62 | 61 | 1 | 11 | 0 |

| | GP | GG | GF | GS | TGR |
|---|---|---|---|---|---|
| 95-96 | 86.84 | 3.00 | 49 | 11 | 22.45 |
| 96-97 | 76.32 | 2.42 | 62 | 12 | 19.35 |
| Averages | 81.58 | 2.71 | 55.50 | 11.50 | 20.90 |

# BERGSSON, Gudni

## Bolton W. ❶❷ CB

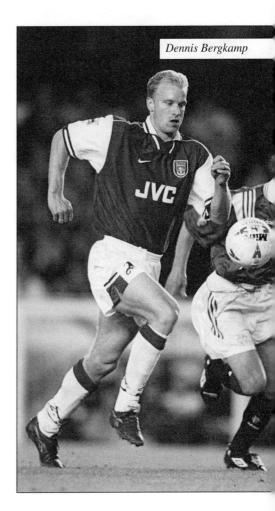

*Dennis Bergkamp*

Fullname: Gudni Bergsson
DOB: 21-07-65 Iceland

The 1997-98 season is the second full season the Icelandic captain and international cap holder experienced in the FA Premier League. He was a near ever-present in the Bolton side that were relegated at the end of 1995-96 and his experience has helped Wanderers to bounce straight back into the top flight.

Only injury prevented the 32-year-old playing in Bolton's complete campaign, featuring in 33 of their 46 games and contributing three goals to their record-breaking century.

Having been spotted by Spurs when playing for Valur in his native Iceland, he moved to White Hart Lane in 1988 but was not able to command a regular first team spot. He moved north in March 1995 and his ability to play anywhere in the back line has made him a valuable asset to Wanderers.

He will need to be in top form to ensure the Bolton defence remains tight in the Premiership.

## Form Factors

| Season | Team | Tot | St | Sb | Y | R |
|---|---|---|---|---|---|---|
| 92-93 | Tottenham | 5 | 0 | 5 | 0 | 0 |
| 95-96 | Bolton W. | 34 | 34 | 0 | 8 | 1 |
| Total | | 39 | 34 | 5 | 8 | 1 |

| | GP | GG | GF | GS | TGR |
|---|---|---|---|---|---|
| 92-93 | 11.90 | 0.00 | 60 | 0 | 0.00 |
| 95-96 | 89.47 | 8.50 | 39 | 4 | 10.26 |
| Averages | 50.69 | 4.25 | 49.50 | 2.00 | 5.13 |

## BERKOVIC, Eyal

# West Ham U.  ❶❷❸❹  M

Fullname: Eyal Berkovic
DOB: 02-04-72 Haifa

Berkovic made an immediate impression in the Premiership when he joined Southampton from Maccabi Haifa. Possesses a terrific first touch which, coupled with his burst of speed through the Saints' midfield, made him an instant crowd pleaser. All this from a player no one had heard of when Souness signed him for £1 million in June 1997.

An Israeli international, he came to national notice with a stunning performance and two goals in Southampton's 6-3 mauling of Manchester United.

A clause in his contract though allowed him to move to West Ham in the summer of 1997 for £1.75 million where he is sure to become a big hit both on and off the field of play.

### Form Factors

| Season | Team | Tot | St | Sb | Y | R |
|---|---|---|---|---|---|---|
| 96-97 | Southampton | 28 | 26 | 2 | 4 | 0 |
| Total | | 28 | 26 | 2 | 4 | 0 |

| | GP | GG | GF | GS | TGR |
|---|---|---|---|---|---|
| 96-97 | 73.68 | 7.00 | 50 | 4 | 8.00 |
| Averages | 73.68 | 7.00 | 50.00 | 4.00 | 8.00 |

## BILIC, Slaven

# Everton  ❶❷❸❹❺  CB

Fullname: Slaven Bilic
DOB: 11-09-68 Croatia

Having been linked with Everton before the transfer deadline in March 1997, the big Croatian centre-half moved to Goodison Park in a £4.5 million deal in the close season.

His departure will be a blow to West Ham where his 35 appearances last season were the most made by any player at Upton Park. He joined the Hammers in February 1994 for £1.3 million from Karlsruhe and became the dominant figure in their defence, where his aerial ability is especially good and combines well with his excellent ball distribution.

Came to the notice of most fans for some excellent performances at the heart of the Croatian defence during Euro '96 and his signature is a major coup for Everton.

### Form Factors

| Season | Team | Tot | St | Sb | Y | R |
|---|---|---|---|---|---|---|
| 95-96 | West Ham | 13 | 13 | 0 | 1 | 0 |
| 96-97 | West Ham | 35 | 35 | 0 | 10 | 0 |
| Total | | 48 | 48 | 0 | 11 | 0 |

| | GP | GG | GF | GS | TGR |
|---|---|---|---|---|---|
| 95-96 | 34.21 | 0.00 | 43 | 0 | 0.00 |
| 96-97 | 92.11 | 17.50 | 39 | 2 | 5.13 |
| Averages | 63.16 | 8.75 | 41.00 | 1.00 | 2.56 |

## BISHOP, Ian

# West Ham U.  ❶❷  M

Fullname: Ian William Bishop
DOB:     29-05-65 Liverpool

Now entering his final years at West Ham, Bishop remained an important and influential figure at Upton Park last season. A creative player who loves to run with the ball at his feet he has a fine temperament that ensures that yellow cards are a rare experience for him.

Apart from a year on the south coast with Bournemouth, Bishop had played most of his football in the north-east before signing for the Hammers from Manchester City in December 1989.

A groin injury curtailed his 1995-96 season and small injuries sidelined him for some of the time last season. At 32 he remains one of the more classy performers in the Premier League but will be under pressure from new arrivals.

## Form Factors

| Season | Team | Tot | St | Sb | Y | R |
|--------|------|-----|-----|-----|-----|-----|
| 94-95 | West Ham | 31 | 31 | 0 | 1 | 0 |
| 95-96 | West Ham | 35 | 35 | 0 | 3 | 0 |
| 96-97 | West Ham | 29 | 26 | 3 | 2 | 0 |
| Total | | 95 | 92 | 3 | 6 | 0 |

| | GP | GG | GF | GS | TGR |
|--------|-----|-----|-----|-----|-----|
| 94-95 | 73.81 | 31.00 | 44 | 1 | 2.27 |
| 95-96 | 92.11 | 35.00 | 43 | 1 | 2.33 |
| 96-97 | 92.11 | 35.00 | 39 | 1 | 2.56 |
| Averages | 86.01 | 33.67 | 42.00 | 1.00 | 2.39 |

## BJORNEBYE, Stig

# Liverpool  ❶❷❸❹❺  FB

Fullname: Stig Inge Bjornebye
DOB:     11-12-69 Norway

An excellent tackler and passer of the ball, the Norwegian international, with more than 50 caps to his name, was an ever-present in 1996-97.

The £600,000 which the club paid for him in December 1992 has proved a sound investment as Bjornebye has made the left wing-back role his own to take his place in a long line of specialist left-backs at Anfield. He can combine in attack and is capable of pulling excellent crosses back from around the corner flag.

His intelligent overlaps give the side width and he scored twice in 1996-97, including the first Premiership goal of the 1996-97 season during a 3-3 draw away at Middlesbrough.

The form book points to an ever-present 1997-98 with a good number of assists and the odd goal.

## Form Factors

| Season | Team | Tot | St | Sb | Y | R |
|--------|------|-----|-----|-----|-----|-----|
| 94-95 | Liverpool | 31 | 31 | 0 | 5 | 0 |
| 95-96 | Liverpool | 2 | 2 | 0 | 0 | 0 |
| 96-97 | Liverpool | 38 | 38 | 0 | 3 | 0 |
| Total | | 71 | 71 | 0 | 8 | 0 |

| | GP | GG | GF | GS | TGR |
|--------|-----|-----|-----|-----|-----|
| 94-95 | 73.81 | 0.00 | 65 | 0 | 0.00 |
| 95-96 | 5.26 | 0.00 | 70 | 0 | 0.00 |
| 96-97 | 100.00 | 19.00 | 62 | 2 | 3.23 |
| Averages | 59.69 | 6.33 | 65.67 | 0.67 | 1.08 |

*Nathan Blake (left) with Per Frandsen*

## BLACKWELL, Dean

# Wimbledon ❶❷❸ CB

Fullname: Dean Robert Blackwell
DOB: 05-12-69 Camden

Blackwell came through the ranks at Wimbledon and has developed into one of their most consistent central defensive players. He made his 100th Premiership appearance last season and would have had many more, but for a number of ongoing injury problems, which saw him miss the 1994-95 season.

In the past two seasons he has developed a good understanding with Chris Perry that has coincided with the improvement of the Dons' fortunes.

Blackwell is especially good in the air, possessing a good heading ability. It is in his own defence that this is used to best effect as he still awaits his first senior goal.

## Form Factors

| Season | Team | Tot | St | Sb | Y | R |
|---|---|---|---|---|---|---|
| 93-94 | Wimbledon | 18 | 16 | 2 | 1 | 0 |
| 95-96 | Wimbledon | 8 | 8 | 0 | 0 | 0 |
| 96-97 | Wimbledon | 27 | 22 | 5 | 4 | 0 |
| Total | | 53 | 46 | 7 | 5 | 0 |

| | GP | GG | GF | GS | TGR |
|---|---|---|---|---|---|
| 93-94 | 42.86 | 0.00 | 56 | 0 | 0.00 |
| 95-96 | 21.05 | 0.00 | 55 | 0 | 0.00 |
| 96-97 | 21.05 | 0.00 | 49 | 0 | 0.00 |
| Averages | 28.32 | 0.00 | 53.33 | 0.00 | 0.00 |

## BLAKE, Nathan

### Bolton W. ❶❷❸ S

Fullname: Nathan Alexander Blake
DOB: 27-01-72 Cardiff

At Cardiff City and Sheffield United
Nathan Blake had developed a reputation
as a goalscorer and that was the reason
which led to Bolton paying £1.5m to
secure his services in December 1995.
The aim was clearly to add fire-power up
front to pull Wanderers away from the
relegation zone of the Premiership.
Despite playing in 18 of the remaining
games, Blake could only contribute a
single goal and Bolton were relegated.

Last season though Blake rediscovered
his touch and his partnership up front
with John McGinlay has blossomed with
the Welsh international striker netting 19
goals in their streak back to the
Premiership.

The question remains to be answered.
Will Blake hit the net as regularly in the
Premier League now that he has a second
chance? It will be harder but he has now
had time to settle in and Wanderers' great
new stadium may be the fitting venue to
make it all happen.

### Form Factors

| Season | Team | Tot | St | Sb | Y | R |
|--------|------|-----|-----|-----|-----|-----|
| 95-96 | Bolton W. | 18 | 14 | 4 | 4 | 0 |
| Total | | 18 | 14 | 4 | 4 | 0 |

| | GP | GG | GF | GS | TGR |
|--------|-----|-----|-----|-----|-----|
| 95-96 | 47.37 | 18.00 | 39 | 1 | 2.56 |
| Averages | 47.37 | 18.00 | 39 | 1 | 2.56 |

Regi Blinker

## BLINKER, Regi

### Sheffield W. ❶❷❸ M

Fullname: Regi Blinker
DOB: 06-04-69 Rotterdam

Exciting player whose transfer to
Sheffield Wednesday in March 1996 was
shrouded in controversy as he had also
signed for Italian side Udinese. Was
suspended and fined as a result but, once
in the Wednesday side, he made his mark
in the best possible fashion with two
goals at Villa Park, but his new side still
lost 3-2. Left sided winger, who has been

capped by his native Holland, and is very distinctive because of his dreadlocks which drew unwanted attention during the 1996-97 season from Arsenal's Ian Wright. Joined Wednesday from Feyenoord for £275,000 when the Dutch side would have lost him for nothing a few months later under the Bosman ruling. Played in 33 of Wednesday's Premiership games last season although 18 were from the subs' bench.

### Form Factors

| Season | Team | Tot | St | Sb | Y | R |
|---|---|---|---|---|---|---|
| 95-96 | Sheffield W. | 9 | 9 | 0 | 1 | 0 |
| 96-97 | Sheffield W. | 33 | 15 | 18 | 6 | 0 |
| Total | | 42 | 24 | 18 | 7 | 0 |

| | GP | GG | GF | GS | TGR |
|---|---|---|---|---|---|
| 95-96 | 23.68 | 4.50 | 48 | 2 | 4.17 |
| 96-97 | 86.84 | 33.00 | 50 | 1 | 2.00 |
| Averages | 55.26 | 18.75 | 49.00 | 1.50 | 3.08 |

## BLUNT, Jason

## Leeds United ❶ M

Fullname:  Jason Blunt
DOB:       16-08-77 Penzance
   England Youth international midfield player and trainee who made his first appearance in the Premiership with Leeds United in March 1996 as a substitute during a 1-0 home defeat by Middlesbrough. Started in two more games that season but made little significant progress during 1996-97 with just one more Premiership game to his credit.
   Was born in Penzance on the day Elvis Presley died.

### Form Factors

| Season | Team | Tot | St | Sb | Y | R |
|---|---|---|---|---|---|---|
| 95-96 | Leeds Utd | 3 | 2 | 1 | 0 | 0 |
| 96-97 | Leeds Utd | 1 | 0 | 1 | 0 | 0 |
| Total | | 4 | 2 | 2 | 0 | 0 |

| | GP | GG | GF | GS | TGR |
|---|---|---|---|---|---|
| 95-96 | 7.89 | 0.00 | 40 | 0 | 0.00 |
| 96-97 | 2.63 | 0.00 | 28 | 0 | 0.00 |
| Averages | 5.26 | 0.00 | 34.00 | 0.00 | 0.00 |

## BOHINEN, Lars

## Blackburn Rovers ❶❷❸ M

Fullname:  Lars Bohinen
DOB:       08-09-69 Vadso, Norway
   A hugely experienced Norwegian international, Bohinen joined Blackburn Rovers mid-way through the 1995-96 season when Rovers realised a clause in his contract meant he could be had for what was a bargain £700,000.
   He arrived at Nottingham Forest via the Swiss-based club Young Boys of Berne before moving to Ewood Park and featured in the majority of Blackburn's remaining games for the 1995-96 season. Last season international call-ups and injury restricted Bohinen's appearances to 23 plus a number of unused bench placements.
   Bohinen is a skilful midfield player who provides goals on a regular basis for those around him. Can strike a deadball to good effect, which makes him dangerous in free-kick situations.

### Form Factors

| Season | Team | Tot | St | Sb | Y | R |
|---|---|---|---|---|---|---|
| 95-96 | N. Forest | 7 | 7 | 0 | 1 | 0 |
| 95-96 | Blackburn | 20 | 18 | 2 | 3 | 0 |
| 96-97 | Blackburn | 23 | 17 | 6 | 6 | 0 |
| Total | | 50 | 42 | 8 | 10 | 0 |

| | GP | GG | GF | GS | TGR |
|---|---|---|---|---|---|
| 95-96 | 18.42 | 0.00 | 50 | 0 | 0.00 |
| 95-96 | 52.63 | 5.00 | 61 | 4 | 6.56 |
| 96-97 | 52.63 | 10.00 | 42 | 2 | 4.76 |
| Averages | 41.23 | 5.00 | 51.00 | 2.00 | 3.77 |

## BOLAND, Willie

# Coventry City ❶ M

**Fullname:** Willie Boland
**DOB:** 06-08-75 Republic of Ireland

A skilful midfield player, Boland has come through the ranks at Highfield Road and established himself as a player for the future with Coventry City and his native Republic of Ireland.

He made his Premiership debut in 1993 at the age of 18 and has since gone on to complete over 50 first team appearances for the Sky Blues.

He seemed to have made a significant breakthrough in 1994-95 with 12 appearances, but he has struggled to make the City side since, managing only four appearances in the past two seasons. Indeed his only Premiership game last season came from the bench, a place where he sat another 13 times without being used.

## Form Factors

| Season | Team | Tot | St | Sb | Y | R |
|--------|------|-----|----|----|----|----|
| 94-95 | Coventry City | 12 | 9 | 3 | 1 | 0 |
| 95-96 | Coventry City | 3 | 2 | 1 | 0 | 0 |
| 96-97 | Coventry City | 1 | 0 | 1 | 0 | 0 |
| Total | | 16 | 11 | 5 | 1 | 0 |

| | GP | GG | GF | GS | TGR |
|--------|------|------|------|------|------|
| 94-95 | 28.57 | 0.00 | 44 | 0 | 0.00 |
| 95-96 | 7.89 | 0.00 | 42 | 0 | 0.00 |
| 96-97 | 2.63 | 0.00 | 38 | 0 | 0.00 |
| Averages | 13.03 | 0.00 | 41.33 | 0.00 | 0.00 |

## BOOTH, Andy

# Sheffield W. ❶❷❸❹ S

**Fullname:** Andrew David Booth
**DOB:** 06-12-73 Huddersfield

Yorkshire born striker who enjoyed a fine first season with Sheffield Wednesday following his £2.7 million transfer from Huddersfield Town in July 1996.

Made his debut in the Premiership on the opening day of the season and three days later, in the derby match at Leeds United, used his pace to score the second goal in a 2-0 victory. Went on to score a further nine league goals during the season, and shows signs of continuing the excellent strike rate achieved with Huddersfield which could see him step up from the England Under-21 squad to the senior set-up.

Missed just three league games during his first season at Hillsborough.

## Form Factors

| Season | Team | Tot | St | Sb | Y | R |
|--------|------|-----|----|----|----|----|
| 96-97 | Sheffield W. | 35 | 32 | 3 | 3 | 0 |
| Total | | 35 | 32 | 3 | 3 | 0 |

| | GP | GG | GF | GS | TGR |
|--------|------|------|------|------|------|
| 96-97 | 92.11 | 3.50 | 50 | 10 | 20.00 |
| Averages | 92.11 | 3.50 | 50.00 | 10.00 | 20.00 |

## BORROWS, Brian

### Coventry City ❶ FB

Fullname: Brian Borrows
DOB: 20-12-60 Liverpool
Liverpool-born defender who will be
37 in December and could find his first
team chances, after a lengthy career,
reduced as the season progresses. Since
joining the club from Bolton Wanderers
in 1985, he has made over 470
appearances in the Sky Blues' defence,
but injury forced him to miss the glorious
1987 FA Cup victory over Spurs.

Has previously played for Everton and
Bristol City (loan) as well as Bolton.
Twice voted Coventry's Player of the Year
and made one appearance for England
'B'. Reliable defender whose last goal for
the club came five years ago. Was an
unused sub eight times last season in
addition to his 20 appearances in the
Premiership.

### Form Factors

| Season | Team | Tot | St | Sb | Y | R |
|--------|------------|-----|----|----|----|---|
| 94-95 | Coventry C. | 35 | 33 | 2 | 8 | 0 |
| 95-96 | Coventry C. | 19 | 19 | 0 | 6 | 0 |
| 96-97 | Coventry C. | 23 | 16 | 7 | 3 | 0 |
| Total | | 77 | 68 | 9 | 17 | 0 |

| | GP | GG | GF | GS | TGR |
|---------|-------|------|-------|------|------|
| 94-95 | 83.33 | 0.00 | 44 | 0 | 0.00 |
| 95-96 | 50.00 | 0.00 | 42 | 0 | 0.00 |
| 96-97 | 60.53 | 0.00 | 38 | 0 | 0.00 |
| Averages | 64.62 | 0.00 | 41.33 | 0.00 | 0.00 |

## BOSANCIC, Jovo

### Barnsley ❶❷ M

Fullname: Jovo Bosancic
DOB: 07-08-70
A former Yugoslavian Under-21
international now playing under the
Croatian flag, this skilful player did
remarkably well in his first year with the
Tykes and, after settling into the pace of
the English game, will be pleased with
his progress.

Signed on a free transfer by Danny
Wilson from the Portuguese second
division side Camponaioir, Bosancic
played in 25 of Barnsley's Nationwide
League games last season, starting 17
times and appearing as a substitute on
eight other occasions. Not a prolific
goalscorer, he broke his Yorkshire duck
with a penalty in the 2-0 win over
Manchester City in the last game of 1996.

May take time to find his feet again in
the Premiership but could well make a
real impact.

## BOSNICH, Mark

### Aston Villa ❶❷❸❹ GK

Fullname: Mark John Bosnich
DOB: 13-01-72 Sydney, Australia
The Australian international
goalkeeper, who today might have been a
Manchester United player had a Home
Office technicality not intervened. Now
though, his displays for Villa over the past
few seasons have earned him a reputation
as an excellent shot-stopper. In 1995-96
he competed in every game and conceded
just 35 goals in 38 games behind what
was an excellent Villa defence and one
that was key to that season's Coca Cola
Cup success.

Mark Bosnich

## Form Factors

| Season | Team | Tot | St | Sb | Y | R |
|---|---|---|---|---|---|---|
| 94-95 | Aston Villa | 30 | 30 | 0 | 4 | 1 |
| 95-96 | Aston Villa | 38 | 38 | 0 | 1 | 0 |
| 96-97 | Aston Villa | 20 | 20 | 0 | 2 | 0 |
| Total | | 88 | 88 | 0 | 7 | 1 |

| | GA | GkA | GAp | CS | SO | Rp |
|---|---|---|---|---|---|---|
| 94-95 | 56 | 43 | 1.43 | 6 | 2 | 0 |
| 95-96 | 35 | 34 | 0.89 | 13 | 2 | 0 |
| 96-97 | 34 | 17 | 0.85 | 9 | 2 | 0 |
| Total | 125 | 94 | 1.07 | 28 | 6 | |

Last season he found himself blighted by injury and his willingness to put country before club enabled Michael Oakes to stake a claim and push him for a first team spot. Nevertheless his nine clean sheets in 20 games was outstanding as he conceded less than a goal a game on average.

The goalkeeper battle at Villa Park will be interesting and if Bosnich gets the nod he will have to play at tip-top form to keep the No. 1 jersey.

## BOULD, Steve

### Arsenal ❶❷❸ CB

Fullname:  Stephen Andrew Bould
DOB:        16-11-62 Stoke

A powerful centre-half whose formidable partnership with Tony Adams provided the fulcrum for Arsenal triumphs during the George Graham reign and led to him winning two England caps during Bruce Rioch's one-year term as manager.

Bould joined Arsenal in 1988 from his home town club Stoke City, for whom he made 212 appearances. He has only scored 13 league goals in total despite his undoubted ability in the air, especially when flicking on near post corners, an ability that came to the fore in the Cup Winners' Cup semi-final, 1st leg, against Sampdoria when he scored twice.

Approaching 250 league games for Arsenal, he was a near ever-present for the Gunners last season. However, he will be 35 towards the end of 1997 and must be considered more and more as a fringe player for the Gunners this season, a fact backed up by the signing of a one-year contract.

May be worth a gamble if the price is right and he remains in Wenger's plans.

Lee Bowyer

# Leeds United ❶❷❸❹ M

Fullname: Lee David Bowyer
DOB: 03-01-77 London

Became one of the hottest properties around in 1996 after an outstanding season with Charlton Athletic which saw him gain recognition by England at Under-21 level to go with the Youth caps won earlier in his fledgling career. Scored eight goals in 46 league games for the Addicks and a further six goals in ten cup ties. Leeds United won the race for his signature paying Charlton £2.6 million for his services, the highest fee paid at that time in English football for a teenager. Appeared in 32 of Leeds 38 Premiership matches last season, scoring a useful four goals from midfield. Should make the step up to the full England side in the not too distant future and will be a cornerstone of the Leeds side for many years to come.

## Form Factors

| Season | Team | Tot | St | Sb | Y | R |
|---|---|---|---|---|---|---|
| 96-97 | Leeds Utd | 32 | 32 | 0 | 6 | 0 |
| Total | | 32 | 32 | 0 | 6 | 0 |

| | GP | GG | GF | GS | TGR |
|---|---|---|---|---|---|
| 96-97 | 84.21 | 8.00 | 28 | 4 | 14.29 |
| Averages | 84.21 | 8.00 | 28.00 | 4.00 | 14.29 |

## Form Factors

| Season | Team | Tot | St | Sb | Y | R |
|---|---|---|---|---|---|---|
| 94-95 | Arsenal | 31 | 30 | 1 | 4 | 0 |
| 95-96 | Arsenal | 19 | 19 | 0 | 7 | 1 |
| 96-97 | Arsenal | 33 | 33 | 0 | 6 | 0 |
| Total | | 83 | 82 | 1 | 17 | 1 |

| | GP | GG | GF | GS | TGR |
|---|---|---|---|---|---|
| 94-95 | 73.81 | 0.00 | 52 | 0 | 0.00 |
| 95-96 | 50.00 | 0.00 | 49 | 0 | 0.00 |
| 96-97 | 86.84 | 0.00 | 62 | 0 | 0.00 |
| Averages | 70.22 | 0.00 | 54.33 | 0.00 | 0.00 |

## BOXALL, Danny

### Crystal Palace ❶ FB

Fullname: Daniel James Boxall
DOB: 24-08-77 Croydon

Injury wrecked Boxall's season in 1996-97. Having made six appearances at the start of the season the defender suffered a cruciate ligament injury which sidelined him for over six months. He made his comeback in the reserves near the end of the season and should be fighting fit for the 1997-98 season.

Born close to Selhurst Park, Boxall joined as a trainee and his speed and skill on the ball have helped establish him as a player for the future.

## BRANAGAN, Keith

### Bolton W. ❶❷ GK

Fullname: Keith Branagan
DOB: 10-07-66 Fulham

Having joined Bolton on a free transfer from Millwall in the summer of 1992, this especially brave goalkeeper has become one of the club's most consistent performers – a fact that didn't go unnoticed at international level when he was awarded his first cap for the Republic of Ireland last season. Injury prevented Branagan from being an ever-present during 1996-97 but didn't stop him recording his 200th senior appearance in Bolton's colours.

He was a member of the 1995-96 season team that had one year in the Premiership, playing in 31 of their 38 games. As a last line of defence there are few better goalkeepers and he will need to be at his tip-top best to hold off the challenge of reserve 'keeper Gavin Ward, and a variety of Premier League strikers.

*Keith Branagan*

### Form Factors

| Season | Team | Tot | St | Sb | Y | R |
|--------|------|-----|-----|-----|-----|-----|
| 95-96 | Bolton W. | 31 | 31 | 0 | 1 | 0 |
| Total | | 31 | 31 | 0 | 1 | 0 |

| | GA | GkA | GAp | CS | SO | Rp |
|--------|-----|-----|-----|-----|-----|-----|
| 95-96 | 71 | 60 | 1.94 | 4 | 2 | 0 |
| Total | 71 | 60 | 1.94 | 4 | 2 | – |

*Michael Branch*

last term all came from his striking partner's nod downs!

Has an excellent turn of pace and will look to establish himself even further during the 1997-98 season.

## Form Factors

| Season | Team | Tot | St | Sb | Y | R |
|---|---|---|---|---|---|---|
| 95-96 | Everton | 3 | 1 | 2 | 0 | 0 |
| 96-97 | Everton | 25 | 13 | 12 | 2 | 0 |
| Total | | 28 | 14 | 14 | 2 | 0 |

| | GP | GG | GF | GS | TGR |
|---|---|---|---|---|---|
| 95-96 | 7.89 | 0.00 | 64 | 0 | 0.00 |
| 96-97 | 65.79 | 8.33 | 44 | 3 | 6.82 |
| Averages | 36.84 | 4.17 | 54.00 | 1.50 | 3.41 |

## BREACKER, Tim

### West Ham U.  ❶❷  FB

Fullname:  Timothy Sean Breacker
DOB:  02-07-65 Bicester

Now in his seventh season at Upton Park, Breacker is an attack minded full-back who normally plays on the right of defence. He joined the Hammers from Luton Town and has been a major influence in the team. Injuries in the past couple of seasons have reduced the number of games he has played, particularly during 1995-96, but his 26 games last term shows that he has re-established himself.

Having scored three goals in his Premiership debut season (1993-94) he has since failed to register one!

Played over 200 games for the Hatters and went through the same landmark for the Hammers last season.

## Form Factors

| Season | Team | Tot | St | Sb | Y | R |
|---|---|---|---|---|---|---|
| 94-95 | West Ham | 33 | 33 | 0 | 8 | 1 |
| 95-96 | West Ham | 22 | 19 | 3 | 6 | 0 |
| 96-97 | West Ham | 26 | 22 | 4 | 2 | 0 |
| Total | | 81 | 74 | 7 | 16 | 1 |

## BRANCH, Michael

### Everton  ❶❷❸❹  S

Fullname:  Michael Paul Branch
DOB:  18-10-78 Liverpool

Former Everton trainee and England Youth player who made his debut for the Toffeemen during the 1995-96 season when he was just 17 years and 126 days old to be precise! In his second season he has become an established member of the Everton squad – of his 25 league appearances a dozen have been as substitute and he was also an unused sub on eight other occasions. He has established a good playing relationship with Duncan Ferguson and his three goals

| | GP | GG | GF | GS | TGR |
|---|---|---|---|---|---|
| 94-95 | 78.57 | 0.00 | 44 | 0 | 0.00 |
| 95-96 | 57.89 | 0.00 | 43 | 0 | 0.00 |
| 96-97 | 57.89 | 0.00 | 39 | 0 | 0.00 |
| Averages | 64.79 | 0.00 | 42.00 | 0.00 | 0.00 |

## BREEN, Gary

## Coventry City ❶❷ CB

**Fullname:** Gary Patrick Breen
**DOB:** 12-12-73 Hendon

Joined Coventry in the early part of 1997 as the Sky Blues looked to shore up a defence leaking goals. It ultimately proved successful as the side won their battle against relegation but Breen took time to settle in and made a number of mistakes that cost his side goals.

He made eight consecutive appearances starting with a goalless draw against Sheffield Wednesday but his next seven games saw 14 goals conceded and just five points secured.

The Sky Blues will be hoping that Republic of Ireland international Breen can settle in at the start of the new season and establish himself as the sort of dominating central defender he can be.

### Form Factors

| Season | Team | Tot | St | Sb | Y | R |
|---|---|---|---|---|---|---|
| 96-97 | Coventry C. | 9 | 8 | 1 | 0 | 0 |
| Total | | 9 | 8 | 1 | 0 | 0 |

| | GP | GG | GF | GS | TGR |
|---|---|---|---|---|---|
| 96-97 | 23.68 | 0.00 | 38 | 0 | 0.00 |
| Averages | 23.68 | 0.00 | 38.00 | 0.00 | 0.00 |

## BRISCOE, Lee

## Sheffield W. ❶ FB

**Fullname:** Lee Stephen Briscoe
**DOB:** 30-09-75 Pontefract

Very promising 22-year-old wide player, who like many of his generation has converted from a winger to the modern wing-back. Briscoe will be looking to break into the first team in a big way this season, having seen injury hinder the forward strides made two years ago when he started in 23 of Sheffield Wednesday's Premiership matches and came on as sub in three more. He played in just six league games last season and, although he has yet to score for Wednesday time is on his side so could yet play an important role down the left flank for the club.

### Form Factors

| Season | Team | Tot | St | Sb | Y | R |
|---|---|---|---|---|---|---|
| 94-95 | Sheffield W. | 6 | 6 | 0 | 0 | 0 |
| 95-96 | Sheffield W. | 25 | 22 | 3 | 1 | 0 |
| 96-97 | Sheffield W. | 6 | 5 | 1 | 0 | 0 |
| Total | | 37 | 33 | 4 | 1 | 0 |

| | GP | GG | GF | GS | TGR |
|---|---|---|---|---|---|
| 94-95 | 14.29 | 0.00 | 49 | 0 | 0.00 |
| 95-96 | 65.79 | 0.00 | 48 | 0 | 0.00 |
| 96-97 | 65.79 | 0.00 | 50 | 0 | 0.00 |
| Averages | 48.62 | 0.00 | 49.00 | 0.00 | 0.00 |

## BROLIN, Tomas

## Leeds United ❶❷ S

**Fullname:** Tomas Brolin
**DOB:** 29-11-69 Hudiksvall, Sweden

Very experienced Swedish international striker who has not shown the most willing attitude towards his employers since making a well-paid move to Leeds United for £4.5 million in November 1995. Has since had loan spells with FC

Zurich and one of his former clubs, Parma. Played 19 times for Leeds during the 1995-96 season, scoring four goals, but is unlikely to inflate that total and therefore be worth precious little in the way of points in your fantasy team, if indeed he remains at Elland Road for any length of time. Previous clubs include the football strongholds of GIF Sundsvall and Norrkoping.

## Form Factors

| Season | Team | Tot | St | Sb | Y | R |
|--------|------|-----|----|----|----|----|
| 95-96 | Leeds Utd | 19 | 17 | 2 | 4 | 0 |
| 96-97 | Leeds Utd | 0 | 0 | 0 | 0 | 0 |
| Total | | 19 | 17 | 2 | 4 | 0 |

| | GP | GG | GF | GS | TGR |
|--|----|----|----|----|----|
| 95-96 | 50.00 | 4.75 | 40 | 4 | 10.00 |
| Averages | 50.00 | 7.74 | 40.00 | 4.00 | 10.00 |

## BULLOCK, Martin

# Barnsley ❶❷❸ M

Fullname: Martin John Bullock
DOB: 05-03-75 Derby

Martin Bullock possesses excellent dribbling skills that enable him to attack defences from his midfield role for Barnsley. However he wasn't able to establish himself in the Tykes' starting line-up and, although he had 30 appearances to his credit last season, 23 came from the bench.

He was spotted playing for non-league side Eastwood Town, and moved to Oakwell for a £10,000 fee in September 1993. Made his 100th league appearance at the end of the season with only 49 of these as a starter, and only one goal in those games.

## BURLEY, Craig

# Chelsea ❶❷❸❹ M

Fullname: Craig William Burley
DOB: 24-09-71 Irvine

The Scottish midfield player and nephew of Ipswich Town manager George Burley played in 30 of Chelsea's Premiership games in 1996-97 and generally had an excellent season. It was all the more gratifying for Burley, given the succession of niggling injuries that inhibited his 1995-96 season.

Burley joined the Blues as a trainee in September 1989 and should make his 150th senior appearance during 1997-98.

Hardworking Burley possesses a tremendous shot and is one of those unique players who has represented their country at every level.

## Form Factors

| Season | Team | Tot | St | Sb | Y | R |
|--------|------|-----|----|----|----|----|
| 94-95 | Chelsea | 25 | 16 | 9 | 5 | 0 |
| 95-96 | Chelsea | 22 | 16 | 6 | 1 | 0 |
| 96-97 | Chelsea | 31 | 26 | 5 | 3 | 0 |
| Total | | 78 | 58 | 20 | 9 | 0 |

| | GP | GG | GF | GS | TGR |
|--|----|----|----|----|----|
| 94-95 | 59.52 | 12.50 | 50 | 2 | 4.00 |
| 95-96 | 57.89 | 8.33 | 46 | 0 | 0.00 |
| 96-97 | 81.58 | 15.50 | 58 | 2 | 3.45 |
| Averages | 66.33 | 12.11 | 51.33 | 1.33 | 2.48 |

## BURROWS, David

### Coventry City  ❶  FB

Fullname: David Burrows
DOB: 25-10-68 Dudley
Arrived at Highfield Road via Liverpool, West Ham and Everton. He was part of a successful Anfield side that won him two championship medals.

Hasn't been able to hold down a regular first team place since signing and this hasn't been helped by injuries, not least hamstring problems in 1995-96 and a hernia operation last season that limited him to under half of City's games. His versatility is a major aspect of his play, being able to play in central defence or midfield.

Has represented England at Under-21 and 'B' levels and there is no doubt that Coventry wouldn't have struggled so much recently had he been fully fit.

### Form Factors

| Season | Team | Tot | St | Sb | Y | R |
|---|---|---|---|---|---|---|
| 94-95 | Everton | 19 | 19 | 0 | 7 | 0 |
| 94-95 | Coventry C. | 11 | 11 | 0 | 4 | 0 |
| 95-96 | Coventry C. | 13 | 13 | 0 | 4 | 0 |
| 96-97 | Coventry C. | 18 | 17 | 1 | 5 | 0 |
| Total | | 61 | 60 | 1 | 20 | 0 |

| | GP | GG | GF | GS | TGR |
|---|---|---|---|---|---|
| 94-95 | 41.43 | 0.00 | 44 | 0 | 0.00 |
| 95-96 | 34.21 | 0.00 | 42 | 0 | 0.00 |
| 96-97 | 47.37 | 0.00 | 38 | 0 | 0.00 |
| Averages | 41.00 | 0.00 | 41.33 | 0.00 | 0.00 |

## BUTT, Nicky

### Manchester U.  ❶❷❸❹  M

Fullname: Nicholas Butt
DOB: 21-01-75 Manchester
This Mancunian fulfilled a boyhood dream by making the grade from trainee. Although not an ever-present, he has established himself as part of the squad and played 26 games in 1996-97. Butt has learned much from Roy Keane in the Reds' midfield – indeed one published statistic suggested he was successful in almost 80% of the tackles he goes into!

He is rarely in the headlines but his committed displays make him a big favourite with the United fans. Like Keane, Butt is a player with stamina and a fierce tackle. His distribution skills are now matched by his dangerous attacking runs which resulted in five goals in the 1996-97.

### Form Factors

| Season | Team | Tot | St | Sb | Y | R |
|---|---|---|---|---|---|---|
| 94-95 | Man. Utd | 22 | 11 | 11 | 4 | 0 |
| 95-96 | Man. Utd | 32 | 31 | 1 | 7 | 1 |
| 96-97 | Man. Utd | 26 | 24 | 2 | 5 | 0 |
| Total | | 80 | 66 | 14 | 16 | 1 |

| | GP | GG | GF | GS | TGR |
|---|---|---|---|---|---|
| 94-95 | 52.38 | 22.00 | 77 | 1 | 1.30 |
| 95-96 | 84.21 | 16.00 | 73 | 2 | 2.74 |
| 96-97 | 68.42 | 5.20 | 76 | 5 | 6.58 |
| Averages | 68.34 | 14.40 | 75.33 | 2.67 | 3.54 |

## CALDERWOOD, Colin

# Tottenham H.  ❶❷❸  CB

Fullname:  Colin Calderwood
DOB:      20-01-65 Stranraer
  Signed for Tottenham Hotspur from
Swindon Town four years ago, during
which time he has become a regular in
the Scotland squad. Formed a useful
partnership with Gary Mabbutt and more
recently Sol Campbell, in the heart of the
Spurs' defence, having initially struggled
when Ossie Ardiles was manager at a
time when defending was not high on the
list of priorities!
  Calderwood is now a permanent fixture
in the Spurs' defence having missed just
four games last season. Made 100 league
appearances for Mansfield Town before
joining Swindon Town and after 330
league games for the Wiltshire club,
signed for Spurs for £1.25m. Has twice
won promotion through the play-offs and
represented the Football League.

### Form Factors

| Season | Team | Tot | St | Sb | Y | R |
|--------|------|-----|----|----|----|---|
| 94-95 | Tottenham | 36 | 35 | 1 | 4 | 1 |
| 95-96 | Tottenham | 29 | 26 | 3 | 6 | 0 |
| 96-97 | Tottenham | 34 | 33 | 1 | 6 | 0 |
| Total |  | 99 | 94 | 5 | 16 | 1 |

|  | GP | GG | GF | GS | TGR |
|--|----|----|----|----|-----|
| 94-95 | 85.71 | 18.00 | 66 | 2 | 3.03 |
| 95-96 | 76.32 | 29.00 | 50 | 1 | 2.00 |
| 96-97 | 76.32 | 0.00 | 44 | 0 | 0.00 |
| Averages | 79.45 | 15.67 | 53.33 | 1.00 | 1.68 |

## CAMPBELL, Sol

# Tottenham H.  ❶❷❸❹❺  CB

Fullname:  Sulzeer Jeremiah Campbell
DOB:      18-09-74 Newham, London
  The 1996-97 campaign may not have
been one of the most memorable in the
history of Tottenham Hotspur but for Sol
Campbell it was a very important season
as he established himself strongly in the
England set-up and looks set to be the
main feature in both defences for many
years to come.
  Committed himself to Spurs at the end
of last season by signing a new contract at
a time when there was transfer
speculation surrounding him.
  Impressive throughout, he completed
the season ever-present taking his total
Spurs' league appearances to 134.
Although renowned for his defensive
capabilities has also revelled in a midfield
position when required. An excellent
reader of the game with a great tackling
ability – should be strongly considered
for any fantasy team.

### Form Factors

| Season | Team | Tot | St | Sb | Y | R |
|--------|------|-----|----|----|----|---|
| 94-95 | Tottenham | 30 | 29 | 1 | 0 | 1 |
| 95-96 | Tottenham | 31 | 31 | 0 | 2 | 0 |
| 96-97 | Tottenham | 38 | 38 | 0 | 1 | 0 |
| Total |  | 99 | 98 | 1 | 3 | 1 |

|  | GP | GG | GF | GS | TGR |
|--|----|----|----|----|-----|
| 94-95 | 71.43 | 0.00 | 66 | 0 | 0.00 |
| 95-96 | 81.58 | 31.00 | 50 | 1 | 2.00 |
| 96-97 | 100.00 | 0.00 | 44 | 0 | 0.00 |
| Averages | 84.34 | 10.33 | 53.33 | 0.33 | 0.67 |

Sol Campbell

## CARBON, Matt

### Derby County ❶ CB

Fullname: Matthew Carbon
DOB: 08-06-75 Nottingham

Nottingham-born central defender whose versatility has also seen him fill several other positions very comfortably. One time England Under-21 international who started his career as a trainee at Lincoln City before scoring ten times in 69 first team appearances at Sincil Bank. He joined Derby for £385,000 during their promotion run-in but was injured early in his career at the Baseball Ground and featured in just ten Premiership matches for the Rams last season, and was an unused sub on eight other occasions. A groin injury troubled him throughout the season. At just 22 years of age he has youth and the talent to make his impact in the coming seasons.

### Form Factors

| Season | Team | Tot | St | Sb | Y | R |
|---|---|---|---|---|---|---|
| 96-97 | Derby Co. | 10 | 6 | 4 | 1 | 0 |
| Total | | 10 | 6 | 4 | 1 | 0 |

| | GP | GG | GF | GS | TGR |
|---|---|---|---|---|---|
| 96-97 | 26.32 | 0.00 | 45 | 0 | 0.00 |
| Averages | 26.32 | 0.00 | 45.00 | 0.00 | 0.00 |

## CARBONE, Benito

### Sheffield W. ❶❷❸ M

Fullname: Benito Carbone
DOB: 14-08-71 Bagnara Calabra, Italy

Diminutive Italian international who is in his second season with Sheffield Wednesday, which is something of an achievement given the frequency with which he moved around his homeland with Torino (twice), Reggina, Casertana, Ascoli, Napoli and Internazionale from where he joined the Owls in October 1996 for £3 million – a record for

Wednesday. A crowd pleaser who is very skilful and elusive with the tight control one expects of Latin players. Scored six times in 25 Premiership outings last season, which is pretty much in keeping with his strike rate during eight years of Italian football. Carbone certainly enhances the case for overseas players playing in England, with his first goal for the club against Nottingham Forest being one of many classic efforts.

### Form Factors

| Season | Team | Tot | St | Sb | Y | R |
|---|---|---|---|---|---|---|
| 93-94 | Tottenham | 1 | 1 | 0 | 0 | 0 |
| 96-97 | Tottenham | 26 | 24 | 2 | 1 | 0 |
| Total | | 27 | 25 | 2 | 1 | 0 |

| | GP | GG | GF | GS | TGR |
|---|---|---|---|---|---|
| 93-94 | 2.38 | 0.00 | 54 | 0 | 0.00 |
| 96-97 | 68.42 | 0.00 | 44 | 0 | 0.00 |
| Averages | 35.40 | 0.00 | 49.00 | 0.00 | 0.00 |

## CARRAGHER, Jamie

## Liverpool ❶ M

**Fullname:** James Carragher
**DOB:** 28-01-78 Bootle

Born in Bootle and a trainee, Carragher made a great start to first team football when he scored against Aston Villa in his first game. However this tough-tackling utility player will find it hard to force his way into the side in 1997-98 after one Premiership start and eight appearances on the subs bench, coming on just once for Bjornebye early in the season, in 1996-97.

Played for the England Under-20 side in Malaysia during the summer of 1997.

### Form Factors

| Season | Team | Tot | St | Sb | Y | R |
|---|---|---|---|---|---|---|
| 96-97 | Liverpool | 2 | 1 | 1 | 1 | 0 |
| Total | | 2 | 1 | 1 | 1 | 0 |

| | GP | GG | GF | GS | TGR |
|---|---|---|---|---|---|
| 96-97 | 5.26 | 2.00 | 62 | 1 | 1.61 |
| Averages | 5.26 | 2.00 | 62.00 | 1.00 | 1.61 |

### Form Factors

| Season | Team | Tot | St | Sb | Y | R |
|---|---|---|---|---|---|---|
| 96-97 | Sheffield W. | 25 | 24 | 1 | 3 | 0 |
| Total | | 25 | 24 | 1 | 3 | 0 |

| | GP | GG | GF | GS | TGR |
|---|---|---|---|---|---|
| 96-97 | 65.79 | 4.17 | 50 | 6 | 12.00 |
| Averages | 65.79 | 4.17 | 50.00 | 6.00 | 12.00 |

## CARR, Stephen

## Tottenham H. ❶ FB

**Fullname:** Stephen Carr
**DOB:** 29-08-76 Dublin

A regular in the Spurs' reserves in recent seasons but propelled himself into the first team in determined fashion during the 1996-97 season, after being called up during one of Tottenham's numerous injury crises.

Carr's defensive displays impressed and he went on to play in almost 70% of Spurs' Premiership matches, forcing former regular Dean Austin onto the sidelines. Will be 21 early in the season and if he maintains the promise shown last season, could well continue to build on an international career which has seen him represent the Republic of Ireland at Schoolboy, Youth and U21 levels.

## CARSLEY, Lee

## Derby County   ①②   FB

Fullname: Lee Kevin Carsley
DOB: 28-04-74 Birmingham
  Although Birmingham-born he joined Derby County as a trainee prior to signing professional forms in July 1992. His first appearance in the Premiership came just a month after Derby began their programme in the top flight and he should play his 100th game for Derby early in 1997-98.

A Republic of Ireland Under-21 international, he made 24 appearances last season although nine of these were from the substitutes' bench.

Carsley can play in midfield but is predominantly a defender. Another young Derby talent who can be expected to play a big role in Derby's 1997-98 campaign.

### Form Factors

| Season | Team | Tot | St | Sb | Y | R |
|---|---|---|---|---|---|---|
| 96-97 | Derby Co. | 24 | 15 | 9 | 2 | 0 |
| Total | | 24 | 15 | 9 | 2 | 0 |

| | GP | GG | GF | GS | TGR |
|---|---|---|---|---|---|
| 96-97 | 63.16 | 0.00 | 45 | 0 | 0.00 |
| Averages | 63.16 | 0.00 | 45.00 | 0.00 | 0.00 |

## CASPER, Chris

## Manchester U.   ①   CB

Fullname: Christopher Martin Casper
DOB: 28-04-75 Burnley
  Young central defender who is the son of the Burnley legend Frank Casper. Cool on the ball especially under pressure, he is already being likened to the man he may replace in the United defence, Gary Pallister.

He went on loan to Bury in 1996-97 but got his taste of the Premiership when he debuted against Tottenham Hotspur just a couple of weeks after coming on as a substitute during United's win in Vienna in the UEFA Champions' League.

One for the future who may get more of a role on the bench this season but who will probably only get a chance if there are injuries to the established back four.

### Form Factors

| Season | Team | Tot | St | Sb | Y | R |
|---|---|---|---|---|---|---|
| 96-97 | Man. Utd | 2 | 0 | 2 | 0 | 0 |
| Total | | 2 | 0 | 2 | 0 | 0 |

| | GP | GG | GF | GS | TGR |
|---|---|---|---|---|---|
| 96-97 | 5.26 | 0.00 | 76 | 0 | 0.00 |
| Averages | 5.26 | 0.00 | 76.00 | 0.00 | 0.00 |

## CASTLEDINE, Stewart

## Wimbledon   ①   M

Fullname: Stewart Mark Castledine
DOB: 22-01-73 Wandsworth
  The majority of Castledine's six appearances for the Dons' last season came in the final stretch of their campaign when Kinnear was using his small squad to the full, as the team battled to two cup semi-finals and a high league position.

A tall, strong central midfield player, Castledine has been utilised almost exclusively as a squad player since making his debut in April 1994. He spent some time on loan at Wycombe Wanderers in 1995-96, where he scored three times in his seven games.

Has come right through the Wimbledon system and may make a bigger impact in the team this season.

### Form Factors

| Season | Team | Tot | St | Sb | Y | R |
|---|---|---|---|---|---|---|
| 94-95 | Wimbledon | 6 | 5 | 1 | 1 | 0 |
| 95-96 | Wimbledon | 4 | 2 | 2 | 0 | 0 |
| 96-97 | Wimbledon | 6 | 4 | 2 | 0 | 0 |
| Total | | 16 | 11 | 5 | 1 | 0 |

| GP | GG | GF | GS | TGR |
|---|---|---|---|---|
| 94-95 | 14.29 | 6.00 | 48 | 1 | 2.08 |
| 95-96 | 10.53 | 4.00 | 55 | 1 | 1.82 |
| 96-97 | 15.79 | 6.00 | 49 | 1 | 2.04 |
| Averages | 13.54 | 5.33 | 50.67 | 1.00 | 1.98 |

## CHARLES, Gary

### Aston Villa ❶❷❸ FB

Fullname: Gary Andrew Charles
DOB: 13-04-70 Newham

A broken ankle kept Charles out of the Villa side last season and meant the arrival of additional cover in his right full-back position. Displaying an attacking instinct that makes him suited for the wing-back role, Charles was enjoying top form during the 1995-96 season until his unfortunate injury against West Ham.

Having made his name at Nottingham Forest and winning two full England caps, he fell out of favour and found himself at Villa Park after spells at Leicester and Derby.

With Fernando Nelson signed from Sporting Lisbon as cover last season and playing well, Charles will have a fight on his hands to win back his first team spot when fully recovered from injury.

### Form Factors

| Season | Team | Tot | St | Sb | Y | R |
|---|---|---|---|---|---|---|
| 92-93 | N. Forest | 14 | 14 | 0 | 0 | 0 |
| 94-95 | Aston Villa | 16 | 14 | 2 | 0 | 0 |
| 95-96 | Aston Villa | 34 | 34 | 0 | 1 | 0 |
| Total | | 64 | 62 | 2 | 1 | 0 |

| | GP | GG | GF | GS | TGR |
|---|---|---|---|---|---|
| 92-93 | 33.33 | 0.00 | 41 | 0 | 0.00 |
| 94-95 | 38.10 | 0.00 | 51 | 0 | 0.00 |
| 95-96 | 89.47 | 34.00 | 52 | 1 | 1.92 |
| Averages | 53.63 | 11.33 | 48.00 | 0.33 | 0.64 |

## CHARLTON, Simon

### Southampton ❶❷ FB

Fullname: Simon Thomas Charlton
DOB: 25-10-71 Huddersfield

Small injuries have conspired to prevent Simon Charlton being a probable ever-present in the Southampton side since he joined them from Huddersfield in March 1993. Nevertheless he made his 100th Premiership appearance towards the end of last season and has established himself as an important member of the Saints squad.

A former England Youth player, Charlton is a left sided player who often competes with Francis Benali for a spot at full-back or in midfield.

A non-stop runner, he possesses a long throw that Southampton sometimes take advantage of.

### Form Factors

| Season | Team | Tot | St | Sb | Y | R |
|---|---|---|---|---|---|---|
| 94-95 | Southampton | 25 | 25 | 0 | 1 | 0 |
| 95-96 | Southampton | 26 | 24 | 2 | 4 | 0 |
| 96-97 | Southampton | 26 | 24 | 2 | 1 | 0 |
| Total | | 77 | 73 | 4 | 6 | 0 |

| | GP | GG | GF | GS | TGR |
|---|---|---|---|---|---|
| 94-95 | 59.52 | 25.00 | 61 | 1 | 1.64 |
| 95-96 | 68.42 | 0.00 | 34 | 0 | 0.00 |
| 96-97 | 68.42 | 0.00 | 50 | 0 | 0.00 |
| Averages | 65.46 | 8.33 | 48.33 | 0.33 | 0.55 |

## CLAPHAM, Jamie

# Tottenham H. ❶ FB

Fullname: James Clapham
DOB: 07-12-75 Lincoln

Although born in Lincoln, he is a former Spurs trainee who turned professional in 1994 but had to wait until the tail end of last season to make his break into the first team with his debut against Coventry City.

He started at Tottenham as a winger but has been converted very successfully into a defender during his time in the reserves. He will be looking to follow in the footsteps of Stephen Carr and hold down a first team place this season, perhaps at the expense of Clive Wilson.

## Form Factors

| Season | Team | Tot | St | Sb | Y | R |
|--------|------|-----|----|----|----|----|
| 96-97 | Tottenham | 1 | 0 | 1 | 0 | 0 |
| Total | | 1 | 0 | 1 | 0 | 0 |

| | GP | GG | GF | GS | TGR |
|--------|------|------|------|------|------|
| 96-97 | 2.63 | 0.00 | 44 | 0 | 0.00 |
| Averages | 2.63 | 0.00 | 44.00 | 0.00 | 0.00 |

## CLARIDGE, Steve

# Leicester City ❶❷❸ S

Fullname: Stephen Edward Claridge
DOB: 10-04-66 Portsmouth

One of the most fascinating players in the Premiership who has scaled the depths of a couple of spells in the non-league game to grab the glory of scoring a vital goal at Wembley. Has been a tremendous success since signing for Leicester City from Birmingham City for £1 million in March 1996 and, after scoring five goals in 14 Division One matches, conjured up the promotion clinching play-off goal to defeat Crystal Palace at Wembley.

He was top scorer in Leicester's first season back in the Premiership and crowned the season with the extra-time winner against Middlesbrough in the Coca Cola Cup replay. In a total of 431 games for Bournemouth, Aldershot, Cambridge United (twice), Luton Town, Birmingham and Leicester, he has scored 122 goals.

Out-and-out striker who could be a shrewd buy if Leicester can build on last season's success.

## Form Factors

| Season | Team | Tot | St | Sb | Y | R |
|--------|------|-----|----|----|----|----|
| 96-97 | Leicester C. | 32 | 29 | 3 | 2 | 0 |
| Total | | 32 | 29 | 3 | 2 | 0 |

| | GP | GG | GF | GS | TGR |
|--------|-------|------|------|------|-------|
| 96-97 | 84.21 | 2.67 | 46 | 12 | 26.09 |
| Averages | 84.21 | 2.67 | 46.00 | 12.00 | 26.09 |

## CLARKE, Andy

# Wimbledon ❶❷ S

Fullname: Andrew Weston Clarke
DOB: 22-07-67 Islington
When Andy Clarke started the first game of last season he set a Premiership record. It was his 100th game in the Premier League and his 50th in the starting line-up – with the other 50 from the bench making him the most used sub in Premier League history!

His role as playing sub didn't change during last season with seven of his 11 appearances coming that way.

Clarke came to the fore playing non-league football for Barnet where he attracted a good deal of attention. But it was Wimbledon who bought his services at the end of the 1990-91 season.

A forward who plays wide on the right, he possesses great pace and excellent dribbling ability. In each of the last three seasons his number of appearances in the first team have waned and he may now be towards the end of his time at Selhurst Park.

## Form Factors

| Season | Team | Tot | St | Sb | | Y | R |
|--------|------|-----|-----|-----|---|---|---|
| 94-95 | Wimbledon | 25 | 8 | 17 | | 2 | 0 |
| 95-96 | Wimbledon | 18 | 9 | 9 | | 0 | 0 |
| 96-97 | Wimbledon | 11 | 4 | 7 | | 1 | 0 |
| Total | | 54 | 21 | 33 | | 3 | 0 |

| | GP | GG | GF | GS | TGR |
|--------|-----|-----|-----|-----|-----|
| 94-95 | 59.52 | 25.00 | 48 | 1 | 2.08 |
| 95-96 | 47.37 | 9.00 | 55 | 2 | 3.64 |
| 96-97 | 28.95 | 11.00 | 49 | 1 | 2.04 |
| Averages | 45.28 | 15.00 | 50.67 | 1.33 | 2.59 |

## CLARKE, Matt

# Sheffield W. ❶ GK

Fullname: Matthew John Clarke
DOB: 03-11-73 Sheffield
Twenty three year old Sheffield born goalkeeper who signed for Wednesday from Yorkshire neighbours Rotherham United for £325,000 (rising to £500,000) in the summer of 1996, but had to wait until the final game of the season before making his Premiership debut. It will certainly be a day he will not forget as he came on as substitute just 17 minutes from the end of Wednesday's home match with Liverpool, but was dismissed nine minutes later by David Elleray for handball outside the penalty area despite many observers doubting whether the whole of the ball had left the box. Will continue as understudy to Pressman but has the class to take his chance when it comes.

## Form Factors

| Season | Team | Tot | St | Sb | Y | R |
|--------|------|-----|-----|-----|---|---|
| 96-97 | Sheffield W. | 1 | 0 | 1 | 0 | 1 |
| Total | | 1 | 0 | 1 | 0 | 1 |

| | GA | GkA | GAp | CS | SO | Rp |
|--------|-----|-----|-----|-----|-----|-----|
| 96-97 | 51 | 0 | 0.00 | 0 | 0 | – |

## CLARKE, Steve

# Chelsea ❶❷❸❹ CB

Fullname: Stephen Clarke
DOB: 29-08-63 Saltcoats

Partnered Frank Leboeuf in the centre of Chelsea's defence last season and as the longest serving player currently playing for the Blues, he is also probably the most underrated.

Having joined from St Mirren in January 1987 for £400,000, he passed his 400th league appearance towards the end of the1996-97 season, and has still to score his first goal in the Premier League. He played as a right-back for a large part of his career and switched to a more central role to allow Dan Petrescu to be accommodated in the team.

A good reader of the game, Clarke's experience and energy have played a major role in his team's growth in the past two seasons. Will need to be at top form to retain his place during 1997-98 and, at 34 years, is in the late stages of his career.

## Form Factors

| Season | Team | Tot | St | Sb | Y | R |
|--------|------|-----|----|----|----|----|
| 94-95 | Chelsea | 29 | 29 | 0 | 3 | 1 |
| 95-96 | Chelsea | 22 | 21 | 1 | 2 | 0 |
| 96-97 | Chelsea | 31 | 31 | 0 | 7 | 0 |
| Total | | 82 | 81 | 1 | 12 | 1 |

| | GP | GG | GF | GS | TGR |
|--------|------|------|------|------|------|
| 94-95 | 69.05 | 0.00 | 50 | 0 | 0.00 |
| 95-96 | 57.89 | 0.00 | 46 | 0 | 0.00 |
| 96-97 | 81.58 | 0.00 | 58 | 0 | 0.00 |
| Averages | 69.51 | 0.00 | 51.33 | 0.00 | 0.00 |

## CLEGG, Michael

# Manchester U. ❶ FB

Fullname: Michael Clegg
DOB: 03-07-77 Tameside

Injuries to Denis Irwin and the Neville brothers allowed Michael Clegg his chance to add his name to the list of youngsters who have made it into the United team in recent years. It came in a 2-2 draw at Middlesbrough and he impressed enough to ensure that he played in several more games before the season was out.

A first choice in the reserves, Clegg is likely to have just limited opportunities again in 1997-98.

## Form Factors

| Season | Team | Tot | St | Sb | Y | R |
|--------|------|-----|----|----|----|----|
| 96-97 | Man. Utd | 4 | 3 | 1 | 0 | 0 |
| Total | | 4 | 3 | 1 | 0 | 0 |

| | GP | GG | GF | GS | TGR |
|--------|------|------|------|------|------|
| 96-97 | 10.53 | 0.00 | 76 | 0 | 0.00 |
| Averages | 10.53 | 0.00 | 76.00 | 0.00 | 0.00 |

# COLE, Andy

## Manchester U. ❶❷❸     S

Fullname: Andrew Alexander Cole
DOB: 15-10-71 Nottingham

Prolific striker who caught the public's imagination in the 1993-94 season when he scored 34 league goals for Newcastle United. After a record, £7 million transfer move to United, he failed to match his former strike rate but his all-round play has improved under the watchful eyes of Brian Kidd and Alex Ferguson. Nevertheless in 72 appearances for United, Cole has contributed 29 goals, scoring about every third game. His overall Premiership record brings him a goal in just under every second game and he is the all-time seventh highest scorer with 72.

Cole was a trainee at Arsenal before playing for Fulham and Bristol City, transferring to Newcastle for £1.75 million. He suffered a broken leg in a reserve team game at Anfield which sidelined the unlucky striker for the first half of the 1996-97 season.

He seemed to relish his return and he scored six in 20 Premiership games (half as substitute) to help the club to the top of the Premiership again. He also looked dangerous in United's European games without quite finding the finishing touch.

He is unlikely to get the chance of scoring five goals in a game, as he did against Ipswich in 1994-95 but he is a possible each way bet for your team, considering his excellent form at the end of 1996-97 which found him back in Glenn Hoddle's England team thoughts.

Andy Cole

## Form Factors

| Season | Team | Tot | St | Sb | Y | R |
|--------|------|-----|----|----|---|---|
| 94-95 | Man. Utd | 18 | 17 | 1 | 1 | 0 |
| 95-96 | Man. Utd | 34 | 32 | 2 | 4 | 0 |
| 96-97 | Man. Utd | 20 | 10 | 10 | 1 | 0 |
| Total | | 72 | 59 | 13 | 6 | 0 |

| | GP | GG | GF | GS | TGR |
|--------|------|------|------|------|------|
| 94-95 | 42.86 | 1.50 | 77 | 12 | 15.58 |
| 95-96 | 89.47 | 3.09 | 73 | 11 | 15.07 |
| 96-97 | 52.63 | 3.33 | 76 | 6 | 7.89 |
| Averages | 61.65 | 2.64 | 75.33 | 9.67 | 12.85 |

## COLEMAN, Chris

### Blackburn Rovers ❶❷❸ CB

Fullname: Christopher Coleman
DOB: 10-06-70 Swansea
Injury in the opening stages of last
season ended Coleman's season after just
eight games when he was hurt against
Coventry City. He had established
himself as a Premiership player with
Crystal Palace in the 1994-95 season and
was signed for £2.8 million in December
1995 as a replacement for the injured Ian
Pearce. He immediately struck up a fine
defensive partnership with Colin Hendry
and missed only one game during the
unsuccessful defences of the
Championship.
   A regular in the Welsh international
side Blackburn will be hoping he is back
to fitness for the 1997-98 season.

### Form Factors

| Season | Team | Tot | St | Sb | Y | R |
|---|---|---|---|---|---|---|
| 94-95 | C. Palace | 35 | 35 | 0 | 4 | 0 |
| 95-96 | Blackburn | 20 | 19 | 1 | 2 | 0 |
| 96-97 | Blackburn | 8 | 8 | 0 | 3 | 0 |
| Total | | 63 | 62 | 1 | 9 | 0 |

| | GP | GG | GF | GS | TGR |
|---|---|---|---|---|---|
| 94-95 | 83.33 | 35.00 | 34 | 1 | 2.94 |
| 95-96 | 52.63 | 0.00 | 61 | 0 | 0.00 |
| 96-97 | 52.63 | 0.00 | 42 | 0 | 0.00 |
| Averages | 62.87 | 11.67 | 45.67 | 0.33 | 0.98 |

## COLLINS, Wayne

### Sheffield W.　　❶　　FB

Fullname: Wayne Collins
DOB: 04-03-69 Manchester
Midfielder who completed the rise from
non-league football, with Winsford
United, to the Premiership with a
£600,000 transfer from Crewe Alexandra
during the close season following the 95-
96 season. Caught the eye of Sheffield
Wednesday boss David Pleat when the
Owls faced Crewe in the Coca Cola Cup
and he slotted in well at Hillsborough
until injuries kept him out of the side.
Scored 11 times in 40 league games for
Crewe during the 1994-95 campaign and
showed he has not lost his touch with his
first goal for Wednesday being a cracking
volley during a 2-2 draw at Derby.

### Form Factors

| Season | Team | Tot | St | Sb | Y | R |
|---|---|---|---|---|---|---|
| 96-97 | Sheffield W. | 12 | 8 | 4 | 0 | 1 |
| Total | | 12 | 8 | 4 | 0 | 1 |

| | GP | GG | GF | GS | TGR |
|---|---|---|---|---|---|
| 96-97 | 31.58 | 12.00 | 50 | 1 | 2.00 |
| Averages | 31.58 | 12.00 | 50.00 | 1.00 | 2.00 |

## COLLYMORE, Stan

### Aston Villa ❶❷❸❹❺    S

Fullname: Stanley Victor Collymore
DOB: 22-01-71 Stone

After a season of speculation, Collymore finally joined Aston Villa in the close season. He broke into the Premiership as a Nottingham Forest signing from Southend in 1994 and his 23 goals in 37 games in his first season prompted Liverpool to make him the most expensive British footballer at the time.

However, his time at Anfield was a curious mixture; despite averaging a goal every 2.5 games, he never really settled in to the Liverpool way so as to make a transfer back to his beloved Midlands simply a matter of time.

His form early on earned him two full England caps and his likely partnership with Dwight Yorke holds much promise. Collymore is big and powerful and his goals are often spectacular. Could prove a big hit at Villa.

### Form Factors

| Season | Team | Tot | St | Sb | Y | R |
|--------|------|-----|-----|-----|-----|-----|
| 94-95 | N. Forest | 37 | 37 | 0 | 4 | 0 |
| 95-96 | Liverpool | 30 | 29 | 1 | 2 | 0 |
| 96-97 | Liverpool | 30 | 25 | 5 | 3 | 0 |
| Total | | 97 | 91 | 6 | 9 | 0 |

| | GP | GG | GF | GS | TGR |
|--------|-----|-----|-----|-----|-----|
| 94-95 | 88.10 | 1.61 | 72 | 23 | 31.94 |
| 95-96 | 78.95 | 2.14 | 70 | 14 | 20.00 |
| 96-97 | 78.95 | 2.50 | 62 | 12 | 19.35 |
| Averages | 82.00 | 2.08 | 68.00 | 16.33 | 23.77 |

*Stan Collymore*

## COUZENS, Andy

### Leeds United    ❶    M

Fullname: Andrew Couzens
DOB: 04-06-75 Shipley

Shipley-born defender who has progressed from being a trainee at Leeds United to the England Under-21 side. Had two years as a professional at Elland Road prior to making his Premiership debut at home to Coventry City in March 1995. That match ended in a 3-0 win and he started in the next game which resulted in a defeat by Nottingham Forest by the same score. Has since been in contention for a regular place in the side, playing in approximately a quarter of the Yorkshire club's matches. Last season saw him score his first goal for the club and he was substituted in each of the seven games he started.

## Form Factors

| Season | Team | Tot | St | Sb | Y | R |
|---|---|---|---|---|---|---|
| 94-95 | Leeds Utd | 4 | 2 | 2 | 1 | 0 |
| 95-96 | Leeds Utd | 14 | 8 | 6 | 1 | 0 |
| 96-97 | Leeds Utd | 10 | 7 | 3 | 2 | 0 |
| Total | | 28 | 17 | 11 | 4 | 0 |

| | GP | GG | GF | GS | TGR |
|---|---|---|---|---|---|
| 94-95 | 9.52 | 0.00 | 59 | 0 | 0.00 |
| 95-96 | 36.84 | 0.00 | 40 | 0 | 0.00 |
| 96-97 | 26.32 | 10.00 | 28 | 1 | 3.57 |
| Averages | 24.23 | 3.33 | 42.33 | 0.33 | 1.19 |

## CROFT, Gary

# Blackburn Rovers ❶ FB

Fullname: Gary Croft
DOB: 17-02-74 Burton on Trent

Signed from Grimsby Town, for whom he played over 150 games, in March 1996 for £1.7 million. A left-sided player who can play a wing-back or defensive role, he made his debut against Coventry City last season, making five appearances in all, but featuring regularly on the Rovers' bench.

Despite being just 23, he has plenty of experience and has represented England at Under-21 level.

## Form Factors

| Season | Team | Tot | St | Sb | Y | R |
|---|---|---|---|---|---|---|
| 96-97 | Blackburn | 5 | 4 | 1 | 0 | 0 |
| Total | | 5 | 4 | 1 | 0 | 0 |

| | GP | GG | GF | GS | TGR |
|---|---|---|---|---|---|
| 96-97 | 13.16 | 0.00 | 42 | 0 | 0.00 |
| Averages | 13.16 | 0.00 | 42.00 | 0.00 | 0.00 |

## CRUYFF, Jordi

# Manchester U. ❶❷❸ S

Fullname: Johan Jordi Cruyff
DOB: 09-02-74 Amsterdam

Son of legendary Dutch star Johan Cruyff, Jordi Cruyff made his own name while at Barcelona where his father was manager. His arrival at Old Trafford during the summer of 1996 for £1 million was one of several high profile signings for Manchester United following Euro '96. The season wasn't the best for the 23-year-old who struggled to find his form and wasn't helped by a reoccurring knee injury that continued to niggle him.

Cruyff can operate in any sector of the attack and has looked lively and skilful in several of his sixteen games in 1996-97 which also provided three goals.

The 1997-98 season will go a long way to deciding the young Cruyff's future at Old Trafford.

## Form Factors

| Season | Team | Tot | St | Sb | Y | R |
|---|---|---|---|---|---|---|
| 96-97 | Man. Utd | 16 | 11 | 5 | 2 | 0 |
| Total | | 16 | 11 | 5 | 2 | 0 |

| | GP | GG | GF | GS | TGR |
|---|---|---|---|---|---|
| 96-97 | 42.11 | 5.33 | 76 | 3 | 3.95 |
| Averages | 42.11 | 5.33 | 76.00 | 3.00 | 3.95 |

## CUNNINGHAM, Kenny

# Wimbledon ❶❷❸❹ FB

Fullname: Kenneth Edward
Cunningham
DOB: 28-06-71 Dublin

A near ever-present at right-back, Cunningham missed just two games last season and has been an increasing influence in the Wimbledon side, since he was signed from Millwall before Christmas in 1994. Immediately established himself in the team and is a near fixture in the crazy-gang's starting line-up.

He started the 1997-98 season needing just three more appearances to reach his Premiership century but he still awaits his first goal in a senior game for Wimbledon.

He played close on 150 games for Millwall and cost Joe Kinnear the Wimbledon manager over £1.3 million.

The lack of goals – just one at Millwall – comes as a surprise, given Cunningham's love to go forward on traditional over-lapping runs.

Solid in defence, he is a Republic of Ireland international.

## Form Factors

| Season | Team | Tot | St | Sb | Y | R |
|---|---|---|---|---|---|---|
| 94-95 | Wimbledon | 28 | 28 | 0 | 1 | 0 |
| 95-96 | Wimbledon | 33 | 32 | 1 | 5 | 0 |
| 96-97 | Wimbledon | 36 | 36 | 0 | 5 | 0 |
| Total | | 97 | 96 | 1 | 11 | 0 |

| | GP | GG | GF | GS | TGR |
|---|---|---|---|---|---|
| 94-95 | 66.67 | 0.00 | 48 | 0 | 0.00 |
| 95-96 | 86.84 | 0.00 | 55 | 0 | 0.00 |
| 96-97 | 94.74 | 0.00 | 49 | 0 | 0.00 |
| Averages | 82.75 | 0.00 | 50.66 | 0.00 | 0.00 |

## CURCIC, Sasa

# Aston Villa ❶❷❸ M

Fullname: Sasa Curcic
DOB: 14-02-72 Belgrade

A Yugoslavian international, Curcic made his Premiership debut with Bolton Wanderers in the 1995-96 season. Following their relegation he remained in top-flight English football, signing for Villa in August 1996.

A highly skilful player, he was like a light in a dim Bolton side. He has the ability to create space and movement and dominate players about him. However, he has failed drastically to establish himself as a goalscorer and at the end of his first full season in a Villa shirt, had failed to notch a Premiership goal, despite 22 appearances.

Unable to maintain a regular first team space, there was some public disgruntlement last season but this seems to have been settled. May need a good season in 1997-98 to ensure he remains a Villa player.

## Form Factors

| Season | Team | Tot | St | Sb | Y | R |
|---|---|---|---|---|---|---|
| 95-96 | Bolton W. | 28 | 28 | 0 | 3 | 0 |
| 96-97 | Aston Villa | 22 | 17 | 5 | 4 | 0 |
| Total | | 50 | 45 | 5 | 7 | 0 |

| | GP | GG | GF | GS | TGR |
|---|---|---|---|---|---|
| 95-96 | 73.68 | 7.00 | 39 | 4 | 10.26 |
| 96-97 | 57.89 | 0.00 | 47 | 0 | 0.00 |
| Averages | 65.79 | 3.50 | 43.00 | 2.00 | 5.13 |

## DAILLY, Christian

# Derby County ❶❷❸❹ M

Fullname: Christian Dailly
DOB: 23-10-73 Dundee
Featured in all but two of Derby's games last season (31 as a starter). He is a tenacious midfielder who spent six years with his home town club of Dundee prior to a £1 million move to the Baseball Ground prior to the 1996-97 season.

Enjoyed a very successful first year with the Rams, making his debut against Leeds on the opening day of the season and following it with his first goal four days later at Tottenham. He went on to score two more league goals. Made 36 appearances in the Premiership overall and by the end of the season had added a senior Scotland cap to his collection of 'B' appearances.

A vital cog in the Derby play.

## Form Factors

| Season | Team | Tot | St | Sb | Y | R |
|--------|------|-----|-----|-----|-----|-----|
| 96-97 | Derby Co. | 36 | 31 | 5 | 6 | 0 |
| Total | | 36 | 31 | 5 | 6 | 0 |

| | GP | GG | GF | GS | TGR |
|--------|-----|-----|-----|-----|-----|
| 96-97 | 94.74 | 12.00 | 45 | 3 | 6.67 |
| Averages | 94.74 | 12.00 | 45.00 | 3.00 | 6.67 |

## DAISH, Liam

# Coventry City ❶❷ CB

Fullname: Liam Sean Daish
DOB: 23-09-68 Portsmouth
Very powerful and commanding central defender who worked his way through the ranks at Portsmouth, his home town club, before spending over six years at Cambridge United. Moved to Birmingham City for £50,000 before Coventry took him to Highfield Road for £1.1 million in February 1996.

His knee problems during the 1996-97 season restricted him to 20 Premiership appearances and he missed out on the final dramatic run-in. Given his build he has scored surprisingly few goals from set pieces. He has played five times for the Republic of Ireland.

When fit, Daish should be a near ever-present in the Coventry starting line-up.

## Form Factors

| Season | Team | Tot | St | Sb | Y | R |
|--------|------|-----|-----|-----|-----|-----|
| 95-96 | Coventry C. | 11 | 11 | 0 | 2 | 0 |
| 96-97 | Coventry C. | 20 | 20 | 0 | 4 | 1 |
| Total | | 31 | 31 | 0 | 6 | 1 |

| | GP | GG | GF | GS | TGR |
|--------|-----|-----|-----|-----|-----|
| 95-96 | 28.95 | 11.00 | 42 | 1 | 2.38 |
| 96-97 | 52.63 | 20.00 | 38 | 1 | 2.63 |
| Averages | 40.79 | 15.50 | 40.00 | 1.00 | 2.51 |

## DE GOEY, Ed

### Chelsea ❶❷❸❹❺ GK

Fullname: Ed de Goey
DOB: 20-12-66

The fact that Chelsea were willing to pay Dutch club Feyenoord £2.5 million to secure his services in June 1997 would seem to indicate that Ruud Gullit sees him as the starting Number One at Stamford Bridge.

De Goey started his career at Sparta Rotterdam before moving across town to neighbours Feyenoord. Since joining them in 1990 he missed just eight games in seven years (a phenomenal record) and these through injury.

The form of rival Edwin van der Sar has meant that De Goey has been the second-string 'keeper for Holland in recent years but, at 31 years old, he has a number of good seasons ahead of him and could prove to be an excellent purchase.

## DE ZEEUW, Arjan

### Barnsley ❶❷ CB

Fullname: Adrianus Johannes De Zeeuw
DOB: 16-04-70 Holland

Signed from Dutch second division side SC Telstar in November 1995, the big Dutch centre half has been impressive throughout his stay at Oakwell. Having won the club's Player of the Year award in his first season, he played in 43 of their Nationwide League games last season, contributing two goals to the cause in the process.

His aerial authority makes him a dominating figure at the back and he has matched that with good timing in tackles and his ability to use the ball when it is at his feet.

## DEANE, Brian

### Leeds United ❶❷❸ S

Fullname: Brian Christopher Deane
DOB: 07-02-68 Leeds

Powerful striker who was Leeds United's top scorer in 1996-97 for the second consecutive season but his cumulative total of 21 Premiership goals from the past three seasons underlines how barren times have been at Elland Road in recent years. In fact his tally of five goals in the Premiership last season was, along with Lee Sharpe's, the most by any one player!

Born in Leeds, he started his career with Yorkshire club Doncaster Rovers where he spent three years before making a £30,000 move to Sheffield United. Built his reputation at Bramall Lane, scoring 104 goals in 227 games, which prompted Leeds to fork out £2.9 million four years ago. Has played in around 85% of Leeds games since moving to Elland Road and is averaging a goal at just under once every five games. Possessor of three England caps, he has historically been used to play a traditional centre forward role, but in recent sides has been playing wide on the right.

### Form Factors

| Season | Team | Tot | St | Sb | Y | R |
|--------|------|-----|-----|-----|-----|-----|
| 94-95 | Leeds Utd | 35 | 33 | 2 | 9 | 0 |
| 95-96 | Leeds Utd | 34 | 30 | 4 | 5 | 0 |
| 96-97 | Leeds Utd | 28 | 27 | 1 | 2 | 0 |
| Total | | 97 | 90 | 7 | 16 | 0 |

| | GP | GG | GF | GS | TGR |
|--------|-----|-----|-----|-----|-----|
| 94-95 | 83.33 | 3.89 | 59 | 9 | 15.25 |
| 95-96 | 89.47 | 4.86 | 40 | 7 | 17.50 |
| 96-97 | 73.68 | 5.60 | 28 | 5 | 17.86 |
| Averages | 82.16 | 4.78 | 42.33 | 7.00 | 16.87 |

Roberto Di Matteo

## DI MATTEO, Roberto

### Chelsea ❶❷❸❹❺ M

Fullname: Roberto Di Matteo
DOB: 29-05-70 Sciaffusa,
Switzerland

A Swiss-born Italian international, Di Matteo was another of the big-name buys orchestrated by Gullit when he took over the managerial reins and was a near ever-present during his first season. More than anything he will go down in Chelsea and Wembley folklore as scoring the quickest ever goal – 42 seconds – in a Wembley FA Cup Final.

A superb play-maker, Di Matteo learnt his football in Switzerland before coming to international recognition at Lazio in Rome. It took nearly £5 million for Chelsea to secure his transfer.

Ruling from the centre of midfield, Di Matteo possesses a highly competitive edge to his play and couples this with an outstanding passing ability.

### Form Factors

| Season Team | | Tot | St | Sb | | Y | R |
|---|---|---|---|---|---|---|---|
| 96-97 Chelsea | | 34 | 33 | 1 | | 5 | 0 |
| Total | | 34 | 33 | 1 | | 5 | 0 |
| | GP | GG | GF | | GS | TGR |
| 96-97 | 89.47 | 5.67 | 58 | | 6 | 10.34 |
| Averages | 89.47 | 5.67 | 58.00 | | 6.00 | 10.34 |

# DICKS, Julian

## West Ham Utd ❶❷❸❹❺   CB

Fullname:   Julian Andrew Dicks
DOB:          08-08-68 Bristol

Dicks has established himself in Upton Park folklore. While he will not rank alongside their World Cup winning stars, he has never given anything less that 100% for the team.

His disciplinary problems in recent years have been the one thing that has held him back from earning a full international cap – something his performances have probably deserved. Cards galore have affected his availability and this is reflected in the fact that he has never been an ever-present in the team.

He spent a one year period at Liverpool but never settled in and it was no surprise to anyone when he returned to his home.

One thing Dicks does well for a defender is to score goals, and not only from the penalty spot.

The 1997-98 season should see him come very close to his 500th senior game.

Should be a first choice for consideration but will miss games through suspension and is likely to miss the start of the season through injury.

## Form Factors

| Season | Team | Tot | St | Sb | Y | R |
|--------|------|-----|-----|-----|-----|-----|
| 94-95 | West Ham | 29 | 29 | 0 | 9 | 0 |
| 95-96 | West Ham | 34 | 34 | 0 | 5 | 1 |
| 96-97 | West Ham | 31 | 31 | 0 | 6 | 0 |
| Total | | 94 | 94 | 0 | 20 | 1 |

| | GP | GG | GF | GS | TGR |
|--------|-----|-----|-----|-----|-----|
| 94-95 | 69.05 | 5.80 | 44 | 5 | 11.36 |
| 95-96 | 89.47 | 3.40 | 43 | 10 | 23.26 |
| 96-97 | 81.58 | 5.17 | 39 | 6 | 15.38 |
| Averages | 80.03 | 4.79 | 42.00 | 7.00 | 16.67 |

*Julian Dicks*

## DIXON, Lee

# Arsenal ❶❷❸ FB

**Fullname:** Lee Michael Dixon
**DOB:** 17-03-64 Manchester

Dixon has had the Arsenal right-back spot to himself for almost eight years. Solid to say the least, he loves the big occasion and big challenge and will invariably come out on top – ask David Ginola!

Holder of 21 England caps, he was one of George Graham's first Arsenal signings from Stoke City where he played alongside Steve Bould, having started his career at Burnley.

Last season he chalked up his 500th career league game and he has played in over 90% of the Gunners' Premiership encounters during the past three years, contributing five goals to their cause.

At 32 years of age, he doesn't seem to have lost any of his pace and he seems ideally suited to the role of wing-back which he has been assuming over the past two years.

Barring any major signings he should be an integral part of the Arsenal side for 1997-98 and could be worth considering provided the price is right.

## Form Factors

| Season | Team | Tot | St | Sb | Y | R |
|---|---|---|---|---|---|---|
| 94-95 | Arsenal | 39 | 39 | 0 | 0 | 0 |
| 95-96 | Arsenal | 38 | 38 | 0 | 2 | 0 |
| 96-97 | Arsenal | 32 | 31 | 1 | 8 | 0 |
| Total | | 109 | 108 | 1 | 10 | 0 |

| | GP | GG | GF | GS | TGR |
|---|---|---|---|---|---|
| 94-95 | 92.86 | 39.00 | 52 | 1 | 1.92 |
| 95-96 | 100.00 | 19.00 | 49 | 2 | 4.08 |
| 96-97 | 84.21 | 16.00 | 62 | 2 | 3.23 |
| Averages | 92.36 | 24.67 | 54.33 | 1.67 | 3.08 |

## DODD, Jason

# Southampton ❶❷❸ FB

**Fullname:** Jason Robert Dodd
**DOB:** 02-11-70 Bath

Ranks amongst one of the most consistent performers in the Premiership but often fails to get the recognition he deserves. A £50,000 purchase from Bath City in March 1989, Dodd has developed into an outstanding reader of the game. Although essentially a right-back, he has also featured in the centre of the Saints' defence when required to do so.

A near ever-present in the 1995-96 campaign, Dodd's 23 outings last season were a reflection on a number of injuries rather than his own form.

An England Under-21 international, he started the 1997-98 season needing just six games to make his 200th league appearance.

## Form Factors

| Season | Team | Tot | St | Sb | Y | R |
|---|---|---|---|---|---|---|
| 94-95 | Southampton | 26 | 24 | 2 | 4 | 0 |
| 95-96 | Southampton | 36 | 36 | 0 | 4 | 0 |
| 96-97 | Southampton | 23 | 23 | 0 | 2 | 1 |
| Total | | 85 | 83 | 2 | 10 | 1 |

| | GP | GG | GF | GS | TGR |
|---|---|---|---|---|---|
| 94-95 | 61.90 | 13.00 | 61 | 2 | 3.28 |
| 95-96 | 94.74 | 18.00 | 34 | 2 | 5.88 |
| 96-97 | 60.53 | 23.00 | 50 | 1 | 2.00 |
| Averages | 72.39 | 18.00 | 48.33 | 1.67 | 3.72 |

## DONALDSON, O'Neill

# Sheffield W. ❶ S

Fullname:  O'Neill McKay Donaldson
DOB:       24-11-69 Birmingham
   Another in the Sheffield Wednesday
squad to have progressed into the
Premiership after starting his career in
non-league football, in his case with
Hinckley. Turned professional with
Shrewsbury Town where he scored four
times in 28 league games. Moved to
Doncaster Rovers where he was
permitted nine first team appearances,
during which he scored twice. Had a very
successful loan spell with Mansfield
Town where he scored six goals in just
four games, but has found his
opportunities limited since moving to
Hillsborough.

### Form Factors

| Season | Team | Tot | St | Sb | Y | R |
|--------|------|-----|-----|-----|-----|-----|
| 94-95 | Sheffield W. | 1 | 0 | 1 | 0 | 0 |
| 95-96 | Sheffield W. | 3 | 1 | 2 | 0 | 0 |
| 96-97 | Sheffield W. | 6 | 3 | 3 | 0 | 0 |
| Total |  | 10 | 4 | 6 | 0 | 0 |

|  | GP | GG | GF | GS | TGR |
|--------|-----|-----|-----|-----|-----|
| 94-95 | 2.38 | 0.00 | 49 | 0 | 0.00 |
| 95-96 | 7.89 | 3.00 | 48 | 1 | 2.08 |
| 96-97 | 15.79 | 3.00 | 50 | 2 | 4.00 |
| Averages | 8.69 | 2.00 | 49.00 | 1.00 | 2.03 |

## DONIS, George

# Blackburn Rovers ❶❷❸ M

Fullname:  Georgio Donis
DOB:       29-10-69 Frankfurt
   A full Greek international who was
born in Germany, Donis joined Blackburn
Rovers at the start of the 1996-97 season
on a free transfer from Panathanikos. He
has wicked pace, a fact that has led to him
being dubbed 'The Athens Express' by
the supporters at Ewood Park.
   Donis featured in 22 of Rovers' games
during the 1996-97 season, with 11
starting appearances and 11 as a playing
substitute in what could be described as a
settling-in period. He was unavailable due
to injury in a number of games. His
ability to deliver perfect crosses could
form an effective relationship with an in-
form Chris Sutton.

### Form Factors

| Season | Team | Tot | St | Sb | Y | R |
|--------|------|-----|-----|-----|-----|-----|
| 96-97 | Blackburn | 22 | 11 | 11 | 0 | 0 |
| Total |  | 22 | 11 | 11 | 0 | 0 |

|  | GP | GG | GF | GS | TGR |
|--------|-----|-----|-----|-----|-----|
| 96-97 | 57.89 | 11.00 | 42 | 2 | 4.76 |
| Averages | 57.89 | 11.00 | 42.00 | 2.00 | 4.76 |

## DORIGO, Tony

# Leeds United ❶❷❸ FB

Fullname:  Anthony Robert Dorigo
DOB:       31-12-65 Melbourne,
           Australia
   Australian-born defender who has spent
all but one season of his 14-year playing
career in the Premiership and old
Division One. Former Aston Villa
apprentice who played 133 times for the
club before making a £475,000 move
south to join Chelsea in July 1987. One
hundred and sixty-four games later he

signed for Leeds United in a £1.3 million transfer and was a member of their 1992 championship winning side. Athletic and good ball-playing full-back who, despite originating from Melbourne, has played 15 times for England. He has featured in less than half of Leeds games over the past two seasons, not least due to injuries.

## Form Factors

| Season | Team | Tot | St | Sb | Y | R |
|--------|------|-----|----|----|---|---|
| 94-95 | Leeds Utd | 28 | 28 | 0 | 1 | 0 |
| 95-96 | Leeds Utd | 17 | 17 | 0 | 2 | 0 |
| 96-97 | Leeds Utd | 18 | 15 | 3 | 5 | 0 |
| Total | | 63 | 60 | 3 | 8 | 0 |

| | GP | GG | GF | GS | TGR |
|--|----|----|----|----|----|
| 94-95 | 66.67 | 0.00 | 59 | 0 | 0.00 |
| 95-96 | 44.74 | 17.00 | 40 | 1 | 2.50 |
| 96-97 | 47.37 | 0.00 | 28 | 0 | 0.00 |
| Averages | 52.92 | 5.67 | 42.33 | 0.33 | 0.83 |

## DOWIE, Iain

# West Ham U.     ❶     S

Fullname:  Iain Dowie
DOB:       09-01-65 Hatfield
    The arrival of Hartson and Kitson at Upton Park may make it difficult for Iain Dowie to secure a regular first team spot during the 1997-98 season. Now in his second spell with the Hammers, Dowie failed to find the net in all of his 23 Premiership appearances last season, which was a big disappointment after having scored eight in 1995-96.
    Strikers don't come more committed to the cause than Iain Dowie, who gives everything to his game. Often criticised for a lack of technique, he may be remembered more for the own goal he scored that saw West Ham crash out of the Coca-Cola Cup at the hands of Stockport County.
    An international who has won over 40 caps for Northern Ireland he also played

Premiership football for Southampton and Crystal Palace.

## Form Factors

| Season | Team | Tot | St | Sb | Y | R |
|--------|------|-----|----|----|---|---|
| 94-95 | C. Palace | 15 | 15 | 0 | 3 | 0 |
| 95-96 | West Ham | 33 | 33 | 0 | 6 | 0 |
| 96-97 | West Ham | 23 | 18 | 5 | 1 | 0 |
| Total | | 71 | 66 | 5 | 10 | 0 |

| | GP | GG | GF | GS | TGR |
|--|----|----|----|----|----|
| 94-95 | 35.71 | 3.75 | 34 | 4 | 11.76 |
| 95-96 | 86.84 | 4.13 | 43 | 8 | 18.60 |
| 96-97 | 60.53 | 0.00 | 39 | 0 | 0.00 |
| Averages | 61.03 | 2.63 | 38.67 | 4.00 | 10.12 |

## DOZZELL, Jason

# Tottenham H.     ❶❷     M

Fullname:  Jason Alvin Winans Dozzell
DOB:       09-12-67 Ipswich
    A midfield player who had an outstanding ten years with Ipswich Town prior to a £1.9m transfer to Tottenham Hotspur in August 1993. After a decent first season in the Spurs' midfield he struggled to impose himself in the side and it was during the 1996-97 season that he again came into favour with manager Gerry Francis.
    With the right application he could feature strongly in the Spurs' line-up and certainly possesses the ability to improve a fairly paltry strike-rate since moving to White Hart Lane.
    Made a sensational start to his career when becoming the youngest ever goalscorer in Division One whilst still a schoolboy. The 1997-98 season could well be make or break for Dozzell.

## Form Factors

| Season | Team | Tot | St | Sb | Y | R |
|--------|------|-----|----|----|---|---|
| 94-95 | Tottenham | 7 | 6 | 1 | 1 | 0 |
| 95-96 | Tottenham | 28 | 24 | 4 | 7 | 0 |
| 96-97 | Tottenham | 17 | 10 | 7 | 2 | 0 |
| Total | | 52 | 40 | 12 | 10 | 0 |

|  | GP | GG | GF | GS | TGR |
|---|---|---|---|---|---|
| 94-95 | 16.67 | 0.00 | 66 | 0 | 0.00 |
| 95-96 | 73.68 | 9.33 | 50 | 3 | 6.00 |
| 96-97 | 44.74 | 8.50 | 44 | 2 | 4.55 |
| Averages | 45.03 | 5.94 | 53.33 | 1.67 | 3.52 |

## DRAPER, Mark

### Aston Villa    ❶❷❸❹    M

Fullname:  Mark Draper
DOB:       11-11-70 Long Eaton

Injury denied Draper the chance to establish himself as one of the country's top midfield players. His performances for Leicester City earned him a transfer to Villa Park when the Filberts were relegated at the end of 1994-95.

An England Under-21 international, he looked set to win his first full cap last season when he was on the bench for England's World Cup encounter in Moldova. But a series of minor injuries caused a loss of form and his place in the England squad. A great reader of the game, he combines this with his non-stop running to win balls and turn defence into attack. He featured in 29 of Villa's games last season but was unable to reproduce any of the long-range shooting that has often got him onto the score sheet in recent years.

When fit and on form, one of the best players in the Premiership.

### Form Factors

| Season | Team | Tot | St | Sb | Y | R |
|---|---|---|---|---|---|---|
| 94-95 | Leicester C. | 39 | 39 | 0 | 5 | 0 |
| 95-96 | Aston Villa | 36 | 36 | 0 | 1 | 0 |
| 96-97 | Aston Villa | 29 | 28 | 1 | 4 | 1 |
| Total |  | 104 | 103 | 1 | 10 | 1 |

|  | GP | GG | GF | GS | TGR |
|---|---|---|---|---|---|
| 94-95 | 92.86 | 7.80 | 45 | 5 | 11.11 |
| 95-96 | 94.74 | 18.00 | 52 | 2 | 3.85 |
| 96-97 | 76.32 | 0.00 | 47 | 0 | 0.00 |
| Averages | 87.97 | 8.60 | 48.00 | 2.33 | 4.99 |

Mark Draper (left) battles for the ball

## Southampton ❶❷❸ CB

Fullname: Richard Andrew Dryden
DOB: 14-06-69 Stroud

During the 1995-96 season Dryden was struggling to get into the Bristol City first team and played in less than half of their league games. On the opening day of last season he was marking Gianluca Vialli as a Premiership player with Southampton. Such are the fortunes of a football player. Dryden played in 29 of Saints' games in 1996-97 and at £150,000 was probably Souness' most astute buy during his year in charge at the Dell. But for injury he would have been an ever-present in their starting line-up.

Not the tallest of central defenders, Dryden is an effective man-marker who times his tackles well.

Having started his career at the other Bristol club, he did the rounds of the clubs in the lower divisions and made his 250th league appearance towards the end of the 1996-97 season.

### Form Factors

| Season | Team | Tot | St | Sb | Y | R |
|---|---|---|---|---|---|---|
| 96-97 | Southampton | 29 | 28 | 1 | 5 | 0 |
| Total | | 29 | 28 | 1 | 5 | 0 |

| | GP | GG | GF | GS | TGR |
|---|---|---|---|---|---|
| 96-97 | 76.32 | 29.00 | 50 | 1 | 2.00 |
| Averages | 76.32 | 29.00 | 50.00 | 1.00 | 2.00 |

## Chelsea ❶❷❸❹ CB

Fullname: Michael Wayne Duberry
DOB: 14-10-75 London

After making his Premiership debut at the end of the 1993-94 season, Duberry got the chance of an extended run in the Chelsea side a season later when the side was hit with a spate of injuries. He played 22 times in all and was widely recognised as a star of the future.

Injuries and the influx of high-profile players limited Duberry's chances in '96-97 to just 15 appearances in the Premiership but he is well suited to the three-man central defensive system that Gullit has installed at Stamford Bridge, having a big physical presence and an outstanding heading ability.

Will only get better training and playing alongside Chelsea's imports and was looking to be fit in time for the start of the 1997-98 season.

### Form Factors

| Season | Team | Tot | St | Sb | Y | R |
|---|---|---|---|---|---|---|
| 93-94 | Chelsea | 1 | 1 | 0 | 0 | 0 |
| 95-96 | Chelsea | 22 | 22 | 0 | 3 | 0 |
| 96-97 | Chelsea | 15 | 13 | 2 | 4 | 0 |
| Total | | 38 | 36 | 2 | 7 | 0 |

| | GP | GG | GF | GS | TGR |
|---|---|---|---|---|---|
| 93-94 | 2.38 | 0.00 | 49 | 0 | 0.00 |
| 95-96 | 57.89 | 0.00 | 46 | 0 | 0.00 |
| 96-97 | 39.47 | 15.00 | 58 | 1 | 1.72 |
| Averages | 33.25 | 5.00 | 51.00 | 0.33 | 0.57 |

## DUBLIN, Dion

### Coventry City ❶❷❸❹ S

Fullname: Dion Dublin
DOB: 22-04-69 Leicester

Without any doubt, Dion Dublin is, with Gordon Strachan, the most influential figure at Highfield Road. Big and powerful as a centre forward, he has been one of City's key signings since joining them from Manchester United for £1.95 million in September 1994.

Dublin was troubled by injury during his brief time at Old Trafford but has become a pivotal figure in Coventry's goal fortunes, having got into double figures to make him top scorer in each of his last three seasons in the Midlands. During the 1996-97 season he also more than proved his worth as a central defender but had to sit on the sidelines for seven games through suspension after being dismissed in two consecutive matches. Will again be a vital part of Coventry's fortunes in 1997-98, especially at home where his presence seems to lift the crowd.

### Form Factors

| Season | Team | Tot | St | Sb | Y | R |
|---|---|---|---|---|---|---|
| 94-95 | Coventry C. | 31 | 31 | 0 | 3 | 0 |
| 95-96 | Coventry C. | 34 | 34 | 0 | 3 | 0 |
| 96-97 | Coventry C. | 34 | 33 | 1 | 5 | 0 |
| Total | | 99 | 98 | 1 | 11 | 0 |

| | GP | GG | GF | GS | TGR |
|---|---|---|---|---|---|
| 94-95 | 73.81 | 2.38 | 44 | 13 | 29.55 |
| 95-96 | 89.47 | 2.43 | 42 | 14 | 33.33 |
| 96-97 | 89.47 | 2.43 | 38 | 14 | 36.84 |
| Averages | 84.25 | 2.41 | 41.33 | 13.67 | 33.24 |

*Dion Dublin*

## DUCROS, Andrew

### Coventry City ❶ S

Fullname: Andrew Ducros
DOB: 16-09-77 Evesham

Evesham-born striker who has represented England Youth and broke into the Coventry City first team during the 1996-97 season, making the first of five appearances when he came on as a substitute against Nottingham Forest.

One-time Coventry trainee who progressed through the ranks at Highfield Road. Likely to take just a squad role during the 1997-98 season.

## Form Factors

| Season | Team | Tot | St | Sb | Y | R |
|---|---|---|---|---|---|---|
| 96-97 | Coventry C. | 5 | 1 | 4 | 0 | 0 |
| Total | | 5 | 1 | 4 | 0 | 0 |

| | GP | GG | GF | GS | TGR |
|---|---|---|---|---|---|
| 96-97 | 13.16 | 0.00 | 38 | 0 | 0.00 |
| Averages | 13.16 | 0.00 | 38.00 | 0.00 | 0.00 |

## DUNNE, Richard

### Everton ❶❷ CB

Fullname: Richard Dunne
DOB: 21-09-79 Dublin

Another of the next generation of Everton youngsters already pushing for a place in the Premiership. Made Everton history when he played against Swindon Town at Goodison Park in the FA Cup in January '97 when he became the youngest ever home debutant for the Blues. Made his Premiership debut a week later during a 2-1 defeat at Sheffield Wednesday and went on to make a further six appearances before the end of the season.

His early form earned him a call-up to the Republic of Ireland squad and he featured in a 'B' international for them. Dublin-born big central defender who will be pushing for a regular first team place in 1997-98.

## Form Factors

| Season | Team | Tot | St | Sb | Y | R |
|---|---|---|---|---|---|---|
| 96-97 | Everton | 7 | 6 | 1 | 2 | 0 |
| Total | | 7 | 6 | 1 | 2 | 0 |

| | GP | GG | GF | GS | TGR |
|---|---|---|---|---|---|
| 96-97 | 18.42 | 0.00 | 44 | 0 | 0.00 |
| Averages | 18.42 | 0.00 | 44.00 | 0.00 | 0.00 |

## DYER, Bruce

### Crystal Palace ❶❷❸ S

Fullname: Bruce Antonio Dyer
DOB: 13-04-75 Ilford

Dyer joined Palace for £1 million in March 1994 after he had completed just 36 games for the Watford first team. He was in and out of the starting line-up in the early stages of his career but was always amongst the goals. The departure of Gareth Taylor during the early part of the 1995-96 season allowed him to

*Bruce Dyer*

*Nicky Eaden*

## Form Factors

| Season | Team | Tot | St | Sb | Y | R |
|--------|------|-----|-----|-----|-----|-----|
| 94-95 | C. Palace | 16 | 7 | 9 | 1 | 0 |
| Total | | 16 | 7 | 9 | 1 | 0 |

| | GP | GG | GF | GS | TGR |
|--------|-----|-----|-----|-----|-----|
| 94-95 | 38.10 | 16.00 | 34 | 1 | 2.94 |
| Averages | 38.10 | 16.00 | 34.00 | 1.00 | 2.94 |

## EADEN, Nicky

### Barnsley   ❶❷❸    FB

Fullname:   Nicholas Jeremy Eaden
DOB:       12-12-72 Sheffield

    Along with goalkeeper Dave Watson, Nick Eaden featured in all 46 of Barnsley's Nationwide League games last season. By far the club's most consistent performer, he has missed just two games in the past three seasons, having made the number two shirt his own in a right wing-back role. His distribution and crossing are the main features of his game and his three goals are a reflection of his willingness to get up in the area where he can use his powerful shooting ability to good effect.

    Joined Barnsley as a junior in the summer of 1991 and, by the end of the 1996-97 season, had made 176 league appearances for the club.

develop a formidable partnership with Dougie Freedman that produced 28 goals last term – 17 notched by Dyer himself.

    The Palace striker is as direct as they come and knows only one way to goal – the most direct route. The England Under-21 international is equally skilful and could prove his potential in the Premiership, having been part of Palace's relegated side in 1994-95 when he scored just one goal in 16 games.

# EARLE, Robbie

## Wimbledon ❶❷❸❹❺ M

*Robbie Earle*

Fullname: Robert Gerald Earle
DOB: 27-01-65
Newcastle-under-Lyme

Last season was without doubt Earle's best for the Dons with most independent observers championing his cause for an England call-up.

Fast and skilful, Earle operates in a midfield role that allows him to join up with the attack at every opportunity – which is reflected by the fact that he finished as the Dons' third top scorer in 1996-97, although his seven strikes was down on his 11 in the 1995-96 season. Many of his goals come from his powerful heading ability and his willingness to have a shot on goal when the chance arises.

Small but powerful, he joined Wimbledon from Port Vale in 1991 where he made over 250 appearances. Last season he played his 200th league game for Wimbledon and interestingly not one of those has come as a substitute!

### Form Factors

| Season | Team | Tot | St | Sb | Y | R |
|---|---|---|---|---|---|---|
| 94-95 | Wimbledon | 9 | 9 | 0 | 0 | 0 |
| 95-96 | Wimbledon | 37 | 37 | 0 | 2 | 1 |
| 96-97 | Wimbledon | 32 | 32 | 0 | 3 | 0 |
| Total | | 78 | 78 | 0 | 5 | 1 |

| | GP | GG | GF | GS | TGR |
|---|---|---|---|---|---|
| 94-95 | 21.43 | 0.00 | 48 | 0 | 0.00 |
| 95-96 | 97.37 | 3.36 | 55 | 11 | 20.00 |
| 96-97 | 84.21 | 4.57 | 49 | 7 | 14.29 |
| Averages | 67.67 | 2.65 | 50.67 | 6.00 | 11.84 |

# EDINBURGH, Justin

## Tottenham H. ❶❷❸ FB

Fullname: Justin Charles Edinburgh
DOB: 18-12-69 Brentwood

A bargain buy for Tottenham back in July 1990 when they snapped him up from Southend United for just £150,000. He had spent four months on loan to Spurs prior to the club making the move permanent. Since then has figured in 65% of the club's Premiership matches and played in the 1991 FA Cup winning side.

*Justin Edinburgh*

## Form Factors

| Season | Team | Tot | St | Sb | | Y | R |
|---|---|---|---|---|---|---|---|
| 94-95 | Tottenham | 31 | 29 | 2 | | 6 | 0 |
| 95-96 | Tottenham | 22 | 15 | 7 | | 5 | 0 |
| 96-97 | Tottenham | 24 | 21 | 3 | | 11 | 0 |
| Total | | 77 | 65 | 12 | | 22 | 0 |

| | GP | GG | GF | GS | TGR |
|---|---|---|---|---|---|
| 94-95 | 73.81 | 0.00 | 66 | 0 | 0.00 |
| 95-96 | 57.89 | 0.00 | 50 | 0 | 0.00 |
| 96-97 | 63.16 | 0.00 | 44 | 0 | 0.00 |
| Averages | 64.95 | 0.00 | 53.33 | 0.00 | 0.00 |

## EDWORTHY, Marc

### Crystal Palace ❶❷❸ FB

Fullname: Marc Edworthy
DOB: 24-12-74 Barnstaple

A £350,000 signing from Plymouth Argyle in the summer of 1995, Edworthy was a main component in Palace's promotion drive last season. A solid right-back, he featured in all 46 of the Eagle's Nationwide Division One games last season, 43 of them in the starting line-up. His displays helped Palace back through the play-offs and made up for the fact that it was he who conceded the penalty kick that helped Leicester City win the Division One final play-off at Wembley at the end of the 1995-96 season.

Powerful with the ball at his feet, Edworthy loves to get forward on over-laps and has occasionally featured in the Palace midfield.

Bookings were a problem last season, his 11 yellows earning him suspension and being his previous two years' total!

Despite his desire to join in with the attack, don't look for Edinburgh to score even the occasional goal for your side; his one and only success came back in his first season at White Hart Lane! Should complete 150 Premiership appearances during 1997-98.

## EHIOGU, Ugo

### Aston Villa ❶❷❸❹❺ CB

Fullname: Ugochuku Ehiogu
DOB: 03-11-72 Hackney

A real linchpin of the mean Villa defence, Ehiogu played in all of Villa's Premiership matches last season and has missed just five games in the past three seasons. Extremely strong and with pace to match, few Premiership strikers manage to get the better of him.

He played just two games for West Bromwich Albion before he was snapped up for what now seems a real give-away at £40,000. He looked likely to win a string of international honours but today still has just the one cap following his appearance as a substitute against China prior to Euro '96. So far though he hasn't featured in Glenn Hoddle's plans.

Good consistent performances in one of the meanest defences in the Premiership make him a defender well worth considering.

### Form Factors

| Season | Team | Tot | St | Sb | Y | R |
|--------|------|-----|-----|-----|-----|-----|
| 94-95 | Aston Villa | 39 | 38 | 1 | 7 | 0 |
| 95-96 | Aston Villa | 36 | 36 | 0 | 7 | 0 |
| 96-97 | Aston Villa | 38 | 38 | 0 | 4 | 0 |
| Total | | 113 | 112 | 1 | 18 | 0 |

| | GP | GG | GF | GS | TGR |
|--------|--------|--------|--------|--------|--------|
| 94-95 | 92.86 | 0.00 | 51 | 0 | 0.00 |
| 95-96 | 94.74 | 36.00 | 52 | 1 | 1.92 |
| 96-97 | 100.00 | 12.67 | 47 | 3 | 6.38 |
| Averages | 95.86 | 16.22 | 50.00 | 1.33 | 2.77 |

## EKOKU, Efan

### Wimbledon ❶❷❸❹ S

Fullname: Efangwu Goziem Ekoku
DOB: 08-06-67 Manchester

A big, strong centre forward who has represented his native Nigeria at full international level. Ekoku started in the non-league game before coming to full recognition at Norwich City, whom he joined from Bournemouth. He made his Premiership debut for the Canaries and was a member of the team that had a memorable UEFA Cup run a few years back.

He joined Wimbledon for £900,000 in October 1994 and has now completed well over 100 Premiership games. He was the Dons' top Premiership scorer last season with 11 goals but was also their most substituted – coming off no less than 17 times in his 30 games!

### Form Factors

| Season | Team | Tot | St | Sb | Y | R |
|--------|------|-----|-----|-----|-----|-----|
| 94-95 | Wimbledon | 24 | 24 | 0 | 6 | 0 |
| 95-96 | Wimbledon | 31 | 28 | 3 | 5 | 0 |
| 96-97 | Wimbledon | 30 | 28 | 2 | 4 | 0 |
| Total | | 85 | 80 | 5 | 15 | 0 |

| | GP | GG | GF | GS | TGR |
|--------|--------|--------|--------|--------|--------|
| 94-95 | 57.14 | 2.67 | 48 | 9 | 18.75 |
| 95-96 | 81.58 | 4.43 | 55 | 7 | 12.73 |
| 96-97 | 78.95 | 2.73 | 49 | 11 | 22.45 |
| Averages | 72.56 | 3.27 | 50.67 | 9.00 | 17.98 |

## ELLIOTT, Matt

### Leicester City ❶❷❸❹❺    CB

Fullname: Matthew Stephen Elliott
DOB:      01-11-68 Wandsworth

One of the great, even if surprising, success stories of the 1996-97 season. Leicester manager Martin O'Neill gambled £1.6 million on Elliott in January 1997 at a time when the Foxes' Premiership position was a touch precarious. At the time the 28-year-old central defender was plying his trade in Division One with Oxford United. Slotted in with astonishing ease and made a mockery of his four previous transfers which totalled just £215,000. Scored the goal which finally secured Leicester's future during the final week of the season. Only had 16 games with Leicester last season but his quality was clear and he should play a major part in their fortunes this season.

A whole-hearted player who never knows when he is beaten, he will be a major influence with City this season. Could be a real bargain.

### Form Factors

| Season | Team | Tot | St | Sb | Y | R |
|--------|------|-----|-----|-----|-----|-----|
| 96-97 | Leicester C. | 16 | 16 | 0 | 3 | 0 |
| Total | | 16 | 16 | 0 | 3 | 0 |

| | GP | GG | GF | GS | TGR |
|--------|-----|-----|-----|-----|-----|
| 96-97 | 42.11 | 4.00 | 46 | 4 | 8.70 |
| Averages | 42.11 | 4.00 | 46.00 | 4.00 | 8.70 |

## ELLIOTT, Robbie

### Bolton W.      ❶❷❸    FB

Fullname: Robert James Elliott
DOB:      25-12-73 Newcastle

Despite playing in 29 of Newcastle's games last season and contributing seven goals, Kenny Dalglish decided to part with the services of Robbie Elliot during the close season which was Bolton's immediate gain.

Although employed as a full-back on Tyneside, Elliott can play in the centre of defence or in midfield with equal effectiveness. He possesses good distribution skill and is very strong in the tackle. When used at left-back he loves to join in the attack and has the ability to deliver pin-point crosses.

### Form Factors

| Season | Team | Tot | St | Sb | Y | R |
|--------|------|-----|-----|-----|-----|-----|
| 94-95 | Newcastle | 14 | 10 | 4 | 4 | 0 |
| 95-96 | Newcastle | 6 | 5 | 1 | 2 | 0 |
| 96-97 | Newcastle | 29 | 29 | 0 | 3 | 0 |
| Total | | 49 | 44 | 5 | 9 | 0 |

| | GP | GG | GF | GS | TGR |
|--------|-----|-----|-----|-----|-----|
| 94-95 | 33.33 | 7.00 | 67 | 2 | 2.99 |
| 95-96 | 15.79 | 0.00 | 66 | 0 | 0.00 |
| 96-97 | 76.32 | 4.14 | 73 | 7 | 9.59 |
| Averages | 41.81 | 5.57 | 68.67 | 3.00 | 6.29 |

## ERANIO, Stefano

### Derby County ❶❷❸❹    M

Fullname: Stefano Eranio
DOB:      29-12-66 Genova

A vastly experienced Italian international, Eranio was snapped up by Derby manager Jim Smith on a free transfer from Milan. He started his career at Tornio and earned what was regarded as a big move to Milan in the summer of 1990. However, he struggled to claim a regular first team spot and he has generally played a squad role in the past few years with his appearances being limited to a dozen or so each season.

Nevertheless he his highly competitive and possesses typical latin skills that could make him a big hit at Pride Park.

## EUELL, Jason

# Wimbledon ❶❷ S

Fullname:  Jason Euell
DOB:        06-02-77 South London

Another product of the Wimbledon youth system, Jason Euell spent much of the summer playing for the England Under-20 side in Malaysia.

He is unlikely to forget his Premier League debut against Southampton in October 1995 when he scored with a brilliant overhead freekick. Although a midfield player, he has an eye for goal as illustrated against Southampton and the fact that he scored twice in his seven appearances last season. Both of those goals came in the final two games of the season – the second being the goal that relegated Sunderland on the last day of the season.

## Form Factors

| Season | Team | Tot | St | Sb | Y | R |
|--------|------|-----|----|----|----|----|
| 95-96 | Wimbledon | 9 | 4 | 5 | 1 | 0 |
| 96-97 | Wimbledon | 7 | 4 | 3 | 0 | 0 |
| Total | | 16 | 8 | 8 | 1 | 0 |

| | GP | GG | GF | GS | TGR |
|--------|-----|-----|-----|-----|-----|
| 95-96 | 23.68 | 4.50 | 55 | 2 | 3.64 |
| 96-97 | 18.42 | 3.50 | 49 | 2 | 4.08 |
| Averages | 21.05 | 4.00 | 52.00 | 2.00 | 7.72 |

## EVANS, Micky

# Southampton ❶ S

Fullname:  Michael James Evans
DOB:        01-01-73 Plymouth

One of Graeme Souness' last signings for Southampton, Evans arrived from Plymouth Argyle for £500,000 before the transfer deadline in March 1997.

Although primarily a striker, he can play wide on the right and he featured in all of Saints' last 12 Premier League games last season, scoring four goals. Evans had a strike rate of about one goal every five games while at Plymouth.

Made an impressive debut against Everton when he came on as a substitute. His four games from that position got him into the starting line-up as the club sought to retain their Premiership status.

## Form Factors

| Season | Team | Tot | St | Sb | Y | R |
|--------|------|-----|----|----|----|----|
| 96-97 | Southampton | 12 | 8 | 4 | 1 | 0 |
| Total | | 12 | 8 | 4 | 1 | 0 |

| | GP | GG | GF | GS | TGR |
|--------|-----|-----|-----|-----|-----|
| 96-97 | 31.58 | 3.00 | 50 | 4 | 8.00 |
| Averages | 31.58 | 3.00 | 50.00 | 4.00 | 8.00 |

## FAIRCLOUGH, Chris

### Bolton W.  ❶❷❸  CB

Fullname:  Courtney Huw Fairclough
DOB:  12-04-64 Nottingham

The heart of the Bolton defence, Fairclough was the only player in the Wanderers' squad to feature in all of their 46 Nationwide Division One games. He is no newcomer to life at the top, having played there for Leeds, Nottingham Forest and Tottenham Hotspur. Indeed he won a championship medal while with Leeds United and made over 200 appearances for the Elland Road club.

He first came to the fore at Nottingham Forest and was widely predicted to win full international honours. England Under-21 and 'B' appearances were made but the ultimate cap was never quite achieved.

He has been a cornerstone of the Bolton side since joining them and he is likely to take on a man-marking role – in which he excels – during 1997-98. If Fairclough has a good season so will Bolton.

### Form Factors

| Season | Team | Tot | St | Sb | Y | R |
|---|---|---|---|---|---|---|
| 93-94 | Leeds Utd | 40 | 40 | 0 | 4 | 0 |
| 94-95 | Leeds Utd | 5 | 1 | 4 | 0 | 0 |
| 95-96 | Bolton W. | 33 | 33 | 0 | 6 | 0 |
| Total | | 78 | 74 | 4 | 10 | 0 |

| | GP | GG | GF | GS | TGR |
|---|---|---|---|---|---|
| 93-94 | 95.24 | 10.00 | 65 | 4 | 6.15 |
| 94-95 | 11.90 | 0.00 | 59 | 0 | 0.00 |
| 95-96 | 13.16 | 0.00 | 39 | 0 | 0.00 |
| Averages | 40.10 | 3.33 | 54.33 | 1.33 | 2.05 |

## FARRELLY, Gareth

### Everton  ❶❷  M

Fullname:  Gareth Farrelly
DOB:  28-08-75 Dublin

A Republic of Ireland international at every level, Farrelly joined Villa as a trainee in 1992. Following a spell on loan at Rotherham United, he made the first of four appearances for Villa during the 1995-96 season. A hard-working midfield player, his chances continued to be limited last season, adding just three more Premiership games to his tally. However he was an unused sub on 15 occasions, proving his worth to the first team squad, something that Everton picked up on in the close season.

### Form Factors

| Season | Team | Tot | St | Sb | Y | R |
|---|---|---|---|---|---|---|
| 95-96 | Aston Villa | 4 | 1 | 3 | 0 | 0 |
| 96-97 | Aston Villa | 3 | 1 | 2 | 0 | 0 |
| Total | | 7 | 2 | 5 | 0 | 0 |

| | GP | GG | GF | GS | TGR |
|---|---|---|---|---|---|
| 95-96 | 10.53 | 0.00 | 52 | 0 | 0.00 |
| 96-97 | 7.89 | 0.00 | 47 | 0 | 0.00 |
| Averages | 9.21 | 0.00 | 49.50 | 0.00 | 0.00 |

## FEAR, Peter

### Wimbledon  ❶❷  M

Fullname:  Peter Stanley Fear
DOB:  10-09-73 Sutton

Fear came through the ranks at Wimbledon and had one of his most productive seasons at Selhurst Park in 96-97. He featured in 29 of the Dons' Premiership games, making 18 appearances and 11 as a non-used substitute.

A midfield player who likes to use his skill to create chances he made his Premier League debut at Arsenal in

February 1993. He looked to have fully established himself the following season, making 23 appearances, but then struggled to make the team prior to last term.

Likely to remain an important squad player this season.

## Form Factors

| Season | Team | Tot | St | Sb | Y | R |
|---|---|---|---|---|---|---|
| 94-95 | Wimbledon | 14 | 8 | 6 | 2 | 0 |
| 95-96 | Wimbledon | 4 | 4 | 0 | 1 | 0 |
| 96-97 | Wimbledon | 18 | 9 | 9 | 3 | 0 |
| Total | | 36 | 21 | 15 | 6 | 0 |

| | GP | GG | GF | GS | TGR |
|---|---|---|---|---|---|
| 94-95 | 33.33 | 14.00 | 48 | 1 | 2.08 |
| 95-96 | 10.53 | 0.00 | 55 | 0 | 0.00 |
| 96-97 | 47.37 | 0.00 | 49 | 0 | 0.00 |
| Averages | 30.41 | 4.67 | 50.67 | 0.33 | 0.69 |

## FENN, Neale

# Tottenham H.  ❶  S

Fullname: Neale Fenn
DOB: 18-01-77 Tottenham

Has scored freely for the Tottenham Hotspur reserve side over the past three seasons and was given his chance to sample life in the Premiership for four games towards the end of last season, making his debut during a 2-1 defeat at Sheffield Wednesday.

Could well become a major figure for years to come if he can repeat his Avon Insurance League goalscoring exploits in the Premiership.

Aged 21, he has played for the Republic of Ireland at Schoolboy and Youth levels.

## Form Factors

| Season | Team | Tot | St | Sb | Y | R |
|---|---|---|---|---|---|---|
| 96-97 | Tottenham | 4 | 0 | 4 | 0 | 0 |
| Total | | 4 | 0 | 4 | 0 | 0 |

| | GP | GG | GF | GS | TGR |
|---|---|---|---|---|---|
| 96-97 | 10.53 | 0.00 | 44 | 0 | 0.00 |
| Averages | 10.53 | 0.00 | 44.00 | 0.00 | 0.00 |

## FENTON, Graham

# Blackburn Rovers ❶❷␣  S

Fullname: Graham Anthony Fenton
DOB: 22-05-74 Wallsend

Fenton is probably best remembered for the two goals he scored at the end of the 1995-96 season that effectively ended Newcastle United's hopes of winning the Premiership.

Unable to establish himself in the Aston Villa side he joined Rovers for £1.5 million in December 1995 playing in 14 games and scoring six goals – an excellent start – despite a nagging hamstring injury. Last season he managed 13 appearances, eight of which came as a substitute. He was also unused as a sub on six occasions.

A strong striker, his bustling style often forces opponents into mistakes, providing opportunities for both himself and those around him. At 23 years old still has plenty of time to establish himself as a first choice selection.

## Form Factors

| Season | Team | Tot | St | Sb | Y | R |
|---|---|---|---|---|---|---|
| 95-96 | Aston Villa | 3 | 0 | 3 | 0 | 0 |
| 95-96 | Blackburn | 14 | 4 | 10 | 2 | 0 |
| 96-97 | Blackburn | 13 | 5 | 8 | 3 | 0 |
| Total | | 30 | 9 | 21 | 5 | 0 |

| | GP | GG | GF | GS | TGR |
|---|---|---|---|---|---|
| 95-96 | 7.89 | 0.00 | 52 | 0 | 0.00 |
| 95-96 | 36.84 | 2.33 | 61 | 6 | 9.84 |
| 96-97 | 34.21 | 13.00 | 42 | 1 | 2.38 |
| Averages | 26.32 | 5.11 | 51.67 | 2.33 | 4.07 |

## FERDINAND, Les

# Newcastle U.  ❶❷❸❹           S

Fullname:  Leslie Ferdinand
DOB:        18-12-66 Acton

Les Ferdinand only came into the professional game late, playing his first regular season for QPR at the age of 23 following a move from non-league side Hayes. He had a loan spell in Turkey as well, with Besiktas. After 163 league games with Queens Park Rangers, Ferdinand shocked nobody when he moved to Newcastle in a £6 million transfer in the summer of 1995. Ferdinand has ably carried out the task of filling the shoes of Newcastle's prolific Andy Cole. Although Cole's season record has yet to be bettered, Ferdinand was certainly up there in that first season up north as he scored 25 league goals from just 37 appearances.

Apart from Alan Shearer, Ferdinand is the only player to have scored more than 100 goals in the Premiership – having notched a total of 101 with QPR and Newcastle. In the 1996-97 season he was second behind Shearer at Newcastle with 16 goals in the Premiership. This was despite a period of injury which kept his appearances down to 31.

A powerful force up front for Newcastle and England, Ferdinand will resume his fruitful partnership with Shearer in the Premiership and the Champions' League for 1997-98 . Both club and country will be looking for a bag of goals and Ferdinand is equipped to deliver. He is strong in the air, certainly, but also quick, inventive and powerful on the ground.

### Form Factors

| Season | Team | Tot | St | Sb | Y | R |
|---|---|---|---|---|---|---|
| 94-95 | QPR | 37 | 37 | 0 | 6 | 1 |
| 95-96 | Newcastle | 37 | 37 | 0 | 4 | 0 |
| 96-97 | Newcastle | 31 | 30 | 1 | 3 | 0 |
| Total | | 105 | 104 | 1 | 13 | 1 |

| | GP | GG | GF | GS | TGR |
|---|---|---|---|---|---|
| 94-95 | 88.10 | 1.54 | 61 | 24 | 39.34 |
| 95-96 | 97.37 | 1.48 | 66 | 25 | 37.88 |
| 96-97 | 81.58 | 1.94 | 73 | 16 | 21.92 |
| Averages | 89.01 | 1.65 | 66.67 | 21.67 | 33.05 |

## FERDINAND, Rio

# West Ham U.  ❶❷❸❹           CB

Fullname:  Rio Gavin Ferdinand
DOB:        07-11-78 London

Second cousin of Newcastle United striker Les, Rio Ferdinand is regarded as one of the best young talents in England, so much so that, after his early performances, the Hammers tied him to a highly lucrative five year contract.

A commanding defender who is cool on the ball, he made his debut from the bench at the end of the 1995-96 season and after a couple of early season positions on the subs bench he made his full team debut against Derby County. With Marc Rieper injured, he was a near ever-present at the end of the season, scoring twice in the process.

An England Youth and Under-21 international, he is expected to play at the highest levels.

### Form Factors

| Season | Team | Tot | St | Sb | Y | R |
|---|---|---|---|---|---|---|
| 95-96 | West Ham | 1 | 0 | 1 | 0 | 0 |
| 96-97 | West Ham | 15 | 11 | 4 | 2 | 0 |
| Total | | 16 | 11 | 5 | 2 | 0 |

| | GP | GG | GF | GS | TGR |
|---|---|---|---|---|---|
| 95-96 | 2.63 | 0.00 | 43 | 0 | 0.00 |
| 96-97 | 39.47 | 7.50 | 39 | 2 | 5.13 |
| Averages | 21.05 | 3.75 | 41.00 | 1.00 | 2.56 |

## FERGUSON, Duncan

### Everton ❶❷❸❹ S

Fullname: Duncan Ferguson
DOB: 27-12-71 Stirling

One of the most powerful and highly respected strikers in the Premiership who also, occasionally, courts indiscipline which has been known to restrict his appearances during a season. Has few peers in the air but has yet to match his reputation with the games per goal ratio of great goalscorers – currently standing at a goal every three games or so. Joined Everton from Rangers for £4 million after a period on loan from the perennial Scottish champions towards the end of 1994. Made himself a hero after moving to Goodison Park with a goal against Liverpool and has since scored 26 times in 84 games for the Blues. Scotland international who made the breakthrough in his native land with Dundee United after playing originally for non-league side Carse Town.

### Form Factors

| Season | Team | Tot | St | Sb | Y | R |
|--------|------|-----|----|----|---|---|
| 94-95 | Everton | 23 | 22 | 1 | 2 | 2 |
| 95-96 | Everton | 18 | 16 | 2 | 4 | 0 |
| 96-97 | Everton | 33 | 31 | 2 | 5 | 1 |
| Total | | 74 | 69 | 5 | 11 | 3 |

| | GP | GG | GF | GS | TGR |
|--------|-----|------|-------|------|-------|
| 94-95 | 54.76 | 3.29 | 44 | 7 | 15.91 |
| 95-96 | 47.37 | 3.60 | 64 | 5 | 7.81 |
| 96-97 | 86.84 | 3.30 | 44 | 10 | 22.73 |
| Averages | 62.99 | 3.40 | 50.67 | 7.33 | 15.48 |

*Duncan Ferguson*

## FILAN, John

### Coventry City ❶ GK

Fullname: John Richard Filan
DOB: 08-02-70 Sydney, Australia

Australian Under-21 international goalkeeper who, due to the great consistency of Steve Ogrizovic, has had only limited opportunities to shine at Highfield Road since signing from Cambridge United during March 1995 for £300,000.

Made his debut during a vital 3-1 win at Tottenham in May 1995 and played 12 games at the start of the 1995-96 season when Ogrizovic was injured, and managed two clean sheets.

Last season Oggy was in such great form that Filan was only able to get one appearance under his belt, which was at Highbury after Ogrizovic had to leave the field of play with a broken nose.

Born in Sydney, Filan began his career with Aussie side St. George Budapest.

## Form Factors

| Season | Team | Tot | St | Sb | Y | R |
|---|---|---|---|---|---|---|
| 94-95 | Coventry C. | 2 | 2 | 0 | 0 | 0 |
| 95-96 | Coventry C. | 13 | 13 | 0 | 0 | 0 |
| 96-97 | Coventry C. | 1 | 0 | 1 | 0 | 0 |
| Total | | 16 | 15 | 1 | 0 | 0 |

| | GA | GkA | GAp | CS | SO | Rp |
|---|---|---|---|---|---|---|
| 95-96 | 60 | 27 | 2.08 | 2 | 1 | 0 |
| 96-97 | 54 | 0 | 0.00 | 0 | 0 | 0 |
| Total | 114 | 27 | 1.93 | 2 | 1 | – |

## FLITCROFT, Garry

## Blackburn Rovers ❶❷❸❹　S

Fullname:　Garry William Flitcroft
DOB:　　　06-11-72 Bolton

It was a surprise when a struggling Manchester City allowed one of their prize assets to move to Blackburn in March 1996 for over £3 million. He immediately made the headlines by getting sent off three minutes from time in his debut game. Following a three-match suspension he played in just two more games prior to the end of the season.

The 1996-97 season saw Flitcroft feature in 28 games but contribute just three goals. A creative player, with excellent stamina, he also has the ability to tackle and win the ball.

## Form Factors

| Season | Team | Tot | St | Sb | Y | R |
|---|---|---|---|---|---|---|
| 95-96 | Man City | 25 | 25 | 0 | 9 | 0 |
| 95-96 | Blackburn | 3 | 3 | 0 | 1 | 1 |
| 96-97 | Blackburn | 28 | 27 | 1 | 1 | 0 |
| Total | | 56 | 55 | 1 | 11 | 1 |

| | GP | GG | GF | GS | TGR |
|---|---|---|---|---|---|
| 95-96 | 65.79 | 0.00 | 33 | 0 | 0.00 |
| 95-96 | 7.89 | 0.00 | 61 | 0 | 0.00 |
| 96-97 | 73.68 | 9.33 | 42 | 3 | 7.14 |
| Averages | 49.12 | 3.11 | 45.33 | 1.00 | 2.38 |

## FLO, Tore Andre

## Chelsea ❶❷❸　S

Fullname:　Tore Andre Flo
DOB:　　　15-06-73 Norway

A tall, gangly striker in the fairly typical Norwegian mould, he signed for the Blues in May 1997, from SK Brann. In 1996 he finished third top scorer in the Norwegian league, with 19 goals in 24 games, and this compares favourably with the 18 goals from 25 games the previous season while playing for Tromso.

A full international, at 6' 2" Flo is strong in the air and like any good striker can use both feet to good effect and, at just 24 years of age, has great promise.

Prior to joining Chelsea, Everton had agreed terms, only for the deal to fall through when the Everton manager at the time, Joe Royle, resigned from the club.

*Tim Flowers*

## FLOWERS, Tim

## Blackburn R. ❶❷❸❹❺  GK

Fullname:  Timothy David Flowers
DOB:        03-02-67 Kenilworth

Tim Flowers became Britain's most expensive goalkeeper when he moved to Ewood Park for £2.4 million from Southampton in 1993. Along with Neville Southall he leads the Premiership in most appearances, having played in 195 games from the 202 possible at the end of the 1996-97 season. In the last three seasons he has conceded just over one goal a game on average and has maintained a clean sheet in nearly 30% of his games.

Not surprisingly he has been a regular member of the England squad and briefly had the number one spot before losing it to David Seaman. A great shot-stopper, like all top 'keepers he has an almost carefree attitude during games.

## Form Factors

| Season | Team | Tot | St | Sb | Y | R |
|--------|------|-----|-----|-----|-----|-----|
| 94-95 | Blackburn | 39 | 39 | 0 | 1 | 1 |
| 95-96 | Blackburn | 37 | 37 | 0 | 3 | 1 |
| 96-97 | Blackburn | 36 | 36 | 0 | 2 | 0 |
| Total | | 112 | 112 | 0 | 6 | 2 |

| | GA | GkA | GAp | CS | SO | Rp |
|--------|-----|-----|-----|-----|-----|-----|
| 94-95 | 39 | 30 | 0.77 | 16 | 4 | 0 |
| 95-96 | 47 | 36 | 0.97 | 9 | 2 | 0 |
| 96-97 | 43 | 42 | 1.17 | 10 | 3 | 0 |
| Total | 129 | 108 | 0.96 | 35 | 9 | – |

## FLYNN, Sean

# Derby County ❶❷ M

Fullname: Sean Michael Flynn
DOB: 13-03-68 Birmingham
Midfielder who joined Derby from
Coventry City in August 1995 after
becoming a regular in the first team at
Highfield Road. Indeed he seldom missed
a match during his final two seasons with
the Sky Blues. Has experienced greater
difficulty in holding down a permanent
place in the Rams' side, having found
himself on the bench on 16 occasions –
seven of which went towards his 17 first
team appearances. Had a spell on loan at
Stoke towards the end of last season but
at the end of the 1996-97 season needed
just eight more outings to complete a
century of Premiership appearances.

Started his career in non-league
football before joining Coventry in
January 1991.

## Form Factors

| Season | Team | Tot | St | Sb | Y | R |
|---|---|---|---|---|---|---|
| 93-94 | Coventry C. | 36 | 33 | 3 | 3 | 0 |
| 94-95 | Coventry C. | 32 | 32 | 0 | 1 | 0 |
| 96-97 | Derby Co. | 17 | 10 | 7 | 3 | 0 |
| Total | | 85 | 75 | 10 | 7 | 0 |

| | GP | GG | GF | GS | TGR |
|---|---|---|---|---|---|
| 93-94 | 85.71 | 12.00 | 43 | 3 | 6.98 |
| 94-95 | 76.19 | 8.00 | 44 | 4 | 9.09 |
| 96-97 | 84.21 | 32.00 | 45 | 1 | 2.22 |
| Averages | 82.04 | 17.33 | 44.00 | 2.67 | 6.10 |

## FORD, Mark

# Leeds United ❶ M

Fullname: Mark Ford
DOB: 10-10-75 Pontefract
Born in nearby Pontefract, he is a
former trainee with Leeds United who
captained the club to success in the FA
Youth Cup before making his mark in the
Premiership. A midfield battler who is
formidable in the tackle but has to curb
certain aspects of his game, having
already served several suspensions,
despite making just 40 first team
appearances to the end of the 1996-97
season. Has made progress at Elland
Road over each of the past three seasons
and could be on the verge of fully
establishing himself in the side. Aged 21
at the start of the season, he has
represented England at Youth and Under-
21 levels.

## Form Factors

| Season | Team | Tot | St | Sb | Y | R |
|---|---|---|---|---|---|---|
| 93-94 | Leeds Utd | 1 | 0 | 1 | 0 | 0 |
| 95-96 | Leeds Utd | 11 | 11 | 0 | 3 | 0 |
| 96-97 | Leeds Utd | 16 | 15 | 1 | 4 | 0 |
| Total | | 28 | 26 | 2 | 7 | 0 |

| | GP | GG | GF | GS | TGR |
|---|---|---|---|---|---|
| 93-94 | 2.38 | 0.00 | 65 | 0 | 0.00 |
| 95-96 | 28.95 | 0.00 | 40 | 0 | 0.00 |
| 96-97 | 42.11 | 16.00 | 28 | 1 | 3.57 |
| Averages | 24.48 | 5.33 | 44.33 | 0.33 | 1.19 |

*Robbie Fowler*

## FOWLER, Robbie

# Liverpool ❶❷❸❹❺ S

Fullname: Robert Bernard Fowler
DOB: 09-04-75 Liverpool

Robbie Fowler is one of the stars of the modern game with a special talent for scoring goals and a big game temperament. He was top scorer in all competitions in 1996-97 with 31, 18 in the Premiership to take his total to 83, the fourth highest all-time. He scored four against Middlesbrough.

A poacher of goals, but maturing as an all-round player, Fowler's competitive nature can get him into trouble and he was sent off towards the end of the 1996-97 season. The rebel also found a cause with a T-shirt supporting the sacked Liverpool dockers being revealed to the cameras.

He is a natural goalscorer the way Liverpool like them. Quick over 10 yards and with a powerful shot. Fowler looks certain to add to his six England caps and his first goal scored against Mexico.

## Form Factors

| Season | Team | Tot | St | Sb | Y | R |
|--------|------|-----|-----|-----|-----|-----|
| 94-95 | Liverpool | 42 | 42 | 0 | 4 | 0 |
| 95-96 | Liverpool | 38 | 36 | 2 | 3 | 0 |
| 96-97 | Liverpool | 32 | 32 | 0 | 4 | 1 |
| Total | | 112 | 110 | 2 | 11 | 1 |

| | GP | GG | GF | GS | TGR |
|--------|------|------|------|------|------|
| 94-95 | 100.00 | 1.68 | 65 | 25 | 38.46 |
| 95-96 | 100.00 | 1.36 | 70 | 28 | 40.00 |
| 96-97 | 84.21 | 2.11 | 62 | 18 | 29.03 |
| Averages | 94.74 | 1.72 | 65.67 | 23.67 | 35.83 |

## FOX, Ruel

## Tottenham H.  ❶❷  M

Fullname: Ruel Adrian Fox
DOB: 14-01-68 Ipswich

Winger who has been involved in transfers totalling around £6.5m since making his debut for Norwich City against Coventry in November 1986. Norwich sold him to Newcastle for £2.25m in February 1994 and less than two years later United transferred him to Spurs for a £2m profit.

Possesses terrific speed and the ability to cross the ball accurately at pace. Scored at around once every four games

with Newcastle but his goal ratio has dropped since joining Spurs to around one goal every 11 games. He seemed to fall out of favour with manager Gerry Francis last year and was often out of the starting line-up, even during Tottenham's injury problems last season.

### Form Factors

| Season | Team | Tot | St | Sb | Y | R |
|--------|------|-----|-----|-----|-----|-----|
| 94-95 | Newcastle | 40 | 40 | 0 | 0 | 0 |
| 95-96 | Newcastle | 4 | 2 | 2 | 0 | 0 |
| 95-96 | Tottenham | 26 | 26 | 0 | 1 | 0 |
| 96-97 | Tottenham | 25 | 19 | 6 | 1 | 0 |
| Total | | 95 | 87 | 8 | 2 | 0 |

| | GP | GG | GF | GS | TGR |
|--------|------|------|------|------|------|
| 94-95 | 95.24 | 4.00 | 67 | 10 | 14.93 |
| 95-96 | 71.43 | 5.00 | 50 | 6 | 12.00 |
| 96-97 | 65.79 | 25.00 | 44 | 1 | 2.27 |
| Averages | 77.49 | 11.33 | 53.66 | 5.66 | 9.73 |

*Dougie Freedman*

## FREEDMAN, Dougie

## Crystal Palace  ❶❷❸  S

Fullname: Douglas Alan Freedman
DOB: 21-01-74 Glasgow

Freedman's performances last season finally earned him a call-up into Craig Brown's Scottish squad. Not bad for a player who was released on a free from QPR and eventually transferred across London for £800,000 from Barnet.

A striker with a real love of goals, scoring 20 in 1995-96 and 11 in his 44 games last season. Although his strike rate had gone down, Freedman started in only 33 of those games, having to fight for his first team place following the arrival of Neil Shipperley.

Possesses a fine first touch and positional sense and can also pass well for a striker!

*Kevin Gallacher*

## GALLACHER, Kevin

### Blackburn Rovers ❶❷❸❹  M

Fullname: Kevin William Gallacher
DOB: 23-11-66 Clydebank

There can be few unluckier players than Kevin Gallacher. Having broken his leg in three places, he fought his way back into the Rovers' first team only to re-break his leg in his first full appearance back. Made another come-back at the start of the 1995-96 season only to suffer a hamstring injury that kept him out until Christmas.

The injury horror looks to be behind him now, having played in 34 of Rovers' games last season and re-establishing himself in the Scottish side. A striker who can play wide, the 10 goals he scored in

1996-97 represented nearly a quarter of his team's total.

### Form Factors

| Season | Team | Tot | St | Sb | Y | R |
|--------|------|-----|-----|-----|-----|-----|
| 94-95 | Blackburn | 1 | 1 | 0 | 0 | 0 |
| 95-96 | Blackburn | 16 | 14 | 2 | 1 | 0 |
| 96-97 | Blackburn | 34 | 34 | 0 | 6 | 0 |
| Total | | 51 | 49 | 2 | 7 | 0 |

| | GP | GG | GF | GS | TGR |
|--------|------|------|------|------|------|
| 94-95 | 2.38 | 1.00 | 80 | 1 | 1.25 |
| 95-96 | 42.11 | 8.00 | 61 | 2 | 3.28 |
| 96-97 | 89.47 | 3.40 | 42 | 10 | 23.81 |
| Averages | 44.65 | 4.13 | 61.00 | 4.33 | 9.45 |

## GARDE, Remi

### Arsenal ❶ M

Fullname: Remi Garde
DOB: 03-04-66 L'Arbesle, France

A former French international with three caps, Garde arrived at Highbury on a free transfer on the eve of the 1996-97 campaign as a prelude to the arrival of Arsène Wenger. He is undoubtedly a cover player and this was the role he played during the 1996-97 season and which he looks likely to fulfil in the 1997-98 season.

First and foremost a midfield player, he is equally comfortable in the centre of the defence and he occupied both these positions during his 11 appearances for Arsenal last season – four coming as substitute.

He was previously with Strasbourg where he played alongside Chelsea's Frank Leboeuf. Will score points when in the Arsenal side, but those opportunities will be limited.

### Form Factors

| Season | Team | Tot | St | Sb | Y | R |
|--------|------|-----|----|----|---|---|
| 96-97 | Arsenal | 11 | 7 | 4 | 2 | 0 |
| Total | | 11 | 7 | 4 | 2 | 0 |

| | GP | GG | GF | GS | TGR |
|--|-----|------|-------|------|------|
| 96-97 | 28.95 | 0.00 | 62 | 0 | 0.00 |
| Averages | 28.95 | 0.00 | 62.00 | 0.00 | 0.00 |

## GAYLE, Marcus

### Wimbledon ❶❷❸❹ S

Fullname: Marcus Anthony Gayle
DOB: 27-09-70 Hammersmith

Tall, powerful midfield player, Gayle operates down the left in Wimbledon's plays and was one of their major successes last season. He has grown in stature in the past three seasons and has missed just six games in that period. It has also been noticeable that he is increasing his goal trawl each season – his eight in the Premier League last season making him the Dons' second highest scorer.

Gayle started his career at Brentford, for whom he played over 150 senior games, and made the short journey across London in March 1994 for what now seems a bargain £250,000.

An England Youth international, Gayle has an exceptional disciplinary record.

### Form Factors

| Season | Team | Tot | St | Sb | Y | R |
|--------|------|-----|----|----|---|---|
| 94-95 | Wimbledon | 23 | 22 | 1 | 0 | 0 |
| 95-96 | Wimbledon | 34 | 21 | 13 | 0 | 0 |
| 96-97 | Wimbledon | 36 | 34 | 2 | 2 | 0 |
| Total | | 93 | 77 | 16 | 2 | 0 |

| | GP | GG | GF | GS | TGR |
|--|-----|------|-------|------|------|
| 94-95 | 54.76 | 11.50 | 48 | 2 | 4.17 |
| 95-96 | 89.47 | 6.80 | 55 | 5 | 9.09 |
| 96-97 | 94.74 | 4.25 | 49 | 8 | 16.33 |
| Averages | 79.66 | 7.52 | 50.67 | 5.00 | 9.86 |

## GERRARD, Paul

## Everton  ❶  GK

Fullname:  Paul William Gerrard
DOB:        22-01-73 Heywood
    England U-21 international goalkeeper
who moved to Goodison Park from
Oldham Athletic in August 1996 for £1.5
million but, despite the high fee, has been
unable to dislodge the evergreen Neville
Southall from between the sticks. During
his first season with the Toffeemen, he
played just five times in the Premiership.
Made 133 appearances for Oldham in just
under five years at Boundary Park, having
been signed by future Everton boss Joe
Royle. Featured as a substitute backup for
Southall on 30 occasions last season and,
aged just 24, he still has plenty of time in
which to further his Everton and
international careers. Nevertheless will be
looking to make the Number One jersey
his own in the course of the next year.

### Form Factors

| Season | Team | Tot | St | Sb | Y | R |
|--------|------|-----|-----|-----|-----|-----|
| 92-93 | Oldham A. | 25 | 25 | 0 | 0 | 0 |
| 93-94 | Oldham A. | 16 | 15 | 1 | 0 | 0 |
| 96-97 | Everton⁻ | 5 | 4 | 1 | 0 | 0 |
| Total | | 46 | 44 | 2 | 0 | 0 |

| | GA | GkA | GAp | CS | SO | Rp |
|--------|-----|-----|-----|-----|-----|-----|
| 92-93 | 74 | 44 | 1.76 | 2 | 1 | 0 |
| 93-94 | 68 | 24 | 1.50 | 2 | 1 | 0 |
| 96-97 | 58 | 6 | 1.20 | 2 | 2 | 0 |
| Total | 200 | 74 | 1.61 | 6 | 4 | – |

## GIGGS, Ryan

## Manchester U. ❶❷❸❹❺  S

Fullname:  Ryan Joseph Giggs
DOB:        29-11-73 Cardiff
    The flying Welsh winger performed
with passion and at speed in 1996-97
against teams like Juventus, but without
much luck. He scored only two goals in
the Premiership and many regard his
failure to find the net more regularly the
only thing stopping him from being one
of the all-time greats.
    Born in Wales but brought up in nearby
Salford, Giggs was on the books of rivals
Manchester City as a youngster but had
no hesitation in signing for the club he
supported as a boy when offered the
chance. In 167 Premiership appearances,
Giggs has scored 37 goals at a goal every
four and a half games.
    He burst into the United side as a
talented 17 year-old and, still only 24, he
is back to his swerving, weaving best
after an injury which kept him down to 25
starts and one substitute appearance last
season. After a rather on/off season,
1997-98 could go either way for Giggs
and he should be treated as a risk in
fantasy terms.

### Form Factors

| Season | Team | Tot | St | Sb | Y | R |
|--------|------|-----|-----|-----|-----|-----|
| 94-95 | Man. Utd | 29 | 29 | 0 | 3 | 0 |
| 95-96 | Man. Utd | 33 | 30 | 3 | 0 | 0 |
| 96-97 | Man. Utd | 26 | 25 | 1 | 2 | 0 |
| Total | | 88 | 84 | 4 | 5 | 0 |

| | GP | GG | GF | GS | TGR |
|--------|-----|-----|-----|-----|-----|
| 94-95 | 69.05 | 29.00 | 77 | 1 | 1.30 |
| 95-96 | 86.84 | 3.00 | 73 | 11 | 15.07 |
| 96-97 | 68.42 | 8.67 | 76 | 3 | 3.95 |
| Averages | 74.77 | 13.56 | 75.33 | 5.00 | 6.77 |

## GILLESPIE, Keith

# Newcastle U. ❶❷❸❹     S

Fullname: Keith Robert Gillespie
DOB: 18-02-75 Bangor

Signed from Manchester United as part of the deal that saw Andy Cole go to Old Trafford. Keith Gillespie, already a full Northern Irish International despite being only 22 years of age, is on his day one of the most electrifying wingers in the game though he hasn't always looked his best when asked to fill a wing-back role.

He is becoming one of the most dangerous crossers of the ball in the Premiership. He has the pace to glide past full-backs and the energy to get up and down the flank to pursue his defensive duties. Chasing opposition wingers can lead to ungainly tackles and Gillespie went one too far in 1996-97 and got his marching orders. Only two yellow cards in 32 games in 1996-97 doesn't look like a problem however. He is set for a full season in a successful Newcastle side leaving his previous manager Alex Ferguson wondering why he let him go.

## Form Factors

| Season | Team | Tot | St | Sb | | Y | R |
|---|---|---|---|---|---|---|---|
| 94-95 | Newcastle | 17 | 15 | 2 | | 2 | 0 |
| 95-96 | Newcastle | 28 | 26 | 2 | | 3 | 0 |
| 96-97 | Newcastle | 32 | 23 | 9 | | 2 | 1 |
| Total | | 77 | 64 | 13 | | 7 | 1 |

| | GP | GG | GF | GS | TGR |
|---|---|---|---|---|---|
| 94-95 | 40.48 | 8.50 | 67 | 2 | 2.99 |
| 95-96 | 73.68 | 7.00 | 66 | 4 | 6.06 |
| 96-97 | 84.21 | 28.00 | 73 | 1 | 1.37 |
| Averages | 66.12 | 14.50 | 68.67 | 2.33 | 3.47 |

## GINOLA, David

# Tottenham H. ❶❷❸     S

Fullname: David Ginola
DOB: 25-01-67 Gassin,
nr St. Tropez, France

The mercurial French winger is often a genius on the football field and perhaps more popular in the Premiership than in his native land (where they remember a mistake which ultimately cost France a World Cup finals place in 1994).

Ginola doesn't confine himself to football, pursuing parallel careers in modelling and motor racing and this could be interpreted as lack of commitment at this stage of his career. He managed 24 appearances, four from the subs bench, in 1996-97.

Plays a stylish game down the left side of the attack but sometimes flatters only to fall flat. When he does get in a cross, it's usually well directed and he's got a powerful shot from dead ball situations or when volleying from around the area. These skills don't translate into goals however, with only six in two Premiership seasons, although when they do arrive they are invariably spectacular.

## Form Factors

| Season | Team | Tot | St | Sb | | Y | R |
|---|---|---|---|---|---|---|---|
| 95-96 | Newcastle | 34 | 34 | 0 | | 5 | 0 |
| 96-97 | Newcastle | 24 | 20 | 4 | | 3 | 0 |
| Total | | 58 | 54 | 4 | | 8 | 0 |

| | GP | GG | GF | GS | TGR |
|---|---|---|---|---|---|
| 95-96 | 89.47 | 6.80 | 66 | 5 | 7.58 |
| 96-97 | 63.16 | 24.00 | 73 | 1 | 1.37 |
| Averages | 76.32 | 15.40 | 69.50 | 3.00 | 4.47 |

## GIVEN, Shay

# Newcastle U.  ❶❷❸❹  GK

Fullname:  Seamus John Givens
DOB:       20-04-76 Lifford,
           Co Donegal

Became one of three players at St
James' Park who played under Kenny
Dalglish when he was signed from
Blackburn Rovers in the summer of 1997.
Given began his league career with first
team loan spells at Swindon Town and
Sunderland – helping the latter to
promotion during the 1995-96 season and
keeping 12 clean sheets in his 17
appearances.

He broke into the Republic of Ireland
team in the 1995-96 season as well, and
in doing so became one of very few who
has played for their country before their
club.

Made his Premiership bow against
Southampton at the back end of 1996, but
couldn't dislodge Tim Flowers from the
regular goalkeeping slot at Ewood Park.
One of the most promising 'keepers to
emerge in the game for quite some time,
Given's contract ran out and the player
decided to link up with his former boss
Kenny Dalglish at St. James' Park.

## Form Factors

| Season | Team | Tot | St | Sb | Y | R |
|--------|------|-----|----|----|----|----|
| 96-97 | Blackburn | 2 | 2 | 0 | 0 | 0 |
| Total |  | 2 | 2 | 0 | 0 | 0 |

|  | GA | GkA | GAp | CS | SO | Rp |
|--------|-----|-----|-----|----|----|----|
| 96-97 | 43 | 1 | 0.50 | 1 | 1 | 0 |
| Total | 43 | 1 | 0.50 | 1 | 1 | – |

## GOODMAN, Jon

# Wimbledon  ❶❷  S

Fullname:  Jonathan Goodman
DOB:       02-06-71 Walthamstow

Joined the Dons from Millwall in
November 1994 but has yet to establish
himself as a regular in the first team. Of
his 13 appearances last season, seven
were as a substitute and he was

*Shay Given*

substituted in each of the six games he started.

Had faired better in 1995-96 when he played in over 70% of the Dons' games. Made over 100 appearances for Millwall who he joined from non-league Bromley in the summer of 1990.

A striker who is willing to run and run, he notched one goal last season.

## Form Factors

| Season | Team | Tot | St | Sb | Y | R |
|---|---|---|---|---|---|---|
| 94-95 | Wimbledon | 19 | 13 | 6 | 0 | 0 |
| 95-96 | Wimbledon | 27 | 9 | 18 | 0 | 0 |
| 96-97 | Wimbledon | 13 | 6 | 7 | 0 | 0 |
| Total | | 59 | 28 | 31 | 0 | 0 |

| | GP | GG | GF | GS | TGR |
|---|---|---|---|---|---|
| 94-95 | 45.24 | 4.75 | 48 | 4 | 8.33 |
| 95-96 | 71.05 | 4.50 | 55 | 6 | 10.91 |
| 96-97 | 34.21 | 13.00 | 49 | 1 | 2.04 |
| Averages | 50.17 | 7.42 | 50.67 | 3.67 | 7.09 |

## GORDON, Dean

# Crystal Palace ❶❷　FB

Fullname:　Dean Dwight Gordon
DOB:　　　10-02-73 Croydon

Despite being just 24 years of age, Dean Gordon already has Premiership experience with Palace, playing in their two previous seasons in the top flight. Indeed he missed only one game in their 1994-95 Premiership campaign.

An England Under-21 international, Gordon is a strong, tall left-back and looks to have a good future ahead of him. Injury limited his appearances during the early part of the 1996-97 season, but even so, he managed 29 outings in Division One and is now close on 200 first team appearances for Crystal Palace.

Gordon also contributes the odd goal and actually scored a hat-trick against WBA in December 1995!

## Form Factors

| Season | Team | Tot | St | Sb | Y | R |
|---|---|---|---|---|---|---|
| 92-93 | C. Palace | 10 | 6 | 4 | 0 | 0 |
| 94-95 | C. Palace | 41 | 38 | 3 | 4 | 0 |
| Total | | 51 | 44 | 7 | 4 | 0 |

| | GP | GG | GF | GS | TGR |
|---|---|---|---|---|---|
| 92-93 | 23.81 | 0.00 | 48 | 0 | 0.00 |
| 94-95 | 97.62 | 20.50 | 34 | 2 | 5.88 |
| Averages | 60.71 | 10.25 | 41.00 | 1.00 | 2.94 |

## GRANT, Tony

# Everton ❶❷　M

Fullname:　Anthony James Grant
DOB:　　　14-11-74 Liverpool

Is in his fifth season as a professional with Everton during which time he has made 42 appearances for the Merseyside club without becoming a permanent fixture in the side. A relatively small but talented midfielder with two good feet. He made his league debut at Newcastle in February 1995 but looked to be on his way from Goodison when loaned to Swindon Town during the following season. Came back strongly last season, making 18 appearances in the Premiership and three more in both the FA and Coca Cola Cups. Born in Liverpool, an England Under-21 player who is on the verge of a big season at Goodison.

## Form Factors

| Season | Team | Tot | St | Sb | Y | R |
|---|---|---|---|---|---|---|
| 94-95 | Everton | 5 | 1 | 4 | 0 | 0 |
| 95-96 | Everton | 13 | 11 | 2 | 1 | 0 |
| 96-97 | Everton | 18 | 11 | 7 | 3 | 0 |
| Total | | 36 | 23 | 13 | 4 | 0 |

| | GP | GG | GF | GS | TGR |
|---|---|---|---|---|---|
| 94-95 | 11.90 | 0.00 | 44 | 0 | 0.00 |
| 95-96 | 34.21 | 13.00 | 64 | 1 | 1.56 |
| 96-97 | 47.37 | 0.00 | 44 | 0 | 0.00 |
| Averages | 31.16 | 4.33 | 50.67 | 0.33 | 0.52 |

## GRAY, Andy

### Leeds United ❶❷ M

Fullname: Andrew David Gray
DOB: 15-11-77 Harrogate

Teenage winger who will have had the best coaching available as he is the son of Frank Gray and the nephew of another Leeds hero, Eddie. Has made inroads into the first team over the past two seasons but has yet to command a regular place in the starting line-up. Gray will be looking to make further progress in 1997-98 after appearing as sub in six of his seven games last season. Was surprisingly called into the side for the Coca Cola Cup Final against Aston Villa in 1995-96 and was one of the few Leeds players to enhance his reputation as Villa ran the show.

### Form Factors

| Season | Team | Tot | St | Sb | Y | R |
|---|---|---|---|---|---|---|
| 95-96 | Leeds Utd | 15 | 12 | 3 | 0 | 0 |
| 96-97 | Leeds Utd | 7 | 1 | 6 | 0 | 0 |
| Total | | 22 | 13 | 9 | 0 | 0 |

| | GP | GG | GF | GS | TGR |
|---|---|---|---|---|---|
| 95-96 | 39.47 | 0.00 | 40 | 0 | 0.00 |
| 96-97 | 18.42 | 0.00 | 28 | 0 | 0.00 |
| Averages | 28.95 | 0.00 | 34.00 | 0.00 | 0.00 |

## GRAYSON, Simon

### Aston Villa ❶❷❸ FB

Fullname: Simon Nicholas Grayson
DOB: 16-12-69 Ripon

A consistent right-back who broke the hearts of Leicester fans (not to mention Martin O'Neill) when he opted to join Aston Villa when his contract was up for renewal in the close season.

A reliable right-back who obviously impressed Brian Little when he was in charge at Filbert Street, not least for his consistent displays. His 36 games for Leicester last season were the most by any City player.

Has scored goals down the years but failed to chalk any up in the Premiership last season.

Started as a trainee at Leeds United and was sold to Leicester for a bargain £50,000 in March 1992 after just two league appearances. Should make his 200th league appearance during 1997-98 and he might also be employed as midfield cover at Villa.

### Form Factors

| Season | Team | Tot | St | Sb | Y | R |
|---|---|---|---|---|---|---|
| 94-95 | Leicester C. | 34 | 34 | 0 | 7 | 1 |
| 96-97 | Leicester C. | 36 | 36 | 0 | 4 | 0 |
| Total | | 70 | 70 | 0 | 11 | 1 |

| | GP | GG | GF | GS | TGR |
|---|---|---|---|---|---|
| 94-95 | 80.95 | 0.00 | 45 | 0 | 0.00 |
| 96-97 | 94.74 | 0.00 | 46 | 0 | 0.00 |
| Averages | 87.84 | 0.00 | 45.50 | 0.00 | 0.00 |

## GRIMANDI, Gilles

### Arsenal ❶❷❸ D

Full name: Gilles Grimandi
DOB: 11-11-70 Gap, France

Grimandi signed a four-year deal with Arsenal in the close season when he arrived from Monaco with fellow team-mate Manu Petit. A talented defender, he is seen as part of Wenger's defence re-building plans and is sure to be pushing for a place in the Gunners' starting line-up. Now 26 years old, he joined Monaco as a 19-year-old and played in their championship winning side last season.

Still awaiting an international cap, Grimandi has the experience of 90 French league games behind him and his speed and technique on the ground will make him an attacking outlet when the Gunners push forward.

Frode Grodas

## GRODAS, Frode

### Chelsea    ❶    GK

Fullname:  Frode Grodas
DOB:       24-10-69 Norway

Grodas signed for Chelsea on a two-year contract after Dmitri Kharine was ruled out with a broken leg in the early part of the 1996-97 season. A Norwegian international, he played in 21 Premiership games and also featured on the bench when Kevin Hitchcock took over the Number One jersey.

A good shot-stopper, he is somewhat suspect with crosses, preferring to fist or claw them away whenever possible and he only managed four clean sheets in his games. Suffered an injury late in the season but recovered to play in the FA Cup Final.

With the arrival of Dutch international Ed De Goey at Stamford Bridge, the Blues seem to have too many goalkeepers and Grodas may well be one to suffer.

### Form Factors

| Season Team |  | Tot | St | Sb | Y | R |
|---|---|---|---|---|---|---|
| 96-97 | Chelsea | 21 | 20 | 1 | 1 | 1 |
| Total |  | 21 | 20 | 1 | 1 | 1 |

|  | GA | GkA | GAp | CS | SO | Rp |
|---|---|---|---|---|---|---|
| 96-97 | 55 | 30 | 1.43 | 4 | 1 | 0 |
| Total | 55 | 30 | 1.43 | 4 | 1 | – |

## GUDMUNDSSON, Niklas

### Blackburn Rovers  ❶    M

Fullname:  Niklas Gudmundsson
DOB:       29-02-72 Halmstads, Sweden

A full international from Sweden Gudmundsson, who plays wide on the left, arrived from Halmstads at the end of

1995, initially on loan. He made three appearances in the final part of the season, doing enough for the club to sign him permanently. Last season he featured mainly in the Blackburn Rovers' reserve team, making just two substitute appearances and five as a sub not used.

Skillful and fast, he has time to establish himself at Ewood Park.

## Form Factors

| Season | Team | Tot | St | Sb | Y | R |
|---|---|---|---|---|---|---|
| 95-96 | Blackburn | 4 | 1 | 3 | 0 | 0 |
| 96-97 | Blackburn | 2 | 0 | 2 | 0 | 0 |
| Total | | 6 | 1 | 5 | 0 | 0 |

| | GP | GG | GF | GS | TGR |
|---|---|---|---|---|---|
| 95-96 | 10.53 | 0.00 | 61 | 0 | 0.00 |
| 96-97 | 5.26 | 0.00 | 42 | 0 | 0.00 |
| Averages | 7.89 | 0.00 | 51.50 | 0.00 | 0.00 |

## GULLIT, Ruud

# Chelsea ❶ M

Fullname: Dil Ruud Gullit
DOB: 01-09-62 Amsterdam, Holland

Injury and a successful team have limited the Chelsea player/manager's appearances in the first team. Given his activity in the transfer market recently, it begs the point as to whether he will be anything more than a squad player in the 1997-98 season.

As a player his record is second to none having achieved just about every major honour with top club sides like PSV, Milan and Sampdoria.

He was signed by Glenn Hoddle in a major coup in June 1995 and was first choice to take over the manager's role when Hoddle left to take control of the England side. He guided Chelsea to an FA Cup win in May 1997 – the first foreign manager to win a major trophy in England.

## Form Factors

| Season | Team | Tot | St | Sb | Y | R |
|---|---|---|---|---|---|---|
| 95-96 | Chelsea | 31 | 31 | 0 | 2 | 0 |
| 96-97 | Chelsea | 12 | 6 | 6 | 1 | 0 |
| Total | | 43 | 37 | 6 | 3 | 0 |

| | GP | GG | GF | GS | TGR |
|---|---|---|---|---|---|
| 95-96 | 81.58 | 10.33 | 46 | 3 | 6.52 |
| 96-97 | 31.58 | 12.00 | 58 | 1 | 1.72 |
| Averages | 56.58 | 11.17 | 52.00 | 2.00 | 4.12 |

## GUPPY, Steve

# Leicester City ❶❷ FB

Fullname: Stephen Guppy
DOB: 29-03-69 Winchester

Signed by Leicester City in the spring of 1997 to bolster their attacking options in a bid, ultimately successful, to stave off relegation. Exciting winger who has had a chequered career since making his Football League debut with Wycombe Wanderers when the club came into the League in 1993. Played under his present boss Martin O'Neill when Wycombe won the Vauxhall Conference. Made an ambitious move to Newcastle United in August 1994 but left three months later after just one Coca Cola Cup appearance. Signed for Port Vale from where he joined Leicester.

A player who lives on confidence – if he starts well he plays well. Might ultimately be a little lightweight for the Premiership.

## Form Factors

| Season | Team | Tot | St | Sb | Y | R |
|---|---|---|---|---|---|---|
| 96-97 | Leicester C. | 13 | 12 | 1 | 2 | 0 |
| Total | | 13 | 12 | 1 | 2 | 0 |

| | GP | GG | GF | GS | TGR |
|---|---|---|---|---|---|
| 96-97 | 34.21 | 0.00 | 46 | 0 | 0.00 |
| Averages | 34.21 | 0.00 | 46.00 | 0.00 | 0.00 |

P.G. & E. Chandler
335 Lakeside Drive
Denton, Texas 76208
Tel. (940) 321-1468

## HALL, Marcus

# Coventry City ❶ FB

Fullname: Marcus Hall
DOB: 24-03-76 Coventry

One-time Coventry City trainee progressed through to the first team in December 1994 and to the end of last season had made 43 appearances in the Premiership.

Hall is a tall strong left-sided full-back who looked to be on the way to fully establishing himself in the Sky Blues' starting line-up during the 1995-96 season in the wake of an injury to David Burrows. Last season he had to be content with a role that was mainly on the bench – 13 times in fact.

A local lad, having been born in Coventry, he has gained England Under-21 honours.

## Form Factors

| Season | Team | Tot | St | Sb | Y | R |
|--------|------|-----|----|----|----|----|
| 94-95 | Coventry C. | 5 | 2 | 3 | 1 | 0 |
| 95-96 | Coventry C. | 25 | 24 | 1 | 1 | 0 |
| 96-97 | Coventry C. | 13 | 10 | 3 | 0 | 0 |
| Total | | 43 | 36 | 7 | 2 | 0 |

| | GP | GG | GF | GS | TGR |
|--------|------|------|------|------|------|
| 94-95 | 11.90 | 0.00 | 44 | 0 | 0.00 |
| 95-96 | 65.79 | 0.00 | 42 | 0 | 0.00 |
| 96-97 | 34.21 | 0.00 | 38 | 0 | 0.00 |
| Averages | 37.30 | 0.00 | 41.33 | 0.00 | 0.00 |

## HALL, Richard

# West Ham U. ❶❷❸ CB

Fullname: Richard Anthony Hall
DOB: 14-03-72 Ipswich

Hall earned his reputation as a possible England player of the future while playing at Southampton. His performances at the Dell persuaded the Hammers to pay £1.9 million for him in the summer of 1996. Unfortunately he had to wait until April 1997 to make his debut for United as a foot injury picked up on a pre-season tour sidelined him for almost nine months. Making his debut against Middlesbrough, Hall played out the final seven games of the Hammers' season as they secured their Premiership place for another year.

A tall central defender, who started his career at Scunthorpe, he captained the England Under-21 side to victory in the 1993 Toulon tournament. He should be a major influence in the West Ham rear-guard during 1997-98 but may miss the start of the season.

## Form Factors

| Season | Team | Tot | St | Sb | Y | R |
|--------|------|-----|----|----|----|----|
| 94-95 | Southampton | 37 | 36 | 1 | 4 | 0 |
| 95-96 | Southampton | 30 | 30 | 0 | 6 | 0 |
| 96-97 | West Ham | 7 | 7 | 0 | 1 | 0 |
| Total | | 74 | 73 | 1 | 11 | 0 |

| | GP | GG | GF | GS | TGR |
|--------|------|------|------|------|------|
| 94-95 | 88.10 | 9.25 | 61 | 4 | 6.56 |
| 95-96 | 78.95 | 30.00 | 34 | 1 | 2.94 |
| 96-97 | 18.42 | 0.00 | 39 | 0 | 0.00 |
| Averages | 61.82 | 13.08 | 44.67 | 1.67 | 3.17 |

## HALLE, Gunnar

# Leeds United ❶❷❸❹ FB

Fullname: Gunnar Halle
DOB: 11-08-65 Oslo, Norway
    Born in the Norwegian capital of Oslo,
he began his career in England in 1991
with Oldham Athletic. Stayed with the
Latics until December 1996 when he was
signed by George Graham for Leeds
United at a cost of £400,000. Has adapted
well to the English game as befitting a
player who has represented his country
on more than 50 occasions. Also settled
quickly at Elland Road, with his arrival
contributing greatly to a defence which
became one of the meanest and most
difficult to break down in the
Premiership. Scored 18 times in 187
games for Oldham but has yet to find the
target for Leeds. He was a near ever-
present after his transfer and his 20
appearances in the Premiership last
season would seem to indicate that
Graham will expect him to play a big role
for Leeds during the 1997-98 season.

## Form Factors

| Season | Team | Tot | St | Sb | Y | R |
|--------|------|-----|-----|-----|-----|-----|
| 92-93 | Oldham At. | 40 | 40 | 0 | 3 | 0 |
| 93-94 | Oldham At. | 23 | 22 | 1 | 0 | 0 |
| 96-97 | Leeds Utd | 20 | 20 | 0 | 2 | 0 |
| Total | | 83 | 82 | 1 | 5 | 0 |

| | GP | GG | GF | GS | TGR |
|--------|------|------|------|------|------|
| 92-93 | 95.24 | 8.00 | 63 | 5 | 7.94 |
| 93-94 | 54.76 | 23.00 | 42 | 1 | 2.38 |
| 96-97 | 52.63 | 0.00 | 28 | 0 | 0.00 |
| Averages | 67.54 | 10.33 | 44.33 | 2.00 | 3.44 |

## HAMILTON, Des

# Newcastle U. ❶❷❸ M

Fullname: Derrick Vivian Hamilton
DOB: 15-08-76 Bradford
    Newcastle United snapped Des
Hamilton up from Bradford City in
March 1997 for £1.5 million, a figure
which could eventually rise to £2 million
after a number of senior appearances.
With a reputation as a strong, aggressive
player, who tackles hard and works
tirelessly and who has also been known to
play in a wing-back role.
    Hamilton didn't make it straight into
Dalglish's side but got onto the bench in
three of their final Premiership games last
season
    Hamilton earned selection for The
Nationwide League Under-21
Representative side and received rave
reviews for his displays for Division One
strugglers Bradford City.

## HARFORD, Mick

# Wimbledon ❶ S

Fullname: Michael Gordon Harford
DOB: 12-02-59 Sunderland
    The joke about having more clubs than
Jack Nicklaus was written for Mick
Harford. At 38 he is one of the oldest
players active in the Premier League but
such is his worth to the Wimbledon squad
that manager Joe Kinnear gave him a new
one year contract for the 1997-98 season.
    By my reckoning Wimbledon are his
12th professional club and he is only a
handful of games short of making his
600th league appearance. Primarily a
striker, he has also covered in defence
where his experience has been invaluable.
Used totally as a squad player, 10 of his

13 appearances last season came from there and he was an unused sub on 15 occasions.

Won two full international caps for England at the height of his game but this must surely be his final season at this level.

## Form Factors

| Season | Team | Tot | St | Sb | Y | R |
|---|---|---|---|---|---|---|
| 94-95 | Wimbledon | 27 | 17 | 10 | 7 | 0 |
| 95-96 | Wimbledon | 21 | 17 | 4 | 6 | 0 |
| 96-97 | Wimbledon | 13 | 3 | 10 | 2 | 0 |
| Total | | 61 | 37 | 24 | 15 | 0 |

| | GP | GG | GF | GS | TGR |
|---|---|---|---|---|---|
| 94-95 | 64.29 | 4.50 | 48 | 6 | 12.50 |
| 95-96 | 55.26 | 10.50 | 55 | 2 | 3.64 |
| 96-97 | 34.21 | 13.00 | 49 | 1 | 2.04 |
| Averages | 51.25 | 9.33 | 52.67 | 3.00 | 6.06 |

# HARKNESS, Steve

## Liverpool ❶❷ FB

Fullname: Steven Harkness
DOB: 27-08-71 Carlisle

A reliable defender and powerful striker of the ball with his left foot, Harkness didn't have much opportunity to shine in the1996-97 season. He appeared only seven times, two from the subs bench and sat out a further five.

He was bought from Carlisle United in 1989 and was most involved in 24 appearances during the 1995-96 season which was tragically cut short when Harkness broke his leg at Coventry in April 1996.

Harkness can play at left-back or in central defence and may play a part as a squad player in 1997-98.

## Form Factors

| Season | Team | Tot | St | Sb | Y | R |
|---|---|---|---|---|---|---|
| 94-95 | Liverpool | 8 | 8 | 0 | 2 | 0 |
| 95-96 | Liverpool | 24 | 23 | 1 | 4 | 0 |
| 96-97 | Liverpool | 7 | 5 | 2 | 0 | 0 |
| Total | | 39 | 36 | 3 | 6 | 0 |

| | GP | GG | GF | GS | TGR |
|---|---|---|---|---|---|
| 94-95 | 19.05 | 8.00 | 65 | 1 | 1.54 |
| 95-96 | 63.16 | 24.00 | 70 | 1 | 1.43 |
| 96-97 | 18.42 | 0.00 | 62 | 0 | 0.00 |
| Averages | 33.54 | 10.67 | 65.67 | 0.67 | 0.99 |

# HARTE, Ian

## Leeds United ❶❷ S

Fullname: Ian Harte
DOB: 31-08-77 Drogheda

Mainly a full-back, he has already shown tremendous versatility and is highly rated at Elland Road. Played four times in the Premiership during the 1995-96 season and made further progress last season with another 14 Premiership outings. Already has two goals to his credit and, despite his relative youth, 20 at the end of August, he has scored a goal at international level for the Republic of Ireland. Further honours at both club and country level are on the cards for a player who is good in the tackle. He will be looking to spend a little less time on the bench during the 1997-98 season – he sat games out on 21 occasions last term!

## Form Factors

| Season | Team | Tot | St | Sb | Y | R |
|---|---|---|---|---|---|---|
| 95-96 | Leeds Utd | 4 | 2 | 2 | 1 | 0 |
| 96-97 | Leeds Utd | 14 | 10 | 4 | 1 | 0 |
| Total | | 18 | 12 | 6 | 2 | 0 |

| | GP | GG | GF | GS | TGR |
|---|---|---|---|---|---|
| 95-96 | 10.53 | 0.00 | 40 | 0 | 0.00 |
| 96-97 | 36.84 | 7.00 | 28 | 2 | 7.14 |
| Averages | 23.68 | 3.50 | 34.00 | 1.00 | 3.57 |

## HARTSON, John

# West Ham Utd ❶❷❸ S

Fullname: John Hartson
DOB: 05-04-75 Swansea

Hartson became West Ham's record signing when he arrived from Arsenal in February 1996. A complicated deal which could cost them £5 million but it ultimately proved worthwhile as his goals in the final stages of the season helped ensure the Hammers another season of Premiership football.

A Welsh international, he started his career as a trainee under David Pleat at Luton. For such a tall striker he possessed a great first touch and has an eye for goal and, as such, is never frightened to unleash a shot. His red hair complements his temper, which can lead to a succession of bookings and he earned the dubious honour of being the first player suspended in the Premiership last season. If he can curb that temper, he has already shown that he can develop a good partnership with Paul Kitson.

### Form Factors

| Season | Team | Tot | St | Sb | Y | R |
|---|---|---|---|---|---|---|
| 95-96 | Arsenal | 19 | 15 | 4 | 3 | 0 |
| 96-97 | Arsenal | 19 | 15 | 4 | 9 | 0 |
| 96-97 | West Ham | 11 | 11 | 0 | 3 | 0 |
| Total | | 49 | 41 | 8 | 15 | 0 |

| | GP | GG | GF | GS | TGR |
|---|---|---|---|---|---|
| 95-96 | 50.00 | 4.75 | 49 | 4 | 8.16 |
| 96-97 | 50.00 | 6.33 | 62 | 3 | 4.84 |
| 96-97 | 28.95 | 3.80 | 39 | 5 | 12.82 |
| Averages | 42.98 | 4.96 | 50.00 | 4.00 | 8.61 |

John Hartson

## HEALD, Paul

# Wimbledon ❶ GK

Fullname: Paul Andrew Heald
DOB: 20-09-68 Wath-on-Dearne

After looking like he could secure the number one spot at Wimbledon, Heald found himself as the Dons' reserve 'keeper last season, behind Neil Sullivan.

Having signed from Sheffield United in the summer of 1995, Heald completed his first full season with 18 Premiership games, ahead of both Sullivan and Hans Segers. A loan spell at Swindon Town, prior to his move to Selhurst Park, had seen the 6' 2" goalkeeper make three Premiership appearances.

Last season Heald saw most of his football from the bench, being a sub on no less than 23 occasions, and making just two appearances.

Likely to remain as Sullivan's back-up again in 1997-98.

## Form Factors

| Season | Team | Tot | St | Sb | Y | R |
|---|---|---|---|---|---|---|
| 93-94 | Swindon Tn | 3 | 2 | 1 | 0 | 0 |
| 95-96 | Wimbledon | 18 | 18 | 0 | 1 | 1 |
| 96-97 | Wimbledon | 2 | 2 | 0 | 0 | 0 |
| Total | | 23 | 22 | 1 | 1 | 1 |

| | GA | GkA | GAp | CS | SO | Rp |
|---|---|---|---|---|---|---|
| 93-94 | 100 | 6 | 3.00 | 0 | 0 | 0 |
| 95-96 | 70 | 26 | 1.44 | 3 | 1 | 0 |
| 96-97 | 48 | 3 | 1.50 | 0 | 0 | 0 |
| Total | 218 | 35 | 1.59 | 3 | 1 | – |

# HELDER, Glenn

## Arsenal ❶ S

Fullname: Glenn Helder
DOB: 28-10-68 Leiden, Holland

One of George Graham's last signings for the club, Helder is an exceptionally fast winger who can produce defence-splitting crosses. He can also be equally infuriating by ballooning balls behind the goal. Seems to panic in front of goal and, despite starting in over half of the Gunners' Premiership games during the 1995-96 season, and has just one goal to his credit.

Last season he didn't feature in Arsène Wenger's plans and spent the season on loan to Portuguese club Benfica. He was recalled by the club for the start of this season but the arrival of Marc Overmars could put his long-term future at the club in some doubt.

## Form Factors

| Season | Team | Tot | St | Sb | Y | R |
|---|---|---|---|---|---|---|
| 94-95 | Arsenal | 13 | 12 | 1 | 0 | 0 |
| 95-96 | Arsenal | 24 | 15 | 9 | 0 | 0 |
| 96-97 | Arsenal | 2 | 0 | 2 | 0 | 0 |
| Total | | 39 | 27 | 12 | 0 | 0 |

| | GP | GG | GF | GS | TGR |
|---|---|---|---|---|---|
| 94-95 | 30.95 | 0.00 | 52 | 0 | 0.00 |
| 95-96 | 63.16 | 24.00 | 49 | 1 | 2.04 |
| 96-97 | 5.26 | 0.00 | 62 | 0 | 0.00 |
| Averages | 33.12 | 8.00 | 54.33 | 0.33 | 0.68 |

# HENDRIE, John

## Barnsley ❶❷ S

Fullname: John Hendrie
DOB: 24-10-63 Lennoxtown

Barnsley's second top scorer in the Premiership with 15 goals from 36 appearances, indicating just how quickly the 33-year-old striker settled in after his £250,000 move to Oakwell from Middlesbrough in October 1996.

Made his Premiership debut with the Teesside club and made 45 appearances for them, scoring ten goals in the process.

His ability to hold the ball up as an out-and-out target man enables him to bring players into the game around him and, coupled with his high work rate, has made him a favourite wherever he has played.

Having started his career at Coventry City, he played for most of his career at Bradford City before moving to Middlesbrough via Leeds United. He has made well over 500 senior appearances.

John Hendrie

## Form Factors

| Season | Team | Tot | St | Sb | Y | R |
|--------|------|-----|-----|-----|-----|-----|
| 92-93 | Middlesbro' | 32 | 31 | 1 | 0 | 0 |
| 95-96 | Middlesbro' | 13 | 7 | 6 | 1 | 0 |
| Total | | 45 | 38 | 7 | 1 | 0 |

| | GP | GG | GF | GS | TGR |
|--------|-----|-----|-----|-----|-----|
| 92-93 | 76.19 | 3.56 | 54 | 9 | 16.67 |
| 95-96 | 34.21 | 13.00 | 35 | 1 | 2.86 |
| Averages | 55.20 | 8.28 | 44.50 | 5.00 | 9.76 |

## HENDRIE, Lee

## Aston Villa ❶ S

Fullname: Lee Hendrie
DOB: 18-05-77 Birmingham
   At 20 years old, Lee Hendrie is just starting his Premiership career. However his debut in December 1995 will be one he wishes to forget after being sent off for a second bookable offence when coming on as a sub at QPR.

Has now completed seven appearances for Villa, five as substitute, but has yet to score for the first team, something he has done regularly in the reserves.
   Small but quick, Lee is the cousin of Barnsley's John Hendrie.

## Form Factors

| Season | Team | Tot | St | Sb | Y | R |
|--------|------|-----|-----|-----|-----|-----|
| 95-96 | Aston Villa | 3 | 2 | 1 | 1 | 1 |
| 96-97 | Aston Villa | 4 | 0 | 4 | 0 | 0 |
| Total | | 7 | 2 | 5 | 1 | 1 |

| | GP | GG | GF | GS | TGR |
|--------|-----|-----|-----|-----|-----|
| 95-96 | 7.89 | 0.00 | 52 | 0 | 0.00 |
| 96-97 | 10.53 | 0.00 | 47 | 0 | 0.00 |
| Averages | 9.21 | 0.00 | 49.50 | 0.00 | 0.00 |

## HENDRY, Colin

### Blackburn R. ❶❷❸❹❺ CB

Fullname: Edward Colin James Hendry
DOB: 07-12-65 Keith

During the past two seasons Hendry has probably been Blackburn's most consistent player. His distinctive blond hair makes him stand out as do his battling performances at centre-half. The key to beating Rovers in the past couple of seasons has been to attack the defence at the point where Hendry is not!

Powerful and dominant in the air, he has lightning reflexes that enable him to make both pin-point tackles and perfect interceptions.

An ever-present in Rovers' championship team, he missed just three games last year due to a groin strain in the early part of the season. A fixture in the Scottish national side.

### Form Factors

| Season | Team | Tot | St | Sb | Y | R |
|---|---|---|---|---|---|---|
| 94-95 | Blackburn | 38 | 38 | 0 | 3 | 0 |
| 95-96 | Blackburn | 33 | 33 | 0 | 9 | 0 |
| 96-97 | Blackburn | 35 | 35 | 0 | 4 | 0 |
| Total | | 106 | 106 | 0 | 16 | 0 |

| | GP | GG | GF | GS | TGR |
|---|---|---|---|---|---|
| 94-95 | 90.48 | 9.50 | 80 | 4 | 5.00 |
| 95-96 | 86.84 | 33.00 | 61 | 1 | 1.64 |
| 96-97 | 92.11 | 35.00 | 42 | 1 | 2.38 |
| Averages | 89.81 | 25.83 | 61.00 | 2.00 | 3.01 |

## HESKEY, Emile

### Leicester City ❶❷❸❹ S

Fullname: Emile Heskey
DOB: 11-01-78 Leicester

Leicester-born striker who it is hard to believe is still only 19 years old. Has enjoyed an almost meteoric rise to the top since playing one game for his home town club at the end of the 1994-95 season. Scored seven goals in 30 Division One matches in 1995-96 as Leicester won promotion and has built upon that record in fine style with ten goals last season in 35 Premiership games, an outstanding return for a highly rated teenager. Heskey is very quick for his size and holds the ball well. Spent much of last season playing a wide right-hand role and is tipped to challenge for senior England honours in the future, having broken into

*Colin Hendry*

Emile Heskey

the Under-21 side over the past year. He will be an important player for Leicester during 1997-98 and should be considered.

## Form Factors

| Season | Team | Tot | St | Sb | Y | R |
|---|---|---|---|---|---|---|
| 94-95 | Leicester C. | 1 | 1 | 0 | 0 | 0 |
| 96-97 | Leicester C. | 35 | 35 | 0 | 8 | 0 |
| Total | | 36 | 36 | 0 | 8 | 0 |

| | GP | GG | GF | GS | TGR |
|---|---|---|---|---|---|
| 94-95 | 2.38 | 0.00 | 45 | 0 | 0.00 |
| 96-97 | 92.11 | 3.50 | 46 | 10 | 21.74 |
| Averages | 47.24 | 1.75 | 45.50 | 5.00 | 10.87 |

## HILLS, John

# Everton ❶ M

Fullname: John Hills
DOB: 21-04-78 Blackpool

One more teenager in the Everton ranks who joined the club from his home town club of Blackpool in the summer of 1996. Hills didn't feature in the first team at Bloomfield Road but made his debut in the Premiership against Wimbledon on 28 December at Goodison Park when coming on as a substitute.

A diminutive midfielder who had three appearances under his belt by the end of the campaign plus three non-appearing ones on the Everton substitutes' bench.

## Form Factors

| Season | Team | Tot | St | Sb | Y | R |
|---|---|---|---|---|---|---|
| 96-97 | Everton | 3 | 1 | 2 | 0 | 0 |
| Total | | 3 | 1 | 2 | 0 | 0 |

| | GP | GG | GF | GS | TGR |
|---|---|---|---|---|---|
| 96-97 | 7.89 | 0.00 | 44 | 0 | 0.00 |
| Averages | 7.89 | 0.00 | 44.00 | 0.00 | 0.00 |

## HINCHCLIFFE, Andy

## Everton   ①②③④⑤    FB

Fullname: Andrew George Hinchcliffe
DOB:      05-02-69 Manchester

Defender in his eighth season at
Goodison Park but has really come to the
fore in recent seasons for the almost
monotonous regularity with which his
dead ball kicks hit their intended target.
Particularly lethal at corners and
contributed greatly to Everton's 1995 FA
Cup victory. England Youth and Under-21
international who was a professional at
Manchester City for four years prior to a
bargain £800,000 transfer to Everton in
July 1990. Has made over 330
appearances for his two clubs and would
have made well over 200 appearances for
Everton alone had injury not restricted
him to just 18 Premiership matches
during 1996-97 and put a hold on his full
England career which began under Glenn
Hoddle last year.

When fit, will be one of the first names
Howard Kendall puts on his teamsheet.

### Form Factors

| Season | Team | Tot | St | Sb | Y | R |
|--------|------|-----|-----|-----|-----|-----|
| 94-95 | Everton | 29 | 28 | 1 | 2 | 0 |
| 95-96 | Everton | 28 | 23 | 5 | 4 | 0 |
| 96-97 | Everton | 18 | 18 | 0 | 2 | 0 |
| Total | | 75 | 69 | 6 | 8 | 0 |

| | GP | GG | GF | GS | TGR |
|--------|------|------|------|-----|------|
| 94-95 | 69.05 | 14.50 | 44 | 2 | 4.55 |
| 95-96 | 73.68 | 14.00 | 64 | 2 | 3.13 |
| 96-97 | 47.37 | 18.00 | 44 | 1 | 2.27 |
| Averages | 63.37 | 15.50 | 50.67 | 1.67 | 3.31 |

## HIRST, David

## Sheffield W.    ❶    S

Fullname: David Eric Hirst
DOB:      07-12-67 Cudworth

One of the most highly respected
strikers in the Premiership although his
goals per game ratio may not always
support his reputation. That said, when
fully fit there are few better forwards in
the Premiership. A former apprentice
with Barnsley, he was snapped up by
Sheffield Wednesday in 1986 for
£200,000 after just one season and nine
goals in 28 games at Oakwell. Between
the start of the 1989-90 and his final
appearance of the 1992-93 season, he
scored 67 goals in just 134 league games,
an effort which earned him three caps

*David Hirst*

with England. If he can avoid injury during 1997-98 then his partnership with Carbone and Booth could be one of the most threatening in the Premiership although speculation of a move, with the likes of Barnsley and Middlesbrough being amongst likely bidders, continued at the time of writing.

## Form Factors

| Season | Team | Tot | St | Sb | Y | R |
|---|---|---|---|---|---|---|
| 94-95 | Sheffield W. | 15 | 13 | 2 | 2 | 0 |
| 95-96 | Sheffield W. | 30 | 29 | 1 | 1 | 1 |
| 96-97 | Sheffield W. | 25 | 20 | 5 | 3 | 1 |
| Total | | 70 | 62 | 8 | 6 | 2 |

| | GP | GG | GF | GS | TGR |
|---|---|---|---|---|---|
| 94-95 | 35.71 | 5.00 | 49 | 3 | 6.12 |
| 95-96 | 78.95 | 2.31 | 48 | 13 | 27.08 |
| 96-97 | 65.79 | 4.17 | 50 | 6 | 12.00 |
| Averages | 60.15 | 3.82 | 49.00 | 7.33 | 15.07 |

## HISLOP, Shaka

# Newcastle U. ❶ GK

Fullname: Neil Hislop
DOB: 22-02-69 London

Named after the African King, Shaka Zulu, the six foot six 'keeper was signed from Reading for £1.5 million in the summer of 1995 as the then manager Kevin Keegan looked to shore up the number one position. Challenging with Pavel Srnicek for the job, neither was able to hold down the position. Considered erratic but often brilliant, he played in the unsuccessful first part of the 1996-97 season when Srnicek was suspended but only managed sixteen appearances in the Premiership and six in the cups.

Started his career at Reading playing over 100 games for the side before his move north. The arrival of Shay Given from Blackburn Rovers must threaten the position of one of United's 'keepers.

## Form Factors

| Season | Team | Tot | St | Sb | Y | R |
|---|---|---|---|---|---|---|
| 95-96 | Newcastle | 24 | 24 | 0 | 0 | 0 |
| 96-97 | Newcastle | 16 | 16 | 0 | 0 | 0 |
| Total | | 40 | 40 | 0 | 0 | 0 |

| | GA | GkA | GAp | CS | SO | Rp |
|---|---|---|---|---|---|---|
| 95-96 | 37 | 19 | 0.79 | 8 | 3 | 0 |
| 96-97 | 40 | 21 | 1.31 | 3 | 1 | 0 |
| Total | 77 | 40 | 1.00 | 11 | 4 | – |

## HITCHCOCK, Kevin

# Chelsea ❶ GK

Fullname: Kevin Joseph Hitchcock
DOB: 05-10-62 Canning Town

Kevin Hitchcock is in danger of becoming known as the Dozen-man given the fact that in the past three seasons he has featured in 12 of Chelsea's Premiership games. He started the 1996-97 season as reserve to Dimitri Kharine, but when the Russian was injured at the start of the season, manager Gullit imported Frode Grodas to take over the first team role.

Having previously played at Nottingham Forest and Mansfield Town, Hitchcock joined Chelsea in March 1988.

## Form Factors

| Season | Team | Tot | St | Sb | Y | R |
|---|---|---|---|---|---|---|
| 94-95 | Chelsea | 12 | 11 | 1 | 0 | 0 |
| 95-96 | Chelsea | 12 | 12 | 0 | 0 | 0 |
| 96-97 | Chelsea | 12 | 10 | 2 | 1 | 0 |
| Total | | 36 | 33 | 3 | 1 | 0 |

| | GA | GkA | GAp | CS | SO | Rp |
|---|---|---|---|---|---|---|
| 94-95 | 55 | 9 | 0.75 | 0 | 0 | 0 |
| 95-96 | 44 | 15 | 1.25 | 2 | 2 | 0 |
| 96-97 | 55 | 18 | 1.50 | 0 | 0 | 0 |
| Total | 154 | 42 | 1.17 | 2 | 2 | – |

## HOLDSWORTH, Dean

# Wimbledon ❶❷❸     S

Fullname: Dean Christopher Holdsworth
DOB: 08-11-68 London

Holdsworth's long-term future at Wimbledon seemed under threat last year. No less than 15 of his 25 appearances came from the substitutes' bench, which will have hindered his contribution of goals – just five. Prior to this he was arguably one of the most sought after strikers in England with his close control and heading ability typifying his general all-round game.

Started his career at Watford where his twin brother, David, was a regular and arrived at Wimbledon from Brentford in 1989 after periods on loan at a variety of lower division clubs.

Back problems have also hindered Holdsworth's performances which might have otherwise resulted in international recognition.

## Form Factors

| Season | Team | Tot | St | Sb | Y | R |
|---|---|---|---|---|---|---|
| 94-95 | Wimbledon | 28 | 27 | 1 | 5 | 0 |
| 95-96 | Wimbledon | 33 | 31 | 2 | 7 | 1 |
| 96-97 | Wimbledon | 25 | 10 | 15 | 0 | 0 |
| Total | | 86 | 68 | 18 | 12 | 1 |

| | GP | GG | GF | GS | TGR |
|---|---|---|---|---|---|
| 94-95 | 66.67 | 4.00 | 48 | 7 | 14.58 |
| 95-96 | 86.84 | 3.30 | 55 | 10 | 18.18 |
| 96-97 | 65.79 | 5.00 | 49 | 5 | 10.20 |
| Averages | 73.10 | 4.10 | 50.67 | 7.33 | 14.32 |

## HOLMES, Matty

# Blackburn Rovers ❶❷     M

Fullname: Matthew Jason Holmes
DOB: 01-08-69 Luton

During the past three years, Holmes has figured less and less in the Premiership. Having made 34 and then 24 appearances for West Ham United in the 1993-94 and 1994-95 seasons respectively. Following just eight appearances in 1995-96 he was confined to the reserves last season, not least because of the acquisition of Lars Bohinen.

A £1.2 million signing from West Ham, he is a hard-running midfield player. Having failed to even make the bench in the Premiership during 1996-97 he will be looking to impress new manager Roy Hodgson early on.

## Form Factors

| Season | Team | Tot | St | Sb | Y | R |
|---|---|---|---|---|---|---|
| 93-94 | West Ham | 34 | 33 | 1 | 1 | 0 |
| 94-95 | West Ham | 24 | 24 | 0 | 4 | 0 |
| 95-96 | Blackburn | 8 | 7 | 1 | 1 | 0 |
| Total | | 66 | 64 | 2 | 6 | 0 |

| | GP | GG | GF | GS | TGR |
|---|---|---|---|---|---|
| 93-94 | 80.95 | 11.33 | 47 | 3 | 6.38 |
| 94-95 | 57.14 | 24.00 | 44 | 1 | 2.27 |
| 95-96 | 21.05 | 8.00 | 61 | 1 | 1.64 |
| Averages | 53.05 | 14.44 | 50.67 | 1.67 | 3.43 |

## HOPKIN, David

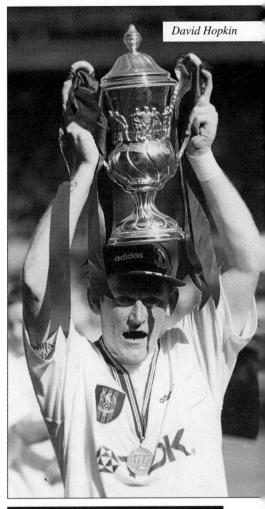

*David Hopkin*

# Crystal Palace ❶❷❸❹　M

Fullname: David Hopkin
DOB:　21-08-70 Greenock
　His performances for Crystal Palace during the later stages of the 1996-97 season have made David Hopkin one of the hottest properties around and it remains to be seen if the Eagles can hang onto one of their gems.
　A deep-lying attacking midfield player with an eye for goal, Hopkin contributed 13 goals in his 41 appearances last season and scored a quite memorable last-minute winner to clinch the play-off final victory over Sheffield United and the Eagles' Premiership spot.
　Started his career in Scotland before moving to Chelsea in September 1992 where he played 40 Premiership games from 1993 to 1995 – but scored only one goal. He moved to Selhurst Park in the 1995 closeseason for £850,000 and has become a firm favourite since, especially with his aggressive style of play. He is Palace's second longest-serving player.

### Form Factors

| Season | Team | Tot | St | Sb | Y | R |
|---|---|---|---|---|---|---|
| 92-93 | Chelsea | 4 | 2 | 2 | 0 | 0 |
| 93-94 | Chelsea | 21 | 12 | 9 | 1 | 0 |
| 94-95 | Chelsea | 15 | 7 | 8 | 0 | 0 |
| Total | | 40 | 21 | 19 | 1 | 0 |

| | GP | GG | GF | GS | TGR |
|---|---|---|---|---|---|
| 92-93 | 9.52 | 0.00 | 51 | 0 | 0.00 |
| 93-94 | 50.00 | 0.00 | 49 | 0 | 0.00 |
| 94-95 | 35.71 | 15.00 | 50 | 1 | 2.00 |
| Averages | 31.75 | 5.00 | 50.00 | 0.33 | 0.67 |

## HOTTIGER, Marc

# Everton ❶❷　FB

Fullname: Marc Hottiger
DOB:　07-11-67 Lausanne, Switzerland
　Very experienced Swiss international defender with more than 60 caps under his belt. Hottiger is a composed full-back, a fact supported by his exemplary disciplinary record, and when going forward a fine crosser of the ball.

*Ray Houghton*

## Form Factors

| Season | Team | Tot | St | Sb | Y | R |
|--------|------|-----|----|----|----|---|
| 95-96 | Newcastle | 1 | 0 | 1 | 0 | 0 |
| 95-96 | Everton | 9 | 9 | 0 | 0 | 0 |
| 96-97 | Everton | 8 | 4 | 4 | 0 | 0 |
| Total | | 18 | 13 | 5 | 0 | 0 |

| | GP | GG | GF | GS | TGR |
|---|----|----|----|----|-----|
| 95-96 | 2.63 | 0.00 | 66 | 0 | 0.00 |
| 95-96 | 23.68 | 9.00 | 64 | 1 | 1.56 |
| 96-97 | 21.05 | 0.00 | 44 | 0 | 0.00 |
| Averages | 15.79 | 3.00 | 58.00 | 0.33 | 0.52 |

## HOUGHTON, Ray

# Crystal Palace ❶❷ M

Fullname: Raymond James Houghton
DOB: 09-01-62 Glasgow

There are few more experienced players than Ray Houghton, who secured numerous medals during his five year stay at Liverpool. Following three seasons at Aston Villa, the Irish international moved to Selhurst Park for £300,000 in March 1995.

Houghton's bustling midfield style and his vast experience have been a key in the development of a young Crystal Palace side. Outstanding during the 1995-96 season, he was troubled by injury throughout the 1996-97 season, a fact that limited his role to 21 Division One appearances.

However, with over 100 Premiership appearances behind him, he is sure to remain a big influence this season, especially on the field, if the injury problems abate.

Born in the Swiss town of Lausanne, he played in over 100 games for the town's club prior to joining Sion from whence, after two seasons, he joined Newcastle United in a £520,000 deal. Just over a season later he switched to Goodison Park at a cost to Everton of £700,000. Injury has restricted his appearances but he also spent much of the season on the Blues' bench – a non-playing sub on no less than 22 occasions.

## Form Factors

| Season | Team | Tot | St | Sb | Y | R |
|--------|------|-----|----|----|----|---|
| 93-94 | Aston Villa | 30 | 25 | 5 | 0 | 0 |
| 94-95 | Aston Villa | 26 | 19 | 7 | 1 | 0 |
| 94-95 | C. Palace | 10 | 10 | 0 | 1 | 0 |
| Total | | 66 | 54 | 12 | 2 | 0 |

*Russell Hoult*

|         | GP    | GG    | GF    | GS   | TGR  |
|---------|-------|-------|-------|------|------|
| 93-94   | 71.43 | 15.00 | 46    | 2    | 4.35 |
| 94-95   | 61.90 | 26.00 | 51    | 1    | 1.96 |
| 94-95   | 61.90 | 13.00 | 34    | 2    | 5.88 |
| Averages| 65.08 | 18.00 | 43.67 | 1.67 | 4.06 |

## HOULT, Russell

# Derby County ❶ GK

Fullname: Russell Hoult
DOB: 28-03-71 Leicester

Goalkeeper who has experienced a remarkable transformation in his fortunes since making a £300,000 move from Leicester City to Derby County in February 1995. During five seasons at Filbert Street he made just ten league appearances for the Foxes and a further 21 whilst on loan to Lincoln City and Bolton. Was immediately installed as first choice 'keeper at the Baseball Ground, missing just five games during their promotion campaign and played 32 times in the Premiership last season, keeping six clean sheets. His 6'4" frame makes him strong in the air and, at 26-years old, he is likely to be behind the Rams' defence for quite some time to come, although he will face stiff competition from the Estonian 'keeper Mart Poom, who arrived at Derby prior to last season's transfer deadline.

## Form Factors

| Season | Team      | Tot | St | Sb | Y | R |
|--------|-----------|-----|----|----|---|---|
| 96-97  | Derby Co. | 32  | 31 | 1  | 0 | 0 |
| Total  |           | 32  | 31 | 1  | 0 | 0 |

|        | GA | GkA | GAp  | CS | SO | Rp |
|--------|----|-----|------|----|----|----|
| 96-97  | 58 | 48  | 1.50 | 6  | 1  | 0  |
| Total  | 58 | 48  | 1.50 | 6  | 1  | –  |

## HOWELLS, David

### Tottenham H. ❶❷❸ M

Fullname: David Howells
DOB: 15-12-67 Guildford

Now in his 13th season at White Hart Lane and seems to grow in stature and influence with every passing season. Plays the defensive role in the Tottenham Hotspur midfield but manages to get forward to score the occasional goal.

Has a quiet, unassuming nature but revels in his tireless midfield duties where he has really come to the fore since Gerry Francis' arrival at the club.

Played in 84% of Spurs' Premiership matches last season and will certainly play a leading role in the 1997-98 as Tottenham look to improve their dipping fortunes. Has played for England at three youth levels but his major honour is an FA Cup winners medal in 1991.

### Form Factors

| Season | Team | Tot | St | Sb | Y | R |
|---|---|---|---|---|---|---|
| 94-95 | Tottenham | 26 | 26 | 0 | 2 | 0 |
| 95-96 | Tottenham | 29 | 29 | 0 | 6 | 0 |
| 96-97 | Tottenham | 32 | 32 | 0 | 7 | 0 |
| Total | | 87 | 87 | 0 | 15 | 0 |

| | GP | GG | GF | GS | TGR |
|---|---|---|---|---|---|
| 94-95 | 61.90 | 26.00 | 66 | 1 | 1.52 |
| 95-96 | 76.32 | 9.67 | 50 | 3 | 6.00 |
| 96-97 | 84.21 | 16.00 | 44 | 2 | 4.55 |
| Averages | 74.14 | 17.22 | 53.33 | 2.00 | 4.02 |

## HOWEY, Steve

### Newcastle U. ❶❷❸❹❺ CB

Fullname: Stephen Norman Howey
DOB: 26-10-71 Sunderland

Steve Howey joined Newcastle as a trainee in December 1989 where he played at centre forward like his older brother Lee at Sunderland. He eventually switched from attack to defence and it resulted in his becoming a regular in both the 1994-95 and 1995-96 seasons.

With four England caps, he was in the squad for Euro '96 but was ruled out of the entire tournament by injury. Only eight appearances followed in the Premiership in 1996-97 as the tall commanding centre half was again troubled by injury – reoccurrence of a calf problem which has required a fourth operation. If he is fit then he will certainly be looking to re-establish his credentials in 1997-98, at which point he is due to become a regular in Kenny Dalglish's team, and perhaps your's for that matter!

### Form Factors

| Season | Team | Tot | St | Sb | Y | R |
|---|---|---|---|---|---|---|
| 94-95 | Newcastle | 30 | 29 | 1 | 5 | 0 |
| 95-96 | Newcastle | 28 | 28 | 0 | 2 | 0 |
| 96-97 | Newcastle | 8 | 8 | 0 | 0 | 0 |
| Total | | 66 | 65 | 1 | 7 | 0 |

| | GP | GG | GF | GS | TGR |
|---|---|---|---|---|---|
| 94-95 | 71.43 | 30.00 | 67 | 1 | 1.49 |
| 95-96 | 73.68 | 28.00 | 66 | 1 | 1.52 |
| 96-97 | 21.05 | 8.00 | 73 | 1 | 1.37 |
| Averages | 55.37 | 22.00 | 68.67 | 1.00 | 1.46 |

## HRISTOV, Georgi

### Barnsley ❶❷❸ S

Fullname: Georgi Hristov
DOB: nk

One of the first summer signings by Danny Wilson, looking to strengthen his side for life in the Premiership. His £1.5 million fee was a record for the club and the 21-year-old FYR Macedonian striker already has a good track record, having led his former club Partizan to a third successive Yugoslav championship.

Already in double figures for international caps, he scored on his national debut against Armenia and also netted the winner in Macedonia's 3-2 win over the Republic of Ireland in the World Cup qualifying competition.

## HUCKERBY, Darren

### Coventry City ❶❷❸❹ S

Fullname: Darren Carl Huckerby
DOB: 27-04-76 Nottingham

Newcastle's decision to dispense with a reserve side last season might well have been Coventry's gain. Not able to secure a first team spot at St. James Park and with little football available to him – just one substitute appearance during 1995-96 – Huckerby tripped south to Highfield Road and was an instant success. His £1 million transfer to Coventry City last November resulted in a flurry of goals and some scintillating performances. He quickly set about repaying the transfer fee with the first installment for Coventry being the opening goal in the Sky Blues' 2-1 win over the Magpies in December. Has an almost unique swash-buckling style and, at just 21 years old, he has the pace, strength and ability to be one of the hot properties of 1997-98. Made his Football League debut with Lincoln City prior to a £400,000 move to Newcastle in November 1995.

### Form Factors

| Season | Team | Tot | St | Sb | Y | R |
|---|---|---|---|---|---|---|
| 95-96 | Newcastle | 1 | 0 | 1 | 0 | 0 |
| 96-97 | Coventry C. | 25 | 21 | 4 | 2 | 0 |
| Total | | 26 | 21 | 5 | 2 | 0 |

| | GP | GG | GF | GS | TGR |
|---|---|---|---|---|---|
| 95-96 | 2.63 | 0.00 | 66 | 0 | 0.00 |
| 96-97 | 65.79 | 5.00 | 38 | 5 | 13.16 |
| Averages | 34.21 | 2.50 | 52.00 | 2.50 | 6.58 |

## HUGHES, David

### Southampton ❶ M

Fullname: David Robert Hughes
DOB: 30-12-72 St Albans

Last season was a disappointing one for Hughes who was sidelined for much of the season with back problems. Joined Southampton as a junior and made his first appearance in the Premiership during the 1993-94 season. With a couple of handfuls of games in each of the following seasons, he was expected to become an important member of the Saints squad last season.

A Welsh under-21 international, he was called into the full squad before his injury changed the course of his season. Of his 29 Premiership appearances, 20 have come from the bench.

A hard-working, skilful midfield player with an eye for goal, Hughes will be looking to the 1997-98 season with the intention of fulfilling his undoubted potential.

## Form Factors

| Season | Team | Tot | St | Sb | Y | R |
|---|---|---|---|---|---|---|
| 94-95 | Southampton | 12 | 2 | 10 | 2 | 0 |
| 95-96 | Southampton | 11 | 6 | 5 | 1 | 0 |
| 96-97 | Southampton | 6 | 1 | 5 | 1 | 0 |
| Total | | 29 | 9 | 20 | 4 | 0 |

| | GP | GG | GF | GS | TGR |
|---|---|---|---|---|---|
| 94-95 | 28.57 | 6.00 | 61 | 2 | 3.28 |
| 95-96 | 28.95 | 11.00 | 34 | 1 | 2.94 |
| 96-97 | 28.95 | 0.00 | 50 | 0 | 0.00 |
| Averages | 28.82 | 5.67 | 48.33 | 1.00 | 2.07 |

| | GP | GG | GF | GS | TGR |
|---|---|---|---|---|---|
| 94-95 | 80.95 | 4.25 | 77 | 8 | 10.39 |
| 95-96 | 81.58 | 3.88 | 46 | 8 | 17.39 |
| 96-97 | 92.11 | 4.38 | 58 | 8 | 13.79 |
| Averages | 84.88 | 4.17 | 60.33 | 8.00 | 13.86 |

## HUGHES, Michael

### West Ham U. ❶❷ M

Fullname: Michael Eamonn Hughes
DOB: 02-08-71 Larne

Missed just five games for the Hammers last season, Hughes is a midfield player who is generally used out wide on either flank where he can also run at opponents defences.

Started his career at Manchester City before moving to French club Strasbourg

## HUGHES, Mark

### Chelsea ❶❷❸❹❺ S

Fullname: Leslie Mark Hughes
DOB: 01-11-63 Wrexham

Despite the arrival of foreign stars Mark 'Sparky' Hughes is without doubt one of Chelsea's best captures and, at 33 years of age, still looks a snip at £1.5 million. After a glittering career at Old Trafford which saw two Premiership titles, three FA Cups, one League Cup and a Cup-Winners' Cup, he moved to Stamford Bridge and added another FA Cup victory to his total within two seasons.

He is a consistent goalscorer in the Premiership and has managed eight in each of the past three seasons. While this may seem a small tally for a striker, his unselfish play results in plenty of assists for players around him.

A down side of his play has been his aggressive nature, but he went some way to curbing the wrath of the referees last season which saw just six yellow cards.

## Form Factors

| Season | Team | Tot | St | Sb | Y | R |
|---|---|---|---|---|---|---|
| 94-95 | Man. Utd | 34 | 33 | 1 | 7 | 1 |
| 95-96 | Chelsea | 31 | 31 | 0 | 12 | 1 |
| 96-97 | Chelsea | 35 | 32 | 3 | 6 | 0 |
| Total | | 100 | 96 | 4 | 25 | 2 |

*Mark Hughes*

where he played for two years before joining West Ham on a loan arrangement that eventually ended with him transferring to East London for £450,000.

On the down side is his apparent shyness in front of goal – his 78 Premiership appearances reaping just five goals.

Born in Larne, Hughes is an established Northern Ireland international and an important member of the West Ham side.

## Form Factors

| Season | Team | Tot | St | Sb | Y | R |
|---|---|---|---|---|---|---|
| 94-95 | West Ham | 17 | 15 | 2 | 0 | 0 |
| 95-96 | West Ham | 28 | 28 | 0 | 1 | 0 |
| 96-97 | West Ham | 33 | 31 | 2 | 5 | 0 |
| Total | | 78 | 74 | 4 | 6 | 0 |

| | GP | GG | GF | GS | TGR |
|---|---|---|---|---|---|
| 94-95 | 40.48 | 8.50 | 44 | 2 | 4.55 |
| 95-96 | 73.68 | 0.00 | 43 | 0 | 0.00 |
| 96-97 | 86.84 | 11.00 | 39 | 3 | 7.69 |
| Averages | 67.00 | 6.50 | 42.00 | 1.67 | 4.08 |

## HUGHES, Paul

# Chelsea    ❶❷    M

Fullname: Paul Hughes
DOB: 19-04-76 Hammersmith

While the news is about Chelsea's international signings, Paul Hughes is another youngster from the Chelsea youth camp who broke through into the Blues' first team last season. Born locally in Hammersmith, Hughes showed that he can be both a tenacious and creative player in his 12 appearances in the Premier League. He certainly made an impact coming on as a substitute against Derby in January and scoring straight away. A case of start as you mean to go on!

*Michael Hughes*

## Form Factors

| Season | Team | Tot | St | Sb | Y | R |
|---|---|---|---|---|---|---|
| 96-97 | Chelsea | 12 | 8 | 4 | 1 | 0 |
| Total | | 12 | 8 | 4 | 1 | 0 |

| | GP | GG | GF | GS | TGR |
|---|---|---|---|---|---|
| 96-97 | 31.58 | 6.00 | 58 | 2 | 3.45 |
| Averages | 31.58 | 6.00 | 58.00 | 2.00 | 3.45 |

## HUGHES, Steve

# Arsenal    ❶❷❸❹    M

Fullname: Stephen John Hughes
DOB: 18-09-76 Reading

A four star rating for a virtually unknown player? Stephen Hughes is highly regarded at Arsenal and there are many pundits in the game that fancy him to break into the full England squad this season, provided he can force himself into the Arsenal starting line-up.

A skilful, pacey left-sided midfield player who possesses a venomous shot, the 20-year-old debuted for the Gunners in 1994-95, but started to become a regular in the Gunners line-up last season when he made 14 appearances and scored his first Premiership goal.

An England Under-21 regular, Hughes could be a worthwhile gamble player who could return his fair share of fantasy points, especially as he is likely to be relatively cheap.

## Form Factors

| Season | Team | Tot | St | Sb | Y | R |
|---|---|---|---|---|---|---|
| 94-95 | Arsenal | 1 | 1 | 0 | 0 | 0 |
| 95-96 | Arsenal | 1 | 0 | 1 | 0 | 0 |
| 96-97 | Arsenal | 14 | 9 | 5 | 1 | 0 |
| Total | | 16 | 10 | 6 | 1 | 0 |

| | GP | GG | GF | GS | TGR |
|---|---|---|---|---|---|
| 94-95 | 2.38 | 0.00 | 52 | 0 | 0.00 |
| 95-96 | 2.63 | 0.00 | 49 | 0 | 0.00 |
| 96-97 | 36.84 | 14.00 | 62 | 1 | 1.61 |
| Averages | 13.95 | 4.67 | 54.33 | 0.33 | 0.54 |

## HUMPHREYS, Ritchie

# Sheffield W.          ❶❷❸          S

Fullname:  Richard John Humphreys
DOB:

Teenager with a terrifically bright future ahead of him providing the vast forward strides made over the past two seasons are maintained. Nurtured through the ranks at Hillsborough, he made his Sheffield Wednesday debut at Queens Park Rangers in September 1995. Only four more league games were played that season but during 1996-97 he announced his arrival in style. His first goal in the Premiership came courtesy of a very

reliable left foot, in a 2-0 victory at county rivals Leeds, and although 15 of his 29 league appearances last season came from the subs' bench, he did well when standing in for the injured David Hirst and may well be his ultimate replacement.

## Form Factors

| Season | Team | Tot | St | Sb | Y | R |
|---|---|---|---|---|---|---|
| 95-96 | Sheffield W. | 5 | 1 | 4 | 0 | 0 |
| 96-97 | Sheffield W. | 29 | 14 | 15 | 2 | 0 |
| Total | | 34 | 15 | 19 | 2 | 0 |

| | GP | GG | GF | GS | TGR |
|---|---|---|---|---|---|
| 95-96 | 13.16 | 0.00 | 48 | 0 | 0.00 |
| 96-97 | 76.32 | 9.67 | 50 | 3 | 6.00 |
| Averages | 44.74 | 4.83 | 49.00 | 1.50 | 3.00 |

## HYDE, Graham

# Sheffield W.          ❶❷❸          M

Fullname:  Graham Hyde
DOB:        10-11-70 Doncaster

Former Sheffield Wednesday youngster who has played over 160 games for the club since breaking into the first team back in 1992. Has not figured as strongly in David Pleat's plans as he did with Trevor Francis but still made 19 Premiership appearances last season, scoring two goals from midfield.

A hard working player, Hyde has improved his game considerably in the past two seasons, not least in his passing which is now reliable and accurate.

Born in Yorkshire, he joined Wednesday as a trainee in the summer of 1988 and is one of the most popular players with the fans at Hillsborough.

## Form Factors

| Season | Team | Tot | St | Sb | Y | R |
|---|---|---|---|---|---|---|
| 93-94 | Sheffield W. | 36 | 27 | 9 | 1 | 0 |
| 94-95 | Sheffield W. | 35 | 33 | 2 | 7 | 0 |
| 95-96 | Sheffield W. | 26 | 14 | 12 | 2 | 0 |
| Total | | 97 | 74 | 23 | 10 | 0 |

| | GP | GG | GF | GS | TGR |
|---|---|---|---|---|---|
| 93-94 | 85.71 | 36.00 | 76 | 1 | 1.32 |
| 94-95 | 83.33 | 7.00 | 49 | 5 | 10.20 |
| 95-96 | 92.11 | 35.00 | 48 | 1 | 2.08 |
| Averages | 87.05 | 26.00 | 57.67 | 2.33 | 4.53 |

## IRWIN, Denis

# Manchester U. ❶❷❸❹❺ FB

Fullname:  Joseph Denis Irwin
DOB:  31-10-65 Cork

It's hard to recall a defensive mistake by Dennis Irwin and difficult to imagine him ever having a bad game for United, such is his consistency. He can operate equally well on either side of defence in the full-back positions and has also deputised in central defence. He currently commands the left flank and puts in accurate passes and crosses to his front men.

A veteran of many a Republic of Ireland campaign, Irwin remains an important part of any defence he performs in and his experience rubs off on younger colleagues. Although at the wrong end of his career (he should complete his 200th Premiership game in 97-98), Irwin is likely to remain a regular performer in what should be an outstanding season for United in 1997-98.

## Form Factors

| Season | Team | Tot | St | Sb | Y | R |
|---|---|---|---|---|---|---|
| 94-95 | Man. Utd | 40 | 40 | 0 | 1 | 0 |
| 95-96 | Man. Utd | 31 | 31 | 0 | 4 | 0 |
| 96-97 | Man. Utd | 31 | 29 | 2 | 1 | 0 |
| Total | | 102 | 100 | 2 | 6 | 0 |

| | GP | GG | GF | GS | TGR |
|---|---|---|---|---|---|
| 94-95 | 95.24 | 20.00 | 77 | 2 | 2.60 |
| 95-96 | 81.58 | 31.00 | 73 | 1 | 1.37 |
| 96-97 | 81.58 | 31.00 | 76 | 1 | 1.32 |
| Averages | 86.13 | 27.33 | 75.33 | 1.33 | 1.76 |

*Stefan Iversen*

## IVERSEN, Steffen

# Tottenham H. ❶❷❸❹ S

Fullname:  Steffen Iversen
DOB:

Tottenham manager Gerry Francis was kept waiting in his efforts to sign the Norwegian international as he pursued a Champions' Cup dream with his former club Rosenborg last season. The wait was justified in the end with the £2.7m striker scoring six times in 16 Premiership matches – a strike rate of about a goal every three games – including a classy hat

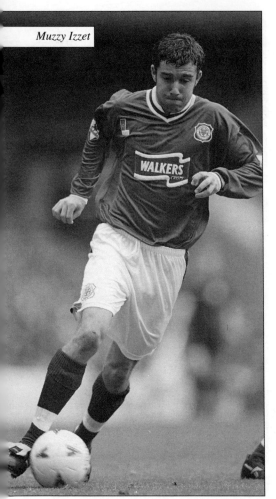

*Muzzy Izzet*

## Form Factors

| Season Team | | Tot | St | Sb | Y | R |
|---|---|---|---|---|---|---|
| 96-97 | Tottenham | 16 | 16 | 0 | 1 | 0 |
| Total | | 16 | 16 | 0 | 1 | 0 |
| | GP | GG | GF | | GS | TGR |
| 96-97 | 42.11 | 2.67 | 44 | | 6 | 13.64 |
| Averages | 42.11 | 2.67 | 44.00 | | 6.00 | 13.64 |

## IZZET, Muzzy

## Leicester City  ❶❷❸  M

Fullname: Mustafa Izzet
DOB: 31-10-74 Mile End, London

Midfielder who blossomed in his first season in the Premiership, having joined Leicester City firstly on loan and then in an £800,000 transfer from Chelsea. Muzzy never made the first team at Stamford Bridge but had already caught the eye of Foxes' manager Martin O'Neill. Scored once in nine games during the promotion run-in and added three more goals in 35 Premiership matches last season. His goal against Watford in May 1996 pretty much secured his future at Leicester as it was the goal which took the club into the play-offs. A good season now could see him gain international recognition with Turkey.

A solid player but not one who is going to score you points in vast quantities.

trick at Roker Park against a struggling Sunderland team. Goals should come easy to Iversen as his father is the all-time top scorer in Norway's first division!

As Spurs go through a transitional period, his few months with the club during last season should prove invaluable experience in 1997-98 when he could well become one of the star players in the Premiership.

## Form Factors

| Season Team | | Tot | St | Sb | Y | R |
|---|---|---|---|---|---|---|
| 96-97 | Leicester C. | 35 | 34 | 1 | 6 | 0 |
| Total | | 35 | 34 | 1 | 6 | 0 |
| | GP | GG | GF | | GS | TGR |
| 96-97 | 92.11 | 11.67 | 46 | | 3 | 6.52 |
| Averages | 92.11 | 11.67 | 46.00 | | 3.00 | 6.52 |

## JACKSON, Mark

# Leeds Utd ❶❷ CB

**Fullname:** Mark Graham Jackson
**DOB:** 30-09-77 Leeds

A product of the Leeds United youth system, Jackson made his breakthrough onto the Premiership scene during 1995-96 when he appeared as a sub against Middlesbrough late in the season. An England Youth international, Jackson furthered his career at the heart of the Leeds defence last season with a further 17 appearances. He was also an unused sub on 11 other occasions which suggests he will play another role as part of the United squad during 1997-98.

## Form Factors

| Season | Team | Tot | St | Sb | Y | R |
|---|---|---|---|---|---|---|
| 95-96 | Leeds Utd | 1 | 0 | 1 | 0 | 0 |
| 96-97 | Leeds Utd | 17 | 11 | 6 | 1 | 0 |
| Total | | 18 | 11 | 7 | 1 | 0 |

|  | GP | GG | GF | GS | TGR |
|---|---|---|---|---|---|
| 95-96 | 2.63 | 0.00 | 40 | 0 | 0.00 |
| 96-97 | 44.74 | 0.00 | 28 | 0 | 0.00 |
| Averages | 23.68 | 0.00 | 34.00 | 0.00 | 0.00 |

## JAMES, David

# Liverpool ❶❷❸❹❺ GK

**Fullname:** David Benjamin James
**DOB:** 01-08-70
Welwyn Garden City

A physically imposing goalkeeper at 6'5", with an excellent record, James ended the 1996-97 season with some less than impressive displays. This was perhaps part of Liverpool's overall decline but it put a question mark against James for the first time in three seasons as an ever-present.

After signing from Watford for £1 million in 1992, James got his chances between Grobbelaar and Hooper before making the spot his own. His goals per

*David James*

game ratio is under 1, which makes him the third most effective Premiership goalkeeper. He has kept a clean sheet in just over a third of all his 161 appearances. His club success has been rewarded with a regular place in Glenn Hoddle's England squad and he was capped for the first time against Mexico in March 1997.

In 1996-97 the stats show that James kept 12 clean sheets, including five in a row, so the impression left by the end of the season performances is probably not to relied upon as a form guide. The likelihood is that James will be a regular player in a tight Liverpool defence and therefore an excellent fantasy team choice.

## Form Factors

| Season | Team | Tot | St | Sb | Y | R |
|---|---|---|---|---|---|---|
| 94-95 | Liverpool | 42 | 42 | 0 | 0 | 0 |
| 95-96 | Liverpool | 38 | 38 | 0 | 1 | 0 |
| 96-97 | Liverpool | 38 | 38 | 0 | 0 | 0 |
| Total | | 118 | 118 | 0 | 1 | 0 |

| | GA | GkA | GAp | CS | SO | Rp |
|---|---|---|---|---|---|---|
| 94-95 | 37 | 37 | 0.88 | 17 | 3 | 0 |
| 95-96 | 34 | 34 | 0.89 | 16 | 3 | 0 |
| 96-97 | 37 | 37 | 0.97 | 12 | 5 | 0 |
| Total | 108 | 108 | 0.92 | 45 | 11 | – |

# JOACHIM, Julian

## Aston Villa ❶❷❸ M

Fullname: Julian Kevin Joachim
DOB: 12-09-74 Peterborough

The England Under-21 international burst onto the scene with Leicester City a few years back. When Brian Little took over at Villa Park, Joachim was one of his first signings. However, since the move, he has failed to hold down any sort of regular spot, despite scoring on his debut. In fact, of his 26 appearances up until the end of last season, only seven were as part of the starting line-up. Employed at Leicester as an out-and-out winger, Villa's style of play has concentrated more on the use of wing-backs rather than dedicated wide flank players.

At just 22 years old the Peterborough-born player has time on his side and may yet prove to be the player that Villa paid £1.5 million for.

## Form Factors

| Season | Team | Tot | St | Sb | Y | R |
|---|---|---|---|---|---|---|
| 94-95 | Leicester C. | 15 | 11 | 4 | 0 | 0 |
| 95-96 | Aston Villa | 11 | 4 | 7 | 0 | 0 |
| 96-97 | Aston Villa | 15 | 3 | 12 | 0 | 0 |
| Total | | 41 | 18 | 23 | 0 | 0 |

| | GP | GG | GF | GS | TGR |
|---|---|---|---|---|---|
| 94-95 | 35.71 | 5.00 | 45 | 3 | 6.67 |
| 95-96 | 28.95 | 11.00 | 52 | 1 | 1.92 |
| 96-97 | 39.47 | 5.00 | 47 | 3 | 6.38 |
| Averages | 34.71 | 7.00 | 48.00 | 2.33 | 4.99 |

## JOBSON, Richard

### Leeds United ❶❷❸ CB

Fullname: Richard Ian Jobson
DOB: 09-05-63 Holderness

Now at the veteran stage of his career, he has found his opportunities limited by injury since making a £1 million move to Elland Road from Oldham Athletic in October 1995. A cruciate knee ligament injury has kept his appearances down to just 22 in two seasons, equating to less than a third of Leeds United's Premiership matches. Reliable and stylish defender whose league career started at Watford, following a move from non-league Burton Albion. He then had lengthy spells with Hull City and Oldham. Has played for England 'B' but the injury curtailed hopes of moving up to the senior squad. His ten appearances last season all came in the opening months before he was forced to have further surgery on his knee. Has played over 500 senior games.

### Form Factors

| Season | Team | Tot | St | Sb | Y | R |
|--------|------|-----|-----|-----|-----|-----|
| 93-94 | Oldham At. | 37 | 37 | 0 | 0 | 0 |
| 95-96 | Leeds Utd | 12 | 12 | 0 | 2 | 0 |
| 96-97 | Leeds Utd | 10 | 10 | 0 | 2 | 0 |
| Total | | 59 | 59 | 0 | 4 | 0 |

| | GP | GG | GF | GS | TGR |
|--------|-----|-----|-----|-----|-----|
| 93-94 | 88.10 | 7.40 | 42 | 5 | 11.90 |
| 95-96 | 31.58 | 12.00 | 40 | 1 | 2.50 |
| 96-97 | 31.58 | 0.00 | 28 | 0 | 0.00 |
| Averages | 50.42 | 6.47 | 36.67 | 2.00 | 4.80 |

## JOHANSEN, Michael

### Bolton W. ❶❷ M

Fullname: Michael Johansen
DOB: 22-07-76 Glostrup, Denmark

Johansen joined Bolton in the summer of 1996 in a £1 million deal that took him to Lancashire from FC Copenhagen in a move that has been successful for both club and player.

Has represented Denmark in Under-18, Under-21 and 'B' internationals and played in 32 of Wanderers' Division One games last season, contributing five goals to their cause.

Started his career with Rosenhoj and KB before signing for B1903 in 1991. The following year he was a member of the team that reached the quarter-finals of the Champions' Cup.

## JOHNSEN, Ronny

### Manchester U. ❶❷❸❹ CB

Fullname: Ronald Johnsen
DOB: 06-10-69

Formally Norway's most expensive player, Johnsen is a composed centre half who has pace and skill. Having built up a good relationship with United's other defenders, Johnsen looks to have the potential to become an integral part of Alex Ferguson's squad.

After his £1.2 million signing from Besiktas of Turkey, Johnsen immediately became a regular part of the Premiership team with 26 starts and five substitute appearances, failing to score but picking up only a couple of yellow cards. He can also play in midfield as he showed against Porto in United's Champions' Cup quarter final. Johnsen will form part of a Manchester United defence (and that of

Norway), which is usually reliable but which suffered a few strange set-backs in 1996-97.

## Form Factors

| Season | Team | Tot | St | Sb | Y | R |
|---|---|---|---|---|---|---|
| 96-97 | Man. Utd | 31 | 26 | 5 | 3 | 0 |
| Total | | 31 | 26 | 5 | 3 | 0 |

| | GP | GG | GF | GS | TGR |
|---|---|---|---|---|---|
| 96-97 | 81.58 | 0.00 | 76 | 0 | 0.00 |
| Averages | 81.58 | 0.00 | 76.00 | 0.00 | 0.00 |

| | GP | GG | GF | GS | TGR |
|---|---|---|---|---|---|
| 94-95 | 33.33 | 3.50 | 51 | 4 | 7.84 |
| 95-96 | 65.79 | 5.00 | 52 | 5 | 9.62 |
| 96-97 | 52.63 | 5.00 | 47 | 4 | 8.51 |
| Averages | 50.58 | 4.50 | 50.00 | 4.33 | 8.66 |

## JONES, Lee

### Liverpool ❶ S

Fullname: Philip Lee Jones
DOB: 29-05-73 Wrexham

Lee Jones is a young striker with exciting speed and potential. He scored regularly for the reserves and whilst on loan with his former club, Wrexham, during 1995-96, scoring 9 goals in 20 league and cup appearances. In 1996-97 he was on the subs' bench on 17 occasions, getting off it to play just twice. If he remains at Anfield he could possibly revive the David Fairclough role of super-sub for 1997-98.

## Form Factors

| Season | Team | Tot | St | Sb | Y | R |
|---|---|---|---|---|---|---|
| 94-95 | Liverpool | 1 | 0 | 1 | 0 | 0 |
| 96-97 | Liverpool | 2 | 0 | 2 | 0 | 0 |
| Total | | 3 | 0 | 3 | 0 | 0 |

| | GP | GG | GF | GS | TGR |
|---|---|---|---|---|---|
| 94-95 | 2.38 | 0.00 | 65 | 0 | 0.00 |
| 96-97 | 5.26 | 0.00 | 62 | 0 | 0.00 |
| Averages | 3.82 | 0.00 | 63.50 | 0.00 | 0.00 |

## JOHNSON, Tommy

### Aston Villa ❶❷❸ M

Fullname: Thomas Johnson
DOB: 15-01-71 Newcastle

When he was at Notts County Johnson had a scoring record that averaged a goal every two games or so. That encouraged Derby County to part with over £1.3 million to secure his services. Villa doubled that figure when he joined them and since that point his average has fallen to a goal every 4.5 games during the past three seasons, contributing less than 10% of their Premiership goals.

His quick reactions and pace always ensure that he is a handful for defenders but last season he struggled to hold down a regular spot, especially after suffering a thigh strain in the final part of the season. Recently he has battled with Savo Milosevic to determine who partners Dwight Yorke in the Villa attack. The arrival of Stan Collymore may make it even more difficult for the Geordie to secure a regular starting place.

## Form Factors

| Season | Team | Tot | St | Sb | Y | R |
|---|---|---|---|---|---|---|
| 94-95 | Aston Villa | 14 | 11 | 3 | 2 | 0 |
| 95-96 | Aston Villa | 25 | 19 | 6 | 5 | 0 |
| 96-97 | Aston Villa | 20 | 10 | 10 | 4 | 0 |
| Total | | 59 | 40 | 19 | 11 | 0 |

## JONES, Rob

### Liverpool ❶❷❸❹ FB

Fullname: Robert Marc Jones
DOB: 05-11-71 Wrexham

A dependable right-back, Jones was a regular in both the 1994-95 and 1995-96 seasons but managed only two starts in 1996-97 due to a long term back injury. He should now have recovered and will be looking to re-establish his name on the team sheet in a 4-4-2 formation. He is more likely to act as cover for the established wing-backs and his chances for Premiership football at Liverpool may be limited initially but he has the skill and pace to force his way back into contention.

These attributes earned him eight international caps and he can operate at left-back. Well-known for not scoring despite his forays into the penalty area.

### Form Factors

| Season | Team | Tot | St | Sb | Y | R |
|--------|------|-----|-----|-----|-----|-----|
| 94-95 | Liverpool | 31 | 31 | 0 | 5 | 0 |
| 95-96 | Liverpool | 33 | 33 | 0 | 2 | 0 |
| 96-97 | Liverpool | 2 | 2 | 0 | 1 | 0 |
| Total | | 66 | 66 | 0 | 8 | 0 |

| | GP | GG | GF | GS | TGR |
|--------|-----|-----|-----|-----|-----|
| 94-95 | 73.81 | 0.00 | 65 | 0 | 0.00 |
| 95-96 | 86.84 | 0.00 | 70 | 0 | 0.00 |
| 96-97 | 5.26 | 0.00 | 62 | 0 | 0.00 |
| Averages | 55.30 | 0.00 | 65.67 | 0.00 | 0.00 |

## JONES, Scott

### Barnsley ❶ FB

Fullname: Scott Jones
DOB: 01-05-75 Sheffield

Jones forced his way into the Barnsley team towards the end of the 1995-96 season and continued to knock on the door for inclusion last season. A left-footed defender, he played his part in 17 of Barnsley's games during 1996-97 including a run of seven consecutive games in the latter part of 1996.

Started as a trainee at Oakwell, signing for the club in the February of 1994.

## JONES, Vinnie

### Wimbledon ❶❷❸ M

Fullname: Vincent Peter Jones
DOB: 05-01-65 Watford

An uncompromising midfielder, the player whom all the opposing fans love to hate. A hard-working, hard-tackling player who always courts controversy and as such his ball-playing ability is often overlooked.

Now in his second spell at the club, following a three year period which saw him wear the colours of Leeds United, Sheffield United and Chelsea.

His disciplinary record invariably leads to a number of suspensions each year, but for which he would have probably been an ever-present in recent seasons. During the 1995-96 season he reached double figures for red cards.

More recently Jones was selected to play for the Welsh national side and was elected captain of his country by his fellow players for a World Cup qualifier against Holland which Wales lost 7-1.

### Form Factors

| Season | Team | Tot | St | Sb | Y | R |
|--------|------|-----|-----|-----|-----|-----|
| 94-95 | Wimbledon | 33 | 33 | 0 | 9 | 2 |
| 95-96 | Wimbledon | 31 | 27 | 4 | 7 | 2 |
| 96-97 | Wimbledon | 29 | 29 | 0 | 5 | 1 |
| Total | | 93 | 89 | 4 | 21 | 5 |

| | GP | GG | GF | GS | TGR |
|--------|-----|-----|-----|-----|-----|
| 94-95 | 78.57 | 11.00 | 48 | 3 | 6.25 |
| 95-96 | 81.58 | 10.33 | 55 | 3 | 5.45 |
| 96-97 | 76.32 | 9.67 | 49 | 3 | 6.12 |
| Averages | 78.82 | 10.33 | 44.00 | 3.00 | 5.94 |

## JUPP, Duncan

# Wimbledon ❶ FB

Fullname: Duncan Jupp
DOB: 25-01-75 Guildford

His performances at Fulham in recent seasons persuaded Wimbledon to seek his signature last summer. At just 22 Jupp has tremendous potential and he gained a small experience of Premier League football last season with six appearances.

At 6' 1" Jupp is big for a right-back, but he possesses pace and a good crossing ability. Loss of concentration was the only real question mark against him during his 100 plus games for the west London club.

A Scottish Under-21 international, he is tipped by many to become a full international.

## Form Factors

| Season | Team | Tot | St | Sb | Y | R |
|---|---|---|---|---|---|---|
| 96-97 | Wimbledon | 6 | 6 | 0 | 1 | 0 |
| Total | | 6 | 6 | 0 | 1 | 0 |

| | GP | GG | GF | GS | TGR |
|---|---|---|---|---|---|
| 96-97 | 15.79 | 0.00 | 49 | 0 | 0.00 |
| Averages | 15.79 | 0.00 | 49.00 | 0.00 | 0.00 |

## KAAMARK, Pontus

# Leicester City ❶❷ M

Fullname: Pontus Kaamark
DOB:

An £840,000 signing from IFK Gothenburg in November 1995 who has not enjoyed the best of fortunes since moving to England. Suffered a cruciate knee ligament injury during a reserve match for Leicester which destroyed most of the past two seasons for him. Battled back to win his place in the side in time for the Coca Cola Cup Final and was richly praised for his efforts in marking

Juninho out of the game in both matches. Should the former Gothenburg captain steer clear of injury this season, he will play a big part in Leicester's achievements and could further add to his tally of Swedish caps.

Primarily a right-back, manager O'Neill, realising his potential as a man-marker, might use him as a special team reserve which could limit his appearances in 1997-98.

## Form Factors

| Season | Team | Tot | St | Sb | Y | R |
|---|---|---|---|---|---|---|
| 96-97 | Leicester C. | 10 | 9 | 1 | 0 | 0 |
| Total | | 10 | 9 | 1 | 0 | 0 |

| | GP | GG | GF | GS | TGR |
|---|---|---|---|---|---|
| 96-97 | 26.32 | 0.00 | 46 | 0 | 0.00 |
| Averages | 26.32 | 0.00 | 46.00 | 0.00 | 0.00 |

## KEANE, Roy

# Manchester U. ❶❷❸❹❺ M

Fullname: Roy Maurice Keane
DOB: 10-08-71 Cork

Keane emerged from the shadow of Paul Ince to become the strong man in the Reds' midfield. His stamina has led to Alex Ferguson describing Keane as having a 'Rolls Royce Engine'. Twenty yellow cards and three red over the past three years is a measure of his occasional indiscipline. He doesn't get on the score sheet these days but he turns defence into attack with surging runs, often after a solid tackle of his own. His disciplinary record meant that there were a few eyebrows raised when Keane was named as the new United skipper. But then the same was true of Cantona.

Keane was signed by Nottingham Forest from Cobh Rangers and paid his dues (114 starts, 22 goals) before setting an English record £3.75 million fee when moving to United.

Kasey Keller

Despite only appearing 21 times, Keane was named in the PFA Premiership team of the year for the 96-97 season, is an automatic choice for the Republic of Ireland and will be an important element of continuity in midfield, with Cantona gone.

## Form Factors

| Season | Team | Tot | St | Sb | Y | R |
|---|---|---|---|---|---|---|
| 94-95 | Man. Utd | 25 | 23 | 2 | 7 | 0 |
| 95-96 | Man. Utd | 29 | 29 | 0 | 7 | 2 |
| 96-97 | Man. Utd | 21 | 21 | 0 | 6 | 1 |
| Total | | 75 | 73 | 2 | 20 | 3 |

| | GP | GG | GF | GS | TGR |
|---|---|---|---|---|---|
| 94-95 | 59.52 | 12.50 | 77 | 2 | 2.60 |
| 95-96 | 76.32 | 4.83 | 73 | 6 | 8.22 |
| 96-97 | 55.26 | 10.50 | 76 | 2 | 2.63 |
| Averages | 63.70 | 9.28 | 75.33 | 3.33 | 4.48 |

## KELLER, Kasey

## Leicester City ❶❷❸❹ GK

Fullname: Kasey Keller
DOB: 27-11-69 Washington USA

American goalkeeper who is a full international with his homeland. After five seasons in England with Millwall, he made a very favourable impression in the Premiership last season, having joined Leicester City for £900,000 just prior to the start of the season. Played in all but seven of the Foxes' Premiership matches, plus 12 cup ties including both games in the Coca Cola Cup Final. Kept nine clean sheets in the league with a best run of two consecutive shut-outs. Joined Millwall on a free transfer in 1992 from Portland University in the States. He is a great shot-stopper and his handling of crosses has improved immeasurably in the past season. Underrated and could therefore be underpriced.

## Form Factors

| Season | Team | Tot | St | Sb | Y | R |
|---|---|---|---|---|---|---|
| 96-97 | Leicester C. | 31 | 31 | 0 | 0 | 0 |
| Total | | 31 | 31 | 0 | 0 | 0 |

| | GA | GkA | GAp | CS | SO | Rp |
|---|---|---|---|---|---|---|
| 96-97 | 54 | 41 | 1.32 | 9 | 2 | 0 |
| Total | 54 | 41 | 1.32 | 9 | 2 | – |

## KELLY, Gary

# Leeds United   ❶❷❸❹   FB

Fullname: Gary Kelly
DOB: 09-07-74 Drogheda

One of two Leeds United players to emanate from Drogheda but joined the club from Republic of Ireland side Home Farm. First forced his way into the senior side during the 1991-92 season but had to wait until the 1993-94 season to fully establish himself. Was then ever-present for two consecutive seasons and only missed two Premiership matches during the 1996-97 campaign. Still only 23 years old, he will quickly add to his impressive tally of caps for the Republic of Ireland and as an attack-minded full-back will remain a vital part of George Graham's rebuilding plans at Elland Road. Starred for the Republic in the World Cup in America in 1994.

## Form Factors

| Season | Team | Tot | St | Sb | Y | R |
|---|---|---|---|---|---|---|
| 94-95 | Leeds Utd | 42 | 42 | 0 | 6 | 0 |
| 95-96 | Leeds Utd | 34 | 34 | 0 | 4 | 1 |
| 96-97 | Leeds Utd | 36 | 34 | 2 | 5 | 0 |
| Total | | 112 | 110 | 2 | 15 | 1 |

| | GP | GG | GF | GS | TGR |
|---|---|---|---|---|---|
| 94-95 | 100.00 | 0.00 | 59 | 0 | 0.00 |
| 95-96 | 89.47 | 0.00 | 40 | 0 | 0.00 |
| 96-97 | 89.47 | 17.00 | 28 | 2 | 7.14 |
| Averages | 92.98 | 5.67 | 42.33 | 0.67 | 2.38 |

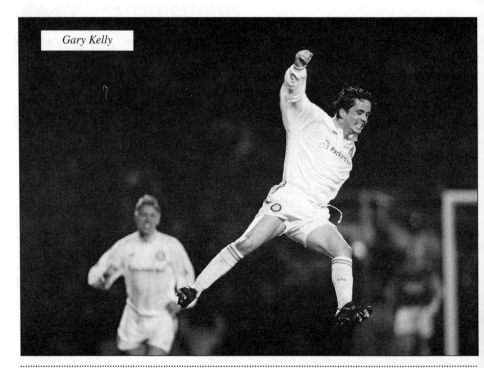

*Gary Kelly*

# KENNA, Jeff

## Blackburn Rovers ❶❷     FB

Fullname: Jeffrey Jude Kenna
DOB: 27-08-70 Dublin
There were a few eyebrows raised when Kenna was signed from Southampton for £1.5 million in March 1995. Since that point he has been a near ever-present, missing only a handful of games in the past two seasons.

An industrious right-back, Kenna played at left-back during the 1995-96 season as cover for the injured Graeme Le Saux. Injury to Chris Coleman saw him back in his more favoured right-back position. He will have to fight hard to maintain his position when Coleman is fit and with Henning Berg looking to establish himself again.

### Form Factors

| Season | Team | Tot | St | Sb | Y | R |
|---|---|---|---|---|---|---|
| 94-95 | Blackburn | 9 | 9 | 0 | 1 | 0 |
| 95-96 | Blackburn | 32 | 32 | 0 | 2 | 0 |
| 96-97 | Blackburn | 37 | 37 | 0 | 2 | 0 |
| Total | | 78 | 78 | 0 | 5 | 0 |

| | GP | GG | GF | GS | TGR |
|---|---|---|---|---|---|
| 94-95 | 21.43 | 9.00 | 80 | 1 | 1.25 |
| 95-96 | 84.21 | 0.00 | 61 | 0 | 0.00 |
| 96-97 | 97.37 | 0.00 | 42 | 0 | 0.00 |
| Averages | 67.67 | 3.00 | 61.00 | 0.33 | 0.42 |

# KENNEDY, Mark

## Liverpool     ❶❷     M

Fullname: Mark Kennedy
DOB: 15-05-76 Dublin,
Republic of Ireland
A promising young midfielder biding his time on the subs' bench, having been signed from Millwall for £1.5 million in March 1995. He was on the bench for 20 games in 1996-97, getting the track suit off just five times.

He has earned regular call-ups to the Republic of Ireland side where he employs his pace and excellent crossing. With the Liverpool old guard fading in midfield, Kennedy may get his chance in 1997-98 although he is just as likely to deputise for Redknapp and Leonhardsen.

### Form Factors

| Season | Team | Tot | St | Sb | Y | R |
|---|---|---|---|---|---|---|
| 94-95 | Liverpool | 6 | 4 | 2 | 1 | 0 |
| 95-96 | Liverpool | 4 | 1 | 3 | 0 | 0 |
| 96-97 | Liverpool | 5 | 0 | 5 | 0 | 0 |
| Total | | 15 | 5 | 10 | 1 | 0 |

| | GP | GG | GF | GS | TGR |
|---|---|---|---|---|---|
| 94-95 | 14.29 | 0.00 | 65 | 0 | 0.00 |
| 95-96 | 10.53 | 0.00 | 70 | 0 | 0.00 |
| 96-97 | 13.16 | 0.00 | 62 | 0 | 0.00 |
| Averages | 12.66 | 0.00 | 65.67 | 0.00 | 0.00 |

## KEOWN, Martin

# Arsenal ❶❷❸❹ CB

**Fullname:** Martin Raymond Keown
**DOB:** 24-07-66 Oxford

There was a time when Martin Keown was booed by Arsenal supporters when he found the ball at his feet. Now he is openly cheered and at the end of the 1995-96 season was voted as their Player of the Year. It shouldn't really be a surprise then that he also found himself back in the England squad during 1997 even if it did end with a broken shoulder during the game with Brazil.

Keown is a player who has literally found his feet. A strong man-marker cum centre-half, he developed a flair for playing in midfield under Bruce Rioch.

Now in his second spell at Arsenal, having cost the club ten times the £200,000 fee they received for him when they brought him back to Highbury from Everton in 1993. He should pass the 200 league appearance mark for Arsenal this season and has the experience of 160 Premiership games under his belt.

Doesn't get as many goals as he should but he can man mark the opposition's players out of the game. That scores points!

### Form Factors

| Season | Team | Tot | St | Sb | Y | R |
|---|---|---|---|---|---|---|
| 94-95 | Arsenal | 31 | 24 | 7 | 6 | 1 |
| 95-96 | Arsenal | 34 | 34 | 0 | 6 | 0 |
| 96-97 | Arsenal | 33 | 33 | 0 | 7 | 0 |
| Total | | 98 | 91 | 7 | 19 | 1 |

| | GP | GG | GF | GS | TGR |
|---|---|---|---|---|---|
| 94-95 | 73.81 | 31.00 | 52 | 1 | 1.92 |
| 95-96 | 89.47 | 0.00 | 49 | 0 | 0.00 |
| 96-97 | 86.84 | 33.00 | 62 | 1 | 1.61 |
| Averages | 83.38 | 21.33 | 54.33 | 0.67 | 1.18 |

## KEWELL, Harry

# Leeds United ❶ M

**Fullname:** Harold Kewell
**DOB:** 22-09-78 Australia

Australian midfielder who has made three first team appearances for Leeds United over the past couple of seasons. Made his debut against Middlesbrough towards the end of the 1995-96 season and also started in the following game against Southampton. Having been substituted in both, Kewell's only appearance last season came from one of his five bench appearances.

Signed from the Australian Academy of Sport, he is highly regarded by staff at Elland Road.

### Form Factors

| Season | Team | Tot | St | Sb | Y | R |
|---|---|---|---|---|---|---|
| 95-96 | Leeds Utd | 2 | 2 | 0 | 0 | 0 |
| 96-97 | Leeds Utd | 1 | 0 | 1 | 0 | 0 |
| Total | | 3 | 2 | 1 | 0 | 0 |

| | GP | GG | GF | GS | TGR |
|---|---|---|---|---|---|
| 95-96 | 5.26 | 0.00 | 40 | 0 | 0.00 |
| 96-97 | 2.63 | 0.00 | 28 | 0 | 0.00 |
| Averages | 3.95 | 0.00 | 34.00 | 0.00 | 0.00 |

## KHARINE, Dmitri

# Chelsea ❶ GK

**Fullname:** Dmitri Kharine
**DOB:** 16-08-68 Moscow, Russia

Injury has pretty much ruined the Chelsea 'keeper's chances in the past two seasons, ending his 1995-96 season as the New Year came and then last season after just five games when he was carried off after only 19 minutes at Sheffield Wednesday.

An excellent shot-stopper who has good distribution skills, he played for Russia in the 1994 World Cup Finals and

Euro '96. He has completed 107 Premiership games for the Blues, with 37 clean sheets.

By the end of last season Kharine was back in training and hoping to make a claim for a first team place during the 1997-98 season, in a position where Chelsea look over-stocked.

## Form Factors

| Season | Team | Tot | St | Sb | Y | R |
|---|---|---|---|---|---|---|
| 94-95 | Chelsea | 31 | 31 | 0 | 0 | 0 |
| 95-96 | Chelsea | 26 | 26 | 0 | 1 | 0 |
| 96-97 | Chelsea | 5 | 5 | 0 | 0 | 0 |
| Total | | 62 | 62 | 0 | 1 | 0 |

| | GA | GkA | GAp | CS | SO | Rp |
|---|---|---|---|---|---|---|
| 94-95 | 55 | 46 | 1.48 | 13 | 3 | 0 |
| 95-96 | 44 | 29 | 1.12 | 10 | 2 | 2 |
| 96-97 | 55 | 3 | 0.60 | 3 | 3 | 0 |
| Total | 154 | 78 | 1.26 | 26 | 8 | – |

## KIMBLE, Alan

# Wimbledon ❶❷❸ FB

Fullname: Alan Frank Kimble
DOB: 06-08-66 Dagenham

At £175,000, Kimble has been a typical Dons' bargain purchase. Made his 100th Premiership appearance towards the tail end of last season, having arrived from Cambridge United with another 250 appearances under his belt.

An attacking left-back, who possesses a powerful shot and a good ability in dead-ball situations, his first few seasons were blighted with injury but the last two seasons have seen him feature in over 80% of the Dons' matches.

Surprisingly for a defender he receives very few cautions, indeed just eight in the past three seasons, which says much about his tackling ability.

*Alan Kimble*

## Form Factors

| Season | Team | Tot | St | Sb | Y | R |
|---|---|---|---|---|---|---|
| 94-95 | Wimbledon | 26 | 26 | 0 | 4 | 1 |
| 95-96 | Wimbledon | 31 | 31 | 0 | 2 | 0 |
| 96-97 | Wimbledon | 31 | 28 | 3 | 2 | 0 |
| Total | | 88 | 85 | 3 | 8 | 1 |

| | GP | GG | GF | GS | TGR |
|---|---|---|---|---|---|
| 94-95 | 61.90 | 0.00 | 48 | 0 | 0.00 |
| 95-96 | 81.58 | 0.00 | 55 | 0 | 0.00 |
| 96-97 | 81.58 | 0.00 | 49 | 0 | 0.00 |
| Averages | 75.02 | 0.00 | 50.66 | 0.00 | 0.00 |

## KITSON, Paul

# West Ham U. ❶❷❸❹ S

Fullname: Paul Kitson
DOB: 09-01-71 Peterlee
  The goals of Paul Kitson and John Hartson in the final weeks of the 1996-97 season ensured West Ham another season of Premiership football. Unable to secure a first team spot at Newcastle, the Hammers parted with £2.3 million to secure his signature in February 1997. Made his debut against Derby County and scored the first of eight goals in 14 games in the next match against Tottenham. His goal streak included a hat-trick against Sheffield Wednesday and only a missed penalty earlier in the season against Everton prevented him getting a second.
  An England Under-21 international, Kitson started his career at Leicester City but it was at Derby County where his record of a goal every three games prompted Newcastle to pay £2.25 million for him.

## Form Factors

| Season | Team | Tot | St | Sb | Y | R |
|---|---|---|---|---|---|---|
| 95-96 | Newcastle | 7 | 2 | 5 | 1 | 0 |
| 96-97 | Newcastle | 3 | 0 | 3 | 0 | 0 |
| 96-97 | West Ham | 14 | 14 | 0 | 2 | 0 |
| Total | | 24 | 16 | 8 | 3 | 0 |

| | GP | GG | GF | GS | TGR |
|---|---|---|---|---|---|
| 95-96 | 18.42 | 3.50 | 66 | 2 | 3.03 |
| 96-97 | 7.89 | 0.00 | 73 | 0 | 0.00 |
| 96-97 | 7.89 | 0.38 | 39 | 8 | 20.51 |
| Averages | 11.40 | 1.29 | 59.33 | 3.33 | 7.85 |

## KRIZAN, Ales

# Barnsley ❶❷❸ S

Fullname: Ales Krizan
DOB:
  A £450,000 summer signing from Maribor Branik, Krizan is a Slovenian international defender. An integral part of the Slovenian champions' side last season, the 24-year-old combines strength, speed and a great left foot, which make him a formidable stopper.

## KVARME, Bjorn Tore

# Liverpool ❶❷❸ D

Fullname: Bjorn Tore Kvarme
DOB: 17-07-72 Trondheim, Norway
  Kvarme was signed on a free transfer in January 1997 to give the Liverpool management an abundance of options on the right flank. He started his career as an attacker and had a trial period with Liverpool late in 1996 before negotiations began. He played fifteen starts and looks likely to link up with new signing Leonhardsen, with whom he played in a successful Rosenborg side.
  A pacy and perceptive defender his performances in the side were probably one of the reasons for Liverpool allowing John Scales to move on to Spurs. Could be available cheaply.

## Form Factors

| Season | Team | Tot | St | Sb | Y | R |
|---|---|---|---|---|---|---|
| 96-97 | Liverpool | 15 | 15 | 0 | 1 | 0 |
| Total | | 15 | 15 | 0 | 1 | 0 |

| | GP | GG | GF | GS | TGR |
|---|---|---|---|---|---|
| 96-97 | 39.47 | 0.00 | 62 | 0 | 0.00 |
| Averages | 39.47 | 0.00 | 62.00 | 0.00 | 0.00 |

## LAMPARD, Frank

# West Ham U.   ❶❷❸   FB

Fullname:   Frank Lampard
DOB:          21-06-78 Romford
   Has come through the ranks at Upton
Park to follow his namesake father who is
one of the Hammers' all-time greats. A
strong tenacious defender, Lampard made
his Premiership debut in the 1995-96
season and became an important member
of the squad last season when he was
named on the bench 25 times in total,
being called upon 10 times.
   An England Youth player, Lampard had
a brief spell on loan in Wales in the final
two months of 1995 where he made nine
appearances for Swansea City. His one
league goal while on loan there remained
his only senior strike at the end of the
1996-97 season.

## Form Factors

| Season | Team | Tot | St | Sb | Y | R |
|--------|------|-----|-----|-----|-----|-----|
| 95-96 | West Ham | 2 | 0 | 2 | 0 | 0 |
| 96-97 | West Ham | 13 | 3 | 10 | 1 | 0 |
| Total | | 15 | 3 | 12 | 1 | 0 |

| | GP | GG | GF | GS | TGR |
|--------|------|------|------|------|------|
| 95-96 | 5.26 | 0.00 | 43 | 0 | 0.00 |
| 96-97 | 34.21 | 0.00 | 39 | 0 | 0.00 |
| Averages | 19.74 | 0.00 | 41.00 | 0.00 | 0.00 |

## LAURENT, Pierre

# Leeds United   ❶❷❸❹   S

Fullname:   Pierre Laurent
DOB:
   French winger who came to Leeds
United late in the 1996-97 season and
made his debut during a dismal 0-0 draw
with Blackburn Rovers at Elland Road.
Cost his new club £500,000 to prise him
away from Bastia, where he scored ten
goals in 49 league matches. Will add

extra width and attacking options to a
side which was criticised for being too
negative during the early months of
George Graham's managerial reign.
Primarily a right-sided winger, he has
good technique and a fast turn of pace.

## Form Factors

| Season | Team | Tot | St | Sb | Y | R |
|--------|------|-----|-----|-----|-----|-----|
| 96-97 | Leeds Utd | 4 | 2 | 2 | 0 | 0 |
| Total | | 4 | 2 | 2 | 0 | 0 |

| | GP | GG | GF | GS | TGR |
|--------|------|------|------|------|------|
| 96-97 | 10.53 | 0.00 | 28 | 0 | 0.00 |
| Averages | 10.53 | 0.00 | 28.00 | 0.00 | 0.00 |

## LAURSEN, Jacob

# Derby County   ❶❷❸❹   FB

Fullname:   Jacob Laursen
DOB:
   Joined Derby County just prior to the
start of last season in a £500,000 move
from Danish side Silkeborg and quickly
settled at the Baseball Ground, missing
just two of their 38 Premiership matches.
In fact his record of 35 starts from the 38
Premier League games was matched only
by team-mates Gary Rowett and Chris
Powell.
   An international defender with
Denmark, who possesses a fine
temperament and picked up just two
bookings during his first season in
England, scored his one league goal
during Derby's home match with
Manchester United.

## Form Factors

| Season | Team | Tot | St | Sb | Y | R |
|--------|------|-----|-----|-----|-----|-----|
| 96-97 | Derby Co. | 36 | 35 | 1 | 2 | 0 |
| Total | | 36 | 35 | 1 | 2 | 0 |

| | GP | GG | GF | GS | TGR |
|--------|------|------|------|------|------|
| 96-97 | 94.74 | 36.00 | 45 | 1 | 2.22 |
| Averages | 94.74 | 36.00 | 45.00 | 1.00 | 2.22 |

## LAWRENCE, Jamie

# Leicester City ➊➋ M

**Fullname:** James Hubert Lawrence
**DOB:** 08-03-70 Balham

Twenty-seven-year-old winger who has played in around 40% of Leicester City's matches since joining the club in January 1995 for £125,000. A handful on his day and a very useful squad member but has struggled to command a place in the starting line-up. His first professional contract was with Sunderland after impressing them whilst with non-league side Cowes. He moved to Doncaster Rovers in the spring of 1994 for just £20,000 and on to Leicester less than a year later. Has scored one Premiership goal, which came during a 4-3 defeat by Wimbledon in April 1995 as Leicester battled unsuccessfully against relegation.

Will probably be another fringe player in 1997-98.

## Form Factors

| Season | Team | Tot | St | Sb | Y | R |
|---|---|---|---|---|---|---|
| 94-95 | Leicester C. | 17 | 9 | 8 | 0 | 0 |
| 96-97 | Leicester C. | 15 | 2 | 13 | 0 | 0 |
| Total | | 32 | 11 | 21 | 0 | 0 |

| | GP | GG | GF | GS | TGR |
|---|---|---|---|---|---|
| 94-95 | 40.48 | 17.00 | 45 | 1 | 2.22 |
| 96-97 | 39.47 | 0.00 | 46 | 0 | 0.00 |
| Averages | 39.97 | 8.50 | 45.50 | 0.50 | 1.11 |

## LAZARIDIS, Stan

# West Ham U. ➊➋ M

**Fullname:** Stanley Lazaridis
**DOB:** 16-08-72 Perth, W.Australia

A fast out-and-out winger, Lazaridis is an Australian international who was noticed by West Ham when they were on a pre-season tour in the summer of 1995. Having previously played for West Adelaide, he made his debut in September 1995 and after a stint in the reserves, had his season cut short when he sustained a broken leg in an FA Cup tie against Grimsby Town.

Last season Lazaridis took the chance to make a bigger impression and ended up appearing in 22 of the Hammers' games, nine as a substitute He also recorded his only goal in the Premier League to date – at Wimbledon in the closing stages of the season.

Having come to terms with the pace of the Premiership, Lazaridis could become a regular member of the Hammers' side.

## Form Factors

| Season | Team | Tot | St | Sb | Y | R |
|---|---|---|---|---|---|---|
| 95-96 | West Ham | 4 | 2 | 2 | 0 | 0 |
| 96-97 | West Ham | 22 | 13 | 9 | 2 | 0 |
| Total | | 26 | 15 | 11 | 2 | 0 |

| | GP | GG | GF | GS | TGR |
|---|---|---|---|---|---|
| 95-96 | 10.53 | 0.00 | 43 | 0 | 0.00 |
| 96-97 | 57.89 | 22.00 | 39 | 1 | 2.56 |
| Averages | 34.21 | 11.00 | 41.00 | 0.50 | 1.28 |

## LE SAUX, Graeme

# Blackburn R. ❶❷❸❹❺     FB

Fullname: Graeme Pierre Le Saux
DOB: 17-10-68 Jersey

Graeme Le Saux is one of those players that even opposing fans like. A skilful attacking full or wing-back, he suffered a serious injury in December 1995 when he broke his ankle and ruptured tendons when playing against Middlesbrough. The injury kept him out until October 1996 when he made his comeback at West Ham.

He quickly re-established himself not only in the Rovers side but also in the England team.

He was a near ever-present in the Blackburn title team and tends to pop up with the occasional goal. A fine crosser of the ball, especially at speed.

## Form Factors

| Season | Team | Tot | St | Sb | Y | R |
|--------|------|-----|-----|-----|-----|-----|
| 94-95 | Blackburn | 39 | 39 | 0 | 6 | 0 |
| 95-96 | Blackburn | 15 | 14 | 1 | 2 | 0 |
| 96-97 | Blackburn | 26 | 26 | 0 | 6 | 0 |
| Total | | 80 | 79 | 1 | 14 | 0 |

| | GP | GG | GF | GS | TGR |
|--------|-----|-----|-----|-----|-----|
| 94-95 | 92.86 | 13.00 | 80 | 3 | 3.75 |
| 95-96 | 39.47 | 15.00 | 61 | 1 | 1.64 |
| 96-97 | 68.42 | 26.00 | 42 | 1 | 2.38 |
| Averages | 66.92 | 18.00 | 61.00 | 1.67 | 2.59 |

## LE TISSIER, Matthew

# Southampton ❶❷❸❹❺     M

Fullname: Matthew Paul Le Tissier
DOB: 14-10-68 Guernsey

The first thing manager Dave Jones did on his arrival at the Dell was to ensure 'Le God' (as he is known on the south coast) signed a new four-year contract. He is a Saints player through and through and fans will never know just how good he might have been at a top side.

When he plays, there are few better club players in the world and his England recall by Glenn Hoddle just hyped up the the Le Tissier-England debate.

*Matt Le Tissier*

*Frank Lebeouf*

## Form Factors

| Season | Team | Tot | St | Sb | Y | R |
|---|---|---|---|---|---|---|
| 94-95 | Southampton | 41 | 41 | 0 | 5 | 0 |
| 95-96 | Southampton | 34 | 34 | 0 | 11 | 1 |
| 96-97 | Southampton | 31 | 25 | 6 | 5 | 0 |
| Total | | 106 | 100 | 6 | 21 | 1 |

| | GP | GG | GF | GS | TGR |
|---|---|---|---|---|---|
| 94-95 | 97.62 | 2.05 | 61 | 20 | 32.79 |
| 95-96 | 89.47 | 4.86 | 34 | 7 | 20.59 |
| 96-97 | 81.58 | 2.38 | 50 | 13 | 26.00 |
| Averages | 89.56 | 3.10 | 48.33 | 13.33 | 26.46 |

## LEBOEUF, Frank

### Chelsea ❶❷❸❹❺ CB

Fullname: Frank Leboeuf
DOB: 22-01-68 Marseille, France

   Possibly the best long-range passer of the ball in the Premiership, Leboeuf was one of Ruud Gullit's first major signings, joining from Strasbourg for £2.5 million. A French international who might have won more caps but for the form of the likes of Blanc and Desailly. Featured in 26 of Chelsea's games last season and might have been an ever-present but for injury and suspension. Chelsea's main penalty taker, four of his six league goals came from the spot.

   A key member of the FA Cup winning side last season with the ability to turn defence into attack with a single pass, he is often at his most dangerous when in possession of the ball in the heart of the Chelsea defence.

## Form Factors

| Season | Team | Tot | St | Sb | Y | R |
|---|---|---|---|---|---|---|
| 96-97 | Chelsea | 26 | 26 | 0 | 7 | 0 |
| Total | | 26 | 26 | 0 | 7 | 0 |

| | GP | GG | GF | GS | TGR |
|---|---|---|---|---|---|
| 96-97 | 68.42 | 4.33 | 58 | 6 | 10.34 |
| Averages | 68.42 | 4.33 | 58.00 | 6.00 | 10.34 |

   Guernsey's most famous export, Le Tissier has missed just 18 Premiership games since it was formed (making him 8th in the all-time apps list) and his 80 goals make him fifth in that particular list. Invariably his goals are spectacular and the majority have probably come from the edge or outside of the area. Tap-ins are simply not his style.

   Was Southampton's top scorer (again) last season and will probably be so again when 1997-98 draws to an end.

## LEE, Dave

# Bolton W. ❶ S

Fullname: David Mark Lee
DOB: 05-11-67 Blackburn

A traditional winger, possessing pace and an accurate crossing ability, Lee was often used from the bench last season, making nearly half of his 25 appearances that way.

After six years at Bury, where he played over 200 times, Lee was picked up by Southampton in 1991 for £350,000. He made his Premiership debut with them, coming on as a substitute against Manchester United. But not long after, he was transferred to Bolton Wanderers. He was a member of the squad in the 1995-96 Premiership season and, like last season, his record then was 18 appearances with nine as substitute.

Now 29-years old, it seems likely that Lee will be an important member of the Wanderers side in his role as a squad player.

## Form Factors

| Season | Team | Tot | St | Sb | Y | R |
|--------|------|-----|-----|-----|-----|-----|
| 92-93 | Southampton | 1 | 0 | 1 | 0 | 0 |
| 95-96 | Bolton W. | 18 | 9 | 9 | 2 | 0 |
| Total | | 19 | 9 | 10 | 2 | 0 |

| | GP | GG | GF | GS | TGR |
|--------|-----|-----|-----|-----|-----|
| 92-93 | 2.38 | 0.00 | 54 | 0 | 0.00 |
| 95-96 | 47.37 | 18.00 | 39 | 1 | 2.56 |
| Averages | 24.87 | 9.00 | 46.50 | 0.50 | 1.28 |

## LEE, Robert

# Newcastle U. ❶❷❸❹❺ M

Fullname: Robert Martin Lee
DOB: 01-02-66 West Ham

Signed by Kevin Keegan from Charlton Athletic for £700,000 in September 1992 as a right winger, the London born player has transformed into an effective attacking midfield player. He joined Charlton on a free transfer from non-league side Hornchurch in the summer of 1983 and played over 300 senior games for the south London side.

He was an important part of the Division One championship winning side and first captained Newcastle in 1994-95. He has put in 104 appearances in the past three seasons and averages a goal every five or so games.

He scored on his England debut against Romania in 1995 and continues to be one of the key midfield players in the international squad, especially since he links with Shearer, Ferdinand and Batty at club level. Last season was perhaps his best as he showed he could go the course of the full season.

He will wish to peak with Newcastle United and England, preferably in France, during the 97-98 season.

## Form Factors

| Season | Team | Tot | St | Sb | Y | R |
|--------|------|-----|-----|-----|-----|-----|
| 94-95 | Newcastle | 35 | 35 | 0 | 5 | 1 |
| 95-96 | Newcastle | 36 | 36 | 0 | 3 | 0 |
| 96-97 | Newcastle | 33 | 32 | 1 | 7 | 0 |
| Total | | 104 | 103 | 1 | 15 | 1 |

| | GP | GG | GF | GS | TGR |
|--------|-----|-----|-----|-----|-----|
| 94-95 | 83.33 | 3.89 | 67 | 9 | 13.43 |
| 95-96 | 94.74 | 4.50 | 66 | 8 | 12.12 |
| 96-97 | 86.84 | 7.20 | 73 | 5 | 6.85 |
| Averages | 88.30 | 5.20 | 68.67 | 7.33 | 9.37 |

## LENNON, Neil

### Leicester City ❶❷❸ M

Fullname: Neil Francis Lennon
DOB: 25-06-71 Lurgan

Only two Leicester City players featured in more of the Foxes' matches during 1996-97 than 26-year-old midfielder Lennon. Has proved a typically excellent piece of work in the transfer market by City manager Martin O'Neill who seized the Irishman from under the noses of several bigger clubs for £750,000 from Crewe Alexandra in February 1996. His career had been under threat at one time at Crewe through a serious back injury. Prior to Crewe he made one appearance during a season with Manchester City and has progressed through the Northern Ireland Under-23 side into the senior set-up.

A hard-working player who loves to run, he played in every minute of his 35 games last season, which confirms his worth.

### Form Factors

| Season | Team | Tot | St | Sb | Y | R |
|---|---|---|---|---|---|---|
| 96-97 | Leicester C. | 35 | 35 | 0 | 8 | 0 |
| Total | | 35 | 35 | 0 | 8 | 0 |

| | GP | GG | GF | GS | TGR |
|---|---|---|---|---|---|
| 96-97 | 92.11 | 35.00 | 46 | 1 | 2.17 |
| Averages | 92.11 | 35.00 | 46.00 | 1.00 | 2.17 |

## LEONHARDSEN, Oyvind

### Liverpool ❶❷❸❹ M

Fullname: Oyvind Leonhardsen
DOB: 17-08-70 Norway

The Norwegian international's performances for the Dons in the past couple of seasons prompted Liverpool to part with £3.5 million to secure his services during the summer of 1997. The non-stop midfield player joined Wimbledon from Rosenborg in November 1994 for £660,000. Since then only injury has prevented him completing more games than he has.

His tireless running normally ensures he pops up in the area from time to time and he is always likely to contribute to the team's goals tally during the course of a season – five last term.

He has also got to grips with the English system and avoided even a single yellow card in his 27 Premiership games last season.

He played with Bjornebye and Kvarme at Rosenborg. Sure to be have a big role to play in Liverpool's quest for honours.

### Form Factors

| Season | Team | Tot | St | Sb | Y | R |
|---|---|---|---|---|---|---|
| 94-95 | Wimbledon | 20 | 18 | 2 | 2 | 0 |
| 95-96 | Wimbledon | 29 | 28 | 1 | 6 | 0 |
| 96-97 | Wimbledon | 27 | 27 | 0 | 0 | 0 |
| Total | | 76 | 73 | 3 | 8 | 0 |

| | GP | GG | GF | GS | TGR |
|---|---|---|---|---|---|
| 94-95 | 47.62 | 5.00 | 48 | 4 | 8.33 |
| 95-96 | 76.32 | 7.25 | 55 | 4 | 7.27 |
| 96-97 | 71.05 | 5.40 | 49 | 5 | 10.20 |
| Averages | 65.00 | 5.88 | 50.67 | 4.33 | 8.54 |

## LEWIS, Neil

## Leicester City ❶ FB

Fullname: Neil Anthony Lewis
DOB: 28-06-74 Wolverhampton

Wolverhampton-born Leicester City midfielder who joined the Foxes as a trainee and has now made 76 appearances for the club. Has scored one goal for the Blues, which came during a 1-1 draw with Reading at Elm Park during City's promotion season. Lewis has excellent close skills but does occasionally fall foul of the laws of the game – 16 bookings in two seasons – and the law of the land, having served a prison sentence during his career. Made just six Premiership appearances during last season but, providing his problems are behind him, could make the right sort of impression in 1997-98.

Possibly a player for the future.

### Form Factors

| Season | Team | Tot | St | Sb | Y | R |
|---|---|---|---|---|---|---|
| 94-95 | Leicester C. | 16 | 13 | 3 | 1 | 1 |
| 96-97 | Leicester C. | 6 | 4 | 2 | 0 | 0 |
| Total | | 22 | 17 | 5 | 1 | 1 |

| | GP | GG | GF | GS | TGR |
|---|---|---|---|---|---|
| 94-95 | 38.10 | 0.00 | 45 | 0 | 0.00 |
| 96-97 | 15.79 | 0.00 | 46 | 0 | 0.00 |
| Averages | 26.94 | 0.00 | 45.50 | 0.00 | 0.00 |

## LIDDELL, Andy

## Barnsley ❶❷ S

Fullname: Andrew Mark Liddell
DOB: 28-06-73 Leeds

Only Neil Redfearn out of the current players on the Barnsley books has scored more goals for the club. Liddle might have hit more than his eight last season had he held his place longer. Having been a regular in the Tykes' starting line-up up until November, he found himself in and out for the remainder of the season. Thirteen of his 25 appearances came from the bench and he was an unused sub in most of the other matches.

A non-stop worker for the cause, Liddle joined Barnsley in the summer of 1991 and has now made over 150 appearances.

## LILLEY, Derek

## Leeds United ❶❷ S

Fullname: Derek Lilley
DOB:

Striker who broke into the Leeds United first team towards the end of the 1996-97 season following a £500,000 transfer from Scottish side Greenock Morton. Top scorer for Morton for the two previous seasons and will prove an invaluable asset and bargain buy if that form can be repeated south of the border. He was spotted by Leeds' Scottish scout John Barr, who sadly died on the day Lilley signed for Leeds. Barr had previously unearthed players of the calibre of Gordon McQueen and Joe Jordan. Lilley will do well to live with that company. He finished the season with six appearances, two from the bench.

### Form Factors

| Season | Team | Tot | St | Sb | Y | R |
|---|---|---|---|---|---|---|
| 96-97 | Leeds Utd | 6 | 4 | 2 | 0 | 0 |
| Total | | 6 | 4 | 2 | 0 | 0 |

| | GP | GG | GF | GS | TGR |
|---|---|---|---|---|---|
| 96-97 | 15.79 | 0.00 | 28 | 0 | 0.00 |
| Averages | 15.79 | 0.00 | 28.00 | 0.00 | 0.00 |

## LINIGHAN, Andy

# Crystal Palace ❶❷❸ CB

**Fullname:** Andrew Linighan
**DOB:** 18-06-62 Hartlepool

Experienced central defender who was signed at what now seems a bargain £110,000 from Arsenal in January 1997. Played in 21 of Palace's remaining Division One games and his experience was a key factor in seeing the Eagles through the play-offs. Was signed by Dave Bassett in a bid to help stop Palace conceding goals from dead-ball plays, which they did on his debut at Southend!

Although Linighan was never able to fully establish himself as a first team regular at Arsenal, he gained considerable experience with extended runs while covering for injuries. He joined Arsenal from Norwich City for £1.25 million seven years ago and played in the 1993 Coca Cola Cup winning side before clinching the domestic cup double when heading home the winning goal in the dying seconds of extra time against Sheffield Wednesday.

## Form Factors

| Season | Team | Tot | St | Sb | Y | R |
|--------|------|-----|-----|-----|-----|-----|
| 94-95 | Arsenal | 20 | 13 | 7 | 1 | 0 |
| 95-96 | Arsenal | 18 | 17 | 1 | 0 | 0 |
| 96-97 | Arsenal | 11 | 10 | 1 | 2 | 0 |
| Total | | 49 | 40 | 9 | 3 | 0 |

| | GP | GG | GF | GS | TGR |
|--------|------|------|------|------|------|
| 94-95 | 47.62 | 10.00 | 52 | 2 | 3.85 |
| 95-96 | 47.37 | 0.00 | 49 | 0 | 0.00 |
| 96-97 | 28.95 | 11.00 | 62 | 1 | 1.61 |
| Averages | 41.31 | 7.00 | 54.33 | 1.00 | 1.82 |

## LOMAS, Stephen

# West Ham U. ❶❷❸ M

**Fullname:** Stephen Martin Lomas
**DOB:** 18-01-74 Hanover

A tough-tackling Northern Ireland international, Lomas moved to Upton Park from Manchester City on transfer deadline day in March 1997. His flame red hair always makes him stand out as can his crunching tackles.

Played three seasons in the Premier League but was unable to save the Maine Road side from relegation and spent nearly a season in the Nationwide League before West Ham signed him.

Played in the final seven games for the Hammers last season and proved to be one of the key signings that helped them maintain their place in the top flight.

Lomas is sure to be an important player for West Ham during 1997-98.

## Form Factors

| Season | Team | Tot | St | Sb | Y | R |
|--------|------|-----|-----|-----|-----|-----|
| 94-95 | Man. City | 20 | 18 | 2 | 3 | 0 |
| 95-96 | Man. City | 33 | 32 | 1 | 8 | 1 |
| 96-97 | West Ham | 7 | 7 | 0 | 0 | 0 |
| Total | | 60 | 57 | 3 | 11 | 1 |

| | GP | GG | GF | GS | TGR |
|--------|------|------|------|------|------|
| 94-95 | 47.62 | 10.00 | 53 | 2 | 3.77 |
| 95-96 | 86.84 | 11.00 | 33 | 3 | 9.09 |
| 96-97 | 18.42 | 0.00 | 39 | 0 | 0.00 |
| Averages | 73.77 | 7.00 | 41.67 | 1.67 | 4.29 |

## LUKIC, John

### Arsenal ❶ GK

Fullname: Jovan Lukic
DOB: 11-12-60 Chesterfield

John Lukic is now in his second spell at Arsenal – following two spells at Leeds United! He first signed for the Gunners in 1983 and collected a championship winners medal in 1989. Having accumulated over 200 appearances he moved back to Leeds for £1 million and helped the Elland Road side to their championship success in 1991-92.

He returned to Highbury during the 1996 close season as cover for David Seaman and quickly found himself thrust back into the Premiership limelight as the England 'keeper suffered with injury.

Despite an erratic start, Lukic provided good cover in his 15 appearances. He will be fighting for a bench place this season, and unless there are further injuries, will have limited first team chances.

### Form Factors

| Season | Team | Tot | St | Sb | Y | R |
|--------|------|-----|----|----|---|---|
| 94-95 | Leeds Utd | 42 | 42 | 0 | 0 | 0 |
| 95-96 | Leeds Utd | 28 | 28 | 0 | 0 | 0 |
| 96-97 | Arsenal | 15 | 15 | 0 | 0 | 0 |
| Total | | 85 | 85 | 0 | 0 | 0 |

| | GA | GkA | GlA | CS | SO | Rp |
|--|----|----|----|----|----|----|
| 94-95 | 38 | 38 | 0.90 | 17 | 3 | 3 |
| 95-96 | 57 | 42 | 1.50 | 7 | 2 | 0 |
| 96-97 | 32 | 17 | 1.13 | 5 | 2 | 0 |
| Total | 127 | 97 | 1.14 | 29 | 7 | – |

## LUNDEKVAM, Claus

### Southampton ❶❷❸ CB

Fullname: Claus Lundekvam
DOB: 22-02-73 Norway

Lundekvam is arguably one of the best ball-playing central defenders to have come out of Norway. At £400,000 he has proved to be a very good investment for the Saints since joining them from SK Brann in the summer of 1996.

He likes to get forward and join in the attacks, although he failed to get off the scoring mark during his 29 appearances in his first season with Southampton.

Missed some games through injury but should be another important player for Southampton during 1997-98.

### Form Factors

| Season | Team | Tot | St | Sb | Y | R |
|--------|------|-----|----|----|---|---|
| 96-97 | Southampton | 29 | 28 | 1 | 6 | 0 |
| Total | | 29 | 28 | 1 | 6 | 0 |

| | GP | GG | GF | GS | TGR |
|--|----|----|----|----|-----|
| 96-97 | 76.32 | 0.00 | 50 | 0 | 0.00 |
| Averages | 76.32 | 0.00 | 50.00 | 0.00 | 0.00 |

## MABBUTT, Gary

### Tottenham H. ❶❷❸ CB

Fullname: Gary Vincent Mabbutt
DOB: 23-08-61 Bristol

A Tottenham defence without Gary Mabbutt seemed unthinkable one year ago but a broken leg on the opening day of the 1996-97 season put him out of action for the rest of the campaign, and his absence was all too evident as a glance at Spurs' results and performances will testify.

An inspirational captain who was capped 16 times by England and has picked up UEFA and FA Cup winners medals in over 570 games since joining

Tottenham from Bristol Rovers back in August 1992.

Mabbutt's playing days could be on the wane but his influence at White Hart Lane will be high, even from behind the scenes. A terrific reader of the game who is fearless and has suffered some horrific and not superficial injuries down the years, and is well known for being a diabetic.

## Form Factors

| Season | Team | Tot | St | Sb | Y | R |
|---|---|---|---|---|---|---|
| 94-95 | Tottenham | 33 | 33 | 0 | 1 | 0 |
| 95-96 | Tottenham | 32 | 32 | 0 | 4 | 0 |
| 96-97 | Tottenham | 1 | 1 | 0 | 0 | 0 |
| Total | | 66 | 66 | 0 | 5 | 0 |

| | GP | GG | GF | GS | TGR |
|---|---|---|---|---|---|
| 94-95 | 78.57 | 0.00 | 66 | 0 | 0.00 |
| 95-96 | 84.21 | 0.00 | 50 | 0 | 0.00 |
| 96-97 | 2.63 | 0.00 | 44 | 0 | 0.00 |
| Averages | 55.14 | 0.00 | 53.33 | 0.00 | 0.00 |

## MAGILTON, Jim

### Southampton ❶❷❸ M

Fullname: James Magilton
DOB: 06-05-69 Belfast, N. Ireland

Magilton featured in all 38 Southampton Premier League games last season – once as a non-playing substitute. A skilful midfield player who has a good playing relationship with Matt le Tissier, he has also established himself as a regular in the Northern Ireland side.

Having started his career as an apprentice at Liverpool, he didn't make the grade there and went on to play 150 league games with Oxford United. His performances prompted the Saints to pay £600,000 for his services in February 1994 and it is arguably some of the best money the club has spent.

Magilton has played in almost 90% of Southampton's games in recent years and

was an ever-present during the 1994-95 season. He was Saints' second most subbed player last season, leaving the pitch on six occasions. His average of a goal every seven or so games is worth recording.

## Form Factors

| Season | Team | Tot | St | Sb | Y | R |
|---|---|---|---|---|---|---|
| 94-95 | Southampton | 42 | 42 | 0 | 3 | 0 |
| 95-96 | Southampton | 31 | 31 | 0 | 2 | 0 |
| 96-97 | Southampton | 37 | 31 | 6 | 4 | 0 |
| Total | | 110 | 104 | 6 | 9 | 0 |

| | GP | GG | GF | GS | TGR |
|---|---|---|---|---|---|
| 94-95 | 100.00 | 7.00 | 61 | 6 | 9.84 |
| 95-96 | 81.58 | 10.33 | 34 | 3 | 8.82 |
| 96-97 | 97.37 | 7.75 | 50 | 4 | 8.00 |
| Averages | 89.77 | 8.36 | 48.33 | 4.33 | 8.89 |

## MARCELLE, Clint

### Barnsley ❶❷❸ S

Fullname: Clint Marcelle
DOB:

One of many arrivals at Oakwell in the summer of 1996 that formed the backbone of Barnsley's promotion push. A Trinidadian international who was born in the West Indies, the striker had an instant success when scoring on his debut at West Bromwich Albion. He followed this up with a goal at home to Huddersfield and a couple more against Manchester City, to make it four goals in his first six games in the red of Barnsley.

In all, Marcelle scored eight times in his 39 Nationwide League appearances – a third of which came off the substitutes' bench. He could prove equally adept in the Premier League.

## MARKER, Nicky

### Blackburn Rovers ❶ M

Fullname: Nicholas R T Marker
DOB: 03-06-65 Budleigh Salterton

Since signing from Plymouth in 1992, Marker has been used mainly as a reserve to come in and cover injuries, most notably standing in for Colin Hendry during the 1995-96 season. A cruciate ligament injury has hindered his appearances and made him miss the 1994-95 season.

Now 32 years old, he made over 200 appearances for both Exeter City and Plymouth Argyle and can play in defence or midfield.

### Form Factors

| Season | Team | Tot | St | Sb | Y | R |
|---|---|---|---|---|---|---|
| 93-94 | Blackburn | 23 | 16 | 7 | 1 | 0 |
| 95-96 | Blackburn | 9 | 8 | 1 | 0 | 0 |
| 96-97 | Blackburn | 7 | 5 | 2 | 0 | 0 |
| Total | | 39 | 29 | 10 | 1 | 0 |

| | GP | GG | GF | GS | TGR |
|---|---|---|---|---|---|
| 93-94 | 54.76 | 0.00 | 63 | 0 | 0.00 |
| 95-96 | 23.68 | 9.00 | 61 | 1 | 1.64 |
| 96-97 | 18.42 | 0.00 | 42 | 0 | 0.00 |
| Averages | 32.29 | 3.00 | 55.33 | 0.33 | 0.55 |

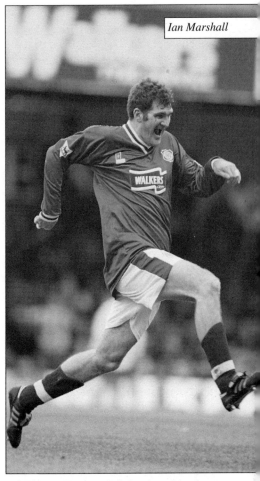

*Ian Marshall*

## MARSHALL, Ian

### Leicester City ❶❷ S

Fullname: Ian Paul Marshall
DOB: 20-03-66 Liverpool

Powerfully built and a whole-hearted character with deceptively good close control to go with plenty of strength in the air. Joined Leicester City at the start of the 1996-97 season to add needed experience to the Foxes' attack and responded with eight Premiership goals in 28 games, nine of which were as substitute. Has previously played in the Premiership with Oldham Athletic and Ipswich Town and scored 23 goals in 102 top flight games. Also had a spell with Everton with whom he played at Wembley in the Charity Shield. During his career he has made a successful conversion from central defender to a striker.

Has shown that he can score goals in the Premier League despite being with two sides that were ultimately relegated.

# Form Factors

| Season | Team | Tot | St | Sb | Y | R |
|---|---|---|---|---|---|---|
| 93-94 | Ipswich T. | 29 | 28 | 1 | 0 | 0 |
| 94-95 | Ipswich T. | 18 | 14 | 4 | 0 | 0 |
| 96-97 | Leicester C. | 28 | 19 | 9 | 1 | 0 |
| Total | | 75 | 61 | 14 | 1 | 0 |

| | GP | GG | GF | GS | TGR |
|---|---|---|---|---|---|
| 93-94 | 69.05 | 2.90 | 35 | 10 | 28.57 |
| 94-95 | 42.86 | 6.00 | 36 | 3 | 8.33 |
| 96-97 | 47.37 | 2.25 | 46 | 8 | 17.39 |
| Averages | 53.09 | 3.72 | 39.00 | 7.00 | 18.10 |

| | GP | GG | GF | GS | TGR |
|---|---|---|---|---|---|
| 92-93 | 4.76 | 0.00 | 40 | 0 | 0.00 |
| 95-96 | 28.95 | 11.00 | 49 | 1 | 2.04 |
| 96-97 | 21.05 | 0.00 | 62 | 0 | 0.00 |
| Averages | 18.25 | 3.67 | 50.33 | 0.33 | 0.68 |

## MARSHALL, Scott

### Arsenal ❶ CB

Fullname: Scott Roderick Marshall
DOB: 01-05-73 Edinburgh

Bred through the Arsenal system to a first team debut in May 1993 but went away to gain further Football League experience with Rotherham United, Oxford United and Sheffield United before injury to key players allowed him an extended run in the first team during the closing weeks of 1995-96.

Looked to be on the way out from Highbury when Bruce Rioch was manager, but injuries last season gave him another chance to prove his worth to Arsène Wenger, and also score his first goal for the club – a bullet header against Newcastle United. A Scottish Under-21 international, he likes to play his way out of defence.

The arrival of new central players at Arsenal will certainly limit his chances during the coming season.

## Form Factors

| Season | Team | Tot | St | Sb | Y | R |
|---|---|---|---|---|---|---|
| 92-93 | Arsenal | 2 | 2 | 0 | 0 | 0 |
| 95-96 | Arsenal | 11 | 10 | 1 | 4 | 0 |
| 96-97 | Arsenal | 8 | 6 | 2 | 1 | 0 |
| Total | | 21 | 18 | 3 | 5 | 0 |

## MARTYN, Nigel

### Leeds United ❶❷❸❹❺ GK

Fullname: Nigel Anthony Martyn
DOB: 11-08-66 St Austell

Enjoyed a personally outstanding first season with Leeds United last season following a £2.25 million move from Crystal Palace to Elland Road in the summer of 1996. Missed just one game for United during 1996-97 and, with 20 clean sheets, including a run of four consecutive games without conceding a goal, he forced his way back into contention for a place in the England squad. His 20 clean sheets represent the second best record of any 'keeper since the launch of the Premiership. One- time goalkeeper with non-leaguers St. Blazey, he played 340 games for Bristol Rovers and Palace before signing for Leeds.

Recent signings by Leeds will further strengthen the defensive wall in front of one of our most reliable 'keepers.

## Form Factors

| Season | Team | Tot | St | Sb | Y | R |
|---|---|---|---|---|---|---|
| 92-93 | C. Palace | 42 | 42 | 0 | 2 | 0 |
| 94-95 | C. Palace | 37 | 37 | 0 | 1 | 0 |
| 96-97 | Leeds Utd | 37 | 37 | 0 | 1 | 0 |
| Total | | 116 | 116 | 0 | 4 | 0 |

| | GA | GkA | GAp | CS | SO | Rp |
|---|---|---|---|---|---|---|
| 92-93 | 61 | 61 | 1.45 | 11 | 3 | 0 |
| 94-95 | 49 | 41 | 1.11 | 14 | 2 | 0 |
| 96-97 | 38 | 38 | 1.03 | 20 | 4 | 0 |
| Total | 148 | 140 | 1.21 | 45 | 9 | – |

*Nigel Martyn*

## MATTEO, Dominic

## Liverpool ❶❷❸❹ CB

Fullname: Dominic Matteo
DOB: 28-04-74 Dumfries

Trainee Matteo made his breakthrough as a regular in the first team during 1996-97 and looks like a good prospect alongside Wright again in 1997-98. He is naturally left sided and can play wing back as well as his more usual central position. An England Under-21 player, Matteo made the full England squad in 1996-97, only to get injured. He will look to consolidate his position at Anfield in 1997-98 in a fairly tight Liverpool's defence where he has shown great awareness and composure on the ball.

### Form Factors

| Season | Team | Tot | St | Sb | Y | R |
|--------|------|-----|----|----|----|----|
| 94-95 | Liverpool | 7 | 2 | 5 | 0 | 0 |
| 95-96 | Liverpool | 5 | 5 | 0 | 0 | 0 |
| 96-97 | Liverpool | 26 | 22 | 4 | 2 | 0 |
| Total | | 38 | 29 | 9 | 2 | 0 |

| | GP | GG | GF | GS | TGR |
|--------|------|------|------|------|------|
| 94-95 | 16.67 | 0.00 | 65 | 0 | 0.00 |
| 95-96 | 13.16 | 0.00 | 70 | 0 | 0.00 |
| 96-97 | 68.42 | 0.00 | 62 | 0 | 0.00 |
| Averages | 32.75 | 0.00 | 65.67 | 0.00 | 0.00 |

# Manchester U. ❶❷❸❹❺ CB

Fullname:  David May
DOB:       24-06-70 Oldham

Central defender May was forced to play many of his early first team games at full-back after a £1.4 million move from Blackburn Rovers. However he has been playing an improved game in the centre of defence and was even called up into the England squad for the friendly international against Mexico in March, although he did not actually make it into the team. That recognition by the England coach just goes to confirm what a superb season May had in the United defence last term.

He started 28 games in 1996-97 and put in a further appearance as substitute, scoring once. Six goals in the last three years fairly reflects May's role and, at the other end of the field, five yellow cards was a little worrying.

There's still competition for the central defenders' places in the United team but May should get a further chance to prove himself in 1997-98 and perhaps force himself into what we hope will be an England side in France during the summer of 1998!

## Form Factors

| Season | Team | Tot | St | Sb | Y | R |
|---|---|---|---|---|---|---|
| 94-95 | Man. Utd | 19 | 15 | 4 | 2 | 0 |
| 95-96 | Man. Utd | 16 | 11 | 5 | 1 | 0 |
| 96-97 | Man. Utd | 29 | 28 | 1 | 5 | 0 |
| Total | | 64 | 54 | 10 | 8 | 0 |

| | GP | GG | GF | GS | TGR |
|---|---|---|---|---|---|
| 94-95 | 45.24 | 9.50 | 77 | 2 | 2.60 |
| 95-96 | 42.11 | 16.00 | 73 | 1 | 1.37 |
| 96-97 | 76.32 | 9.67 | 76 | 3 | 3.95 |
| Averages | 54.55 | 11.72 | 75.33 | 2.00 | 2.64 |

# Wimbledon ❶❷❸ CB

Fullname:  Brian McAllister
DOB:       30-11-70 Glasgow

Brian McAllister started to make a breakthrough into the Wimbledon defence last season. Having joined the Dons in 1989 as a trainee, he had generally made no more than a couple of handfuls of appearances each season with the exception of 1992-93 when he made 27.

Injury halted progress in the 1995-96 season and it finished with a loan spell at Crewe. However, last season McAllister was either in the team or playing a supporting role on the bench.

Tough and uncompromising, McAllister can hit long range balls from the centre of the Dons' defence and often turns defence into attack in the traditional Wimbledon style.

## Form Factors

| Season | Team | Tot | St | Sb | Y | R |
|---|---|---|---|---|---|---|
| 93-94 | Wimbledon | 13 | 13 | 0 | 2 | 0 |
| 95-96 | Wimbledon | 2 | 2 | 0 | 0 | 0 |
| 96-97 | Wimbledon | 23 | 19 | 4 | 2 | 0 |
| Total | | 38 | 34 | 4 | 4 | 0 |

| | GP | GG | GF | GS | TGR |
|---|---|---|---|---|---|
| 93-94 | 30.95 | 0.00 | 56 | 0 | 0.00 |
| 95-96 | 5.26 | 0.00 | 55 | 0 | 0.00 |
| 96-97 | 60.53 | 0.00 | 49 | 0 | 0.00 |
| Averages | 32.25 | 0.00 | 53.33 | 0.00 | 0.00 |

## McALLISTER, Gary

# Coventry City ❶❷❸❹    M

**Fullname:** Gary McAllister
**DOB:** 25-12-64 Motherwell

Over the past few seasons Gary McAllister has been one of the most highly rated midfield players in England. It came as a surprise when the Scotland captain left Leeds United for Highfield Road for £3 million in the summer of 1996.

The cultured left foot of McAllister first saw the professional football scene with his home town club of Motherwell before moving to Leicester City, from where he joined Leeds United and won a Premiership championship medal in 1992.

Although 32 in December 1996, he is still one of the finest ball players in the Premiership and is deadly from set plays – penalties in Euro '96 excluded! The Sky Blues record signing, he was ever present in 1996-97, playing in every minute of those games, and will play a leading role if the club is to shake off its reputation as perennial strugglers.

*Gary McAllister*

## Form Factors

| Season | Team | Tot | St | Sb | Y | R |
|---|---|---|---|---|---|---|
| 94-95 | Leeds Utd | 41 | 41 | 0 | 1 | 0 |
| 95-96 | Leeds Utd | 36 | 36 | 0 | 1 | 0 |
| 96-97 | Coventry C. | 38 | 38 | 0 | 1 | 0 |
| Total | | 115 | 115 | 0 | 3 | 0 |

| | GP | GG | GF | GS | TGR |
|---|---|---|---|---|---|
| 94-95 | 97.62 | 6.83 | 59 | 6 | 10.17 |
| 95-96 | 94.74 | 7.20 | 40 | 5 | 12.50 |
| 96-97 | 100.00 | 6.33 | 38 | 6 | 15.79 |
| Averages | 97.45 | 6.79 | 45.67 | 5.67 | 12.82 |

## McANESPIE, Steve

# Bolton W.    ❶    FB

**Fullname:** Steve McAnespie
**DOB:** 01-02-72 Kilmarnock

McAnespie joined Bolton shortly after the start of their first Premiership campaign, coming south of the border as a £900,000 signing from Raith, where he had won both the Division One title and the Scottish League Cup.

He came into the team in his normal right-back position and played six consecutive games before he was dropped

*Jason McAteer*

in favour of Scott Green and he didn't get another chance until the very end of the season, by which time the team were already consigned to a season in Nationwide Division One.

In 1996-97 he had another run of games in the early part of the season covering for injuries, but again found himself limited to 13 appearances in total.

A Scottish Youth player who, at 25 years old, will be looking to try to establish a more regular position in the Bolton side.

## Form Factors

| Season | Team | Tot | St | Sb | Y | R |
|--------|------|-----|----|----|----|----|
| 95-96 | Bolton W. | 9 | 7 | 2 | 0 | 0 |
| Total | | 9 | 7 | 2 | 0 | 0 |

| | GP | GG | GF | GS | TGR |
|--------|------|------|------|------|------|
| 95-96 | 23.68 | 0.00 | 39 | 0 | 0.00 |
| Averages | 23.68 | 0.00 | 39.00 | 0.00 | 0.00 |

## McATEER, Jason

### Liverpool ❶❷❸❹ FB

Fullname: Jason McAteer
DOB: 18-06-71 Birkenhead

The flying winger was signed from Bolton Wanderers at the start of the 1995-96 season as a winger or midfielder but Roy Evans converted him to an attacking right wing-back. McAteer proved to have the talent to adapt to this role and he's lost none of his pace. His defensive awareness has improved but he did pick up six bookings in 1996-97.

He is often the channel out of defence and he combines well with McManaman and Fowler up front. He started 36 times, came on once as sub in 1996-97 and scored once. Birkenhead-born, McAteer is also a regular for the Republic of Ireland.

## Form Factors

| Season | Team | Tot | St | Sb | Y | R |
|---|---|---|---|---|---|---|
| 95-96 | Bolton W. | 4 | 4 | 0 | 1 | 0 |
| 95-96 | Liverpool | 29 | 27 | 2 | 4 | 0 |
| 96-97 | Liverpool | 37 | 36 | 1 | 6 | 0 |
| Total | | 70 | 67 | 3 | 11 | 0 |

| | GP | GG | GF | GS | TGR |
|---|---|---|---|---|---|
| 95-96 | 10.53 | 0.00 | 39 | 0 | 0.00 |
| 95-96 | 76.32 | 0.00 | 70 | 0 | 0.00 |
| 96-97 | 97.37 | 37.00 | 62 | 1 | 1.61 |
| Averages | 61.40 | 12.33 | 57.00 | 0.33 | 0.54 |

## McCLAIR, Brian

# Manchester U.   ❶❷         S

Fullname:  Brian John McClair
DOB:         08-12-63 Bellshill

McClair is United's number one substitute and Alex Ferguson often puts him on to wrap up a winning game or to try to work a winning goal in a close encounter. His United career and scoring record, built up over a decade at United, speaks volumes. He has played in over 300 games in all and over 100 in the Premiership.

McClair's appearances are becoming less frequent and more and more from the bench. This trend will continue so he isn't going to see much action during 1997-98, having had his contract renewed for one year.

## Form Factors

| Season | Team | Tot | St | Sb | Y | R |
|---|---|---|---|---|---|---|
| 94-95 | Man. Utd | 40 | 35 | 5 | 1 | 0 |
| 95-96 | Man. Utd | 22 | 12 | 10 | 1 | 0 |
| 96-97 | Man. Utd | 19 | 4 | 15 | 1 | 0 |
| Total | | 81 | 51 | 30 | 3 | 0 |

| | GP | GG | GF | GS | TGR |
|---|---|---|---|---|---|
| 94-95 | 95.24 | 8.00 | 77 | 5 | 6.49 |
| 95-96 | 57.89 | 7.33 | 73 | 3 | 4.11 |
| 96-97 | 50.00 | 0.00 | 76 | 0 | 0.00 |
| Averages | 67.71 | 5.11 | 75.33 | 2.67 | 3.53 |

## McGINLAY, John

# Bolton W.       ❶❷❸        S

Fullname:  John McGinlay
DOB:         08-04-64 Inverness

John McGinlay contributed nearly a quarter of Bolton's 100 Division One goals last season, notching 24 times from 34 games – that's an average of about two goals every three games. He will be looking to be amongst the scorers during 1997-98 and make up for the six he scored in the 1995-96 campaign – a time when he often played as the only man up front.

*John McGinlay*

Started in his native Scotland with Elgin City before moving to Bolton for £125,000 from Millwall, after having spells at Shrewsbury and Bury.

At just 5' 9" McGinlay gets the majority of his goals with his feet and has developed a predatory instinct around the opponents' penalty area. His partnership with Nathan Blake was one of the bonuses from Bolton's season last term and his performances earned him a place not only in the Scottish squad but also in their World Cup side.

## Form Factors

| Season | Team | Tot | St | Sb | Y | R |
|---|---|---|---|---|---|---|
| 95-96 | Bolton W. | 32 | 29 | 3 | 4 | 0 |
| Total | | 32 | 29 | 3 | 4 | 0 |

| | GP | GG | GF | GS | TGR |
|---|---|---|---|---|---|
| 95-96 | 84.21 | 5.33 | 39 | 6 | 15.38 |
| Averages | 84.21 | 5.33 | 39.00 | 6.00 | 15.38 |

## McGOWAN, Gavin

# Arsenal ❶ FB

Fullname: Gavin Gregory McGowan
DOB: 16-01-76 Blackheath

At 21 years old, McGowan will be looking to make a breakthrough into the Arsenal side in the next season. He made his debut three seasons ago, coming in for the injured Nigel Winterburn. Since then he has managed one appearance per season. He can play in either full-back position or in midfield, and is comfortable on either flank.

A former England Youth international it may be another season before he makes a real impact in the Premiership and in your fantasy team.

## Form Factors

| Season | Team | Tot | St | Sb | Y | R |
|---|---|---|---|---|---|---|
| 94-95 | Arsenal | 1 | 1 | 0 | 0 | 0 |
| 95-96 | Arsenal | 1 | 1 | 0 | 0 | 0 |
| 96-97 | Arsenal | 1 | 1 | 0 | 0 | 0 |
| Total | | 3 | 3 | 0 | 0 | 0 |

| | GP | GG | GF | GS | TGR |
|---|---|---|---|---|---|
| 94-95 | 2.38 | 0.00 | 52 | 0 | 0.00 |
| 95-96 | 2.63 | 0.00 | 49 | 0 | 0.00 |
| 96-97 | 2.63 | 0.00 | 62 | 0 | 0.00 |
| Averages | 2.55 | 0.00 | 54.33 | 0.00 | 0.00 |

## McKENZIE, Leon

# Crystal Palace ❶ S

Fullname: Leon Mark McKenzie
DOB: 17-05-78 Croydon

From the famous boxing family that includes Clinton (his father) and Duke (his cousin), Leon McKenzie was a key substitute for Palace last season, coming on 17 times in his 21 appearances. At just 19 he is a small but powerful striker with a great turn of speed.

He came to the fore through the Eagles' reserve team where his performances as a 17 year old, which included a spell of 14 goals in eight games, earned him his full debut.

With Shipperley, Freedman and Dyer vying for the two main striking positions, McKenzie will probably need to make his mark on the Premiership from the bench once again during 1997-98.

## McKINLAY, Billy

## Blackburn Rovers ❶❷    M

Fullname: William McKinlay
DOB: 22-04-69 Glasgow
  A £1.75 million buy from Dundee United, McKinlay has not quite established himself as a first team starter at Ewood Park. In his two full seasons he has figured in just over half of Rovers' games. As an attack-minded central midfield player his tally of three goals in that period is disappointing.
  A full international, McKinlay featured in the Scottish Euro '96 squad. His sometimes aggressive play keeps him in the eyes of most referees and his consistent accumulation of yellow cards means that he invariably suffers suspension.

## Form Factors

| Season | Team | Tot | St | Sb | Y | R |
|---|---|---|---|---|---|---|
| 95-96 | Blackburn | 19 | 13 | 6 | 5 | 1 |
| 96-97 | Blackburn | 25 | 23 | 2 | 12 | 0 |
| Total | | 44 | 36 | 8 | 17 | 1 |

| | GP | GG | GF | GS | TGR |
|---|---|---|---|---|---|
| 95-96 | 50.00 | 9.50 | 61 | 2 | 3.28 |
| 96-97 | 65.79 | 25.00 | 42 | 1 | 2.38 |
| Averages | 57.89 | 17.25 | 51.50 | 1.50 | 2.83 |

## McMANAMAN, Steve

## Liverpool    ❶❷❸❹❺    M

Fullname: Steven McManaman
DOB: 11-02-72 Bootle
  Originally a winger McManaman has played more recently played in free role in front of the midfield. Having been ever-present in 1995-96, he started 37 games in 1996-97 and scored seven times. Now with 18 caps for England, there's no better sight than international

*Steve McManaman*

defences retreating in the face of a McManaman marauding run. He hasn't got the killer instinct of a striker but takes his chances while setting up even more.

He picks up his share of bookings but seems to dodge injury in the same way that he dodges defenders. Should therefore perform regularly in a winning Liverpool side as their creative schemer.

### Form Factors

| Season | Team | Tot | St | Sb | Y | R |
|---|---|---|---|---|---|---|
| 94-95 | Liverpool | 40 | 40 | 0 | 5 | 0 |
| 95-96 | Liverpool | 38 | 38 | 0 | 1 | 0 |
| 96-97 | Liverpool | 37 | 37 | 0 | 5 | 0 |
| Total | | 115 | 115 | 0 | 11 | 0 |

| | GP | GG | GF | GS | TGR |
|---|---|---|---|---|---|
| 94-95 | 95.24 | 5.71 | 65 | 7 | 10.77 |
| 95-96 | 100.00 | 6.33 | 70 | 6 | 8.57 |
| 96-97 | 97.37 | 5.29 | 62 | 7 | 11.29 |
| Averages | 97.54 | 5.78 | 65.67 | 6.67 | 10.21 |

## McVEIGH, Paul

# Tottenham H.  ❶  M

Fullname:  Paul McVeigh
DOB:  06-12-77 Belfast

One of several youngster to make his first team debut for Tottenham Hotspur towards the end of the 1996-97 season. Notched his first Premiership goal on the final day of the season, when he headed Spurs' consolation goal against Coventry City, a goal which almost condemned the Sky Blues to relegation.

McVeigh has worked his way through from the ranks of the youth at Tottenham and enjoyed a good amount of success along the way. Born in Belfast in December 1977 and he will be looking to establish himself during the 1997-98 season.

### Form Factors

| Season | Team | Tot | St | Sb | Y | R |
|---|---|---|---|---|---|---|
| 96-97 | Tottenham | 3 | 2 | 1 | 0 | 0 |
| Total | | 3 | 2 | 1 | 0 | 0 |

| | GP | GG | GF | GS | TGR |
|---|---|---|---|---|---|
| 96-97 | 7.89 | 3.00 | 44 | 1 | 2.27 |
| Averages | 7.89 | 3.00 | 44.00 | 1.00 | 2.27 |

## MIKLOSKO, Ludek

# West Ham U.  ❶❷❸❹  GK

Fullname:  Ludek Miklosko
DOB:  09-12-61 Protesov, Czechoslovakia

Known as 'Ludo' to West Ham supporters, the former Czech international has been one of the Hammers' most consistent players. He has missed just four games in three seasons and only one United player has more than his 156 Premiership appearances. Indeed, until he suffered a one match suspension in the 1995-96 season, he had not missed a game for four years!

In his Premiership career he has kept 47 clean sheets and concedes on average 1.28 goals per game.

At 6'5" and 14 stone he is one of the most imposing goalkeepers in the Premier League but remains remarkably agile. Would earn more fantasy points if he played behind a more watertight defence.

### Form Factors

| Season | Team | Tot | St | Sb | Y | R |
|---|---|---|---|---|---|---|
| 94-95 | West Ham | 42 | 42 | 0 | 1 | 0 |
| 95-96 | West Ham | 36 | 36 | 0 | 1 | 1 |
| 96-97 | West Ham | 36 | 36 | 0 | 0 | 0 |
| Total | | 114 | 114 | 0 | 2 | 1 |

| | GA | GkA | GAp | CS | SO | Rp |
|---|---|---|---|---|---|---|
| 94-95 | 48 | 48 | 1.14 | 13 | 2 | 2 |
| 95-96 | 52 | 47 | 1.31 | 11 | 3 | 0 |
| 96-97 | 48 | 46 | 1.28 | 9 | 1 | 0 |
| Total | 148 | 141 | 1.24 | 33 | 6 | – |

*Ludek Miklosko*

## MILOSEVIC, Savo

# Aston Villa ❶❷❸ S

Fullname: Savo Milosevic
DOB: 02-09-73 Bijeljina,
Yugoslavia

Ever since joining Villa as a £3.5 million signing from Partizan Belgrade in the summer of 1995, Savo Milosevic has been the centre of transfer speculation. Nevertheless he has featured in the majority of Villa's games and in the past two seasons has contributed nearly a quarter of their goals. That's after he had to wait nearly four months for his first goal which came as the first in a hat-trick against Coventry City.

He is a Yugoslav international who is strong on the ball and has a powerful left foot. His play is often characterised by strong surging runs, although the final product isn't always the one required.

A move to Italian side Perugia last season fell through at the last moment and the arrival of Stan Collymore at Villa Park must put another question mark against his long-term future at Villa.

## Form Factors

| Season | Team | Tot | St | Sb | Y | R |
|--------|------|-----|-----|-----|-----|-----|
| 95-96 | Aston Villa | 37 | 36 | 1 | 6 | 0 |
| 96-97 | Aston Villa | 30 | 29 | 1 | 6 | 0 |
| Total | | 67 | 65 | 2 | 12 | 0 |

| | GP | GG | GF | GS | TGR |
|--------|-----|-----|-----|-----|-----|
| 95-96 | 97.37 | 3.08 | 52 | 12 | 23.08 |
| 96-97 | 78.95 | 3.00 | 47 | 10 | 21.28 |
| Averages | 88.16 | 3.04 | 49.50 | 11.00 | 22.18 |

## MOLENAAR, Robert

# Leeds United ❶❷❸ CB

Fullname: Robert Molenaar
DOB: 27-02-69 Zaandam, Holland

A £1 million signing by Leeds United manager George Graham in the winter of 1996 from Dutch side Volendam where he scored three goals in 107 league games. Quickly proved himself as ideally suited to the English game with some robust challenges but his availability for a complete season looks suspect after he picked up five yellow cards in just a dozen games for the Yorkshire club. His first goal, a match winner, was a powerful header against Everton and his dominance in the air and strength on the ground was another good reason for Leeds' high total of clean sheets. Already nicknamed 'The Terminator' by Leeds fans, he will be a big influence throughout the 1997-98 campaign.

## Form Factors

| Season | Team | Tot | St | Sb | Y | R |
|--------|------|-----|-----|-----|-----|-----|
| 96-97 | Leeds Utd | 12 | 12 | 0 | 5 | 0 |
| Total | | 12 | 12 | 0 | 5 | 0 |

| | GP | GG | GF | GS | TGR |
|--------|-----|-----|-----|-----|-----|
| 96-97 | 31.58 | 12.00 | 28 | 1 | 3.57 |
| Averages | 31.58 | 12.00 | 28.00 | 1.00 | 3.57 |

## MONCUR, John

# West Ham U. ❶❷❸ M

Fullname: John Frederick Moncur
DOB: 22-09-66 Stepney

Having started his career at Tottenham, Moncur made his mark in the Premier League at Swindon. He played in 41 of their 42 games in their only season in the top flight but did enough to impress the powers at Upton Park to spend £900,000 to secure his signature.

A succession of injuries and an occasional suspension have limited his availability in each of his three seasons since the move and in the past two seasons he has featured in only slightly more than half of the Hammers' games.

A creative midfield player he finds it difficult to get amongst the goals having scored just nine in his 135 Premiership appearances at the end of last season.

## Form Factors

| Season | Team | Tot | St | Sb | Y | R |
|--------|------|-----|-----|-----|-----|-----|
| 94-95 | West Ham | 30 | 30 | 0 | 7 | 0 |
| 95-96 | West Ham | 20 | 19 | 1 | 4 | 0 |
| 96-97 | West Ham | 27 | 26 | 1 | 8 | 0 |
| Total | | 77 | 75 | 2 | 19 | 0 |

| | GP | GG | GF | GS | TGR |
|--------|-----|-----|-----|-----|-----|
| 94-95 | 71.43 | 15.00 | 44 | 2 | 4.55 |
| 95-96 | 52.63 | 0.00 | 43 | 0 | 0.00 |
| 96-97 | 71.05 | 13.50 | 39 | 2 | 5.13 |
| Averages | 65.04 | 19.25 | 42.00 | 1.33 | 3.22 |

## MONKOU, Ken

### Southampton ❶ CB

**Fullname:** Kenneth John Monkou
**DOB:** 29-11-64 Necare, Surinam

Injury and the failure to impress the then new Southampton manager Graeme Souness, mean that Monkou wasn't the regular he had been in the side since joining them for £750,000 from Chelsea in August 1992.

Born in Surinam, and a Dutch Under-21 international, Monkou is a powerful centre half who can compete in both the air and on the ground. These attributes of his game tend to distract from the fact that he is also quite handy at passing the ball. Having started his career at Feyenoord, he played over 100 senior games at Chelsea before moving to the Dell. Last season, five of his 13 appearances came as a substitute and his six yellow cards in that period was not an impressive record.

May well have a clean slate at the start of the season with new manager Dave Jones but indiscipline remains a problem.

### Form Factors

| Season | Team | Tot | St | Sb | Y | R |
|---|---|---|---|---|---|---|
| 94-95 | Southampton | 31 | 31 | 0 | 11 | 0 |
| 95-96 | Southampton | 32 | 31 | 1 | 7 | 0 |
| 96-97 | Southampton | 13 | 8 | 5 | 6 | 0 |
| Total | | 76 | 70 | 6 | 24 | 0 |

| | GP | GG | GF | GS | TGR |
|---|---|---|---|---|---|
| 94-95 | 73.81 | 31.00 | 61 | 1 | 1.64 |
| 95-96 | 84.21 | 16.00 | 34 | 2 | 5.88 |
| 96-97 | 34.21 | 0.00 | 50 | 0 | 0.00 |
| Averages | 64.08 | 15.67 | 48.33 | 1.00 | 2.51 |

## MORRIS, Jody

### Chelsea ❶❷❸ M

**Fullname:** Jody Morris
**DOB:** 22-12-78 London

A former England under-17 captain, Morris added further to his international career by playing in the World Under-20 competition held in Malaysia during June 1997. He became one of the youngest players to play in the Premier League when he played against Middlesbrough in February 1996 – just six weeks after turning 17.

A creative and skilful midfield player who can play a holding role when required, he is clearly being moulded for the future, playing a dozen times in the Premiership last time – six from the subs bench. He was also a non-playing substitute on a further eight occasions.

Set to make a big impact at Stamford Bridge in the coming seasons.

### Form Factors

| Season | Team | Tot | St | Sb | Y | R |
|---|---|---|---|---|---|---|
| 95-96 | Chelsea | 1 | 0 | 1 | 0 | 0 |
| 96-97 | Chelsea | 12 | 6 | 6 | 1 | 0 |
| Total | | 13 | 6 | 7 | 1 | 0 |

| | GP | GG | GF | GS | TGR |
|---|---|---|---|---|---|
| 95-96 | 2.63 | 0.00 | 46 | 0 | 0.00 |
| 96-97 | 31.58 | 0.00 | 58 | 0 | 0.00 |
| Averages | 17.11 | 0.00 | 52.00 | 0.00 | 0.00 |

## MOSES, Adrian

### Barnsley ❶❷ CB

Fullname: Adrian Paul Moses
DOB: 04-05-75 Doncaster

A central defender who started as a trainee at Oakwell, breaking into the first team in the 1994-95 season. Last season was the 22-year-old's best by far with 28 appearances and two goals.

Often employed as an out-and-out marker where he can use his undoubted tackling ability to good effect. Made his 50th appearance last term.

## MURRAY, Scott

### Aston Villa ❶ FB

Fullname: Scott George Murray
DOB: 26-05-74 Aberdeen

A 23-year-old full-back who joined Villa in March 1994 from Scottish non-league side Fraserburgh for £35,000. He made his Villa debut in the 1995-96 season when Gary Charles suffered a broken ankle, but the arrival of Nelson has once again left Murray looking for appearances.

A player with potential but unlikely to feature during 1997-98 unless as injury cover.

### Form Factors

| Season | Team | Tot | St | Sb | Y | R |
|---|---|---|---|---|---|---|
| 95-96 | Aston Villa | 3 | 3 | 0 | 0 | 0 |
| 96-97 | Aston Villa | 1 | 1 | 0 | 0 | 0 |
| Total | | 4 | 4 | 0 | 0 | 0 |

| | GP | GG | GF | GS | TGR |
|---|---|---|---|---|---|
| 95-96 | 7.89 | 0.00 | 52 | 0 | 0.00 |
| 96-97 | 2.63 | 0.00 | 47 | 0 | 0.00 |
| Averages | 5.26 | 0.00 | 49.50 | 0.00 | 0.00 |

## MUSCAT, Kevin

### Crystal Palace ❶ FB

Fullname: Kevin Muscat
DOB: 07-08-73 Bolton

Having been born in Bolton, Muscat arrived at Selhurst Park via Australia where he made his name playing for South Melbourne.

A defender, signed in June 1996, he has played at both full-back and sweeper during his first full season in English football.

He has proved a more than valuable signing for Palace and featured in 44 of their Nationwide Division One games last season, contributing two goals in the process.

Although primarily a right-back, he has made an impression as an attacking left-back who packs a venomous shot. Quick and strong, his aggressive nature inevitably leads to referees brandishing a yellow card.

## MYERS, Andy

### Chelsea ❶❷❸ CB

Fullname: Andrew John Myers
DOB: 03-11-73 Hounslow

A small, energetic player who can play in defence and/or midfield, he has found it hard to establish himself in the Chelsea first team and has not been helped by a spate of injuries. The first of these struck during the 1995-96 season, limiting him to just 20 of Chelsea's Premiership games, and again in the early part of last season. His 18 games came largely as part of the starting line-up but he was one of the players who Gullit subbed most of all.

His goal against Sheffield Wednesday at Hillsborough was his first and only one in

the Premiership at the end of last season.
   Fast and skilful, Myers may well find
that he is utilised as a squad player during
the 1997-98 season.

## Form Factors

| Season | Team | Tot | St | Sb | Y | R |
|---|---|---|---|---|---|---|
| 94-95 | Chelsea | 10 | 9 | 1 | 1 | 0 |
| 95-96 | Chelsea | 20 | 20 | 0 | 2 | 0 |
| 96-97 | Chelsea | 18 | 15 | 3 | 2 | 0 |
| Total | | 48 | 44 | 4 | 5 | 0 |

| | GP | GG | GF | GS | TGR |
|---|---|---|---|---|---|
| 94-95 | 23.81 | 0.00 | 50 | 0 | 0.00 |
| 95-96 | 52.63 | 0.00 | 46 | 0 | 0.00 |
| 96-97 | 47.37 | 18.00 | 58 | 1 | 1.72 |
| Averages | 41.27 | 6.00 | 51.33 | 0.33 | 0.57 |

## NASH, Carlo

### Crystal Palace   ❶❷   GK

Fullname:  Carlo Nash
DOB:        13-09-73
   For Carlo Nash read 'Roy of the
Rovers'. During 1995-96 he was playing
non-league football for Clitheroe before
signing for Crystal Palace for £35,000.
Nash signed in time for Palace's pre-
season tour but the departure of Nigel
Martyn to Leeds saw Chris Day arrive
from Spurs. Nash was seen as cover but,
when Day was on Under-21 duty, the then
manager Dave Bassett elected for Bobby
Mimms as a stand-in. Later, following
injury to Day in September, Nash made
his debut and then established himself as
first choice for the final 18 games of the
league season and the play-offs
themselves.
   The battle for the Number One jersey at
Selhurst Park will continue during 1997-
98.

*Kevin Muscat*

## NDAH, George

### Crystal Palace   ❶❷   M

Fullname:  George Ndah
DOB:        23-12-74 Dulwich
   Ndah has struggled to become a regular
in the Crystal Palace team. He played in
only 25 games in total during Palace's
two previous Premiership seasons and the
drop to Division One failed to help his
cause. Indeed he found himself on loan to
Bournemouth at one point when Dave
Bassett was in charge. Last season saw
Ndah as a semi-permanent fixture on the
bench and 20 of his 25 appearances came

as a result of joining the play as a substitute.

The departure of John Salako to Coventry City at the start of the 1995-96 season looked to be the ideal opportunity for the skilful winger cum striker to establish himself. It didn't happen and things will only be harder in the Premiership.

## Form Factors

| Season | Team | Tot | St | Sb | Y | R |
|---|---|---|---|---|---|---|
| 92-93 | C. Palace | 13 | 4 | 9 | 0 | 0 |
| 94-95 | C. Palace | 12 | 5 | 7 | 0 | 0 |
| Total | | 25 | 9 | 16 | 0 | 0 |

| | GP | GG | GF | GS | TGR |
|---|---|---|---|---|---|
| 92-93 | 30.95 | 0.00 | 48 | 0 | 0.00 |
| 94-95 | 28.57 | 12.00 | 34 | 1 | 2.94 |
| Averages | 29.76 | 6.00 | 41.00 | 0.50 | 1.47 |

## NEILSON, Alan

# Southampton ❶❷❸ CB

Fullname: Alan Bruce Neilson
DOB: 26-09-72 Wegburg, Germany

Despite his name, Neilson is a Welsh intentional defender who was born in Germany. He started his career at Newcastle United as a trainee, before moving to the Dell for £500,000 in the summer of 1995. Made his debut in the Premier League with Newcastle but in the past two seasons has established himself as a major influence in the Saints side.

Known as a hard tackler, he had his best season during 1996-97, playing in 29 of the Saints games but still awaits his first senior goal for the club.

Had a particularly bad week in mid November playing in the Welsh side that lost 7-1 to Holland in a World Cup qualifier, and then the Southampton side that lost 7-1 at Everton.

## Form Factors

| Season | Team | Tot | St | Sb | Y | R |
|---|---|---|---|---|---|---|
| 94-95 | Newcastle | 6 | 5 | 1 | 0 | 0 |
| 95-96 | Southampton | 18 | 15 | 3 | 3 | 0 |
| 96-97 | Southampton | 29 | 24 | 5 | 4 | 0 |
| Total | | 53 | 44 | 9 | 7 | 0 |

| | GP | GG | GF | GS | TGR |
|---|---|---|---|---|---|
| 94-95 | 14.29 | 0.00 | 67 | 0 | 0.00 |
| 95-96 | 47.37 | 0.00 | 34 | 0 | 0.00 |
| 96-97 | 76.32 | 0.00 | 50 | 0 | 0.00 |
| Averages | 56.56 | 0.00 | 50.33 | 0.00 | 0.00 |

## NELSON, Fernando

# Aston Villa ❶❷❸❹ FB

Fullname: Fernando Nelson
DOB: 11-05-71

Nelson was brought to Villa Park last summer when Gary Charles broke his ankle. A left-sided defender who operates as an attacking wing-back, he was a £1.75 million signing from Portuguese club Sport Lisbon, for whom he made over 120 appearances. A member of the full international Portuguese side he was a regular first-choice selection for Villa, featuring in 34 of Villa's 38 Premiership games. He still awaits his first Premiership goal for the club and it will be interesting to watch the competition between him and a fit Gary Charles.

## Form Factors

| Season | Team | Tot | St | Sb | Y | R |
|---|---|---|---|---|---|---|
| 96-97 | Aston Villa | 34 | 33 | 1 | 6 | 0 |
| Total | | 34 | 33 | 1 | 6 | 0 |

| | GP | GG | GF | GS | TGR |
|---|---|---|---|---|---|
| 96-97 | 89.47 | 0.00 | 47 | 0 | 0.00 |
| Averages | 89.47 | 0.00 | 47.00 | 0.00 | 0.00 |

## NETHERCOTT, Stuart

# Tottenham H. ❶ CB

Fullname: Stuart David Nethercott
DOB: 21-03-73 Ilford

A central defender who has been on the fringe of the Spurs' first team for a number of years but has yet to make a permanent claim for a regular place in the side.

He is a very strong and competitive player who can dominate in the air. He has showed his versatility at times by playing in the Tottenham midfield, especially during the 1995-96 season when he acted as cover for David Howells.

Despite his aerial presence he has yet to score in the Premiership but has chalked up a goal for Spurs in the FA Cup. He played eight times for England U21 and to gain Football League experience had loan spells with Maidstone United and Barnet. Actually started his football career as a schoolboy for north London rivals Arsenal.

## Form Factors

| Season | Team | Tot | St | Sb | Y | R |
|--------|----------|-----|----|----|---|---|
| 94-95 | Tottenham | 17 | 8 | 9 | 0 | 0 |
| 95-96 | Tottenham | 13 | 9 | 4 | 2 | 0 |
| 96-97 | Tottenham | 9 | 2 | 7 | 2 | 0 |
| Total | | 39 | 19 | 20 | 4 | 0 |

| | GP | GG | GF | GS | TGR |
|--------|-------|------|-------|------|------|
| 94-95 | 40.48 | 0.00 | 66 | 0 | 0.00 |
| 95-96 | 34.21 | 0.00 | 50 | 0 | 0.00 |
| 96-97 | 23.68 | 0.00 | 44 | 0 | 0.00 |
| Averages | 32.79 | 0.00 | 53.33 | 0.00 | 0.00 |

## NEVILLE, Gary

# Manchester U. ❶❷❸❹❺ FB

Fullname: Gary Alexander Neville
DOB: 18-02-75 Bury

Neville G, a product of the Reds' successful youth policy, established himself as a regular in the United side half way through the 1994-95 season. He has completed two further seasons, each made up of 30 starts and one substitute appearance.

After making his full England debut against Japan in the Umbro Cup in the same season he broke into the United side, Neville has carried his form into

*Gary Neville*

regular appearances for England, at right-back and in central defence when required. His performances in Euro '96 illustrated his skill and assurance.

The 22-year old scored his first goal in the Premiership in 1996-97. His looping crosses and excellent long throw contribute to the Reds' attacking options.

He was included in the PFA Premiership team of the year for the 1996-97 season and may hold down that place for a number of years to come. An excellent fantasy player.

## Form Factors

| Season | Team | Tot | St | Sb | Y | R |
|---|---|---|---|---|---|---|
| 94-95 | Man. Utd | 18 | 16 | 2 | 5 | 0 |
| 95-96 | Man. Utd | 31 | 30 | 1 | 7 | 0 |
| 96-97 | Man. Utd | 31 | 30 | 1 | 4 | 0 |
| Total | | 80 | 76 | 4 | 16 | 0 |

| | GP | GG | GF | GS | TGR |
|---|---|---|---|---|---|
| 94-95 | 42.86 | 0.00 | 77 | 0 | 0.00 |
| 95-96 | 81.58 | 0.00 | 73 | 0 | 0.00 |
| 96-97 | 81.58 | 31.00 | 76 | 1 | 40.79 |
| Averages | 68.67 | 31.00 | 75.33 | 0.33 | 13.60 |

## NEVILLE, Phil

# Manchester U. ❶❷❸❹    FB

Fullname:  Philip John Neville
DOB:        21-01-77 Bury

The younger brother of Gary, this 20-year old can play anywhere across the back four at Old Trafford. Philip Neville has made remarkable progress from trainee and a couple of games in 1994-95, to regular in both the United and England set-up.

The youngster suffered a career setback mid way through the 1996-97 season when glandular fever struck. He managed 15 starts and three substitute appearances and his recent performances suggest he is back to his best. A best that brother Gary says makes him the better player!

## Form Factors

| Season | Team | Tot | St | Sb | Y | R |
|---|---|---|---|---|---|---|
| 94-95 | Man. Utd | 2 | 1 | 1 | 0 | 0 |
| 95-96 | Man. Utd | 24 | 21 | 3 | 2 | 0 |
| 96-97 | Man. Utd | 18 | 15 | 3 | 2 | 0 |
| Total | | 44 | 37 | 7 | 4 | 0 |

| | GP | GG | GF | GS | TGR |
|---|---|---|---|---|---|
| 94-95 | 4.76 | 0.00 | 77 | 0 | 0.00 |
| 95-96 | 63.16 | 0.00 | 73 | 0 | 0.00 |
| 96-97 | 47.37 | 0.00 | 76 | 0 | 0.00 |
| Averages | 38.43 | 0.00 | 75.33 | 0.00 | 0.00 |

## NEWSOME, Jon

# Sheffield W.    ❶    CB

Fullname:  Jonathan Newsome
DOB:        06-09-70 Sheffield

Tall central defender who is back for his second spell at Hillsborough. He worked his way through from the youth team with the Owls but joined Leeds United in a £150,000 deal after just ten first team games. Made his name with Leeds as a defender in the side which won the championship under Howard Wilkinson but departed in June 1994 in a £1 million move to Norwich City. As Norwich wallowed in the bottom half of Division One, he rejoined Wednesday at a cost of £1.6 million but injury has limited him to 10 Premier League outings last season. Will face stiff competition to get a regular place during 1997-98.

## Form Factors

| Season | Team | Tot | St | Sb | Y | R |
|---|---|---|---|---|---|---|
| 94-95 | Norwich City | 35 | 35 | 0 | 4 | 0 |
| 95-96 | Sheffield W. | 8 | 8 | 0 | 1 | 0 |
| 96-97 | Sheffield W. | 10 | 10 | 0 | 1 | 0 |
| Total | | 53 | 53 | 0 | 6 | 0 |

| | GP | GG | GF | GS | TGR |
|---|---|---|---|---|---|
| 94-95 | 83.33 | 11.67 | 37 | 3 | 8.11 |
| 95-96 | 21.05 | 8.00 | 48 | 1 | 2.08 |
| 96-97 | 26.32 | 10.00 | 50 | 1 | 2.00 |
| Averages | 43.57 | 9.89 | 45.00 | 1.67 | 4.06 |

## NEWTON, Eddie

# Chelsea ❶❷❸ M

Fullname: Edward John Ikem Newton
DOB: 13-12-71 Hammersmith
Scored the goal, eight minutes from time, that made sure of Chelsea's FA Cup victory at the end of the 1996-97 season, a reward for his fight-back from injury.

An astute midfield player who adds balance to the Chelsea side especially when playing alongside more adventurous midfield players.

He joined Chelsea as a trainee in May 1990 and won England Under-21 caps. Apart from a short spell on loan at Cardiff, he has played all his football at Stamford Bridge, making his 150th senior appearance last season. Played in 30 games during the 1994-95 season, but a broken shin limited his availability during 1995-96. Newton had an operation on a cartilage problem in the close season but is expected to be fit for the start of the 1997-98 season.

Jon Newsome

## Form Factors

| Season | Team | Tot | St | Sb | Y | R |
|---|---|---|---|---|---|---|
| 94-95 | Chelsea | 30 | 22 | 8 | 0 | 0 |
| 95-96 | Chelsea | 24 | 21 | 3 | 2 | 0 |
| 96-97 | Chelsea | 15 | 13 | 2 | 2 | 0 |
| Total | | 69 | 56 | 13 | 4 | 0 |

| | GP | GG | GF | GS | TGR |
|---|---|---|---|---|---|
| 94-95 | 71.43 | 30.00 | 50 | 1 | 2.00 |
| 95-96 | 63.16 | 24.00 | 46 | 1 | 2.17 |
| 96-97 | 39.47 | 0.00 | 58 | 0 | 0.00 |
| Averages | 58.02 | 18.00 | 51.33 | 0.67 | 1.39 |

## NICOL, Steve

# Sheffield W. ❶❷ CB

Fullname: Stephen Nicol
DOB: 01-12-61 Irvine
Timeless player who has excelled in defence and midfield during a glittering career which has seen him play in four championship winning sides and one Champions' Cup success with Liverpool. Made his Liverpool debut in 1981 after a £300,000 move from Ayr United and went on to play 434 games for the Reds before joining Notts County on a free transfer in January 1995. He has

Allan Nielsen

| | GP | GG | GF | GS | TGR |
|---|---|---|---|---|---|
| 94-95 | 9.52 | 0.00 | 65 | 0 | 0.00 |
| 95-96 | 50.00 | 0.00 | 48 | 0 | 0.00 |
| 96-97 | 60.53 | 0.00 | 50 | 0 | 0.00 |
| Averages | 40.02 | 0.00 | 54.33 | 0.00 | 0.00 |

## NIELSEN, Allan

## Tottenham H.  ❶❷❸  M

Fullname:  Allan Nielsen
DOB:  13-03-71

Twenty six year old Danish international midfielder who hit the headlines in his native land when he was signed by crack German side Bayern Munich when just 17-years of age. However, the young Nielsen didn't live up to the hype and he returned home to play his football in Esbjerg after just one appearance in three years for Bayern. He progressed through the ranks of Danish club football, moving to Odense, FC Copenhagen and then Brondby.

A Danish international, who scored within a minute of making his debut for Denmark – this is believed to be a world record.

Nielsen went some way to showing his potential in his first season with Spurs, scoring six times in 29 Premiership appearances from his midfield role, and is sure to be a major influence on those around him in the coming seasons.

### Form Factors

| Season | Team | Tot | St | Sb | Y | R |
|---|---|---|---|---|---|---|
| 96-97 | Tottenham | 29 | 28 | 1 | 6 | 0 |
| Total | | 29 | 28 | 1 | 6 | 0 |

| | GP | GG | GF | GS | TGR |
|---|---|---|---|---|---|
| 96-97 | 76.32 | 4.83 | 44 | 6 | 13.64 |
| Averages | 76.32 | 4.83 | 44.00 | 6.00 | 13.64 |

continued to show his versatility during his time with Sheffield Wednesday, playing in a number of different positions since having his career rejuvenated by manager David Pleat. A model professional who should again be integral in Wednesday's plans for 1997-98 although maybe more from the bench.

### Form Factors

| Season | Team | Tot | St | Sb | Y | R |
|---|---|---|---|---|---|---|
| 94-95 | Liverpool | 4 | 4 | 0 | 0 | 0 |
| 95-96 | Sheffield W. | 19 | 18 | 1 | 1 | 0 |
| 96-97 | Sheffield W. | 23 | 19 | 4 | 0 | 0 |
| Total | | 46 | 41 | 5 | 1 | 0 |

## NOLAN, Ian

# Sheffield W.   ❶❷❸❹   FB

Fullname:  Ian Robert Nolan
DOB:       09-07-70 Liverpool
  Defender who has proved to be a very shrewd purchase at £1.5 million, having been ever-present in two of his three seasons at Hillsborough. His right foot is the stronger of the two although he has mainly been used down the left side of the Sheffield Wednesday back line. Was past his 20th birthday when he came into the professional game with Tranmere Rovers after spells with Northwich Victoria and Marine. The £10,000 Tranmere gambled on his signature was handsomely repaid with his move to Hillsborough where he has become firmly entrenched at full-back.
  Was an ever present in the Wednesday side last season and was only substituted in one of those 38 games. Expect a similar performance again for 1997-98.

## Form Factors

| Season | Team | Tot | St | Sb | Y | R |
|--------|------|-----|-----|-----|-----|-----|
| 94-95 | Sheffield W. | 42 | 42 | 0 | 4 | 0 |
| 95-96 | Sheffield W. | 29 | 29 | 0 | 1 | 0 |
| 96-97 | Sheffield W. | 38 | 38 | 0 | 1 | 0 |
| Total | | 109 | 109 | 0 | 6 | 0 |

| | GP | GG | GF | GS | TGR |
|--------|-----|-----|-----|-----|-----|
| 94-95 | 100.00 | 14.00 | 49 | 3 | 6.12 |
| 95-96 | 76.32 | 0.00 | 48 | 0 | 0.00 |
| 96-97 | 100.00 | 38.00 | 50 | 1 | 2.00 |
| Averages | 92.11 | 17.33 | 49.00 | 1.33 | 2.71 |

## OAKES, Michael

# Aston Villa   ❶❷❸   GK

Fullname:  Michael Oakes
DOB:       30-10-73 Northwich
  The England Under-21 international seized his chance last season when Villa's established No. 1 Mark Bosnich was injured and unable to start the season. The son of former Manchester City hero and record appearance holder Alan Oakes, he competed in 20 of Villa's games last term, twice as a substitute, and equalled Bosnich's achievement of nine clean sheets in his run – twice managing shut-outs in three consecutive games.
  Like Bosnich he conceded just 17 goals last term and, although Bosnich regained his place on each occasion he was fit, it is clear that Oakes, who is just 23 and joined the club as a trainee, looks set to have a glittering future ahead of him. He will see that future as being owner of the No. 1 shirt at Villa Park.
  Oakes will do well when he is in the team but the battle for top honcho at Villa may make him one to avoid for the time being.

## Form Factors

| Season | Team | Tot | St | Sb | Y | R |
|--------|------|-----|-----|-----|-----|-----|
| 96-97 | Aston Villa | 20 | 18 | 2 | 0 | 0 |
| Total | | 20 | 18 | 2 | 0 | 0 |

| | GA | GkA | GAp | CS | SO | Rp |
|--------|-----|-----|-----|-----|-----|-----|
| 96-97 | 34 | 17 | 0.85 | 9 | 3 | 2 |
| Total | 34 | 17 | 0.85 | 9 | 3 | – |

## OAKES, Scott

# Sheffield W. ❶❷ S

Fullname: Scott John Oakes
DOB: 05-08-72 Leicester

Played under present manager David Pleat whilst with Luton Town and Leicester City and it was Pleat who snapped up the Leicester born striker from the Hatters with a £450,000 bid in the summer of 1996. Made only three appearances in the league with his hometown club but caught the eye as a member of the Luton side which reached the last four of the FA Cup. Was almost ever-present in the Luton side until injury forced him out and has yet to fully establish himself at Hillsborough, having been used as a substitute in 12 of his 19 Premiership run outs last season. A tricky, pacey winger, Oakes likes to run at defenders with the ball.

## Form Factors

| Season | Team | Tot | St | Sb | Y | R |
|--------|------|-----|-----|-----|-----|-----|
| 96-97 | Sheffield W. | 19 | 7 | 12 | 1 | 0 |
| Total | | 19 | 7 | 12 | 1 | 0 |

| | GP | GG | GF | GS | TGR |
|--------|-----|-----|-----|-----|-----|
| 96-97 | 50.00 | 19.00 | 50 | 1 | 2.00 |
| Averages | 50.00 | 19.00 | 50.00 | 1.00 | 2.00 |

## OAKLEY, Matthew

# Southampton ❶❷ M

Fullname: Matthew Oakley
DOB: 17-08-77 Peterborough

A midfield player with great energy, Oakley made his entry into the Premiership at the end of the 1994-95 season, coming on as a sub against Everton. Since then he has developed his game and seems especially at home playing wide on either flank.

Having played a five and five season making 10 appearances in 1995-96, he was one of the Saints' most consistent players last term, chalking up 28 appearances and scoring three goals. At just 20, it was not surprising he was substituted 11 times (joint most with Berkovic).

Joined Southampton as a trainee in the summer of 1995.

## Form Factors

| Season | Team | Tot | St | Sb | Y | R |
|--------|------|-----|-----|-----|-----|-----|
| 94-95 | Southampton | 1 | 0 | 1 | 0 | 0 |
| 95-96 | Southampton | 10 | 5 | 5 | 0 | 0 |
| 96-97 | Southampton | 28 | 23 | 5 | 0 | 0 |
| Total | | 39 | 28 | 11 | 0 | 0 |

| | GP | GG | GF | GS | TGR |
|--------|-----|-----|-----|-----|-----|
| 94-95 | 2.38 | 0.00 | 61 | 0 | 0.00 |
| 95-96 | 26.32 | 0.00 | 34 | 0 | 0.00 |
| 96-97 | 73.68 | 9.33 | 50 | 3 | 6.00 |
| Averages | 34.13 | 3.11 | 48.33 | 1.00 | 2.00 |

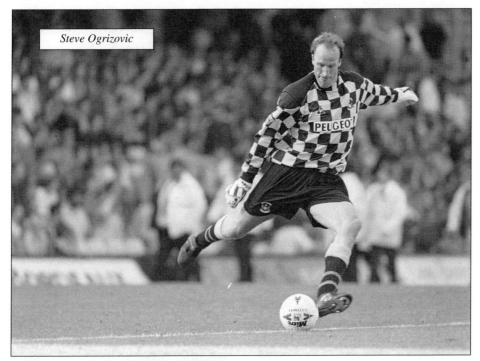

*Steve Ogrizovic*

## OGRIZOVIC, Steve

## Coventry City ❶❷❸❹ GK

Fullname: Steven Ogrizovic
DOB: 12-09-57 Mansfield
Will be 40 early in the new season but such is his consistency, fitness and agility, he is likely to be around for many years to come. Was ever present behind the Coventry defence in 1996-97 and only a broken nose sustained in the final ten minutes of the match at Arsenal prevented him from completing a 100% season. Needless to say he was between the sticks in the very next match!

Oggy was outstanding in the final match of the season to help secure the three points needed at Tottenham to ensure Coventry's survival for another year. Missed only two league games from the start of 1982-83 to the end of 1991-

92. Joined Coventry from Shrewsbury in 1984 after spells with Liverpool and Chesterfield. Won an FA Cup winners medal in 1987 and is unlucky not to have won the greater number of honours he fully deserves.

### Form Factors

| Season | Team | Tot | St | Sb | Y | R |
|--------|---------|-----|----|----|----|---|
| 94-95 | Coventry C. | 33 | 33 | 0 | 1 | 0 |
| 95-96 | Coventry C. | 25 | 25 | 0 | 0 | 0 |
| 96-97 | Coventry C. | 38 | 38 | 0 | 1 | 0 |
| Total | | 96 | 96 | 0 | 2 | 0 |

| | GA | GkA | GAp | CS | SO | Rp |
|-------|-----|-----|------|----|----|----|
| 94-95 | 62 | 55 | 1.67 | 11 | 2 | 0 |
| 95-96 | 60 | 33 | 1.32 | 8 | 4 | 0 |
| 96-97 | 54 | 54 | 1.42 | 2 | 2 | 0 |
| Total | 176 | 142 | 1.48 | 21 | 8 | – |

## OSTENSTAD, Egil

### Southampton  ❶❷❸  S

Fullname:  Egil Ostenstad
DOB:  02-01-72 Haugesund, Norway
  Another of Graeme Souness' early signings during his one year reign as manager at the Dell. Ostenstad averaged a goal every three games for the Saints last season and his hat-trick in the 6-3 win over Manchester United gained him initial recognition nationally.
  A Norwegian international, he is a tall striker in the normal Norwegian ilk.

*Egil Ostenstad*

Quick, he can use either foot and was Southampton's second top scorer in the Premier League last season.

### Form Factors

| Season | Team | Tot | St | Sb | | Y | R |
|---|---|---|---|---|---|---|---|
| 96-97 | Southampton | 30 | 29 | 1 | | 3 | 0 |
| Total | | 30 | 29 | 1 | | 3 | 0 |

| | GP | GG | GF | GS | TGR |
|---|---|---|---|---|---|
| 96-97 | 78.95 | 3.00 | 50 | 10 | 20.00 |
| Averages | 78.95 | 3.00 | 50.00 | 10.00 | 20.00 |

## OVERMARS, Marc

### Arsenal  ❶❷❸❹❺  S

Fullname:  Marc Overmars
DOB:  29-3-73 Emst, Holland
  If you rate your players by their speed then Arsenal's £7 million man will come top of your charts. Overmars is not a product of the Ajax youth scene but broke into their first team in the 1992-93 season after being spotted playing in the Dutch second division with Tilburg-based club Willem II.
  Such was his impact he made it straight into the Dutch international side, scoring within five minutes of his debut against Turkey. Most England fans will remember him as the player Des Walker dragged back to concede a penalty during the 1990 World Cup qualifier at Wembley.
  Since then he has been the subject of transfer speculation but a cruciate ligament injury forced him to miss Euro '96 and much of last season. He is now back to full fitness and will be the scourge of full-backs throughout the Premiership.

## OWEN, Michael

# Liverpool    ❶    S

Fullname: Michael Owen
DOB:

Only played in the last two games of 1996-97 but considered a hot prospect at Anfield. With Collymore gone, there's room for a striker to make the grade, although at 17 years of age neither Owen or manager Evans are in any hurry.

Owen scored a goal on his debut (substitute) appearance against Wimbledon and, if he starts, he's always likely to score. One to watch or gamble on.

## Form Factors

| Season | Team | Tot | St | Sb | Y | R |
|--------|------|-----|----|----|----|----|
| 96-97 | Liverpool | 2 | 1 | 1 | 0 | 0 |
| Total | | 2 | 1 | 1 | 0 | 0 |

| | GP | GG | GF | GS | TGR |
|--------|------|------|------|------|------|
| 96-97 | 5.26 | 2.00 | 62 | 1 | 1.61 |
| Averages | 5.26 | 2.00 | 62.00 | 1.00 | 1.61 |

## PAATELAINEN, Mixu

# Bolton W.    ❶    S

Fullname: Mixu Paatelainen
DOB: 03-02-67 Helsinki, Finland

Paatelainen found himself coming on from the Bolton subs' bench towards the end of last season, with seven of his 10 appearances coming in that fashion.

A strong, physical striker, he has mainly deputised for John McGinlay, which was often the case during the 1995-96 season when he made 15 Premiership appearances. Injuries also inhibited his presence during Bolton's last spell in the top flight.

Born in Helsinki, the Finnish international moved to Scotland for his first experience of football in Britain and had successful spells with both Dundee United and Aberdeen.

Now aged 30, he will find it difficult to dislodge the McGinlay/Blake partnership.

## Form Factors

| Season | Team | Tot | St | Sb | Y | R |
|--------|------|-----|----|----|----|----|
| 95-96 | Bolton W. | 15 | 12 | 3 | 1 | 0 |
| Total | | 15 | 12 | 3 | 1 | 0 |

| | GP | GG | GF | GS | TGR |
|--------|------|------|------|------|------|
| 95-96 | 39.47 | 15.00 | 39 | 1 | 2.56 |
| Averages | 39.47 | 15.00 | 39.00 | 1.00 | 2.56 |

## PALLISTER, Gary

# Manchester U. ❶❷❸❹ CB

**Fullname:** Gary Andrew Pallister
**DOB:** 30-06-65 Ramsgate

Alex Ferguson paid a record £2.3 million for Pallister in 1989 and the ex Middlesbrough player, after a shaky start, formed a solid partnership with Steve Bruce which amazingly never transferred to the England central defence.

At 6' 4" not too many strikers can cause him problems in the air and he is quick on the turn. Pallister could break the 300 league and Premiership game barrier in the 1997-98 season. Experience counts for much in a defensive role, so expect Pallister to continue making a strong case for his presence in a winning United team.

Injury, which has reduced Pallister's involvement in international football, is the only thing between Pallister and another successful season.

## Form Factors

| Season | Team | Tot | St | Sb | Y | R |
|--------|------|-----|-----|-----|-----|-----|
| 94-95 | Man. Utd | 42 | 42 | 0 | 0 | 0 |
| 95-96 | Man. Utd | 21 | 21 | 0 | 3 | 0 |
| 96-97 | Man. Utd | 27 | 27 | 0 | 4 | 0 |
| Total | | 90 | 90 | 0 | 7 | 0 |

| | GP | GG | GF | GS | TGR |
|--------|------|------|------|------|------|
| 94-95 | 100.00 | 21.00 | 77 | 2 | 2.60 |
| 95-96 | 55.26 | 21.00 | 73 | 1 | 1.37 |
| 96-97 | 71.05 | 9.00 | 76 | 3 | 3.95 |
| Averages | 75.44 | 17.00 | 75.33 | 2.00 | 2.64 |

## PALMER, Carlton

# Leeds United ❶ M

**Fullname:** Carlton Lloyd Palmer
**DOB:** 05-12-65 Rowley Regis

Possibly not one of the most naturally gifted players ever to have won 18 caps for England but would be an asset to any club midfield. Missed just six Premiership matches during his first two seasons at Elland Road but a total of 25 bookings over the past three seasons does equal a good number of suspensions for a tenacious midfielder who made his breakthrough back in 1985 with West Bromwich Albion. Joined Sheffield Wednesday for £750,000 in 1989 and five years later moved across the county in a £2.6 million transfer to Leeds. More noted for his defensive holding work in midfield, he has still managed to score six goals in 126 games for United. May not be a permanent fixture in the Leeds side any more.

## Form Factors

| Season | Team | Tot | St | Sb | Y | R |
|--------|------|-----|-----|-----|-----|-----|
| 94-95 | Leeds Utd | 39 | 39 | 0 | 7 | 0 |
| 95-96 | Leeds Utd | 35 | 35 | 0 | 8 | 0 |
| 96-97 | Leeds Utd | 28 | 26 | 2 | 10 | 1 |
| Total | | 102 | 100 | 2 | 25 | 1 |

| | GP | GG | GF | GS | TGR |
|--------|------|------|------|------|------|
| 94-95 | 92.86 | 13.00 | 59 | 3 | 5.08 |
| 95-96 | 92.11 | 17.50 | 40 | 2 | 5.00 |
| 96-97 | 73.68 | 0.00 | 28 | 0 | 0.00 |
| Averages | 86.22 | 10.17 | 42.33 | 1.67 | 3.36 |

## PARKER, Garry

### Leicester City ❶❷❸❹    M

Fullname: Garry Stuart Parker
DOB: 07-09-65 Oxford

Experienced and well-respected midfielder who has scored a number of top quality goals during his successful career although his main attribute is creating chances for those around him. A fine reader of the game, he joined Leicester City for £300,000 in February 1995 and missed just six games during the Foxes' promotion campaign. On his return to the Premiership with Leicester last season he played in more than 81% of their matches. England Youth, 'B' and Under-21 international who never quite made it to the senior side, but will continue to be an influential figure at Filbert Street. Began his career with Luton Town and has since played for Hull City, Nottingham Forest and Aston Villa, from whom he joined City.

Hard-working and is amongst the top passers of the ball in the game – either short or long he invariably finds his man.

### Form Factors

| Season | Team | Tot | St | Sb | Y | R |
|--------|------|-----|-----|-----|-----|-----|
| 94-95 | Aston Villa | 14 | 12 | 2 | 1 | 0 |
| 94-95 | Leicester C. | 14 | 14 | 0 | 0 | 0 |
| 96-97 | Leicester C. | 31 | 22 | 9 | 0 | 0 |
| Total | | 59 | 48 | 11 | 1 | 0 |

| | GP | GG | GF | GS | TGR |
|--------|------|------|------|------|------|
| 94-95 | 33.33 | 14.00 | 51 | 1 | 1.96 |
| 94-95 | 33.33 | 7.00 | 45 | 2 | 4.44 |
| 96-97 | 81.58 | 15.50 | 46 | 2 | 4.35 |
| Averages | 49.42 | 12.17 | 47.33 | 1.67 | 3.58 |

## PARKINSON, Joe

### Everton ❶❷❸    M

Fullname: Joseph Simon Parkinson
DOB: 11-06-71 Eccles

Former Wigan Athletic trainee who left the club for Bournemouth after 139 games but spent less than a year at Dean Court before being propelled into the Premiership with a £250,000 transfer to Everton in March 1994. In less than a year Bournemouth turned round a healthy profit of over £200,000 for a defender who is calm on the ball and uses possession to good effect. Settled quickly at Goodison Park and has played in around 75% of the Blues' games since moving north, including the 1995 FA Cup success. Unfortunately has found yellow cards easier to come by than goals since joining Everton but still a major force in the team.

### Form Factors

| Season | Team | Tot | St | Sb | Y | R |
|--------|------|-----|-----|-----|-----|-----|
| 94-95 | Everton | 34 | 32 | 2 | 6 | 0 |
| 95-96 | Everton | 28 | 28 | 0 | 9 | 0 |
| 96-97 | Everton | 28 | 28 | 0 | 4 | 0 |
| Total | | 90 | 88 | 2 | 19 | 0 |

| | GP | GG | GF | GS | TGR |
|--------|------|------|------|------|------|
| 94-95 | 80.95 | 0.00 | 44 | 0 | 0.00 |
| 95-96 | 73.68 | 9.33 | 64 | 3 | 4.69 |
| 96-97 | 73.68 | 0.00 | 44 | 0 | 0.00 |
| Averages | 76.11 | 3.11 | 50.67 | 1.00 | 1.56 |

## PARLOUR, Ray

# Arsenal ❶❷❸ M

**Fullname:** Raymond Parlour
**DOB:** 07-03-73 Romford

A ball-winning midfielder whose style is characterised by his almost incessant running and penetration down the right flank. His attitude reflects his tremendous appetite for the game and ensures that he is a player the crowd notice.

At the start of the 1997-98 season he had played in 130 games and needed just one more starting appearance to chalk up his century in that category. Goals though have been hard to come by and his two last season were his first for well over two years.

An England Under-21 player, Parlour came through the ranks at Highbury and was a key part of the side in the 1994-95 campaign. A spate of injuries in recent times has thwarted his first team opportunities, but his energy and industry make him a player that the current manager cannot ignore. Even so his first team chances may be limited with the arrival of a number of new midfield players at Highbury.

## Form Factors

| Season | Team | Tot | St | Sb | Y | R |
|---|---|---|---|---|---|---|
| 94-95 | Arsenal | 30 | 22 | 8 | 0 | 0 |
| 95-96 | Arsenal | 22 | 20 | 2 | 7 | 0 |
| 96-97 | Arsenal | 30 | 17 | 13 | 6 | 0 |
| Total | | 82 | 59 | 23 | 13 | 0 |

| | GP | GG | GF | GS | TGR |
|---|---|---|---|---|---|
| 94-95 | 71.43 | 0.00 | 52 | 0 | 0.00 |
| 95-96 | 57.89 | 0.00 | 49 | 0 | 0.00 |
| 96-97 | 78.95 | 15.00 | 62 | 2 | 3.23 |
| Averages | 69.42 | 5.00 | 54.33 | 0.67 | 1.08 |

## PEACOCK, Darren

# Newcastle U. ❶❷❸ CB

**Fullname:** Darren Peacock
**DOB:** 03-02-68 Bristol

Darren Peacock began his career at Newport County and Hereford United before a 126 league game stint at Queens Park Rangers. Since signing for Newcastle United in March 1994 for £2.7 million, Peacock has been a regular at St James' Park and his composure in possession and his aerial ability soon became apparent.

It's sometimes difficult to work out whether it's Newcastle's style which leaves Peacock sometimes exposed at the back or whether his reading of the play isn't as good as his skills on the ball and his pace. Makes telling runs into the opponents' area at corners and free kicks but doesn't find the mark himself, having scored only once for Newcastle in the Premiership. Tall and powerful Peacock is characterised by his ponytail hair.

## Form Factors

| Season | Team | Tot | St | Sb | Y | R |
|---|---|---|---|---|---|---|
| 94-95 | Newcastle | 35 | 35 | 0 | 6 | 0 |
| 95-96 | Newcastle | 34 | 33 | 1 | 3 | 0 |
| 96-97 | Newcastle | 35 | 35 | 0 | 2 | 0 |
| Total | | 104 | 103 | 1 | 11 | 0 |

| | GP | GG | GF | GS | TGR |
|---|---|---|---|---|---|
| 94-95 | 83.33 | 35.00 | 67 | 1 | 1.49 |
| 95-96 | 89.47 | 0.00 | 66 | 0 | 0.00 |
| 96-97 | 92.11 | 35.00 | 73 | 1 | 1.37 |
| Averages | 88.30 | 23.33 | 68.67 | 0.67 | 0.95 |

## PEARCE, Ian

## Blackburn Rovers ❶❷❸  CB

Fullname:  Ian Anthony Pearce
DOB:  07-05-74 Bury St Edmunds
  Pearce established himself in the centre of Blackburn's Premiership winning defence of 1994-95, having been signed from Chelsea a year or so earlier. However, by November 1995 a piece of floating bone in one leg effectively ended his season. By the end of last season Pearce was back and challenging for his place in the Rovers' side.
  Although used as a defender, Pearce is one of those players that can play in midfield, and if required in attack where his ability in the air and close control are always effective.

### Form Factors

| Season | Team | Tot | St | Sb | Y | R |
|---|---|---|---|---|---|---|
| 94-95 | Blackburn | 28 | 22 | 6 | 1 | 0 |
| 95-96 | Blackburn | 12 | 12 | 0 | 1 | 0 |
| 96-97 | Blackburn | 12 | 7 | 5 | 0 | 1 |
| Total | | 52 | 41 | 11 | 2 | 1 |

| | GP | GG | GF | GS | TGR |
|---|---|---|---|---|---|
| 94-95 | 66.67 | 0.00 | 80 | 0 | 0.00 |
| 95-96 | 31.58 | 12.00 | 61 | 1 | 1.64 |
| 96-97 | 31.58 | 0.00 | 42 | 0 | 0.00 |
| Averages | 43.27 | 4.00 | 61.00 | 0.33 | 0.55 |

## PEDERSEN, Per

## Blackburn Rovers ❶❷  S

Fullname:  Per Pedersen
DOB:  30-03-69 Aalberg, Norway
  A striker who has been seen as a replacement signing for Alan Shearer, Pedersen joined Rovers from Odense for £2.4 million in February 1997. Made his debut at Anfield as a substitute and made a total of 11 appearances, five as substitute. At 28 he will need to establish

himself in the Blackburn side during 1997-98 and add to the one goal he scored against Chelsea.

### Form Factors

| Season | Team | Tot | St | Sb | Y | R |
|---|---|---|---|---|---|---|
| 96-97 | Blackburn | 11 | 6 | 5 | 0 | 0 |
| Total | | 11 | 6 | 5 | 0 | 0 |

| | GP | GG | GF | GS | TGR |
|---|---|---|---|---|---|
| 96-97 | 28.95 | 11.00 | 42 | 1 | 2.38 |
| Averages | 28.95 | 11.00 | 42.00 | 1.00 | 2.38 |

## PEMBRIDGE, Mark

## Sheffield W.  ❶❷❸  M

Fullname:  Mark Anthony Pembridge
DOB:  29-11-70 Merthyr Tydfil
  Welsh international midfielder who despite scoring just once in his first season with Sheffield Wednesday has always scored a useful number of goals. Missed just four of Wednesday's Premiership games during the 1996-97 season and chipped in with six goals. Possesses a sweet left foot which persuaded David Pleat to take him from Derby County in exchange for £900,000 in July 1995, initially to fill the spot left by the departure of Chris Bart-Williams to Nottingham Forest. Pembridge was previously a member of Pleat's Luton Town side around the turn of the decade. Joined Derby from Luton for £1.25 million and scored a creditable 32 goals in 125 league and cup games.

### Form Factors

| Season | Team | Tot | St | Sb | Y | R |
|---|---|---|---|---|---|---|
| 95-96 | Sheffield W. | 25 | 24 | 1 | 0 | 9 |
| 96-97 | Sheffield W. | 34 | 33 | 1 | 7 | 0 |
| Total | | 59 | 57 | 2 | 7 | 9 |

| | GP | GG | GF | GS | TGR |
|---|---|---|---|---|---|
| 95-96 | 65.79 | 12.50 | 48 | 2 | 4.17 |
| 96-97 | 89.47 | 5.67 | 50 | 6 | 12.00 |
| Averages | 77.63 | 9.08 | 49.00 | 4.00 | 8.08 |

## PERRY, Chris

# Wimbledon ❶❷❸❹ CB

Fullname: Christopher John Perry
DOB: 26-04-73 Surrey

Without a doubt, Chris Perry was Wimbledon's most outstanding player last season. A cultured central defender, he can read situations perfectly and has that uncanny ability to be able to nip in and whip a ball away from an opposing attacker. Also confident in the air it would seem only a matter of time until Perry gets international recognition.

Started as a trainee with the Dons in July 1991 and has missed just one game in each of the last two seasons. At the end of the 1996-97 season he needed just two more appearances to record his 100th in the Premier League.

His goal at Manchester United last season was his first in the Premiership and only his second for the club at senior level.

### Form Factors

| Season | Team | Tot | St | Sb | Y | R |
|--------|------|-----|-----|-----|-----|-----|
| 94-95 | Wimbledon | 22 | 17 | 5 | 2 | 0 |
| 95-96 | Wimbledon | 37 | 36 | 1 | 8 | 0 |
| 96-97 | Wimbledon | 37 | 37 | 0 | 0 | 0 |
| Total | | 96 | 90 | 6 | 10 | 0 |

| | GP | GG | GF | GS | TGR |
|--------|-----|-----|-----|-----|-----|
| 94-95 | 52.38 | 0.00 | 48 | 0 | 0.00 |
| 95-96 | 97.37 | 0.00 | 55 | 0 | 0.00 |
| 96-97 | 97.37 | 37.00 | 49 | 1 | 2.04 |
| Averages | 82.37 | 12.33 | 50.67 | 0.33 | 0.68 |

## PETIT, Emmanuel

# Arsenal ❶❷❸❹ M

Full name: Emmanuel Petit
DOB: 22-09-70 Dieppe, France

Signed as part of a £5 million package that also saw fellow Monaco team-mate Gilles Grimandi move to Highbury, 'Manu' opted for the red half of North London in preference to Spurs so that he could be reunited with his former boss Arsène Wenger. Wenger gave Petit his debut at Monaco in 1989 and from that point he became a first team regular over the next eight seasons.

A left-sided midfield player, Petit was part of the Monaco side that won the French championship last season and, at 26 years old, will be looking to recapture the form that earned him 15 international caps.

But while he will be looking to pull the strings in the Gunners' midfield, alongside fellow Frenchman Patrick Vierra, don't expect him to be amongst the goals – Petit, who was Monaco's longest serving player, scored just four times in 213 league appearances.

## PETRESCU, Dan

# Chelsea ❶❷❸❹ FB

Fullname: Dan Vasile Petrescu
DOB: 22-12-67 Bucharest, Romania

After joining Sheffield Wednesday for £1.25 million in July 1993 (having also played for no less than four clubs in his native Romania), a move from Hillsborough always looked likely given that he was unable to hold down a first team spot. Many thought that it would be a move away from England but instead £2.3 million lured him to Stamford

Bridge where he has been one of their most consistent players.

Having arrived in November 1995 he was a near ever-present, missing just two games. His contribution to the Blues 1996-97 was even greater, missing just four games, and providing an attacking outlet with his forages forward from a right wing-back position. His accurate passing is another positive asset of his game and it is not surprising that he is also a fixture in the Romanian national side.

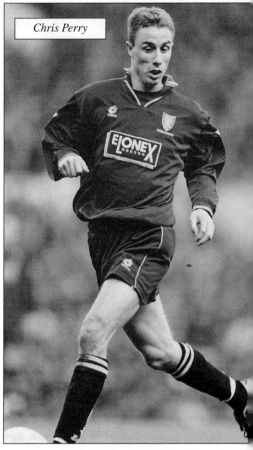

Chris Perry

## Form Factors

| Season | Team | Tot | St | Sb | Y | R |
|--------|------|-----|-----|-----|-----|-----|
| 95-96 | Sheffield W. | 8 | 8 | 0 | 2 | 0 |
| 95-96 | Chelsea | 24 | 22 | 2 | 3 | 0 |
| 96-97 | Chelsea | 34 | 34 | 0 | 4 | 0 |
| Total | | 66 | 64 | 2 | 9 | 0 |

| | GP | GG | GF | GS | TGR |
|--------|-----|-----|-----|-----|-----|
| 95-96 | 21.05 | 0.00 | 48 | 0 | 0.00 |
| 95-96 | 63.16 | 12.00 | 46 | 2 | 4.35 |
| 96-97 | 89.47 | 8.00 | 58 | 3 | 5.17 |
| Averages | 57.89 | 6.67 | 50.67 | 1.67 | 3.17 |

## PHELAN, Terry

## Everton ❶❷ FB

Fullname: Terence Michael Phelan
DOB: 16-03-67 Manchester

In his 13th season of a Football League career which began in 1985 with Leeds United and went via Wimbledon, Manchester City and Chelsea to Everton in December 1996.

Joined Swansea on a free transfer but cost Wimbledon £100,000 which proved to be chicken feed compared to the £2.5 million they pocketed from his move to Maine Road. Three years later Chelsea parted with a more modest £900,000 and Joe Royle reduced that to £850,000 when taking him to Goodison Park. Not one of

the tallest defenders in the Premiership but has excellent pace to go with a fine reading of the game when playing as a full-back or wing-back.

Played for the Republic of Ireland at four different levels before winning 35 full caps.

## Form Factors

| Season | Team | Tot | St | Sb | Y | R |
|--------|------|-----|-----|-----|-----|-----|
| 94-95 | Man. City | 27 | 26 | 1 | 7 | 1 |
| 95-96 | Man. City | 9 | 9 | 0 | 5 | 0 |
| 95-96 | Chelsea | 12 | 12 | 0 | 1 | 0 |
| 96-97 | Chelsea | 4 | 3 | 1 | 0 | 0 |
| 96-97 | Everton | 15 | 15 | 0 | 0 | 0 |
| Total | | 67 | 65 | 2 | 13 | 1 |

| | GP | GG | GF | GS | TGR |
|---|---|---|---|---|---|
| 94-95 | 64.29 | 0.00 | 53 | 0 | 0.00 |
| 95-96 | 55.26 | 0.00 | 46 | 0 | 0.00 |
| 96-97 | 50.00 | 0.00 | 58 | 0 | 0.00 |
| Averages | 56.52 | 0.00 | 52.33 | 0 | 0.00 |

## PHILLIPS, Jimmy

## Bolton W.　❶❷❸　FB

Fullname: James Neil Phillips
DOB: 08-02-66 Bolton

An experienced left-back who has the rather unwanted record of having suffered relegation from the Premiership with two different clubs – Middlesbrough in 1992-93, when he played 40 games and Bolton in 1995-96 when he played 37 games.

Featured as a starter in all of his 36 appearances for Wanderers in their Division One championship last season. He was the subject of some criticism last season, but having conceded 53 goals last year the team's eye was obviously always on offence!

Started his career in his native Bolton before spending a season at Celtic. Moved onto Oxford United and then to Middlesbrough before re-joining his home town team for £250,000 in the summer of 1993.

### Form Factors

| Season | Team | Tot | St | Sb | Y | R |
|---|---|---|---|---|---|---|
| 92-93 | Middlesbro' | 40 | 40 | 0 | - | - |
| 95-96 | Bolton W. | 37 | 37 | 0 | 4 | 0 |
| Total | | 77 | 77 | 0 | 4 | 0 |

| | GP | GG | GF | GS | TGR |
|---|---|---|---|---|---|
| 92-93 | 95.24 | 20.00 | 54 | 2 | 3.70 |
| 95-96 | 97.37 | 0.00 | 39 | 0 | 0.00 |
| Averages | 96.30 | 10.00 | 46.50 | 1.00 | 1.85 |

## PITCHER, Darren

## Crystal Palace　❶❷❸　M

Fullname: Darren Edward Pitcher
DOB: 12-10-69 Stepney

Pitcher has always been an important player to the Eagles since joining them from Charlton Athletic for £700,000 in the summer of 1994. A hard-tackling defence-minded midfield player, injury forced him to miss most of last season – he made just three starting appearances. His midfield partnership with Ray Houghton was most effective during their run to the play-off final in the 1995-96 season.

He made his mark for Palace in their 1994-95 Premiership season and his influence will be vital to them during their third attempt to remain a Premier League side in 1997-98.

### Form Factors

| Season | Team | Tot | St | Sb | Y | R |
|---|---|---|---|---|---|---|
| 94-95 | C. Palace | 25 | 21 | 4 | 5 | 0 |
| Total | | 25 | 21 | 4 | 5 | 0 |

| | GP | GG | GF | GS | TGR |
|---|---|---|---|---|---|
| 94-95 | 59.52 | 0.00 | 34 | 0 | 0.00 |
| Averages | 59.52 | 0.00 | 34.00 | 0.00 | 0.00 |

## PLATT, David

# Arsenal ❶❷❸ M

Fullname: David Andrew Platt
DOB: 10-06-66 Oldham

Combined transfer fees made David Platt the world's most expensive footballer when Bruce Rioch signed him for Arsenal at the start of the 1996-97 season. The former England captain made a name for himself with a last minute extra time goal against Belgium in the 1990 World Cup finals.

He established himself in England with Aston Villa before playing in Italy with Bari, Juventus and Sampdoria. His non-stop running game would seem ideally suited to the Premiership but a nagging knee injury and a more restrictive role placed on him by Rioch and then Wenger has limited his chances in front of goal. Indeed in his 57 games for the Gunners prior to the start of the season he was averaging just one goal every ten games.

The current season will be a make-or-break one for Platt and it may be worth waiting to see how he fits into the new style Arsenal before adding him to your roster.

## Form Factors

| Season | Team | Tot | St | Sb | Y | R |
|---|---|---|---|---|---|---|
| 95-96 | Arsenal | 29 | 27 | 2 | 3 | 0 |
| 96-97 | Arsenal | 28 | 27 | 1 | 4 | 0 |
| Total | | 57 | 54 | 3 | 7 | 0 |

| | GP | GG | GF | GS | TGR |
|---|---|---|---|---|---|
| 95-96 | 76.32 | 4.83 | 49 | 6 | 12.24 |
| 96-97 | 73.68 | 7.00 | 62 | 4 | 6.45 |
| Averages | 75.00 | 5.92 | 55.50 | 5.00 | 9.35 |

## POBORSKY, Karel

# Manchester U. ❶❷❸ M

Fullname: Karel Poborsky
DOB: 30-03-72 Trebon, Czech Rep.

It was a frustrating first season for both Poborsky and United with more starts on the bench than on the field. Poborsky scored one of the most audacious chips ever seen, against Portugal in the quarter finals of Euro '96. Ferguson won the battle for the Czech Republic international's signature. Nicknamed the 'Express Train', Poborsky has yet to use this turn of speed to good effect in the Premiership. However the midfielder got on seven times from the bench and kicked off fifteen times. Towards the end of the season the long-haired Czech set up many chances through his tenacity, although his three goals is a strike rate below that indicated by his Euro '96 performances.

However, after a year to settle in there could be bigger things to come from the player during 1997-98

## Form Factors

| Season | Team | Tot | St | Sb | Y | R |
|---|---|---|---|---|---|---|
| 96-97 | Man. Utd | 22 | 15 | 7 | 1 | 0 |
| Total | | 22 | 15 | 7 | 1 | 0 |

| | GP | GG | GF | GS | TGR |
|---|---|---|---|---|---|
| 96-97 | 57.89 | 7.33 | 76 | 3 | 3.95 |
| Averages | 57.89 | 7.33 | 76.00 | 3.00 | 3.95 |

## POLLOCK, Jamie

# Bolton W. ❶❷ M

Fullname: Jamie Pollock
DOB: 16-02-74 Stockton

Had two years of Premiership experience on Teesside with Middlesbrough where he was a product of their youth team. Played 20 times in their first relegation season but was a more established player in their return season, 1995-96, turning out on 31 occasions.

Made his move to Bolton via Spanish club Osasuna where he spent just two months.

A hustling, bustling central midfield player, Pollock was a vital cog in Bolton's Premiership push last season, being a near ever-present from his arrival. It left him with 20 appearances and four goals, three of which came in successive games.

A former England Under-21 captain, he should have a major role to play in Bolton's side during the 1997-98 season.

## Form Factors

| Season | Team | Tot | St | Sb | Y | R |
|--------|------|-----|----|----|----|----|
| 92-93 | Middlesbro' | 20 | 15 | 5 | - | - |
| 95-96 | Middlesbro' | 31 | 31 | 0 | 10 | 0 |
| Total | | 51 | 46 | 5 | 10 | 0 |

| | GP | GG | GF | GS | TGR |
|--|----|----|----|----|-----|
| 92-93 | 47.62 | 20.00 | 54 | 1 | 1.85 |
| 95-96 | 81.58 | 31.00 | 35 | 1 | 2.86 |
| Averages | 64.60 | 25.50 | 44.50 | 1.00 | 2.35 |

## POOLE, Kevin

# Leicester City ❶ GK

Fullname: Kevin Poole
DOB: 21-07-63 Bromsgrove

Goalkeeper who has been at Filbert Street for six seasons, during which time he has seen off several contenders for his position between the sticks. Despite Leicester City's relegation in 1995 he won the Player of the Year award and missed just one Division

One match as the Foxes returned to the top flight at the first attempt the following year. Unfortunately for him City again got the cheque book out and he had to play second fiddle to Kasey Keller during the 1996-97 campaign, limiting his appearances in the Premiership to just seven games. A more than fine 'keeper to have in reserve, who has also seen service with Aston Villa, Northampton Town, Middlesbrough and Hartlepool United.

Poole was on the bench for 31 games last season and that is where he will probably remain in 1997-98.

## Form Factors

| Season | Team | Tot | St | Sb | Y | R |
|--------|------|-----|----|----|----|----|
| 94-95 | Leicester C. | 36 | 36 | 0 | 0 | 0 |
| 96-97 | Leicester C. | 7 | 7 | 0 | 0 | 0 |
| Total | | 43 | 43 | 0 | 0 | 0 |

| | GA | GkA | GAp | CS | SO | Rp |
|--|----|-----|-----|----|----|----|
| 94-95 | 80 | 67 | 1.86 | 4 | 1 | 0 |
| 96-97 | 54 | 13 | 1.86 | 0 | 0 | 0 |
| Total | 134 | 80 | 1.86 | 4 | 1 | – |

## POOM, Mart

# Derby County ❶❷❸ GK

Fullname: Mart Poom
DOB: 03-02-72 Tallinn, Estonia

Snapped up by Derby County manager Jim Smith for £500,000, prior to the 1996-97 transfer deadline, from FC Flora Tallinn.

He replaced Russell Hoult for four games towards the end of the season with his debut coming during Derby's remarkable 3-2 win over Manchester United at Old Trafford. Has previous experience of English conditions, having played four games for Portsmouth in 1995-96. Poom has also played in the Swiss league with FC Wil during the Estonian winter break. He has made over 40 appearances for Estonia and was part of the Estonian team that failed to turn up for the World Cup qualifying match against Scotland in Tallinn last season.

It remains to be seen who Derby manager Jim Smith will favour as his number one choice in goal.

## Form Factors

| Season | Team | Tot | St | Sb | Y | R |
|--------|------|-----|----|----|----|----|
| 96-97 | Derby Co. | 4 | 4 | 0 | 0 | 0 |
| Total | | 4 | 4 | 0 | 0 | 0 |

| | GA | GkA | GAp | CS | SO | Rp |
|--|----|-----|-----|----|----|----|
| 96-97 | 58 | 7 | 1.75 | 0 | 0 | 0 |
| Total | 58 | 7 | 1.75 | 0 | 0 | – |

## POTTS, Steve

# West Ham U. ❶❷ CB

Fullname: Steven John Potts
DOB: 07-05-67 Hartford, USA

Having missed only one game during the first two Premiership seasons, Potts has seen his number of appearances drop drastically to 20 last season.

Came through the Hammer's youth system and represented England at that level early on. Born in the USA, Potts has been one of West Ham's most consistent players down the years.

Very aware on the field – a fact which allows him to play an effective central defence role despite being just 5' 7" tall.

A former Hammers' skipper, last season was his testimonial year. Equally at home as a right-back, he could well record his 400th appearance for the Hammers first team during 1997-98.

## Form Factors

| Season | Team | Tot | St | Sb | Y | R |
|--------|------|-----|----|----|----|----|
| 94-95 | West Ham | 42 | 42 | 0 | 4 | 0 |
| 95-96 | West Ham | 34 | 34 | 0 | 3 | 0 |
| 96-97 | West Ham | 20 | 17 | 3 | 2 | 0 |
| Total | | 96 | 93 | 3 | 9 | 0 |

| | GP | GG | GF | GS | TGR |
|--|----|----|----|----|-----|
| 94-95 | 100.00 | 0.00 | 44 | 0 | 0.00 |
| 95-96 | 89.47 | 0.00 | 43 | 0 | 0.00 |
| 96-97 | 89.47 | 0.00 | 39 | 0 | 0.00 |
| Averages | 92.98 | 0.00 | 42.00 | 0.00 | 0.00 |

## POWELL, Chris

### Derby County ❶❷❸❹ FB

Fullname: Christopher George Robin
Powell
DOB: 08-09-69 Lambeth

Astute purchase by Jim Smith who took
left-back Powell from Southend United to
Derby for £750,000 in January 1996 and
has not been disappointed. Gave Derby's
promotion push renewed impetus and
missed just three games during their first
season back in the top flight. Is equally
comfortable with the ball at either foot
and has an assurance unusual amongst
defenders. Born in Lambeth, he began his
career with nearby Crystal Palace but also
had a brief loan spell with Aldershot.
Don't look for him to move forward to
get you extra points in front of goal as he
last found the target in December 1992.
He won Derby's Player of the Year award
for last season.

## Form Factors

| Season | Team | Tot | St | Sb | Y | R |
|--------|------|-----|----|----|----|----|
| 96-97 | Derby Co. | 35 | 35 | 0 | 4 | 0 |
| Total | | 35 | 35 | 0 | 4 | 0 |

| | GP | GG | GF | GS | TGR |
|--------|------|------|-------|------|------|
| 96-97 | 92.11 | 0.00 | 45 | 0 | 0.00 |
| Averages | 92.11 | 0.00 | 45.00 | 0.00 | 0.00 |

## POWELL, Darryl

### Derby County ❶❷❸❹ M

Fullname: Darryl Anthony Powell
DOB: 15-11-71 Lambeth

South Londoner who spent seven years
on the south coast with Portsmouth
before joining Derby County in a
£750,000 deal in July 1995. Midfielder
who played a powerful part in Derby's
promotion at the end of the 1995-96
season. Successfully made the step up to
the Premiership, having appeared in 87%
of the Rams' league games last season,
and he made his 200th league appearance

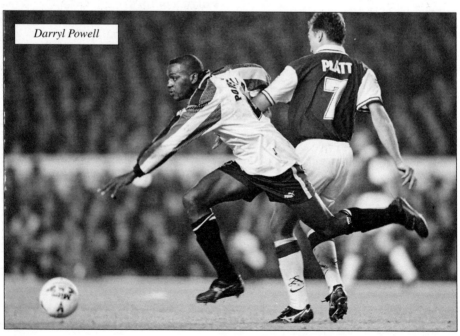

Darryl Powell

at the tail end of the season.

Mainly a left-sided player, Darryl Powell is a good ball-winner with a determined attitude in the tackle and is very quick off the mark. Derby have yet to lose a league match in which he has scored!

## Form Factors

| Season | Team | Tot | St | Sb | Y | R |
|---|---|---|---|---|---|---|
| 96-97 | Derby Co. | 33 | 27 | 6 | 7 | 0 |
| Total | | 33 | 27 | 6 | 7 | 0 |

| | GP | GG | GF | GS | TGR |
|---|---|---|---|---|---|
| 96-97 | 86.84 | 33.00 | 45 | 1 | 2.22 |
| Averages | 86.84 | 33.00 | 45.00 | 1.00 | 2.22 |

## POYET, Gustavo

# Chelsea ❶❷❸❹ CB

Fullname: Gustavo Poyet
DOB: 15-11-67 Montevideo, Uruguay

A dominating 6' 1" midfield player who joined Chelsea in the close season from Spanish side Real Zaragoza, where he was skipper. A Uruguayan international, he joined Zaragoza in 1990 and has since played over 240 times, scoring 60 goals with the large percentage of them coming via his considerable heading ability!

He was part of the triumphant 1995 Cup Winners' Cup side that beat Arsenal in the final, having also disposed of, ironically, Chelsea in the semi-finals. His international performances in the Copa de America in 1995 earned him the Player of the Tournament award.

The Chelsea player will have no work permit problems having qualified as a Spanish national and therefore having freedom of movement in the EU!

## PRESSMAN, Kevin

# Sheffield W. ❶❷❸❹ GK

Fullname: Kevin Paul Pressman
DOB: 06-11-67 Fareham

Born in Fareham, Hampshire, he grew up in Sheffield and progressed through the ranks at Hillsborough before making his debut with Wednesday during a 1-1 draw away to Southampton in September 1987. Was in and out of the side over the next five years before finally establishing his claim to the goalkeeper's jersey in the 1993-94 season, by which time he had

*Kevin Pressman*

already had a spell on loan to Stoke City. Has since played for England 'B' and in 137 appearances in the Premiership kept 34 clean sheets and conceded goals at a rate of 1.40 per game, which puts him in 16th place since the inception of the Premier League. Started in every Premiership game last season and played all but 17 minutes of the season. Expect a similar set of stats during 1997-98.

## Form Factors

| Season | Team | Tot | St | Sb | Y | R |
|--------|------|-----|-----|-----|-----|-----|
| 94-95 | Sheffield W. | 34 | 34 | 0 | 1 | 1 |
| 95-96 | Sheffield W. | 30 | 30 | 0 | 0 | 0 |
| 96-97 | Sheffield W. | 38 | 38 | 0 | 0 | 0 |
| Total | | 102 | 102 | 0 | 1 | 1 |

| | GA | GkA | GAp | CS | SO | Rp |
|--------|-----|-----|-----|-----|-----|-----|
| 94-95 | 57 | 52 | 1.53 | 9 | 2 | 0 |
| 95-96 | 61 | 48 | 1.60 | 6 | 1 | 0 |
| 96-97 | 51 | 50 | 1.32 | 10 | 2 | 2 |
| Total | 169 | 150 | 1.47 | 25 | 5 | – |

# PRIOR, Spencer

## Leicester City ❶❷❸ CB

Fullname: Spencer Justin Prior
DOB: 22-04-71 Hockley

No stranger to his current manager at Leicester City, having played under Martin O'Neill when the duo were at Norwich City. Spent three seasons at Carrow Road and after being voted Player of the Year at the end of his final season there, 1995-96, he moved to Filbert Street in a £600,000 deal. Prior missed just four games during 1996-97, his third season in the Premiership, having previously been there with Norwich. Has proved an excellent acquisition with his aerial strength and assured touch on the ground helping to shore up the Foxes. In 280 games he has scored just four times but he does like to get forward whenever possible.

## Form Factors

| Season | Team | Tot | St | Sb | Y | R |
|--------|------|-----|-----|-----|-----|-----|
| 93-94 | Norwich City | 13 | 13 | 0 | 1 | 0 |
| 94-95 | Norwich City | 17 | 12 | 5 | 2 | 0 |
| 96-97 | Leicester C. | 34 | 33 | 1 | 4 | 0 |
| Total | | 64 | 58 | 6 | 7 | 0 |

| | GP | GG | GF | GS | TGR |
|--------|-----|-----|-----|-----|-----|
| 93-94 | 30.95 | 0.00 | 65 | 0 | 0.00 |
| 94-95 | 40.48 | 0.00 | 37 | 0 | 0.00 |
| 96-97 | 89.47 | 0.00 | 46 | 0 | 0.00 |
| Averages | 53.63 | 0.00 | 49.33 | 0.00 | 0.00 |

# QUINN, Robert

## Crystal Palace ❶❷ CB

Fullname: Robert John Quinn
DOB: 08-11-76 Sidcup

Coming through the ranks as a Palace trainee, Quinn made his debut towards the end of the 1995-96 season and featured in all three of the Eagles' play-off games that term.

Despite being under six foot, Quinn is a composed central defender who played in 22 of Palace's games last season often at the expense of more experienced squad members, most notably Leif Andersen. Much of this was under the reign of Dave Bassett and Quinn featured mainly as a substitute under Steve Coppell in the run in to making the play-offs.

Made his debut for the Republic of Ireland Under-21 side last season.

## RADEBE, Lucas

## Leeds United ❶❷❸ CB

Fullname: Lucas Radebe
DOB: 12-04-69 Johannesburg, SA
   Born in South Africa (Johannesburg to be precise), this defender has come on leaps and bounds since some shaky early performances for Leeds United three years ago. His settling-in period was seriously hampered by a broken leg which kept his total of appearances for the first two years down to just 25 Premiership outings but missed just six games during the 1996-97 season. Has proved himself to be a very versatile player at Elland Road and has even twice played in goal conceding just one goal. Yet to score for Leeds but his defensive abilities more than counter that fact. Cost Leeds just £250,000 to take him from Kaiser Chiefs in his native country, where he is a full international.

### Form Factors

| Season | Team | Tot | St | Sb | Y | R |
|---|---|---|---|---|---|---|
| 94-95 | Leeds Utd | 12 | 9 | 3 | 2 | 0 |
| 95-96 | Leeds Utd | 13 | 10 | 3 | 2 | 0 |
| 96-97 | Leeds Utd | 32 | 28 | 4 | 6 | 0 |
| Total | | 57 | 47 | 10 | 10 | 0 |

| | GP | GG | GF | GS | TGR |
|---|---|---|---|---|---|
| 94-95 | 28.57 | 0.00 | 59 | 0 | 0.00 |
| 95-96 | 34.21 | 0.00 | 40 | 0 | 0.00 |
| 96-97 | 84.21 | 0.00 | 28 | 0 | 0.00 |
| Averages | 49.00 | 0.00 | 42.33 | 0.00 | 0.00 |

## REDFEARN, Neil

## Barnsley ❶❷❸ M

Fullname: Neil David Redfearn
DOB: 20-06-65 Dewsbury
   Skipper of the Barnsley team that won promotion in 1996-97, Redfearn played in all but three of Barnsley's 46 Nationwide League games last season and was the club's leading scorer in that competition with 17 goals from midfield, six of which came from the penalty spot.
   A captain who leads by example, he is the leading scorer out of the current crop of players with more than 60 goals from his 250-plus senior appearances.

*Neil Redfearn*

He started his career as a junior at Nottingham Forest and having been released, did the rounds of a variety of clubs including Bolton, Lincoln, Doncaster, Crystal Palace, Watford and Oldham before signing for the Tykes in the summer of 1991. Has now played over 600 senior games.

## REDKNAPP, Jamie

## Liverpool ❶❷❸❹ M

**Fullname:** Jamie Frank Redknapp
**DOB:** 25-06-73 Barton on Sea

The talented midfielder has established himself as a key figure in the Liverpool set-up. Unfortunately, after putting in an ever-present performance in 1994-95, he suffered injuries to restrict him to 23 games in 1995-96 and 23 in 1996-97, five from the subs' bench. He also sat out six games on the bench.

Redknapp, son of West Ham boss Harry, was signed by Kenny Dalglish in 1991 from Bournemouth. He was selected for Terry Venables' England squad for Euro '96, and helped change the game against Scotland when he came on as sub. Glen Hoddle has him pencilled in as England sweeper if he can get injury free.

Well known for his passing abilities, and skill, teams fear Jamie's ability from set pieces, particularly free kicks within range of the goal.

A fractured ankle will keep Redknapp out of contention for the first half of the 1997-98 season following an injury against Scotland in Euro '96 where he virtually turned the game England's way.

One of the pin-up boys of the Premiership and also one of the most popular in fantasy football selections.

## Form Factors

| Season | Team | Tot | St | Sb | Y | R |
|--------|------|-----|-----|-----|-----|-----|
| 94-95 | Liverpool | 40 | 36 | 4 | 5 | 0 |
| 95-96 | Liverpool | 23 | 19 | 4 | 1 | 0 |
| 96-97 | Liverpool | 23 | 18 | 5 | 0 | 0 |
| Total | | 86 | 73 | 13 | 6 | 0 |

| | GP | GG | GF | GS | TGR |
|--------|-----|-----|-----|-----|-----|
| 94-95 | 95.24 | 13.33 | 65 | 3 | 4.62 |
| 95-96 | 60.53 | 7.67 | 70 | 3 | 4.29 |
| 96-97 | 60.53 | 7.67 | 62 | 3 | 4.84 |
| Averages | 72.10 | 9.56 | 65.67 | 3.00 | 4.58 |

## RICHARDSON, Kevin

## Coventry City ❶❷ M

**Fullname:** Kevin Richardson
**DOB:** 04-12-62 Newcastle

One of the ever-lasting players of English football and his non-stop commitment has often earned him the nickname of Mr Reliable. Always gives 100 per cent, never stops running and is always making vital tackles and interceptions – none more so that starting the move that ultimately won Arsenal the championship in 1989 with Michael Thomas' last gasp goal at Anfield.

A Geordie, he has great vision and is now relying ever more on his experience to ensure he continues to compete at the top level of the game. His clubs include Everton, Watford, Arsenal and Aston Villa and he has won two championship medals and one England cap.

## Form Factors

| Season | Team | Tot | St | Sb | Y | R |
|--------|------|-----|-----|-----|-----|-----|
| 94-95 | Coventry C. | 14 | 14 | 0 | 2 | 0 |
| 95-96 | Coventry C. | 33 | 33 | 0 | 6 | 1 |
| 96-97 | Coventry C. | 28 | 25 | 3 | 2 | 0 |
| Total | | 75 | 72 | 3 | 10 | 1 |

| | GP | GG | GF | GS | TGR |
|--------|-----|-----|-----|-----|-----|
| 94-95 | 33.33 | 0.00 | 44 | 0 | 0.00 |
| 95-96 | 86.84 | 0.00 | 42 | 0 | 0.00 |
| 96-97 | 73.68 | 0.00 | 38 | 0 | 0.00 |
| Averages | 64.62 | 0.00 | 41.33 | 0.00 | 0.00 |

## RIDEOUT, Paul

# Everton    ❶❷    S

Fullname:  Paul David Rideout
DOB:        14-08-64 Bournemouth

Although his Premiership career may be on the wane, his place in Everton folklore is assured after scoring the goal which defeated Manchester United at Wembley in the 1995 FA Cup Final. Has scored at a reasonable rate throughout his career although only one of his five seasons at Goodison Park has been truly productive. He has enjoyed a lengthy career which has taken him from his native Bournemouth to Swindon Town (twice), Aston Villa, Bari in Italy, Southampton, Notts County and six months in Scotland with Rangers before making a £500,000 move to Everton. An England Under-21 international, his transfer fees total close on £2.5 million.

## Form Factors

| Season | Team | Tot | St | Sb | Y | R |
|--------|------|-----|-----|-----|-----|-----|
| 94-95 | Everton | 29 | 25 | 4 | 1 | 0 |
| 95-96 | Everton | 25 | 19 | 6 | 2 | 0 |
| 96-97 | Everton | 9 | 4 | 5 | 2 | 0 |
| Total | | 63 | 48 | 15 | 5 | 0 |

| | GP | GG | GF | GS | TGR |
|--------|------|------|------|------|------|
| 94-95 | 69.05 | 2.07 | 44 | 14 | 31.82 |
| 95-96 | 65.79 | 4.17 | 64 | 6 | 9.38 |
| 96-97 | 23.68 | 0.00 | 44 | 0 | 0.00 |
| Averages | 52.84 | 2.08 | 50.67 | 6.67 | 13.73 |

## RIEPER, Marc

# West Ham U.    ❶❷❸    CB

Fullname:  Marc Rieper
DOB:        05-06-68 Rodoure, Denmark

A Danish international who made over 100 appearances for Brondby before signing for West Ham in December 1994. A tall central defender, who despite setting a Danish record of 37 consecutive caps for his country during Euro '96, cannot command a regular first team spot at Upton Park!

The 1995-96 season was undoubtedly his best, missing just two games, but he played in less that 75% of the Hammers' games during 1996-97 and found himself on the bench on several occasions. Rieper may be under pressure to retain his place with Richard Hall back to full fitness.

## Form Factors

| Season | Team | Tot | St | Sb | Y | R |
|--------|------|-----|-----|-----|-----|-----|
| 94-95 | West Ham | 21 | 17 | 4 | 0 | 0 |
| 95-96 | West Ham | 36 | 35 | 1 | 2 | 0 |
| 96-97 | West Ham | 28 | 26 | 2 | 3 | 1 |
| Total | | 85 | 78 | 7 | 5 | 1 |

| | GP | GG | GF | GS | TGR |
|--------|------|------|------|------|------|
| 94-95 | 50.00 | 21.00 | 44 | 1 | 2.27 |
| 95-96 | 94.74 | 18.00 | 43 | 2 | 4.65 |
| 96-97 | 73.68 | 28.00 | 39 | 1 | 2.56 |
| Averages | 72.81 | 22.33 | 42.00 | 1.33 | 3.16 |

## RIPLEY, Stuart

# Blackburn Rovers ❶❷    M

Fullname:  Stuart Edward Ripley
DOB:        20-11-67 Middlesbrough

A flying winger with tight control and the ability to deliver driven crosses from the right. Ripley's success at Middlesbrough earned him a move to Blackburn. He was another key player in the Rovers' championship side, a fact that earned him his only England cap. But since that time his form has dipped dramatically and last season he played in just 13 of their Premiership games.

His lack of form is also matched by a lack of goals. He has managed just 11 in the league since joining and did not find the net in any competition during the past two seasons.

Will remain under pressure for a place from Greek international George Donis – the 1997-98 season could be a make-or-break one for him.

### Form Factors

| Season | Team | Tot | St | Sb | Y | R |
|--------|------|-----|-----|-----|-----|-----|
| 94-95 | Blackburn | 37 | 36 | 1 | 0 | 0 |
| 95-96 | Blackburn | 28 | 28 | 0 | 1 | 0 |
| 96-97 | Blackburn | 13 | 5 | 8 | 0 | 0 |
| Total | | 78 | 69 | 9 | 1 | 0 |

| | GP | GG | GF | GS | TGR |
|--------|-----|-----|-----|-----|-----|
| 94-95 | 88.10 | 0.00 | 80 | 0 | 0.00 |
| 95-96 | 73.68 | 0.00 | 61 | 0 | 0.00 |
| 96-97 | 34.21 | 0.00 | 42 | 0 | 0.00 |
| Averages | 65.33 | 0.00 | 61.00 | 0.00 | 0.00 |

## ROBERTS, Andy

### Crystal Palace ❶ M

Fullname: Andrew James Roberts
DOB: 20-03-74 Dartford

Andy Roberts became Crystal Palace's record signing when he joined them for £2.5 million in July 1995. His first full season was effective enough and, in addition to being named as the club's Player of the Year, he also scored the goal that gave Palace the early lead in the 1995-96 season play-off final at Wembley. It was his first goal for the club. Last season he again featured in all but one of the Nationwide Division One games – after being sent off in the 6-1 win at Reading in the early part of the season.

Initially a midfield player, he has played many of his games as a sweeper and at 23 years old is sure to feature strongly for Palace in the coming seasons. A former England Under-21 international.

## ROBINS, Mark

### Leicester City ❶ S

Fullname: Mark Gordon Robins
DOB: 22-12-69 Ashton-under-Lyne

Probably still best remembered for a burst of goals early in his career with Manchester United but has since been in and out of the first team of whichever club he is with at the time, as highlighted by his total of 18 unused substitute appearances in the Premiership with Leicester City last season.

A small, lively, one time England Under-21 international who left Manchester United for Norwich City in exchange for £800,000 and notched a healthy 21 goals in 78 games before joining Leicester for £1 million in January 1995. Scored the goal which took Leicester through to the Coca Cola Cup semi-final last season. His goals per game ratio has dropped in recent years but he retains the ability to get back to the top.

### Form Factors

| Season | Team | Tot | St | Sb | Y | R |
|--------|------|-----|-----|-----|-----|-----|
| 94-95 | Norwich C. | 17 | 14 | 3 | 0 | 0 |
| 94-95 | Leicester C. | 17 | 16 | 1 | 0 | 0 |
| 96-97 | Leicester C. | 8 | 5 | 3 | 0 | 0 |
| Total | | 42 | 35 | 7 | 0 | 0 |

| | GP | GG | GF | GS | TGR |
|--------|-----|-----|-----|-----|-----|
| 94-95 | 40.48 | 4.25 | 37 | 4 | 10.81 |
| 95-96 | 40.48 | 3.40 | 45 | 5 | 11.11 |
| 96-97 | 21.05 | 8.00 | 46 | 1 | 2.17 |
| Averages | 34.00 | 5.22 | 42.67 | 3.33 | 8.03 |

## RODGER, Simon

### Crystal Palace &#x2460;&#x2461; M

Fullname: Simon Rodger
DOB: 03-10-71 Shoreham
A midfielder who joined Crystal Palace from non-league side Bognor Regis, he has found it difficult to re-establish himself in the Eagles' side following a bad back injury in 1994. He started to make his comeback during the later stages of the 1995-96 season but was used mainly as a squad player during 1996-97 with just 11 appearances. The strong-tackling, left-sided midfield player found himself on loan at Manchester City and Stoke City during the early part of last season and may yet have a role to play under Steve Coppell. He remains Palace's longest-serving player.

## ROLLING, Frank

### Leicester City &#x2460; CB

Fullname: Frank Rolling
DOB: 23-08-68 Colnar
Central defender who was Mark McGee's last signing when he joined Leicester City early in the 1995-96 season and played 17 Division One games during the Foxes' promotion season. Predominantly a right-sided player, he featured in just one match in the Premiership last season, that game being the final 90 minutes of the season which saw Leicester storm to a remarkable 4-2 victory away to Blackburn Rovers.
Joined Leicester from Scottish club Ayr United, having previously played for FC Pau. He was an unused sub on six other occasions and will be looking to impress current manager Martin O'Neill given the arrival of new defensive players at Filbert Street.

### Form Factors

| Season | Team | Tot | St | Sb | Y | R |
|---|---|---|---|---|---|---|
| 96-97 | Leicester C. | 1 | 1 | 0 | 0 | 0 |
| Total | | 1 | 1 | 0 | 0 | 0 |

| | GP | GG | GF | GS | TGR |
|---|---|---|---|---|---|
| 96-97 | 2.63 | 0.00 | 46 | 0 | 0.00 |
| Averages | 2.63 | 0.00 | 46.00 | 0.00 | 0.00 |

## ROSENTHAL, Ronny

### Tottenham H. &#x2460; M

Fullname: Ronny Rosenthal
DOB: 11-10-63 Haifa, Israel
Experienced striker who can play in midfield, he has scaled the heights of winning league championships in Israel, Belgium and England, the latter with Liverpool, from whom he joined Tottenham in January 1994 for £250,000.
Although a regular first teamer at White Hart Lane since signing for the club, he has always been considered something of a luxury with a less than killer instinct, although the memory of one televised open goal gaff was offset by a hat-trick in an FA Cup replay at Southampton.
Has found his role at White Hart Lane change somewhat in the past couple of seasons. Having been a near ever-present during the 1995-96 season, he became more of a bench player last season with no less than 16 of his 20 appearances coming as a substitute. At over 33-years of age he is undoubtedly in the later stages of his career at Spurs.

### Form Factors

| Season | Team | Tot | St | Sb | Y | R |
|---|---|---|---|---|---|---|
| 94-95 | Tottenham | 20 | 14 | 6 | 4 | 0 |
| 95-96 | Tottenham | 33 | 26 | 7 | 2 | 0 |
| 96-97 | Tottenham | 20 | 4 | 16 | 0 | 0 |
| Total | | 73 | 44 | 29 | 6 | 0 |

| | GP | GG | GF | GS | TGR |
|---|---|---|---|---|---|
| 94-95 | 47.62 | 0.00 | 66 | 0 | 0.00 |
| 95-96 | 86.84 | 33.00 | 50 | 1 | 2.00 |
| 96-97 | 52.63 | 20.00 | 44 | 1 | 2.27 |
| Averages | 62.36 | 17.67 | 53.33 | 0.67 | 1.42 |

## ROWETT, Gary

# Derby County ❶❷❸❹   CB

Fullname:  Gary Rowett
DOB:       06-03-74 Bromsgrove

Twenty-three-year-old central defender who has excelled to rebuild his career since completing a £300,000 transfer from Everton to Derby County in July 1995. Rowett joined Everton for £200,000 after playing 77 times for Cambridge United but could not command a regular place at Goodison Park – playing just four times for them in the Premier League – and had a spell on loan to Blackpool prior to joining Derby. Has become an integral part of Jim Smith's side over the past two years, mostly in the heart of the defence, but has also been used on the right of the midfield. He started 35 times last season, a feat matched only by team-mates Chris Powell and Jacob Laursen.

### Form Factors

| Season | Team | Tot | St | Sb | Y | R |
|---|---|---|---|---|---|---|
| 93-94 | Everton | 2 | 0 | 2 | 0 | 0 |
| 94-95 | Everton | 2 | 2 | 0 | 0 | 0 |
| 96-97 | Derby Co. | 35 | 35 | 0 | 2 | 6 |
| Total | | 39 | 37 | 2 | 2 | 6 |

| | GP | GG | GF | GS | TGR |
|---|---|---|---|---|---|
| 93-94 | 4.76 | 0.00 | 42 | 0 | 0.00 |
| 94-95 | 4.76 | 0.00 | 44 | 0 | 0.00 |
| 96-97 | 92.11 | 17.50 | 45 | 2 | 4.44 |
| Averages | 33.88 | 5.83 | 43.67 | 0.67 | 1.48 |

## ROWLAND, Keith

# West Ham U.   ❶❷   FB

Fullname:  Keith Rowland
DOB:       01-09-71 Portadown,
           Northern Ireland

Keith Rowland is pretty much a squad player at Upton Park and in many respects an understudy for the role played in the Hammers side by Julian Dicks. This was emphasised last season when he was substituted in eight of the 11 games he started in the Premiership. He made four appearances from the bench and remained on it on 11 other occasions.

An international player with Northern Ireland, Rowland joined West Ham from Bournemouth in the summer of 1993, having already made his Premiership debut by playing twice as a substitute for Coventry City. The Sky Blues declined to take him on and it was the Hammers who gained his services, for whom he has now figured in 73 Premier League games.

### Form Factors

| Season | Team | Tot | St | Sb | Y | R |
|---|---|---|---|---|---|---|
| 94-95 | West Ham | 12 | 11 | 1 | 1 | 0 |
| 95-96 | West Ham | 23 | 19 | 4 | 4 | 0 |
| 96-97 | West Ham | 15 | 11 | 4 | 5 | 0 |
| Total | | 50 | 41 | 9 | 10 | 0 |

| | GP | GG | GF | GS | TGR |
|---|---|---|---|---|---|
| 94-95 | 28.57 | 0.00 | 44 | 0 | 0.00 |
| 95-96 | 60.53 | 0.00 | 43 | 0 | 0.00 |
| 96-97 | 39.47 | 15.00 | 39 | 1 | 2.56 |
| Averages | 42.86 | 5.00 | 42.00 | 0.33 | 0.85 |

## RUDDOCK, Neil

### Liverpool ❶❷❸ CB

Fullname: Neil Ruddock
DOB: 09-05-68 Wandsworth
Very strong in the air and also in the tackle, Ruddock is a match for most Premiership strikers. Spent his early career swapping between Millwall and Tottenham. Settled at Southampton and then spent another season at Tottenham before a £2.5 million move to Anfield.

He is comfortable on the ball and often fires 40 yard passes to team-mates with his left foot. The 29-year old also gets a fair share of goals for a defender, usually at set pieces or corners.

Ruddock is not guaranteed first team starts, having only 15 starts in 1996-97, picking up one goal. He was on the subs' bench for another 17 games, getting off onto the pitch twice. Ruddock will probably spend 1997-98 competing with Wright and Matteo for a place but he played well at the back end of 1996-97 and has worked on his fitness. Could be a make or break season with Liverpool.

### Form Factors

| Season | Team | Tot | St | Sb | Y | R |
|---|---|---|---|---|---|---|
| 94-95 | Liverpool | 37 | 37 | 0 | 5 | 0 |
| 95-96 | Liverpool | 20 | 18 | 2 | 7 | 0 |
| 96-97 | Liverpool | 17 | 15 | 2 | 2 | 0 |
| Total | | 74 | 70 | 4 | 14 | 0 |

| | GP | GG | GF | GS | TGR |
|---|---|---|---|---|---|
| 94-95 | 88.10 | 18.50 | 65 | 2 | 3.08 |
| 95-96 | 52.63 | 4.00 | 70 | 5 | 7.14 |
| 96-97 | 44.74 | 17.00 | 62 | 1 | 1.61 |
| Averages | 61.82 | 13.17 | 65.67 | 2.67 | 3.94 |

## RUSH, Ian

### Leeds United ❶ S

Fullname: Ian James Rush
DOB: 20-10-61 St Asaph
Ian Rush was arguably the greatest goalscorer ever known to wear a Liverpool shirt. Despite a brief spell in Italy with Juventus he spent his greatest days at Anfield for whom he played over 500 senior games in his two spells there and won nearly every honour in the game.

He was granted a free transfer by Liverpool and moved to Leeds United in the summer of 1996 and, following Gary McAllister's departure to Coventry, he was make Leeds' captain. Amazingly it took him15 games before he netted his first goal for the club in the 2-0 home win over Chelsea as he suffered to find his feet in his new surroundings.

Rush scored just three times in his 36 Premiership outings last season and the arrival of George Graham as a manager at Elland Road may have put a cloud over his future there.

He holds the record for the highest Welsh goalscorer with 28 goals in 73 internationals.

### Form Factors

| Season | Team | Tot | St | Sb | Y | R |
|---|---|---|---|---|---|---|
| 94-95 | Liverpool | 36 | 36 | 0 | 1 | 0 |
| 95-96 | Liverpool | 20 | 10 | 10 | 0 | 0 |
| 96-97 | Leeds Utd | 36 | 34 | 2 | 6 | 0 |
| Total | | 92 | 80 | 12 | 7 | 0 |

| | GP | GG | GF | GS | TGR |
|---|---|---|---|---|---|
| 94-95 | 85.71 | 3.00 | 65 | 12 | 18.46 |
| 95-96 | 52.63 | 4.00 | 70 | 5 | 7.14 |
| 96-97 | 94.74 | 12.00 | 28 | 3 | 10.71 |
| Averages | 77.69 | 6.33 | 54.33 | 6.67 | 12.11 |

# SALAKO, John

## Coventry City  ❶❷❸  M

Fullname:  John Akin Salako
DOB:  11-02-69 Nigeria

Exciting and talented wide player who made five appearances for England before having his career ravaged by injury.

Salako had nine years as a professional with Crystal Palace, with whom he played in the 1990 FA Cup Final, having worked his way up from a trainee at Selhurst Park under Terry Venables.

He cost Coventry an initial £1.5 million, rising to a possible £3 million, and when clear of injury justifies that high price.

Not regarded as an out-and-out goal scorer, just eight in his last 100 Premiership appearances, he is more renowned for his high number of assists.

### Form Factors

| Season | Team | Tot | St | Sb | Y | R |
|---|---|---|---|---|---|---|
| 94-95 | C. Palace | 39 | 39 | 0 | 2 | 0 |
| 95-96 | Coventry C. | 37 | 34 | 3 | 3 | 0 |
| 96-97 | Coventry C. | 24 | 23 | 1 | 0 | 0 |
| Total | | 100 | 96 | 4 | 5 | 0 |

| | GP | GG | GF | GS | TGR |
|---|---|---|---|---|---|
| 94-95 | 92.86 | 9.75 | 34 | 4 | 11.76 |
| 95-96 | 97.37 | 12.33 | 42 | 3 | 7.14 |
| 96-97 | 63.16 | 24.00 | 38 | 1 | 2.63 |
| Averages | 84.46 | 15.36 | 38.00 | 2.67 | 7.18 |

# SCALES, John

## Tottenham H.  ❶❷❸❹  CB

Fullname:  John Robert Scales
DOB:  04-07-66 Harrogate

Former Bristol Rovers defender who went via Wimbledon (280 games) and Liverpool (89) to Tottenham Hotspur last December for £2.6million, taking his total transfer fees to well over £6million.

Having found it difficult to establish a regular place in the Liverpool first team during the early months of last season, he looked set to join Leeds United before opting for White Hart Lane at the 11th hour. Made a couple of early substitute appearances in December 1996 before the Tottenham injury bug struck, sidelining him for a number of games and limiting the central defender to 12 appearances.

A sound first touch, speed and a good reading of the game, his early performances at Tottenham earned him a call-up into the England squad where he was used as a non-playing sub in Le Tournoi.

### Form Factors

| Season | Team | Tot | St | Sb | Y | R |
|---|---|---|---|---|---|---|
| 94-95 | Liverpool | 35 | 35 | 0 | 3 | 0 |
| 95-96 | Liverpool | 27 | 27 | 0 | 3 | 0 |
| 96-97 | Liverpool | 3 | 3 | 0 | 0 | 0 |
| 96-97 | Tottenham | 12 | 10 | 2 | 0 | 0 |
| Total | | 77 | 75 | 2 | 6 | 0 |

| | GP | GG | GF | GS | TGR |
|---|---|---|---|---|---|
| 94-95 | 83.33 | 17.50 | 65 | 2 | 3.08 |
| 95-96 | 71.05 | 0.00 | 70 | 0 | 0.00 |
| 96-97 | 39.47 | 0.00 | 44 | 0 | 0.00 |
| Averages | 64.62 | 38.50 | 59.67 | 0.67 | 1.03 |

*Peter Schmeichel*

## SCHMEICHEL, Peter

# Manchester U. ❶❷❸❹❺ GK

Fullname: Peter Boleslaw Schmeichel
DOB: 18-11-68 Glodsone, Denmark

The Danish International goalkeeper puts his formidable frame about a bit, and has even been known to sprint up the pitch for his side's corners. Back in his own area he is dominant at corners and a vocal marshaller of the United defence. His competitive edge resulted in a feud with Arsenal's Ian Wright in 96-97 but Schmeichel's goalkeeping skills have often saved United when one on one with opposing strikers and his long accurate throws are capable of turning defence into attack in a matter of seconds.

Alex Ferguson bought the 'Great Dane' for £550,000 from Brondby in August 1991 and he has matured in the style of a Shilton or Jennings. In the Premiership there are only three 'keepers with a goals per appearance ratio of less than one and Schmeichel's record is 0.88 (163 goals conceded in 186 appearances), just 0.08 behind David Seaman. He holds the record for total number of clean sheets with 88 (24 in 1994-95), nearly half his appearances! In 1996-97 Schmeichel kept 13 clean sheets, including four consecutive shut-outs.

## Form Factors

| Season | Team | Tot | St | Sb | Y | R |
|--------|------|-----|-----|-----|-----|-----|
| 94-95 | Man. Utd | 32 | 32 | 0 | 0 | 0 |
| 95-96 | Man. Utd | 36 | 36 | 0 | 1 | 0 |
| 96-97 | Man. Utd | 36 | 36 | 0 | 2 | 0 |
| Total | | 104 | 104 | 0 | 3 | 0 |

| | GA | GkA | GAp | CS | SO | Rp |
|--------|-----|-----|------|-----|-----|-----|
| 94-95 | 28 | 22 | 0.69 | 24 | 4 | 2 |
| 95-96 | 35 | 30 | 0.83 | 18 | 4 | 0 |
| 96-97 | 44 | 42 | 1.17 | 13 | 4 | 0 |
| Total | 107 | 94 | 0.90 | 55 | 12 | – |

## SCHOLES, Paul

# Manchester U. ❶❷❸❹❺ M

**Fullname:** Paul Scholes
**DOB:** 16-11-74 Salford

The 1996-97 season started slowly for Paul Scholes but finished at whirlwind pace. Having been confined to the subs bench for much of the first part of the season, the ginger haired striker finally got into the side and enjoyed a run of ten successive games over the Christmas period. At the other end when the dust was settling on another United Premiership title, Scholes found himself playing against Italy in France and scoring a sensational goal for England and making his partner Ian Wright's goal.

Scholes signed for United as a trainee in July 1991 and first broke into their first team during the 1994-95 season. He still hasn't quite managed to secure a regular spot in the Reds' side despite his England call-up.

A full-running striker he works hard in and around the penalty area, often making runs from deep and scoring some vital goals. In many respects the 1996-97 could perhaps be considered a disappointment with just three Premiership goals after the ten he scored in 1995-96.

### Form Factors

| Season | Team | Tot | St | Sb | Y | R |
|---|---|---|---|---|---|---|
| 94-95 | Man. Utd | 17 | 6 | 11 | 0 | 0 |
| 95-96 | Man. Utd | 26 | 16 | 10 | 2 | 0 |
| 96-97 | Man. Utd | 24 | 16 | 8 | 6 | 0 |
| Total | | 67 | 38 | 29 | 8 | 0 |

| | GP | GG | GF | GS | TGR |
|---|---|---|---|---|---|
| 94-95 | 40.48 | 3.40 | 77 | 5 | 6.49 |
| 95-96 | 68.42 | 2.60 | 73 | 10 | 13.70 |
| 96-97 | 63.16 | 8.00 | 76 | 3 | 3.95 |
| Averages | 57.35 | 4.67 | 75.33 | 6.00 | 8.05 |

## SCIMECA, Ricky

# Aston Villa ❶❷❸ CB

**Fullname:** Riccardo Scimeca
**DOB:** 13-08-75 Leamington

Despite the name, Scimeca is English through and through and has representative honours at Under-21 level, and was part of the Under-21 side that played in the Under-21 European Championships last season.

Scimeca broke into the Villa first team during the 1995-96 season and appeared 17 times both last season and the one before. A consistent goalscorer in the reserves while playing in midfield he has yet to make his scoring mark in the Premiership where he has been mainly used as defensive cover.

At 21 he looks to have a good future ahead of him and he will be looking to establish a more regular starting role at Villa during the 1997-98 season.

### Form Factors

| Season | Team | Tot | St | Sb | Y | R |
|---|---|---|---|---|---|---|
| 95-96 | Aston Villa | 17 | 7 | 10 | 1 | 0 |
| 96-97 | Aston Villa | 17 | 11 | 6 | 1 | 0 |
| Total | | 34 | 18 | 16 | 2 | 0 |

| | GP | GG | GF | GS | TGR |
|---|---|---|---|---|---|
| 95-96 | 44.74 | 0.00 | 52 | 0 | 0.00 |
| 96-97 | 44.74 | 0.00 | 47 | 0 | 0.00 |
| Averages | 44.74 | 0.00 | 49.50 | 0.00 | 0.00 |

## SEAMAN, David

# Arsenal ❶❷❸❹❺ GK

**Fullname:** David Andrew Seaman
**DOB:** 19-09-63 Rotherham

Now established as England's number one, he missed a significant part of Arsenal's 1996-97 season through injury. An ever-present in 1995-96, his calmness and almost jocular manner instill

David Seaman

confidence in the defence in front of him. During Euro '96 he was arguably England's best player and has built a reputation as an ace penalty saver especially on the big occasions, his stops taking England to a semi-final spot in 1996 and Arsenal to a Cup-Winners' Cup Final in 1996.

He is widely regarded as one of the world's best 'keepers and the debate as to whether he or Peter Schmeichel is best will continue.

Has played for Peterborough, Birmingham and QPR before joining the Gunners in May 1990. This season should see him close in on his 600th league appearance.

Now looks to have recovered from injury and, with a solid defence in front

of him, will always end up with a positive points tally.

## Form Factors

| Season | Team | Tot | St | Sb | Y | R |
|--------|------|-----|----|----|----|----|
| 94-95 | Arsenal | 31 | 31 | 0 | 0 | 0 |
| 95-96 | Arsenal | 38 | 38 | 0 | 0 | 0 |
| 96-97 | Arsenal | 22 | 22 | 0 | 0 | 0 |
| Total | | 91 | 91 | 0 | 0 | 0 |

| | GA | GkA | GAp | CS | SO | Rp |
|--------|----|-----|-----|----|----|----|
| 94-95 | 49 | 31 | 1.00 | 11 | 2 | 0 |
| 95-96 | 32 | 32 | 0.84 | 16 | 2 | 4 |
| 96-97 | 32 | 15 | 0.68 | 10 | 5 | 0 |
| Total | 113 | 78 | 0.86 | 37 | 9 | – |

## SELLARS, Scott

### Bolton W. ❶❷❸ M

Fullname: Scott Sellars
DOB: 27-11-65 Sheffield

Sellars has done the rounds of northern clubs but seems to have found a home in the Bolton line-up, where he was absent on just four occasions. Happy to play either a central or left-sided midfield role, he is very skilful and can be very effective from dead ball situations.

While he is more often than not creating goals for forwards he weighed in with eight of his own last season in Division One.

Had it not been for Keegan's cheque book spending during the summer of 1995, he might still have had a key role to play at Newcastle. He started his career as an apprentice with Leeds United and returned to Elland Road after making over 200 appearances for Blackburn Rovers, before moving to Tyneside.

Will have a large role to play in Bolton's season during 1997-98.

### Form Factors

| Season | Team | Tot | St | Sb | Y | R |
|--------|------|-----|-----|-----|-----|-----|
| 94-95 | Newcastle | 12 | 12 | 0 | 2 | 0 |
| 95-96 | Newcastle | 6 | 2 | 4 | 0 | 0 |
| 95-96 | Bolton W. | 22 | 22 | 0 | 2 | 0 |
| Total | | 40 | 36 | 4 | 4 | 0 |

| | GP | GG | GF | GS | TGR |
|--------|-----|-----|-----|-----|-----|
| 94-95 | 28.57 | 0.00 | 67 | 0 | 0.00 |
| 95-96 | 15.79 | 0.00 | 66 | 0 | 0.00 |
| 95-96 | 57.89 | 7.33 | 39 | 3 | 7.69 |
| Averages | 34.09 | 2.44 | 57.33 | 1.00 | 2.56 |

## SELLEY, Ian

### Arsenal ❶❷ M

Fullname: Ian Selley
DOB: 14-06-74 Chertsey

A strong-tackling midfield player with good technique, Ian Selley broke into the Arsenal first team squad for the 1992-93 FA and Coca Cola Cup winning season. An England Under-21 international deemed to be a precocious talent, injury has plagued his career which has seen just 41 Premiership appearances in five years. Last year was the worst but a substitute appearance in the final five minutes of the 3-0 win at Chelsea signalled what will hopefully be the resurrection of a promising career.

*Scott Sellars*

The 1997-98 season will be one in which Selley will be looking to get back to being a bench regular at the very least. As a fantasy player it may take another season before he can be considered a points investment – injuries permitting.

## Form Factors

| Season | Team | Tot | St | Sb | Y | R |
|---|---|---|---|---|---|---|
| 93-94 | Arsenal | 18 | 16 | 2 | 3 | 0 |
| 94-95 | Arsenal | 13 | 10 | 3 | 3 | 0 |
| 96-97 | Arsenal | 1 | 0 | 1 | 0 | 0 |
| Total | | 32 | 26 | 6 | 6 | 0 |

| | GP | GG | GF | GS | TGR |
|---|---|---|---|---|---|
| 93-94 | 42.86 | 0.00 | 53 | 0 | 0.00 |
| 94-95 | 30.95 | 0.00 | 52 | 0 | 0.00 |
| 96-97 | 2.63 | 0.00 | 62 | 0 | 0.00 |
| Averages | 25.48 | 0.00 | 55.67 | 0.00 | 0.00 |

# SHARPE, Lee

# Leeds United ❶❷❸ M

*Lee Sharpe*

Fullname:  Lee Stuart Sharpe
DOB:        27-05-71 Halesowen

Picked up numerous honours during eight glorious years with Manchester United before signing for Leeds United in exchange for £4.5 million in July 1996. Originally joined the Reds for just £185,000 from Torquay United after just 14 games for the Devon club. Struggled to find his best form during his early days at Elland Road but regained his touch as the season wore on and featured in almost 70% of United's Premiership matches. Scored five times for Leeds which represents his best campaign for four years. Has played for England on five occasions and should make his 150th Premiership appearance during the 1997-98 season.

## Form Factors

| Season | Team | Tot | St | Sb | Y | R |
|---|---|---|---|---|---|---|
| 94-95 | Man. Utd | 28 | 26 | 2 | 7 | 0 |
| 95-96 | Man. Utd | 31 | 21 | 10 | 3 | 0 |
| 96-97 | Leeds Utd | 26 | 26 | 0 | 1 | 0 |
| Total | | 85 | 73 | 12 | 11 | 0 |

| | GP | GG | GF | GS | TGR |
|---|---|---|---|---|---|
| 94-95 | 66.67 | 9.33 | 77 | 3 | 3.90 |
| 95-96 | 81.58 | 7.75 | 73 | 4 | 5.48 |
| 96-97 | 68.42 | 5.20 | 28 | 5 | 17.86 |
| Averages | 72.22 | 7.43 | 59.33 | 4.00 | 9.08 |

## Arsenal ❶❷ M

Fullname: Paul Shaw
DOB: 04-09-73 Burnham

For the Gunners' reserve side Shaw has proved to be a free-scoring midfielder cum attacker. He was on the verge of the Arsenal first team last season and proved his worth by scoring twice in just eight Premiership appearances – seven of those as a substitute!

The 23-year-old has spent several periods on loan with Burnley and Cardiff but his most notable success came with Peterborough, where he brought a new dimension to the side and picked up five goals during his 14 games there.

The 1997-98 season will probably see him a regular on the bench once again but he is always likely to come off it and score a goal. Not quite a super-sub but perhaps not far from it!

### Form Factors

| Season | Team | Tot | St | Sb | Y | R |
|---|---|---|---|---|---|---|
| 94-95 | Arsenal | 1 | 0 | 1 | 0 | 0 |
| 95-96 | Arsenal | 3 | 0 | 3 | 0 | 0 |
| 96-97 | Arsenal | 8 | 1 | 7 | 0 | 0 |
| Total | | 12 | 1 | 11 | 0 | 0 |

| | GP | GG | GF | GS | TGR |
|---|---|---|---|---|---|
| 94-95 | 2.38 | 0.00 | 52 | 0 | 0.00 |
| 95-96 | 7.89 | 0.00 | 49 | 0 | 0.00 |
| 96-97 | 21.05 | 4.00 | 62 | 2 | 3.23 |
| Averages | 10.44 | 1.33 | 54.33 | 0.67 | 1.08 |

## Coventry City ❶❷ CB

Fullname: Richard Edward Shaw
DOB: 11-09-68 Brentford

Defender who is equally happy at full-back or in the heart of the back line, he has settled in well at Highfield Road since a £1 million move from Crystal Palace in November 1995.

He made over 200 league appearances for Palace and was a member of their FA Cup Final side and was the unfortunate player against whom Eric Cantona kicked out prior to his sending off and kung-fu kick at Selhurst Park during the 1995-96 season.

He missed just three Premiership games last season and was a non-playing substitute in another two.

### Form Factors

| Season | Team | Tot | St | Sb | Y | R |
|---|---|---|---|---|---|---|
| 94-95 | C. Palace | 41 | 41 | 0 | 4 | 0 |
| 95-96 | Coventry C. | 21 | 21 | 0 | 2 | 1 |
| 96-97 | Coventry C. | 35 | 35 | 0 | 3 | 0 |
| Total | | 97 | 97 | 0 | 9 | 1 |

| | GP | GG | GF | GS | TGR |
|---|---|---|---|---|---|
| 94-95 | 97.62 | 0.00 | 34 | 0 | 0.00 |
| 95-96 | 55.26 | 0.00 | 42 | 0 | 0.00 |
| 96-97 | 92.11 | 0.00 | 38 | 0 | 0.00 |
| Averages | 81.66 | 0.00 | 38.00 | 0 | 0.00 |

## SHEARER, Alan

# Newcastle U. ❶❷❸❹❺     S

Fullname: Alan Shearer
DOB:     13-08-70 Newcastle

Became the world's most expensive player, when he signed for Newcastle and is rapidly paying back the £15 million Kevin Keegan paid for him. The first top flight player to fire in 30 Premiership goals in three successive seasons, Shearer is a mobile six-foot centre-forward in the classic mould. Just one of his outstanding records is the seven consecutive Premiership games – between September 14th and November 30th 1996 – in which he scored goals.

Shearer is the all-time Premiership top scorer, with 137 from 169 games for Blackburn and Newcastle. He was the leading scorer in the Premiership in 1996-97 with 25 (including his ninth Premiership hat-trick), and notched 28 in all competitions. Although not quite at as pure as a Gary Lineker, Shearer keeps clear of yellow cards. An injury, which twice required an operation, kept him on the sidelines in 1996-97.

Shearer's unselfish philosophy that it's not important if he scores so long as the team wins, plus the respect which his utter professionalism earns him amongst other players, made him an ideal choice to be England captain. He scored in four out of England's five games in Euro '96, taking the Golden boot award.

Once again he was in the PFA Premiership team and was chosen PFA Player of the Year. He was Football Writers' Player of the Year in 1993-94. Shearer is yet to find a defence which can tame him and there's no reason to think that 1997-98 won't be a profitable season

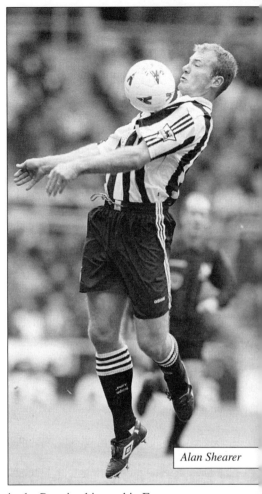

*Alan Shearer*

in the Premiership, and in Europe as Shearer leads the way to World Cup '98.

## Form Factors

| Season | Team | Tot | St | Sb | Y | R |
|--------|------|-----|-----|-----|-----|-----|
| 94-95 | Blackburn | 42 | 42 | 0 | 4 | 0 |
| 95-96 | Blackburn | 35 | 35 | 0 | 4 | 0 |
| 96-97 | Newcastle | 31 | 31 | 0 | 5 | 0 |
| Total | | 108 | 108 | 0 | 13 | 0 |

| | GP | GG | GF | GS | TGR |
|--------|-----|-----|-----|-----|-----|
| 94-95 | 100.00 | 1.24 | 80 | 34 | 42.50 |
| 95-96 | 92.11 | 1.13 | 61 | 31 | 50.82 |
| 96-97 | 81.58 | 1.24 | 73 | 25 | 34.25 |
| Averages | 91.23 | 1.20 | 71.33 | 30.00 | 42.52 |

## SHERIDAN, Darren

# Barnsley ❶ M

Fullname: Darren Stephen Sheridan
DOB: 01-10-64 Stretford

Sheridan played in all but five of Barnsley's Nationwide League games last season and his undoubted passing ability was one of the features of both his and the team's games. In only his second full season in professional football, he provided manager Danny Wilson with a variety of options thanks to his ability to operate either in his preferred central midfield role or as an attacking wing-back – the latter often as a stand-in for the injury-struck Neil Thompson.

Joined the club in the summer of 1993 – a £10,000 buy from non-league Winsford United, and has now made over 120 senior appearances for the club. Could attract the attention of the bigger clubs if he continues his form in the Premiership.

## SHERIDAN, John

# Bolton W. ❶❷ M

Fullname: John Joseph Sheridan
DOB: 01-10-64 Manchester

Sheridan has had long spells at both Leeds United and Sheffield Wednesday, making over 200 appearances for both clubs at senior level. His move to Bolton came after he fell out of favour with the Wednesday management in the early part of last season, not least when a spate of injuries affected his availability.

He looked to be on his way to Birmingham City but his loan spell ended without the offer of a contract, at which point Colin Todd, the Wanderers' manager, stepped in to secure his signature.

A full international with the Republic of Ireland, he has vast experience that will benefit Bolton in their return to the Premiership from the centre of midfield, where he has often taken on the role of playmaker, using his accurate passing ability to best effect.

Played in 19 of Bolton's games last season, contributing two goals, and will be remembered by fans at Hillsborough for scoring the winning goal in the League Cup final at Wembley in 1991.

### Form Factors

| Season | Team | Tot | St | Sb | Y | R |
|---|---|---|---|---|---|---|
| 94-95 | Sheffield W. | 36 | 34 | 2 | 3 | 0 |
| 95-96 | Sheffield W. | 17 | 13 | 4 | 4 | 0 |
| 96-97 | Sheffield W. | 2 | 0 | 2 | 0 | 0 |
| Total | | 55 | 47 | 8 | 7 | 0 |

| | GP | GG | GF | GS | TGR |
|---|---|---|---|---|---|
| 94-95 | 85.71 | 36.00 | 49 | 1 | 2.04 |
| 95-96 | 44.74 | 0.00 | 48 | 0 | 0.00 |
| 96-97 | 5.26 | 0.00 | 50 | 0 | 0.00 |
| Averages | 45.24 | 12.00 | 49.00 | 0.33 | 0.68 |

## SHERINGHAM, Teddy

*Tim Sherwood*

# Manchester U. ❶❷❸❹     S

Fullname:  Edward Paul Sheringham
DOB:       02-04-66 Walthamstow
   International class striker whose reputation was wholly enhanced by Euro '96 when he linked to deadly effect with Alan Shearer. He joined Spurs in August 1992 and for each of the next four seasons scored freely hitting the back of the net 68 times in just 137 Premiership matches. Managed 29 appearances last season despite injury but with injury ruling out Chris Armstrong and Darren Anderton for much of the campaign, his supply lines were less than flowing.

   He was an ever-present in the Tottenham side during the 1994-95 and 1995-96 season and he has a distinctive style of play which often involves linking midfield and attack. Often criticised for a lack of pace, Alan Shearer defended him by saying that he had two yards of extra pace in his head. A highly intelligent player and terrific passer of the ball, he ended his association with Spurs at the end of June 1997, joining Manchester United for £3.5 million.

   Despite being 31, he looks to have a number of seasons ahead of him at the top flight and is expected to fulfil the role left by the retirement of Eric Cantona.

## Form Factors

| Season | Team | Tot | St | Sb | Y | R |
|--------|------|-----|-----|-----|-----|-----|
| 94-95 | Tottenham | 42 | 41 | 1 | 3 | 0 |
| 95-96 | Tottenham | 38 | 38 | 0 | 2 | 0 |
| 96-97 | Tottenham | 29 | 29 | 0 | 6 | 0 |
| Total | | 109 | 108 | 1 | 11 | 0 |

| | GP | GG | GF | GS | TGR |
|--------|-----|-----|-----|-----|-----|
| 94-95 | 100.00 | 2.47 | 66 | 17 | 25.76 |
| 95-96 | 100.00 | 2.38 | 50 | 16 | 32.00 |
| 96-97 | 76.32 | 4.14 | 44 | 7 | 15.91 |
| Averages | 92.11 | 3.00 | 53.33 | 13.33 | 24.56 |

## SHERWOOD, Tim

# Blackburn R. ❶❷❸❹    M

Fullname:  Timothy Alan Sherwood
DOB:       06-02-69 St Albans
   It wouldn't be an exaggeration to say that Tim makes Blackburn Rovers tick. When he plays well the team invariably does too, and it is not surprising that he wears the captain's armband. Has missed just six games in the past three seasons – mainly due to suspension – weighing in with 12 goals in the same period. Indeed only five players have chalked up more Premier League appearances than him since it began.

Speculation has been rife in the past year that he would be leaving Ewood Park but he seems to have started to recapture the form that helped bring Rovers the title in 1994-95.

Formerly with Watford and Norwich City, he has played at England Under-21 and 'B' level.

## Form Factors

| Season | Team | Tot | St | Sb | Y | R |
|---|---|---|---|---|---|---|
| 94-95 | Blackburn | 38 | 38 | 0 | 8 | 0 |
| 95-96 | Blackburn | 33 | 33 | 0 | 8 | 0 |
| 96-97 | Blackburn | 37 | 37 | 0 | 7 | 1 |
| Total | | 108 | 108 | 0 | 23 | 1 |

| | GP | GG | GF | GS | TGR |
|---|---|---|---|---|---|
| 94-95 | 90.48 | 6.33 | 80 | 6 | 7.50 |
| 95-96 | 86.84 | 11.00 | 61 | 3 | 4.92 |
| 96-97 | 97.37 | 12.33 | 42 | 3 | 7.14 |
| Averages | 91.56 | 9.89 | 61.00 | 4.00 | 6.52 |

## SHIPPERLEY, Neil

# Crystal Palace ❶❷❸ S

Fullname:  Neil Shipperley
DOB:        30-10-74 Chatham

For a centre forward Shipperley possesses all-round attributes. However he has found it hard to settle at any one club – his £1 million move to Crystal Palace in October 1996 making it his third club in four years.

His contribution to Palace's cause was huge, with 12 goals in 32 appearances. He started last season at the Dell, playing in ten games early on before his move.

Good on the ball and an accurate passer who packs a powerful shot in both feet, he started his career as a trainee at Chelsea and was briefly loaned out at Watford before Southampton paid £1.25 million to secure his services in January 1995.

Now has the chance to prove himself as a Premier League class striker once again.

## Form Factors

| Season | Team | Tot | St | Sb | Y | R |
|---|---|---|---|---|---|---|
| 94-95 | Southampton | 19 | 19 | 0 | 3 | 0 |
| 95-96 | Southampton | 37 | 37 | 0 | 1 | 0 |
| 96-97 | Southampton | 10 | 9 | 1 | 0 | 0 |
| Total | | 66 | 65 | 1 | 4 | 0 |

| | GP | GG | GF | GS | TGR |
|---|---|---|---|---|---|
| 94-95 | 45.24 | 4.75 | 61 | 4 | 6.56 |
| 95-96 | 97.37 | 4.63 | 34 | 8 | 23.53 |
| 96-97 | 26.32 | 10.00 | 50 | 1 | 2.00 |
| Averages | 56.31 | 6.46 | 48.33 | 4.33 | 10.70 |

## SHORT, Craig

# Everton ❶❷❸ CB

Fullname:  Craig Short
DOB:        25-06-68 Bridlington

Dominating central defender whose height has earned him a good number of goals down the years and should continue to be an asset to Everton for some time to come. Moved to Goodison Park from Derby County in a £2.75 million deal in July 1995 and has since played in 60% of the Blues' Premiership matches scoring four goals and picking up a dozen cautions along the way.

His career kicked off with non-leaguers Pickering Town before he was snapped up by Scarborough in 1987, from where he joined Notts County in a £100,000 deal. County recouped their outlay many times over when he signed for Derby in exchange for £2.5 million three years later.

## Form Factors

| Season | Team | Tot | St | Sb | Y | R |
|---|---|---|---|---|---|---|
| 95-96 | Everton | 23 | 22 | 1 | 6 | 0 |
| 96-97 | Everton | 23 | 19 | 4 | 6 | 0 |
| Total | | 46 | 41 | 5 | 12 | 0 |

| | GP | GG | GF | GS | TGR |
|---|---|---|---|---|---|
| 95-96 | 60.53 | 11.50 | 64 | 2 | 3.13 |
| 96-97 | 60.53 | 11.50 | 44 | 2 | 4.55 |
| Averages | 60.53 | 11.50 | 54.00 | 2.00 | 3.84 |

## SIMPSON, Paul

### Derby County ❶❷ M

Fullname: Paul David Simpson
DOB: 26-07-66 Carlisle

Paul Simpson was getting used to life on the bench last season, starting an incredible 31 games seated on the sidelines. It was an important role though as he was County's most used sub, coming on no less than 19 times and notching two goals as well – one an equaliser two minutes from time against Leeds United on the opening day of the season.

A striker who can play wide or through the middle, Simpson has played well over a century of games at each of his clubs – Manchester City, Oxford United and Derby. Is close on his 200th league appearance for Derby but may have to do it from the bench again in 1997-98.

### Form Factors

| Season | Team | Tot | St | Sb | Y | R |
|---|---|---|---|---|---|---|
| 96-97 | Derby Co. | 19 | 0 | 19 | 0 | 0 |
| Total | | 19 | 0 | 19 | 0 | 0 |

| | GP | GG | GF | GS | TGR |
|---|---|---|---|---|---|
| 96-97 | 50.00 | 9.50 | 45 | 2 | 4.44 |
| Averages | 50.00 | 9.50 | 45.00 | 2.00 | 4.44 |

## SINCLAIR, Frank

### Chelsea ❶❷❸ CB

Fullname: Frank Mohammed Sinclair
DOB: 03-12-71 Lambeth

Twenty Premier League games in the heart of the Chelsea defence last season may prove that Sinclair has a future in manager Ruud Gullit's plans, despite the influx of defenders.

Having joined Chelsea as a trainee in May 1990, he has played in over 150 senior games and, but for shin splint problems in the 1995-96 season, might have further entrenched himself at Stamford Bridge.

A ball-playing defender who is equally good in the air, he has been prone to errors which have cost his team. The 1997-98 season will be a big one for him and especially as a squad player.

### Form Factors

| Season | Team | Tot | St | Sb | Y | R |
|---|---|---|---|---|---|---|
| 94-95 | Chelsea | 35 | 35 | 0 | 9 | 0 |
| 95-96 | Chelsea | 13 | 12 | 1 | 5 | 1 |
| 96-97 | Chelsea | 20 | 17 | 3 | 5 | 0 |
| Total | | 68 | 64 | 4 | 19 | 1 |

| | GP | GG | GF | GS | TGR |
|---|---|---|---|---|---|
| 94-95 | 83.33 | 11.67 | 50 | 3 | 6.00 |
| 95-96 | 34.21 | 13.00 | 46 | 1 | 2.17 |
| 96-97 | 52.63 | 20.00 | 58 | 1 | 1.72 |
| Averages | 56.73 | 14.89 | 51.33 | 1.67 | 3.30 |

## SINTON, Andy

# Tottenham H.    ❶❷❸    M

Fullname:  Andrew Sinton
DOB:        19-03-66 Newcastle

Andy Sinton took a long time to make his mark at Tottenham but finished the 1996-97 season with six goals from 33 Premiership matches, making it his most successful campaign since his final season with Queens Park Rangers in 1992-93.

The player played under Gerry Francis at QPR and, after a less than fruitful two and a half years at Sheffield Wednesday, joined Tottenham to again be under Francis' leadership.

Predominantly a left-sided midfield player, be can also play a wider attacking role and picked up 12 England caps during the Graham Taylor era.

## Form Factors

| Season | Team | Tot | St | Sb | Y | R |
|---|---|---|---|---|---|---|
| 95-96 | Sheffield W. | 10 | 7 | 3 | 1 | 0 |
| 95-96 | Tottenham | 9 | 8 | 1 | 1 | 0 |
| 96-97 | Tottenham | 33 | 32 | 1 | 5 | 0 |
| Total | | 52 | 47 | 5 | 7 | 0 |

| | GP | GG | GF | GS | TGR |
|---|---|---|---|---|---|
| 95-96 | 26.32 | 0.00 | 48 | 0 | 0.00 |
| 95-96 | 23.68 | 0.00 | 50 | 0 | 0.00 |
| 96-97 | 86.84 | 5.50 | 44 | 6 | 13.64 |
| Averages | 45.61 | 1.83 | 47.33 | 2.00 | 4.55 |

## SLATER, Robbie

# Southampton    ❶❷    S

Fullname:  Robert David Slater
DOB:        22-11-64 Skelmersdale

A full Australian international player, Robbie Slater first came to the notice of English managers when he was playing in France for the French clubs Lens. A fast, pacy winger, Slater is very competitive but also struggles to find the consistency that would make him into one of the top players in English football.

He was signed by Blackburn Rovers in August 1994 and after 18 games was traded to West Ham United in a swap deal for Matty Holmes. Having completed just 25 games for the Hammers he found himself on the South coast with Southampton shortly after the 1996-97 season has started.

He had probably his best run of games in England under Graeme Souness featuring in 30 games but scoring just two goals.

*Robbie Slater*

## Form Factors

| Season | Team | Tot | St | Sb | Y | R |
|---|---|---|---|---|---|---|
| 95-96 | West Ham | 22 | 16 | 6 | 1 | 0 |
| 96-97 | West Ham | 3 | 2 | 1 | 1 | 0 |
| 96-97 | Southampton | 30 | 22 | 8 | 5 | 0 |
| Total | | 55 | 40 | 15 | 7 | 0 |

| | GP | GG | GF | GS | TGR |
|---|---|---|---|---|---|
| 95-96 | 57.89 | 11.00 | 43 | 2 | 4.65 |
| 96-97 | 7.89 | 0.00 | 39 | 0 | 0.00 |
| 96-97 | 78.95 | 15.00 | 50 | 2 | 4.00 |
| Averages | 48.24 | 13.00 | 44.00 | 1.33 | 2.88 |

## SMALL, Bryan

# Bolton W.  ❶❷  FB

Fullname: Bryan Small
DOB: 15-11-71 Birmingham

Small looks the likely long-term replacement for Jimmy Phillips at left-back. Made 10 of his 11 appearances as a starter in the middle of the 1996-97 season.

Very strong, and equally quick, he joined Bolton after being unable to hold down a regular place in the Aston Villa team he had joined as a trainee. He played one Premiership game in Bolton's last spell in the top division.

Spent a brief period on loan at Villa's cross-town rivals Birmingham City and has a dozen England Under-21 caps to his credit.

Although primarily a full-back, he has played in midfield and provides Bolton with several options in this area.

## Form Factors

| Season | Team | Tot | St | Sb | Y | R |
|---|---|---|---|---|---|---|
| 93-94 | Aston Villa | 14 | 10 | 4 | 0 | 0 |
| 94-95 | Aston Villa | 5 | 5 | 0 | 0 | 0 |
| 95-96 | Bolton W. | 1 | 1 | 0 | 0 | 0 |
| Total | | 20 | 16 | 4 | 0 | 0 |

| | GP | GG | GF | GS | TGR |
|---|---|---|---|---|---|
| 93-94 | 33.33 | 0.00 | 46 | 0 | 0.00 |
| 94-95 | 11.90 | 0.00 | 51 | 0 | 0.00 |
| 95-96 | 2.63 | 0.00 | 39 | 0 | 0.00 |
| Averages | 15.95 | 0.00 | 45.33 | 0.00 | 0.00 |

## SOLIS, Mauricio

# Derby County  ❶❷  M

Fullname: Mauricio Solis
DOB:

Signed in the spring of 1997 along with Paulo Wanchope from CS Heridiano for a combined fee of £600,000 and made his debut for the final eleven minutes of Derby's 2-1 win at Aston Villa in April, a result which just about confirmed County's Premiership status for another season. Also played as a substitute against Newcastle United and was also an unused sub on two other occasions.

Looks likely to be part of Jim Smith's plans for the 1997-98 season.

## Form Factors

| Season | Team | Tot | St | Sb | Y | R |
|---|---|---|---|---|---|---|
| 96-97 | Derby Co. | 2 | 0 | 2 | 0 | 0 |
| Total | | 2 | 0 | 2 | 0 | 0 |

| | GP | GG | GF | GS | TGR |
|---|---|---|---|---|---|
| 96-97 | 5.26 | 0.00 | 45 | 0 | 0.00 |
| Averages | 5.26 | 0.00 | 45.00 | 0.00 | 0.00 |

*Ole Gunnar Solskjaer*

## SOLSKJAER, Ole Gunnar

# Manchester U. ❶❷❸❹❺    S

Fullname:   Ole Gunnar Solskjaer

DOB:      26-02-73 Kristiansund, Norway

Of the three major overseas signings in the summer of 1996, Ole Gunnar Solskjaer has been by far the most successful. His combination with Eric Cantona was just one of the reasons he finished as their top scorer in the Premiership with 18 goals. At just 5' 8" he is good in the air and a star with ball at his feet. A £1.5 million signing from Molde, the Norwegian looks like an alternative to Andy Cole for the centre forward position but the two of them also combined to good effect.

Still has youth on his side at 24, and is already a favourite with the fans after a solid season of 25 starts and eight substitute appearances.

Just two seasons ago Solskjaer was playing in the Norwegian third division with FK Clausenengen – how quickly a footballer's fortunes can change.

Now, if Solskjaer can perform in the lofty company of the Champions' League then United have hit gold. Expect more goals during the 1997-98 season.

## Form Factors

| Season | Team | Tot | St | Sb | Y | R |
|---|---|---|---|---|---|---|
| 96-97 | Man. Utd | 33 | 25 | 8 | 1 | 0 |
| Total | | 33 | 25 | 8 | 1 | 0 |

| | GP | GG | GF | GS | TGR |
|---|---|---|---|---|---|
| 96-97 | 86.84 | 1.83 | 76 | 18 | 23.68 |
| Averages | 86.84 | 1.83 | 76.00 | 18.00 | 23.68 |

## SOUTHALL, Neville

### Everton ❶❷❸❹❺ GK

Fullname: Neville Southall
DOB: 16-09-58 Llandudno

Goalkeeper who, along with Tim Flowers, has made more Premiership appearances than any other player. Has kept 59 clean sheets in his 195 league games for Everton and can look to further improve that record in 1997-98 following Everton's capture of Bilic. Llandudno-born, he is edging towards 100 caps for Wales and has played an astonishing 700 games for Everton since joining the club for a paltry £150,000 in July 1981! Cost Bury just £6,000 when they took him from non-league outfit Winsford. Has won League Championship, FA Cup and European Cup Winners' Cup medals during his highly distinguished career. Not the tallest goalkeeper in the Premiership but has great agility and exceptional handling ability. He will be under pressure from Paul Gerrard this season to retain his place between the sticks.

### Form Factors

| Season | Team | Tot | St | Sb | Y | R |
|--------|------|-----|-----|-----|-----|-----|
| 94-95 | Everton | 41 | 41 | 0 | 3 | 0 |
| 95-96 | Everton | 38 | 38 | 0 | 0 | 0 |
| 96-97 | Everton | 34 | 34 | 0 | 2 | 0 |
| Total | | 113 | 113 | 0 | 5 | 0 |

| | GA | GkA | GAp | CS | SO | Rp |
|--------|-----|-----|-----|-----|-----|-----|
| 94-95 | 51 | 51 | 1.24 | 14 | 7 | 0 |
| 95-96 | 44 | 44 | 1.16 | 15 | 2 | 5 |
| 96-97 | 58 | 51 | 1.50 | 8 | 1 | 0 |
| Total | 153 | 146 | 1.29 | 37 | 10 | – |

Neville Southall

## SOUTHGATE, Gareth

### Aston Villa ❶❷❸❹❺ CB

Fullname: Gareth Southgate
DOB: 03-09-70 Watford

Will always be remembered for *that* miss! Southgate remains one of the best central defenders in England, if not world football. Having started his career as a trainee with Crystal Palace, his performances in their 1994-95 relegation side earned him a requested move to Villa Park and the chance to continue to play at the top level. His performances quickly

earned him his England call-up and he won his first cap in December 1995 against Portugal.

Since that point he has been plagued by nagging injuries. A knee injury forced him to miss the 1996 Coca Cola win and last season he missed ten games of the campaign due to a recurrent ankle problem. He recovered in time to feature in England's close season games and, provided he can retain his fitness, will add further to the depth of an already strong Aston Villa defence.

### Form Factors

| Season | Team | Tot | St | Sb | Y | R |
|--------|------|-----|-----|-----|-----|-----|
| 94-95 | C. Palace | 42 | 42 | 0 | 5 | 0 |
| 95-96 | Aston Villa | 31 | 31 | 0 | 1 | 0 |
| 96-97 | Aston Villa | 28 | 28 | 0 | 1 | 0 |
| Total | | 101 | 101 | 0 | 7 | 0 |

| | GP | GG | GF | GS | TGR |
|--------|-----|-----|-----|-----|-----|
| 94-95 | 100.00 | 14.00 | 34 | 3 | 8.82 |
| 95-96 | 81.58 | 31.00 | 52 | 1 | 1.92 |
| 96-97 | 73.68 | 28.00 | 47 | 1 | 2.13 |
| Averages | 85.09 | 24.33 | 44.33 | 1.67 | 4.29 |

*Gareth Southgate*

## SPEED, Gary

### Everton ❶❷❸❹ M

Fullname: Gary Andrew Speed
DOB: 08-09-69 Hawarden

Served Leeds United for eight years as a professional before switching across the Pennines to Everton for £3.5 million in July 1996. A midfielder, he missed just one Premiership game last season and had his most productive campaign in front of goal for four seasons, finding the back of the net eleven times in all competitions. Fast left-sided player and fine crosser of the ball who is deceptively useful in the air. Scored 55 goals during his 295 games at Elland Road. Veteran of almost 40 Welsh caps and could improve that figure considerably given that he is only 28 in September.

## Form Factors

| Season | Team | Tot | St | Sb | Y | R |
|---|---|---|---|---|---|---|
| 94-95 | Leeds Utd | 39 | 39 | 0 | 5 | 0 |
| 95-96 | Leeds Utd | 29 | 29 | 0 | 2 | 0 |
| 96-97 | Everton | 37 | 37 | 0 | 8 | 0 |
| Total | | 105 | 105 | 0 | 15 | 0 |

| | GP | GG | GF | GS | TGR |
|---|---|---|---|---|---|
| 94-95 | 92.86 | 13.00 | 59 | 3 | 5.08 |
| 95-96 | 76.32 | 14.50 | 40 | 2 | 5.00 |
| 96-97 | 97.37 | 4.11 | 44 | 9 | 20.45 |
| Averages | 88.85 | 10.54 | 47.67 | 4.67 | 10.18 |

*Gary Speed*

## SRNICEK, Pavel

# Newcastle U.    ❶    GK

Fullname:  Pavel Srnicek
DOB:       10-03-68 Ostrava,
           Czechoslovakia

A Czech international who sat out Euro '96 to West Ham United's Ludo Miklosko, 'Pav' joined the St James' Park brigade in February 1991 when Newcastle paid Banik Ostrava £350,000, to secure his services. In 1994-95 Srnicek established himself as first choice keeper and played 38 games, conceded 43 goals, and kept 13 clean sheets. During both the 1995-96 and 1996-97 seasons Srnicek had to fight for his place especially when Shaka Hislop arrived from Reading in the summer of 1995 from which point they have largely shared the 'keeping duties.

The arrival of Shay Given from Blackburn Rovers must put a serious question mark over Srnicek's future on Tyneside.

In the Premiership he has kept 33 clean sheets in 96 appearances in total, and he achieved a sequence of four games without conceding amongst his 22 appearances in the 1996-97 season.

## Form Factors

| Season | Team | Tot | St | Sb | Y | R |
|---|---|---|---|---|---|---|
| 94-95 | Newcastle | 38 | 38 | 0 | 1 | 2 |
| 95-96 | Newcastle | 15 | 14 | 1 | 0 | 0 |
| 96-97 | Newcastle | 22 | 22 | 0 | 0 | 0 |
| Total | | 75 | 74 | 1 | 1 | 2 |

| | GA | GkA | GAp | CS | SO | Rp |
|---|---|---|---|---|---|---|
| 94-95 | 47 | 43 | 1.13 | 13 | 2 | 0 |
| 95-96 | 37 | 18 | 1.20 | 5 | 2 | 0 |
| 96-97 | 40 | 19 | 0.86 | 7 | 4 | 0 |
| Total | 124 | 80 | 1.07 | 25 | 8 | – |

## STAUNTON, Steve

# Aston Villa ❶❷❸ FB

Fullname: Stephen Staunton
DOB: 19-01-69 Drogheda

Steve Staunton is perhaps one of the most under-rated players in the Premiership. Having served as an apprentice at Liverpool, he looked to have been packed off early when he was loaned out to Bradford by the Anfield club in November 1987. Villa though were quick to react and snapped up a bargain.

Played much of his time at Villa as a full-back but last season formed a three-man defence alongside Ugo Ehiogu and Gareth Southgate, which conceded just 34 goals – the second best record in the Premiership.

His sweet left foot has provided crosses for numerous goals and it packs a fierce drive that will always ensure the odd goal here and there.

Staunton has been a major factor in the Republic of Ireland's success in recent years and he is well on his way to becoming the most capped Irish player of all time.

A serious contender for any fantasy team.

## Form Factors

| Season | Team | Tot | St | Sb | Y | R |
|---|---|---|---|---|---|---|
| 94-95 | Aston Villa | 35 | 34 | 1 | 7 | 0 |
| 95-96 | Aston Villa | 13 | 11 | 2 | 0 | 0 |
| 96-97 | Aston Villa | 30 | 30 | 0 | 5 | 1 |
| Total | | 78 | 75 | 3 | 12 | 1 |

| | GP | GG | GF | GS | TGR |
|---|---|---|---|---|---|
| 94-95 | 83.33 | 7.00 | 51 | 5 | 9.80 |
| 95-96 | 34.21 | 0.00 | 52 | 0 | 0.00 |
| 96-97 | 78.95 | 15.00 | 47 | 2 | 4.26 |
| Averages | 65.50 | 7.33 | 50.00 | 2.33 | 4.69 |

## STEFANOVIC, Dejan

# Sheffield W. ❶❷❸ CB

Fullname: Dejan Stefanovic
DOB: 20-10-74 Yugoslavia

Arrived at Hillsborough in December 1995 and, after a shaky start last season, showed more promise. Was part of a £4.5 million deal with Red Star Belgrade which also saw his team-mate Darko Kovacevic move to Yorkshire. Kovacevic went but Stefanovic remained and formed a good understanding with Des Walker at the heart of the Wednesday defence.

The Yugoslavian international played in 29 of the Owls' Premiership games last season and scored his first goals against Chelsea and Sunderland. Tall and imposing, he has excellent skills in his left foot and should continue to add to the English game during 1997-98.

## Form Factors

| Season | Team | Tot | St | Sb | Y | R |
|---|---|---|---|---|---|---|
| 95-96 | Sheffield W. | 6 | 5 | 1 | 0 | 0 |
| 96-97 | Sheffield W. | 29 | 27 | 2 | 6 | 0 |
| Total | | 35 | 32 | 3 | 6 | 0 |

| | GP | GG | GF | GS | TGR |
|---|---|---|---|---|---|
| 95-96 | 15.79 | 0.00 | 48 | 0 | 0.00 |
| 96-97 | 76.32 | 14.50 | 50 | 2 | 4.00 |
| Averages | 46.05 | 7.25 | 49.00 | 1.00 | 2.00 |

## Derby County ❶❷❸ CB

Fullname: Igor Stimac
DOB: 09-06-67 Croatia

Thirty-year-old Croatian international defender who has been a huge success since signing for Derby County from Hadjuk Split in October 1995 for a bargain £1.5 million. Very strong, consistent and influential, he scored on his Derby debut at Tranmere in November 1995, although his new club still went down 5-1. Since then he has become one of the most respected overseas players in the Premiership although the frequency with which he falls foul of match officials restricted him to just 55% of the Rams' Premiership games. Derby will need all his experience to complete another successful campaign in 1997-98.

*Igor Stimac*

### Form Factors

| Season | Team | Tot | St | Sb | Y | R |
|--------|------|-----|----|----|----|---|
| 96-97 | Derby Co. | 21 | 21 | 0 | 9 | 0 |
| Total | | 21 | 21 | 0 | 9 | 0 |

| | GP | GG | GF | GS | TGR |
|--------|-----|-----|-----|-----|-----|
| 96-97 | 55.26 | 21.00 | 45 | 1 | 2.22 |
| Averages | 55.26 | 21.00 | 45.00 | 1.00 | 2.22 |

## Coventry City ❶ M

Fullname: Gordon David Strachan
DOB: 09-02-57 Edinburgh

One of the greatest midfield players of his era, which extended into a 23rd year of professional football when he made a handful of inspirational performances for his ailing Coventry side.

It may be unlikely for him to feature in too many games during 1997-98 as he concentrates on the position of manager which he acquired during last season.

Capped 50 times by Scotland, he played for Dundee and Aberdeen before moving south of the border to spend five years with Manchester United and six years with Leeds United, prior to joining Coventry in March 1995.

Exudes infectious enthusiasm and his passing still remains a highlight of his game. Many feel it was his performances in the latter stages of the season which ensured the Sky Blues could maintain their presence in the Premiership.

### Form Factors

| Season | Team | Tot | St | Sb | Y | R |
|--------|------|-----|----|----|----|---|
| 94-95 | Coventry C. | 5 | 5 | 0 | 1 | 0 |
| 95-96 | Coventry C. | 12 | 5 | 7 | 1 | 0 |
| 96-97 | Coventry C. | 9 | 3 | 6 | 1 | 0 |
| Total | | 26 | 13 | 13 | 3 | 0 |

Dean Sturridge

| | GP | GG | GF | GS | TGR |
|---|---|---|---|---|---|
| 94-95 | 11.90 | 0.00 | 44 | 0 | 0.00 |
| 95-96 | 31.58 | 0.00 | 42 | 0 | 0.00 |
| 96-97 | 23.68 | 0.00 | 38 | 0 | 0.00 |
| Averages | 22.39 | 0.00 | 41.33 | 0.00 | 0.00 |

## STUART, Graham

## Everton    ❶❷❸    S

Fullname:  Graham Charles Stuart
DOB:     24-10-70 Tooting
   Born in Tooting, he joined Chelsea as a
youngster and played 105 games for the
club before heading north to sign for
Everton in an £850,000 deal in August
1993. Two-footed striker who plays wide
and turned out for England at Under-21
level whilst with Chelsea, but the high
point of his career to date came as a
member of Everton's FA Cup winning
side. Has become a linchpin in the

Everton side in his four years at Goodison
Park, featuring in around 80% of the
Blues' Premiership matches and scoring
at a rate of one goal in less than every
seven games. Made his 150th Premiership
appearance last season and is only a
handful of games short of his 250th
senior appearance.

### Form Factors

| Season | Team | Tot | St | Sb | Y | R |
|---|---|---|---|---|---|---|
| 94-95 | Everton | 28 | 20 | 8 | 0 | 0 |
| 95-96 | Everton | 29 | 27 | 2 | 3 | 0 |
| 96-97 | Everton | 35 | 29 | 6 | 4 | 0 |
| Total | | 92 | 76 | 16 | 7 | 0 |

| | GP | GG | GF | GS | TGR |
|---|---|---|---|---|---|
| 94-95 | 66.67 | 9.33 | 44 | 3 | 6.82 |
| 95-96 | 76.32 | 3.22 | 64 | 9 | 14.06 |
| 96-97 | 92.11 | 7.00 | 44 | 5 | 11.36 |
| Averages | 78.36 | 6.52 | 50.67 | 5.67 | 10.75 |

## STURRIDGE, Dean

# Derby County ❶❷❸❹    S

Fullname: Dean Constantine Sturridge
DOB: 27-07-73 Birmingham

Possesses the speed, strength, skill and sharpness in front of goal to become one of the hottest properties in the Premiership. Scored some stunning goals in his first season of Premier League football with Derby County in 1996-97 and, with 11 goals from 30 games, went a long way towards ensuring the Rams' survival. Moved through the ranks at the Baseball Ground having joined the club as a trainee but had a spell on loan to Torquay United, where he scored five goals in ten games, before fully establishing himself under Jim Smith at Derby. Then proved himself at a higher level with 20 league goals during Derby's promotion season.

He made his 100th senior appearance in the 2-3 defeat by Leicester City at Filbert Street and it may be just a matter of time before he is lured away to richer pastures.

## Form Factors

| Season | Team | Tot | St | Sb | Y | R |
|---|---|---|---|---|---|---|
| 96-97 | Derby Co. | 30 | 29 | 1 | 9 | 0 |
| Total | | 30 | 29 | 1 | 9 | 0 |

| | GP | GG | GF | GS | TGR |
|---|---|---|---|---|---|
| 96-97 | 78.95 | 2.73 | 45 | 11 | 24.44 |
| Averages | 78.95 | 2.73 | 45.00 | 11.00 | 24.44 |

## SULLIVAN, Neil

# Wimbledon ❶❷❸❹    GK

Fullname: Neil Sullivan
DOB: 24-02-70 Sutton

Sullivan made the headlines for all the wrong reasons last season. In a dismal opening three games he found himself beaten by David Beckham from the half way line, only to be lobbed again in

*Neil Sullivan*

*Chris Sutton*

almost similar fashion, albeit nearer his goal, at Newcastle in the very next game.

The Sutton born 'keeper, who joined the Dons as a trainee, missed just two Premiership games last season and had his best season, maintaining a clean sheet 11 times and conceding just 43 goals.

At just six foot tall, he is not the tallest of 'keepers and some may point to that as the reason for him being beaten twice early on by lobs. Nevertheless he is very agile and produced several outstanding performances in Wimbledon's run to two cup semi-finals last season.

Has now established himself as the Dons' number one over Paul Heald.

## Form Factors

| Season | Team | Tot | St | Sb | Y | R |
|--------|------|-----|-----|-----|-----|-----|
| 94-95 | Wimbledon | 11 | 11 | 0 | 0 | 0 |
| 95-96 | Wimbledon | 16 | 16 | 0 | 0 | 0 |
| 96-97 | Wimbledon | 36 | 36 | 0 | 0 | 0 |
| Total | | 63 | 63 | 0 | 0 | 0 |

|  | GA | GkA | GAp | CS | SO | Rp |
|--------|-----|-----|------|-----|-----|-----|
| 94-95 | 65 | 11 | 1.00 | 6 | 3 | 2 |
| 95-96 | 70 | 35 | 2.19 | 3 | 1 | 0 |
| 96-97 | 48 | 43 | 1.19 | 11 | 3 | 0 |
| Totals | 183 | 89 | 1.41 | 20 | 7 | – |

## SUTTON, Chris

### Blackburn Rovers ❶❷❸❹  S

Fullname:  Christopher Roy Sutton
DOB:  10-03-73 Nottingham

Sutton was a member of what was regarded as the SAS in the Premiership winning side. Shearer And Sutton – a potent attacking force. Yet Sutton started life at Norwich as a defender and having converted to a free-scoring attacker, moved to Blackburn Rovers for £5 million. He scored 15 goals in the championship-winning campaign but the Rovers' injury blight struck the following season as he was limited to just 13 appearances – some as defensive cover.

Last season he was starting to get back to top form and his 11 goals came at a rate of just over one every other game.

## Form Factors

| Season | Team | Tot | St | Sb | Y | R |
|---|---|---|---|---|---|---|
| 94-95 | Blackburn | 40 | 40 | 0 | 7 | 0 |
| 95-96 | Blackburn | 13 | 9 | 4 | 3 | 0 |
| 96-97 | Blackburn | 25 | 24 | 1 | 4 | 0 |
| Total | | 78 | 73 | 5 | 14 | 0 |

| | GP | GG | GF | GS | TGR |
|---|---|---|---|---|---|
| 94-95 | 95.24 | 2.67 | 80 | 15 | 18.75 |
| 95-96 | 34.21 | 0.00 | 61 | 0 | 0.00 |
| 96-97 | 65.79 | 2.27 | 42 | 11 | 26.19 |
| Averages | 65.08 | 1.65 | 61.00 | 8.67 | 14.98 |

## TAGGART, Gerry

# Bolton W.  ❶  CB

Fullname: Gerald Paul Taggart
DOB: 18-10-70 Belfast

An experienced Northern Ireland international who had a major role to play in Bolton's return to the Premiership. His 43 appearances in the centre of the defence provided the backbone for many of the team's victories. Injury severely limited his appearances in the 1995-96 season but 1997-98 gives him a chance to see if he can ensure Bolton maintain Premiership status.

Started his career with Manchester City as a trainee and moved to Barnsley in 1990, going on to make over 200 league appearances for them before becoming Bolton's record purchase at the time when he joined them for £1.5 million in the summer of 1995.

Tall and commanding, he is a threat at set-pieces and for a defender can strike the ball well.

## Form Factors

| Season | Team | Tot | St | Sb | Y | R |
|---|---|---|---|---|---|---|
| 95-96 | Bolton W. | 11 | 11 | 0 | 6 | 0 |
| Total | | 11 | 11 | 0 | 6 | 0 |

| | GP | GG | GF | GS | TGR |
|---|---|---|---|---|---|
| 95-96 | 28.95 | 11.00 | 39 | 1 | 2.56 |
| Averages | 28.95 | 11.00 | 39.00 | 1.00 | 2.56 |

## TAYLOR, Ian

# Aston Villa  ❶❷❸  M

Fullname: Ian Kenneth Taylor
DOB: 04-06-68 Birmingham

Ian Taylor's position looked the most under threat when Sasa Curcic arrived from Bolton Wanderers in the summer of 1996. However, the former Port Vale and Sheffield Wednesday player took to the challenge and held his place in the starting line-up for most of the season.

Although classified as a midfield player, Taylor can perform in the defence when required. Always looks comfortable on the ball despite his hard-tackling reputation and can hit some spectacular, if rare, goals.

This season will see him battling it out with Curcic for a midfield role.

## Form Factors

| Season | Team | Tot | St | Sb | Y | R |
|---|---|---|---|---|---|---|
| 94-95 | Aston Villa | 22 | 22 | 0 | 2 | 0 |
| 95-96 | Aston Villa | 25 | 24 | 1 | 5 | 0 |
| 96-97 | Aston Villa | 34 | 29 | 5 | 4 | 0 |
| Total | | 81 | 75 | 6 | 11 | 0 |

| | GP | GG | GF | GS | TGR |
|---|---|---|---|---|---|
| 94-95 | 52.38 | 22.00 | 51 | 1 | 1.96 |
| 95-96 | 65.79 | 8.33 | 52 | 3 | 5.77 |
| 96-97 | 89.47 | 17.00 | 47 | 2 | 4.26 |
| Averages | 69.21 | 15.78 | 50.00 | 2.00 | 4.00 |

## TAYLOR, Maik

### Southampton ❶❷❸ GK

Fullname: Maik Stefan Taylor
DOB: 04-09-71 Germany

Having been linked with a number of clubs, Taylor signed for the Saints in December 1996 – a £500,000 purchase from Nationwide Division Three side Barnet. He made his debut against Middlesbrough the following month and was then an ever-present in the Southampton line-up, playing 18 straight games to see the season out.

Taylor was one of four goalkeepers used by the Saints during 1996-97 but was by far the most successful, conceding on average slightly over a goal a game and just 19 goals out of Southampton's 56 conceded. He also kept seven clean sheets and would seem to have established himself as the number one choice at the Dell.

At 6' 5" he physically dominates his area and missed just one game in his season with Barnet.

### Form Factors

| Season | Team | Tot | St | Sb | Y | R |
|---|---|---|---|---|---|---|
| 96-97 | Southampton | 18 | 18 | 0 | 1 | 0 |
| Total | | 18 | 18 | 0 | 1 | 0 |

| | GA | GkA | GAp | CS | SO | Rp |
|---|---|---|---|---|---|---|
| 96-97 | 56 | 19 | 1.06 | 7 | 2 | 2 |
| Total | 56 | 19 | 1.06 | 7 | 2 | – |

## TAYLOR, Scott

### Bolton W. ❶ S

Fullname: Scott James Taylor
DOB: 05-05-76 Chertsey

Bolton Wanderers paid Millwall £150,000 to secure Taylor's services just before the transfer deadline in 1996. He made one substitute appearance in the Premiership as the club were relegated back to Division One.

Seen as an investment for the future, he is a compact striker who has both good close control and a fast turn of speed. Played in 11 of Wanderers' games last season with seven of those being from the bench. During this spell he also scored his first senior goal for the club.

Was spotted playing non-league football with Staines and turned 21 years old during the close season.

### Form Factors

| Season | Team | Tot | St | Sb | Y | R |
|---|---|---|---|---|---|---|
| 95-96 | Bolton W. | 1 | 0 | 1 | 0 | 0 |
| Total | | 1 | 0 | 1 | 0 | 0 |

| | GP | GG | GF | GS | TGR |
|---|---|---|---|---|---|
| 95-96 | 2.63 | 0.00 | 39 | 0 | 0.00 |
| Averages | 2.63 | 0.00 | 39.00 | 0.00 | 0.00 |

## TELFER, Paul

### Coventry City ❶❷❸ M

Fullname: Paul Norman Telfer
DOB: 12-10-91 Edinburgh

Has become a central figure in the Coventry City midfield since making a £1.5 million move from Luton Town in the summer of 1995. Has figured in over 85% of the Sky Blues' Premiership matches and, although predominantly a right-sided player, he is known for his versatility.

Telfer was a regular scorer during his last two seasons with Luton but goals have been scarcer since stepping up to the Premiership – just one in fact against Manchester City in August 1995.

Born in Edinburgh, Telford has Scottish Under-21 and 'B' appearances to his credit.

### Form Factors

| Season | Team | Tot | St | Sb | Y | R |
|--------|------|-----|-----|-----|-----|-----|
| 95-96 | Coventry C. | 31 | 31 | 0 | 4 | 0 |
| 96-97 | Coventry C. | 34 | 31 | 3 | 6 | 0 |
| Total | | 65 | 62 | 3 | 10 | 0 |

| | GP | GG | GF | GS | TGR |
|--------|-----|-----|-----|-----|-----|
| 95-96 | 81.58 | 31.00 | 42 | 1 | 2.38 |
| 96-97 | 89.47 | 0.00 | 38 | 0 | 0.00 |
| Averages | 85.53 | 15.50 | 40.00 | 0.50 | 1.19 |

## THATCHER, Ben

### Wimbledon ❶❷❸❹ FB

Fullname: Benjamin David Thatcher
DOB: 30-11-75 Swindon

It marked a change in Wimbledon's buying policy when they paid Millwall a club record fee of £2 million for Thatcher. Unfortunately injury limited the England Under-21 player to just nine appearances last season so it remains to be seen how well the young left-back come central defender can do in the Premier League.

His consistency and performances while with Millwall attracted attention from a wide range of clubs and ultimately led to Dons' manager Joe Kinnear making his purchase.

Hard tackling, good in the air and a good distributor of the ball, he represented the Football League against an Italian Serie B XI in 1995-96 and is widely predicted to go on to achieve full international honours with England.

### Form Factors

| Season | Team | Tot | St | Sb | Y | R |
|--------|------|-----|-----|-----|-----|-----|
| 96-97 | Wimbledon | 9 | 9 | 0 | 2 | 0 |
| Total | | 9 | 9 | 0 | 2 | 0 |

| | GP | GG | GF | GS | TGR |
|--------|-----|-----|-----|-----|-----|
| 96-97 | 23.68 | 0.00 | 49 | 0 | 0.00 |
| Averages | 23.68 | 0.00 | 49.00 | 0.00 | 0.00 |

play a full part in Liverpool's midfield, especially with Redknapp injured. A reliable fantasy choice.

He will always be remembered for the last second goal he scored for Arsenal at Anfield that gave the Gunners the championship in May 1989. A hard running, often under-rated midfield player, he has a knack of running from deep without detection and scoring great goals.

## Form Factors

| Season | Team | Tot | St | Sb | Y | R |
|---|---|---|---|---|---|---|
| 94-95 | Liverpool | 23 | 16 | 7 | 2 | 0 |
| 95-96 | Liverpool | 27 | 18 | 9 | 3 | 0 |
| 96-97 | Liverpool | 30 | 28 | 2 | 4 | 0 |
| Total | | 80 | 62 | 18 | 9 | 0 |

| | GP | GG | GF | GS | TGR |
|---|---|---|---|---|---|
| 94-95 | 54.76 | 0.00 | 65 | 0 | 0.00 |
| 95-96 | 71.05 | 27.00 | 70 | 1 | 1.43 |
| 96-97 | 78.95 | 10.00 | 62 | 3 | 4.84 |
| Averages | 68.25 | 12.33 | 65.67 | 1.33 | 2.09 |

*Alan Thompson*

# THOMAS, Michael

## Liverpool ❶❷ M

Fullname: Michael Lauriston Thomas
DOB: 24-08-67 Lambeth

Thomas signed a further three year deal in summer 1996 and was rewarded with 28 starts and two subs appearances in 1996-97, grabbing three goals in the process.

Thomas was signed from Arsenal for £1.5 million in the summer of 1991 but had a dreadful time with injuries to restrict his chances until a good run in 1995-96. He'll celebrate his 30th birthday as the season begins and looks likely to

# THOMPSON, Alan

## Bolton W. ❶❷❸ M

Fullname: Alan Thompson
DOB: 22-12-73 Newcastle

A tall, left-sided midfield player who possesses crafty skill and a good turn of speed. He contributed 11 goals in 34 games last season. After starting out as a trainee at Newcastle he moved to Bolton for £250,000 after making only a handful of appearances for the St James' Park side.

Injury and the need for a hernia operation inhibited his input into the 1995-96 season for Bolton and he might have expected more than one goal from his 26 outings.

Most Bolton fans will long remember him for the brilliant 30-yard shot he scored against Liverpool in the 1995

Coca Cola Cup Final and will be hoping he can maintain his form of the past year. If so, he could become one of the brightest young players around.

## Form Factors

| Season | Team | Tot | St | Sb | Y | R |
|--------|------|-----|-----|-----|-----|-----|
| 95-96 | Bolton W. | 26 | 23 | 3 | 8 | 0 |
| Total | | 26 | 23 | 3 | 8 | 0 |

| | GP | GG | GF | GS | TGR |
|--------|------|------|------|------|------|
| 95-96 | 68.42 | 26.00 | 39 | 1 | 2.56 |
| Averages | 68.42 | 26.00 | 39.00 | 1.00 | 2.56 |

## THOMPSON, Neil

# Barnsley ❶❷❸ FB

Fullname: Neil Thompson
DOB: 02-10-63 Beverly

Injury hindered Neil Thompson's season in 1996-97, just as it had in 1995-96, but he still managed to contribute five goals in his 24 appearances. One of the few players who was part of last season's promotion campaign who has experience of the Premier League. Thompson made 72 appearances for Ipswich Town from 1992 to 1995.

Started his career at Hull City, having been at Nottingham Forest as a junior. He moved on to Scarborough and then Ipswich before signing for Barnsley in the summer of 1996.

## THOMSEN, Claus

# Everton ❶❷❸ M

Fullname: Claus Thomsen
DOB: 31-05-70 Aarhus, Denmark

Danish international from the town of Aarhus who joined Ipswich Town for £250,000 in June 1994 from his home town club. Tall, solid midfielder, he moved up to the Premiership in January 1997 in a deal which cost Everton

*Neil Thompson*

£900,000. Made 16 Premiership appearances for the Toffeemen before the season was out and is almost certain to play a leading role at Goodison Park during the 1997-98 season. Has yet to score for his new club but in 33 Premiership appearances in a struggling Ipswich side, he found the back of the net five times. Played in all three of Denmark's Euro '96 matches in England.

## Form Factors

| Season | Team | Tot | St | Sb | Y | R |
|--------|------|-----|-----|-----|-----|-----|
| 94-95 | Ipswich T. | 33 | 31 | 2 | 3 | 0 |
| 96-97 | Everton | 16 | 15 | 1 | 3 | 0 |
| Total | | 49 | 46 | 3 | 6 | 0 |

| | GP | GG | GF | GS | TGR |
|---|---|---|---|---|---|
| 94-95 | 78.57 | 6.60 | 36 | 5 | 13.89 |
| 96-97 | 42.11 | 0.00 | 44 | 0 | 0.00 |
| Averages | 60.34 | 3.30 | 40.00 | 2.50 | 6.94 |

## THORNLEY, Ben

# Manchester U. ❶ S

Fullname: Benjamin Lindsay Thornley
DOB: 21-04-75 Bury

Winger Thornley has played just four games in the Premiership but spent time on the subs bench in a further five games during 1996-97. He was a big crowd favourite at Huddersfield Town, but was sent off twice during his loan spell with the Yorkshire club. He has also spent time at Stockport County but his career has been severely disrupted by cruciate ligament damage. He is probably talented enough to deputise for Giggs on the left wing but the competition is hot. His temperament came under further question when he was again dismissed in March playing for the United reserve team.

## Form Factors

| Season | Team | Tot | St | Sb | Y | R |
|---|---|---|---|---|---|---|
| 93-94 | Man. Utd | 1 | 0 | 1 | 0 | 0 |
| 95-96 | Man. Utd | 1 | 0 | 1 | 0 | 0 |
| 96-97 | Man. Utd | 2 | 1 | 1 | 0 | 0 |
| Total | | 4 | 1 | 3 | 0 | 0 |

| | GP | GG | GF | GS | TGR |
|---|---|---|---|---|---|
| 93-94 | 2.38 | 0.00 | 80 | 0 | 0.00 |
| 95-96 | 2.63 | 0.00 | 73 | 0 | 0.00 |
| 96-97 | 5.26 | 0.00 | 76 | 0 | 0.00 |
| Averages | 3.43 | 0.00 | 76.33 | 0.00 | 0.00 |

## TINKLER, Eric

# Barnsley ❶❷❸ M

Fullname: Eric Tinkler
DOB: 24-10-74 Bishop Auckland

This South African international, who is cast in very much the same role as Paul Ince, was one of several summer signings by manager Danny Wilson. A £650,000 purchase from Italian side Cagliari, he has earned the plaudits of players such as Pele, who picked him in his all-star African XI side.

Hard-tackling, strong-running with a touch and free-kick to match, Tinkler will almost certainly be a feature of any Barnsley line-up. He opted out of Serie B when Cagliari lost out in an end of season relegation play-off against Piacenza and now gets his chance in England, after being refused a permit to join Coventry City when he was a 16-year-old. Started his career in Portugal with Vitoria Setubal, playing alongside new team-mate Clint Marcelle.

Capped 25 times by Bafana Bafana, he was one of the players who was part of their African Nations Cup win in 1996 and looks certain to feature in the World Cup in France next summer. He was in the team that was beaten 2-1 by England at Old Trafford last season.

# TODD, Andy

## Bolton W. ❶ CB

Fullname: Andrew John James Todd
DOB: 21-09-74 Derby

Will always have to carry the burden of being the son of the Bolton manager. Andy Todd started his defensive career at Middlesbrough. He was signed for £250,000 in the summer of 1995 and went on to play in 12 of Bolton's Premiership games that season. Last season he was used primarily as a squad player and nine of his 15 appearances in Wanderers' championship season came from the bench.

At just 5' 9" tall he is small for a central defender and has often been used as a holding midfield player.

### Form Factors

| Season | Team | Tot | St | Sb | Y | R |
|--------|------|-----|----|----|----|----|
| 95-96 | Bolton W. | 12 | 9 | 3 | 2 | 0 |
| Total | | 12 | 9 | 3 | 2 | 0 |

| | GP | GG | GF | GS | TGR |
|--------|-------|------|-------|------|------|
| 95-96 | 31.58 | 6.00 | 39 | 2 | 5.13 |
| Averages | 31.58 | 6.00 | 39.00 | 2.00 | 5.13 |

# TOWNSEND, Andy

## Aston Villa ❶❷❸❹ M

Fullname: Andrew David Townsend
DOB: 23-07-63 Maidstone

The Villa captain looks to have been one of the club's best signings when he was captured from Chelsea in the summer of 1990. A skilful but hard-grafting midfielder, he generally plays the anchor role at Villa, thus allowing the likes of Mark Draper and Sasa Curcic to move forward and support the attack. This would seem to be borne out by his goals tally for the club – disappointingly just five in the past three seasons.

Hasn't missed many games in recent years and his appearance record is getting better, not least because he seems to have curbed his tendency to get dismissed. On the other hand, he has still accumulated 24 yellow cards in the past three seasons.

Having started his career at Southampton and also played for Norwich, the Republic of Ireland international has over 60 international caps to his name and is sure to be a regular performer for the Villa during the 1997-98 season.

### Form Factors

| Season | Team | Tot | St | Sb | Y | R |
|--------|------|-----|----|----|----|----|
| 94-95 | Aston Villa | 32 | 32 | 0 | 7 | 2 |
| 95-96 | Aston Villa | 31 | 30 | 1 | 9 | 1 |
| 96-97 | Aston Villa | 34 | 34 | 0 | 8 | 0 |
| Total | | 97 | 96 | 1 | 24 | 3 |

| | GP | GG | GF | GS | TGR |
|--------|-------|-------|-------|------|------|
| 94-95 | 76.19 | 32.00 | 51 | 1 | 1.96 |
| 95-96 | 81.58 | 15.50 | 52 | 2 | 3.85 |
| 96-97 | 89.47 | 17.00 | 47 | 2 | 4.26 |
| Averages | 82.41 | 21.50 | 50.00 | 1.67 | 3.35 |

## TROLLOPE, Paul

# Derby County ❶ M

Fullname: Paul Jonathan Trollope
DOB: 03-06-72 Swindon

In his fourth season with Derby County since completing a £100,000 transfer from Torquay United in January 1995 after a month on loan from the Devon club.

Despite featuring in Derby's promotion-winning side he has not been a regular in their Premiership line-up, but remains a more than useful squad member. Had a spell on loan to Crystal Palace during the early part of winter 1996 where he made nine appearances as a substitute. He is closing in on his 200th senior appearance but may find his opportunities limited at Pride Park.

## Form Factors

| Season | Team | Tot | St | Sb | Y | R |
|--------|------|-----|----|----|----|----|
| 96-97 | Derby Co. | 14 | 13 | 1 | 3 | 0 |
| Total | | 14 | 13 | 1 | 3 | 0 |

| | GP | GG | GF | GS | TGR |
|--|-----|-----|-----|-----|-----|
| 96-97 | 36.84 | 14.00 | 45 | 1 | 2.22 |
| Averages | 36.84 | 14.00 | 45.00 | 1.00 | 2.22 |

## TRUSTFULL, Orlando

# Sheffield W. ❶❷ M

Fullname: Orlando Trustfull
DOB:

Hard-working Dutch midfielder who struggled to hold down a place in the Sheffield Wednesday starting line-up during 1996-97, with 10 of his 19 league appearances coming from the substitutes' bench. Nonetheless, he still played in half of Wednesday's Premiership games and will be looking to work closer with his Dutch comrade Regi Blinker during the 1997-98 season. Arrived at Hillsborough in the summer of 1996, following a £750,000 transfer, with a good pedigree. He scored 13 goals in Holland for Feyenoord in 78 games and still managed three goals from limited starts with the Owls.

## Form Factors

| Season | Team | Tot | St | Sb | Y | R |
|--------|------|-----|----|----|----|----|
| 96-97 | Sheffield W. | 19 | 9 | 10 | 3 | 0 |
| Total | | 19 | 9 | 10 | 3 | 0 |

| | GP | GG | GF | GS | TGR |
|--|-----|-----|-----|-----|-----|
| 96-97 | 50.00 | 6.33 | 50 | 3 | 6.00 |
| Averages | 50.00 | 6.33 | 50.00 | 3.00 | 6.00 |

## TUTTLE, David

### Crystal Palace ❶❷❸ CB

Fullname: David Philip Tuttle
DOB: 06-02-72 Reading
Played five times for Tottenham in their 1992-93 Premiership season before making a move to Sheffield United where he featured in 31 of their Premiership games the following season.

Having played under Dave Bassett at Bramall Lane he was one of the manager's Eagles signings when he joined them in March 1996 for £300,000, having recovered from a knee injury.

Regarded as the organiser of the defence, he played in all but five of Palace's Division One games and will not be overawed by playing in the Premier League.

### Form Factors

| Season | Team | Tot | St | Sb | Y | R |
|--------|------|-----|-----|-----|-----|-----|
| 92-93 | Tottenham | 5 | 4 | 1 | 0 | 0 |
| 93-94 | Sheffield U. | 31 | 31 | 0 | 0 | 0 |
| Total | | 36 | 35 | 1 | 0 | 0 |

| | GP | GG | GF | GS | TGR |
|--------|------|------|------|------|------|
| 92-93 | 11.90 | 0.00 | 60 | 0 | 0.00 |
| 93-94 | 73.81 | 0.00 | 42 | 0 | 0.00 |
| Averages | 42.86 | 0.00 | 51.00 | 0.00 | 0.00 |

## ULLATHORNE, Robert

### Leicester City ❶❷❸ FB

Fullname: Robert Ullathorne
DOB: 11-10-71 Wakefield
Quite possibly the unluckiest player last season, having joined Leicester City early in 1997 from Spanish club Osasuna for £600,000 and making his debut during City's home Coca Cola Cup semi final with Wimbledon. He was put out of action for the rest of the season after just 12 minutes when he suffered a broken ankle when turning awkwardly. A midfielder who also plays in a wing-back role, he joined Osasuna from Norwich City in 1996 under the terms of the Bosman ruling after scoring eight goals in 114 games for the Canaries. Should prove to be a useful acquisition once back to full fitness and his presence should be a boost to Leicester.

### Form Factors

| Season | Team | Tot | St | Sb | Y | R |
|--------|------|-----|-----|-----|-----|-----|
| 93-94 | Norwich C. | 16 | 11 | 5 | 1 | 0 |
| 94-95 | Norwich C. | 27 | 27 | 0 | 5 | 0 |
| Total | | 43 | 38 | 5 | 6 | 0 |

| | GP | GG | GF | GS | TGR |
|--------|------|------|------|------|------|
| 93-94 | 38.10 | 8.00 | 65 | 2 | 3.08 |
| 94-95 | 64.29 | 13.50 | 37 | 2 | 5.41 |
| Averages | 51.20 | 10.75 | 51 | 2 | 3.92 |

## UNSWORTH, David

# Everton ❶❷❸ CB

**Fullname:** David Gerald Unsworth
**DOB:** 16-10-73 Chorley
Defender who has become one of the most consistent and resolute players in the Premiership since making his debut with Everton back in December 1992 in the home derby match with Liverpool. Was blended into the side very gently for three years but since the start of the 1994-95 season has been a vital cog in the Blues' back line. His consistent performances for Everton have seen him gain England recognition and, with his strength in the tackle, coupled with an ability to play happily with either foot, further honours will surely follow. Should complete his 150th match for Everton by Christmas.

## Form Factors

| Season | Team | Tot | St | Sb | | Y | R |
|--------|------|-----|----|----|----|---|---|
| 94-95 | Everton | 38 | 37 | 1 | | 7 | 0 |
| 95-96 | Everton | 31 | 28 | 3 | | 3 | 1 |
| 96-97 | Everton | 34 | 32 | 2 | | 5 | 1 |
| Total | | 103 | 97 | 6 | | 15 | 2 |

| | GP | GG | GF | GS | TGR |
|--------|------|-------|-------|----|------|
| 94-95 | 90.48 | 12.67 | 44 | 3 | 6.82 |
| 95-96 | 81.58 | 15.50 | 64 | 2 | 3.13 |
| 96-97 | 89.47 | 6.80 | 44 | 5 | 11.36 |
| Averages | 87.18 | 11.66 | 50.67 | 3.33 | 7.10 |

*David Unsworth*

## VAN DER GOUW, Raimond

# Manchester U. ❶ GK

**Fullname:** Raimond Van der Gouw
**DOB:**
Signed as an experienced cover for Peter Schmeichel in July 1996 and a constant stand-by on the bench. If injury strikes Schmeichel then Van Der Gouw will be thrust into the limelight, as he was against Borussia Dortmund in the first leg of the Champions' League semi-final in Germany. His performance in that game demonstrated his experience and skill.

Born in Holland he has previously played for Go Ahead Eagles and Vitesse Arnhem before arriving at Old Trafford in a £200,000 deal in the summer of 1996. Will remain on the bench again unless an injury to Schmeichel gives him his chance.

## Form Factors

| Season | Team | Tot | St | Sb | Y | R |
|--------|------|-----|-----|-----|-----|-----|
| 96-97 | Man. Utd | 2 | 2 | 0 | 0 | 0 |
| Total | | 2 | 2 | 0 | 0 | 0 |

| | GA | GkA | GAp | CS | SO | Rp |
|--------|-----|-----|-----|-----|-----|-----|
| 96-97 | 44 | 2 | 1.00 | 1 | 1 | 0 |
| Total | 44 | 2 | 1.00 | 1 | 1 | – |

# *Van Der LAAN, Robin*

# Derby County    ❶    M

Fullname: Robertus Petrus
Van Der Laan
DOB: 05-09-68 Schiedam, Holland

Dutchman who moved to this country in 1991 to join Port Vale from Wageningen for just £80,000. Less than five years later, after scoring 26 times in 198 games, his value had increased six-fold with a transfer to Derby County where he played a leading role in the promotion campaign of 1995-96. The high point of his career to date came in the penultimate match of the season when he scored the promotion-winning goal against now Premiership rivals Crystal Palace. Appeared in 42% of County's Premiership matches last season and was a non-playing sub on seven other occasions. Originally a striker, he has also played in midfield where he has a crunching tackle.

## Form Factors

| Season | Team | Tot | St | Sb | Y | R |
|--------|------|-----|-----|-----|-----|-----|
| 96-97 | Derby Co. | 16 | 15 | 1 | 1 | 0 |
| Total | | 16 | 15 | 1 | 1 | 0 |

| | GP | GG | GF | GS | TGR |
|--------|-----|-----|-----|-----|-----|
| 96-97 | 42.11 | 8.00 | 45 | 2 | 4.44 |
| Averages | 42.11 | 8.00 | 45.00 | 2.00 | 4.44 |

# *VAN GOBBEL, Ulrich*

# Southampton    ❶❷❸    CB

Fullname: Ulrich Van Gobbel
DOB: 16-01-71 Surinam

Having played under Souness at Galatasaray, the then Saints manager brought him to the Dell for a club record £1.3 million.

Born in Surinam, Van Gobbel is a Dutch international who started his career with Feyenoord, for whom he played over 100 senior games before moving to Turkey.

*Ulrich Van Gobbel*

Probably one of the fastest players in the Premiership, he would certainly have played more than the 30 times he did, had 10 yellow cards and a sending off at Blackburn Rovers not earned him suspensions.

Primarily a defender, he can play in midfield and, if he can curb his bookability and finds favour with the new managerial regime, he should be one of the mainstays of the Saints' side.

## Form Factors

| Season | Team | Tot | St | Sb | Y | R |
|--------|------|-----|-----|-----|-----|-----|
| 96-97 | Southampton | 25 | 24 | 1 | 10 | 1 |
| Total | | 25 | 24 | 1 | 10 | 1 |

| | GP | GG | GF | GS | TGR |
|--------|------|------|------|------|------|
| 96-97 | 65.79 | 25.00 | 50 | 1 | 2.00 |
| Averages | 65.79 | 25.00 | 50.00 | 1.00 | 2.00 |

# VEART, Carl

## Crystal Palace ❶❷❸ S

Fullname: Carl Thomas Veart
DOB: 21-05-70 Whyalla, Australia

An Australian striker who has a whole-hearted style of play and is an excellent target man who is more than capable of holding up the ball for others around him, a fact that may reflect why he only scored six Nationwide goals last season, despite making 39 appearances.

He began his career with Adelaide City before joining Sheffield United in the summer of 1994 for £250,000, for whom he played over 60 games. He became an Eagles' player in March 1996 in a deal that took Gareth Taylor to Bramall Lane.

Having scored the winner for United in an FA Cup game against Arsenal in 1996, he will feel that he has what it takes to play against some of the best defences in the world.

# VEGA, Ramon

## Tottenham H. ❶❷❸❹ CB

Fullname: Ramon Vega
DOB: 14-06-71

Swiss international who signed for Spurs from Italian club Cagliari in January 1997 for £3.75m. Made his Tottenham debut during a home defeat by Manchester United on 12 January and picked up his first suspension on these shores a week later when sent off as Spurs lost at Nottingham Forest. If that wasn't bad enough, he pulled a hamstring in his next match and was ruled out through suspension and injury!

As such he had only eight games in which to get used to Premiership football last season but scored Spurs' goal in a 1-1 draw at Villa Park and is expected to form a top quality partnership with Sol Campbell and John Scales. Played in all three of Switzerland's Euro '96 games in England.

## Form Factors

| Season | Team | Tot | St | Sb | Y | R |
|--------|------|-----|-----|-----|-----|-----|
| 96-97 | Tottenham | 8 | 8 | 0 | 2 | 0 |
| Total | | 8 | 8 | 0 | 2 | 0 |

| | GP | GG | GF | GS | TGR |
|--------|------|------|------|------|------|
| 96-97 | 21.05 | 8.00 | 44 | 1 | 2.27 |
| Averages | 21.05 | 8.00 | 44.00 | 1.00 | 2.27 |

## VENISON, Barry

# Southampton ❶❷ M

Fullname: Barry Venison
DOB: 16-08-64 Consett

An experienced midfielder who has played at the top and his knowledge of the game has seen him used in the TV studios in the past year. He joined Southampton from Turkish side Galatasary in October 1995, having previously played over 100 league games for Liverpool, Newcastle and Sunderland.

Last season he only played in the first two Saints games, having been sent off for a second bookable offence against Leicester City.

Back problems also hindered his return last season and he may feel he now has a role to play under new manager Dave Jones who may look to his experience and willingness to play any role. Former Saints' manager Graeme Souness has twice sold him, while manager at both Liverpool and Galatasary!

## Form Factors

| Season | Team | Tot | St | Sb | Y | R |
|--------|------|-----|-----|-----|-----|-----|
| 94-95 | Newcastle | 28 | 28 | 0 | 3 | 0 |
| 95-96 | Southampton | 22 | 21 | 1 | 6 | 0 |
| 96-97 | Southampton | 2 | 2 | 0 | 1 | 1 |
| Total | | 52 | 51 | 1 | 10 | 1 |

| | GP | GG | GF | GS | TGR |
|--------|-----|-----|-----|-----|-----|
| 94-95 | 66.67 | 28.00 | 67 | 1 | 1.49 |
| 95-96 | 57.89 | 0.00 | 34 | 0 | 0.00 |
| 96-97 | 5.26 | 0.00 | 50 | 0 | 0.00 |
| Averages | 43.27 | 52.00 | 50.33 | 0.33 | 0.66 |

## VIALLI, Gianluca

# Chelsea ❶❷❸❹ S

Fullname: Gianluca Vialli
DOB: 09-07-64 Cremona, Italy

For one reason or another Vialli was never out of the headlines last season. His arrival at Stamford Bridge was nothing short of sensational. His last game for previous club Juventus had been to help win the Champions' Cup with a victory over Ajax and his performances in the early part of the season were of the expected calibre. Nevertheless he fell out of favour with Gullit and his outbursts to the press seemed to be heading for his departure from the Bridge. The 32-year old had a similar situation occur with Arrigo Sacchi which led to him being excluded from the Italian national side.

Despite all this, he still recorded 25 appearances and only five of these came from the substitutes' bench where he was also an unused sub for a similar number of times.

A striker that possesses great skill and the ability to score goals from nothing, he averaged a goal every three games last season and could still be a vital player to the team.

## Form Factors

| Season | Team | Tot | St | Sb | Y | R |
|--------|------|-----|-----|-----|-----|-----|
| 96-97 | Chelsea | 28 | 23 | 5 | 5 | 0 |
| Total | | 28 | 23 | 5 | 5 | 0 |

| | GP | GG | GF | GS | TGR |
|--------|-----|-----|-----|-----|-----|
| 96-97 | 73.68 | 3.11 | 58 | 9 | 15.52 |
| Averages | 73.68 | 3.11 | 58.00 | 9.00 | 15.52 |

## VIEIRA, Patrick

## Arsenal ❶❷❸❹ M

Fullname: Patrick Vieira
DOB: 23-06-76 Dakar, Senegal

Most Arsenal supporters regard Patrick Vieira as the midfield player they have been lacking since the days of Liam Brady. He was signed from Milan in August 1996 on the advice of Arsène Wenger, who had coached him as a junior at AS Cannes. His performances during last season earned him his first full French cap and by the end of the season he had become a regular in the squad.

At just 21 he is a very exciting prospect and combines a strong tackle with excellent distribution. An anchor in midfield, he also showed his versatility by playing in the middle of the Arsenal defence when required. Despite his willingness to burst forward with the ball, he does not seem to have a real eye for goal, preferring to provide rather than take a chance.

Providing he can quell his over-zealousness that leads to inevitable bookings, he looks set for a glittering career at all levels of the game.

### Form Factors

| Season | Team | Tot | St | Sb | Y | R |
|--------|------|-----|-----|-----|-----|-----|
| 96-97 | Arsenal | 31 | 30 | 1 | 11 | 0 |
| Total | | 31 | 30 | 1 | 11 | 0 |

| | GP | GG | GF | GS | TGR |
|--------|-----|-----|-----|-----|-----|
| 96-97 | 81.58 | 15.50 | 62 | 2 | 3.23 |
| Averages | 81.58 | 15.50 | 62.00 | 2.00 | 3.23 |

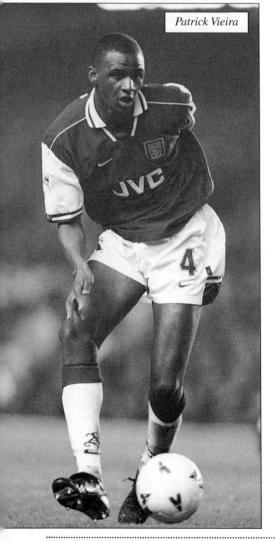

*Patrick Vieira*

## WALKER, Des

## Sheffield W. ❶❷❸❹ CB

Fullname: Desmond Sinclair Walker
DOB: 26-11-65 Hackney

Once the most highly-rated defender in England he suffered a cruel loss of form which denied him the opportunity to add to his 59 England caps in a quantity his undoubted talent deserves. Cemented his reputation with superb displays during the 1990 World Cup. Became an international star during nine seasons in the Nottingham Forest first team, where he scored his only senior goal, and has resurrected his career over the past four years with Sheffield Wednesday. He remains one of the quickest thinking and coolest defenders in the Premiership and has missed just four league games in four years since his move to Hillsborough from Sampdoria for a then club record fee of £2.7 million.

Played in 36 of Wednesday's games last season, missing just two following a sending off at Highbury when The Owls went down 4-1 in the early part of the season.

## Form Factors

| Season | Team | Tot | St | Sb | Y | R |
|---|---|---|---|---|---|---|
| 94-95 | Sheffield W. | 38 | 38 | 0 | 2 | 1 |
| 95-96 | Sheffield W. | 36 | 36 | 0 | 2 | 0 |
| 96-97 | Sheffield W. | 36 | 36 | 0 | 1 | 1 |
| Total | | 110 | 110 | 0 | 5 | 2 |

| | GP | GG | GF | GS | TGR |
|---|---|---|---|---|---|
| 94-95 | 90.48 | 0.00 | 49 | 0 | 0.00 |
| 95-96 | 94.74 | 0.00 | 48 | 0 | 0.00 |
| 96-97 | 94.74 | 0.00 | 50 | 0 | 0.00 |
| Averages | 93.32 | 0.00 | 49.00 | 0.00 | 0.00 |

## WALKER, Ian

# Tottenham H. ❶❷❸❹❺    GK

**Fullname:** Ian Michael Walker
**DOB:** 31-10-71 Watford

Outstanding goalkeeper whose reputation soared in the two seasons leading up to the 1996-97 campaign, but he suffered more than his fair share of knocks last term. Had to withstand criticism for Italy's goal at Wembley, a deflected shot, a cruel bounce for a Liverpool goal at Tottenham and the humiliation of having 13 goals put past him in trips to Bolton and Newcastle. Despite those setbacks, he is a regular in the England squad and a model of consistency. He has missed just two games in the past three seasons, being an ever-present in between the Spurs' sticks

*Ian Walker*

in the 1995-96 season. Walker should make his 200th Spurs appearance in the 1997-98 season.

## Form Factors

| Season | Team | Tot | St | Sb | Y | R |
|---|---|---|---|---|---|---|
| 94-95 | Tottenham | 41 | 41 | 0 | 1 | 0 |
| 95-96 | Tottenham | 38 | 38 | 0 | 1 | 0 |
| 96-97 | Tottenham | 37 | 37 | 0 | 0 | 0 |
| Total | | 116 | 116 | 0 | 2 | 0 |

| | GA | GkA | GAp | CS | SO | Rp |
|---|---|---|---|---|---|---|
| 94-95 | 58 | 57 | 1.39 | 11 | 5 | 0 |
| 95-96 | 38 | 38 | 1.00 | 11 | 5 | 0 |
| 96-97 | 51 | 49 | 1.32 | 13 | 2 | 2 |
| Total | 147 | 144 | 1.24 | 35 | 12 | – |

## WALLACE, Rod

# Leeds United  ❶❷❸  M

Fullname: Rodney Seymour Wallace
DOB: 02-10-69 Greenwich

Winger who, in his 358 games for Southampton and Leeds United, has often hinted at greatness worthy of an international call-up whilst remaining completely anonymous on other occasions. Although best known as a creator of goals for others, he scored freely, at better than a goal every three games, during his time at the Dell. Has not quite managed to match that ratio at Elland Road with just eight league goals from the past three seasons, but his speed down the flank and the quality of his crosses have seen him hold down a place in around 66% of Leeds matches. Became Leeds' record signing when he joined the club for £1.6 million in June 1991.

### Form Factors

| Season | Team | Tot | St | Sb | Y | R |
|---|---|---|---|---|---|---|
| 94-95 | Leeds Utd | 32 | 30 | 2 | 5 | 0 |
| 95-96 | Leeds Utd | 24 | 12 | 12 | 1 | 0 |
| 96-97 | Leeds Utd | 22 | 17 | 5 | 5 | 0 |
| Total | | 78 | 59 | 19 | 11 | 0 |

| | GP | GG | GF | GS | TGR |
|---|---|---|---|---|---|
| 94-95 | 76.19 | 8.00 | 59 | 4 | 6.78 |
| 95-96 | 63.16 | 24.00 | 40 | 1 | 2.50 |
| 96-97 | 57.89 | 7.33 | 40 | 3 | 7.50 |
| Averages | 65.75 | 13.11 | 46.33 | 2.67 | 5.59 |

## WALSH, Steve

# Leicester City  ❶❷❸  CB

Fullname: Steven Walsh
DOB: 03-11-64 Preston

Long-serving central defender, renowned for his aerial strength, who joined Leicester City in June 1986 for a knock-down £100,000 and has since played more than 350 games for the club. Although a source of inspiration from his defensive position, he scored 15 times in 40 Division One games in 1992-93 as Leicester reached the play-off final, where he scored again.

Born in Preston, he started his career with four years at Wigan Athletic before joining the Foxes. Had his testimonial season last year and, despite troublesome knee injuries and the fact that he will turn 33 early in the 1997-98 season, it is hard to believe that he will again be anything other than a leading figure as Leicester head for Europe in the UEFA Cup.

### Form Factors

| Season | Team | Tot | St | Sb | Y | R |
|---|---|---|---|---|---|---|
| 94-95 | Leicester C. | 5 | 5 | 0 | 0 | 0 |
| 96-97 | Leicester C. | 22 | 22 | 0 | 3 | 1 |
| Total | | 27 | 27 | 0 | 3 | 1 |

| | GP | GG | GF | GS | TGR |
|---|---|---|---|---|---|
| 94-95 | 11.90 | 0.00 | 45 | 0 | 0.00 |
| 96-97 | 57.89 | 11.00 | 46 | 2 | 4.35 |
| Averages | 34.90 | 5.50 | 45.50 | 1.00 | 2.17 |

## WANCHOPE, Paulo

# Derby County  ❶❷❸❹  S

Fullname: Paulo Wanchope
DOB:

Has Derby manager Jim Smith unearthed another bargain? Wanchope, a Costa Rican international, joined County from CS Heridiano for £600,000 along with Mauricio Solis. He enjoyed a Premiership debut with Derby in April 1997 which was nothing short of sensational as he scored the Rams' second goal during a shock 3-2 victory over Manchester United at Old Trafford. He had joined Derby a week earlier on transfer deadline and his goal came at the end of a twisting run through the heart of the United defence. Made a total of five

*Steve Walsh*

appearances, three as sub, before the season was out but is expected to make a big impact during the 1997-98 campaign.

## Form Factors

| Season | Team | Tot | St | Sb | Y | R |
|---|---|---|---|---|---|---|
| 96-97 | Derby Co. | 5 | 2 | 3 | 0 | 0 |
| Total | | 5 | 2 | 3 | 0 | 0 |

| | GP | GG | GF | GS | TGR |
|---|---|---|---|---|---|
| 96-97 | 13.16 | 5.00 | 45 | 1 | 2.22 |
| Averages | 13.16 | 5.00 | 45.00 | 1.00 | 2.22 |

## WARD, Ashley

## Derby County ❶❷❸     S

Fullname: Ashley Stuart Ward
DOB: 24-11-70 Manchester

Well-travelled striker whose reputation has soared over the past three years. His career began quietly with a limited number of appearances for Manchester City, Wrexham, Leicester City and Blackpool. An upturn came his way with an £80,000 move to Crewe Alexandra where, under Dario Gradi's guidance, he scored 31 times in just 67 games. Two years later Norwich City took him to Carrow Road for £500,000 and in March 1996 a bid of £1 million secured his services for Derby County. Has continued to justify the rise in his fee and averaged a goal every three games in his 30 appearances last season despite suffering from injury. His striking partnership with Dean Sturridge last season was one of the big pluses for the Rams.

## Form Factors

| Season | Team | Tot | St | Sb | Y | R |
|---|---|---|---|---|---|---|
| 94-95 | Norwich C. | 25 | 25 | 0 | 5 | 0 |
| 96-97 | Derby Co. | 30 | 25 | 5 | 2 | 0 |
| Total | | 55 | 50 | 5 | 7 | 0 |

| | GP | GG | GF | GS | TGR |
|---|---|---|---|---|---|
| 94-95 | 59.52 | 3.13 | 37 | 8 | 21.62 |
| 96-97 | 78.95 | 3.00 | 45 | 10 | 22.22 |
| Averages | 69.24 | 3.06 | 41.00 | 9.00 | 21.92 |

## WARHURST, Paul

## Blackburn Rovers ❶❷❸    M

Fullname: Paul Warhurst
DOB: 26-09-69 Stockport

Possibly the most skilful player on Rovers' books, he has suffered at the hands of the Rovers' injury curse. Like team-mate Kevin Gallacher, he suffered two broken legs in the space of 12 months plus broken ribs and a variety of illnesses.

Started life as a centre half and was converted into a free-scoring centre forward while at Sheffield Wednesday. So convincing was his change to attack, he forced his way into the England squad only to be denied a chance by injury.

Purchased as a striker, Warhurst has been a successful utility player at Ewood Park. Last season he spent much of the time on the bench in a bid to regain the form that made him such an exciting player during Rovers' Premiership-winning year.

### Form Factors

| Season | Team | Tot | St | Sb | Y | R |
|--------|----------|-----|----|----|---|---|
| 94-95 | Blackburn | 27 | 20 | 7 | 5 | 0 |
| 95-96 | Blackburn | 10 | 1 | 9 | 0 | 0 |
| 96-97 | Blackburn | 11 | 5 | 6 | 1 | 0 |
| Total | | 48 | 26 | 22 | 6 | 0 |

| | GP | GG | GF | GS | TGR |
|--------|-------|-------|-------|------|------|
| 94-95 | 64.29 | 13.50 | 80 | 2 | 2.50 |
| 95-96 | 26.32 | 0.00 | 61 | 0 | 0.00 |
| 96-97 | 28.95 | 5.50 | 42 | 2 | 4.76 |
| Averages | 39.85 | 6.33 | 61.00 | 1.33 | 2.42 |

## WARNER, Tony

## Liverpool    ❶    GK

Fullname: Anthony Warner
DOB: 11-05-74 Liverpool

Warner spent the season on the subs' bench as James had an ever-present season. Goalkeeping coach Joe Corrigan has been very impressed with Warner and the 20-year old 6'4" trainee looks to have the confidence of his manager as back-up in goal. Yet to be tested.

## WATSON, Dave

## Everton    ❶❷    CB

Fullname: David Watson
DOB: 20-11-61 Liverpool

Veteran defender and Everton die-hard who took his first steps into management towards the end of the 1996-97 season when handed the caretaker player/manager's role following the resignation of Joe Royle. Reverts to being a player under Howard Kendall but at 35 years old will have a tough battle to extend his outstanding record of 381 league appearances, 169 of which have been in the Premiership, during which time he has played in around 85% of the Blues' matches. An England Under-21 and full international whose career began across Stanley Park with Liverpool, although he moved to Norwich City for £100,000 without playing in the Reds' first team. Signed for Everton in a £900,000 deal in August 1986.

### Form Factors

| Season | Team | Tot | St | Sb | Y | R |
|--------|---------|-----|-----|----|----|---|
| 94-95 | Everton | 38 | 38 | 0 | 5 | 0 |
| 95-96 | Everton | 34 | 34 | 0 | 6 | 1 |
| 96-97 | Everton | 29 | 29 | 0 | 4 | 0 |
| Total | | 101 | 101 | 0 | 15 | 1 |

*Steve Watson*

| | GP | GG | GF | GS | TGR |
|---|---|---|---|---|---|
| 94-95 | 90.48 | 19.00 | 44 | 2 | 4.55 |
| 95-96 | 89.47 | 34.00 | 64 | 1 | 1.56 |
| 96-97 | 76.32 | 29.00 | 44 | 1 | 2.27 |
| Averages | 85.42 | 27.33 | 50.67 | 1.33 | 2.79 |

## WATSON, David

### Barnsley ❶❷❸ GK

Fullname: David Neil Watson
DOB: 10-11-73 Barnsley

An ever-present in the Barnsley goal last season, Watson joined the Oakwell clan as a trainee in the summer of 1992. A former England Youth and Under-21 international, he has developed a reputation as an excellent shot-stopper.

Watson maintained 17 clean sheets last season – four in succession during December, and conceded not much more than a goal a game on average – 55 in 46 games. At just 24 years of age, as a goalkeeper he has plenty of time on his side and could be an England international of the future.

## WATSON, Steve

### Newcastle U. ❶❷❸❹ FB

Fullname: Stephen Craig Watson
DOB: 01-04-74 North Shields

A trainee at Newcastle and a consistent performer with 86 appearances over the past three seasons, 16 of which have come from the subs bench. Watson has been capped at England Youth and Under-21 and the 1996-97 season was a breakthrough year with 33 starts and three from the subs bench.

Having played in a variety of positions he seems to have managed to displace big money signing Warren Barton. Has shown his versatility which makes him so popular at St James' Park having played at full-back, centre-half and in midfield. He also has the ability to score screamers which makes him a crowd-pleaser.

He was the youngest ever Newcastle player when he made his first team debut against Wolverhampton Wanderers in November 1990. Very composed on the ball and a must for consideration by any fantasy team manager.

## Form Factors

| Season | Team | Tot | St | Sb | Y | R |
|--------|------|-----|-----|-----|-----|-----|
| 94-95 | Newcastle | 27 | 22 | 5 | 2 | 0 |
| 95-96 | Newcastle | 23 | 15 | 8 | 0 | 0 |
| 96-97 | Newcastle | 36 | 33 | 3 | 3 | 0 |
| Total | | 86 | 70 | 16 | 5 | 0 |

| | GP | GG | GF | GS | TGR |
|--------|-----|-----|-----|-----|-----|
| 94-95 | 64.29 | 6.75 | 67 | 4 | 5.97 |
| 95-96 | 60.53 | 7.67 | 66 | 3 | 4.55 |
| 96-97 | 94.74 | 36.00 | 73 | 1 | 1.37 |
| Averages | 73.19 | 16.81 | 68.67 | 2.67 | 3.96 |

## WATTS, Julian

## Leicester City ❶❷ CB

Fullname: Julian Watts
DOB: 17-03-71 Sheffield

Central defender who had his most successful season to date when making 35 league and cup appearances for Leicester City during 1996-97 but missed out in both matches in the Coca Cola Cup Final. Signed for Leicester from Sheffield Wednesday in March 1996 for £210,000 after making just 17 appearances for the Owls during four years at Hillsborough. He began his career with Rotherham. Also had a spell on loan to Shrewsbury Town whilst with Wednesday. Has regularly got on the scoreboard during the past two seasons.

The arrival of Matt Elliott may mean that Watts' chances at Filbert Street are more limited during the 1997-98 season.

## Form Factors

| Season | Team | Tot | St | Sb | Y | R |
|--------|------|-----|-----|-----|-----|-----|
| 93-94 | Sheffield W. | 1 | 1 | 0 | 0 | 0 |
| 95-96 | Sheffield W. | 11 | 9 | 2 | 3 | 0 |
| 96-97 | Leicester C. | 26 | 22 | 4 | 3 | 0 |
| Total | | 38 | 32 | 6 | 6 | 0 |

| | GP | GG | GF | GS | TGR |
|--------|-----|-----|-----|-----|-----|
| 93-94 | 21.05 | 0.00 | 40 | 0 | 0.00 |
| 95-96 | 55.26 | 2.63 | 42 | 8 | 19.05 |
| 96-97 | 92.11 | 5.83 | 38 | 6 | 15.79 |
| Averages | 56.14 | 2.82 | 40.00 | 4.67 | 11.61 |

## WETHERALL, David

## Leeds United ❶❷❸❹❺ CB

Fullname: David Wetherall
DOB: 14-03-71 Sheffield

Sheffield-born central defender who was on the books of Sheffield Wednesday before switching his allegiance across the county to Leeds United in July 1991. After a couple of seasons bedding in at Elland Road, he became a rock in the heart of the United defence and over the past four seasons has featured in approximately 80% of Leeds' Premiership matches.

The strength of his game is his heading ability and the competence with which he deals with big bustling strikers. Failed to score during the 1996-97 season which was his first shut-out in five years. A very under rated player who should be given serious consideration.

Should make his 200th appearance for Leeds during the 1997-98 season.

## Form Factors

| Season | Team | Tot | St | Sb | Y | R |
|--------|------|-----|-----|-----|-----|-----|
| 94-95 | Leeds Utd | 38 | 38 | 0 | 6 | 0 |
| 95-96 | Leeds Utd | 34 | 34 | 0 | 5 | 0 |
| 96-97 | Leeds Utd | 29 | 25 | 4 | 7 | 0 |
| Total | | 101 | 97 | 4 | 18 | 0 |

| | GP | GG | GF | GS | TGR |
|---|---|---|---|---|---|
| 94-95 | 90.48 | 12.67 | 59 | 3 | 5.08 |
| 95-96 | 89.47 | 8.50 | 40 | 4 | 10.00 |
| 96-97 | 76.32 | 0.00 | 28 | 0 | 0.00 |
| Averages | 85.42 | 7.06 | 42.33 | 2.33 | 5.03 |

## WHELAN, Noel

# Coventry City ❶❷❸ S

Fullname: Noel Whelan
DOB: 30-12-74 Leeds

Leeds-born striker who made 48 Premiership appearances for his home town club before moving to Coventry City in a £2 million deal in December 1995. He made an immediate impact, scoring seven goals in his first eleven games but after that managed just one more strike in 14 games. Last season the goals were even harder to get, despite the fact that he was a near ever-present.

When the mood takes him he can be one of the most exciting players to watch. Possesses great close, tight control which can produce some mazey dribbles deep into opponents' penalty areas.

Consistency has been his problem and he was subbed nine times by Coventry last season. He has the ability to add to his England Under-21 and Youth honours.

## Form Factors

| Season | Team | Tot | St | Sb | Y | R |
|---|---|---|---|---|---|---|
| 95-96 | Leeds Utd | 8 | 3 | 5 | 0 | 0 |
| 95-96 | Coventry C. | 21 | 21 | 0 | 3 | 0 |
| 96-97 | Coventry C. | 35 | 34 | 1 | 9 | 0 |
| Total | | 64 | 58 | 6 | 12 | 0 |

| | GP | GG | GF | GS | TGR |
|---|---|---|---|---|---|
| 95-96 | 21.05 | 0.00 | 40 | 0 | 0.00 |
| 95-96 | 55.26 | 2.63 | 42 | 8 | 19.05 |
| 96-97 | 92.11 | 5.83 | 38 | 6 | 15.79 |
| Averages | 56.14 | 2.82 | 40.00 | 4.67 | 11.61 |

## WHITLOW, Mike

# Leicester City ❶❷ FB

Fullname: Michael William Whitlow
DOB: 13-01-68 Liverpool

Liverpool-born left-back who has become an integral part of the Leicester City side since a £250,000 transfer from Leeds United in March 1992. He joined Leeds four years earlier for just £10,000 from non-leaguers Witton Albion. Despite problems with injury and sickness he has played in more than half of Leicester's games since signing for the Foxes, although his 17 Premiership appearances in 1996-97 is his lowest total in five years at Filbert Street. Consistent and reliable defender who can normally be called upon to score a goal or two during a season but 1996-97 proved to be the first shut-out of his career.

## Form Factors

| Season | Team | Tot | St | Sb | Y | R |
|---|---|---|---|---|---|---|
| 94-95 | Leicester C. | 28 | 28 | 0 | 7 | 1 |
| 96-97 | Leicester C. | 17 | 14 | 3 | 2 | 0 |
| Total | | 45 | 42 | 3 | 9 | 1 |

| | GP | GG | GF | GS | TGR |
|---|---|---|---|---|---|
| 94-95 | 66.67 | 14.00 | 45 | 2 | 4.44 |
| 96-97 | 44.74 | 0.00 | 46 | 0 | 0.00 |
| Averages | 55.70 | 7.00 | 45.50 | 1.00 | 2.22 |

## WHITTINGHAM, Guy

### Sheffield W. ❶❷❸ M

Fullname: Guy Whittingham
DOB: 10-11-64 Evesham

Versatile player whose career was revived by David Pleat with a simple change of position at Sheffield Wednesday, at a time when his fortunes were none too bright. Has been a regular goalscorer during various stages of his career but when the goals dried up at Hillsborough after a bright opening, Pleat switched him to midfield with such success that he missed just five Premiership matches last season. Scored 103 goals in 179 games for Portsmouth, after buying his way out of the army. He joined Aston Villa in a £1.2m deal but went on to a successful period with Wolves after less than a year, and joined Wednesday for £700,000 almost three years ago.

### Form Factors

| Season | Team | Tot | St | Sb | Y | R |
|--------|------|-----|-----|-----|-----|-----|
| 94-95 | Sheffield W. | 21 | 16 | 5 | 0 | 0 |
| 95-96 | Sheffield W. | 29 | 27 | 2 | 4 | 0 |
| 96-97 | Sheffield W. | 33 | 29 | 4 | 1 | 0 |
| Total | | 83 | 72 | 11 | 5 | 0 |

| | GP | GG | GF | GS | TGR |
|--------|-----|-----|-----|-----|-----|
| 94-95 | 50.00 | 2.33 | 49 | 9 | 18.37 |
| 95-96 | 76.32 | 4.83 | 48 | 6 | 12.50 |
| 96-97 | 86.84 | 11.00 | 50 | 3 | 6.00 |
| Averages | 71.05 | 6.06 | 49.00 | 6.00 | 12.29 |

## WILCOX, Jason

### Blackburn Rovers ❶❷❸ M

Fullname: Jason Malcolm Wilcox
DOB: 15-03-71 Farnworth

Jason Wilcox is almost unique at Ewood Park. In amongst all of the club's multi-million pound signings he came through the youth scheme and won his only England cap to date when he played against Hungary prior to Euro '96.

Yet another Blackburn player to have suffered serious injury – cruciate ligament trouble – he played in 27 of Rovers' title winning games, contributing five goals. He had a similar season in 1996-97 although the goals were harder to come by.

Wilcox prefers to play wide on the left where his pace and willingness to track back and help defend make him a formidable player.

### Form Factors

| Season | Team | Tot | St | Sb | Y | R |
|--------|------|-----|-----|-----|-----|-----|
| 94-95 | Blackburn | 27 | 27 | 0 | 4 | 2 |
| 95-96 | Blackburn | 10 | 10 | 0 | 0 | 0 |
| 96-97 | Blackburn | 28 | 26 | 2 | 3 | 0 |
| Total | | 65 | 63 | 2 | 7 | 2 |

| | GP | GG | GF | GS | TGR |
|--------|-----|-----|-----|-----|-----|
| 94-95 | 64.29 | 5.40 | 80 | 5 | 6.25 |
| 95-96 | 26.32 | 3.33 | 61 | 3 | 4.92 |
| 96-97 | 73.68 | 14.00 | 42 | 2 | 4.76 |
| Averages | 54.76 | 7.58 | 61.00 | 3.33 | 5.31 |

## WILKINSON, Paul

# Barnsley ❶❷❸ S

**Fullname:** Paul Wilkinson
**DOB:** 30-10-64 Louth

Missed just one Nationwide League game last season and was the club's top scorer in the league with nine goals. A give-all front-runner, he was able to renew his Middlesbrough striking partnership when John Hendrie arrived in October.

Very good in the air, he can create plenty of knock-down opportunities and has the ability to hold the ball up in attack.

Started his career as a trainee at Grimsby and had spells at Everton, Forest and Watford before going to Teesside in the summer of 1991. After 164 league games there he averaged a goal every three games. He had spells on loan at Oldham, Watford and Luton before being offered a contract at Oakwell.

## Form Factors

| Season | Team | Tot | St | Sb | Y | R |
|--------|------|-----|-----|-----|-----|-----|
| 92-93 | Middlesbro' | 41 | 41 | 0 | 3 | 0 |
| 95-96 | Middlesbro' | 2 | 1 | 1 | 0 | 0 |
| Total | | 43 | 42 | 1 | 3 | 0 |

| | GP | GG | GF | GS | TGR |
|--------|-----|-----|-----|-----|-----|
| 92-93 | 97.62 | 2.73 | 54 | 15 | 27.78 |
| 95-96 | 5.26 | 0.00 | 35 | 0 | 0.00 |
| Averages | 51.44 | 1.37 | 44.50 | 7.50 | 13.89 |

## WILLEMS, Ron

# Derby County ❶❷❸❹ S

**Fullname:** Ron Willems
**DOB:**

Experienced Dutch striker who played 175 league games in Holland for PEC Zwolle, FC Twente and Ajax before spending two seasons in Switzerland with Grasshopper Club. His career has flourished relatively late in the day and he came to the fore in England with a £300,000 move to Derby County in July 1995 at the age of 28.

A prominent part of the Rams' promotion squad but was restricted to just 16 Premiership games last season and was not helped by injuries. The form of Ward and Sturridge in the Derby attack may well continue to banish Willems to a supporting role during the 1997-98 season.

## Form Factors

| Season | Team | Tot | St | Sb | Y | R |
|--------|------|-----|-----|-----|-----|-----|
| 96-97 | Derby Co. | 16 | 7 | 9 | 0 | 0 |
| Total | | 16 | 7 | 9 | 0 | 0 |

| | GP | GG | GF | GS | TGR |
|--------|-----|-----|-----|-----|-----|
| 96-97 | 42.11 | 8.00 | 45 | 2 | 4.44 |
| Averages | 42.11 | 8.00 | 45.00 | 2.00 | 4.44 |

## WILLIAMS, Mike

### Sheffield W.    ❶    M

Fullname: Michael Anthony Williams
DOB: 21-11-69 Bradford
  Midfielder who has been with Sheffield Wednesday since stepping up from non-league football with Maltby in 1991 but has never enjoyed a lengthy run in the Owls' first team. Made his debut back in April 1993 during a home match with Southampton and his first goal followed two years later in a 4-1 win over Ipswich Town at Hillsborough. Also scored once in nine games on loan to Halifax Town during the 1992-93 season. The reason for his lack of Premiership action can quite simply be put down to him having suffered the tragedy of two broken legs.

### Form Factors

| Season | Team | Tot | St | Sb | Y | R |
|--------|------|-----|----|----|----|----|
| 94-95 | Sheffield W. | 10 | 8 | 2 | 0 | 0 |
| 95-96 | Sheffield W. | 5 | 2 | 3 | 2 | 0 |
| 96-97 | Sheffield W. | 1 | 0 | 1 | 0 | 0 |
| Total | | 16 | 10 | 6 | 2 | 0 |

| | GP | GG | GF | GS | TGR |
|--------|-----|-----|-----|----|-----|
| 94-95 | 23.81 | 10.00 | 49 | 1 | 2.04 |
| 95-96 | 13.16 | 0.00 | 48 | 0 | 0.00 |
| 96-97 | 2.63 | 0.00 | 50 | 0 | 0.00 |
| Averages | 13.20 | 3.33 | 49.00 | 0.33 | 0.68 |

## WILLIAMS, Paul

### Coventry City    ❶❷❸❹    CB

Fullname: Paul Darren Williams
DOB: 26-03-71 Burton
  England Under-21 international who has gained hero status at Highfield Road after scoring the second of Coventry City's two goals at Tottenham on the final day of the 1996-97 season to pull off one more almost unbelievable escape act. Ironically his first Coventry goal was also against Spurs in November 1995.
  A talented and consistent defender who is used to playing in midfield, from where he does show a keen eye for goal. Williams spent six years with Derby County before moving to Coventry in August 1995, where he was voted the supporters' Player of the Year at the first attempt. He has played in just 85% of Coventry's games in the past two seasons – those absences coming from suspensions.

*Paul Williams*

## Form Factors

| Season | Team | Tot | St | Sb | Y | R |
|---|---|---|---|---|---|---|
| 95-96 | Coventry C. | 32 | 30 | 2 | 9 | 1 |
| 96-97 | Coventry C. | 32 | 29 | 3 | 7 | 0 |
| Total | | 64 | 59 | 5 | 16 | 1 |

| | GP | GG | GF | GS | TGR |
|---|---|---|---|---|---|
| 95-96 | 84.21 | 16.00 | 42 | 2 | 4.76 |
| 96-97 | 84.21 | 16.00 | 38 | 2 | 5.26 |
| Averages | 84.21 | 16.00 | 40.00 | 2.00 | 5.01 |

# WILLIAMSON, Danny

# West Ham U.  ❶❷  M

Fullname: Daniel Alan Williamson
DOB: 05-12-73 Newham

A product of the West Ham youth scheme, Williamson is a talented midfield player who should have a long career ahead of him. The Newham born player made his Premiership debut in the 1993-94 season, coming on as a substitute at Arsenal. After just seven appearances in two seasons, he took advantage of an injury hit Hammers in 1995-96 to establish himself in the side and scored four goals in his 29 games.

Last season saw him make 15 appearances in a side that struggled to find its true form, but it took him through his half century of games.

Likely to have a role to play during the course of the 1997-98 season.

## Form Factors

| Season | Team | Tot | St | Sb | Y | R |
|---|---|---|---|---|---|---|
| 94-95 | West Ham | 4 | 4 | 0 | 1 | 0 |
| 95-96 | West Ham | 29 | 28 | 1 | 5 | 0 |
| 96-97 | West Ham | 15 | 13 | 2 | 0 | 0 |
| Total | | 48 | 45 | 3 | 6 | 0 |

| | GP | GG | GF | GS | TGR |
|---|---|---|---|---|---|
| 94-95 | 9.52 | 0.00 | 44 | 0 | 0.00 |
| 95-96 | 76.32 | 7.25 | 43 | 4 | 9.30 |
| 96-97 | 39.47 | 0.00 | 39 | 0 | 0.00 |
| Averages | 41.77 | 12.00 | 42.00 | 1.33 | 3.17 |

# WILSON, Clive

# Tottenham H.  ❶❷  FB

Fullname: Clive Euclid Aklana Wilson
DOB: 13-11-61 Manchester

Wilson resurrected his Premiership career with Tottenham two years ago after being given a free transfer by Queens Park Rangers and has figured in around 70% of Tottenham's matches since switching across London.

Will be 36 in November 1997 but could further extend his career by staying clear of injury as, unusually for a defender, he seldom gets booked, as just one yellow card in 54 league games for Spurs testifies. Although primarily used as a full-back he can also operate as wing-back. Left-footed, he can produce high-calibre crosses at the end of surging runs.

Started his career with Manchester City in 1979, had a spell on loan at Chester before moving to Chelsea and then QPR. He will be under pressure from the younger players at Tottenham to retain his place.

## Form Factors

| Season | Team | Tot | St | Sb | Y | R |
|---|---|---|---|---|---|---|
| 94-95 | QPR | 36 | 36 | 0 | 4 | 1 |
| 95-96 | Tottenham | 28 | 28 | 0 | 1 | 0 |
| 96-97 | Tottenham | 26 | 23 | 3 | 0 | 0 |
| Total | | 90 | 87 | 3 | 5 | 1 |

| | GP | GG | GF | GS | TGR |
|---|---|---|---|---|---|
| 94-95 | 85.71 | 0.00 | 61 | 0 | 0.00 |
| 95-96 | 73.68 | 0.00 | 50 | 0 | 0.00 |
| 96-97 | 68.42 | 26.00 | 44 | 1 | 2.27 |
| Averages | 75.94 | 8.67 | 51.67 | 0.33 | 0.76 |

## WINTERBURN, Nigel

### Arsenal ❶❷❸ FB

Fullname: Nigel Winterburn
DOB: 11-12-63 Nuneaton
Long-serving Arsenal defender who joined the club in 1987 after four seasons with Wimbledon and has been an integral part of their success. The only Gunner to have played in all 38 of their Premiership games last season, Winterburn is a near ever-present, appearing in 95% of their games during the past three years, and has accumulated over 500 career league appearances.

Has picked up two England caps and a sack full of honours with Arsenal including two league championships, an FA Cup winners medal, and winners and runners-up medals in both the Cup Winners' Cup and the Coca Cola Cup.

Used to be Arsenal's regular penalty taker until he missed one in the League Cup Final against Luton Town – and so his goals tally has fallen drastically in recent years.

He signed a one-year contract with Arsenal at the start of the season but it is clear that the Arsenal management are looking for a replacement. If that happens his appearances could be limited but would be a good buy otherwise.

### Form Factors

| Season | Team | Tot | St | Sb | Y | R |
|--------|------|-----|-----|-----|-----|-----|
| 94-95 | Arsenal | 39 | 39 | 0 | 8 | 0 |
| 95-96 | Arsenal | 36 | 36 | 0 | 6 | 0 |
| 96-97 | Arsenal | 38 | 38 | 0 | 5 | 0 |
| Total | | 113 | 113 | 0 | 19 | 0 |

| | GP | GG | GF | GS | TGR |
|--------|------|------|------|------|------|
| 94-95 | 92.86 | 0.00 | 52 | 0 | 0.00 |
| 95-96 | 94.74 | 18.00 | 49 | 2 | 4.08 |
| 96-97 | 100.00 | 0.00 | 62 | 0 | 0.00 |
| Averages | 95.86 | 6.00 | 54.33 | 0.67 | 1.36 |

## WISE, Dennis

### Chelsea ❶❷❸❹ M

Fullname: Dennis Frank Wise
DOB: 15-12-66 Kensington
The diminutive Chelsea skipper has been a consistent performer for them ever since joining from Wimbledon for £1.6 million in the summer of 1990. His non-stop, powerpack play makes him a major contributor to his side's cause. Classed as a midfield player, he can play on either flank and is an accurate crosser and passer of the ball and will always be involved when dead ball situations occur around the opponents' penalty area. Not surprisingly, these attributes were recognised by Terry Venables when he was England coach and Wise has been on the fringes of Hoddle's international squad.

In the 1996-97 season he made his 200th league appearance for Chelsea and the 1997-98 season should see him make his 400th senior appearance.

### Form Factors

| Season | Team | Tot | St | Sb | Y | R |
|--------|------|-----|-----|-----|-----|-----|
| 94-95 | Chelsea | 19 | 18 | 1 | 4 | 1 |
| 95-96 | Chelsea | 35 | 34 | 1 | 10 | 0 |
| 96-97 | Chelsea | 31 | 27 | 4 | 7 | 0 |
| Total | | 85 | 79 | 6 | 21 | 1 |

| | GP | GG | GF | GS | TGR |
|--------|------|------|------|------|------|
| 94-95 | 45.24 | 3.17 | 50 | 6 | 12.00 |
| 95-96 | 92.11 | 5.00 | 46 | 7 | 15.22 |
| 96-97 | 81.58 | 7.75 | 58 | 4 | 6.90 |
| Averages | 72.97 | 5.31 | 51.33 | 5.67 | 11.37 |

## WRIGHT, Alan

### Aston Villa ❶❷❸❹ FB

Fullname: Alan Geoffrey Wright
DOB: 28-09-71 Ashton-under-Lyne

Alan Wright hasn't missed a
Premiership game in the past two seasons
and has only missed one game since
joining Villa in March 1995 for a £1
million fee. His arrival at Villa was
sparked by Blackburn's signing of
Graeme Le Saux who of course missed
most of last season through injury!

A left-sided defender who loves to get
forward, he has revelled in Villa's use of a
system that employs wing-backs. His
pace and ability to deliver searching
crosses make him a favourite with the
Villa crowd.

He won two England Under-21 caps
and still has time to force himself into the
England spotlight.

### Form Factors

| Season | Team | Tot | St | Sb | Y | R |
|---|---|---|---|---|---|---|
| 94-95 | Aston Villa | 8 | 8 | 0 | 0 | 0 |
| 95-96 | Aston Villa | 38 | 38 | 0 | 2 | 0 |
| 96-97 | Aston Villa | 38 | 38 | 0 | 2 | 0 |
| Total | | 84 | 84 | 0 | 4 | 0 |

| | GP | GG | GF | GS | TGR |
|---|---|---|---|---|---|
| 94-95 | 19.05 | 0.00 | 51 | 0 | 0.00 |
| 95-96 | 100.00 | 19.00 | 52 | 2 | 3.85 |
| 96-97 | 100.00 | 38.00 | 47 | 1 | 2.13 |
| Averages | 73.02 | 19.00 | 50.00 | 1.00 | 1.99 |

## WRIGHT, Ian

### Arsenal ❶❷❸❹❺ S

Fullname: Ian Edward Wright
DOB: 03-11-63 Woolwich

Love him or hate him there can be no
denying Ian Wright's talent as a
goalscorer. With 94 Premiership goals at
the end of last season, he is the third
highest Premiership scorer of all time. He
has been Arsenal's top scorer over the

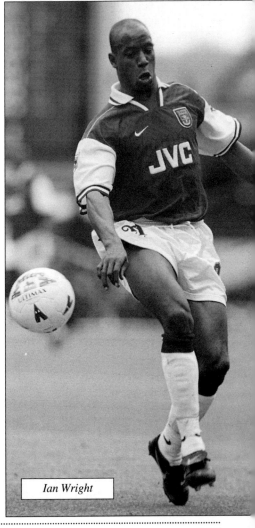

*Ian Wright*

past four seasons and his strike against Middlesbrough last season was his 200th league goal.

Started his career at Crystal Palace and came on in their Cup Final defeat to Manchester United and nearly turned the game in their favour. A real bundle of speed and skill, he will always try the unexpected that inevitably leads to some thrilling goals.

At 33 he is one of the oldest attackers in the Premiership and his total commitment to the cause invariably leads to cautions and subsequent suspensions – something that hit him hard last season.

For 1997-98 he will be looking for the five goals that will bring his tally to 179 and install him as Arsenal's top goalscorer of all-time. Such form has taken him right back into the England squad. A top fantasy striker for any team.

## Form Factors

| Season | Team | Tot | St | Sb | Y | R |
|--------|------|-----|----|----|----|----|
| 94-95 | Arsenal | 31 | 30 | 1 | 8 | 0 |
| 95-96 | Arsenal | 31 | 31 | 0 | 8 | 0 |
| 96-97 | Arsenal | 35 | 30 | 5 | 10 | 1 |
| Total | | 97 | 91 | 6 | 26 | 1 |

| | GP | GG | GF | GS | TGR |
|--------|------|------|------|------|------|
| 94-95 | 73.81 | 1.72 | 52 | 18 | 34.62 |
| 95-96 | 81.58 | 2.07 | 49 | 15 | 30.61 |
| 96-97 | 92.11 | 1.52 | 62 | 23 | 37.10 |
| Averages | 82.50 | 1.77 | 54.33 | 18.67 | 34.11 |

## WRIGHT, Mark

### Liverpool ❶❷❸❹ CB

Fullname: Mark Wright
DOB: 01-08-63
Dorchester on Thames

Still going strong and with a year of his contract to serve, Wright continues his resurgence of form with 33 starts in 1996-97. After a career with Oxford United, Southampton and Derby County, he was signed by Graeme Souness for £2.2 million in 1991. He managed only six appearances in 1994-95 but came back strongly in 1995-96 when others were injured.

His composure and strength have earned him 45 England caps but injury in the run up to the World Cup finals and Euro '96 caused him to miss out on showing his skills on a world stage. He only scored once in the Coca-Cola Cup in 1996-97 but performed stoutly in defence. Wright will be looking to serve out his contract in style in 1997-98.

## Form Factors

| Season | Team | Tot | St | Sb | Y | R |
|--------|------|-----|----|----|----|----|
| 94-95 | Liverpool | 6 | 5 | 1 | 1 | 0 |
| 95-96 | Liverpool | 28 | 28 | 0 | 7 | 0 |
| 96-97 | Liverpool | 33 | 33 | 0 | 6 | 0 |
| Total | | 67 | 66 | 1 | 14 | 0 |

| | GP | GG | GF | GS | TGR |
|--------|------|------|------|------|------|
| 94-95 | 14.29 | 0.00 | 65 | 0 | 0.00 |
| 95-96 | 73.68 | 14.00 | 70 | 2 | 2.86 |
| 96-97 | 86.84 | 0.00 | 62 | 0 | 0.00 |
| Averages | 58.27 | 4.67 | 65.67 | 0.67 | 0.95 |

## YATES, Dean

### Derby County ❶❷ CB

Fullname: Dean Richard Yates
DOB: 26-10-67 Leicester

Having played in 38 games of Derby's promotion campaign in 1995-96, Yates featured in just 10 Premier League matches last season although injury problems inhibited his availability for the Rams.

Now 29 years old, Yates made it into the big time late on and was in his eleventh year with Notts County when he moved to Derby County for £350,000 at the end of January 1995.

He made 314 league appearances for the Nottingham side before enjoying success with promotion in his second season at the Baseball Ground.

Competition for places may limit central defender Yates to a squad role in the 1997-98 season.

### Form Factors

| Season | Team | Tot | St | Sb | Y | R |
|--------|------|-----|-----|-----|-----|-----|
| 96-97 | Derby Co. | 10 | 8 | 2 | 0 | 0 |
| Total | | 10 | 8 | 2 | 0 | 0 |

| | GP | GG | GF | GS | TGR |
|--------|-----|-----|-----|-----|-----|
| 96-97 | 26.32 | 0.00 | 45 | 0 | 0.00 |
| Averages | 26.32 | 0.00 | 45.00 | 0.00 | 0.00 |

## YEBOAH, Anthony

### Leeds United ❶❷❸ S

Fullname: Anthony Yeboah
DOB: 06-06-66 Kumasi, Ghana

Ghanaian international who made a sensational impact on his arrival in the Premiership in 1995, having joined Leeds United for £3.4 million from German side Eintracht Frankfurt.

Scored at a phenomenal rate from the start with many of his strikes being Goal of the Season contenders. Not surprisingly his first full season saw him win United's Player of the Year award.

Sadly knee ligament problems have since severely hindered his progress at Elland Road and he made just seven, goalless, appearances during 1996-97. His absence cost Leeds dearly as they amassed just 28 Premiership goals during the season.

### Form Factors

| Season | Team | Tot | St | Sb | Y | R |
|--------|------|-----|-----|-----|-----|-----|
| 94-95 | Leeds Utd | 18 | 16 | 2 | 0 | 0 |
| 95-96 | Leeds Utd | 23 | 23 | 0 | 1 | 0 |
| 96-97 | Leeds Utd | 7 | 6 | 1 | 2 | 0 |
| Total | | 48 | 45 | 3 | 3 | 0 |

| | GP | GG | GF | GS | TGR |
|--------|-----|-----|-----|-----|-----|
| 94-95 | 42.86 | 1.50 | 59 | 12 | 20.34 |
| 95-96 | 60.53 | 1.92 | 40 | 12 | 30.00 |
| 96-97 | 18.42 | 0.00 | 28 | 0 | 0.00 |
| Averages | 40.60 | 1.14 | 42.33 | 8.00 | 16.78 |

## YORKE, Dwight

### Aston Villa ❶❷❸❹❺ S

Fullname: Dwight Yorke
DOB: 03-11-71 Tobago, West Indies

Yorke plays with a smile on his face that reflects the confidence he has in his own ability and which is borne out by his being consistently amongst the goals. A full international from Tobago he first appeared in a Villa shirt in the 1994-95 season and contributed 6 goals to Villa's Premiership season. It is the last two seasons though that have seen Yorke blossom, miss just four games, and strike 17 times in each campaign

Yorke's fine close control and speed of foot is the major feature of his game

capped with clinical finishing. Prefers to place the ball rather than blasting it even from the edge of the area. Took time to get the goalscoring back into rhythm last term but he managed a hat-trick at Newcastle only to finish on the losing side.

If he can get amongst the goals early on then he is very capable of scoring 20 plus in the Premiership during 1997-98 and that makes him a real asset to any team.

### Form Factors

| Season | Team | Tot | St | Sb | Y | R |
|---|---|---|---|---|---|---|
| 94-95 | Aston Villa | 37 | 33 | 4 | 3 | 0 |
| 95-96 | Aston Villa | 35 | 35 | 0 | 0 | 0 |
| 96-97 | Aston Villa | 37 | 37 | 0 | 2 | 0 |
| Total | | 109 | 105 | 4 | 5 | 0 |

| | GP | GG | GF | GS | TGR |
|---|---|---|---|---|---|
| 94-95 | 88.10 | 6.17 | 51 | 6 | 11.76 |
| 95-96 | 92.11 | 2.06 | 52 | 17 | 32.69 |
| 96-97 | 97.37 | 2.18 | 47 | 17 | 36.17 |
| Averages | 92.52 | 3.47 | 50.00 | 13.33 | 26.88 |

## ZOLA, Gianfranco

### Chelsea ❶❷❸❹❺ S

Fullname: Gianfranco Zola
DOB: 05-07-66 Oliena, Sardinia

Of all Ruud Gullit's signings, Zola must be the most significant, opting to leave his native Italy for West London in October 1996. He made an immediate impact and, with some outstanding performances and his ability to deal with the press in an elegant manner, it was no real surprise that he was elected as the football writers' Footballer of the Year in May 1997.

Born in Sardinia, he came to the fore with Parma, helping the club to their first Italian championship three seasons ago.

Physically small, he has one of the wickedest free-kicks in the Premiership and it is unlikely that any of his eight

*Dwight Yorke*

Gianfranco Zola

Premiership goals were anything but spectacular.

An important player in the Italian national side, he scored the goal that beat England at Wembley in the first part of 1997.

Would feature in anyone's side, be it fantasy or real!

## Form Factors

| Season | Team | Tot | St | Sb | Y | R |
|--------|------|-----|-----|-----|-----|-----|
| 96-97 | Chelsea | 23 | 22 | 1 | 0 | 0 |
| Total | | 23 | 22 | 1 | 0 | 0 |

| | GP | GG | GF | GS | TGR |
|--------|------|------|------|------|------|
| 96-97 | 60.53 | 2.88 | 58 | 8 | 13.79 |
| Averages | 60.53 | 2.88 | 58.00 | 8.00 | 13.79 |

# Appearance Files

# Player Appearance Fact File

APPEARANCE FIGURES taken on their own can be very deceptive. Numbers most often quoted are those for the games played – but football these days, especially in the FA Premier League, is ever more a squad game. Thus very few players indeed actually get to compete in every minute of every season. Goalkeepers are about the only exception.

Equally a player might be seen to make 20 or so appearances but he might never have made the original starting line-up. Indeed his appearances might all have been in the last ten minutes of every game. For example, take Sheffield Wednesday's Regi Blinker. During the 1996-97 season he made 33 appearances, appearing therefore in all but five of the Owls' Premiership campaign. But more than half of these appearances – 18 in fact – came from the bench. His team mate Ritchie Humphreys, who had such a spectacular start last term, was in a similar situation, having made 15 of his 29 appearances off the bench.

A player may also start many games but never actually complete them and this could also affect their ability to score points in your team. Efan Ekoku, for instance, played in 30 of the Dons' games during 1996-97 but was substituted in no less than 17 games!

The following pages contain a detailed analysis of every player who featured in first team league football last season for each of the 20 clubs playing in the 1997-98 Premiership season and provide the information behind the figures as related above. Use this, in conjunction with the information provided at the start of this handbook, to assist you in making your fantasy team selections.

| | |
|---|---|
| Tot | Total number of appearances – this is St+Sb |
| St | Start – the number of times a player started the game. |
| Sb | Sub – the number of times the player came on as a substitute. |
| Snu | Sub Not Used – the number of times the player was on the bench but didn't get used. |
| Ps | Player Subbed – the number of times the player was substituted. |
| Gls | Number or league goals scored. |
| Y | Number of cautions. † |
| R | Number of dismissals. † |
| Lg | League – the league they played in last season, P = Premier, N = Nationwide League. |

The teams indicated are the ones where the player played last season.

† Not for Nationwide League teams.

| Player | Team | Tot | St | Sb | Snu | PS | Gls | Y | R | Lge |
|--------|------|-----|----|----|-----|----|----|---|---|-----|
| ADAMS | Arsenal | 28 | 27 | 1 | 0 | 2 | 3 | 5 | 2 | P |
| ALBERT | Newcastle U. | 27 | 27 | 0 | 5 | 1 | 2 | 6 | 0 | P |
| ALLEN | Everton | 1 | 0 | 1 | 8 | 1 | 0 | 0 | 0 | P |
| ALLEN | Tottenham H. | 12 | 9 | 3 | 12 | 3 | 2 | 4 | 0 | P |
| ANDERSON | C.Palace | 14 | 7 | 7 | 1 | 2 | 1 | - | - | N |
| ANDERTON | Tottenham H. | 16 | 14 | 2 | 0 | 7 | 3 | 4 | 0 | P |
| ANDREWS | Leicester City | 0 | 0 | 0 | 3 | 0 | 0 | 0 | 0 | P |
| ANELKA | Arsenal | 4 | 0 | 4 | 1 | 0 | 0 | 0 | 0 | P |
| APPLEBY | Barnsley | 35 | 35 | 0 | 0 | 6 | 0 | - | - | N |
| APPLETON | Manchester U. | 0 | 0 | 0 | 2 | 0 | 0 | 0 | 0 | P |
| ARBER | Tottenham H. | 0 | 0 | 0 | 1 | 0 | 0 | 0 | 0 | P |
| ARDLEY | Wimbledon | 34 | 33 | 1 | 1 | 4 | 2 | 1 | 0 | P |
| ARMSTRONG | Tottenham H. | 12 | 12 | 0 | 0 | 2 | 5 | 2 | 0 | P |
| ASANOVIC | Derby County | 34 | 34 | 0 | 0 | 11 | 6 | 3 | 0 | P |
| ASPRILLA | Newcastle U. | 24 | 17 | 7 | 4 | 12 | 4 | 1 | 0 | P |
| ATHERTON | Sheffield W. | 37 | 37 | 0 | 0 | 1 | 2 | 7 | 0 | P |
| AUSTIN | Tottenham H. | 15 | 13 | 2 | 8 | 2 | 0 | 3 | 0 | P |
| | | | | | | | | | | |
| BAARDSEN | Tottenham H. | 2 | 1 | 1 | 36 | 0 | 0 | 0 | 0 | P |
| BABB | Liverpool | 22 | 21 | 1 | 2 | 4 | 1 | 5 | 0 | P |
| BALL | Everton | 5 | 2 | 3 | 3 | 1 | 0 | 1 | 0 | P |
| BARMBY | Everton | 25 | 22 | 3 | 1 | 5 | 4 | 0 | 0 | P |
| BARNES | Liverpool | 35 | 34 | 1 | 2 | 2 | 4 | 0 | 0 | P |
| BARRETT | Everton | 36 | 36 | 0 | 0 | 0 | 0 | 1 | 0 | P |
| BARTON | Newcastle U. | 18 | 14 | 4 | 10 | 0 | 1 | 1 | 0 | P |
| BARTRAM | Arsenal | 0 | 0 | 0 | 9 | 0 | 0 | 0 | 0 | P |
| BASHAM | Southampton | 6 | 1 | 5 | 14 | 0 | 0 | 0 | 0 | P |
| BATTY | Newcastle U. | 32 | 32 | 0 | 0 | 1 | 1 | 10 | 1 | P |
| BEARDSLEY | Newcastle U. | 25 | 22 | 3 | 12 | 4 | 5 | 3 | 0 | P |
| BEASANT | Southampton | 14 | 13 | 1 | 20 | 0 | 0 | 0 | 0 | P |
| BEATTIE | Blackburn R. | 1 | 1 | 0 | 0 | 0 | 0 | 0 | 0 | P |
| BECKHAM | Manchester U. | 36 | 33 | 3 | 1 | 3 | 8 | 6 | 0 | P |
| BEENEY | Leeds U. | 1 | 1 | 0 | 37 | 0 | 0 | 0 | 0 | P |
| BEESLEY | Leeds U. | 12 | 11 | 1 | 4 | 1 | 0 | 5 | 0 | P |
| BENALI | Southampton | 18 | 14 | 4 | 4 | 2 | 0 | 3 | 1 | P |
| BERESFORD | Newcastle U. | 19 | 18 | 1 | 5 | 0 | 0 | 4 | 0 | P |
| BERG | Blackburn R. | 36 | 36 | 0 | 0 | 0 | 2 | 3 | 0 | P |
| BERGER | Liverpool | 23 | 13 | 10 | 9 | 5 | 6 | 0 | 0 | P |
| BERGKAMP | Arsenal | 29 | 28 | 1 | 0 | 8 | 12 | 6 | 0 | P |
| BERGSSON | Bolton W. | 33 | 30 | 3 | 0 | 4 | 3 | - | - | N |
| BERKOVIC | Southampton | 28 | 26 | 2 | 2 | 11 | 4 | 4 | 0 | P |
| BILLIC | West Ham U. | 35 | 35 | 0 | 0 | 3 | 2 | 10 | 0 | P |
| BISHOP | West Ham U. | 29 | 26 | 3 | 2 | 9 | 1 | 2 | 0 | P |

| Player | Team | Tot | St | Sb | Snu | PS | Gls | Y | R | Lge |
|--------|------|-----|-----|-----|-----|-----|-----|-----|-----|-----|
| BJORNEBYE | Liverpool | 38 | 38 | 0 | 0 | 3 | 2 | 3 | 0 | P |
| BLACKWELL | Wimbledon | 27 | 22 | 5 | 2 | 0 | 0 | 4 | 0 | P |
| BLAKE | Bolton W. | 34 | 34 | 0 | 0 | 7 | 19 | - | - | N |
| BLINKER | Sheffield W. | 33 | 15 | 18 | 2 | 5 | 1 | 6 | 0 | P |
| BLUNT | Leeds U. | 1 | 0 | 1 | 2 | 0 | 0 | 0 | 0 | P |
| BOHINEN | Blackburn R. | 23 | 17 | 6 | 7 | 0 | 2 | 6 | 0 | P |
| BOLAND | Coventry City | 1 | 0 | 1 | 13 | 0 | 0 | 0 | 0 | P |
| BOOTH | Sheffield W. | 35 | 32 | 3 | 0 | 7 | 10 | 3 | 0 | P |
| BORROWS | Coventry City | 23 | 16 | 7 | 8 | 4 | 0 | 3 | 0 | P |
| BOSANCIC | Barnsley | 25 | 17 | 8 | 20 | 9 | 1 | - | - | N |
| BOSNICH | Aston Villa | 20 | 20 | 0 | 3 | 2 | 0 | 2 | 0 | P |
| BOULD | Arsenal | 33 | 33 | 0 | 1 | 2 | 0 | 6 | 0 | P |
| BOWEN | West Ham U. | 17 | 15 | 2 | 5 | 5 | 1 | 2 | 0 | P |
| BOWYER | Leeds U. | 32 | 32 | 0 | 0 | 4 | 4 | 6 | 0 | P |
| BOXALL | C.Palace | 6 | 4 | 2 | 1 | 3 | 0 | - | - | N |
| BOYLE | Leeds U. | 1 | 0 | 1 | 1 | 0 | 0 | 0 | 0 | P |
| BOYLIN | West Ham U. | 1 | 0 | 1 | 0 | 0 | 0 | 0 | 0 | P |
| BRADY | Tottenham H. | 0 | 0 | 0 | 3 | 0 | 0 | 0 | 0 | P |
| BRANAGAN | Bolton W. | 36 | 36 | 0 | 2 | 1 | 0 | - | - | N |
| BRANCH | Everton | 25 | 13 | 12 | 7 | 7 | 3 | 2 | 0 | P |
| BRAYSON | Newcastle U. | 0 | 0 | 0 | 4 | 0 | 0 | 0 | 0 | P |
| BREACKER | West Ham U. | 26 | 22 | 4 | 1 | 5 | 0 | 2 | 0 | P |
| BREEN | Coventry City | 9 | 8 | 1 | 4 | 0 | 0 | 0 | 0 | P |
| BRIGHT | Sheffield W. | 1 | 0 | 1 | 0 | 0 | 0 | 0 | 0 | P |
| BRISCOE | Sheffield W. | 6 | 5 | 1 | 5 | 1 | 0 | 0 | 0 | P |
| BROCK | Aston Villa | 0 | 0 | 0 | 2 | 0 | 0 | 0 | 0 | P |
| BROOMES | Blackburn R. | 0 | 0 | 0 | 3 | 0 | 0 | 0 | 0 | P |
| BROWN | Tottenham H. | 0 | 0 | 0 | 1 | 0 | 0 | 0 | 0 | P |
| BROWN | West Ham U. | 0 | 0 | 0 | 2 | 0 | 0 | 0 | 0 | P |
| BULLOCK | Barnsley | 30 | 7 | 23 | 15 | 4 | 0 | - | - | N |
| BURLEY | Chelsea | 31 | 26 | 5 | 1 | 8 | 2 | 3 | 0 | P |
| BURNETT | Bolton W. | 1 | 0 | 1 | 0 | 0 | 0 | - | - | N |
| BURROWS | Coventry City | 18 | 17 | 1 | 6 | 3 | 0 | 5 | 0 | P |
| BURTON | C.Palace | 0 | 0 | 0 | 2 | 0 | 0 | - | - | N |
| BUTT | Manchester U. | 26 | 24 | 2 | 0 | 8 | 5 | 5 | 0 | P |
| | | | | | | | | | | |
| CADAMARTERI | Everton | 1 | 0 | 1 | 0 | 0 | 0 | 0 | 0 | P |
| CALDERWOOD | Tottenham H. | 34 | 33 | 1 | 1 | 0 | 0 | 6 | 0 | P |
| CAMPBELL | Leicester City | 10 | 4 | 6 | 10 | 2 | 0 | 0 | 0 | P |
| CAMPBELL | Tottenham H. | 38 | 38 | 0 | 0 | 2 | 0 | 1 | 0 | P |
| CANTONA | Manchester U. | 36 | 36 | 0 | 0 | 1 | 11 | 5 | 0 | P |
| CARBON | Derby County | 9 | 6 | 4 | 8 | 4 | 0 | 1 | 0 | P |
| CARBONE | Sheffield W. | 25 | 24 | 1 | 0 | 11 | 6 | 3 | 0 | P |

| Player | Team | Tot | St | Sb | Snu | PS | Gls | Y | R | Lge |
|--------|------|-----|-----|-----|-----|-----|-----|-----|-----|-----|
| CARR | Tottenham H. | 26 | 24 | 2 | 7 | 3 | 0 | 1 | 0 | P |
| CARRAGHER | Liverpool | 2 | 1 | 1 | 7 | 0 | 1 | 1 | 0 | P |
| CARSLEY | Derby County | 24 | 15 | 9 | 4 | 3 | 0 | 2 | 0 | P |
| CASPER | Manchester U. | 2 | 0 | 2 | 3 | 0 | 0 | 0 | 0 | P |
| CASSIDY | Liverpool | 0 | 0 | 0 | 1 | 0 | 0 | 0 | 0 | P |
| CASTLEDINE | Wimbledon | 6 | 4 | 2 | 0 | 0 | 1 | 0 | 0 | P |
| CHARLTON | Southampton | 26 | 24 | 2 | 1 | 8 | 0 | 1 | 0 | P |
| CHARNOCK | Liverpool | 0 | 0 | 0 | 0 | 0 | 0 | 0 | 0 | P |
| CLAPHAM | Tottenham H. | 1 | 0 | 1 | 1 | 0 | 0 | 0 | 0 | P |
| CLARIDGE | Leicester City | 32 | 29 | 3 | 1 | 7 | 12 | 2 | 0 | P |
| CLARKE | Chelsea | 31 | 31 | 0 | 1 | 1 | 0 | 7 | 0 | P |
| CLARK | Newcastle U. | 25 | 9 | 16 | 12 | 2 | 2 | 1 | 0 | P |
| CLARKE | Sheffield W. | 38 | 0 | 1 | 37 | 0 | 0 | 0 | 1 | P |
| CLARKE | Wimbledon | 11 | 4 | 7 | 9 | 2 | 1 | 1 | 0 | P |
| CLEGG | Manchester U. | 4 | 3 | 1 | 1 | 1 | 0 | 0 | 0 | P |
| CLEMENT | Chelsea | 1 | 1 | 0 | 5 | 1 | 0 | 1 | 0 | P |
| COLE | Manchester U. | 20 | 10 | 10 | 3 | 2 | 6 | 1 | 0 | P |
| COLEMAN | Blackburn R. | 8 | 8 | 0 | 0 | 2 | 0 | 3 | 0 | P |
| COLEMAN | Bolton W. | 0 | 0 | 0 | 2 | 0 | 0 | - | - | N |
| COLGAN | Chelsea | 1 | 1 | 0 | 15 | 0 | 0 | 0 | 0 | P |
| COLLINS | Sheffield W. | 12 | 8 | 4 | 7 | 3 | 1 | 1 | 0 | P |
| COLLYMORE | Liverpool | 30 | 25 | 5 | 5 | 9 | 12 | 3 | 0 | P |
| COOKE | Manchester U. | 0 | 0 | 0 | 0 | 0 | 0 | 0 | 0 | P |
| COOPER | Derby County | 0 | 0 | 0 | 3 | 0 | 0 | 0 | 0 | P |
| CORT | Wimbledon | 1 | 0 | 1 | 0 | 0 | 0 | 0 | 0 | P |
| COSTELLO | Coventry City | 0 | 0 | 0 | 1 | 0 | 0 | 0 | 0 | P |
| COTTEE | West Ham U. | 3 | 2 | 1 | 0 | 2 | 0 | 1 | 0 | P |
| COUZENS | Leeds U. | 10 | 7 | 3 | 4 | 7 | 1 | 2 | 0 | P |
| CRAWFORD | Newcastle U. | 2 | 0 | 2 | 6 | 0 | 0 | 0 | 0 | P |
| CROFT | Blackburn R. | 5 | 4 | 1 | 10 | 0 | 0 | 0 | 0 | P |
| CRUYFF | Manchester U. | 16 | 11 | 5 | 8 | 6 | 3 | 2 | 0 | P |
| CUNNINGHAM | Wimbledon | 36 | 36 | 0 | 0 | 2 | 0 | 5 | 0 | P |
| CURCIC | Aston Villa | 22 | 17 | 5 | 6 | 10 | 0 | 4 | 0 | P |
| CYRUS | C.Palace | 1 | 1 | 0 | 2 | 1 | 0 | - | - | N |
| | | | | | | | | | | |
| DAILLY | Derby County | 36 | 31 | 5 | 0 | 6 | 3 | 6 | 0 | P |
| DAISH | Coventry City | 20 | 20 | 0 | 0 | 2 | 1 | 4 | 1 | P |
| DALGLISH | Liverpool | 0 | 0 | 0 | 0 | 0 | 0 | 0 | 0 | P |
| DAVIES | Barnsley | 24 | 24 | 0 | 0 | 1 | 3 | - | - | N |
| DAVIES | C.Palace | 6 | 5 | 1 | 0 | 1 | 0 | - | - | N |
| DAVIES | Manchester U. | 0 | 0 | 0 | 0 | 0 | 0 | 0 | 0 | P |
| DAVIS | Aston Villa | 0 | 0 | 0 | 1 | 0 | 0 | 0 | 0 | P |
| DAY | C.Palace | 24 | 24 | 0 | 0 | 0 | 0 | - | - | N |

| Player | Team | Tot | St | Sb | Snu | PS | Gls | Y | R | Lge |
|--------|------|-----|-----|-----|------|-----|-----|-----|-----|------|
| DE ZEEUW | Barnsley | 43 | 43 | 0 | 0 | 0 | 2 | - | - | N |
| DEANE | Leeds U. | 28 | 27 | 1 | 0 | 4 | 5 | 2 | 0 | P |
| DI MATTEO | Chelsea | 34 | 33 | 1 | 3 | 5 | 6 | 5 | 0 | P |
| DIA | Southampton | 1 | 0 | 1 | 0 | 1 | 0 | 0 | 0 | P |
| DICKOV | Arsenal | 1 | 0 | 1 | 0 | 0 | 0 | 0 | 0 | P |
| DICKS | West Ham U. | 31 | 31 | 0 | 0 | 0 | 6 | 6 | 0 | P |
| DIXON | Arsenal | 32 | 31 | 1 | 0 | 3 | 2 | 8 | 0 | P |
| DODD | Southampton | 23 | 23 | 0 | 0 | 3 | 1 | 2 | 1 | P |
| DONALDSON | Sheffield W. | 5 | 2 | 3 | 4 | 0 | 2 | 0 | 0 | P |
| DONIS | Blackburn R. | 22 | 11 | 11 | 9 | 4 | 2 | 0 | 0 | P |
| DORIGO | Leeds U. | 18 | 15 | 3 | 0 | 1 | 0 | 5 | 0 | P |
| DOWIE | West Ham U. | 23 | 18 | 5 | 6 | 0 | 0 | 1 | 0 | P |
| DOZZELL | Tottenham H. | 17 | 10 | 7 | 7 | 2 | 2 | 2 | 0 | P |
| DRAPER | Aston Villa | 29 | 28 | 1 | 2 | 10 | 0 | 4 | 1 | P |
| DRYDEN | Southampton | 29 | 28 | 1 | 4 | 3 | 1 | 5 | 0 | P |
| DUBERRY | Chelsea | 15 | 13 | 2 | 4 | 0 | 1 | 4 | 0 | P |
| DUBLIN | Coventry City | 34 | 33 | 1 | 0 | 2 | 14 | 5 | 0 | P |
| DUCROS | Coventry City | 5 | 1 | 4 | 4 | 0 | 0 | 0 | 0 | P |
| DUFF | Blackburn R. | 1 | 1 | 0 | 4 | 0 | 0 | 0 | 0 | P |
| DUMITRESCU | West Ham U. | 7 | 3 | 4 | 5 | 2 | 0 | 0 | 0 | P |
| DUNNE | Everton | 7 | 6 | 1 | 4 | 1 | 0 | 2 | 0 | P |
| DYER | C.Palace | 43 | 39 | 4 | 0 | 23 | 17 | - | - | N |
| | | | | | | | | | | |
| EADEN | Barnsley | 46 | 46 | 0 | 0 | 2 | 3 | - | - | N |
| EARLE | Wimbledon | 32 | 32 | 0 | 0 | 4 | 7 | 3 | 0 | P |
| EATON | Everton | 0 | 0 | 0 | 1 | 0 | 0 | 0 | 0 | P |
| EBBRELL | Everton | 7 | 7 | 0 | 3 | 2 | 0 | 2 | 0 | P |
| EDINBURGH | Tottenham H. | 24 | 21 | 3 | 6 | 2 | 0 | 11 | 0 | P |
| EDWORTHY | C.Palace | 46 | 43 | 3 | 0 | 5 | 0 | - | - | N |
| EHIOGU | Aston Villa | 38 | 38 | 0 | 0 | 0 | 3 | 4 | 0 | P |
| EKOKU | Wimbledon | 30 | 28 | 2 | 0 | 17 | 11 | 4 | 0 | P |
| ELLIOTT | Leicester City | 16 | 16 | 0 | 0 | 0 | 4 | 3 | 0 | P |
| ELLIOTT R. | Newcastle U. | 29 | 29 | 0 | 6 | 1 | 7 | 3 | 0 | P |
| ELLIOTT S. | Newcastle U. | 0 | 0 | 0 | 1 | 0 | 0 | 0 | 0 | P |
| EUELL | Wimbledon | 7 | 4 | 3 | 2 | 0 | 2 | 0 | 0 | P |
| EUSTACE | Coventry City | 0 | 0 | 0 | 1 | 0 | 0 | 0 | 0 | P |
| EVANS | Leeds U. | 0 | 0 | 0 | 1 | 0 | 0 | 0 | 0 | P |
| EVANS | Southampton | 12 | 8 | 4 | 0 | 0 | 4 | 1 | 0 | P |
| EVTUSHOK | Coventry City | 3 | 3 | 0 | 4 | 2 | 0 | 0 | 0 | P |
| | | | | | | | | | | |
| FAIRCLOUGH | Bolton W. | 46 | 46 | 0 | 0 | 1 | 8 | - | - | N |
| FARRELLY | Aston Villa | 3 | 1 | 2 | 15 | 0 | 0 | 0 | 0 | P |
| FEAR | Wimbledon | 17 | 9 | 9 | 11 | 0 | 0 | 3 | 0 | P |

| Player | Team | Tot | St | Sb | Snu | PS | Gls | Y | R | Lge |
|--------|------|-----|-----|-----|-----|-----|-----|-----|-----|-----|
| FENN | Tottenham H. | 4 | 0 | 4 | 3 | 0 | 0 | 0 | 0 | P |
| FENTON | Blackburn R. | 13 | 5 | 8 | 6 | 0 | 1 | 3 | 0 | P |
| FERDINAND | Newcastle U. | 31 | 30 | 1 | 1 | 8 | 16 | 3 | 0 | P |
| FERDINAND | West Ham U. | 15 | 11 | 4 | 2 | 3 | 2 | 2 | 0 | P |
| FERGUSON | Everton | 33 | 31 | 2 | 1 | 0 | 10 | 5 | 1 | P |
| FILAN | Coventry City | 1 | 0 | 1 | 37 | 0 | 0 | 0 | 0 | P |
| FLAHAVAN | Southampton | 0 | 0 | 0 | 2 | 0 | 0 | 0 | 0 | P |
| FLITCROFT | Blackburn R. | 28 | 27 | 1 | 2 | 8 | 3 | 1 | 0 | P |
| FLOWERS | Blackburn R. | 36 | 36 | 0 | 2 | 0 | 0 | 2 | 0 | P |
| FLYNN | Derby County | 17 | 10 | 7 | 8 | 3 | 1 | 3 | 0 | P |
| FORD | Leeds U. | 16 | 15 | 1 | 13 | 6 | 1 | 4 | 0 | P |
| FORREST | Chelsea | 3 | 2 | 1 | 1 | 0 | 0 | 0 | 0 | P |
| FOWLER | Liverpool | 32 | 32 | 0 | 0 | 4 | 18 | 4 | 1 | P |
| FOX | Leicester City | 0 | 0 | 0 | 1 | 0 | 0 | 0 | 0 | P |
| FOX | Tottenham H. | 25 | 19 | 6 | 3 | 6 | 1 | 1 | 0 | P |
| FRANDSEN | Bolton W. | 41 | 40 | 1 | 0 | 8 | 5 | - | - | N |
| FREEDMAN | C.Palace | 44 | 33 | 11 | 0 | 12 | 11 | - | - | N |
| FUTRE | West Ham U. | 9 | 4 | 5 | 0 | 2 | 0 | 0 | 0 | P |
| GABBIADINI | Derby County | 14 | 5 | 9 | 1 | 4 | 0 | 1 | 0 | P |
| GALLACHER | Blackburn R. | 34 | 34 | 0 | 0 | 10 | 10 | 6 | 0 | P |
| GARDE | Arsenal | 11 | 7 | 4 | 2 | 5 | 0 | 2 | 0 | P |
| GAYLE | Wimbledon | 36 | 34 | 2 | 0 | 12 | 8 | 2 | 0 | P |
| GENAUX | Coventry City | 4 | 3 | 1 | 6 | 1 | 0 | 2 | 0 | P |
| GERRARD | Everton | 5 | 4 | 1 | 30 | 0 | 0 | 0 | 0 | P |
| GIBSON | Manchester U. | 0 | 0 | 0 | 1 | 0 | 0 | 0 | 0 | P |
| GIGGS | Manchester U. | 26 | 25 | 1 | 1 | 6 | 3 | 2 | 0 | P |
| GILLESPIE | Newcastle U. | 32 | 23 | 9 | 5 | 8 | 1 | 2 | 1 | P |
| GINOLA | Newcastle U. | 24 | 20 | 4 | 7 | 6 | 1 | 3 | 0 | P |
| GIVEN | Blackburn R. | 2 | 2 | 0 | 36 | 0 | 0 | 0 | 0 | P |
| GOODMAN | Wimbledon | 13 | 6 | 7 | 6 | 6 | 1 | 0 | 0 | P |
| GOODWIN | Coventry City | 0 | 0 | 0 | 1 | 0 | 0 | 0 | 0 | P |
| GORDON | C.Palace | 29 | 25 | 4 | 0 | 2 | 3 | - | - | N |
| GRANT | Everton | 18 | 11 | 7 | 4 | 3 | 0 | 3 | 0 | P |
| GRANVILLE | Chelsea | 5 | 3 | 2 | 2 | 0 | 0 | 0 | 0 | P |
| GRAY | Leeds U. | 7 | 1 | 6 | 4 | 1 | 0 | 0 | 0 | P |
| GRAYSON | Leicester City | 36 | 36 | 0 | 0 | 1 | 0 | 4 | 0 | P |
| GREEN | Bolton W. | 12 | 7 | 5 | 3 | 2 | 1 | - | - | N |
| GRODAS | Chelsea | 21 | 20 | 1 | 9 | 1 | 0 | 1 | 1 | P |
| GUDMUNDSSON | Blackburn R. | 2 | 0 | 2 | 5 | 0 | 0 | 0 | 0 | P |
| GULLIT | Chelsea | 12 | 6 | 6 | 2 | 2 | 1 | 1 | 0 | P |
| GUPPY | Leicester City | 13 | 12 | 1 | 0 | 1 | 0 | 2 | 0 | P |

| Player | Team | Tot | St | Sb | Snu | PS | Gls | Y | R | Lge |
|--------|------|-----|-----|-----|-----|-----|-----|-----|-----|-----|
| HALL | Coventry City | 13 | 10 | 3 | 6 | 2 | 0 | 0 | 0 | P |
| HALL | West Ham U. | 7 | 7 | 0 | 0 | 0 | 0 | 1 | 0 | P |
| HALLE | Leeds U. | 20 | 20 | 0 | 0 | 0 | 0 | 2 | 0 | P |
| HAMILTON | Newcastle U. | 0 | 0 | 0 | 3 | 0 | 0 | 0 | 0 | P |
| HARFORD | Wimbledon | 13 | 3 | 10 | 15 | 1 | 1 | 2 | 0 | P |
| HARKNESS | Liverpool | 7 | 5 | 2 | 5 | 0 | 0 | 0 | 0 | P |
| HARPER | Arsenal | 1 | 1 | 0 | 9 | 0 | 0 | 0 | 0 | P |
| HARRINGTON | Leicester City | 0 | 0 | 0 | 0 | 0 | 0 | 0 | 0 | P |
| HARRIS | C.Palace | 2 | 0 | 2 | 0 | 0 | 0 | - | - | N |
| HARTE | Leeds U. | 14 | 10 | 4 | 21 | 0 | 2 | 1 | 0 | P |
| HARTSON | Arsenal | 19 | 14 | 5 | 2 | 8 | 3 | 9 | 0 | P |
| HARTSON | West Ham U. | 11 | 11 | 0 | 0 | 0 | 5 | 3 | 0 | P |
| HATLEY | Leeds U. | 6 | 5 | 1 | 1 | 1 | 0 | 0 | 0 | P |
| HEALD | Wimbledon | 3 | 2 | 0 | 23 | 0 | 0 | 0 | 0 | P |
| HEANEY | Southampton | 8 | 4 | 4 | 0 | 5 | 1 | 1 | 0 | P |
| HELDER | Arsenal | 2 | 0 | 2 | 3 | 0 | 0 | 0 | 0 | P |
| HENDRIE | Aston Villa | 4 | 0 | 4 | 12 | 0 | 0 | 0 | 0 | P |
| HENDRIE | Barnsley | 36 | 36 | 0 | 0 | 5 | 15 | - | - | N |
| HENDRY | Blackburn R. | 35 | 35 | 0 | 0 | 3 | 1 | 4 | 0 | P |
| HESKEY | Leicester City | 35 | 35 | 0 | 0 | 4 | 10 | 8 | 0 | P |
| HILL | Leicester City | 7 | 6 | 1 | 9 | 4 | 0 | 2 | 0 | P |
| HILL | Tottenham H. | 0 | 0 | 0 | 3 | 0 | 0 | 0 | 0 | P |
| HILLIER | Arsenal | 2 | 0 | 2 | 0 | 0 | 0 | 0 | 0 | P |
| HILLS | Everton | 3 | 1 | 2 | 4 | 0 | 0 | 0 | 0 | P |
| HINCHCLIFFE | Everton | 18 | 18 | 0 | 0 | 2 | 1 | 2 | 0 | P |
| HIRST | Sheffield W. | 25 | 20 | 5 | 0 | 11 | 6 | 3 | 1 | P |
| HISLOP | Newcastle U. | 16 | 16 | 0 | 22 | 0 | 0 | 0 | 0 | P |
| HITCHCOCK | Chelsea | 12 | 10 | 2 | 9 | 1 | 0 | 1 | 0 | P |
| HODGES | West Ham U. | 0 | 0 | 0 | 1 | 0 | 0 | 0 | 0 | P |
| HOLDSWORTH | Wimbledon | 25 | 10 | 15 | 1 | 3 | 5 | 0 | 0 | P |
| HOPKIN | C.Palace | 41 | 38 | 3 | 0 | 4 | 13 | - | - | N |
| HOTTIGER | Everton | 8 | 4 | 4 | 22 | 1 | 0 | 0 | 0 | P |
| HOUGHTON | C.Palace | 21 | 18 | 3 | 0 | 4 | 1 | - | - | N |
| HOULT | Derby County | 32 | 31 | 1 | 5 | 0 | 0 | 0 | 0 | P |
| HOWELLS | Tottenham H. | 32 | 32 | 0 | 0 | 6 | 2 | 7 | 0 | P |
| HOWEY | Newcastle U. | 8 | 8 | 0 | 1 | 0 | 1 | 0 | 0 | P |
| HUCKERBY | Coventry City | 25 | 21 | 4 | 0 | 7 | 5 | 2 | 0 | P |
| HUGHES | Arsenal | 14 | 9 | 5 | 3 | 6 | 1 | 1 | 0 | P |
| HUGHES | Aston Villa | 7 | 4 | 3 | 5 | 1 | 0 | 1 | 0 | P |
| HUGHES | Newcastle U. | 0 | 0 | 0 | 1 | 0 | 0 | 0 | 0 | P |
| HUGHES | Southampton | 6 | 1 | 5 | 1 | 0 | 0 | 1 | 0 | P |
| HUGHES | West Ham U. | 33 | 31 | 2 | 0 | 1 | 3 | 5 | 0 | P |
| HUGHES M. | Chelsea | 35 | 32 | 3 | 0 | 5 | 8 | 6 | 0 | P |

| Player | Team | Tot | St | Sb | Snu | PS | Gls | Y | R | Lge |
|--------|------|-----|-----|-----|-----|-----|-----|-----|-----|-----|
| HUGHES P. | Chelsea | 12 | 8 | 4 | 3 | 6 | 2 | 1 | 0 | P |
| HUMPHREYS | Sheffield W. | 29 | 14 | 15 | 8 | 11 | 3 | 2 | 0 | P |
| HURST | Barnsley | 1 | 0 | 1 | 1 | 0 | 0 | - | - | N |
| HYDE | Leicester City | 0 | 0 | 0 | 3 | 0 | 0 | 0 | 0 | P |
| HYDE | Sheffield W. | 19 | 15 | 4 | 0 | 3 | 2 | 4 | 0 | P |
| | | | | | | | | | | |
| IRWIN | Manchester U. | 31 | 29 | 2 | 3 | 2 | 1 | 1 | 0 | P |
| ISAIAS | Coventry City | 1 | 0 | 1 | 1 | 0 | 0 | 0 | 0 | P |
| IVERSEN | Tottenham H. | 16 | 16 | 0 | 0 | 1 | 6 | 1 | 0 | P |
| IZZET | Leicester City | 35 | 34 | 1 | 0 | 6 | 3 | 6 | 0 | P |
| | | | | | | | | | | |
| JACKSON | Everton | 0 | 0 | 0 | 2 | 0 | 0 | 0 | 0 | P |
| JACKSON | Leeds U. | 17 | 11 | 6 | 11 | 1 | 0 | 1 | 0 | P |
| JAMES | Liverpool | 38 | 38 | 0 | 0 | 0 | 0 | 0 | 0 | P |
| JESS | Coventry City | 27 | 19 | 8 | 7 | 10 | 0 | 0 | 0 | P |
| JOACHIM | Aston Villa | 15 | 3 | 12 | 21 | 2 | 3 | 0 | 0 | P |
| JOBSON | Leeds U. | 10 | 10 | 0 | 0 | 0 | 0 | 2 | 0 | P |
| JOHANSEN | Bolton W. | 32 | 24 | 8 | 8 | 11 | 5 | - | - | N |
| JOHNSEN | Chelsea | 18 | 14 | 4 | 7 | 3 | 0 | 3 | 0 | P |
| JOHNSEN | Manchester U. | 31 | 26 | 5 | 2 | 6 | 0 | 3 | 0 | P |
| JOHNSON | Aston Villa | 20 | 10 | 10 | 6 | 2 | 4 | 4 | 0 | P |
| JONES | Barnsley | 17 | 12 | 5 | 6 | 3 | 0 | - | - | N |
| JONES | West Ham U. | 8 | 5 | 3 | 3 | 3 | 0 | 0 | 0 | P |
| JONES | Wimbledon | 29 | 29 | 0 | 0 | 7 | 3 | 5 | 1 | P |
| JONES L. | Liverpool | 2 | 0 | 2 | 15 | 0 | 0 | 0 | 0 | P |
| JONES R. | Liverpool | 2 | 2 | 0 | 4 | 1 | 0 | 1 | 0 | P |
| JUPP | Wimbledon | 6 | 6 | 0 | 9 | 2 | 0 | 1 | 0 | P |
| | | | | | | | | | | |
| KAAMARK | Leicester City | 10 | 9 | 1 | 2 | 3 | 0 | 0 | 0 | P |
| KANCHELSKIS | Everton | 20 | 20 | 0 | 0 | 5 | 4 | 0 | 0 | P |
| KAVANAGH | Derby County | 0 | 0 | 0 | 0 | 0 | 0 | 0 | 0 | P |
| KEANE | Manchester U. | 21 | 21 | 0 | 0 | 1 | 2 | 6 | 1 | P |
| KELLER | Leicester City | 31 | 31 | 0 | 0 | 0 | 0 | 0 | 0 | P |
| KELLY | Leeds U. | 36 | 34 | 2 | 0 | 2 | 2 | 5 | 0 | P |
| KENNA | Blackburn R. | 37 | 37 | 0 | 0 | 3 | 0 | 2 | 0 | P |
| KENNEDY | Liverpool | 5 | 0 | 5 | 20 | 0 | 0 | 0 | 0 | P |
| KEOWN | Arsenal | 33 | 33 | 0 | 0 | 2 | 1 | 7 | 0 | P |
| KERSLAKE | Tottenham H. | 0 | 0 | 0 | 3 | 0 | 0 | 0 | 0 | P |
| KEWELL | Leeds U. | 1 | 0 | 1 | 4 | 0 | 0 | 0 | 0 | P |
| KHARINE | Chelsea | 5 | 5 | 0 | 0 | 1 | 0 | 0 | 0 | P |
| KIMBLE | Wimbledon | 31 | 28 | 3 | 4 | 0 | 0 | 2 | 0 | P |
| KITSON P. | Newcastle U. | 3 | 0 | 3 | 9 | 0 | 0 | 0 | 0 | P |
| KITSON P. | West Ham U. | 14 | 14 | 0 | 0 | 2 | 8 | 2 | 0 | P |

| Player | Team | Tot | St | Sb | Snu | PS | Gls | Y | R | Lge |
|--------|------|-----|----|----|-----|----|----|----|---|-----|
| KVARME | Liverpool | 15 | 15 | 0 | 0 | 2 | 0 | 1 | 0 | P |
| | | | | | | | | | | |
| LAMPARD | West Ham U. | 13 | 3 | 10 | 15 | 2 | 0 | 1 | 0 | P |
| LAURENT | Leeds U. | 4 | 2 | 2 | 2 | 1 | 0 | 0 | 0 | P |
| LAURSEN | Derby County | 36 | 35 | 1 | 0 | 7 | 1 | 2 | 0 | P |
| LAWRENCE | Leicester City | 15 | 2 | 13 | 16 | 0 | 0 | 0 | 0 | P |
| LAZARIDIS | West Ham U. | 22 | 13 | 9 | 3 | 6 | 1 | 2 | 0 | P |
| Le SAUX | Blackburn R. | 26 | 26 | 0 | 0 | 1 | 1 | 6 | 0 | P |
| Le TISSIER | Southampton | 31 | 25 | 6 | 0 | 8 | 13 | 5 | 0 | P |
| LEBOEUF | Chelsea | 26 | 26 | 0 | 1 | 1 | 6 | 7 | 0 | P |
| LEE | Bolton W. | 25 | 13 | 12 | 6 | 6 | 2 | - | - | N |
| LEE | Chelsea | 1 | 1 | 0 | 5 | 1 | 1 | 0 | 0 | P |
| LEE | Newcastle U. | 33 | 32 | 1 | 0 | 7 | 5 | 7 | 0 | P |
| LENNON | Leicester City | 35 | 35 | 0 | 0 | 0 | 1 | 8 | 0 | P |
| LEONHARDSEN | Wimbledon | 27 | 27 | 0 | 1 | 8 | 5 | 0 | 0 | P |
| LEWIS | Leicester City | 6 | 4 | 2 | 2 | 4 | 0 | 0 | 0 | P |
| LIDDELL | Barnsley | 38 | 25 | 13 | 9 | 10 | 8 | - | - | N |
| LILLEY | Leeds U. | 6 | 4 | 2 | 0 | 0 | 0 | 0 | 0 | P |
| LIMPAR | Everton | 2 | 1 | 1 | 10 | 1 | 0 | 0 | 0 | P |
| LINIGHAN | Arsenal | 11 | 10 | 1 | 11 | 1 | 1 | 2 | 0 | P |
| LINIGHAN | C.Palace | 21 | 19 | 2 | 0 | 0 | 0 | - | - | N |
| LINIGHAN | Sheffield W. | 0 | 0 | 0 | 1 | 0 | 0 | 0 | 0 | P |
| LOMAS | West Ham U. | 7 | 7 | 0 | 0 | 1 | 0 | 0 | 0 | P |
| LUKIC | Arsenal | 15 | 15 | 0 | 20 | 0 | 0 | 0 | 0 | P |
| LUNDEKVAM | Southampton | 29 | 28 | 1 | 1 | 3 | 0 | 6 | 0 | P |
| | | | | | | | | | | |
| MABBUTT | Tottenham H. | 1 | 1 | 0 | 0 | 1 | 0 | 0 | 0 | P |
| MADDISON | Southampton | 17 | 14 | 3 | 16 | 5 | 1 | 4 | 0 | P |
| MAGILTON | Southampton | 37 | 31 | 6 | 1 | 7 | 4 | 4 | 0 | P |
| MARCELLE | Barnsley | 39 | 26 | 13 | 1 | 10 | 8 | - | - | N |
| MARKER | Blackburn R. | 7 | 5 | 2 | 22 | 0 | 0 | 0 | 0 | P |
| MARSHALL | Arsenal | 8 | 6 | 2 | 10 | 1 | 0 | 1 | 0 | P |
| MARSHALL | Leicester City | 28 | 19 | 9 | 1 | 4 | 8 | 1 | 0 | P |
| MARTYN | Leeds U. | 37 | 37 | 0 | 0 | 0 | 0 | 1 | 0 | P |
| MATTEO | Liverpool | 26 | 22 | 4 | 7 | 1 | 0 | 2 | 0 | P |
| MAUTONE | West Ham U. | 1 | 1 | 0 | 7 | 0 | 0 | 0 | 0 | P |
| MAY | Manchester U. | 29 | 28 | 1 | 1 | 2 | 3 | 5 | 0 | P |
| McALLISTER | Coventry City | 38 | 38 | 0 | 0 | 0 | 6 | 1 | 0 | P |
| McALLISTER | Wimbledon | 23 | 19 | 4 | 8 | 2 | 0 | 2 | 0 | P |
| McANESPIE | Bolton W. | 13 | 11 | 2 | 0 | 0 | 0 | - | - | N |
| McATEER | Liverpool | 37 | 36 | 1 | 0 | 2 | 1 | 6 | 0 | P |
| McCANN | Everton | 0 | 0 | 0 | 1 | 0 | 0 | 0 | 0 | P |
| McCLAIR | Manchester U. | 19 | 4 | 15 | 16 | 0 | 0 | 1 | 0 | P |

| Player | Team | Tot | St | Sb | Snu | PS | Gls | Y | R | Lge |
|--------|------|-----|-----|-----|-----|-----|-----|-----|-----|-----|
| McGINLAY | Bolton W. | 43 | 43 | 0 | 0 | 6 | 24 | - | - | N |
| McGOWAN | Arsenal | 1 | 1 | 0 | 0 | 1 | 0 | 0 | 0 | P |
| McGRATH P. | Aston Villa | 0 | 0 | 0 | 7 | 0 | 0 | 0 | 0 | P |
| McGRATH P. | Derby County | 24 | 23 | 1 | 1 | 4 | 0 | 2 | 0 | P |
| McKENZIE | C.Palace | 21 | 4 | 17 | 3 | 3 | 2 | - | - | N |
| McKINLAY | Blackburn R. | 25 | 23 | 2 | 4 | 3 | 1 | 12 | 0 | P |
| McMAHON | Leicester City | 0 | 0 | 0 | 1 | 0 | 0 | 0 | 0 | P |
| McMAHON | Tottenham H. | 0 | 0 | 0 | 1 | 0 | 0 | 0 | 0 | P |
| McMANAMAN | Liverpool | 37 | 37 | 0 | 0 | 1 | 7 | 5 | 0 | P |
| McMENAMIN | Coventry City | 0 | 0 | 0 | 1 | 0 | 0 | 0 | 0 | P |
| McVEIGH | Tottenham H. | 3 | 2 | 1 | 2 | 2 | 1 | 0 | 0 | P |
| MEAN | West Ham U. | 0 | 0 | 0 | 2 | 0 | 0 | 0 | 0 | P |
| MERSON | Arsenal | 32 | 32 | 0 | 2 | 5 | 6 | 1 | 0 | P |
| MIKLOSKO | West Ham U. | 36 | 36 | 0 | 0 | 1 | 0 | 0 | 0 | P |
| MILOSEVIC | Aston Villa | 30 | 29 | 1 | 0 | 8 | 10 | 6 | 0 | P |
| MIMMS | C.Palace | 1 | 1 | 0 | 0 | 0 | 0 | - | - | N |
| MINTO | Chelsea | 25 | 24 | 1 | 4 | 6 | 4 | 6 | 0 | P |
| MOLENAAR | Leeds U. | 12 | 12 | 0 | 4 | 0 | 1 | 5 | 0 | P |
| MONCUR | West Ham U. | 27 | 26 | 1 | 1 | 7 | 2 | 8 | 0 | P |
| MONKOU | Southampton | 13 | 8 | 5 | 1 | 0 | 0 | 6 | 0 | P |
| MORRIS | Chelsea | 12 | 6 | 6 | 8 | 3 | 0 | 1 | 0 | P |
| MORROW | Arsenal | 14 | 5 | 9 | 12 | 3 | 0 | 1 | 0 | P |
| MOSES | Barnsley | 28 | 25 | 3 | 5 | 0 | 2 | - | - | N |
| MOSS | Southampton | 3 | 3 | 0 | 14 | 0 | 0 | 0 | 0 | P |
| MULLINS | C.Palace | 0 | 0 | 0 | 1 | 0 | 0 | - | - | N |
| MURPHY | Wimbledon | 0 | 0 | 0 | 13 | 0 | 0 | 0 | 0 | P |
| MURRAY | Aston Villa | 1 | 1 | 0 | 8 | 1 | 0 | 0 | 0 | P |
| MUSCAT | C.Palace | 44 | 42 | 2 | 0 | 5 | 2 | - | - | N |
| MYERS | Chelsea | 18 | 15 | 3 | 6 | 6 | 1 | 2 | 0 | P |
| | | | | | | | | | | |
| NASH | C.Palace | 21 | 21 | 0 | 0 | 3 | 0 | - | - | N |
| NDAH | C.Palace | 25 | 5 | 20 | 3 | 0 | 3 | - | - | N |
| NDLOVU | Coventry City | 20 | 10 | 10 | 1 | 4 | 1 | 1 | 0 | P |
| NEILSON | Southampton | 29 | 24 | 5 | 3 | 2 | 0 | 4 | 0 | P |
| NELSON | Aston Villa | 34 | 33 | 1 | 1 | 4 | 0 | 6 | 0 | P |
| NETHERCOTT | Tottenham H. | 9 | 2 | 7 | 19 | 2 | 0 | 2 | 0 | P |
| NEVILLE G. | Manchester U. | 31 | 30 | 1 | 3 | 2 | 1 | 4 | 0 | P |
| NEVILLE P. | Manchester U. | 18 | 15 | 3 | 5 | 1 | 0 | 2 | 0 | P |
| NEWELL | West Ham U. | 7 | 6 | 1 | 0 | 2 | 0 | 2 | 0 | P |
| NEWSOME | Sheffield W. | 10 | 10 | 0 | 1 | 0 | 1 | 1 | 0 | P |
| NEWTON | Chelsea | 15 | 13 | 2 | 2 | 2 | 0 | 2 | 0 | P |
| NICHOLLS | Chelsea | 8 | 3 | 5 | 8 | 2 | 0 | 0 | 0 | P |
| NICOL | Sheffield W. | 23 | 19 | 4 | 9 | 8 | 0 | 0 | 0 | P |

| Player | Team | Tot | St | Sb | Snu | PS | Gls | Y | R | Lge |
|--------|------|-----|----|----|-----|----|----|---|---|-----|
| NIELSEN | Tottenham H. | 29 | 28 | 1 | 1 | 8 | 6 | 6 | 0 | P |
| NOLAN | Sheffield W. | 38 | 38 | 0 | 0 | 1 | 1 | 1 | 0 | P |
| | | | | | | | | | | |
| O'CONNOR | Everton | 0 | 0 | 0 | 3 | 0 | 0 | 0 | 0 | P |
| O'KANE | Manchester U. | 1 | 1 | 0 | 0 | 1 | 0 | 0 | 0 | P |
| O'NEILL | Coventry City | 1 | 1 | 0 | 3 | 1 | 0 | 0 | 0 | P |
| O'TOOLE | Coventry City | 0 | 0 | 0 | 0 | 0 | 0 | 0 | 0 | P |
| OAKES | Aston Villa | 20 | 18 | 2 | 17 | 0 | 0 | 0 | 0 | P |
| OAKES | Sheffield W. | 19 | 7 | 12 | 9 | 5 | 1 | 1 | 0 | P |
| OAKLEY | Southampton | 28 | 23 | 5 | 0 | 11 | 3 | 0 | 0 | P |
| OGRIZOVIC | Coventry City | 38 | 38 | 0 | 0 | 1 | 0 | 1 | 0 | P |
| OMOYINMI | West Ham U. | 1 | 0 | 1 | 0 | 0 | 0 | 0 | 0 | P |
| OSTENSTAD | Southampton | 30 | 29 | 1 | 0 | 5 | 10 | 3 | 0 | P |
| OWEN | Liverpool | 2 | 1 | 1 | 2 | 0 | 1 | 0 | 0 | P |
| | | | | | | | | | | |
| PAATELAINEN | Bolton W. | 10 | 3 | 7 | 3 | 1 | 2 | - | - | N |
| PALLISTER | Manchester U. | 27 | 27 | 0 | 1 | 4 | 3 | 4 | 0 | P |
| PALMER | Leeds U. | 28 | 26 | 2 | 1 | 1 | 0 | 10 | 1 | P |
| PARKER | Chelsea | 4 | 1 | 3 | 2 | 1 | 0 | 0 | 0 | P |
| PARKER | Derby County | 4 | 4 | 0 | 2 | 1 | 0 | 1 | 0 | P |
| PARKER | Leicester City | 31 | 22 | 9 | 1 | 5 | 2 | 0 | 0 | P |
| PARKINSON | Everton | 28 | 28 | 0 | 0 | 4 | 0 | 4 | 0 | P |
| PARLOUR | Arsenal | 30 | 17 | 13 | 4 | 2 | 2 | 6 | 0 | P |
| PEACOCK | Chelsea | 0 | 0 | 0 | 2 | 0 | 0 | 0 | 0 | P |
| PEACOCK | Newcastle U. | 35 | 35 | 0 | 3 | 0 | 1 | 2 | 0 | P |
| PEARCE | Blackburn R. | 12 | 7 | 5 | 3 | 1 | 0 | 1 | 0 | P |
| PEDERSEN | Blackburn R. | 11 | 6 | 5 | 1 | 8 | 1 | 0 | 0 | P |
| PEMBRIDGE | Sheffield W. | 34 | 33 | 1 | 0 | 2 | 6 | 7 | 0 | P |
| PERRY | Wimbledon | 37 | 37 | 0 | 0 | 2 | 1 | 0 | 0 | P |
| PETRESCU | Chelsea | 34 | 34 | 0 | 0 | 4 | 3 | 4 | 0 | P |
| PHELAN T. | Chelsea | 3 | 1 | 2 | 2 | 0 | 0 | 0 | 0 | P |
| PHELAN T. | Everton | 15 | 15 | 0 | 0 | 3 | 0 | 1 | 0 | P |
| PHILLIPS | Bolton W. | 36 | 36 | 0 | 1 | 1 | 0 | - | - | N |
| PILKINGTON | Manchester U. | 0 | 0 | 0 | 1 | 0 | 0 | 0 | 0 | P |
| PITCHER | C.Palace | 3 | 3 | 0 | 0 | 0 | 2 | - | - | N |
| PLATT | Arsenal | 28 | 27 | 1 | 0 | 5 | 4 | 4 | 0 | P |
| POBORSKY | Manchester U. | 22 | 15 | 7 | 15 | 10 | 3 | 1 | 0 | P |
| POLLOCK | Bolton W. | 20 | 18 | 2 | 3 | 3 | 4 | - | - | N |
| POOLE | Leicester City | 7 | 7 | 0 | 31 | 0 | 0 | 0 | 0 | P |
| POOM | Derby County | 4 | 4 | 0 | 0 | 1 | 0 | 0 | 0 | P |
| PORFIRIO | West Ham U. | 23 | 15 | 8 | 2 | 5 | 2 | 6 | 0 | P |
| POTTER | Southampton | 8 | 2 | 6 | 6 | 1 | 0 | 0 | 0 | P |
| POTTS | West Ham U. | 20 | 17 | 3 | 5 | 3 | 0 | 2 | 0 | P |

| Player | Team | Tot | St | Sb | Snu | PS | Gls | Y | R | Lge |
|--------|------|-----|-----|-----|-----|-----|-----|-----|-----|-----|
| POWELL C. | Derby County | 35 | 35 | 0 | 0 | 4 | 0 | 4 | 0 | P |
| POWELL D. | Derby County | 33 | 27 | 6 | 0 | 5 | 1 | 7 | 0 | P |
| PRESSMAN | Sheffield W. | 38 | 38 | 0 | 0 | 1 | 0 | 0 | 0 | P |
| PRINDERVILLE | Coventry City | 0 | 0 | 0 | 1 | 0 | 0 | 0 | 0 | P |
| PRIOR | Leicester City | 34 | 33 | 1 | 1 | 4 | 0 | 4 | 0 | P |
| QUINN | C.Palace | 22 | 17 | 5 | 8 | 7 | 1 | - | - | N |
| QUY | Derby County | 0 | 0 | 0 | 3 | 0 | 0 | 0 | 0 | P |
| RACHEL | Aston Villa | 0 | 0 | 0 | 14 | 0 | 0 | 0 | 0 | P |
| RADEBE | Leeds U. | 32 | 28 | 4 | 2 | 3 | 0 | 6 | 0 | P |
| RADUCIOIU | West Ham U. | 11 | 6 | 5 | 2 | 4 | 2 | 0 | 0 | P |
| RAHMBERG | Derby County | 1 | 0 | 1 | 3 | 0 | 0 | 0 | 0 | P |
| RANKIN | Arsenal | 0 | 0 | 0 | 3 | 0 | 0 | 0 | 0 | P |
| REDFEARN | Barnsley | 43 | 43 | 0 | 0 | 1 | 17 | - | - | N |
| REDKNAPP | Liverpool | 23 | 18 | 5 | 6 | 0 | 3 | 0 | 0 | P |
| REEVES | Wimbledon | 2 | 0 | 2 | 11 | 0 | 0 | 0 | 0 | P |
| REGIS | Barnsley | 4 | 0 | 4 | 3 | 0 | 0 | - | - | N |
| RICHARDSON | Coventry City | 28 | 25 | 3 | 7 | 2 | 0 | 2 | 0 | P |
| RIDEOUT | Everton | 9 | 4 | 5 | 15 | 2 | 0 | 2 | 0 | P |
| RIEPER | West Ham U. | 28 | 26 | 2 | 3 | 3 | 1 | 3 | 1 | P |
| RIPLEY | Blackburn R. | 13 | 5 | 8 | 4 | 3 | 0 | 0 | 0 | P |
| ROBERTS | C.Palace | 46 | 45 | 1 | 0 | 0 | 0 | - | - | N |
| ROBINS | Leicester City | 8 | 5 | 3 | 18 | 4 | 1 | 0 | 0 | P |
| ROBINSON | Southampton | 7 | 3 | 4 | 1 | 1 | 0 | 0 | 0 | P |
| RODGER | C.Palace | 11 | 9 | 2 | 2 | 3 | 0 | - | - | N |
| ROLLING | Leicester City | 1 | 1 | 0 | 6 | 1 | 0 | 0 | 0 | P |
| ROSE | Arsenal | 1 | 1 | 0 | 12 | 1 | 0 | 0 | 0 | P |
| ROSENTHAL | Tottenham H. | 20 | 4 | 16 | 6 | 0 | 1 | 0 | 0 | P |
| ROWETT | Derby County | 35 | 35 | 0 | 0 | 2 | 2 | 6 | 0 | P |
| ROWLAND | West Ham U. | 15 | 11 | 4 | 11 | 8 | 1 | 5 | 0 | P |
| RUDDOCK | Liverpool | 17 | 15 | 2 | 17 | 3 | 1 | 2 | 0 | P |
| RUSH | Leeds U. | 36 | 34 | 2 | 0 | 4 | 3 | 6 | 0 | P |
| SALAKO | Coventry City | 24 | 23 | 1 | 0 | 2 | 1 | 0 | 0 | P |
| SCALES J. | Liverpool | 3 | 3 | 0 | 1 | 2 | 0 | 0 | 0 | P |
| SCALES J. | Tottenham H. | 12 | 10 | 2 | 0 | 1 | 0 | 0 | 0 | P |
| SCHMEICHEL | Manchester U. | 36 | 36 | 0 | 0 | 0 | 0 | 2 | 0 | P |
| SCHOLES | Manchester U. | 24 | 16 | 8 | 7 | 7 | 3 | 6 | 0 | P |
| SCIMECA | Aston Villa | 17 | 11 | 6 | 9 | 0 | 0 | 1 | 0 | P |
| SCULLY | C.Palace | 1 | 0 | 1 | 0 | 0 | 0 | - | - | N |
| SEALEY | West Ham U. | 2 | 1 | 1 | 22 | 0 | 0 | 0 | 0 | P |
| SEAMAN | Arsenal | 22 | 22 | 0 | 0 | 0 | 0 | 0 | 0 | P |

| Player | Team | Tot | St | Sb | Snu | PS | Gls | Y | R | Lge |
|--------|------|-----|-----|-----|-----|-----|-----|-----|-----|-----|
| SELLARS | Bolton W. | 42 | 40 | 2 | 0 | 7 | 8 | - | - | N |
| SELLEY | Arsenal | 1 | 0 | 1 | 3 | 0 | 0 | 0 | 0 | P |
| SHARPE | Leeds U. | 26 | 26 | 0 | 3 | 4 | 5 | 1 | 0 | P |
| SHAW | Arsenal | 8 | 1 | 7 | 17 | 1 | 2 | 0 | 0 | P |
| SHAW | Coventry City | 35 | 35 | 0 | 2 | 2 | 0 | 3 | 0 | P |
| SHEARER | Newcastle U. | 31 | 31 | 0 | 0 | 1 | 25 | 5 | 0 | P |
| SHEERIN | Chelsea | 1 | 0 | 1 | 0 | 0 | 0 | 0 | 0 | P |
| SHEPHERD | Leeds U. | 1 | 1 | 0 | 0 | 0 | 0 | 0 | 0 | P |
| SHERIDAN | Barnsley | 41 | 39 | 2 | 0 | 6 | 2 | - | - | N |
| SHERIDAN J. | Bolton W. | 19 | 12 | 7 | 7 | 1 | 2 | - | - | N |
| SHERIDAN J. | Sheffield W. | 2 | 0 | 2 | 2 | 0 | 0 | 0 | 0 | P |
| SHERINGHAM | Tottenham H. | 29 | 29 | 0 | 0 | 0 | 7 | 6 | 0 | P |
| SHERWOOD | Blackburn R. | 37 | 37 | 0 | 0 | 3 | 3 | 7 | 1 | P |
| SHILTON P. | Coventry City | 0 | 0 | 0 | 2 | 0 | 0 | 0 | 0 | P |
| SHILTON P. | West Ham U. | 0 | 0 | 0 | 8 | 0 | 0 | 0 | 0 | P |
| SHIPPERLEY N. | C.Palace | 32 | 29 | 3 | 1 | 8 | 12 | - | - | N |
| SHIPPERLEY N. | Southampton | 10 | 9 | 1 | 0 | 3 | 1 | 0 | 0 | P |
| SHIRTLIFF | Barnsley | 13 | 12 | 1 | 0 | 3 | 0 | - | - | N |
| SHORT | Everton | 23 | 19 | 4 | 6 | 4 | 2 | 6 | 0 | P |
| SIMPSON | Derby County | 19 | 0 | 19 | 12 | 0 | 2 | 0 | 0 | P |
| SINCLAIR | Chelsea | 20 | 17 | 3 | 6 | 0 | 1 | 5 | 0 | P |
| SINTON | Tottenham H. | 33 | 32 | 1 | 0 | 9 | 6 | 5 | 0 | P |
| SLATER | Leicester City | 0 | 0 | 0 | 1 | 0 | 0 | 0 | 0 | P |
| SLATER R. | Southampton | 30 | 22 | 8 | 1 | 3 | 2 | 5 | 0 | P |
| SLATER R. | West Ham U. | 3 | 2 | 1 | 0 | 1 | 0 | 1 | 0 | P |
| SMALL | Bolton W. | 11 | 10 | 1 | 3 | 1 | 0 | - | - | N |
| SOLIS | Derby County | 2 | 0 | 2 | 2 | 0 | 0 | 0 | 0 | P |
| SOLSKJAER | Manchester U. | 33 | 25 | 8 | 2 | 11 | 18 | 1 | 0 | P |
| SORENSEN | Southampton | 0 | 0 | 0 | 0 | 0 | 0 | 0 | 0 | P |
| SOUTHALL | Everton | 34 | 34 | 0 | 4 | 1 | 0 | 2 | 0 | P |
| SOUTHGATE | Aston Villa | 28 | 28 | 0 | 0 | 1 | 1 | 1 | 0 | P |
| SPEARE | Everton | 0 | 0 | 0 | 3 | 0 | 0 | 0 | 0 | P |
| SPEED | Everton | 37 | 37 | 0 | 0 | 0 | 9 | 8 | 0 | P |
| SPENCER | Chelsea | 4 | 0 | 4 | 5 | 0 | 0 | 2 | 0 | P |
| SRNICEK | Newcastle U. | 22 | 22 | 0 | 16 | 0 | 0 | 0 | 0 | P |
| STAUNTON | Aston Villa | 30 | 30 | 0 | 0 | 5 | 2 | 5 | 1 | P |
| STEFANOVIC | Sheffield W. | 29 | 27 | 2 | 5 | 3 | 2 | 6 | 0 | P |
| STIMAC | Derby County | 21 | 21 | 0 | 0 | 1 | 1 | 9 | 0 | P |
| STRACHAN | Coventry City | 9 | 3 | 6 | 9 | 3 | 0 | 1 | 0 | P |
| STUART | Everton | 35 | 29 | 6 | 2 | 3 | 5 | 4 | 0 | P |
| STURRIDGE | Derby County | 30 | 29 | 1 | 0 | 5 | 11 | 9 | 0 | P |
| SULLIVAN | Wimbledon | 36 | 36 | 0 | 1 | 0 | 0 | 1 | 0 | P |
| SUTTON | Blackburn R. | 25 | 24 | 1 | 0 | 3 | 11 | 4 | 0 | P |

Fantasy Football Handbook

| Player | Team | Tot | St | Sb | Snu | PS | Gls | Y | R | Lge |
|--------|------|-----|-----|-----|-----|-----|-----|-----|-----|-----|
| TAGGART | Bolton W. | 43 | 43 | 0 | 0 | 0 | 3 | - | - | N |
| TAYLOR | Aston Villa | 34 | 29 | 5 | 0 | 2 | 2 | 4 | 0 | P |
| TAYLOR | Bolton W. | 11 | 2 | 9 | 13 | 0 | 1 | - | - | N |
| TAYLOR | Derby County | 3 | 3 | 0 | 28 | 0 | 0 | 0 | 0 | P |
| TAYLOR | Leicester City | 25 | 20 | 5 | 4 | 9 | 0 | 2 | 0 | P |
| TAYLOR | Southampton | 18 | 18 | 0 | 0 | 0 | 0 | 1 | 0 | P |
| TELFER | Coventry City | 34 | 31 | 3 | 1 | 2 | 0 | 6 | 0 | P |
| TEN HEUVEL | Barnsley | 2 | 0 | 2 | 3 | 0 | 0 | - | - | N |
| THATCHER | Wimbledon | 9 | 9 | 0 | 0 | 1 | 0 | 2 | 0 | P |
| THOMAS | Liverpool | 30 | 28 | 2 | 3 | 2 | 3 | 4 | 0 | P |
| THOMPSON | Barnsley | 24 | 24 | 0 | 1 | 4 | 5 | - | - | N |
| THOMPSON | Bolton W. | 34 | 34 | 0 | 0 | 3 | 11 | - | - | N |
| THOMPSON | Liverpool | 3 | 1 | 2 | 2 | 0 | 0 | 2 | 0 | P |
| THOMSEN | Everton | 16 | 15 | 1 | 0 | 5 | 0 | 3 | 0 | P |
| THORNLEY | Manchester U. | 2 | 1 | 1 | 5 | 1 | 0 | 0 | 0 | P |
| TILER | Aston Villa | 11 | 9 | 2 | 7 | 1 | 1 | 1 | 0 | P |
| TINKLER | Leeds U. | 3 | 1 | 2 | 1 | 1 | 0 | 0 | 0 | P |
| TODD | Bolton W. | 15 | 6 | 9 | 10 | 1 | 0 | - | - | N |
| TOWNSEND | Aston Villa | 34 | 34 | 0 | 0 | 2 | 2 | 8 | 0 | P |
| TROLLOPE | C.Palace | 9 | 0 | 9 | 1 | 0 | 0 | - | - | N |
| TROLLOPE | Derby County | 14 | 13 | 1 | 2 | 1 | 1 | 3 | 0 | P |
| TRUSTFULL | Sheffield W. | 19 | 9 | 10 | 7 | 8 | 3 | 3 | 0 | P |
| TUTTLE | C.Palace | 41 | 39 | 2 | 0 | 6 | 0 | - | - | N |
| | | | | | | | | | | |
| UNSWORTH | Everton | 34 | 32 | 2 | 0 | 3 | 5 | 5 | 1 | P |
| VAN DER GOUW | Manchester U. | 2 | 2 | 0 | 34 | 0 | 0 | 0 | 0 | P |
| VAN DER LAAN | Derby County | 16 | 15 | 1 | 7 | 7 | 2 | 1 | 0 | P |
| VAN DER VELDEN | Barnsley | 2 | 1 | 1 | 0 | 1 | 0 | - | - | N |
| VAN GOBBEL | Southampton | 25 | 24 | 1 | 1 | 3 | 1 | 10 | 1 | P |
| VEART | C.Palace | 39 | 35 | 4 | 5 | 8 | 6 | - | - | N |
| VEGA | Tottenham H. | 8 | 8 | 0 | 0 | 2 | 1 | 2 | 0 | P |
| VENISON | Southampton | 2 | 2 | 0 | 0 | 0 | 0 | 1 | 1 | P |
| VIALLI | Chelsea | 28 | 23 | 5 | 5 | 3 | 9 | 5 | 0 | P |
| VIEIRA | Arsenal | 31 | 30 | 1 | 0 | 3 | 2 | 11 | 0 | P |
| | | | | | | | | | | |
| WALKER | Sheffield W. | 36 | 36 | 0 | 0 | 1 | 0 | 1 | 1 | P |
| WALKER | Tottenham H. | 37 | 37 | 0 | 0 | 1 | 0 | 0 | 0 | P |
| WALLACE | Leeds U. | 22 | 17 | 5 | 8 | 7 | 3 | 5 | 0 | P |
| WALSH | Leicester City | 22 | 22 | 0 | 0 | 0 | 2 | 3 | 1 | P |
| WANCHOPE | Derby County | 5 | 2 | 3 | 0 | 2 | 1 | 0 | 0 | P |
| WARD | Bolton W. | 11 | 10 | 1 | 3 | 0 | 0 | - | - | N |
| WARD | Derby County | 30 | 25 | 5 | 1 | 7 | 10 | 2 | 0 | P |
| WARHURST | Blackburn R. | 11 | 5 | 6 | 10 | 3 | 2 | 1 | 0 | P |

| Player | Team | Tot | St | Sb | Snu | PS | Gls | Y | R | Lge |
|--------|------|-----|-----|-----|-----|-----|-----|-----|-----|-----|
| WARNER | Liverpool | 0 | 0 | 0 | 38 | 0 | 0 | 0 | 0 | P |
| WARREN | Southampton | 1 | 0 | 1 | 1 | 0 | 0 | 0 | 0 | P |
| WASSALL | Derby County | 0 | 0 | 0 | 0 | 0 | 0 | 0 | 0 | P |
| WATKINSON | Southampton | 2 | 0 | 2 | 1 | 0 | 0 | 0 | 0 | P |
| WATSON | Barnsley | 46 | 46 | 0 | 0 | 0 | 0 | - | - | N |
| WATSON | Everton | 29 | 29 | 0 | 0 | 2 | 1 | 4 | 0 | P |
| WATSON | Newcastle U. | 36 | 33 | 3 | 2 | 3 | 1 | 3 | 0 | P |
| WATSON | Southampton | 15 | 7 | 8 | 3 | 6 | 2 | 0 | 0 | P |
| WATTS | Leicester City | 26 | 22 | 4 | 8 | 4 | 1 | 3 | 0 | P |
| WETHERALL | Leeds U. | 29 | 25 | 4 | 7 | 3 | 0 | 7 | 0 | P |
| WHELAN | Coventry City | 35 | 34 | 1 | 0 | 9 | 6 | 9 | 0 | P |
| WHITLOW | Leicester City | 17 | 14 | 3 | 5 | 1 | 0 | 2 | 0 | P |
| WHITTINGHAM | Sheffield W. | 33 | 29 | 4 | 1 | 10 | 3 | 1 | 0 | P |
| WILCOX | Blackburn R. | 28 | 26 | 2 | 2 | 5 | 2 | 3 | 0 | P |
| WILKINSON | Barnsley | 45 | 45 | 0 | 0 | 8 | 9 | - | - | N |
| WILLEMS | Derby County | 16 | 7 | 9 | 8 | 7 | 2 | 0 | 0 | P |
| WILLIAMS | Sheffield W. | 1 | 0 | 1 | 0 | 0 | 0 | 0 | 0 | P |
| WILLIAMS P. | Coventry City | 32 | 29 | 3 | 2 | 1 | 2 | 7 | 0 | P |
| WILLIAMSON | West Ham U. | 15 | 13 | 2 | 0 | 2 | 0 | 0 | 0 | P |
| WILLIS | Coventry City | 0 | 0 | 0 | 2 | 0 | 0 | 0 | 0 | P |
| WILSON | Leicester City | 2 | 0 | 2 | 2 | 0 | 1 | 0 | 0 | P |
| WILSON | Tottenham H. | 26 | 23 | 3 | 3 | 1 | 1 | 0 | 0 | P |
| WINTERBURN | Arsenal | 38 | 38 | 0 | 0 | 3 | 0 | 5 | 0 | P |
| WISE | Chelsea | 31 | 27 | 4 | 0 | 4 | 4 | 7 | 0 | P |
| WOODS | Southampton | 4 | 4 | 0 | 0 | 1 | 0 | 0 | 0 | P |
| WRIGHT | Arsenal | 35 | 30 | 5 | 0 | 4 | 23 | 10 | 1 | P |
| WRIGHT | Aston Villa | 38 | 38 | 0 | 0 | 0 | 1 | 2 | 0 | P |
| WRIGHT | Derby County | 0 | 0 | 0 | 2 | 0 | 0 | 0 | 0 | P |
| WRIGHT | Liverpool | 33 | 33 | 0 | 0 | 3 | 0 | 6 | 0 | P |
| | | | | | | | | | | |
| YATES | Derby County | 10 | 8 | 2 | 3 | 2 | 0 | 0 | 0 | P |
| YEBOAH | Leeds U. | 7 | 6 | 1 | 4 | 3 | 0 | 2 | 0 | P |
| YORKE | Aston Villa | 37 | 37 | 0 | 0 | 3 | 17 | 2 | 0 | P |
| ZOLA | Chelsea | 23 | 22 | 1 | 1 | 4 | 8 | 0 | 0 | P |

**Fantasy Football Handbook**

# Sorted Appearances

THE FOLLOWING final few pages of lists arrange players by virtue of where they make a large number of their appearances from. The pages immediately following outline details for the 17 clubs from last season that are in the Premier League for the 1997-98 season. The final pages provide details for those clubs who have been promoted into the Premiership namely, Barnsley, Bolton Wanderers and Crystal Palace. The main reason these are dealt with on a separate basis is that the promoted clubs played 46 games in the Nationwide Division One compared to the 38 of the Premiership clubs and would provided an unbalanced view if included in the original sort.

The first list provide details of players who have feature in 30 or more games – this is total appearances. As you can see only ten players started in every game last season and only three of those completed all 38 games (Ehiogu, James and McAllister)!

The second set detail players who were subbed the most – notice the top two are both Wimbledon players. Manager Joe Kinnear loves to protect leads late on in games by throwing on defence minded players for his attack force.

The next list details players who were used most from the bench – Paul Simpson of Derby County had the overall honour in 1997-98 – in fact he didn't start a single game as the stats show.

Finally we can identify who were the most unused subs, ie, who spent the most time on the bench without getting off of it. The answer to such a question would be the Liverpool reserve 'keeper, Tony Warner.

These figures are repeated for the promoted clubs.

# Players Who Played in 30+ Games 1996-97

| Player | Team | Tot | St | Sb | Snu | PS | Gls | Y | R | Lge |
|--------|------|-----|-----|-----|-----|-----|-----|-----|-----|-----|
| BJORNEBYE | Liverpool | 38 | 38 | 0 | 0 | 3 | 2 | 3 | 0 | P |
| CAMPBELL | Tottenham H. | 38 | 38 | 0 | 0 | 2 | 0 | 1 | 0 | P |
| EHIOGU | Aston Villa | 38 | 38 | 0 | 0 | 0 | 3 | 4 | 0 | P |
| JAMES | Liverpool | 38 | 38 | 0 | 0 | 0 | 0 | 0 | 0 | P |
| McALLISTER | Coventry City | 38 | 38 | 0 | 0 | 0 | 6 | 1 | 0 | P |
| NOLAN | Sheffield W. | 38 | 38 | 0 | 0 | 1 | 1 | 1 | 0 | P |
| OGRIZOVIC | Coventry City | 38 | 38 | 0 | 0 | 1 | 0 | 1 | 0 | P |
| PRESSMAN | Sheffield W. | 38 | 38 | 0 | 0 | 1 | 0 | 0 | 0 | P |
| WINTERBURN | Arsenal | 38 | 38 | 0 | 0 | 3 | 0 | 5 | 0 | P |
| WRIGHT | Aston Villa | 38 | 38 | 0 | 0 | 0 | 1 | 2 | 0 | P |
| CLARKE | Sheffield W. | 38 | 0 | 1 | 37 | 0 | 0 | 0 | 1 | P |
| ATHERTON | Sheffield W. | 37 | 37 | 0 | 0 | 1 | 2 | 7 | 0 | P |
| KENNA | Blackburn R. | 37 | 37 | 0 | 0 | 3 | 0 | 2 | 0 | P |
| MARTYN | Leeds U. | 37 | 37 | 0 | 0 | 0 | 0 | 1 | 0 | P |
| McMANAMAN | Liverpool | 37 | 37 | 0 | 0 | 1 | 7 | 5 | 0 | P |
| PERRY | Wimbledon | 37 | 37 | 0 | 0 | 2 | 1 | 0 | 0 | P |
| SHERWOOD | Blackburn R. | 37 | 37 | 0 | 0 | 3 | 3 | 7 | 1 | P |
| SPEED | Everton | 37 | 37 | 0 | 0 | 0 | 9 | 8 | 0 | P |
| WALKER | Tottenham H. | 37 | 37 | 0 | 0 | 1 | 0 | 0 | 0 | P |
| YORKE | Aston Villa | 37 | 37 | 0 | 0 | 3 | 17 | 2 | 0 | P |
| McATEER | Liverpool | 37 | 36 | 1 | 0 | 2 | 1 | 6 | 0 | P |
| MAGILTON | Southampton | 37 | 31 | 6 | 1 | 7 | 4 | 4 | 0 | P |
| BARRETT | Everton | 36 | 36 | 0 | 0 | 0 | 0 | 1 | 0 | P |
| BERG | Blackburn R. | 36 | 36 | 0 | 0 | 0 | 2 | 3 | 0 | P |
| CANTONA | Manchester U. | 36 | 36 | 0 | 0 | 1 | 11 | 5 | 0 | P |
| CUNNINGHAM | Wimbledon | 36 | 36 | 0 | 0 | 2 | 0 | 5 | 0 | P |
| FLOWERS | Blackburn R. | 36 | 36 | 0 | 2 | 0 | 0 | 2 | 0 | P |
| GRAYSON | Leicester City | 36 | 36 | 0 | 0 | 1 | 0 | 4 | 0 | P |
| MIKLOSKO | West Ham U. | 36 | 36 | 0 | 0 | 1 | 0 | 0 | 0 | P |
| SCHMEICHEL | Manchester U. | 36 | 36 | 0 | 0 | 0 | 0 | 2 | 0 | P |
| SULLIVAN | Wimbledon | 36 | 36 | 0 | 1 | 0 | 0 | 1 | 0 | P |
| WALKER | Sheffield W. | 36 | 36 | 0 | 0 | 1 | 0 | 1 | 1 | P |
| LAURSEN | Derby County | 36 | 35 | 1 | 0 | 7 | 1 | 2 | 0 | P |
| GAYLE | Wimbledon | 36 | 34 | 2 | 0 | 12 | 8 | 2 | 0 | P |
| KELLY | Leeds U. | 36 | 34 | 2 | 0 | 2 | 2 | 5 | 0 | P |
| RUSH | Leeds U. | 36 | 34 | 2 | 0 | 4 | 3 | 6 | 0 | P |
| BECKHAM | Manchester U. | 36 | 33 | 3 | 1 | 3 | 8 | 6 | 0 | P |
| WATSON | Newcastle U. | 36 | 33 | 3 | 2 | 3 | 1 | 3 | 0 | P |
| DAILLY | Derby County | 36 | 31 | 5 | 0 | 6 | 3 | 6 | 0 | P |
| BILIC | West Ham U. | 35 | 35 | 0 | 0 | 3 | 2 | 10 | 0 | P |
| HENDRY | Blackburn R. | 35 | 35 | 0 | 0 | 3 | 1 | 4 | 0 | P |

| Player | Team | Tot | St | Sb | Snu | PS | Gls | Y | R | Lge |
|--------|------|-----|-----|-----|-----|-----|-----|-----|-----|-----|
| HESKEY | Leicester City | 35 | 35 | 0 | 0 | 4 | 10 | 8 | 0 | P |
| LENNON | Leicester City | 35 | 35 | 0 | 0 | 0 | 1 | 8 | 0 | P |
| PEACOCK | Newcastle U. | 35 | 35 | 0 | 3 | 0 | 1 | 2 | 0 | P |
| POWELL C. | Derby County | 35 | 35 | 0 | 0 | 4 | 0 | 4 | 0 | P |
| ROWETT | Derby County | 35 | 35 | 0 | 0 | 2 | 2 | 6 | 0 | P |
| SHAW | Coventry City | 35 | 35 | 0 | 2 | 2 | 0 | 3 | 0 | P |
| BARNES | Liverpool | 35 | 34 | 1 | 2 | 2 | 4 | 0 | 0 | P |
| IZZET | Leicester City | 35 | 34 | 1 | 0 | 6 | 3 | 6 | 0 | P |
| WHELAN | Coventry City | 35 | 34 | 1 | 0 | 9 | 6 | 9 | 0 | P |
| BOOTH | Sheffield W. | 35 | 32 | 3 | 0 | 7 | 10 | 3 | 0 | P |
| HUGHES M. | Chelsea | 35 | 32 | 3 | 0 | 5 | 8 | 6 | 0 | P |
| WRIGHT | Arsenal | 35 | 30 | 5 | 0 | 4 | 23 | 10 | 1 | P |
| STUART | Everton | 35 | 29 | 6 | 2 | 3 | 5 | 4 | 0 | P |
| ASANOVIC | Derby County | 34 | 34 | 0 | 0 | 11 | 6 | 3 | 0 | P |
| GALLACHER | Blackburn R. | 34 | 34 | 0 | 0 | 10 | 10 | 6 | 0 | P |
| PETRESCU | Chelsea | 34 | 34 | 0 | 0 | 4 | 3 | 4 | 0 | P |
| SOUTHALL | Everton | 34 | 34 | 0 | 4 | 1 | 0 | 2 | 0 | P |
| TOWNSEND | Aston Villa | 34 | 34 | 0 | 0 | 2 | 2 | 8 | 0 | P |
| ARDLEY | Wimbledon | 34 | 33 | 1 | 1 | 4 | 2 | 1 | 0 | P |
| CALDERWOOD | Tottenham H. | 34 | 33 | 1 | 1 | 0 | 0 | 6 | 0 | P |
| DI MATTEO | Chelsea | 34 | 33 | 1 | 3 | 5 | 6 | 5 | 0 | P |
| DUBLIN | Coventry City | 34 | 33 | 1 | 0 | 2 | 14 | 5 | 0 | P |
| NELSON | Aston Villa | 34 | 33 | 1 | 1 | 4 | 0 | 6 | 0 | P |
| PEMBRIDGE | Sheffield W. | 34 | 33 | 1 | 0 | 2 | 6 | 7 | 0 | P |
| PRIOR | Leicester City | 34 | 33 | 1 | 1 | 4 | 0 | 4 | 0 | P |
| UNSWORTH | Everton | 34 | 32 | 2 | 0 | 3 | 5 | 5 | 1 | P |
| TELFER | Coventry City | 34 | 31 | 3 | 1 | 2 | 0 | 6 | 0 | P |
| TAYLOR | Aston Villa | 34 | 29 | 5 | 0 | 2 | 2 | 4 | 0 | P |
| BOULD | Arsenal | 33 | 33 | 0 | 1 | 2 | 0 | 6 | 0 | P |
| KEOWN | Arsenal | 33 | 33 | 0 | 0 | 2 | 1 | 7 | 0 | P |
| WRIGHT | Liverpool | 33 | 33 | 0 | 0 | 3 | 0 | 6 | 0 | P |
| LEE | Newcastle U. | 33 | 32 | 1 | 0 | 7 | 5 | 7 | 0 | P |
| SINTON | Tottenham H. | 33 | 32 | 1 | 0 | 9 | 6 | 5 | 0 | P |
| FERGUSON | Everton | 33 | 31 | 2 | 1 | 0 | 10 | 5 | 1 | P |
| HUGHES | West Ham U. | 33 | 31 | 2 | 0 | 1 | 3 | 5 | 0 | P |
| WHITTINGHAM | Sheffield W. | 33 | 29 | 4 | 1 | 10 | 3 | 1 | 0 | P |
| POWELL D. | Derby County | 33 | 27 | 6 | 0 | 5 | 1 | 7 | 0 | P |
| SOLSKJAER | Manchester U. | 33 | 25 | 8 | 2 | 11 | 18 | 1 | 0 | P |
| BLINKER | Sheffield W. | 33 | 15 | 18 | 2 | 5 | 1 | 6 | 0 | P |
| BATTY | Newcastle U. | 32 | 32 | 0 | 0 | 1 | 1 | 10 | 1 | P |
| BOWYER | Leeds U. | 32 | 32 | 0 | 0 | 4 | 4 | 6 | 0 | P |
| EARLE | Wimbledon | 32 | 32 | 0 | 0 | 4 | 7 | 3 | 0 | P |
| FOWLER | Liverpool | 32 | 32 | 0 | 0 | 4 | 18 | 4 | 1 | P |

| | | | | | | | | | |
|---|---|---|---|---|---|---|---|---|---|
| HOWELLS | Tottenham H. | 32 | 32 | 0 | 0 | 6 | 2 | 7 | 0 | P |
| MERSON | Arsenal | 32 | 32 | 0 | 2 | 5 | 6 | 1 | 0 | P |
| DIXON | Arsenal | 32 | 31 | 1 | 0 | 3 | 2 | 8 | 0 | P |
| HOULT | Derby County | 32 | 31 | 1 | 5 | 0 | 0 | 0 | 0 | P |
| CLARIDGE | Leicester City | 32 | 29 | 3 | 1 | 7 | 12 | 2 | 0 | P |
| WILLIAMS P. | Coventry City | 32 | 29 | 3 | 2 | 1 | 2 | 7 | 0 | P |
| RADEBE | Leeds U. | 32 | 28 | 4 | 2 | 3 | 0 | 6 | 0 | P |
| GILLESPIE | Newcastle U. | 32 | 23 | 9 | 5 | 8 | 1 | 2 | 1 | P |
| CLARKE | Chelsea | 31 | 31 | 0 | 1 | 1 | 0 | 7 | 0 | P |
| DICKS | West Ham U. | 31 | 31 | 0 | 0 | 0 | 6 | 6 | 0 | P |
| KELLER | Leicester City | 31 | 31 | 0 | 0 | 0 | 0 | 0 | 0 | P |
| SHEARER | Newcastle U. | 31 | 31 | 0 | 0 | 1 | 25 | 5 | 0 | P |
| FERDINAND | Newcastle U. | 31 | 30 | 1 | 1 | 8 | 16 | 3 | 0 | P |
| NEVILLE G. | Manchester U. | 31 | 30 | 1 | 3 | 2 | 1 | 4 | 0 | P |
| VIEIRA | Arsenal | 31 | 30 | 1 | 0 | 3 | 2 | 11 | 0 | P |
| IRWIN | Manchester U. | 31 | 29 | 2 | 3 | 2 | 1 | 1 | 0 | P |
| KIMBLE | Wimbledon | 31 | 28 | 3 | 4 | 0 | 0 | 2 | 0 | P |
| WISE | Chelsea | 31 | 27 | 4 | 0 | 4 | 4 | 7 | 0 | P |
| BURLEY | Chelsea | 31 | 26 | 5 | 1 | 8 | 2 | 3 | 0 | P |
| JOHNSEN | Manchester U. | 31 | 26 | 5 | 2 | 6 | 0 | 3 | 0 | P |
| Le TISSIER | Southampton | 31 | 25 | 6 | 0 | 8 | 13 | 5 | 0 | P |
| PARKER | Leicester City | 31 | 22 | 9 | 1 | 5 | 2 | 0 | 0 | P |
| STAUNTON | Aston Villa | 30 | 30 | 0 | 0 | 5 | 2 | 5 | 1 | P |
| MILOSEVIC | Aston Villa | 30 | 29 | 1 | 0 | 8 | 10 | 6 | 0 | P |
| OSTENSTAD | Southampton | 30 | 29 | 1 | 0 | 5 | 10 | 3 | 0 | P |
| STURRIDGE | Derby County | 30 | 29 | 1 | 0 | 5 | 11 | 9 | 0 | P |
| EKOKU | Wimbledon | 30 | 28 | 2 | 0 | 17 | 11 | 4 | 0 | P |
| THOMAS | Liverpool | 30 | 28 | 2 | 3 | 2 | 3 | 4 | 0 | P |
| COLLYMORE | Liverpool | 30 | 25 | 5 | 5 | 9 | 12 | 3 | 0 | P |
| WARD | Derby County | 30 | 25 | 5 | 1 | 7 | 10 | 2 | 0 | P |
| SLATER R. | Southampton | 30 | 22 | 8 | 1 | 3 | 2 | 5 | 0 | P |
| PARLOUR | Arsenal | 30 | 17 | 13 | 4 | 2 | 2 | 6 | 0 | P |

## Players Who Were Subbed The Most

| Player | Team | PS | Tot | St | Sbs | Snu | Gls | Y | R | Lge |
|---|---|---|---|---|---|---|---|---|---|---|
| EKOKU | Wimbledon | 17 | 30 | 28 | 2 | 0 | 11 | 4 | 0 | P |
| GAYLE | Wimbledon | 12 | 36 | 34 | 2 | 0 | 8 | 2 | 0 | P |
| ASPRILLA | Newcastle U. | 12 | 24 | 17 | 7 | 4 | 4 | 1 | 0 | P |
| ASANOVIC | Derby County | 11 | 34 | 34 | 0 | 0 | 6 | 3 | 0 | P |
| SOLSKJAER | Manchester U. | 11 | 33 | 25 | 8 | 2 | 18 | 1 | 0 | P |
| HUMPHREYS | Sheffield W. | 11 | 29 | 14 | 15 | 8 | 3 | 2 | 0 | P |
| BERKOVIC | Southampton | 11 | 28 | 26 | 2 | 2 | 4 | 4 | 0 | P |
| OAKLEY | Southampton | 11 | 28 | 23 | 5 | 0 | 3 | 0 | 0 | P |
| CARBONE | Sheffield W. | 11 | 25 | 24 | 1 | 0 | 6 | 3 | 0 | P |

| Player | Team | PS | Tot | St | Sbs | Snu | Gls | Y | R | Lge |
|---|---|---|---|---|---|---|---|---|---|---|
| HIRST | Sheffield W. | 11 | 25 | 20 | 5 | 0 | 6 | 3 | 1 | P |
| GALLACHER | Blackburn R. | 10 | 34 | 34 | 0 | 0 | 10 | 6 | 0 | P |
| WHITTINGHAM | Sheffield W. | 10 | 33 | 29 | 4 | 1 | 3 | 1 | 0 | P |
| DRAPER | Aston Villa | 10 | 29 | 28 | 1 | 2 | 0 | 4 | 1 | P |
| JESS | Coventry City | 10 | 27 | 19 | 8 | 7 | 0 | 0 | 0 | P |
| CURCIC | Aston Villa | 10 | 22 | 17 | 5 | 6 | 0 | 4 | 0 | P |
| POBORSKY | Manchester U. | 10 | 22 | 15 | 7 | 15 | 3 | 1 | 0 | P |
| WHELAN | Coventry City | 9 | 35 | 34 | 1 | 0 | 6 | 9 | 0 | P |
| SINTON | Tottenham H. | 9 | 33 | 32 | 1 | 0 | 6 | 5 | 0 | P |
| COLLYMORE | Liverpool | 9 | 30 | 25 | 5 | 5 | 12 | 3 | 0 | P |
| BISHOP | West Ham U. | 9 | 29 | 26 | 3 | 2 | 1 | 2 | 0 | P |
| TAYLOR | Leicester City | 9 | 25 | 20 | 5 | 4 | 0 | 2 | 0 | P |
| GILLESPIE | Newcastle U. | 8 | 32 | 23 | 9 | 5 | 1 | 2 | 1 | P |
| BURLEY | Chelsea | 8 | 31 | 26 | 5 | 1 | 2 | 3 | 0 | P |
| FERDINAND | Newcastle U. | 8 | 31 | 30 | 1 | 1 | 16 | 3 | 0 | P |
| Le TISSIER | Southampton | 8 | 31 | 25 | 6 | 0 | 13 | 5 | 0 | P |
| MILOSEVIC | Aston Villa | 8 | 30 | 29 | 1 | 0 | 10 | 6 | 0 | P |
| BERGKAMP | Arsenal | 8 | 29 | 28 | 1 | 0 | 12 | 6 | 0 | P |
| NIELSEN | Tottenham H. | 8 | 29 | 28 | 1 | 1 | 6 | 6 | 0 | P |
| FLITCROFT | Blackburn R. | 8 | 28 | 27 | 1 | 2 | 3 | 1 | 0 | P |
| LEONHARDSEN | Wimbledon | 8 | 27 | 27 | 0 | 1 | 5 | 0 | 0 | P |
| BUTT | Manchester U. | 8 | 26 | 24 | 2 | 0 | 5 | 5 | 0 | P |
| CHARLTON | Southampton | 8 | 26 | 24 | 2 | 1 | 0 | 1 | 0 | P |
| NICOL | Sheffield W. | 8 | 23 | 19 | 4 | 9 | 0 | 0 | 0 | P |
| HARTSON | Arsenal | 8 | 19 | 14 | 5 | 2 | 3 | 9 | 0 | P |
| TRUSTFULL | Sheffield W. | 8 | 19 | 9 | 10 | 7 | 3 | 3 | 0 | P |
| ROWLAND | West Ham U. | 8 | 15 | 11 | 4 | 11 | 1 | 5 | 0 | P |
| PEDERSEN | Blackburn R. | 8 | 11 | 6 | 5 | 1 | 1 | 0 | 0 | P |
| MAGILTON | Southampton | 7 | 37 | 31 | 6 | 1 | 4 | 4 | 0 | P |
| LAURSEN | Derby County | 7 | 36 | 35 | 1 | 0 | 1 | 2 | 0 | P |
| BOOTH | Sheffield W. | 7 | 35 | 32 | 3 | 0 | 10 | 3 | 0 | P |
| LEE | Newcastle U. | 7 | 33 | 32 | 1 | 0 | 5 | 7 | 0 | P |
| CLARIDGE | Leicester City | 7 | 32 | 29 | 3 | 1 | 12 | 2 | 0 | P |
| WARD | Derby County | 7 | 30 | 25 | 5 | 1 | 10 | 2 | 0 | P |
| JONES | Wimbledon | 7 | 29 | 29 | 0 | 0 | 3 | 5 | 1 | P |
| MONCUR | West Ham U. | 7 | 27 | 26 | 1 | 1 | 2 | 8 | 0 | P |
| BRANCH | Everton | 7 | 25 | 13 | 12 | 7 | 3 | 2 | 0 | P |
| HUCKERBY | Coventry City | 7 | 25 | 21 | 4 | 0 | 5 | 2 | 0 | P |
| SCHOLES | Manchester U. | 7 | 24 | 16 | 8 | 7 | 3 | 6 | 0 | P |
| WALLACE | Leeds U. | 7 | 22 | 17 | 5 | 8 | 3 | 5 | 0 | P |
| ANDERTON | Tottenham H. | 7 | 16 | 14 | 2 | 0 | 3 | 4 | 0 | P |
| VAN DER LAAN | Derby County | 7 | 16 | 15 | 1 | 7 | 2 | 1 | 0 | P |
| WILLEMS | Derby County | 7 | 16 | 7 | 9 | 8 | 2 | 0 | 0 | P |

| Player | Team | PS | Tot | St | Sbs | Snu | Gls | Y | R | Lge |
|--------|------|----|-----|----|----|----|----|---|---|-----|
| COUZENS | Leeds U. | 7 | 10 | 7 | 3 | 4 | 1 | 2 | 0 | P |
| DAILLY | Derby County | 6 | 36 | 31 | 5 | 0 | 3 | 6 | 0 | P |
| IZZET | Leicester City | 6 | 35 | 34 | 1 | 0 | 3 | 6 | 0 | P |
| HOWELLS | Tottenham H. | 6 | 32 | 32 | 0 | 0 | 2 | 7 | 0 | P |
| JOHNSEN | Manchester U. | 6 | 31 | 26 | 5 | 2 | 0 | 3 | 0 | P |
| GIGGS | Manchester U. | 6 | 26 | 25 | 1 | 1 | 3 | 2 | 0 | P |
| FOX | Tottenham H. | 6 | 25 | 19 | 6 | 3 | 1 | 1 | 0 | P |
| MINTO | Chelsea | 6 | 25 | 24 | 1 | 4 | 4 | 6 | 0 | P |
| GINOLA | Newcastle U. | 6 | 24 | 20 | 4 | 7 | 1 | 3 | 0 | P |
| LAZARIDIS | West Ham U. | 6 | 22 | 13 | 9 | 3 | 1 | 2 | 0 | P |
| MYERS | Chelsea | 6 | 18 | 15 | 3 | 6 | 1 | 2 | 0 | P |
| CRUYFF | Manchester U. | 6 | 16 | 11 | 5 | 8 | 3 | 2 | 0 | P |
| FORD | Leeds U. | 6 | 16 | 15 | 1 | 13 | 1 | 4 | 0 | P |
| WATSON | Southampton | 6 | 15 | 7 | 8 | 3 | 2 | 0 | 0 | P |
| HUGHES | Arsenal | 6 | 14 | 9 | 5 | 3 | 1 | 1 | 0 | P |
| GOODMAN | Wimbledon | 6 | 13 | 6 | 7 | 6 | 1 | 0 | 0 | P |
| HUGHES P. | Chelsea | 6 | 12 | 8 | 4 | 3 | 2 | 1 | 0 | P |
| HUGHES M. | Chelsea | 5 | 35 | 32 | 3 | 0 | 8 | 6 | 0 | P |
| DI MATTEO | Chelsea | 5 | 34 | 33 | 1 | 3 | 6 | 5 | 0 | P |
| BLINKER | Sheffield W. | 5 | 33 | 15 | 18 | 2 | 1 | 6 | 0 | P |
| POWELL D. | Derby County | 5 | 33 | 27 | 6 | 0 | 1 | 7 | 0 | P |
| MERSON | Arsenal | 5 | 32 | 32 | 0 | 2 | 6 | 1 | 0 | P |
| PARKER | Leicester City | 5 | 31 | 22 | 9 | 1 | 2 | 0 | 0 | P |
| OSTENSTAD | Southampton | 5 | 30 | 29 | 1 | 0 | 10 | 3 | 0 | P |
| STAUNTON | Aston Villa | 5 | 30 | 30 | 0 | 0 | 2 | 5 | 1 | P |
| STURRIDGE | Derby County | 5 | 30 | 29 | 1 | 0 | 11 | 9 | 0 | P |
| PLATT | Arsenal | 5 | 28 | 27 | 1 | 0 | 4 | 4 | 0 | P |
| WILCOX | Blackburn R. | 5 | 28 | 26 | 2 | 2 | 2 | 3 | 0 | P |
| BREACKER | West Ham U. | 5 | 26 | 22 | 4 | 1 | 0 | 2 | 0 | P |
| BARMBY | Everton | 5 | 25 | 22 | 3 | 1 | 4 | 0 | 0 | P |
| BERGER | Liverpool | 5 | 23 | 13 | 10 | 9 | 6 | 0 | 0 | P |
| PORFIRIO | West Ham U. | 5 | 23 | 15 | 8 | 2 | 2 | 6 | 0 | P |
| KANCHELSKIS | Everton | 5 | 20 | 20 | 0 | 0 | 4 | 0 | 0 | P |
| OAKES | Sheffield W. | 5 | 19 | 7 | 12 | 9 | 1 | 1 | 0 | P |
| BOWEN | West Ham U. | 5 | 17 | 15 | 2 | 5 | 1 | 2 | 0 | P |
| MADDISON | Southampton | 5 | 17 | 14 | 3 | 16 | 1 | 4 | 0 | P |
| THOMSEN | Everton | 5 | 16 | 15 | 1 | 0 | 0 | 3 | 0 | P |
| GARDE | Arsenal | 5 | 11 | 7 | 4 | 2 | 0 | 2 | 0 | P |
| HEANEY | Southampton | 5 | 8 | 4 | 4 | 0 | 1 | 1 | 0 | P |

Fantasy Football Handbook

# Players Who Were The Most Used Subs

| Player | Team | Sbs | Tot | St | Snu | PS | Gls | Y | R | Lge |
|---|---|---|---|---|---|---|---|---|---|---|
| SIMPSON | Derby County | 19 | 19 | 0 | 12 | 0 | 2 | 0 | 0 | P |
| BLINKER | Sheffield W. | 18 | 33 | 15 | 2 | 5 | 1 | 6 | 0 | P |
| CLARKE | Newcastle U. | 16 | 25 | 9 | 12 | 2 | 2 | 1 | 0 | P |
| ROSENTHAL | Tottenham H. | 16 | 20 | 4 | 6 | 0 | 1 | 0 | 0 | P |
| HUMPHREYS | Sheffield W. | 15 | 29 | 14 | 8 | 11 | 3 | 2 | 0 | P |
| HOLDSWORTH | Wimbledon | 15 | 25 | 10 | 1 | 3 | 5 | 0 | 0 | P |
| McCLAIR | Manchester U. | 15 | 19 | 4 | 16 | 0 | 0 | 1 | 0 | P |
| PARLOUR | Arsenal | 13 | 30 | 17 | 4 | 2 | 2 | 6 | 0 | P |
| LAWRENCE | Leicester City | 13 | 15 | 2 | 16 | 0 | 0 | 0 | 0 | P |
| BRANCH | Everton | 12 | 25 | 13 | 7 | 7 | 3 | 2 | 0 | P |
| OAKES | Sheffield W. | 12 | 19 | 7 | 9 | 5 | 1 | 1 | 0 | P |
| JOACHIM | Aston Villa | 12 | 15 | 3 | 21 | 2 | 3 | 0 | 0 | P |
| DONIS | Blackburn R. | 11 | 22 | 11 | 9 | 4 | 2 | 0 | 0 | P |
| BERGER | Liverpool | 10 | 23 | 13 | 9 | 5 | 6 | 0 | 0 | P |
| COLE | Manchester U. | 10 | 20 | 10 | 3 | 2 | 6 | 1 | 0 | P |
| JOHNSON | Aston Villa | 10 | 20 | 10 | 6 | 2 | 4 | 4 | 0 | P |
| NDLOVU | Coventry City | 10 | 20 | 10 | 1 | 4 | 1 | 1 | 0 | P |
| TRUSTFULL | Sheffield W. | 10 | 19 | 9 | 7 | 8 | 3 | 3 | 0 | P |
| HARFORD | Wimbledon | 10 | 13 | 3 | 15 | 1 | 1 | 2 | 0 | P |
| LAMPARD | West Ham U. | 10 | 13 | 3 | 15 | 2 | 0 | 1 | 0 | P |
| GILLESPIE | Newcastle U. | 9 | 32 | 23 | 5 | 8 | 1 | 2 | 1 | P |
| PARKER | Leicester City | 9 | 31 | 22 | 1 | 5 | 2 | 0 | 0 | P |
| MARSHALL | Leicester City | 9 | 28 | 19 | 1 | 4 | 8 | 1 | 0 | P |
| CARSLEY | Derby County | 9 | 24 | 15 | 4 | 3 | 0 | 2 | 0 | P |
| LAZARIDIS | West Ham U. | 9 | 22 | 13 | 3 | 6 | 1 | 2 | 0 | P |
| FEAR | Wimbledon | 9 | 17 | 9 | 11 | 0 | 0 | 3 | 0 | P |
| WILLEMS | Derby County | 9 | 16 | 7 | 8 | 7 | 2 | 0 | 0 | P |
| GABBIADINI | Derby County | 9 | 14 | 5 | 1 | 4 | 0 | 1 | 0 | P |
| MORROW | Arsenal | 9 | 14 | 5 | 12 | 3 | 0 | 1 | 0 | P |
| SOLSKJAER | Manchester U. | 8 | 33 | 25 | 2 | 11 | 18 | 1 | 0 | P |
| SLATER R. | Southampton | 8 | 30 | 22 | 1 | 3 | 2 | 5 | 0 | P |
| JESS | Coventry City | 8 | 27 | 19 | 7 | 10 | 0 | 0 | 0 | P |
| SCHOLES | Manchester U. | 8 | 24 | 16 | 7 | 7 | 3 | 6 | 0 | P |
| PORFIRIO | West Ham U. | 8 | 23 | 15 | 2 | 5 | 2 | 6 | 0 | P |
| WATSON | Southampton | 8 | 15 | 7 | 3 | 6 | 2 | 0 | 0 | P |
| FENTON | Blackburn R. | 8 | 13 | 5 | 6 | 0 | 1 | 3 | 0 | P |
| RIPLEY | Blackburn R. | 8 | 13 | 5 | 4 | 3 | 0 | 0 | 0 | P |
| ASPRILLA | Newcastle U. | 7 | 24 | 17 | 4 | 12 | 4 | 1 | 0 | P |
| BORROWS | Coventry City | 7 | 23 | 16 | 8 | 4 | 0 | 3 | 0 | P |
| POBORSKY | Manchester U. | 7 | 22 | 15 | 15 | 10 | 3 | 1 | 0 | P |
| GRANT | Everton | 7 | 18 | 11 | 4 | 3 | 0 | 3 | 0 | P |
| DOZZELL | Tottenham H. | 7 | 17 | 10 | 7 | 2 | 2 | 2 | 0 | P |

| Player | Team | Sbs | Tot | St | Snu | PS | Gls | Y | R | Lge |
|--------|------|-----|-----|----|----|----|----|----|----|-----|
| FLYNN | Derby County | 7 | 17 | 10 | 8 | 3 | 1 | 3 | 0 | P |
| GOODMAN | Wimbledon | 7 | 13 | 6 | 6 | 6 | 1 | 0 | 0 | P |
| CLARKE | Wimbledon | 7 | 11 | 4 | 9 | 2 | 1 | 1 | 0 | P |
| NETHERCOTT | Tottenham H. | 7 | 9 | 2 | 19 | 2 | 0 | 2 | 0 | P |
| SHAW | Arsenal | 7 | 8 | 1 | 17 | 1 | 2 | 0 | 0 | P |
| MAGILTON | Southampton | 6 | 37 | 31 | 1 | 7 | 4 | 4 | 0 | P |
| STUART | Everton | 6 | 35 | 29 | 2 | 3 | 5 | 4 | 0 | P |
| POWELL D. | Derby County | 6 | 33 | 27 | 0 | 5 | 1 | 7 | 0 | P |
| Le TISSIER | Southampton | 6 | 31 | 25 | 0 | 8 | 13 | 5 | 0 | P |
| FOX | Tottenham H. | 6 | 25 | 19 | 3 | 6 | 1 | 1 | 0 | P |
| BOHINEN | Blackburn R. | 6 | 23 | 17 | 7 | 0 | 2 | 6 | 0 | P |
| JACKSON | Leeds U. | 6 | 17 | 11 | 11 | 1 | 0 | 1 | 0 | P |
| SCIMECA | Aston Villa | 6 | 17 | 11 | 9 | 0 | 0 | 1 | 0 | P |
| GULLIT | Chelsea | 6 | 12 | 6 | 2 | 2 | 1 | 1 | 0 | P |
| MORRIS | Chelsea | 6 | 12 | 6 | 8 | 3 | 0 | 1 | 0 | P |
| WARHURST | Blackburn R. | 6 | 11 | 5 | 10 | 3 | 2 | 1 | 0 | P |
| CAMPBELL | Leicester City | 6 | 10 | 4 | 10 | 2 | 0 | 0 | 0 | P |
| STRACHAN | Coventry City | 6 | 9 | 3 | 9 | 3 | 0 | 1 | 0 | P |
| POTTER | Southampton | 6 | 8 | 2 | 6 | 1 | 0 | 0 | 0 | P |
| GRAY | Leeds U. | 6 | 7 | 1 | 4 | 1 | 0 | 0 | 0 | P |
| DAILLY | Derby County | 5 | 36 | 31 | 0 | 6 | 3 | 6 | 0 | P |
| WRIGHT | Arsenal | 5 | 35 | 30 | 0 | 4 | 23 | 10 | 1 | P |
| TAYLOR | Aston Villa | 5 | 34 | 29 | 0 | 2 | 2 | 4 | 0 | P |
| BURLEY | Chelsea | 5 | 31 | 26 | 1 | 8 | 2 | 3 | 0 | P |
| JOHNSEN | Manchester U. | 5 | 31 | 26 | 2 | 6 | 0 | 3 | 0 | P |
| COLLYMORE | Liverpool | 5 | 30 | 25 | 5 | 9 | 12 | 3 | 0 | P |
| WARD | Derby County | 5 | 30 | 25 | 1 | 7 | 10 | 2 | 0 | P |
| NEILSON | Southampton | 5 | 29 | 24 | 3 | 2 | 0 | 4 | 0 | P |
| OAKLEY | Southampton | 5 | 28 | 23 | 0 | 11 | 3 | 0 | 0 | P |
| VIALLI | Chelsea | 5 | 28 | 23 | 5 | 3 | 9 | 5 | 0 | P |
| BLACKWELL | Wimbledon | 5 | 27 | 22 | 2 | 0 | 0 | 4 | 0 | P |
| HIRST | Sheffield W. | 5 | 25 | 20 | 0 | 11 | 6 | 3 | 1 | P |
| TAYLOR | Leicester City | 5 | 25 | 20 | 4 | 9 | 0 | 2 | 0 | P |
| DOWIE | West Ham U. | 5 | 23 | 18 | 6 | 0 | 0 | 1 | 0 | P |
| REDKNAPP | Liverpool | 5 | 23 | 18 | 6 | 0 | 3 | 0 | 0 | P |
| CURCIC | Aston Villa | 5 | 22 | 17 | 6 | 10 | 0 | 4 | 0 | P |
| WALLACE | Leeds U. | 5 | 22 | 17 | 8 | 7 | 3 | 5 | 0 | P |
| HARTSON | Arsenal | 5 | 19 | 14 | 2 | 8 | 3 | 9 | 0 | P |
| CRUYFF | Manchester U. | 5 | 16 | 11 | 8 | 6 | 3 | 2 | 0 | ˙P |
| HUGHES | Arsenal | 5 | 14 | 9 | 3 | 6 | 1 | 1 | 0 | P |
| MONKOU | Southampton | 5 | 13 | 8 | 1 | 0 | 0 | 6 | 0 | P |
| PEARCE | Blackburn R. | 5 | 12 | 7 | 3 | 1 | 0 | 1 | 0 | P |
| PEDERSEN | Blackburn R. | 5 | 11 | 6 | 1 | 8 | 1 | 0 | 0 | P |

| RADUCIOIU | West Ham U. | 5 | 11 | 6 | 2 | 4 | 2 | 0 | 0 | P |
| FUTRE | West Ham U. | 5 | 9 | 4 | 0 | 2 | 0 | 0 | 0 | P |
| RIDEOUT | Everton | 5 | 9 | 4 | 15 | 2 | 0 | 2 | 0 | P |
| NICHOLLS | Chelsea | 5 | 8 | 3 | 8 | 2 | 0 | 0 | 0 | P |
| BASHAM | Southampton | 5 | 6 | 1 | 14 | 0 | 0 | 0 | 0 | P |
| HUGHES | Southampton | 5 | 6 | 1 | 1 | 0 | 0 | 1 | 0 | P |
| KENNEDY | Liverpool | 5 | 5 | 0 | 20 | 0 | 0 | 0 | 0 | P |

# Players Who Were The Most Unused Subs

| Player | Team | Snu | Tot | St | Sbs | PS | Gls | Y | R | Lge |
|---|---|---|---|---|---|---|---|---|---|---|
| WARNER | Liverpool | 38 | 0 | 0 | 0 | 0 | 0 | 0 | 0 | P |
| CLARKE | Sheffield W. | 37 | 38 | 0 | 1 | 0 | 0 | 0 | 1 | P |
| BEENEY | Leeds U. | 37 | 1 | 1 | 0 | 0 | 0 | 0 | 0 | P |
| FILAN | Coventry City | 37 | 1 | 0 | 1 | 0 | 0 | 0 | 0 | P |
| BAARDSEN | Tottenham H. | 36 | 2 | 1 | 1 | 0 | 0 | 0 | 0 | P |
| GIVEN | Blackburn R. | 36 | 2 | 2 | 0 | 0 | 0 | 0 | 0 | P |
| VAN DER GOUW | Manchester U. | 34 | 2 | 2 | 0 | 0 | 0 | 0 | 0 | P |
| POOLE | Leicester City | 31 | 7 | 7 | 0 | 0 | 0 | 0 | 0 | P |
| GERRARD | Everton | 30 | 5 | 4 | 1 | 0 | 0 | 0 | 0 | P |
| TAYLOR | Derby County | 28 | 3 | 3 | 0 | 0 | 0 | 0 | 0 | P |
| HEALD | Wimbledon | 23 | 3 | 2 | 0 | 0 | 0 | 0 | 0 | P |
| HISLOP | Newcastle U. | 22 | 16 | 16 | 0 | 0 | 0 | 0 | 0 | P |
| HOTTIGER | Everton | 22 | 8 | 4 | 4 | 1 | 0 | 0 | 0 | P |
| MARKER | Blackburn R. | 22 | 7 | 5 | 2 | 0 | 0 | 0 | 0 | P |
| SEALEY | West Ham U. | 22 | 2 | 1 | 1 | 0 | 0 | 0 | 0 | P |
| JOACHIM | Aston Villa | 21 | 15 | 3 | 12 | 2 | 3 | 0 | 0 | P |
| HARTE | Leeds U. | 21 | 14 | 10 | 4 | 0 | 2 | 1 | 0 | P |
| LUKIC | Arsenal | 20 | 15 | 15 | 0 | 0 | 0 | 0 | 0 | P |
| BEASANT | Southampton | 20 | 14 | 13 | 1 | 0 | 0 | 0 | 0 | P |
| KENNEDY | Liverpool | 20 | 5 | 0 | 5 | 0 | 0 | 0 | 0 | P |
| NETHERCOTT | Tottenham H. | 19 | 9 | 2 | 7 | 2 | 0 | 2 | 0 | P |
| ROBINS | Leicester City | 18 | 8 | 5 | 3 | 4 | 1 | 0 | 0 | P |
| OAKES | Aston Villa | 17 | 20 | 18 | 2 | 0 | 0 | 0 | 0 | P |
| RUDDOCK | Liverpool | 17 | 17 | 15 | 2 | 3 | 1 | 2 | 0 | P |
| SHAW | Arsenal | 17 | 8 | 1 | 7 | 1 | 2 | 0 | 0 | P |
| SRNICEK | Newcastle U. | 16 | 22 | 22 | 0 | 0 | 0 | 0 | 0 | P |
| McCLAIR | Manchester U. | 16 | 19 | 4 | 15 | 0 | 0 | 1 | 0 | P |
| MADDISON | Southampton | 16 | 17 | 14 | 3 | 5 | 1 | 4 | 0 | P |
| LAWRENCE | Leicester City | 16 | 15 | 2 | 13 | 0 | 0 | 0 | 0 | P |
| POBORSKY | Manchester U. | 15 | 22 | 15 | 7 | 10 | 3 | 1 | 0 | P |
| HARFORD | Wimbledon | 15 | 13 | 3 | 10 | 1 | 1 | 2 | 0 | P |
| LAMPARD | West Ham U. | 15 | 13 | 3 | 10 | 2 | 0 | 1 | 0 | P |
| RIDEOUT | Everton | 15 | 9 | 4 | 5 | 2 | 0 | 2 | 0 | P |
| FARRELLY | Aston Villa | 15 | 3 | 1 | 2 | 0 | 0 | 0 | 0 | P |

| Player | Team | Snu | Tot | St | Sbs | PS | Gls | Y | R | Lge |
|--------|------|-----|-----|-----|-----|-----|-----|-----|-----|-----|
| JONES L. | Liverpool | 15 | 2 | 0 | 2 | 0 | 0 | 0 | 0 | P |
| COLGAN | Chelsea | 15 | 1 | 1 | 0 | 0 | 0 | 0 | 0 | P |
| BASHAM | Southampton | 14 | 6 | 1 | 5 | 0 | 0 | 0 | 0 | P |
| MOSS | Southampton | 14 | 3 | 3 | 0 | 0 | 0 | 0 | 0 | P |
| RACHEL | Aston Villa | 14 | 0 | 0 | 0 | 0 | 0 | 0 | 0 | P |
| FORD | Leeds U. | 13 | 16 | 15 | 1 | 6 | 1 | 4 | 0 | P |
| BOLAND | Coventry City | 13 | 1 | 0 | 1 | 0 | 0 | 0 | 0 | P |
| MURPHY | Wimbledon | 13 | 0 | 0 | 0 | 0 | 0 | 0 | 0 | P |
| BEARDSLEY | Newcastle U. | 12 | 25 | 22 | 3 | 4 | 5 | 3 | 0 | P |
| CLARK | Newcastle U. | 12 | 25 | 9 | 16 | 2 | 2 | 1 | 0 | P |
| SIMPSON | Derby County | 12 | 19 | 0 | 19 | 0 | 2 | 0 | 0 | P |
| MORROW | Arsenal | 12 | 14 | 5 | 9 | 3 | 0 | 1 | 0 | P |
| ALLEN | Tottenham H. | 12 | 12 | 9 | 3 | 3 | 2 | 4 | 0 | P |
| HENDRIE | Aston Villa | 12 | 4 | 0 | 4 | 0 | 0 | 0 | 0 | P |
| ROSE | Arsenal | 12 | 1 | 1 | 0 | 1 | 0 | 0 | 0 | P |
| FEAR | Wimbledon | 11 | 17 | 9 | 9 | 0 | 0 | 3 | 0 | P |
| JACKSON | Leeds U. | 11 | 17 | 11 | 6 | 1 | 0 | 1 | 0 | P |
| ROWLAND | West Ham U. | 11 | 15 | 11 | 4 | 8 | 1 | 5 | 0 | P |
| LINIGHAN | Arsenal | 11 | 11 | 10 | 1 | 1 | 1 | 2 | 0 | P |
| REEVES | Wimbledon | 11 | 2 | 0 | 2 | 0 | 0 | 0 | 0 | P |
| BARTON | Newcastle U. | 10 | 18 | 14 | 4 | 0 | 1 | 1 | 0 | P |
| WARHURST | Blackburn R. | 10 | 11 | 5 | 6 | 3 | 2 | 1 | 0 | P |
| CAMPBELL | Leicester City | 10 | 10 | 4 | 6 | 2 | 0 | 0 | 0 | P |
| MARSHALL | Arsenal | 10 | 8 | 6 | 2 | 1 | 0 | 1 | 0 | P |
| CROFT | Blackburn R. | 10 | 5 | 4 | 1 | 0 | 0 | 0 | 0 | P |
| LIMPAR | Everton | 10 | 2 | 1 | 1 | 1 | 0 | 0 | 0 | P |

Fantasy Football Handbook

# Promoted Clubs

## Players Who Played in 40+ Games 1996-97

| Player | Team | Tot | St | Sbs | Snu | PS | Gls | Y | R | Lge |
|---|---|---|---|---|---|---|---|---|---|---|
| EADEN | Barnsley | 46 | 46 | 0 | 0 | 2 | 3 | - | - | N |
| FAIRCLOUGH | Bolton W. | 46 | 46 | 0 | 0 | 1 | 8 | - | - | N |
| WATSON | Barnsley | 46 | 46 | 0 | 0 | 0 | 0 | - | - | N |
| ROBERTS | C.Palace | 46 | 45 | 1 | 0 | 0 | 0 | - | - | N |
| EDWORTHY | C.Palace | 46 | 43 | 3 | 0 | 5 | 0 | - | - | N |
| WILKINSON | Barnsley | 45 | 45 | 0 | 0 | 8 | 9 | - | - | N |
| MUSCAT | C.Palace | 44 | 42 | 2 | 0 | 5 | 2 | - | - | N |
| FREEDMAN | C.Palace | 44 | 33 | 11 | 0 | 12 | 11 | - | - | N |
| DE ZEEUW | Barnsley | 43 | 43 | 0 | 0 | 0 | 2 | - | - | N |
| McGINLAY | Bolton W. | 43 | 43 | 0 | 0 | 6 | 24 | - | - | N |
| REDFEARN | Barnsley | 43 | 43 | 0 | 0 | 1 | 17 | - | - | N |
| TAGGART | Bolton W. | 43 | 43 | 0 | 0 | 0 | 3 | - | - | N |
| DYER | C.Palace | 43 | 39 | 4 | 0 | 23 | 17 | - | - | N |
| SELLARS | Bolton W. | 42 | 40 | 2 | 0 | 7 | 8 | - | - | N |
| FRANDSEN | Bolton W. | 41 | 40 | 1 | 0 | 8 | 5 | - | - | N |
| SHERIDAN | Barnsley | 41 | 39 | 2 | 0 | 6 | 2 | - | - | N |
| TUTTLE | C.Palace | 41 | 39 | 2 | 0 | 6 | 0 | - | - | N |
| HOPKIN | C.Palace | 41 | 38 | 3 | 0 | 4 | 13 | - | - | N |
| VEART | C.Palace | 39 | 35 | 4 | 5 | 8 | 6 | - | - | N |
| MARCELLE | Barnsley | 39 | 26 | 13 | 1 | 10 | 8 | - | - | N |
| LIDDELL | Barnsley | 38 | 25 | 13 | 9 | 10 | 8 | - | - | N |
| BRANAGAN | Bolton W. | 36 | 36 | 0 | 2 | 1 | 0 | - | - | N |
| HENDRIE | Barnsley | 36 | 36 | 0 | 0 | 5 | 15 | - | - | N |
| PHILLIPS | Bolton W. | 36 | 36 | 0 | 1 | 1 | 0 | - | - | N |
| APPLEBY | Barnsley | 35 | 35 | 0 | 0 | 6 | 0 | - | - | N |
| BLAKE | Bolton W. | 34 | 34 | 0 | 0 | 7 | 19 | - | - | N |
| THOMPSON | Bolton W. | 34 | 34 | 0 | 0 | 3 | 11 | - | - | N |
| BERGSSON | Bolton W. | 33 | 30 | 3 | 0 | 4 | 3 | - | - | N |
| SHIPPERLEY | C.Palace | 32 | 29 | 3 | 1 | 8 | 12 | - | - | N |
| JOHANSEN | Bolton W. | 32 | 24 | 8 | 8 | 11 | 5 | - | - | N |
| BULLOCK | Barnsley | 30 | 7 | 23 | 15 | 4 | 0 | - | - | N |

## Players Who Were Subbed The Most

| Player | Team | PS | Tot | St | Sbs | Snu | Gls | Y | R | Lge |
|---|---|---|---|---|---|---|---|---|---|---|
| DYER | C.Palace | 23 | 43 | 39 | 4 | 0 | 17 | - | - | N |
| FREEDMAN | C.Palace | 12 | 44 | 33 | 11 | 0 | 11 | - | - | N |
| JOHANSEN | Bolton W. | 11 | 32 | 24 | 8 | 8 | 5 | - | - | N |
| MARCELLE | Barnsley | 10 | 39 | 26 | 13 | 1 | 8 | - | - | N |
| LIDDELL | Barnsley | 10 | 38 | 25 | 13 | 9 | 8 | - | - | N |

| Player | Team | PS | Tot | St | Sbs | Snu | Gls | Y | R | Lge |
|--------|------|----|-----|----|----|-----|-----|---|---|-----|
| BOSANCIC | Barnsley | 9 | 25 | 17 | 8 | 20 | 1 | - | - | N |
| WILKINSON | Barnsley | 8 | 45 | 45 | 0 | 0 | 9 | - | - | N |
| FRANDSEN | Bolton W. | 8 | 41 | 40 | 1 | 0 | 5 | - | - | N |
| VEART | C.Palace | 8 | 39 | 35 | 4 | 5 | 6 | - | - | N |
| SHIPPERLEY | C.Palace | 8 | 32 | 29 | 3 | 1 | 12 | - | - | N |
| SELLARS | Bolton W. | 7 | 42 | 40 | 2 | 0 | 8 | - | - | N |
| BLAKE | Bolton W. | 7 | 34 | 34 | 0 | 0 | 19 | - | - | N |
| QUINN | C.Palace | 7 | 22 | 17 | 5 | 8 | 1 | - | - | N |
| McGINLAY | Bolton W. | 6 | 43 | 43 | 0 | 0 | 24 | - | - | N |
| SHERIDAN | Barnsley | 6 | 41 | 39 | 2 | 0 | 2 | - | - | N |
| TUTTLE | C.Palace | 6 | 41 | 39 | 2 | 0 | 0 | - | - | N |
| APPLEBY | Barnsley | 6 | 35 | 35 | 0 | 0 | 0 | - | - | N |
| LEE | Bolton W. | 6 | 25 | 13 | 12 | 6 | 2 | - | - | N |
| EDWORTHY | C.Palace | 5 | 46 | 43 | 3 | 0 | 0 | - | - | N |
| MUSCAT | C.Palace | 5 | 44 | 42 | 2 | 0 | 2 | - | - | N |
| HENDRIE | Barnsley | 5 | 36 | 36 | 0 | 0 | 15 | - | - | N |

## Players Who Were The Most Used Subs

| Player | Team | Subs | Tot | St | Snu | PS | Gls | Y | R | Lge |
|--------|------|------|-----|----|-----|----|-----|---|---|-----|
| BULLOCK | Barnsley | 23 | 30 | 7 | 15 | 4 | 0 | - | - | N |
| NDAH | C.Palace | 20 | 25 | 5 | 3 | 0 | 3 | - | - | N |
| McKENZIE | C.Palace | 17 | 21 | 4 | 3 | 3 | 2 | - | - | N |
| MARCELLE | Barnsley | 13 | 39 | 26 | 1 | 10 | 8 | - | - | N |
| LIDDELL | Barnsley | 13 | 38 | 25 | 9 | 10 | 8 | - | - | N |
| LEE | Bolton W. | 12 | 25 | 13 | 6 | 6 | 2 | - | - | N |
| FREEDMAN | C.Palace | 11 | 44 | 33 | 0 | 12 | 11 | - | - | N |
| TODD | Bolton W. | 9 | 15 | 6 | 10 | 1 | 0 | - | - | N |
| TAYLOR | Bolton W. | 9 | 11 | 2 | 13 | 0 | 1 | - | - | N |
| TROLLOPE | C.Palace | 9 | 9 | 0 | 1 | 0 | 0 | - | - | N |
| JOHANSEN | Bolton W. | 8 | 32 | 24 | 8 | 11 | 5 | - | - | N |
| BOSANCIC | Barnsley | 8 | 25 | 17 | 20 | 9 | 1 | - | - | N |
| SHERIDAN | Bolton W. | 7 | 19 | 12 | 7 | 1 | 2 | - | - | N |
| ANDERSON | C.Palace | 7 | 14 | 7 | 1 | 2 | 1 | - | - | N |
| PAATELAINEN | Bolton W. | 7 | 10 | 3 | 3 | 1 | 2 | - | - | N |
| QUINN | C.Palace | 5 | 22 | 17 | 8 | 7 | 1 | - | - | N |
| JONES | Barnsley | 5 | 17 | 12 | 6 | 3 | 0 | - | - | N |
| GREEN | Bolton W. | 5 | 12 | 7 | 3 | 2 | 1 | - | - | N |

## Players Who Were The Most Unused Subs

| Player | Team | SNU | Tot | St | Sbs | PS | Gls | Y | R | Lge |
|--------|------|-----|-----|----|-----|----|-----|---|---|-----|
| BOSANCIC | Barnsley | 20 | 25 | 17 | 8 | 9 | 1 | - | - | N |
| BULLOCK | Barnsley | 15 | 30 | 7 | 23 | 4 | 0 | - | - | N |

| Player | Team | SNU | Tot | St | Sbs | PS | Gls | Y | R | Lge |
|--------|------|-----|-----|----|----|----|-----|---|---|-----|
| TAYLOR | Bolton W. | 13 | 11 | 2 | 9 | 0 | 1 | - | - | N |
| TODD | Bolton W. | 10 | 15 | 6 | 9 | 1 | 0 | - | - | N |
| LIDDELL | Barnsley | 9 | 38 | 25 | 13 | 10 | 8 | - | - | N |
| JOHANSEN | Bolton W. | 8 | 32 | 24 | 8 | 11 | 5 | - | - | N |
| QUINN | C.Palace | 8 | 22 | 17 | 5 | 7 | 1 | - | - | N |
| SHERIDAN | Bolton W. | 7 | 19 | 12 | 7 | 1 | 2 | - | - | N |
| LEE | Bolton W. | 6 | 25 | 13 | 12 | 6 | 2 | - | - | N |
| JONES | Barnsley | 6 | 17 | 12 | 5 | 3 | 0 | - | - | N |
| VEART | C.Palace | 5 | 39 | 35 | 4 | 8 | 6 | - | - | N |
| MOSES | Barnsley | 5 | 28 | 25 | 3 | 0 | 2 | - | - | N |
| NDAH | C.Palace | 3 | 25 | 5 | 20 | 0 | 3 | - | - | N |
| McKENZIE | C.Palace | 3 | 21 | 4 | 17 | 3 | 2 | - | - | N |
| POLLOCK | Bolton W. | 3 | 20 | 18 | 2 | 3 | 4 | - | - | N |
| GREEN | Bolton W. | 3 | 12 | 7 | 5 | 2 | 1 | - | - | N |
| SMALL | Bolton W. | 3 | 11 | 10 | 1 | 1 | 0 | - | - | N |
| WARD | Bolton W. | 3 | 11 | 10 | 1 | 0 | 0 | - | - | N |
| PAATELAINEN | Bolton W. | 3 | 10 | 3 | 7 | 1 | 2 | - | - | N |
| REGIS | Barnsley | 3 | 4 | 0 | 4 | 0 | 0 | - | - | N |
| TEN HEUVEL | Barnsley | 3 | 2 | 0 | 2 | 0 | 0 | - | - | N |
| BRANAGAN | Bolton W. | 2 | 36 | 36 | 0 | 1 | 0 | - | - | N |
| RODGER | C.Palace | 2 | 11 | 9 | 2 | 3 | 0 | - | - | N |
| CYRUS | C.Palace | 2 | 1 | 1 | 0 | 1 | 0 | - | - | N |
| BURTON | C.Palace | 2 | 0 | 0 | 0 | 0 | 0 | - | - | N |
| COLEMAN | Bolton W. | 2 | 0 | 0 | 0 | 0 | 0 | - | - | N |

# Team Notes

# Team Notes

# Team Notes